PRINCIPLES OF
MANAGEMENT
INFORMATION
SYSTEMS

McGraw-Hill Series in Management Information Systems

Gordon B. Davis, *Consulting Editor*

PRINCIPLES OF MANAGEMENT INFORMATION SYSTEMS

George M. Scott, Ph.D., C.P.A.

University of Connecticut

McGraw-Hill Book Company

New York St. Louis San Francisco Auckland Bogotá Hamburg
Johannesburg London Madrid Mexico Montreal New Delhi
Panama Paris São Paulo Singapore Sydney Tokyo Toronto

PRINCIPLES OF MANAGEMENT INFORMATION SYSTEMS

1234567890 DOCDOC 898765

ISBN 0-07-056103-6

This book was set in Palatino by Ruttle, Shaw & Wetherill, Inc.
The editors were Christina Mediate, Scott Amerman, Phillip E. McCaffrey, and Linda A. Mittiga;
the designer was Charles A. Carson;
the production supervisor was Leroy A. Young.
The drawings were done by Wellington Studios Ltd. and the author.
The photo editor was Lorinda Morris/Photo Researchers.
R. R. Donnelley & Sons Company was printer and binder.

Library of Congress Cataloging in Publication Data
Scott, George M.
    Principles of management information systems.

    (McGraw-Hill series in management information systems)
    Includes bibliographies and index.
    1. Management information systems. I. Title.
II. Series.
T58.6.S38 1986   658.4'0388   84-21849
ISBN 0-07-056103-6

To my mother, Doris Scott,
for her infinite patience and understanding,
to Kristin and Heather, who are the
lights of my life, and to Ada
for the good years we had together.

CONTENTS

SECTION II
FUNDAMENTALS OF COMPUTER SYSTEMS

SECTION III
DEVELOPING INFORMATION SYSTEMS

PREFACE

This textbook is written for all business school students. However, it is also intended to be useful to all other persons—whether formally enrolled as students or not—who want to acquire a manager's overall understanding of computers and of management information systems.

The major distinguishing characteristics of this textbook are that it presents the "core" of systems knowledge that all business school students should study (except for the topic of programming) and that it presents this material from the perspective of managers rather than that of technical persons. This approach reflects the philosophy that all business school students—whatever their major—should complete a "principles" information systems course, in the same way that they complete principles courses in accounting, finance, management, marketing, and other business areas. The text is comprehensive in its breadth and is oriented toward principles, concepts, and ideas rather than primarily toward the technical, or "data processing," aspects of information systems.

Many management professors and other professors with an interest in information systems who do not believe they have the technical computer background needed to teach information systems should feel comfortable teaching with this text.

The major theme of the text is information systems for managerial purposes and the implications of computer technology for the management processes. The text is intended to serve students equally well for a first and only course in information systems, for a follow-up course to a programming course, or for a required background course for students who are continuing to a programming or to a more advanced information systems course.

There are advantages to completing a principles course rather than a programming course as the first information systems course. One is that a principles course provides most of the full range of knowledge about business information systems that all business school students should possess as a minimum, whereas a programming course as a first course provides a primarily narrow and technical perspective on information systems.

Additionally, the overview provided by a principles course helps students decide early whether they wish to take additional systems courses. A programming course often conveys the strong impression to students that programming is what information systems is all about and that if they do not enjoy or are not proficient at programming, no further studies in information systems are warranted. Without doubt, many students who would have found careers in information systems activities highly interesting and rewarding have been "turned off" by their first systems course because it was a programming course.

Perhaps the greatest advantage of completing a course in the principles of management information systems in advance of taking a programming course is that, as indicated by research into the workings of the human mind, individuals' permanent mind patterns—their "view of the world"—are heavily weighted by early perceptions. The proper view of the world should therefore be established first. It is the author's opinion that in the area of information systems, the proper view for business school students is an overview of information systems. If students are taught programming before they learn about information systems, they run the real risk of forever viewing information systems through the eyes of programmers and technicians, which is too restricted a perspective for managers, who should think in terms of management information systems rather than computer programming.

Students with no background in computer programming can expect to do as well in an initial course using this text as students who have taken a previous course in programming. Indeed, many of the author's best students in courses based on the material presented in this text have had no background whatsoever in computer systems.

Computerized business data processing now is found in even small organizations. Companies and other organizations with even two clerical employees often can profitably use a computer for business purposes. This textbook is intended to serve students equally well whether they join small, medium-sized, or large organizations; the functioning of large computers is similar to that of small computers, and students should be equally knowledgeable about both. The general principles and techniques of systems analysis and design are also similar, no matter what the computer or project size.

However, there are important differences between large and small systems, and the textbook makes a special effort to note these differences. The text also gives extensive attention to microcomputers and small business computer systems. Much of the discussion about computers uses microcomputers as a frame of reference.

The textbook can serve for a one-semester course at the junior, senior, or graduate level for all business school students and for students of public administration, library science, and other scientific areas. The text also provides an excellent introduction to information systems for computer science and engineering students, who can benefit from a counterpoint to their technical computer courses and who should understand the perspectives from which managers view information systems. Liberal arts students who are contemplating a career in data processing can do no better than to be introduced to information systems through study of this text.

The several chapters of Section I examine the management and control processes of organizations and deal with the nature of management information systems. Section II describes the computer industry from the point of view of career opportunities available in the industry and then presents the fundamentals of computer systems. Several chapters give attention to specialized computer systems topics, and two chapters deal with functional information systems.

Section III examines the topic of how to organize for and conduct a systems project and the way in which computers (both large and small) are selected, again from a manager's point of view. The emphasis in this section is on how managers can usefully participate in systems projects.

The material in this textbook has been developed over several years and is the consequence of three major dimensions of the author's activities. The first is extensive teaching in the systems area. The second is management consulting; as a management consultant, the author generally served senior managers in the capacity of intermediary between them and the computer group.

The third dimension is the author's long-term interest in, and study of, general management processes. The entire textbook is intended to reflect this managerial orientation.

The objectives of the textbook are to provide enough information systems, computer technology, and systems development knowledge to enable the student to:

1. Communicate effectively with data processing personnel.
2. Recognize and specify an information systems problem.
3. Participate usefully as a member of a systems project team.
4. Interpret new information technology developments as these occur and fit them into an overall information systems framework.
5. Anticipate and help shape the structure of an organization's information system in recognition of the technology that will be important for the next five years.

The author is indebted to many people for assistance with this text. Foremost among these is Dr. Ronald Teichman of the Pennsylvania State University who critically reviewed the entire manuscript and offered innumerable useful suggestions. Other reviewers to whom the author is indebted include Dr. Gordon Davis of the University of Minnesota, Dr. Paul R. Watkins of the University of Southern California, Dr. Warren J.

Bow of the University of Iowa, Dr. Andrew Varanelli, Jr., of Pace University, Dr. Grover M. Rodich, Visiting Professor at the University of Colorado, Dr. Edward A. Christensen of California State University (Sacramento), and Dr. Virginia Gibson at the University of Maine. At McGraw-Hill Book Company, three editors who have been particularly helpful, each in succession, are James Vastyan, Eric Munson, and Christina Mediate. On the homefront, Blanche Boucher has provided outstanding editorial assistance, and Denise Yphantis has performed stellar service in the word processing system.

George M. Scott

PRINCIPLES OF

MANAGEMENT

INFORMATION

SYSTEMS

SECTION ONE

MANAGEMENT INFORMATION SYSTEMS

This textbook is divided into three sections: Management Information Systems, Fundamentals of Computer Systems, and Developing Information Systems. This section is concerned with the nature of information and the information needs of managers. The first three chapters present a series of information-related concepts, and, building on these concepts, Chapter 4 defines and discusses management information systems. The background provided in the first three chapters enables the student to understand and appreciate the full meaning of the term "management information system."

Chapter 1

THE ORGANIZATION: ITS MANAGERS, STRUCTURE, AND ACTIVITIES

PAYOFF THOUGHT

To work effectively in an organization requires an understanding of how the organization functions. An important way to achieve this understanding is by analyzing the organization's information flows, which requires an examination of its structure and activities and of the style of its managers. These are examined in this chapter.

CHAPTER OBJECTIVES

1. To show the dynamics of an organization's environment, structure, and activities and to demonstrate how they relate to information flows within the organization

2. To illustrate how management style and management processes influence the development of an organization's information system

INTRODUCTION

This text covers the three major areas of information systems knowledge that are essential to managers: computer systems, information systems, and information systems development.

Computer Systems

Computer systems are pervasive in business and commerce, and an understanding of computer technology is necessary for an understanding of information systems. In particular, an understanding of microcomputer systems has become increasingly important to all managers and professional personnel in business organizations.

Information Systems

Of even greater importance to managers than knowledge about computer technology is knowledge about information systems—those systems which are created by analysts and managers to perform specific tasks that are essential to the functioning of the organization. These tasks range from simple data processing, such as preparing customer invoices, to providing sophisticated managerial analyses on which the management of the organization is based. The knowledge that managers require about information systems falls into two general categories:

1. *Business data processing.* Most organizations carry out a tremendous number (possibly several million per day) and a wide variety of business transactions. Accurately recording and processing these transactions is known as "business data processing."

2. *Management information systems (MISs.).* Managers at all levels must receive summaries of the organization's business transactions as well as extensive information about many other matters. Extensive and complex information systems are required to satisfy managers' needs for information.

Information Systems Development

The development of suitable information systems requires a blending of computer systems knowledge, information systems knowledge, and knowledge of how to design and implement an information system and how to acquire the needed computer system. Managers must participate in these processes and for this reason must have a knowledge of the processes.

ORGANIZATION OF THE TEXTBOOK

The underlying theme of this textbook is what managers at all levels of organizations should know about computer systems and about information systems in order to ensure that their information requirements will be satisfactorily met.

The four chapters of Section I explain the interactions between the organization, its managers, and its information systems. Organizational considerations, management processes, managerial style, human information processing concepts, and managers' information needs and their sources of information are discussed in relation to the information systems of the organization; the concept of an MIS is also developed and defined.

Section II explores the fundamentals of computer technology and functional information systems. Included are data base, telecommunications, and microprocessing technologies, as well as two chapters that examine accounting, marketing, and manufacturing information systems.

Systems development activities—systems analysis, systems design, and systems implementation—are dealt with in Section III. Section III also includes chapters on equipment and software selection, with special emphasis on the selection of microcomputer systems.

WHY STUDY MANAGEMENT INFORMATION SYSTEMS?

Beyond the need to understand computer-based business information systems, there are two additional, compelling reasons for studying the material presented in this text:

1. By many accounts, the information technology industry, which consists of the computer industry and related industries, is the largest commercial industry in the world. It is also the fastest-growing of the world's major industries. Information technology is transforming our economic and recreational activities, and it merits careful attention as one of the most important sociological phenomena of the century.

2. The information technology industry is creating job opportunities in dozens of fields for today's business school students. Today's students will have little competition from yesterday's graduates, who do not have an adequate grasp of the nature and implications of computer technology.

THE ENVIRONMENT OF ORGANIZATIONS

A natural beginning for a textbook on information systems is an analysis of the environment of organizations. An organization's environment largely determines what information must be provided by its information systems, the preferred format of the information, and how the information systems should be organized.

The environment of an organization includes economic, cultural, and political forces that affect the organization. These forces include interest-rate changes, inflation levels, employment levels, demographic shifts, social mores, the results of political elections, and a host of other factors that affect product demand and other characteristics of marketplaces. While economic, cultural, and political forces are usually beyond the control of an individual organization, an organization must receive and process extensive information about them.

Individuals and external organizations also influence an organization. These include its customers (the users of the services or products that the organization provides), its competitors, its investors and creditors, and its employees, who may be represented by trade unions. Each group both provides information to, and receives information from, the organization. Additionally, an endless variety of government agencies supply regulatory information to the organization or receive regulatory reports from it. Many companies file more than 1000 reports annually with local, state, and federal government agencies.

The more rapidly an organization's environment changes, the shorter the period of time the organization has in which to adapt to its changed environment before it incurs serious damage. For a number of reasons, the pace of change in most organizations' environments has been accelerating; thus organizations now need more information faster about their changed environments in order to adapt successfully to these environments. This information must be systematically collected, and the organization must also generate and provide information to other organizations and individuals with which it interacts. In general, the more complex and dynamic the environment of an organization, the greater must be the proportion of the organization's total effort and resources that it devotes to its information system.

HIERARCHY IN THE ORGANIZATION STRUCTURE

Hierarchy is the existence of superior/subordinate relationships, resulting in a "chain of command"; this means that multiple "levels" of personnel exist in an organization. In a small organization perhaps there are only two levels: the owner-boss and a few employees. In a large organization there may be many levels: at the lowest level are workers, who carry out the primary activities; at a second level are group leaders, department heads, or supervisors; at the middle level there is a series of managers; and at the highest level there is a superstructure of division heads, vice presidents, senior vice presidents, and president, who are collectively called "top management." The president reports to the board of directors, the highest level of a company.

In a large organization a dozen or more hierarchical levels may be present. A chart of organization for medium-sized company is shown in Exhibit 1.1; only the marketing, accounting, and information systems functions are portrayed in detail. It can be seen that marketing and accounting each have eight levels in their hierarchy and that information systems has nine levels, when the workers at the bottom are included as a level.

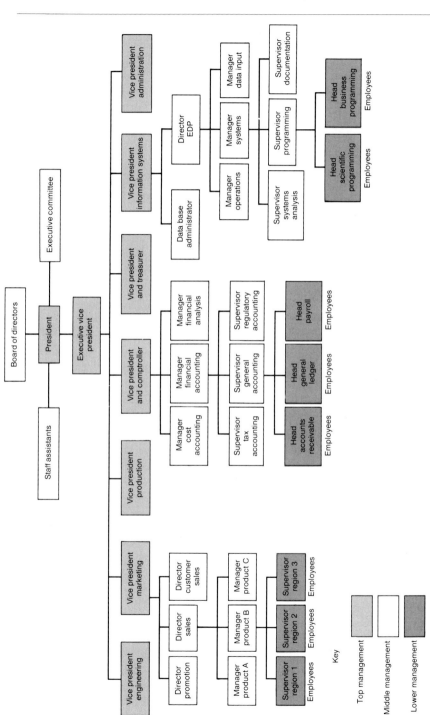

EXHIBIT 1.1 A chart of organization.

Board of directors

Executive committee

President

Staff assistants

Executive vice president

Vice president engineering

Vice president marketing

Vice president production

Vice president and comptroller

Vice president and treasurer

Vice president information systems

Vice president administration

Director promotion

Director sales

Director customer sales

Manager cost accounting

Manager financial accounting

Manager financial analysis

Data base administrator

Director EDP

Manager product A

Manager product B

Manager product C

Supervisor tax accounting

Supervisor general accounting

Supervisor regulatory accounting

Manager operations

Manager systems

Manager data input

Supervisor region 1

Supervisor region 2

Supervisor region 3

Head accounts receivable

Head general ledger

Head payroll

Supervisor systems analysis

Supervisor programming

Supervisor documentation

Employees

Employees

Employees

Employees

Employees

Employees

Head scientific programming

Head business programming

Employees

Employees

Key

Top management

Middle management

Lower management

7

Information Flows

The hierarchy of an organization affects its information system; the hierarchical structure is the fundamental framework around which the information system is organized. With few exceptions and without regard to what other information flows may also exist, the information system is organized to pass information upward along the lines of the hierarchy. Information is usually summarized at each level as it flows up; information provided by organization units at one level is combined at that level and then flows up to the next level, and at that next level a similar combining and upward flow takes place. Thus fewer details are provided to each successively higher level.

Information also flows downward along hierarchical lines in the form of directives, policies, and action guidelines; these types of information are less likely to be generated by the computer system and are usually less voluminous than the upward information flows. Nevertheless, the downward flows constitute an important part of information and communication systems because they channel and direct the activities of managers at each lower level.

The major organization unit that is concerned with the development of information systems usually is the computer information systems department, which is often unaware of the importance of downward-flowing information and which devotes none of its systems development efforts to this information flow. When these downward flows are not properly developed, managers at each level usually are consistent in their criticism of "the lack of communication from above." Downward-flowing information systems merit more attention on the part of both managers and informations systems specialists.

Information flows are not restricted to paths up and down the hierarchy. Information also flows laterally within an organization, particularly in transactions processing information systems. These lateral information flows are often extensive, and they help explain the complexity of information systems in organizations.

Managerial Spans of Control

"Span of control" refers to the number of persons reporting directly to a manager. Referring to Exhibit 1.1 if the comptroller and the treasurer reported to a senior vice president of finance, the span of control of the executive vice president would be reduced by one. Increasing spans of control can have the effect of reducing the number of levels in an organization's hierarchy, as would be the case if the executive vice president position in Exhibit 1.1 were eliminated. The consequence might be reduced organizational complexity and reduced managerial costs because the organization structure would be simplified and fewer managers would be employed. However, these advantages could be offset by a decreased effectiveness of the organization caused by an information and decision "bottleneck," whereby a particular manager receives too much information to analyze, must make too many decisions, and must direct the activities of too many subordinates.

Two major factors affect an organization's ability to increase managerial span of control. The first is that face-to-face contact with subordinates is essential. Managers must interact on a personal basis about personnel problems and other matters, and the time required for this imposes an inherent limitation on the number of subordinates, or span of control, that is practical.

The other factor relates to the control and evaluation of the operations of each subordinate and each subunit of the organization; these activities are highly dependent on information provided by the information system. If less time can be devoted to control and evaluation activities because better information is available from the information system, the span of control can be increased. Thus, the quality of the information system is a critical element here: a greater span of control due to a better information system means that fewer personnel are required, and this means that an effective information system can reduce the administrative costs of an organization.

Information Summarization

Information summarization involves reducing the details reported about activities so that a "big-picture" perspective can be acquired. As a simple example, if two sales are made for $12 and $8 each, these sales can be summarized as total sales of $20. Summarization results in the loss of detail; for example, the $20 summary figure provides no information about the total number of sales or the amount of each sale.

Summarization is necessary because a manager cannot absorb and utilize all the details about the operations of the organization units at lower levels. Additionally, better decisions usually can be made if they are based on analyses of only the highlights of lower-level operations as presented in summaries. For example, often patterns or trends in operations can be clearly seen in summarized information, but without summarization these trends would be obscured by the mass of details.

Hierarchy in and Complexity of Organizations

As a general rule, the greater the number of hierarchical levels, the more complex the information system. Each organization unit at each level generates information that must be summarized and provided to the next higher level; thus as the number of levels increases, the complexity of the information system also increases. Complexity by itself is a major determinant of the cost of an information system; complex systems are more difficult to design, more costly to implement, and also more costly to operate. Complexity in information systems also introduces greater opportunities for data processing errors and systems malfunctions.

Too many levels in the hierarchy may mean that information from lower levels of the organization takes so long to reach higher levels where it is needed that decision making at those higher levels is delayed. To a great extent this problem is caused by the increased time required to complete additional summarizations of the information; these additional summarizations usually require manual intervention in the computer data processing activities. Manual intervention also provides additional opportunities for data processing errors, and therefore additional delay may be caused by the need for error corrections.

FILTERING INFORMATION

Information summarization causes each level in a hierarchy to become a "filter station" at which a choice is made about the extent of detail to include in summaries provided to the next higher level; what is not provided is "filtered out." In a computerized system most of the decisions about filtering are made formally as a part of the systems design, and these decisions are included as a part of the computer programs.

However, noncomputerized information is also summarized at each level and is reported to the next higher level. Here managers make a continuing series of decisions about the information that is not forwarded to their superiors, and they implement these decisions by simply not sending this information. This filtering process can be either useful or harmful. On the one hand, it enables lower-level managers to eliminate information that managers at the next higher level would find too trivial or irrelevant. On the other hand, filtering is harmful to the organization when managers withhold information because it reflects unfavorably upon them or because of their own personal biases.

To minimize the potential for damage resulting from improper filtering of information, as well as to acquire additional information that immediate subordinates do not have, managers develop "windows" so that they can "see" into the lower levels of the organization. A simple window is direct observation of operations at the lower levels; for example, touring the plant and talking to shop floor personnel can provide managers with information which they need but which has been filtered out of the reports they receive. Direct observations can also provide information that is difficult to include in formal reports, such as information about workers' morale and loyalty or their opinions about the need for a plant safety program.

Another window approach is that of having the computer system keep the full detail of unfiltered information so that this information is available "on call" (whenever it is asked for). This detail can be examined at the option of managers if they want assurance that the information received from subordinates accurately portrays the situation or if they feel a need to analyze further details. For example, if a manager wants further information about a summary cost variance, the system design can permit the manager to examine details about the several variances that constitute the summary variance. These details can be requested from a subordinate, but they may also be secured directly by a request to data processing or by direct access to the files via a computer terminal if the information system has been tailored to make backup detail readily available.

Often, managers use windows to test the validity of the information they receive through the formal information system, even if they have no particular reason to doubt it. This provides them with an indication of the reliability of information from the formal information system.

CONCENTRATION OF AUTHORITY

The management literature normally presents a two-way classification of how much authority is given to different levels in the organization; the terms usually used are "centralized management" and "decentralized management." With centralized management, top management is responsible for most or all of the important decisions, and little decision-making authority is left to the lower levels of management. With decentralized management, at some lower level (usually the division level) managers have the authority to make the major decisions that directly affect the performance of their organization units.

Viewing organizations as if they were either centralized or decentralized is an oversimplification because organizations seldom adhere closely to either form. The many different managerial activities and decision-making responsibilities which define the location of policy making and administrative power in an organization can be organized in a wide variety of ways other than by centralized management or decentralized management. At least a third dimension is useful; for the most part, those forms of management which are not clearly centralized or decentralized can be described as "coordinative management," which is sometimes also called "collegial management," "joint management," "collaborative management," or "collective management." Centralized management, decentralized management, and coordinative management will be discussed here.

Centralized Management

Centralized management imposes heavy demands on an information system. In a large company with several thousand different products sold in several geographic markets, voluminous amounts of information relating to just one type of decision-making activity, such as product pricing, must be received and analyzed by senior managers. For many decision-making activities, this detailed information must be received frequently, perhaps as often as weekly, and must be in a standardized form; thus all branches or subsidiaries must maintain a high degree of standardization of their information systems. For example, the information needed by senior managers for each product pricing decision would usually include, as a minimum, information about (1) product demand for each product at each location, (2) production rates and costs, and (3) competitors' prices, sales terms, and sales activities.

The information system of a centrally managed organization must be structured to funnel tremendous quantities of detailed information about operations and product markets to top management. The result is often an information bottleneck of massive proportions. Not only is the information system overburdened, but also top managers suffer from "information overload," a condition in which so much information is communicated to the decision-making managers that they cannot analyze it quickly enough to make timely decisions. The consequent delay in decision making means that the entire organization does not react quickly enough to changed circumstances, such as price reductions by competitors, a costly inventory buildup, or a shortage of some inventory items.

A general rule is that the smaller and less complex the organization, the more likely it is that the information needed for centralized management can be provided to the decision makers in a timely manner and that these managers will be able to use this information effectively. In part this is due to the fact that small organizations have fewer levels in the hierarchy through which the information must pass and where it will perhaps be distorted, delayed, or improperly filtered, and in part it is due to the fact that less total information is involved and that it is less difficult to organize and utilize the information effectively.

A corollary to this general rule is that the better the information system, the greater the extent of centralized management that an organization can have and remain effective. The introduction of computerized business information systems during the 1960s and their continuous improvement since then have meant that, all else being equal, organizations can now have greater centralization of management than previously, if they so choose.

Decentralized Management

Most large organizations have delegated (decentralized) decision-making activities to subunits, which are often called "divisions" and are organized as profit centers. In large organizations this decentralization usually permits faster adaptation to changes in the environment because the decisions can be made by the managers who first become aware of new operating conditions.

This difference in the location of decision making changes the complexion of the required information system. First and most important, the information system of a decentralized organization does not have the burden of providing headquarters with massive amounts of information about operations on a continuous basis. This simplifies the information system. Second, the operations information systems of the divisions of a decentralized organization need not be standardized but instead can be tailored to the needs of each division, which may vary widely among the divisions.

Although detailed information in standardized form is not required by headquarters from decentralized divisions, division managers are nevertheless accountable to headquarters for their performance. Management control by headquarters is based on periodic summary reports provided to headquarters by the information system. As a minimum, these reports will include a monthly position statement and income statement and other summary financial statements, as well as managerial accounting statements. Each division's information system must be designed to provide this periodic performance evaluation information, which may be required in a standardized format, even though it is generated by nonstandard information systems.

Coordinative Management

This form of management involves extensive collaborative efforts in management activities; thus multiple managers who are often at different levels in the organization participate in making the major decisions. Coordinative management is useful when both lower-level and senior managers possess information that is vital to the decision processes and when this information must be pooled for effective management. Most commonly the lower-level managers possess information about a subunit's operations and environments, and senior managers understand the organization's overall goals and have a big-picture knowledge of the entire organization's activities and status. This is often the case in international operations, for example, where local-country managers have an intimate knowledge of the local countries' markets and where headquarters managers have an understanding of global goals, global economic conditions, and the international money markets. The information possessed by both the local and the headquarters managers must be pooled so that decisions that are optimum for the entire enterprise can be made.

The information system required for coordinative management is complex. One reason for this is that for a given management activity, overlapping sets of information may need to be provided by the system to the several participating managers. Another reason relates to performance evaluation, which is more difficult in coordinative organizations because multiple managers may participate in a particular decision, which makes it the shared responsibility of all participants. In this milieu the information provided for performance evaluation must have an extra dimension of sophistication—a dimension that facilitates making a fine distinction between the results of operations that are attributable to a particular manager and those which are attributable to all participants in shared decisions.

The sharing of responsibilities in coordinative organizations is sometimes formalized by establishing a matrix form of organization in which functions such as production and marketing are managed hierarchically and in which product lines are managed laterally across functional lines (or vice versa). A matrix form of organization for a simple organization is shown in Exhibit 1.2. The functional managers in marketing, production, and finance have overall responsibility for all product lines, and each shares the responsibility for a particular product line with a specialized manager within that product line. To illustrate, marketing decisions for product line A are made jointly by the functional marketing manager and the product line A marketing manager, production decisions are made jointly by the functional production manager and the product line A production manager, and so on. Each pair of decision-making managers requires similar information about product line A from the information system, but each also requires different background information. For example, the functional marketing manager must be familiar with the marketing activities of all other product lines, and the product line A marketing manager needs information about the marketplace for product line A products.

Although many organizations have adopted formal matrix management systems, almost all these use matrix management for only a part of their operations. To the extent that matrix management is used in an organization, a virtual complete redundancy of information system is required; thus one complete information system is in existence for the func-

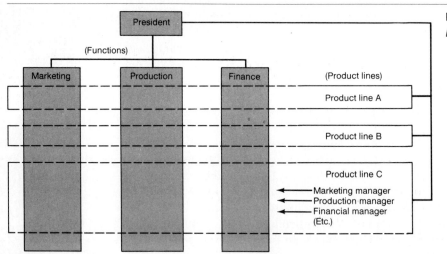

EXHIBIT 1.2
Matrix management.

tional organizations, and another is in existence for the product lines. Each must provide information to, and receive information from, the other; therefore, they are not separate but instead are interrelated in complex ways.

A matrix structure could not work without the processing power of computers and the recent advances in the ability to create sophisticated information systems. Further, as information systems technology continues to improve, matrix management will become more feasible than it is at present. Distributed data processing systems enhance the effectiveness of matrix management because they make the same information more readily available to managers at different locations.

THE ORGANIZATION'S FUNCTIONS

A series of activities that are closely related are collectively called a "function" of the organization. Keeping track of the current addresses of employees, maintaining an up-to-date record of their job experience, and managing other factual data about employees are activities that are considered to be part of the personnel function, for example.

Organizations have several major functions. While these may be organized differently in different organizations, the typical functions of most manufacturing organizations are those shown in Exhibit 1.3. Numerous other functional activities may also exist in companies.

Each function usually has its own quasi-separate information system. The typical manufacturing company has a least 15 major functional information systems and a host of lesser ones. Exhibit 1.4 shows that each functional area has its own hierarchy; each function's information system will parallel that hierarchy.

Cross-functional information flows also can be quite extensive; for example, purchasing managers must receive information from the manufacturing function about the future production schedule for each product as well as about the quantities of materials and components used during production. The extent to which information from one functional area is transmitted to another functional area's information system, as well as the ease with which this is accomplished, is considered a measure of the degree of "integration" of the organization's information systems.

MANAGEMENT STYLE

Management style and management processes are the major determinants of an organization's internal environment. Together they determine how an organization operates, they establish its "personality," and they influence its performance. Styles and processes also influence the structure of the information system needed by an organization.

The Major Functions of a Manufacturing Company   EXHIBIT 1.3

Personnel:
 Involves recruiting, training, and counseling employees as well as maintaining employee records and work-force
 planning.

Production:
 Includes all activities directly involving the manufacture of products.

Marketing:
 Generally consists of the sales and sales promotion activities; in a larger company the marketing function may
 include a market research activity. Marketing also usually has a major responsibility for product pricing.

Engineering:
 Where the products are reasonably complex and sophisticated, an engineering function exists to design the
 products, develop the specifications that must be followed during manufacture, and design the production system.

Distribution:
 Is concerned primarily with the movement of the company's products to its marketing outlets.

Accounting:
 Maintains the records for the financial transactions, assets, and liabilities; produces the financial statements; and
 runs the financial control systems. Accounting activities include transactions processing, accounts receivable billing
 and collection, payroll preparation, and stockholder records maintenance.

Purchasing:
 Is concerned with the acquisition of raw materials, components, and supplies; it includes maintaining vendor history
 files and selecting vendors, preparing purchase orders, and establishing and maintaining EOQ (economic order
 quantity) formulas that automatically determine optimum purchase order size.

Inventory management:
 Maintains physical control over supplies, materials, components, and finished products.

Information management:
 Involves developing, operating, and maintaining the computer information system that accomplishes the data
 processing.

Treasury:
 Handles the organization's financing activities, is concerned with its capital structure, and usually manages its cash.

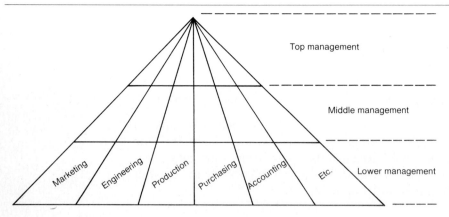

EXHIBIT 1.4
Functions and hierarchy
in a manufacturing
company.

Top management

Middle management

Lower management

Marketing Engineering Production Purchasing Accounting Etc.

Management style consists of the "personalized" aspects of a manager's activities while participating in the management processes. One important ingredient of style is how managers spend their time; for example, a manager who carefully analyzes production reports has a different style from that of another manager who instead takes frequent plant tours. Another important aspect of managerial style is the way a manager conducts interpersonal relationships.

Management style is a consequence of the qualities of the manager's mind and of the past experiences and training that have shaped the manager's thought processes. Two managers with quite different styles may reach the same conclusion, or two managers with similar styles may reach different conclusions, given similar circumstances. However, management style influences the information needed by the manager. The production manager who carefully analyzes production reports must be supported by an extensive formal information system, whereas the production manager who tours the plant, talks extensively to supervisors, counts the products in the scrap bins, and asks the workers what their problems are may need little in the way of a formal information system.

The Nature of Human Minds

Management style is greatly influenced by the qualities of a manager's mind. Basic aptitudes, the information processing characteristics of the mind, and the effects of past experiences on establishing patterns of thinking must be considered.

Basic aptitudes can be collectively termed "native intelligence." Native intelligence strongly influences a person's ability to give meaning to data, interpret work situations and instructions, follow instructions in a work environment, and analyze complex problems. Information systems must be designed in consideration of the probable level of the users' native intelligence. An employee with average intelligence will be unable to utilize a complex information system; a simplified information system is needed instead. Where the work environment dictates that the information system be complex, the persons using the information system must have an appropriately high level of native intelligence.

Human minds also differ with respect to types of information processing abilities. One experiment indicated that there may be four fundamentally different qualities of the human mind, as indicated in Exhibit 1.5.

In this exhibit, the horizontal dimension relates to how a manager evaluates information. A manager with a systematic mind is inclined to deal with a problem by structuring it in terms of a definite and systematic solution method, which, if followed through, leads to an acceptable solution. This kind of manager is good at solving problems which have an inherent underlying structure. For instance, the problems in an accounting

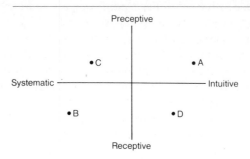

EXHIBIT 1.5
Characteristics of
human minds.

textbook usually have an inherent underlying structure; all or most of the information needed to solve these problems is included, and they can be solved readily by an accountant with a systematic mind. For a manager with a systematic mind, the information system should anticipate the solution method that will be used and should provide the information in the form needed for that method. For example, if a decision involves analysis of the net income components of a division's product line, the information system should provide the information needed to prepare an income statement, or it should actually provide the income statement. Sometimes the method itself might be a part of the information system; for example, the method of analysis may be a computer model that analyzes data and provides the results to the manager. Accountants, engineers, and technical computer personnel, such as professional programmers and analysts, usually have systematic minds.

Managers with intuitive minds are likely to use trial and error to test various solutions. They are able to approach ill-structured problems and quickly find reasonable solutions on the basis of judgment developed through previous experience. Such managers have less need for precise computer models and specific solution algorithms than managers with systematic minds, and they are less likely to use specific methods if they are available.

The vertical dimension of Exhibit 1.5 relates to whether a manager's mind deals most effectively with details or with the big picture. Some managers become deeply immersed in the details of data during an analysis and build a solution based on extensive use of detailed information. These are the managers with receptive minds. They are often criticized because they "can't see the forest for the trees."

Managers with preceptive minds tend to focus on the relationships between elements of data as they gather and process information. They are likely to quickly examine any details provided to find the most relevant way to synthesize data and to establish relationships between data elements. These managers then develop a solution on the basis of a few key relationships which provide the big picture. Managers with preceptive minds don't know what kind of trees are in the forest.

Managers with receptive minds are more likely to possess extensive technical training and experience; those with preceptive minds are more likely to have broader and more general training and experience, such as a liberal arts education and an MBA degree. The distinctly different approaches to problem solving of these two types of managers should be reflected in the information systems designed for them. The manager with a receptive mind desires detailed information in order to carefully develop and document a solution that is based on extensive information. On the other hand, for a manager with a preceptive mind, the information system should be designed to highlight relationships (for example, financial ratios) rather than to provide a large quantity of detailed information.

In Exhibit 1.5, manager A has a mind that combines intuitive and preceptive characteristics. A mind such as this perceives relationships and synthesizes them into an overall perspective about an ill-structured problem that often involves consideration of several alternatives. This manager's mind does not build a step-by-careful-step solution, but instead skips many intermediate steps that are intuitively seen as probably not useful in order to proceed more rapidly. This step skipping is sometimes referred to as an "intuitive leap." General line or staff managers are likely to have intuitive, preceptive minds; they seek an overview, and thus it is the forest rather than the trees which they observe and evaluate. The information system should be tailored to provide this overview.

Manager B, with a mind that is a combination of systematic and receptive, processes large amounts of detailed data in a systematic manner and prefers using a well-developed analysis method. This type of manager, who may be a systems analyst, engineer, librarian, or accountant, needs an information system that provides voluminous amounts of detailed information. If the information system does not provide the analysis method, manager B must have the high level of problem-solving training necessary to structure the detailed information.

Some managers' minds may possess the combinations of attributes shown by points C and D in Exhibit 1.5. Manager C, for example, combines the systematic mind's preference for a specific approach to, or method of, structuring a problem with the preceptive mind's tendency to deal with relationships. For example, psychologists who specialize in developing or using general approaches to explain, measure, or analyze social relationships between people, as exemplified by Freudian psychology, have this kind of mind.

Managers who work with detailed information and are good at dealing with ill-structured problems are like manager D. Unlike manager A, who uses a minimum amount of data and relies on experience to form judgments and make decisions, manager D bases judgments and decisions on the underlying data rather than on personal experience. Manager D is especially good at dealing with unstructured situations in which there is no unequivocally "right" decision but in which there is a wealth of facts

Information Processing by Four Types of Managers*   EXHIBIT 1.6

Manager A: Intuitive, Preceptive	Manager B: Systematic Receptive	Manager C: Preceptive Systematic	Manager D: Receptive, Intuitive
Analysis method: Uses rules of thumb such as "the candidate must interrelate well" and "the candidate must not have made any serious blunders," thereby eliminating most contenders. Makes judgmental evaluations about the two or three remaining candidates with respect to how close a "fit" they are to the new position's requirements.	Analysis method: Reviews the job description to establish the specific attributes needed in the new position and evaluates the extent to which each candidate possesses these, perhaps by preparing a comparative chart or spreadsheet. Performs detailed comparative analyses of the performance of each candidate in former positions. The decision is based on who emerges from this analysis as "best."	Analysis method: Considers the "big picture" and systematically structures a cohesive framework that includes a careful specification of what attributes the winning candidate should possess; reviews but does not rely on the job description for these attributes. Does not analyze the records of candidates who clearly do not have the attributes. A composite profile of each candidate possessing these attributes serves as the basis for the promotion decision; these attributes, as well as others possessed by the candidates, are subjectively weighted.	Analysis method: Sifts through all available information in an unstructured way and without a clear idea in advance of what information is needed. A conclusion gradually emerges from this detailed analysis that certain of the candidates are clearly preferable to others, and the manager then relies upon past experience with these candidates or with similar situations to determine which of the acceptable candidates is the best fit to the new position.
Information used: Personal experience with the candidates, a few bits of information from the personnel files, and the job description. While information from the formal information system may be decisive, little is needed.	Information used: Complete personnel files for each candidate, the job description, and amplifying details. The formal information system must provide extensive information.	Information used: Needs an information system that provides a few relevant bits of information which can be used to minimize the extent of detailed analysis required and which can serve as a systematic basis for making a decision.	Information used: Full detail of information available is used, but because this information usually is not organized into a structure by manager D and because no specific analysis method is employed, it is not always clear what role the information played in the decision process.

* Each of the four types of managers described above must decide which of several candidates should be promoted to fill a managerial vacancy.

on which to base an opinion. Attorneys are likely to have this type of mind—the problem area in a legal case is often ill-structured, and a legal position must be built upon an analysis of large amounts of factual information about precedent cases.

Managers with different types of minds require different types of information systems, as is illustrated in Exhibit 1.6. It is usually true that many of the information systems at the lower levels of the organization should provide highly structured, carefully formatted, detailed information because the greatest concentration of decision makers with systematic, receptive minds is at the lower levels. Similarly, senior managers are more likely to have intuitive, preceptive minds, and information systems designed for them usually should provide a minimum of detail while facilitating the recognition of relationships among the information elements given.

The fundamentally different thought processes of the systematic, receptive mind and of the intuitive, preceptive mind have direct effects on the design and development of information systems. Individuals whose minds process information and who reach decisions in completely different ways often have difficulty communicating with each other. Most systems analysts and programmers—the persons who design and build the information systems—have systematic, receptive minds, whereas senior managers (and, to a lesser extent, middle managers) are more likely to have intuitive, preceptive minds. Because these two groups of persons think differently, they have trouble comprehending each other's perspective on problems. Lacking a thorough understanding of the information systems needs of senior managers, and not being able to communicate effectively with the managers about these needs analysts and programmers tend to design information systems for senior managers that the analysts and programmers would want if they were senior managers. These information systems provide extensive detail, which most senior managers do not wish to have, and they assume highly systematic analysis methods, which most senior managers do not use. This problem usually is greatest at the highest levels of the organization, although it is still present at the other managerial levels.

Human Information Processing and Thought Patterns

A rudimentary portrayal of information processing by the human mind appears in Exhibit 1.7. As indicated in the exhibit, there are two types of memory—short-term and long-term. Long-term memory consists of a large number—thousands or millions—of interrelated "patterns" of information, each of which contains one or more "impressions." Each impression includes a collection of related elements of information.

A pattern is based on past experiences in a particular area. For example, one pattern may contain impressions based on past experiences in

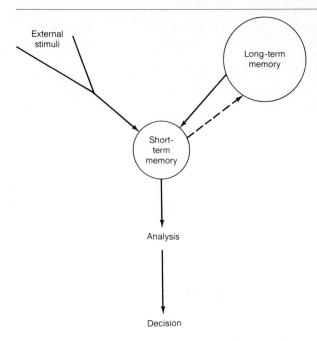

EXHIBIT 1.7
Information processing by the mind.

purchasing automobiles, and another pattern might consist of impressions based on past experiences involving the relative advantages and disadvantages of financing a plant expansion by borrowing rather than by selling capital stock. Impressions usually are composed of a combination of factual information, subjective information, opinions provided by other persons, and inbred biases and prejudices. Racial and sexual prejudices, for example, can profoundly influence a manager's impressions of, and opinions about, the expected productivity of particular employees.

Short-term memory includes very recently acquired elements of data and impressions received from the external environment. These serve as stimuli for long-term memory. These stimuli could be data being read from a production report, data based on observation of machinists at work, data provided orally by the department supervisor, or data from a wide variety of other sources.

A stimulus entering short-term memory triggers a complex associative capability that is unique to each mind; this associative capability recalls to short-term memory patterns from long-term memory that are related to (associated with) the stimulus that entered short-term memory. This recall is selective, incomplete, and capricious. Relevant patterns may not be recalled, irrelevant patterns may be recalled, and important parts of patterns may have been temporarily or permanently forgotten ("memory failure") and thus are not recalled. The external stimuli (the new information received) and the existing patterns are compared and combined in short-term memory, and the combination is then analyzed by the mind.

Then a decision is made, for example, a decision to take an action or a "default decision" to take no action. Thus, decision-making activity is based on both current information (the external stimuli) and past experiences (the patterns recalled to short-term memory).

As these thought processes take place, the patterns in short-term memory are enriched; they may be revised or extended on the basis of new information added by the external stimuli and the mind's analysis of the current situation. A new, enriched pattern is the result, and this is returned to long-term memory to await a subsequent recall. In the interim, portions of the patterns may be forgotten or scrambled, with the result that a subsequent recall may be incomplete or inaccurate.

Short-term memory has a limited capacity and can easily be overloaded by the input of too many new data items. The nature of the data items is critical to managerial decision making. For example, large quantities of "facts" as external stimuli, such as financial statement figures, might consume all the short-term memory capacity and be analyzed in isolation from the patterns in long-term memory; this would be lean fare for decision making. Alternatively, several patterns, each a "data item" that synthesizes several impressions, could be processed simultaneously along with a fewer number of external stimuli facts; this would provide a much richer basis for decision making by drawing extensively on the past experiences of the manager. This suggests that a decision maker should be provided relatively few external stimuli and that these stimuli should be selected partly for their ability to evoke the manager's long-term memory patterns so that past experiences embodied in the patterns can be a major influence in the decision making of the manager.

At present there are no systems design techniques that can deal specifically with ensuring that the stimuli provided will evoke the appropriate long-term memory patterns. The best assurance that a system will have this ability appears to be to have it designed by persons whose minds process data in a manner similar to the way in which the managers who will use the information system process data or to have it designed by the user-managers themselves. Usually, however, this is an unrealistic expectation, although it is realistic to expect managers to articulate their information needs to systems designers. A cardinal rule of systems design is that user-managers must be deeply involved in the design process. A system designed without the involvement of user-managers probably will not provide the external stimuli required and therefore is unlikely to be successful.

Another consideration is that information systems should be designed as much as possible to compensate for managers' inability to fully and accurately recall patterns from long-term memory. Many of the patterns that are particularly important are those which are composed in part of information previously provided by the information system. While the information system should not routinely provide information already pro-

Forms of Information Preferences of Selected Types of Managers   EXHIBIT 1.8

Managerial Group	Information Format Preferred
Accountants	Financial tabulations and financial statements
Financial managers	Charts and financial tabulations
Engineers	Graphs
General managers	Narrative descriptions
Attorneys	Narrative briefs in case form
Management scientists	Mathematical problem formulations and models

vided in the past, it should be structured so that this information is readily available to managers who need it to "refresh" their memories.

The way in which external stimuli are presented to a manager can greatly affect how efficiently the manager processes information. Experiments have established that financial information presented in graphic form is more readily assimilated and understood by most managers than the same information presented in the form of financial statements. Computer graphics is the reporting of computerized information in the form of graphs, and it is an aspect of information systems that is now receiving extensive attention.

For some managers, information presented in narrative form is also more readily understood than information presented in the form of financial statements. Exhibit 1.8 shows the forms of information that have been traditionally preferred by managers with different educational backgrounds and experience. Systems designers should be sensitive to the preferences of the managers for whom they are designing a system.

The impressions that constitute patterns in long-term memory are, as has been noted, subjective. An impression entering as an external stimulus is interpreted on the basis of existing patterns; thus several managers' perceptions of the same situation can vary widely, depending on their backgrounds and biases. For example, a salesperson may perceive that achieving 95 percent of the sales goal is good ("I nearly reached the goal!"), whereas the sales supervisor may perceive this same achievement as inadequate ("Jane didn't reach the sales goal assigned"). To avoid different interpretations of the same facts, the information system should be designed, where feasible, to reduce ambiguity about the information presented. In the example above, for instance, the information system should have made it clear that the supervisor's interpretation was that less than 100 percent of sales goal was unsatisfactory performance.

CHARACTERISTICS OF MANAGERS

Managers have personal characteristics that influence their attitudes toward information systems, their information needs, and the ways in which they interact with systems. While reading the discussion which follows, the student should keep in mind that although few, if any, managers conform fully to the mold of the "typical" manager, nevertheless some general statements can be made.

Managers tend to avoid relying on anything they do not understand, and most managers do not understand computer systems and therefore distrust them. For similar reasons, managers also distrust computerized corporate models offered to them as decision aids. Accordingly, computer systems and models may not be utilized fully by managers, who may instead gather and process their own information from their own sources. Managers should be encouraged to understand their organization's computer systems because, if they do acquire this understanding, they will be more willing to use those systems.

To facilitate this managerial understanding, information systems should be as simple as possible. Simple systems are much less intimidating to both clerical and managerial personnel. Computer models, for example, preferably should be small so that they can be more easily understood, and they also should process information in ways that the manager can readily understand.

Another characterisitc of managers is that most of them are "people-oriented." Managers prefer to interact with people rather than with machines, and they accomplish their tasks through other people. This characteristic is pervasive and helps explain why many managers encourage good information systems for their technical and clerical personnel but are not themselves extensive direct users of formal information systems.

An overriding concern of managers is that they use their time efficiently. Managers avoid tasks that they can delegate unless by doing the task they can acquire useful insights. For example, managers are disinclined to use a computer or a terminal directly or to develop a computer program personally. Managers are especially unlikely to undertake these tasks if doing so would compel them first to devote significant time to learning about the computer or terminal or to learning how to program. Younger managers often have the advantage of having had experience with computers when they were students, and they are more often inclined to interact directly with computer systems.

In trying to use their time efficiently, managers often prioritize and dynamically reschedule their activities so that they are always working on the highest-priority task. Keeping the work of others flowing smoothly is a high managerial priority; thus when a subordinate requires a few minutes of a manager's time, the manager's schedule is usually reorganized to provide it. Also, as a task becomes more critical because of an approaching deadline or a new perception of its importance, managers put aside uncompleted tasks to take up the priority one. A consequence of this continuous task reprioritization is that managers have many tasks in process stimultaneously, some of which they will not work on for days or weeks, although only a small effort is required for completion. Meanwhile, other, higher-priority tasks have been started and completed. One implication of this for information systems is that managers prefer to have needed information continuously available because they often cannot predict when they will be working on a particular task. However, this is frustrating to systems personnel, who are asked to satisfy a manager's demand for information immediately and then observe that the information remains unused for several days.

Systems personnel are also frustrated when they attempt to get a manager to assist in systems analysis and design. Managers too often agree to assist and make an initial effort, only to turn to new matters that have just become high-priority tasks.

Another related characteristic of managers is their tendency to become caught up in the tempo of their work activities. Partly because they are people-oriented, partly because of their typical system of prioritization, and partly because they are always curious about what the next telephone call or knock on the door will bring, managers will usually interrupt their work activities to provide time to another manager. A manager's work structure, then, depends greatly upon how many persons wish to talk to that manager; usually, the higher the manager's position in the organization, the more people there are who want to talk to that manager, and the less time is available for each. Lower-level managers usually spend several minutes with each of a few persons during a day and still have time for tasks that do not involve personal interaction, but senior managers are likely to talk with a great many persons very briefly and to spend most of their remaining hours in formal meetings. Senior managers have little time left for independent managerial analysis.

Because managers' workdays tend to be so fragmented, managers in general, and senior managers in particular, can devote only short periods of time to systems analysts. The analysts, on the other hand, prefer to reserve large blocks of time for a particular task, such as talking to a manager about information system needs, so a natural conflict results.

A characteristic that most managers have in common is that they do not like unpleasant surprises; most managers also think that "good" surprises that could have been anticipated are also unpleasant. Managers prefer the comfortable feeling that they are in control of the organization's activities and that the information system will forewarn them of both unfavorable and favorable situations. For example, a severe cash shortage that gradually develops can cause the organization (and the manager) acute embarrassment and necessitate hasty and expensive arrangements to cover it. Conversely, an unanticipated large cash excess also causes embarrassment and consternation because the manager was not able to prepare a plan in advance to achieve a maximum yield from the investment of the excess cash.

One unpleasant surprise is belatedly seeing a developing trend, such as a deteriorating financial position that was not observed until the financial statements were completed well after the end of the period. Managers want to monitor trends as they develop.

The information system plays the primary role in identifying trends and eliminating surprises. This is accomplished through good systems design and the incorporation of a number of technical features into the information system. Managers must communicate this "no-surprise" philosophy to systems personnel and must follow up with participation in the design of the information system to ensure that a no-surprise system emerges.

A final characteristic of managers relates to their roles as leaders of the organization. Within the part of the organization that they manage, they are looked to for effective leadership by clerical personnel and by other managers who report to them. Any action that would erode their leadership ability is naturally avoided because it is harmful to both the organization and their own careers. Since "losing face" in front of their employees, their peers, or more senior managers damages their leadership position, managers at all levels attempt to keep up appearances by avoiding situations in which they might be embarrassed.

Computer information systems are intuitively viewed by most managers as infinitely complex and difficult to understand. Managers prefer to avoid working closely with technical persons such as systems analysts and designers because they know that their ignorance about computer systems will be exposed, causing them embarrassment. This concern about maintaining their leadership image is one reason why many managers do not participate in the development of their organization's information systems.

The characteristics of managers that affect information systems are summarized in Exhibit 1.9. Several of these characteristics are powerful influences working against the manager's development and use of information systems. These characteristics of managers have a great deal to do with why the managerial information systems of even many of the largest organizations are underdeveloped.

THE MANAGER AS PART OF THE INFORMATION SYSTEM

The mind of a manager has attributes that are similar in certain respects to those of a computer information system. A manager's mind receives data from a variety of sources, processes and stores this as information, and then often communicates the information to other managers; these characteristics of the human mind are shared by computer systems. Computer systems and managers jointly process, store, and communicate the organization's information, and for this reason managers are viewed here as integral parts of their organization's information systems.

The human mind differs in certain respects from other types of information systems, however. One of its most valuable characteristics is its

Managerial Characteristics and the Information System   EXHIBIT 1.9

Managerial Characteristic	Impact on the Information System
1. Managers will not rely on a system they do not understand.	The system must be simple and understandable.
2. Managers are people-oriented.	If given their choice, managers prefer to receive information from people rather than from information systems.
3. Managers are concerned with efficient use of their time.	Managers are disinclined to interact directly with the information system.
4. Managers prioritize and re-prioritize.	Managers need information for a problem to be continuously available so that they can use it when they have time to address the problem. Managers who initially agree to become involved in designing a system often reorder their priorities, to the frustration of systems personnel.
5. Managers' work is fragmented.	Systems analysts are frustrated by the small amounts of time devoted to them by managers.
6. Managers dislike surprises.	The information system must be designed to prevent surprises by providing information about trends and key events.
7. As leaders, managers are unwilling to display their ignorance.	Managers often avoid all but the most superficial discussions of systems with systems personnel.

ability to synthesize large amounts of information. This characteristic comes into play, for example, when a student writes an answer to an essay question on an exam. The student often utilizes information from a variety of sources, including a textbook, lectures, other courses taken in the past, and even personal experiences. All this information is quickly retrieved from memory, albeit with less than total recall, and is synthesized into a narrative essay answer. This synthesis of information by the mind is evidenced by the way new information is incorporated into a manager's experience and assists the manager in making judgments and estimates about risk or the probable outcome of a decision.

Another attribute of the human mind is that it can make more complex associations than a computer can. A manager's mind can often perceive more possible implications of information received than can be placed in a computer program. For example, a manager's mind might see the relationship of a report of an inventory shortage of a raw material to recent demand for that product and to the recent delivery service of vendors of the material. The manager might then judge that the finished goods inventory will be depleted and that sales will be lost before the needed raw materials can be secured. The human mind can make such inferences instantly, in a variety of circumstances, whereas even a sophisticated computer system is likely to be programmed for only a limited number of the most probable circumstances.

Another important attribute of a manager's mind is selective communication of information based on extremely complex thought processes. For example, by talking briefly with another manager, a manager usually can rapidly decipher what information the other manager is seeking, not only from what the other manager says, but also from voice inflections, the urgency or casualness of speech, facial expressions, and a variety of other interpersonal "cues." The manager can then respond efficiently without providing unsought information. The mind is much more capable of this selective communication than a computer system is.

The preceding discussion shows that managers, as a part of an information system, reduce the complexity and increase the efficiency of the entire information system. For the most part, the computer system provides information that is processed in simple, straightforward ways and reported in an established format, all according to detailed computer programs that have only a rudimentary ability to react to unusual conditions. The human mind, on the other hand, instantly synthesizes information in very complex ways in response to an infinite variety of conditions; if the mind did not have this capability, much more elaborate computer systems would be needed. Further, the mind associates information received with past experience patterns in ways that are far too complicated for computer systems, and it also makes inferences on the basis of these associations. The mind also selectively receives and selectively communicates information. No computer system comes even close to being able to perform these complex tasks, which the mind can do quickly and efficiently.

However, managers' minds have drawbacks; as has been noted, managers' feelings, beliefs, and biases influence the way information is perceived and processed, and no two minds process information in exactly the same way; thus, given the same facts about a situation, two managers may reach completely different conclusions. Managers with different backgrounds may also interpret the same information differently. Further, human information processing is notoriously error-prone, compared with computer information processing. Managers forget or overlook relevant information and make frequent mechanical errors in their calculations.

Another limitation of the human mind as compared with a computer information system is evidenced when extensive, detailed information is transmitted informally between managers. Even though a manager's mind can contain a voluminous amount of information, the communications process rapidly breaks down because a manager cannot absorb details as rapidly as another manager can transmit them. Whereas a computer print-out can be retained and referred to as necessary to refresh a manager's memory, details provided orally by another manager usually cannot be recalled completely—they are likely to be forgotten or remembered incorrectly.

Mindful of these shortcomings of human information processing, managers like to establish the reliability of information received from another manager by double-checking it with related information from another source. If the information from the second source differs from that from the original source, further information may be sought to validate or invalidate the information from both sources. Particular managers establish "track records" of being reliable or unreliable sources of information, and accordingly they are consulted more often or less often.

Students of information systems should understand the part that managers play in information systems, both in reducing the complexity of the systems and in introducing biases and errors into them. Information systems depend upon the participation of managers as integral parts of the systems, but systems must be designed to protect against managers' biases and errors.

PROBLEM SOLVING BY MANAGERS

Most administrative processes involve several activities. These usually include problem and or opportunity identification, information search, choosing from among alternatives, and decision making. With clerical processes such as transactions processing, these activities are similar but may be fully automated: the problem is self-defined (e.g., to process transactions, update records, and prepare documents such as checks and invoices), and the information needed is completely specified and readily available. For the managerial processes, however, each step of problem solving requires the explicit attention of managers.

Problem and Opportunity Identification

Certain managerial problems may be difficult to identify. Even in small organizations, problems may not be known to exist until they threaten the entire organization. The information systems should be designed as "early warning systems" that provide information that clearly indicates the nature and severity of managerial problems. For example, the information systems should provide advance warning of a prospective inventory shortage so that inventory can be ordered in time to avert the shortage. This is consistent with the no-surprise approach to information systems.

Opportunity identification is usually more difficult. For example, it is difficult to be aware of revenue lost because of a missed sales opportunity if the revenue was not expected in the first place. The information system can spotlight opportunities; for example, it can highlight the ways in which costs vary as production procedures change and thus can point the way toward a least-cost organization of production activities.

The information system can also play a major role in helping the organization identify external opportunities. An "intelligence information system" can be designed to systematically monitor the environment and report significant changes that may provide opportunities to the organization. An intelligence system is equally important for detecting how the organization might be harmed by changes in its environment.

Information Search

After a problem has been identified, a manager usually must search for additional information that will be useful in analyzing it. Voluminous amounts of information may be readily at hand in the computer files, but additional, noncomputerized information also is usually required. The search time may be significant in terms of both the amount of the manager's time that is devoted to the search and the usually much greater amount of time that elapses before the information is gathered.

For some problems, the information search time may include several worker-months of writing programs to retrieve the needed data from the computer files. Within the last decade, two major technological developments have accelerated this activity. One is data base technology, which involves specialized data file designs and a new approach to developing applications programs, and the other is "productivity programming languages," which permit data retrieval programs to be written more rapidly.

The information sought can be factual or nonfactual. Where there is general agreement about its validity, information is factual. Nonfactual information includes estimates based on related facts and is usually considered the best form of information in the absence of facts. For example, an estimate of the year's sales based on actual sales for the first 11 months is likely to be accepted as fairly reliable by an organization's managers.

Estimates, which may be about the present, the past, or the future, are not usually provided directly by formal information systems but instead are formulated directly by managers and are based on all relevant information received by them from the formal information system and from other sources, including other persons whose opinions are unsupported. Future inflation rates; future costs; future interest rates; competitors' past, present, and future profits; costs and revenues; and the quantity of a new product that can be sold at a given price are often estimated. Forecasts are one form of estimates that involve careful and usually formal analyses of related facts. Increasingly, forecasts are provided by the formal information system.

Managers may expend considerable effort to find facts or make estimates. Designing the information system so that it will reduce the manager's information search effort is important. Studies indicate that if the information system makes the information more readily available, the manager spends more time on problem analysis.

Choosing from among Alternatives

Choosing from among proposed alternative problem solutions involves synthesizing and analyzing data from all sources to perform costs/benefits analysis. Certain aspects of managerial problem analysis can be computerized by utilizing preprogrammed algorithms and models. For example, rates of return, discounted present-value analyses, and asset depreciation schedules for the proposed alternatives can be routinely calculated and reported in comparative form by computer programs. Nevertheless, the critical element in managerial analysis is not the computer-performed calculations and comparisons, but rather the managerial judgment required for knowing which analytic methods should be applied and for interpreting the results. Computerizing a portion of the analysis permits the manager to focus more carefully on interpretation.

Decision Making

Decision making, the climax of the managerial problem-solving process, is dependent almost entirely on the manager's judgment. After the analysis has been completed, the role of the computer in making managerial decisions is usually nil. Frequently, however, the computer plays a major follow-up function by providing information that shows the consequences of the decisions, which often permits judging whether particular past decisions were good ones.

SUMMARY

An organization's information systems are complex and diverse, and the development of these systems is challenging and difficult. The organization's information systems must provide information about its various environments to its managers, and the more dynamic these environments are, the more critical this information becomes. Often, however, systems that gather information about the external environment are not as well developed as they should be.

Organizations are hierarchical, and this hierarchy provides the basic framework for information systems. Information is summarized on the basis of functions and levels within this hierarchy; thus each organizational level of each functional area usually has its own set of reports. The need for extensive cross-functional information flows and the need for information for general management activities must also be accommodated.

Changes in the organization structure require that information systems be changed so that they will continue to parallel the structure of the organization. Information systems must be tailored to managers' spans of control, and the quality of the information system is one determinant of how large a span of control can be.

The basic structure of the information system is influenced by the general type of management of the organization, that is, whether it is centralized management, decentralized management, or coordinative management. Each type of management requires a distinctly different organization of information systems. If the organization, or a part of it, has authority relationships in the form of a matrix, overlapping information systems are needed to serve each functional area a well as to serve each product line.

Management style is the personalized aspect of management, including such considerations as how managers spend their time and how they interact with other personnel. The qualities of the human mind are a major influence on management style; as a group, managers have minds with different qualities from those of systems analysts, and this difference explains in part why analysts often have difficulty designing systems that are acceptable to managers.

Managers' thought and analysis processes are a part of their management style. Thought patterns in long-term memory that reflect past experiences are retrieved and then modified by external stimuli entering short-term memory. The modified thought patterns are the information on which managers base decisions. The information system must be designed to take account of the shortcomings of managers' thought processes.

Most managers share certain personal characteristics. They are reluctant to rely on information systems they do not understand, they prefer to receive information from people than from computers, and they are concerned with their own efficiency. Managers' time is fragmented, they dislike surprises, and as leaders they try to avoid being embarrassed by their ignorance about information systems. Each of these characteristics affects the design or operation of the organization's information system.

KEY TERMS

intelligence information system: an information system oriented toward gathering and processing external information primarily for long-range planning purposes.

management style: the "personalized" aspects of a manager's actions with respect to the myriad of tasks that constitute the management processes.

management processes: the usually well-defined and prescribed sets of procedures or steps that are used to accomplish management tasks; they are often performed sequentially and are usually undertaken by multiple managers. Budgeting is an example of a management process.

intuitive mind: a mind that is likely to use trial and error to test various solutions.

systematic mind: a mind that is inclined to deal with a problem by structuring it in terms of some method or approach which, if followed through, leads to an acceptable solution.

preceptive mind: a mind which tends to focus on the relationships between data elements in the gathering and processing of information and which attempts to grasp the "big picture."

receptive mind: a mind that tends to become deeply immersed in the details of data and to build solutions on the basis of massive use of detailed information.

short-term memory: memory consisting primarily of very recently acquired impressions, along with memory patterns retrieved from long-term memory.

long-term memory: the permanent storage location in the mind for patterns of information developed from past experiences.

REFERENCES

McKenney, James L., and Peter G. W. Keen, "How Managers' Minds Work," *Harvard Business Review,* May–June 1974, p. 79.

Mintzberg, Henry, "The Manager's Job: Folklore or Fact?" *Harvard Business Review,* July–August 1975, p. 49.

Radford, K. J., *Information Systems for Strategic Decisions,* Reston, VA: Reston Publishing Company, 1978.

REVIEW QUESTIONS

1. Why does a more dynamic environment mean that an organization should have a more sophisticated information system?

2. What factors indicate that the environments of most organizations are more dynamic now than they have been in past decades?

3. What is the purpose of hierarchy in an organization? Why do large organizations usually have more levels in their hierarchy than small organizations?

4. How does hierarchy affect the information system?

5. What is meant by "filtering" of information at a level in the hierarchy? Is filtering good or bad?

6. How does the information system influence the span of control?

7. What is information summarization?

8. What are the characteristics of a decentralized organization's information system?

9. Why can a managerially centralized organization be managed more effectively now than a similar organization could be 30 years ago?

10. Why is the information system of a highly coordinative organization more complex than that of a decentralized organization?

11. What cross-functional information flows would you expect to find between marketing and production? Between personnel and payroll? Between engineering and production? Between personnel and production?

12. What is management style?

13. What kind of information system will probably be best for a manager who has a receptive, intuitive mind?

14. Referring to Exhibit 1.5, do you believe that manager B can or will change management style so that in 20 years that manager might have a style like that of manager A? Why or why not?

15. Discuss the characteristics of the person at point D in Exhibit 1.5. Is this person likely to be a business manager?

16. Why are senior managers in large organizations likely to have preceptive, intuitive management styles?

17. Why might a manager with a degree in law who has a position as a low-level manager in an organization be frustrated with the information received from the information system?

18. How are thought patterns developed in the mind?

19. What implications do thought-pattern development processes have for information systems development?

20. What characteristics do many managers possess that tend to inhibit the development of information systems?

21. Distinguish between the planning and control processes of an organization.

22. How do short-term memory and long-term memory differ?

23. Summarize the insights provided in the chapter about the development of information systems.

CASE 1

San Francisco—While the shortage of trained data processing professionals multiplies, universities continue to give students the wrong kind of data processing training, Al Strong, president and founder of Commercial Programming Systems Inc., said here recently.

"Almost every student they graduate comes to us ready to begin work on scientific applications— moon shots, research in the physical sciences— when what we need are business applications programmers," Strong said at a symposium on "Finding Solutions to the EDP Personnel Shortage."

"While data processing for the scientific community has been steadily growing in importance since the 1950s, it has little effect on the EDP personnel shortage as it is today. It is the business applications of the computer—and the development of computers most businesses could afford— that are a hundred times more significant," he said.

"For want of a better solution, our biggest DP users hire these people anyway and promptly send them back to school for retraining in business principles as well as business programming," he said, adding that they finally become useful in six months to two years after being hired. . . .

Source: Software News, June 1982.

Case Question

Try to obtain information about the need in your locality for busines school graduates who have studied information systems to work as programmers, systems analysts, and office automation experts, as well as in other information systems positions. How does this need compare with the need for business school graduates with other backgrounds, and how do starting salaries compare? (Possible sources of information include the chamber of commerce, state employment offices, and the classified advertisement sections of local newspapers.)

CASE 2

Court Sentences Information System to Oblivion

by Tim Scannell, CW Staff

Grand Rapids, Mich.—After nearly seven years of planning and expenditures of more than $400,000, the Grand Rapids District Court here has decided to abandon its computer-based court information system.

Plagued by delays, operational deficiencies and bureaucratic disinterest, the Comprehensive Lower Court Information System (Colocis)—which never actually came out of the testing phase—will be permanently tabled in favor of the court's present manual system.

"We had so many [administrative] people we had to deal with, so many other people that controlled the destiny of that effort, that is was doomed to fail," according to James Farrar, a former court administrator here and now a senior staff attorney with the National Center for State Courts in St. Paul, Minn.

Developed on the city's Burroughs Corp. 3500 mainframe, Colocis was eventually supposed to keep track of parking and traffic fines, generate court date notices and generally speed up the whole traffic court process. However, although the system was fully program-tested, had a trained staff and was prepared to run parallel to the city's manual operation, the multi-thousand-dollar system never got off the ground, Farrar said.

In fact, the most the controversial system ever did was prepare standard operational reports for the court's traffic bureau.

System Collapse

While opinions vary on why the system collapsed, most sources agree that plans for the court computer began to fall apart midway through the project.

For example, just as the project was building up speed, the city temporarily lost interest when the State Court Administrator's office in Detroit announced it was expanding its data center and would be offering services to limited jurisdiction courts like the one in Grand Rapids. This action had a "substantial impact on the momentum of the project" and delayed things by about six months, Farrar claimed.

Friction between the city and the court eventually resulted in a legal suit, initiated by the court, contesting the city's sudden distinterest in Colocis. The suit also protested the city's desire to fire Colocis' only programmer/analyst, Howard Friar, because he did not meet certain residency requirements, Farrar noted.

Although the court subsequently won the support portion of the suit, the city dismissed Friar because of the residency question.

"Once [Friar] was gone, the system started going downhill," Josef Sopper, who replaced Farrar as court administrator, said.

Like Farrar, Sopper admitted that Colocis failed because there were too many bureaucratic hands in the pot and no clear administrative control of system development.

When Colocis was first proposed, computer-based criminal justice systems, which were fairly new at the time, adhered to the current state of the art—an interrelated-type architecture. By comparison, today's systems are modular and made up of related but independently operating parts.

(Early in the game, Grand Rapids' court officials also considered installing the computerized prosecutor's management information system [Promis], but decided against it because the system is too broad-based for a smaller court's judicial needs.)

Basically, the Colocis interrelated architecture had a lot to do with its demise. When parts of the court system began to fail, the whole system collapsed like so many dominoes, court administrator Sopper explained: "An error in one place screwed up all of the [system's] reactions on down the line."

In addition, when the court was developing and testing Colocis on the city's Burroughs Corp. 3500 mainframe, it found that the computer and the city's DP staff could never keep up with the demands of the batch-oriented judicial system, Farrar said. In fact, even though the city was billing the court about $130,000 annually for its computer time, the court was using computer time worth only a fraction of that amount.

One reason for this billing inconsistency was that while the city was using the computer to process necessary water, tax and other bills, it was also trying to develop a fairly extensive police information system, Farrar stated. All of the city's background computer work reportedly limited the time available to the court to develop Colocis.

Source: Computerworld, Aug. 11, 1980, p. 17.

Case Questions

1. What lessons can be learned from this failure?

2. Colocis was started in about 1974; do you think that such a failure could occur in the case of a system started today? Why or why not?

Chapter 2

THE INFORMATION NEEDS AND SOURCES OF MANAGERS

PAYOFF THOUGHT

The information systems required for the lowest level of an organization differ dramatically from those needed for other levels. For the top levels, summarized information about lower-level operations is only a part of the information needed; a very important type of information at the top levels relates to planning, and a high proportion of this comes from other sources. Middle management has a great need for summarized information about operations for management control purposes as well as planning-related information similar to that utilized by top-management levels; to a great extent, middle management's information systems should integrate information from both the operations-level and the top-management-level information systems.

CHAPTER OBJECTIVES

1. To show how the information needs of top-, middle-, and lower-level managers, as well as those of technical and professional personnel, spring from the activities performed and types of decisions made at each level

2. To examine the sources of the information needed at each level

3. To show how the needs for and sources of information relate to the overall design of an organization's information system

INTRODUCTION

The nature of the information systems required by an organization depends primarily on the kinds of activities performed and the types of decisions made by the information users, who may be managers, technical and professional specialists, or clerical or operations personnel. The information needs of managers tend to vary with the level of the organization because the nature of managerial activities tends to differ at different levels. As might be expected, the different types of information required at each level tend to come from different sources.

ACTIVITIES OF THE ORGANIZATION

Exhibit 2.1 portrays the typical organization. The personnel shown at the lowest level of the exhibit are of two general types: operations personnel, whose jobs involve primary activities related to providing a product or service, and clerical personnel, who process transactions and participate clerically in the administrative tasks of the organization. Operating personnel include machine operators, inventory clerks, warehouse workers, salespersons, repairers, bookkeepers, secretaries, typists, and data processing input-output clerks, to name but a few. Most of the personnel at the operating level have minimal or no supervisory or managerial responsibilities and are involved only with the operations information systems of the organization.

Many operations personnel provide input to the computer system or process or analyze individual transactions in the course of their work, but their tasks generally do not involve analysis of information output. Normally, persons in operations or clerical activities are involved with the information systems in only a limited way; for example, they may originate only a few types of transactions, which are then processed by the information system.

At the next level—the first of the managerial levels—the predominant activity in most organizations is supervision of operation personnel. This requires extensive interaction with these personnel about operations or for the purpose of resolving personnel problems. Supervisory personnel are less likely to process transactions as input to the information systems and are more likely to utilize summary output from the systems. Supervisory personnel may become deeply involved with systems design, sometimes even to the extent of being temporarily reassigned to a systems development project team; for example, an accounts receivable supervisor may be assigned to a team that is designing an accounts receivable information system.

The middle managerial level in Exhibit 2.1 involves two general types of activities, as shown. The technical and professional activities are conducted by specialists who work either independently or as part of a group

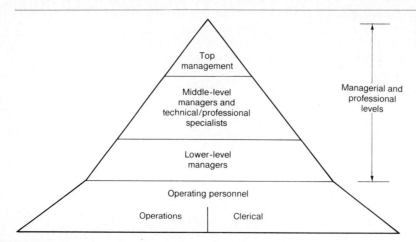

EXHIBIT 2.1
The typical
organization.

of similarly specialized professionals. The duties of these specialists are not managerial in nature; the managing they do, if any, seldom extends beyond supervision of a few clerical or quasi-professional staff members. Showing these specialists at the middle-management level is arbitrary and has been done only because their salaries are typically comparable to those of middle-level managers. In fact, these specialist groups do not fit into any particular "level," although most frequently they are managed by an upper-middle-level manager. Examples of these specialists are engineers, research scientists, accountants, systems analysts, lawyers, actuaries, market analysts, buyers, staff planners, product designers, and advertising and sales promotion personnel.

In many organizations, the tasks performed by one or more groups of these technical and professional specialists are the most critical tasks of the organization. Systems designers must give a great deal of attention to the information systems that support these tasks.

The information systems needs of technical and professional specialists depend upon the nature of their specialization. The tasks of certain research scientists, for instance, require little support in the way of a formal information system, while the tasks of other research scientists require extensive computer models to process data and provide research results.

Two generalizations about the information systems needs of technical and professional specialists can be made. First, they usually require raw, unsummarized data because their specialties generally involve detailed analyses; for instance, it is of little value for a corporate attorney to be told that 67 percent of all legal cases dealing with sex discrimination are settled in favor of the litigant, because the attorney must review the details of cases similar to those facing the corporation, even to the point of analyzing the phrasing of each opinion.

Second, the information systems needed by technical and professional personnel tend to depend upon whether their activity involves (1) rapid, time-critical, and often high-pressure decision making based upon specialized knowledge and professional judgment; (2) careful, methodical, or reflective analysis; or (3) creative activity. The information system for specialists whose duties fall into the first category is likely to provide a few critical elements of information that are rapidly absorbed and mentally analyzed. Stock brokerage and futures trading firms' specialists usually require this kind of information.

Usually at the other extreme are information systems for the second category of specialists. For instance, drug companies' research scientists conduct carefully controlled experiments that require careful and methodical analysis of massive amounts of detailed data, such as data from previous related experiments that have been completed.

The information systems required by specialists involved in creative activity usually must provide information that helps establish a general background or framework that inspires new ideas. This information—for example, information about the marketplace or information about competitors' products—is likely to come from outside the organization. Product designers, for instance, review current fashions in a variety of products that are unrelated to their firm's products, and they also study the designs of competitors' products. An extensive formal information system based on data from within the organization may do little to assist this type of specialist.

The information systems of specialists can be complex and interesting. However, the subsequent discussion will relate to managers' rather than specialists' information needs.

MANAGERIAL ACTIVITIES

Planning

Exhibit 2.2 shows the general types of activities performed by each level of management. The diagonal line indicates the approximate emphasis that each level of management places on each activity. It can be seen, for example, that strategic and long-range planning is assigned primarily to top management, although even lower-level management does have a modest involvement with this activity.

Planning activities are intended to establish a plan that will enable the organization to maneuver itself toward a desired future position; this future position may be defined in terms of market position, in terms of earnings, and in other ways.

The organization's first step is to assess its present status; this step should include an evaluation of the resources available to the organization and of the environment as it affects the organization. The primary source of information about the organization's present status is its own operations. One important source is summarized transactions information, in-

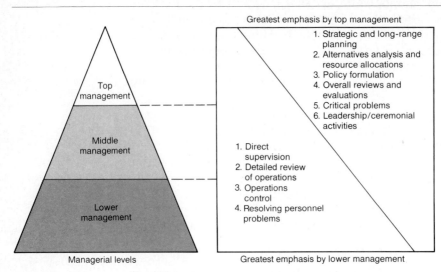

Greatest emphasis by top management

Top management

Middle management

Lower management

Managerial levels

1. Strategic and long-range planning
2. Alternatives analysis and resource allocations
3. Policy formulation
4. Overall reviews and evaluations
5. Critical problems
6. Leadership/ceremonial activities

1. Direct supervision
2. Detailed review of operations
3. Operations control
4. Resolving personnel problems

Greatest emphasis by lower management

Activities at each managerial level

EXHIBIT 2.2
General types of managerial activities performed at each level of the organization.

cluding financial statements. Information about the status of the organization's environment may be received informally by its managers or may be provided by a formal information system that is organized to gather this information. The organization's customers and vendors can also provide important planning information.

The present status of the organization becomes the context for further planning activities. As a part of these activities, an organization establishes specific goals that indicate desired levels and types of achievement. Goals are usually based on a reasonable assessment of what is possible within the long-range planning period, given the current status of the organization and its environment. One task of the information system is to monitor and report progress toward what may be thousands of individual goals of organization units at different levels and geographic locations within the organization; for each goal, the information system must report both the goal and the actual performance, as well as deviations from expectations (variances).

Strategies are then established to achieve the organization's goals. Decisions about strategies, or "strategic decisions," are decisions that determine the actions that will be taken to maneuver the organization in particular directions to achieve the position desired in the long-term future. Examples of strategic decisions, sometimes also called "action strategies," are decisions concerning whether and how to diversify, whether to add related product lines, and whether to seek financing through stock issue or borrowing.

There are many strategies that might achieve a goal, and often several strategies are simultaneously followed to achieve a particular goal. For example, a sales revenue increase of 50 percent for product C might be achieved by (1) hiring 100 more salespersons, (2) improving product quality (3) reducing price by 10 percent to stimulate demand, (4) improving the training of salespersons, (5) advertising, or (6) using some combination of these or other ways.

Two major types of planning activities usually take place. The first is long-range planning, which establishes a multiyear plan, typically for 5 years. The second is short-range planning, often referred to as "profit planning," which is similar to long-range planning and is done within the framework of the long-range plan.

Information systems for planning are difficult to design and implement. One reason for this is that information about the organization's operations is seldom in the form needed for planning—it must be recast and reprocessed. Planning concerns the future; therefore, the organization's information about its past activities is useful for planning only to the extent that it is relevant to the future, and it is relevant only insofar as it can be used to predict the future. Accordingly, the primary use of the organization's information about operations is for forecasting, but to be useful for forecasting, the information usually must be reorganized and adjusted.

Another reason why information systems for planning are difficult to design and implement is that much of the information required is about the external environment and does not originate within the organization. Systems analysts seldom have an extensive understanding of the nature of the systems required to gather information about the external environment.

Overall Reviews and Evaluations (Management Control)

Management control regulates the organization to ensure that activities remain consistent with the goals established in its plans. Management control relates directly to the organization's goals and strategies, allocating resources to the strategies and subsequently assessing the strategies' effectiveness and efficiency in achieving the goals. Management control is a major responsibility of both top and middle management, as indicated in Exhibit 2.2.

Management control depends to a great extent on highly summarized reports provided by the information system; these reports compare operating results with the goals stated in the long- and short-range plans. Managers analyze these reports to determine variances from plans and the reasons for these variances.

Some of the information required for management control must come from outside the organization; for example, overall productivity of operations should be compared with competitors' productivity or with industry averages. If formal information systems are used for gathering this external information, these must be especially designed for this purpose. Even some of the information needed from inside the organization must be provided by specialized information systems that are largely independent of transactions processing systems or by special reports that process routinely acquired data in a nonroutine manner. For example, monitoring the effectiveness of employee training programs is an important ingredient of management control, but the transactions processing systems gather little data that sheds light on this activity.

Critical-Problem Analysis

Another general management activity is "crisis management" of what are called "critical problems" in Exhibit 2.2. Top- and middle-level managers devote a great deal of their time to these critical problems. Examples are customer concerns about a new product's design or safety, decreasing effectiveness of an R&D activity, a precipitous and serious decline in worker productivity, or a precipitous decline in consumer demand for particular products. Because these problems are unexpected, it would be only by a fortunate chance that the organization's information systems could quickly provide complete, fully relevant information.

Special problems must be analyzed in a nonroutine manner, and information bearing on these problems must be specially developed. Often, much or most of the information required for a special problem exists within the organization, but is scattered among the many data files of several different information systems; the required information must first be identified, then located and retrieved, and finally restructured through processing to a suitable form, all of which may be a massive task in an organization with hundreds or even thousands of data files that must be searched to find the required information.

Gathering information needed for special problems can be facilitated by an information system with a structure that allows rapid identification and retrieval of information from all the organization's data files. Achieving this structure is a great challenge; data base technology can provide the required information systems structure.

Leadership and Ceremonial Activities

Senior managers spend a great deal of time carrying out leadership and ceremonial activities. These include social activities both within and outside the organization, speechmaking, and civic activities. For many of these an information system can be of little value, and for others routine reports will provide the needed information.

Direct Supervision

The first activity among those dominated by lower-level managers, shown on the left of the diagonal line at the right of Exhibit 2.2, is that of direct supervision. This activity does not utilize the information system directly because it consists of personal observation of employees. The next activity, detailed review of operations, may utilize the full detail of information in routine reports provided by the operations information systems. One example of a detailed review is the review of an aged customer accounts receivable report to assess the organization's bad debts and its credit practices. Operations information systems are tailored to provide a wide variety of reports on which these detailed reviews are based.

Operations Control

Operations control consists of measuring the efficiency with which each individual task is completed and of initiating remedial action to improve this efficiency where necessary. Whereas management control focuses on a range of activities directly relating to progress toward the organization's goals, operations control relates to a single task at a time. Operations control utilizes detailed rather than highly summarized information from the information system.

An example of operations control is control of the cost of production of one component of one of the organization's products. The cost accounting information system provides an "expected cost" (usually known as a "standard cost"), which may be based on an engineering estimate or on past experience. The information system collects actual costs incurred in the manufacture of this component and at the end of the accounting period (usually 1 month) reports a detailed comparison of actual costs with expected costs and calculates variances for costs of each type from the expected cost. By analyzing these variances, the manager can take corrective action.

Operations control is exercised almost entirely by managers who directly supervise the operations; they use a combination of direct observation and detailed reports of operations. The reports consist primarily of transactions listings and summaries of transactions provided by the formal information system.

Managers at the middle and lower levels of an organization devote a great deal of their time—typically 50 percent or more—to personnel matters, many of which involve dealing with the personal problems of employees. This is largely a matter of applying interpersonal relations techniques. Most of the information for resolving personnel problems that an information system can provide is likely to be routinely available from the personnel information system.

Analysis of Exhibit 2.2 shows a clear pattern. The information needs for the activities of lower-level managers tend to be satisfied by routine information systems designed for that purpose. On the other hand, much of the information needed for the higher-level managerial activity of planning is not available from within the organization, and the information needed for critical-problem analysis cannot be readily predicted, with the consequence that information systems cannot be designed to provide information for critical problems immediately. A recurring theme of this text is the difficulty of providing the information needed by higher-level managers, and the preceding discussion gives indications of the nature of this difficulty.

THE TIME ORIENTATION OF MANAGERIAL INFORMATION

Exhibit 2.3 shows the time orientation of most of the activities at the various levels of an organization. As indicated, a high proportion of senior-management activities are oriented toward dealing with the future of the organization, whereas all the principal lower-level managerial activities relate to present or past operations. In particular, strategic and long-range planning alternatives analysis and resource allocation policy formulation, and dealing with special problems are activities specifically undertaken to influence and change the future. Of the senior-management activities indicated in Exhibit 2.3, only the overall review and evaluation focuses on the past. As suggested by the exhibit, middle managers need substantial amounts of information bearing on the future as well as substantial amounts about the past.

This difference in time orientation between low- and top-level managerial activities means that details and summaries of past transactions have little relevance to top managers, other than for their overall review and evaluation activities. However, these details and summaries are one ingredient of forecasting, and forecasting information systems are important for top management. Forecast information, such as forecasts of sales, costs, the future character of the marketplace, and the economy, is important to senior managers. Some forecasting systems rely on simple projections of the organization's past trends. Others, generally more satisfactory, merge external and internal data to provide forecasts.

TYPES OF MANAGEMENT DECISIONS AND INFORMATION NEEDS

Many managerial activities encompass or ultimately culminate in significant decisions by managers. As Exhibit 2.4 shows, the decisions made at the top and lower levels of an organization are quite different in nature. Decisions made at the lower level tend to be repetitive; for example, credit decisions may be made for thousands of customers. These decisions also tend to be structured, in that the required analysis is standardized, a specific methodology is applied routinely, and the kind of information needed for the analysis is known and is the same for each type of decision.

Information systems can be readily developed to provide the information needed for highly structured decisions. The repetitive nature of these decisions makes it well worthwhile to develop efficient information

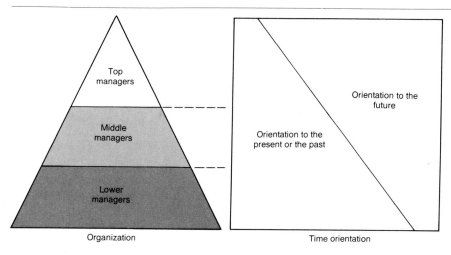

EXHIBIT 2.3
The time orientation of managerial activities.

systems for this purpose. Many decisions are so structured that they can be, and often are, made by computer programs. One example is programmed inventory reorder formulas that automatically decide how many units of particular items of inventory to order.

Managers still participate in most programmed decision situations in that they usually monitor and can override the programmed decisions; in the case of inventory reorder, for example, a manager usually could alter the number of items that would be ordered by the computer program. This "manager override" capability is essential because often the manager has information that the computer system does not have; for instance, the inventory manager may be aware of an additional need for the inventory items that is not considered by the computer algorithm.

A computer program may make only a part of a set of decisions

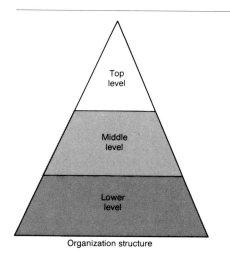
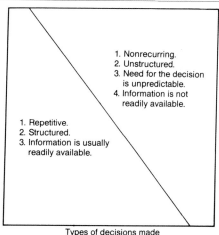

EXHIBIT 2.4
Kinds of decisions made in organizations.

required for a particular activity. It may determine, for example, the quantity of each inventory item that should be purchased; the manager then selects the most appropriate vendor on the basis of price and such service criteria as percentage of defects and estimated delivery dates. Systems designers continuously attempt to further structure managers' activities so that more of the decision processes can be efficiently programmed.

While there is a cyclical nature to some of the top-management activities (for example, planning processes follow a long-term, repetitive cycle of usually 1 year), nevertheless the decisions relating to these activities tend to be unique and not highly structured. To illustrate, the problem of "Shall we buy XYZ Company or ABC Company?" is a unique and non-recurring one. It is also relatively unstructured because (1) no universally accepted methodology can be applied; (2) multiple alternatives are involved (including no purchase, whether to buy with stock or cash, and so on); and (3) the variables, as well as their relationships to one another, are too many and too complex to specify fully (for example, all the ways in which each company might help or detract from the sales of the purchasing company should be identified and evaluated, but they cannot be). Such a decision also requires extensive managerial judgment because all the future cost and revenue information needed must be estimated.

The managers of an organization, and particularly the senior managers, face countless unstructured problems that require the exercise of managerial judgment. Determining product quality, assessing market demand, and deciding whether to add a company cafeteria are examples of this type of problem.

It is apparent that the unstructured nature and unpredictable occurrence of problems at the higher levels of organizations make it difficult to construct information systems that routinely provide information useful for most top-management decision making. The cost of an information system that is tailored to one decision must be justified by the benefits associated with that one decision, and thus a special information system often is not justified. On the other hand, with repetitive decisions, the cost of the information system can be justified by the benefits which flow from having better information for many decisions.

TYPES OF INFORMATION NEEDED

The information needs at different levels in the organization can be examined in light of the preceding discussion. Exhibit 2.5 portrays this. As shown, most of the information utilized by lower-level managers, but only a small part of that utilized by top managers, is factual and detailed in nature, such as that provided by the transactions processing activities. Exception reports—reports that are tailored to highlight out-of-control conditions, such as inventory shortages—are important to lower- and middle-level managers. Exception reports can also be important to top

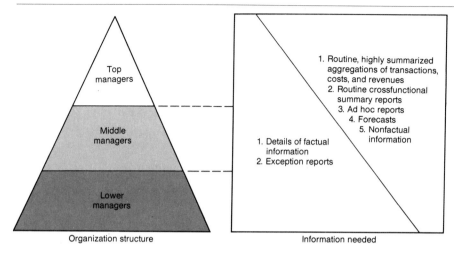

1. Routine, highly summarized
   aggregations of transactions,
   costs, and revenues
2. Routine crossfunctional
   summary reports
3. Ad hoc reports
4. Forecasts
5. Nonfactual
   information

1. Details of factual
   information
2. Exception reports

Organization structure   Information needed

EXHIBIT 2.5
Types of information
needed at different
levels in the
organizations.

management if the condition that is out of control is critical to the overall success of the organization.

For their tasks of overall review and evaluation, top managers utilize information generated by operations and transactions processing primarily in one of two ways: either functionally or cross-functionally. An example of functional use would be the marketing manager's receiving highly summarized reports of marketing costs aggregated for all levels of the marketing function. This type of summarization is useful for cost control at every level in the hierarchy.

Preparation of cross-functional summaries generally entails data processing that merges and combines similar types of costs and revenues across functions. Accounting financial statements, which are presented using general types of costs and revenues rather than by functional areas of the organization, are well-known type of cross-functional reporting. Administrative costs are shown as one summary total that includes all functional areas of the organization, as are many other costs and revenues. This type of summariztion, and variations of it, is considered to be particularly useful for overall profitability and cash flow analyses, which are a part of top management's review and evaluation activities.

The ad hoc reports indicated in Exhibit 2.5 provide information that is intended to be useful in dealing with unanticipated special problems. The difficulty of retrieving this information from multiple sources for ad hoc usage has already been noted.

Top management requires forecasts to help assess the future. As was previously noted, although forecasting often is based partly on information generated by operations-level information systems, it seldom relies exclusively on this source. Separate forecasting information systems are often useful and can frequently be designed to access information within operations-level information systems automatically.

SOURCES OF INFORMATION

Exhibit 2.6 illustrates managers' sources of information in a typical large organization; Exhibit 2.7 summarizes the important points of Exhibit 2.6. The word "typical" must be emphasized because information sources can vary widely from one organization to another, depending on the organization's size, the styles of its managers, the industry and its technology, and the sophistication of the organization's information systems. Also, managers' sources of information at any level of an organization could differ widely among functions. Finally, it should be recognized that most managers spend a great deal of time on personnel problems, an activity not considered in this discussion of information sources.

Exhibit 2.6 indicates that a relatively small proportion (15 to 20 per-

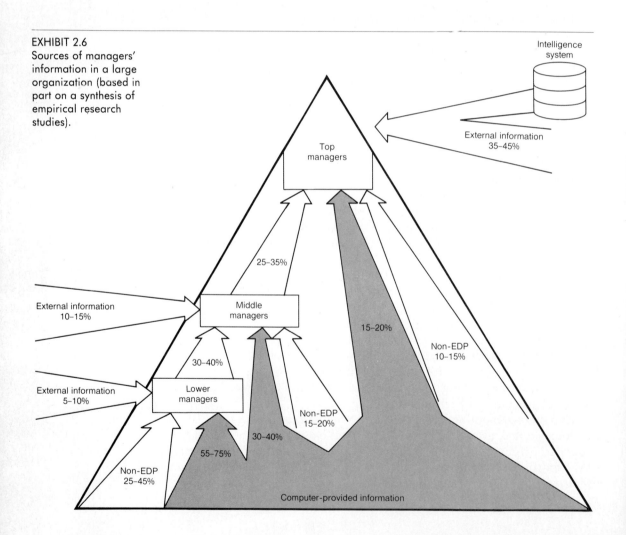

EXHIBIT 2.6
Sources of managers'
information in a large
organization (based in
part on a synthesis of
empirical research
studies).

cent) of the information that is useful to top management is provided directly by the computerized internal information systems; this percentage would tend to be higher in medium-sized organizations. This low proportion is one of the several reasons why top management is often unhappy with its information system—senior managers frequently believe that they are not served well by the computer because they receive so little useful information from it. Without doubt, computerized information systems for top management are usually at rudimentary stages of development; in part, however, this problem is due to the fact that the types of information needed for the planning and special-problem activities of top management cannot be readily provided by computer information systems.

About 30 to 40 percent of the information that is useful to middle managers is received directly from the computer system. Lower managers receive the majority of their information from the computer system (55 to 75 percent). This information is mostly detailed information about operations or transactions processing or summary information about these activities.

Exhibit 2.6 also shows noncomputerized information sources within the organization; these consist of a variety of sources of information, including direct observation (such as a tour of the production centers), the organization's newsletter or journal, manual information systems, and the important informal information system that develops in every organization. Information from this latter source may run the gamut from the "grapevine" to informal, "chatty" lunch meetings that include discussions of particular situations or problems. The informal information network is an important source of information for managers in organizations of every size and should be recognized as such.

Lower managers, whose positions entail direct responsibility for supervision of operations, utilize noncomputerized internal sources for 25 to 45 percent of their information. Middle managers receive less of their information (15 to 20 percent) from internal noncomputerized sources (excluding other managers as a source). Top managers receive the least amount of information from internal sources (10 to 15 percent, excluding other managers as a source); they are effectively cut off from direct contact with operations activities and rely almost entirely on other sources of information.

Summary of Managers' Major Sources of Information   EXHIBIT 2.7

Top Managers	Middle Managers	Lower Managers
External information	The computer system	The computer system
Middle managers	Lower managers	Noncomputerized internal sources

Managers also receive relevant information from outside the organization, as indicated in Exhibit 2.6. The use of this external information is modest at the lower levels, where the primary need is for internally generated information about operations. At the top-management level, however, the information utilized from outside the organization, for planning purposes especially, is both substantial in quantity and critical to top-management activities.

Lower managers provide middle managers with about one-third of their information, as shown in Exhibit 2.6. In turn, middle managers provide almost as much (25 to 35 percent) of the information received by top managers. The computer system is the original source of much of the information communicated in written or oral reports by each level of management to the next higher level. This fact may not be fully realized by managers who look at the small amount of information they receive directly from the computer and lament the computer information system's lack of effectiveness.

UNCERTAINTY ABSORPTION

The process by which information is provided to managers at each level by their subordinates merits special attention because of its implications for information systems. This process, often referred to as "uncertainty absorption," was studied by March and Simon.

Managers at every level in organizations have multiple and competing demands on their time. They must devote time and attention to consumers and representatives of the business community, to stockholders, and to government representatives and regulators, to name but a few. Managers must also perform ceremonial and leadership duties, and even top managers must deal directly with certain personnel problems, such as those arising from jurisdictional disputes among subordinate managers. Finally, each manager has several subordinates who have claims on the manager's time.

Therefore, managers—and especially senior managers, whose time is the most precious—must carefully ration the time devoted to each task and to each subordinate. They cannot take the time to be informed by subordinates about the full details of a particular problem or situation. Subordinates realize this and "capsulize" the information they provide to their superiors. For the most part, this is accomplished not by providing only the most relevant facts and details, but instead by synthesizing the available information. Since this information is often incomplete and (in the case of nonfactual information) since its reliability is unknown, the managers integrate their facts, assumptions, and estimates and then form and opinion on the basis of the overall situation. Managers then communicate these overall opinions, rather than the detailed information, to their superiors. This creates an essential efficiency in the management processes by reducing both the total amount of information that a receiving manager must assimilate and the time required to receive it.

One consequence of this process is that managers rarely communicate fully the uncertainties that result from the nonfactual information on which they base their opinions. If called upon to do so, managers may be unable to explain how the available information was synthesized or the nature of extent of the managerial judgment involved. The effect of this is that the communicating managers "absorb" the uncertainty about these matters, rather than pass the uncertainty along; this process is known as "uncertainty absorption." Uncertainty absorption takes place in formal, written communications to a degree, but it is most common in the informal, face-to-face interactions between managers that are such an important part of the communications processes of organizations.

The following scenario illustrates the uncertainty-absorption process. A middle-level manager is asked to investigate the cause of last month's decreased productivity in plant A. The manager reviews detailed cost and production reports, various personnel reports, and labor grievances filed and talks to the plant A supervisor as well as selected other managers and workers who might have information about the problem. The verbally communicated report by the middle-level manager to a senior manager might consist of little more than stating: "The productivity problem in plant A last month appears to be primarily the result of reorganization of the production line, which necessitated reassignment of production personnel to new tasks. This caused employee discontent, which resulted in some work slowdowns. The problems appear to be resolved now, and we should see normal productivity this month." The senior manager then may or may not ask for elaborations on particular aspects of the verbal report.

Note that in the above scenario, several hours or days of analysis by the middle-level manager may be encapsulated by this verbal report taking less than 5 minutes; note also that the senior manager receives very little or no detailed information. Further, little of what is communicated is factual; the manager cannot know for certain that the plant reorganization was the *primary* problem or that it *caused* the slowdown. The reorganization may have been only the last straw after a series of management actions that alienated employees and will continue to do so, or it could have been an excuse for a slowdown in a situation in which employees did not mind the reorganization but were unhappy for other reasons or wanted to "test" management. It remains to be seen how well the middle manager absorbed the uncertainty and provided a valid analysis.

While this example involves a special problem, a similar uncertainty-absorption process takes place with routine matters. Additionally, uncertainty absorption can occur at all levels in an organization. For instance, what is communicated to a higher level may consist of a combination of facts and judgments from two or more lower levels; the manager just one level below may have received opinions from subordinates and in turn may have added these to information from other sources to form the basis for a report to a higher-level manager.

The impact of this process of synthesis, judgment formation, and uncertainty absorption on information systems is significant in two respects. First, it enables the information system to be simplified—the detailed information provided to one managerial level need not also be provided to the next higher level. If a manager at one level receives enough detailed information to form a judgment, then only summaries or no information at all may be provided to the manager at the next higher level. The subordinate manager's communication of synthesized facts and estimates from multiple sources in the form of an opinion acts as a substitute for a more elaborate information system for the manager at the next higher level.

The second implication relates to managers' desires to cross-check and confirm information provided to them, which is a common desire whether this information is provided by a formal system, another manager, or an outsider. Discovering that they are receiving erroneous or misleading information is one of the surprises that managers like least. Managers attempt to protect themselves from these surprises in several ways. One is simply by seeking a second opinion, and managers will often use even outside acquaintances with no knowledge of a specific situation as sounding boards if they have reason to wonder about an opinion they have received from another manager. Managers may also attempt to verify the judgments of others by seeking and examining the related details of the information available within the information system. Information systems can be designed so that fully detailed information is available on call and can be rapidly retrieved for a manager who wishes to examine the detail

With systems like the Sperry Univac SPERRYLINK executive workstation, managers can have immediate access to computer data while interacting with other executives. *(Courtesy of Sperry Corporation.)*

rather than rely on a synthesized opinion provided by another manager. Programmed search capabilities can be established that greatly facilitate this process. However, this additional capability increases the complexity of the information system.

THE DESIGN OF INFORMATION SYSTEMS FOR MANAGERS

The general information needs of managers follow a pattern based on the nature of the managerial activities at their level. Yet, in the past, formal information systems for managers at all levels have often been based primarily on the operations information systems. For middle-level managers to some extent, but especially for top managers, these information systems sometimes have been ineffective because they have not recognized the nature of the tasks and the management processes at these levels. A general methodology for information systems development at each management level is illustrated in Exhibit 2.8.

Most information systems for lower-level managers must be based on the operations activities and the information systems that process the transactions of these activities for the organization; this is known as "bottom-up" design and is indicated by the arrows linking the transactions and lower-management information systems in Exhibit 2.8. Transactions processing systems and lower-level management information systems should be, and usually are, developed in an interrelated manner.

Most of top management's information systems, on the other hand, must have an essentially external and future focus. The planning information system should be tailored to the needs of top management, which means that they should be developed more or less independently of the transactions processing systems and the operations control systems.

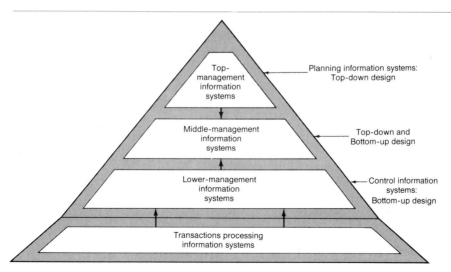

EXHIBIT 2.8
The design of management information systems.

Developing information for planning systems requires a completely different breed of systems designer from that which is required for the lower-level information systems. The primary requirement of the planning systems designer is a knowledge of the management and planning processes at the senior-management level; the secondary requirement is an understanding of information systems and their design. Designers of lower-level systems, on the other hand, must have strong technical information systems skills as well as good knowledge of operations activities.

At the middle-management level the information systems design should be strongly influenced by both the top-level planning information systems (top-down design) and the lower control information systems (bottom-up design). The planning information systems designed for top management should be extended down to provide disaggregated planning information to the middle-management level, where it is further disaggregated to provide the planning information needed by lower-level managers.

In the other direction, management control information is primarily summarized operations control information. The lower level's information systems that are concerned with internal information about the past and the present should provide summary information to serve middle management's management control needs. At the middle-management level, control information is further summarized or differently structured to satisfy much of top management's information needs for overall evaluation and review of operations. At the top level, information from outside the organization will also play a role in the overall evaluation and review of operations.

SUMMARY

Transactions derived from operations and clerical activities are what drive the organization's information systems that provide information to the lower management level. At the middle level of the organization are two general classes of personnel: middle-level managers and technical and professional specialists, who are primarily nonmanagerial. The major principle of information systems for technical and professional specialists is that the technology of each specialist group should be analyzed and that the information system for that group should be tailored to that technology.

Information is defined as data in useful form. Quantitative information is usually more easily interpreted than narrative information, and graphically presented information is often more easily interpreted than quantitative information presented in other forms. Both factual information and nonfactual information are useful to managers.

The activities of managers at different levels in typical organizations tend to differ in a systematic way. Lower-level managers usually spend a great deal of time supervising operations and subordinates and performing detailed reviews of operating results. Middle managers usually spend less time on these activities, and top managers spend very little time on them. Middle managers exert most of their energy on management control activities.

Top managers devote most of their attention to planning activities, overall reviews based on summary information, special problems that are critical to the organization's well-being, and leadership and ceremonial activities. Middle managers spend less of their time on these activities, and lower managers spend very little of their time on them.

Managerial levels also vary with respect to their time orientation. Lower-level managers are concerned primarily with the results of past operations and with conducting current operations, whereas top managers are preoccupied with the future of the organization. Middle managers' time orientation is in the range between that of lower management and that of top management.

The managerial levels also vary with respect to the types of decisions made. Lower manager's decisions usually are repetitive and structured. Top management, on the other hand, is concerned with decisions about goals and strategies as well as with one-of-a-kind decisions about nonrecurring problems or conditions. For decisions of these types, relevant and complete information generally is not easily available and must be provided by special reports, forecasts, estimates, and operations. The information that is readily available to top managers about operations is usually highly summarized and is relevant primarily only to the overall evaluations and reviews conducted by senior managers.

Similarly, the sources of information for different levels of management vary dramatically. Whereas information from sources external to the organization is critical to top management, it has much less importance for middle management and has little importance for lower management. On the other hand, whereas top management utilizes little information directly from the computer system, this source is much more important for middle management and is most important for lower management.

These differences suggest that the information systems required at the various levels are quite different. This has proved to be a stumbling block in the development of information systems above the lower levels in organizations; there has been a tendency for systems personnel to develop information systems for higher-level managers that are basically extensions or modifications of the transactions processing and operations control systems provided for clerical operations and lower managers. However, the differences in the nature and orientation of information needed by the various levels of an organization demonstrate that the information systems required by the various levels must be quite different in structure. In general, lower-level and top-level information systems should be independently developed, and middle-level information systems should be in great part a combination of top- and lower-level systems.

KEY TERMS

technical and professional specialists: employees, such as accountants, engineers, and actuaries, whose specialized duties require that they have a technical or professional background.

quantitative information: information consisting of numeric data or numeric data transformed into graphs.

qualitative information: information consisting of descriptive data.

graphical information: numeric information in picture (schematic) form.

factual information: information which is generally considered valid.

estimate: a type of nonfactual information that is based on related facts; it is usually considered the best form of information in the absence of full factual information.

critical (special) problems: managerial problems which are important, unanticipated, and usually nonrecurring.

exception reports: reports that are tailored to highlight out-of-control conditions.

functional reports: reports that are organized according to functions of the organization, for example, marketing reports.

cross-functional reports: reports that combine information about similar types of costs, revenues, or other matters across functions of the organization; accounting financial statements are an example.

uncertainty absorption: the process by which a manager "absorbs" and does not pass along to other managers the uncertainty surrounding a topic; the uncertainty results from incomplete and possibly unreliable information.

bottom-up design: a way of designing information systems that begins by analyzing the information needed at the lowest levels of the organization.

top-down design: a way of designing information systems that begins by analyzing the information required by top management.

REFERENCE

March, J. G., and H. A., Simon, *Organizations*, New York: Wiley, 1958, p. 165.

REVIEW QUESTIONS

1. What information would probably be useful to a specialist marketing research group that is not likely to be available from the company's operations information systems? How would the information needed be different from that needed by the specialist group charged with brainstorming promotion schemes?

2. What kind of information would an agency specializing in consumer protection in the area of food be likely to utilize for its food-testing function?

3. Try to remember several decisions you have made recently that have not been based on factual information. Classify each according to whether you used estimates, consensus opinion, opinion, conjecture, rumor, or a combination of these as a basis for making the decisions. Can you recall instances in which rumor, conjecture, or someone else's opinion caused you to search for additional information?

4. What is usually the difference between the kinds of problems that lower- and top-level managers deal with, and how does this affect the information needed and managers at each of these levels?

5. Why doesn't top management do a great deal of direct supervision?

6. On the basis of the discussion in this chapter only, explain why information systems for top managers are difficult to design and build.

7. Provide several examples of repetitive and structured decisions made by lower-level managers.

8. Should information systems for middle- and top-level managers be primarily extensions and adaptations of those for lower-level managers? Why or why not?

9. How would you go about designing an information system for top management?

10. What is "external information", and how is it used in an organization?

11. How useful is computer-provided information to each level of management?

12. What is the nature of informal information systems? Are they useful?

13. Why is it important for someone who designs information systems to understand the sources of managers' information?

14. When a top manager tours the manufacturing plant and stops in to talk to the plant superintendent or a department supervisor, what is the top manager probably attempting to accomplish? Does this relate in any way to inadequacies of the information systems for top management?

15. Have you ever been employed in an organization and had occasion to say, "If the people in management ever found out about this, it would blow their minds"? Describe the situation and suggest what kind of information system, if any, would have enabled top management to know what was happening.

16. Everyone absorbs uncertainty as described in this chapter. Try to remember instances in which you possessed factual and other information but passed along to someone else opinions based on this information rather than the details of the information. In each case, what was your motivation for doing so? If you cannot recall any such instances, for the next few days pay particular attention to your dealings with friends and associates and try to spot an example of uncertainty absorption on your part or on the part of someone else. Then describe the situation.

17. Is uncertainty absorption useful? In what ways is it potentially harmful?

18. Explain how each of the following may help account for the fact that a small proportion of the information used by top managers is provided directly to them by computers:

   (a) Some of the information provided by computers reaches top management indirectly.

   (b) Information systems for top management have often been extensions and adaptations of the transactions processing information systems of the organization.

(c) Top managers are usually over 50, and many are 60 years of age. (*Hint*: When did business computer systems become widespread?)

(d) Communications between systems personnel and senior managers are usually poor.

(e) Systems analysts often do not understand the management processes.

CASE

A Computer at the NFL Draft

By Robert Parker

"Tampa Bay selects Ricky Bell, running back, Unviersity of Southern California."

From the 482 names that paper the right wall, a BLESTO scout lifts the strip with Bell's name from the halfback column and transfers it across the room to the Tampa Bay heading on the opposite wall. The 1977 National Football League player draft has begun, and by the following night 336 names—defensive players in red, offensive in black—will be transferred across the room to the 28 NFL teams which selected them.

It is May 3, 1977, at Veterans Stadium, Philadelphia. The Philadelphia Eagles are hosting the nine NFL teams which belong to BLESTO, one of the league's two major scouting combines. At a long table in the center of the room sit BLESTO scouts who have seen the players perform, while adjoining rooms house assistant coaches of the nine teams, each linked by phone to his NFL city.

To fans of non-playoff teams, the build-up to the NFL draft is as suspenseful as are the final games of the regular season. For a club's fortunes are directly linked to how it uses its draft choices over a three- to five-year period.

"We have a trade. The Seattle Seahawks send their first-round pick to Dallas . . . and the Cowboys take Tony Dorsett, halfback, University of Pittsburgh."

The room buzzes. Who got the edge? How do you evaluate a player? How do you match his speed, size, intelligence, and desire to your own needs? And how do you compare his position and his level of competition with that of 1,000 other seniors to decide which man's ability, which man's position is most important to your team? Pro football personnel people tackle such complex data the same way it is done in business: on a computer.

Thus, one "civilian" also sits at the long table. He is Jim Renouf, a stocky, deep-voiced computer specialist from Western Publishing Company, which sells computer services to BLESTO. In front of Renouf sits a 29-pound computer terminal with a keyboard and printout. The phone piece tucked into its back provides BLESTO a direct line during the entire draft with a mineload of information stored in a Univac 1110 computer in Racine, Wis.

The scouts sit facing the wall of players' names, recording the order in which they are selected. (A fan would face the wall with team listings, to see who selected whom.) "Allllright," says one, "the first seven picks are players BLESTO rated best in their position."

At the head of the long table sits the director of BLESTO, Jack Butler. A former Pittsburgh defensive back who had 52 interceptions during his 9-year career in the 1950s, Butler has the square jaw and bright eyes of a man who was strong against both the run and the pass. Both here and in his two-room headquarters in downtown Pittsburgh, he is continually sought for advice, and his gentle voice does not conceal the toughness of his opinions.

Origins of BLESTO

BLESTO was organized in 1963 as the Bears, Lions, Eagles, Steelers Talent Organization—it was later joined by the Bills, Chiefs, Colts, Dolphins, and Vikings—but its scouting reports were rather primitive when the owners hired Butler in 1966 and suggested he look into the computer.

"I didn't know what computers, what programming were all about," he says. "One consultant asked exactly what was it I wanted. I didn't know—exactly! And there were language problems, such as when they talked of core storage and down time and COBOL. I decided to go to night college."

That first year's printout was equally primitive. Butler describes the four categories of speed: excellent, good, average, and slow. Good men could be spotted—Ron Yary, still a Viking tackle, was the top-rated of 977 athletes—but "general comments" was the catchall heading for most information.

Today, BLESTO records a man's speed in hundredths of a second and the conditions, the weather, the time of day, the track surface, and who did the timing. It also records height, weight, injuries, a dozen abilities based on position, and if ratings are based on coaches' comments or personal observation of practice, games, or film. Each player's record is filed under a combination of the code number of his school and his jersey number.

Butler sends one of eight area scouts to see a potential pro in the spring and fall. The better of these seniors are also observed by one of three regional scouts and possibly BLESTO's national scout. Copies of their written reports go to each BLESTO team, but the material is also key-punched in Racine, Wis. and entered on a computer disk.

Twice each year, complete computer printouts on the seniors are sent to each BLESTO team (supplemented by semi-annual meetings in which the scouts talk directly to the coaches of BLESTO teams). Many lists are printed:

—Alphabetical by name.
—Alphabetical by school.
—Overall athletic ability, all positions, nationwide.
—Ranking by ability for each position, nationwide.
—Overall ability, all positions, in each scout's area.
—Ranking by ability, for each position, in each scout's area.

—Ranking by position, nationally, according to speed.
—Ranking by position, nationally, according to size.
—A name and address listing.

Each athlete's combined statistical information is printed out in one line in these listings. In addition,

—A history file, a two-page printout on each player includes as well the written comment by each scout.

Grading of Players

In the first 30 minutes of the May draft, 11 players are chosen. At about this point in any draft, the blue chip players are gone, and each team begins to use more of the 15 minutes it is allotted for the balancing act between its needs and the best athletes remaining. Thus, the key to BLESTO's service is the grading it gives to each player.

Ratings range from .4 to 3.1. Very few players are rated from .4 to .9; such an athlete could start his first year for any team in the league. Most high round draft picks rate from 1.0 to 1.5, the lower the number the earlier the pick; these are eventual starters. Above 1.8 means an athlete may have size, speed, and talent but not all three; these will be free agents, with a potential to make the club.

The first round has ended after three hours. Watching closely is the Steelers' Art Rooney, Sr., whose son, Art, Jr. originated BLESTO. He is a short man, with white hair and a cigar stuck into the side of his mouth. He says little, but the affection he has for the draft process is clear, as is the affection that these football men have for him.

"That was a tought first round, Mr. Rooney," says Jack Butler. "Some teams really took a gamble.

A scout always has questions. He knows he is judging another human being. He also knows his rating may differ from the computer's, which is programmed to interpret cold statistics: the school's level of competition, the quality of its coaching, the player's size and speed relative to his position, an injury record, his performance record.

Thus, scout and machine complement one another.

"How can the computer evaluate the performance of a defensive end who is projected as a pro linebacker?" asks Butler. "He has never played linebacker, and it will reject him as a lineman because he is too light. Another thing," he taps his heart, "how do you put this on a computer?"

Jim Renouf agrees that emotions are difficult to quantify. But the close to 40,000 lines of instruction he has given to the Univac 1110 cover everything from body and leg structure to home telephone numbers. Last year, operators at Western Publishing key-punched 3,500 separate reports on 1,004 seniors.

Renouf has set up the computer so that information may be retrieved in 15 seconds or less. This is a far cry from the 25 hours it sometimes required under the original system in 1966. That was an alphabetized sequentially batched system using a scientific computer language, FORTRAN, explains Renouf. "It just wasn't geared to BLESTO's needs. Jack needed a random access system, so he could ask for the 10 fastest players, over six feet six inches, or whatever criteria he had, and receive a response quickly. He also needed COBOL, a computer language better suited for file manipulation; and it was clear that identifying players by a code number would increase the computer's efficiency.

Renouf worked 16 hours a day for six months in 1970 to set up 20 basic programs for BLESTO's needs. Not only did he set up an "online, mass-storage-oriented, random access system," he also had to design a report form that would be simple for not only the scouts to follow but also the key-punch operators.

The highly sophisticated system is key-word driven. Thus, Renouf enters the word "draft" when a player is chosen. He types the name on the keyboard, and the computer files the player under the proper round and team and is able to print his basic scouting statistics on request. Once a player is selected, he is coded ineligible for the draft; his name is not purged, since the online system is designed to print an up-to-the-minute status of the draft by position, by round, or by team.

In order to answer requests for the top remaining players by such categories as BLESTO rating, speed, weight, or position, the player master file is randomly organized according to an interlocking coding system. In coding the retrieval criteria, for example, defensive corner back is position code 16. When this retrieval code is matched to a table code that provides access to the data stored in the computer, the information on a player is ready for printing. All information remains in the computer so that draft choices by round and by team can be printed in subsequent years.

Team Criteria

The selection process has slowed to a crawl. Like certain recent Super Bowls, there is more excitement in the buildup than in the event itself. And the NFL draft also prompts more second-guessing, for the process is not actually over at the end of two days. Which team chose better players? Which team better filled its needs?

"First of all, you have to pick a player that fits your system, even if other players are rated higher, points out Herman Ball, Eagles' director of player personnel. "Then, you can't really evaluate a draft for three years, until you see how a player matures. Is he contributing more each year? Does he make it more difficult each year for another player to make the team?"

If recent Super Bowl appearances are any criteria, BLESTO teams, which represent but one-third of the NFL, are breaking in the right players. "The key," says Dick Haley of the Steelers, "is judging a player's potential development. For you need new players each year, even if you have won the Super Bowl. And each team will go at it with different standards. The Steelers, for example, don't require defensive linemen to be as tall as some teams do. We've had success with men 6-2 or so, and other teams won't consider that height.

The Steelers, of course, built themselves through wise draft choices in the early 70s. They enter the draft with 300 men on their list and a room full of information. They begin with the BLESTO reports, then follow up with their own scouting reports on players or positions in which they have an interest. "At any point in the draft," Haley says, "we know pretty much the size and speed of everyone who is left.

Other teams acknowledge a greater reliance on BLESTO's computer during the draft. Les Miller of the Kansas City Chiefs describes how his office of player personnel often calls after a round for both the top 10 athletes remaining, and the top offensive linemen, and then checks the information with its own records. "The round in which you draft a player is vital. You don't take a player in the second round who will still be there in the fifth round, but you do take a player who will be gone before your third round turn comes."

Thus, Jack Butler says, "for all the information we have stored, we don't deal with facts and figures only. We are making judgments. We can time a player exactly, but when a scout says, 'this man is quick,' what the hell is quickness? It's subjective. So the computer is a great tool, and without it we would need 200 clerks to keep track of our records—if we could—but I don't want to over-emphasize its role. Because when you get down to it, what matters is how well a player fills a need and how well we have judged the intangibles, like quickness."

Future Applications

Between the slow rounds on the second day of the draft—when one team is not requesting the name of all linemen who are 6-4 and 240, with 4.9 speed, or another is not asking for all players with 4.6 speed, whatever position—Renouf occasionally needles Butler on the further use that could be made of the computer. Why, for example, cannot the same data be entered for pro players?

In all competitive situations, there is a certain secretiveness—as TEMPO faced when it agreed not to publish BLESTO ratings of specific players—and one wonders if coaches would release such vital information as weight and speed. But Butler has obviously considered the question. For he would like to add minutes played as a pro to such a record. But he is obviously working under budget constraints. At the moment, the next practical step, he believes, will be to review a scout's work—to see how well he has predicted pro potential and if he is more accurate with certain types of players.

You cannot quiet a creative computer man easily, however. Many NFL teams use computer systems for ticketing, budgeting, personnel, and some teams use the machine in formulating their game plan. They analyze the tendencies of their opponents as well as themselves. What does an offense (or defense) tend to do on third down, when the ball is on the 40 yard line, when there is one minute to play in the half, when the team is ahead (or behind), when five yards are needed for a first down? If a given tendency can be found, the defense (or offense) can attack somewhere else.

Knowing this, Renouf has a vision of himself on the sidelines with his 29-pound computer terminal. "There is no question that I could call every play in a game based on past tendencies, and I bet I would win more than my share." But, alas, the NFL has a rule prohibiting such machines on the sidelines. "They want to keep the human element as part of the game, and I have to admit they're right," says Renouf.

"The Oakland Raiders choose Rolf Benirshke, kicker, University of California at Davis."

The last of 336 selections has been made. It is early evening on May 4. It has been a long, slow two days, spiced by the speculation over certain picks. The BLESTO scouts are leaving.

But the assistant coaches from each BLESTO team remain. As they wait, the computer terminal is chattering away. The machine is printing BLESTO's rating of the top 25 unselected athletes in each position. These seniors are now free agents, and some of the scouts will be hopping planes to their university in hopes of signing them.

From now on, BLESTO teams are once again in competition.

Source: Touche Ross Tempo, Vol. 24, no. 1.

Case Question

Analyze the role of the computer in the NFL draft with respect to:
(1) Operations control information
(2) Management control information
(3) Strategic and long-range planning information
(4) The extent to which it is used for structured versus unstructured problems.

Chapter 3

THE CONCEPT OF A MANAGEMENT INFORMATION SYSTEM

PAYOFF THOUGHT

The development of a management information system (MIS) requires, first, a full understanding and appreciation of the idea of an MIS and, second, a long-range plan which outlines the general nature of the MIS sought and establishes specific development goals.

CHAPTER OBJECTIVE

To examine the elements of, and the concepts associated with, an MIS

INTRODUCTION

Expectations concerning what an MIS can accomplish for an organization should not be overinflated. An MIS is not and cannot be a "total information system" in the 1960s sense of the term; that is, not all information in an organization can be within one massive and completely automated system. The computer information systems of an organization can be neither fully automated nor totally comprehensive. Major aspects of the information system will always remain outside the computer system. Even if the technology existed to build totally computerized information systems, doing so would not be cost-effective.

Nevertheless, a very sophisticated computer-based MIS is possible and practical. The development of such an MIS requires the continuous attention of a great many highly skilled systems personnel over several years; it also requires the wholehearted participation of the managers of the organization. Many organizations that have set out to build a sophisticated MIS have committed the necessary monetary resources but have failed. They lacked proper organization, a good overall plan, qualified systems personnel, or, most important, adequate management participation as evidenced by the assistance of managers in designing the systems, controlling the systems development efforts, and motivating all the personnel involved. Lavish spending on information systems does not guarantee quality; a study by McKinsey & Company, a well-known management consulting firm, showed little correlation between yearly expenditures on information systems and managers' satisfaction with the systems.

Whether a sophisticated MIS is ultimately achieved or not, the attempt to develop one is costly. An objective costs/benefits tradeoff assessment may indicate that a particular organization should plan for an information system that is less than the best. While a good information system can produce cost savings, revenue increases, and intangible benefits that spring from having more useful information, nevertheless for most organizations the quest should not be for the "best possible" information system, but rather for an information system that strikes a proper balance between its cost and the benefits it provides.

Despite these cautions, however, organizations should realize that if they are realistic about their needs, careful in designing and implementing an MIS to fit those needs, and reasonable in establishing cost limits in view of expected benefits, the resulting MIS will be well worth the effort and money. This entire text is intended to help students understand how such an MIS is developed.

A full discussion of the MIS concept is deferred to the following chapter. For the purposes of this chapter, the following greatly simplified definition of an MIS is put forward:

An MIS is a collection of interacting information systems that provide information for both operations and managerial needs.

The most important aspect of this definition is its inclusiveness. An MIS encompasses *all* the information-providing systems at all levels of the organization; however, it must be stressed that this is a collection of information systems rather than one "total" system.

In theory, a computer is not necessarily an ingredient of an MIS, but in practice it is unlikely that a sophisticated MIS could exist without the processing capabilities of a computer. Nevertheless, every MIS includes noncomputer elements. The word "interacting" in the definition implies some degree of integration of the multiple information systems involved, a thought that is developed in this chapter. This conception of an MIS, though broader than that of many experts, is fully justified because the information systems of all the organization's functions are increasingly tied together in a suprasystem of quasi-independent information systems, such that no one information system can be viewed as entirely separate from the others.

THE ELEMENTS OF A SIMPLE INFORMATION SYSTEM

All information systems involve three primary activities: They receive data as input; they process data by performing calculations, combining data elements, updating accounts, and so on; and they provide information as output. This is true of manual, electromechanical, and computerized information systems. These three functions are illustrated in Exhibit 3.1.

Thus an information system receives and processes *data* and transforms this data into *information*. A data processing system could instead be called an "information-generating system"; this term actually is preferable because it accents the purpose of the system. Although the term "data processing" will be used in this text because of its general acceptance, the student should think of an MIS as an information-generating system.

TRANSACTIONS PROCESSING INFORMATION SYSTEMS

Exhibit 3.2 illustrates a data processing system that is primarily an operations-level transactions processing system, but is not an MIS. The exhibit shows a variety of transactions input from two general sources: outside the organization and within the organization. Externally generated transactions are from customers, vendors, and other groups. Any internal event

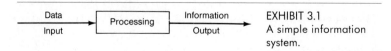

EXHIBIT 3.1
A simple information
system.

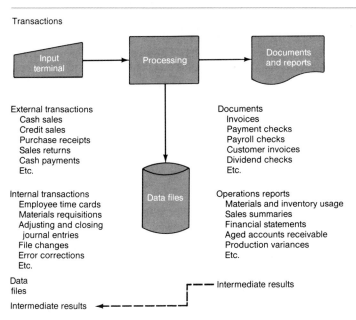

that is recorded by the information system is considered to be a transaction; examples include transferring materials to processing, transferring work in process from one stage of production to the next, recording depreciation on equipment, making routine file changes such as adding or deleting records or changing an employee's address, and correcting errors in previous input data.

Existing data files are also used as input to data processing systems. In a computer processing system, for example, the customer's account "master file" (the file that includes all the data about the customer) is input to the computer system along with sales transactions for processing together.

"Intermediate results" are also a type of input to the processing system. Shown as the last category of output, intermediate results are processed results which may serve one purpose but which must undergo further processing before they can provide useful information for another purpose. Usually this output is in " machine-readable" form; that is, it can be easily read and processed by a computer. A large proportion of data processing activity involves the production of intermediate results, which must then be further processed.

The output of a data processing system may be of several different types. One type of output is revised data files which have been corrected for errors, have had records added or deleted, or have had record status such as employee name or address altered in some fashion. Updated data files are files against which transactions have been processed and which typically then include the details added and reflect the new balances in the records. A master file is usually established for each category of transactions, such as for all transactions affecting sales.

Data processing systems, particularly transactions processing systems, also produce numerous types of documents; Exhibit 3.2 shows several types of output documents. Additionally, summary reports for managers are routine outputs from data processing systems. An additional output not shown in Exhibit 3.2 is a simple listing of the transactions processed, which is quite commonly produced to serve as the basis for further processing involving those transactions or as a "backup" to facilitate reconstruction of the master file if it is destroyed or lost.

Although managers may review some of the transactions processing reports, the system shown in Exhibit 3.2 is essentially an operations-level system. The materials inventory usage reports, for instance, which contain full details of materials requisitioned, are useful to clerks for checking inventory levels but are unlikely to be useful to managers. The summary reports from one group of transactions, such as sales of product D for the day, provide summary totals of all the transactions of this type for this period. Such reports are used for controlling the transactions, making entries in the accounting records, and documenting data processing, but they are not likely to be used for managerial purposes.

The master file shown in Exhibit 3.2 serves two primary purposes. First, since the transactions master file for a category of transactions is updated each time more transactions in this category are processed, it is a complete record of all transactions processed during the time period. Second, each master file serves as a basis for the preparation of management reports. In the case of credit sales transactions, for example, the sales master file accumulates the details about sales and related transactions (such as sales returns) for each customer for a certain time period. The sales master file may then be used for the further operations-level activity of preparing customer statements containing an itemized listing of at least the transactions that took place since the last statement. Additionally, the sales master file is processed, perhaps monthly, to prepare both an aged accounts receivable report for analysis by a manager and highly summarized management reports for use by more senior managers.

There are several types of transactions processing information systems. The ones found in a manufacturing company, for instance, are likely to include those shown in Exhibit 3.3. Each information system shown in the exhibit processes several types of transactions in addition to those indicated.

INFORMATION SYSTEMS FOR MANAGERS

Exhibit 3.4 illustrates the structure of an information system for managers. Four general types of computer-generated information are shown, starting at the top lefthand corner. This information may be for control of opera-

Transactions Processing Information Systems of a Manufacturing Company   EXHIBIT 3.3

Transactions Information Systems	Typical Transactions
Sales	Sales orders and sales returns
Accounts receivable	Credit sales and credit slips
Disbursing	Vendor payments
Cash	Cash receipts and cash disbursements
Cost accounting	Accounting for labor and materials used in production
Materials inventory	Materials receipts and disbursements
Finished products inventory	Product completions and product shipments
Plant and machinery	Depreciation, additions, and dispositions
Engineering	Engineering changes
Payroll	Pay-rate changes and withholding changes
Personnel	Employee additions and employee status changes
Purchasing	Purchase orders
Marketing research	Consumer survey results

tions, strategic and long-range planning, short-range planning, management control, and special-problem solving. Exception reports are the first type of computer-generated information; they may be based directly on transactions files. In a computerized system, computer programs may continuously monitor incoming transactions which are being processed or which were recently processed to identify and automatically report exceptional circumstances that require a manager's attention. For example, out-of-stock inventory conditions caused by a sales transaction, or a credit sales transaction that has been accepted for processing even though the customer has already exceeded an alloted amount of credit, may be reported automatically as an exception by the information system. Most reports for management control are based primarily on summaries from transactions master files, rather than directly on the transactions.

The external information files shown in Exhibit 3.4 could be data files provided for a fee by data vending service companies, or they could be intelligence files maintained by the organization's personnel. Noncomputerized sources of information are also shown in the exhibit as the two categories of formal (but not computer-based) reports and informally received information.

The files shown in Exhibit 3.4 as "nontransactions master files" consist of data files which are not the result of transactions processing but which instead are created within the organization for special purposes that are

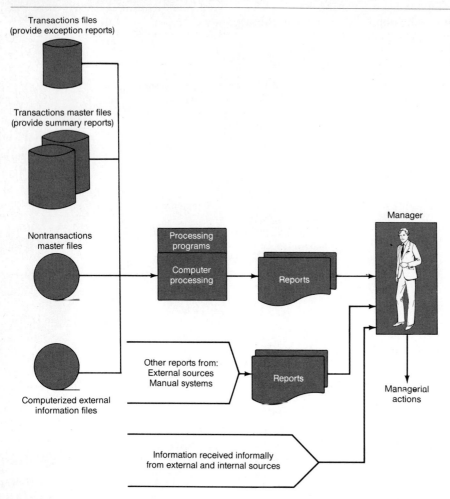

EXHIBIT 3.4
The components of an
information system for
managers.

usually related to operations and management control. One example is a budget (profit planning) file that is especially created to contain budget information, such as cost and revenue standards. At a later point, data from actual transactions contained in the master files is processed with the budget file to generate budget reports for management. Higher levels of management are also likely to use externally provided information for management control purposes. Comparisons of the organization's performance with summary statistics on competitors or with industry averages are especially important.

A typical budgeting information system is shown in greatly simplified form in Exhibit 3.5. The budget "transactions" are not actual business transactions but instead are entries that result from short-range planning; they are the expected costs and revenues of all types for each month of the budget year. This data is processed by the budget assembly programs, which place the data in the same structure and format that the organization's accounting system uses to accumulate costs and revenues.

This creates, in advance of the budget period, a budget file of month-by-month expected costs and revenues. At the end of each month a set of budget programs processes the master files containing that month's actual costs and revenues and compares these with the expected costs and revenues to determine the extent to which each type of actual cost and revenue conformed to expectations. A new budget–actual monthly file is produced which consists of pairs (a budget figure and an actual figure

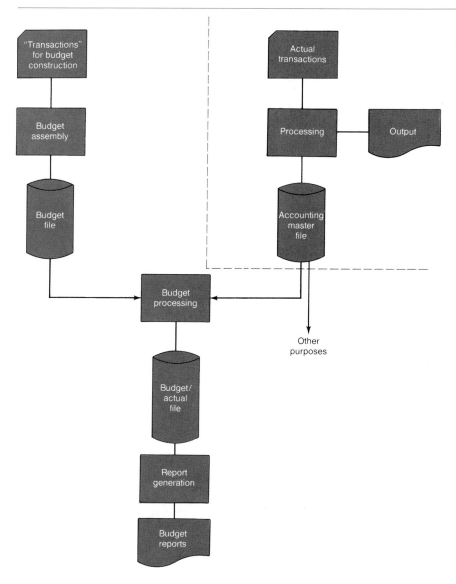

EXHIBIT 3.5
A budgeting
information system.

representing summarized transactions) of data costs and revenues in each detailed cost and revenue category of the accounting system. The computer budget programs then calculate the difference between the amounts in each pair and produce budget reports which show the variances. Managers use variance reports for control purposes by investigating the causes of the variances and taking corrective action where necessary. During the processing the accounting master files are not altered and are later processed for other reporting purposes.

EXTERNAL FINANCIAL REPORTING INFORMATION SYSTEMS

Almost all organizations must prepare finanacial reports for distribution to persons outside the organization and to other organizations; this is one of the ways in which an organization interacts with its environment. For example, reports must be provided to government agencies for regulatory purposes, to major creditors who wish to assess the probability that the money due them will be paid, and to shareholders to inform them of the financial status of the company.

These external reports are either limited-purpose reports (reports sent to government agencies about withheld social security or income taxes are prime examples) or general-purpose financial statements—company balance sheets and income statements. Frequently a special subsystem must be designed to generate limited-purpose reports, such as those sent to government agencies; hundreds of information subsystems may exist in an organization to provide these specialized reports. General-purpose financial statements usually conform to "generally accepted accounting principles," which prescribe the accounting treatment of hundreds of different types of transactions as well as the content and format of the financial statements. The information systems that provide data for external reporting purposes may be extensive and complex, and often they contain very detailed information.

In a smaller organization the information systems that generate the general-purpose financial statements often are the dominant information system of the organization. There is a great deal of overlap between these systems and the managerial information systems, even though their purposes are different. Indeed, because much of the financial information needed by managers and by external information users is similar, some organizations, especially smaller ones, design information systems for external financial reporting and use the resulting information for mangerial purposes as well; this practice deprives their managers of internal reporting systems tailored to their needs. While this practice decreases considerably the complexity of the organization's information systems, more often than not the utility of the information that is available to managers is decreased more than proportionately, and therefore the internal managerial decision-making and control processes are less effective. While there is a strong temptation in small organizations to "take the easy way" and develop only an external reporting information system, managers should take special care to ensure that their managerial information needs are met, and most often this requires information systems that are tailored to managerial purposes.

Exhibit 3.6 shows an information system for external reporting purposes. Typically in larger organizations these information systems are "piggybacked" on the transactions processing systems and on the master files prepared for the managerial information systems; that is, they receive their information from these transactions processing systems and master files. During processing of the organization's transactions, the data needed for both internal and external reporting is captured. The master files created with the processed transactions are primarily for the organization's

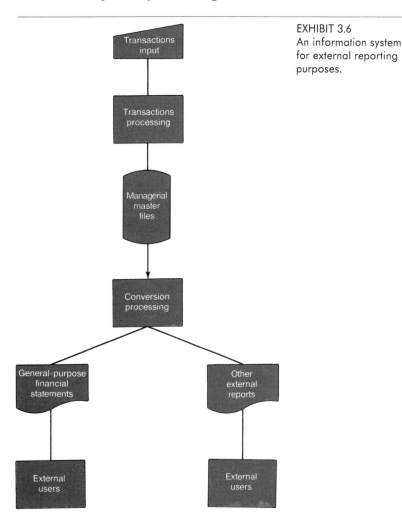

EXHIBIT 3.6
An information system for external reporting purposes.

managers, but additional data needed exclusively for external reporting, such as for regulatory reporting, is also captured at this point to avoid the need to subsequently gather and process additional data. Up to this point the information systems are no different from the combined transactions processing and managerial information systems shown in Exhibits 3.2 and 3.4, except that additional data is collected that is needed only for external reporting.

The master files are then processed, using different sets of programs, to prepare both managerial and external reports separately. For external reporting the data in the master files often must be converted from its managerial format in the files to a quite different format.

A comparison of Exhibits 3.6 and 3.4 shows differences between the managerial and the external reporting information systems. First, only the formal information systems are shown as providing information for external reporting; generally, external reports are not based on informally received information, although manual information systems may be used to generate certain external reports. Second, it is external users rather than managers who receive and use the external reports.

A third difference between the managerial and the external reporting information systems relates to timing. External reports are almost all provided on a periodic basis—usually monthly, quarterly, or annually—and reasonable delay in their preparation after the end of the period can be tolerated. On the other hand, much of the information that is useful to managers should be kept up to date continuously and should be available whenever it is needed, rather than only after the end of the period. Further, to increase the effectiveness of their control activities, managers should receive periodic managerial reports as quickly as possible after the end of the period.

Certain reports are valuable both for external users and for managerial analysis. For example, this is usually true of the general-purpose financial statements. While required for external purposes, they are often used by the organization's managers for anlysis, such as for analysis of return on investment and other overall financial ratios. Additionally, managers use these statements to assess overall trends by comparing current financial statements with those of preceding periods; typical trends analyzed are income and cost of sales.

INTELLIGENCE INFORMATION SYSTEMS

In most organizations that have a long-range plan, it is a master plan in the sense that several other planning systems are subordinate to, and integrated with, the long-range planning system, as indicated in Exhibit 3.7. Other planning activities occur within the framework and guidelines established by the long-range plan.

Of the systems shown in Exhibit 3.7, capital budgets, operations

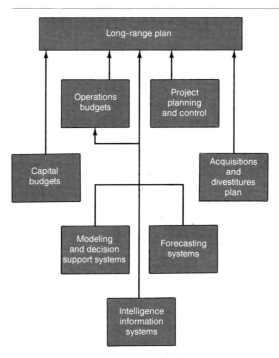

EXHIBIT 3.7
The system of planning systems.

budgets, forecasting, project planning and control, and the acquisitions and divestitures plan may each be thought of as being a combination of managerial system and an information system. The activities of each are performed within the guidelines established by the long-range plan and are carefully timed to dovetail with the long-range planning process.

The modeling and decision support systems and the intelligence information systems are primarily information systems that in and of themselves do not encompass managerial processes. Rather, they are managerial support systems in that their emphasis is on providing information to the planning processes, principally to the long-range planning and operations budgeting processes, as suggested in Exhibit 3.7. Decision support systems are discussed in the next section.

A business intelligence information system systematically gathers and analyzes information about the social, political, legal, regulatory, and economic environments of one or more countries, as well as about the health and future prospects of the industry that the company is in and about its competitors. Patterns may be uncovered, for example, which indicate an impending shift in a government's attitude toward regulation of companies or which suggest the long-range strategies of competing companies.

Intelligence information systems provide planning information that managers might not receive otherwise. These systems also reduce the amount of time that managers must spend collecting planning information, which leaves them more time to devote to the planning itself.

Intelligence information Categories   EXHIBIT 3.8

Government regulations
Social and cultural trends
The economic environment
The political environment
Industry practices and trends
Product markets
Competitors
Technology

An intelligence information system usually is quasi-independent of other information systems. Most of the information gathered is usually directed to strategic planning, although some may be useful for short-term planning or for operations activities.

Despite the frequent association of the word "intelligence" with clandestine military operations, corporate espionage is not included in the concept of intelligence information systems. Most of the information gathered by intelligence systems is available from government agencies, industry trade associations, and private market research companies or appears in journals and newspapers. The remainder comes from special studies commissioned by the organization, which usually relate to specialized market research or technology forecasts.

The kinds of information gathered by intelligence information systems typically fit into the categories listed in Exhibit 3.8. Information is gathered in each of these categories to serve as general background information for managers who are responsible for planning, to establish trends, or to aid in forecasting. The information gathered may relate to significant past events or to probable future events, or it may be seemingly trivial information gathered in the hope that several bits of such information can be pieced together to reveal a competitor's strategy, a subtle shift in consumer preferences, or some other important pattern.

Intelligence information systems may be on a small scale and either formal or informal, or they may be comprehensive and formal. The concept of intelligence information systems for nonmilitary organizations is relatively new, and the methodology for their implementation is not widespread; thus while many large organizations, and particularly multinational enterprises, have comprehensive intelligence information systems, most medium-sized and small organizations, as well as some large ones, have only small, informal intelligence information systems or none at all.

Exhibit 3.9 lists the major components of a comprehensive intelligence information system. Whether large or small, the system is usually managed independently of the organization's data processing operations by a manager who reports directly to a vice president, the planning director, or even the president. The intelligence information system may depend

The Major Components of a Comprehensive Intelligence Information System	EXHIBIT 3.9
Intelligence needs profiles of managers The intelligence gathering system The coding and storage system The data analysis system Special studies The reporting system Data purging guidelines	

on the organization's central computer system, or it may be based on a separate microcomputer system.

The key element of an intelligence information system is the first item in the exhibit: managers establish "profiles" by specifying their intelligence information needs. A manager's profile might, for example, indicate that the manager would like to receive all available information about world bauxite production and about the production and marketing activities of specified companies that use bauxite as a raw material.

The intelligence gathering system, as outlined in the exhibit, systematically gathers data about the external environment from both internal and external sources. Members of the organization who are in direct contact with the environment—such as salespersons—are excellent sources of information. The intelligence information system should systematically gather information from these persons. Equally important, government reports, trade journals, newspapers, and other information sources should be monitored for information about the topics identified in managers' profiles.

The information collected is then coded. For example, bauxite production statistics might be coded with the key words "bauxite—production," or information about a key competitor that uses bauxite might be coded as "bauxite—ABC Company." The information is then placed in a computer or in other files from which it can be easily retrieved when needed by use of its key-word code.

More than 300 United States companies and many government agencies are in the business of selling over 3000 computer-readable data files containing intelligence information. The usual areas that these "data banks" cover are marketing, business and finance, industry statistics, and various aspects of the economy. Many of these services provide their data by subscription (usually on a monthly basis). Since the data is in the computer-readable form (usually on magnetic tape), key words can be used to identify information that is of interest to particular managers. Exhibit 3.10 shows an example of information provided by a commercial intelligence service; note that use of these services requires the definition of a "user profile" that is established by the subscriber.

An Example of Information Provided by a Commercial Intelligence Service   EXHIBIT 3.10

B3 Printed Extracts, to Customers' Editing Specifications

A subsidiary of McGraw-Hill publishes the Dodge Reports, an excellent example of a customized printed report. The Dodge reports field organization collects information on all proposed construction activity in the United States. It considers activities of all sizes, from single-family homebuilding on up to the construction of large industrial and commercial complexes. The field reporters follow the progress of each project, from the issuance of specifications and the letting of bids to the completion of construction.

Dodge mechanizes the information and keeps it up to date. Subscribers, largely contractors and building products manufacturers, ask Dodge to keep them informed of all developments within a subset of Dodge's data bank. The subscriber chooses the subset by specifying the geographic regions, dollar range, types of construction (e.g., brick, wood, or concrete), and the building's purpose (e.g., school or factory). Each day, Dodge produces and mails a printout of changes that occurred in that subset of its databank.

Source: Joel W. Darrow and James R. Belilowe, "The Growth of Databank Sharing," *Harvard Business Review*, November–December 1978, p. 188.

Data bank directories are also available; the National Technical Information Service (NTIS) publishes a federal government directory listing the information offerings of over 100 federal agencies, and the Association of Timesharing Users has an applications directory that briefly describes a great many data banks that are available to anyone with a computer terminal.

If a manager wishes, a trained analyst can retrieve related kinds of data—usually on a key-word basis—and analyze this data for patterns. To continue the preceding example, all recent entries during the current period about worldwide bauxite production, as well as about competitors' purchases of bauxite, might be analyzed together to permit study of purchasing patterns, such as whether each competitor is purchasing more or less bauxite than previously, whether the source of competitors' purchases is shifting significantly, or whether pricing patterns or practices are changing. Identifying trends in these areas could encourage an organization to change its own purchasing pattern, it could enable the organization to anticipate a competitor's efforts to expand a product's market share and thus allow time to develop a counterstrategy, or it could indicate the wisdom of entering into long-term contracts with producers of necessary raw materials.

Special studies may be conducted by intelligence information systems personnel or by an outside intelligence vending company commissioned by the organization. Typically these studies are narrowly focused on a problem area closely related to the activities of the organization for which current information is not readily available through its normal intelligence acquisition channels. A company whose senior executives will be meeting for discussions with a foreign head of state or a high government minister, for example, may wish a complete report on the dignitary's political persuasions and history in order to better understand the probable position of that government on matters that are scheduled for negotiation. As another example, a company may seek a detailed analysis of the recent economic history of a particular country in which it is considering going into business. Several companies, such as Business International, have extensive resources available for conducting a variety of specialized intelligence studies.

Intelligence may be reported to managers in many ways. For noncritical areas which a manager is monitoring, periodic updates, such as monthly reports, may be supplied. Often, managers will want to interrogate the intelligence files directly about a particular matter. For example, if sales levels of a product in one region decline dramatically, a manager may wish to inquire immediately about a competitor's recent activity in that region.

Another option is including a priority system in managers' profiles so that when intelligence information of a particular type is received, it is immediately reported to the manager rather than filed for later periodic reporting.

Purging is the systematic removal of outdated data from intelligence files. Specific guidelines must be established for this activity to ensure that data does not accumulate indefinitely but that noncurrent data that is still valuable is not discarded.

Small organizations with only meager financial resources can also have an effective intelligence information system. Large amounts of intelligence information about market and other aspects of the environment cost almost nothing, and much is modestly priced. Feedback about competitors' activities is almost cost-free, for example. The federal Freedom of Information Act makes a wealth of information available at no cost. A company can easily determine the competitors about whom information is available under the act by requiring from its own departments a list of reports that each must submit to federal agencies; the company then knows that its competitors' departments must also submit these reports. There are also many small market research firms that sell reasonably priced intelligence in competition with the larger and usually more costly firms.

A small or medium-sized company can also set up a small intelligence unit inexpensively by hiring one experienced market researcher to establish and maintain permanent files about the marketplace and competitors. Subscriptions to selected journals and information services, as well as to a clipping service that scans newspapers, are modest but worthwhile expenses for small organizations.

DECISION SUPPORT SYSTEMS

Decision support systems (DSSs) differ from most traditional information systems in that usually each decision support system is distinct from the other information systems (and often utilizes its own microcomputer) and is entirely within the jurisdiction of managers. Decision support systems, although they are created and run by managers, are nevertheless a part of the organization's MIS.

A decision support system is one of several approaches to establishing an information system for an organizational or managerial key task; indeed, a decision support system typically is tailored to a specific managerial task or special problem, and its use is limited to that task or problem. Decision support systems tend to be designed primarily to serve middle and senior managers, although they can be created to serve a manager at any level of the organization.

Typically, a decision support system uses a small, simple, computerized "model," in the sense that it models a managerial activity. The model is a set of programs, usually consisting of mathematical equations, that represent a particular management problem or task. Altering the model or its data input slightly, which is easily accomplished, offers alternative solutions to a managerial problem, each of which can then be evaluated. For example, altering the sales price within a model might permit an instantaneous determination of the profitability of that product if the actual sales price were changed.

The elements of a decision support system include the model, a specialized data file in the nature of a "data base," and a manager who interacts directly with the model through a terminal to test possible solutions to a managerial problem. The data in the data base typically is a combination of data extracted from the organization's transactions or master files and data from external sources, although all the data may come from only one of these sources.

A good example of a decision support system is one used by bank loan officers at a midwestern bank to evaluate potential customer loans. The system was developed, designed, and implemented by the loan officers who use it. The model's processing parallels closely the way in which the loan managers previously made loan decisions; thus the criteria that the model uses to make loan recommendations are essentially the same as those which the loan officers would use if they did not have the model. The system uses a computer terminal at each loan officer's desk. As a loan applicant provides information about financial status, the type of loan requested, why the loan is needed, and so on, the manager enters this information into the model through the terminal. The model contains lending formulas that consider such variables as loan duration and type, collateral provided, and applicants' creditworthiness as judged by bank policies. The data base already contains both externally provided data (such as data about national and local interest rates for debt securities and for loans of different types and durations) and internally provided data (such as current information about the amount of funds the bank has available for making different types of loans); most of this data is entered on a weekly basis.

The decision support system model calculates a recommended interest rate and payout schedule, recommends that the applicant's request be declined, or suggests a loan of another type or duration to the applicant. The loan manager can accept the recommendation of the model or can make another decision. Often the loan officer possesses additional information that cannot be accommodated by the model, which may justify a different decision. In such a case, the model output serves as useful input to the manager, who combines it with the additional information for further analysis.

Using this decision support system accelerates the loan processes, enabling each loan officer to serve more customers each day. An additional advantage is that while the model makes only recommendations, these are often followed, and therefore loan officers apply evaluating criteria— the criteria included in the loan evaluation formula—more consistently. The structure of the model is simple and easily changed, allowing loan officers to alter the model's formulas slightly every few days, as the structure of the economy and the bank's lending policies change.

Exhibit 3.11 enumerates the characteristics of a typical decision support system. The concept of a decision support system is of recent origin; only a few decision support systems were implemented before the late 1970s. Often a rudimentary decision support system is assembled after just a few hours of analysis and programming to deal with a special problem of management and is discarded when the crisis is over.

Several special-purpose computer software packages are available to help non-data processing personnel develop a decision support system quickly. These language packages usually include several prewritten analysis routines such as interest calculation formulas, discounted cash flow calculation routines, internal rates of return, and time-series analysis rou-

---

Characteristics of a Typical Decision Support System　　　　　　　　　　　　　EXHIBIT 3.11

1. Focuses on decision processes rather than transactions processing.

2. Is easily designed, simple in structure, and quickly implemented and altered.

3. Is designed and run by managers.

4. Provides information that is useful in a subsequent managerial analysis, rather than providing "the answer" or making a decision.

5. Is concerned with only one relatively small area of analysis or a small part of a large problem; more than one decision support system may be used for a large problem or task.

6. Has logic that attempts to mimic the way a manager would analyse the same situation.

7. Has a data base that contains information extracted from the organization's other files and information from the external environment.

8. Permits the manager to test the probable results of alternative decisions, enabling the manager to answer such questions as, "What would be the effect on total sales and profits if I changed the sales discount?"

tines. These routines can be easily integrated into a decision support system requiring that particular calculating function, thereby eliminating the need for the decision support system's developers to write computer programs for that task. Prewritten report preparation routines also greatly ease the programming burden. Interactive Financial Planning Systems (IFPS) and Simplan are two well-known decision support system software packages for use on large computers. VisiCalc, SuperCalc, Context MBA, Lotus 1-2-3, Symphony, and DSS-F provide similar but less extensive assistance in developing decision support systems on microcomputers; IFPS is also now available for microcomputers.

KEY-TASK ORGANIZATION OF INFORMATION SYSTEMS

Each organization has some tasks that must be managed extremely well in order for the organization to succeed in accomplishing its overall goals and even to survive. Typically, an organization has three to seven such key tasks, or what Rokart calls "critical success factors." These are usually determined by the nature of the organization's environment, by the rapidity of the changes within that environment, and by the nature of the industry of which the organization is a part and its position within that industry. For example, a key task for the National Rifle Association (NRA) is to assure that the nation's political climate does not change to favor tough gun control laws, which could adversely affect the market for small arms. To accomplish this key task, the NRA maintains a political lobbying group and an active public relations program.

Other examples of key tasks are (1) cost control in industries in which the products are similar and in which price increases would dramatically decrease market share, such as the supermarket and automobile industries, and (2) fashion design and inventory control in high-fashion industries, in which the design determines whether a product is successful and in which excess inventory cannot be sold at any reasonable price after the fashion changes. In the automobile industry, other key tasks beside cost control include maintaining strong dealer networks, controlling production costs (because these largely determine profit margins), and projecting an image of quality, reliability, and fuel economy for the manufacturers' products.

Most of an organization's key tasks are cross-functional in nature, in that information pertaining to several functional areas is essential for their successful accomplishment. Cost control, for example, involves information from all functions.

Product pricing is a good example of a cross-functional key task that is critical for many companies. Product prices may be set in any of a number of ways, and how they are set depends upon the circumstances. Most approaches to pricing, however, include a consideration of production costs, administrative costs, product R&D costs, and competitors' prices and pricing strategies; thus information for pricing decisions is required from several different functional areas, not just marketing, and information is also required from outside the organization.

Managers must identify the organization's critical tasks and devote the organization's best resources to ensuring that these tasks are done extremely well. A primary principle of information systems design is that the organization's information systems must be carefully tailored to serve its key tasks. Key-task information systems should have priority for development over other information systems and should be revised and improved frequently in response to changes in the environment or changes in managers' needs.

It can be seen that, while at the lower levels of the organization the principle structure around which the information system is organized is the hierarchical structure, at the higher levels, where senior- and middle-level managers must deal with the organization's key tasks, these key tasks become the primary structure around which the information systems should be organized. It is only in recent years that organizations have begun to shift their systems development efforts at the top of the organization from hierarchical information systems that are organized by function to cross-functional information systems that are organized around key tasks. The key tasks of the organization must be systematically identified, and the managerial information systems should be tailored to them; usually, there should be a more or less separate information system for each key task.

In some organizations the information system itself is critical to the success of the organization, and establishing and maintaining an outstanding information system is a key task. This is true of organizations that are "information-intensive," in that the availability of useful information is absolutely essential for managing other key tasks, for example when there is a natural "distance" between the managers and the activity that must be managed. This is the case in an airline company in which the key task of booking passengers for each flight takes place at many locations spread over thousands of miles. The response of airlines to this distance problem has been to develop a sophisticated computerized information system that permits reservations agents in distant cities to access a central computer to determine flight status and to establish passenger reservations on a flight.

Some organizations become information-intensive by their own choice: they elect to develop a better information system than other companies in the industry in order to gain a competitive advantage. This explicit attempt to use information systems as a competitive strategy is quite a different approach from the one, followed by most organizations, of designing an information system at the lowest possible cost that satisfies some perceived level of information needs, with no attention given to whether the information system is superior to that of competitors. When an organization seeks a competitive advantage through its information systems, it is electing to use a strategy of greater information intensity than its competitors.

INTEGRATION OF INFORMATION SYSTEMS

Integration of information systems is one of the key concepts associated with a management information system. Systems can relate to one another in several ways that underline the need for their integration. One way is through potential or actual flows of data between them. Information flows between systems are useful when data in the files of one system is needed by another system but when it would be impossible for the second system to generate that data or when this approach would be more costly, slower, or less accurate than using data from the first system's files.

Data flows between systems are commonly encountered where multiple systems need to access the same data elements from a common source or where the output of one system must be the input of another, such as when information from a transactions processing system is input to a managerial information system. Systems can also be related through their need to provide data for the same task or because each system utilizes the same data from another source.

When any of the above types of relationships are present, the systems are said to "interact." Interactions between systems are taken into account by establishing internal "linkages" between data elements in different systems that are related, for example, data elements that are utilized for the same reporting tasks. These linkages enable data to flow along "data paths" to wherever in the entire information system the data is required for calculating or reporting purposes. When these linkages are established, the systems are said to be "integrated."

Thus, integration is the interlocking of systems so that data from one system can be routinely passed to, or retrieved by, one or more other systems. With manual systems, a degree of integration can be accomplished, for example, by physically carrying data from one workstation to another workstation, where clerical personnel will combine it with data from other systems. Computerized systems can pass data automatically among systems, permitting a much higher degree of integration and greatly speeding up the data integration activities. With most computerized information systems, some of the data integration is accomplished automatically by the computer and some is accomplished by the data processing or clerical personnel. Usually, a major objective of systems development activities is to automate additional aspects of data integration, and, in general, the more automated the data transfers of an information system are, the more sophisticated and advanced that system is.

Integrating systems first requires identification of potentially useful interactions; managers associated with the systems usually must make this identification. However, managers may be unaware that certain kinds of data within their system would be useful to another system, or they may not know that data exists in another system that would be useful for their own activities. Interactions are best identified by planning and designing the systems together, rather than by planning and designing them one by one in isolation from the others. The most effective way of identifying potentially useful but often unsuspected interactions between systems is through a systems investigation that is not limited to just one system.

Integration of information systems may be hierarchical; transactions-level systems feed data to managerial-level systems, or, less often, vice versa. Hierarchical interactions are the most likely to be identified and integrated because managers know that information must be summarized along hierarchical lines, because the systems involved are under one chain of command, and because the managers in a functional area are much more apt to know what data is available from their own systems than from systems entirely outside their jurisdiction.

Exhibit 3.12 illustrates a rudimentary type of hierarchical integration, accomplished by having information from the transactions systems of three sales departments flow into a higher-level managerial information system. The flows depicted in the exhibit are common in organizations; often transactions master files from several operations systems feed data to a higher-level system. This type of data transfer, although it may be fully automated for certain sectors of some organizations, most often results from further processing of intermediate output by computer operations personnel. Data processing departments are responsible for consolidating transactions files to prepare management reports, and this usually also involves additional processing for further preparation of summarized reports to still higher levels of management and for preparation of a variety of different types of managerial reports. These activities

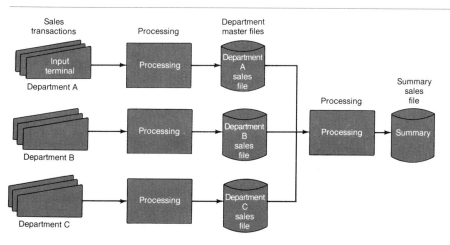

EXHIBIT 3.12
Hierarchical integration of information subsystems.

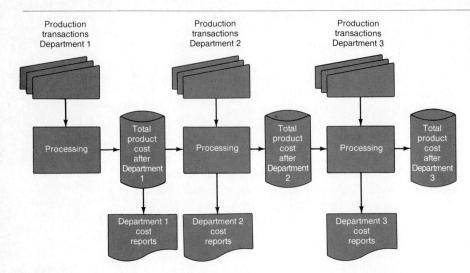

are performed according to a carefully orchestrated schedule of data processing operations and can be quite time-consuming and error-prone. A separate schedule may be followed to correct errors made during integration of the files.

Another type of integration is horizontal integration within a chain of command. In the example shown in Exhibit 3.13, data is passed among the information systems of several production departments as the products move from department to department. The departmental information systems are likely to be integrated so that information about the units of product in the process of manufacture is transferred routinely from one system to the next.

Cross-functional integration involves information systems that are associated with different functional areas. Cross-functional interaction occurs, for example, when the marketing information system routinely transmits information to the inventory control information system about sales lost because of inventory shortages. Often the desirability of cross-functional integration is not easily recognized.

Exhibit 3.14 suggests the complexity of the interactions of information flows in an organization by showing a combination of horizontal and vertical data flows. Despite its complexity, the exhibit is greatly simplified relative to the situation in an actual company, where many more interactions would be found. Each of the arrows in the exhibit may be viewed as the pathway for several types of information flows between information systems, which are represented as rectangles.

Integration can be accomplished by a number of different mechanisms. An elementary way is by establishing standard procedures, such as procedures for ensuring that data is physically transported from one information system to another. In a manual system, for example, a clerk

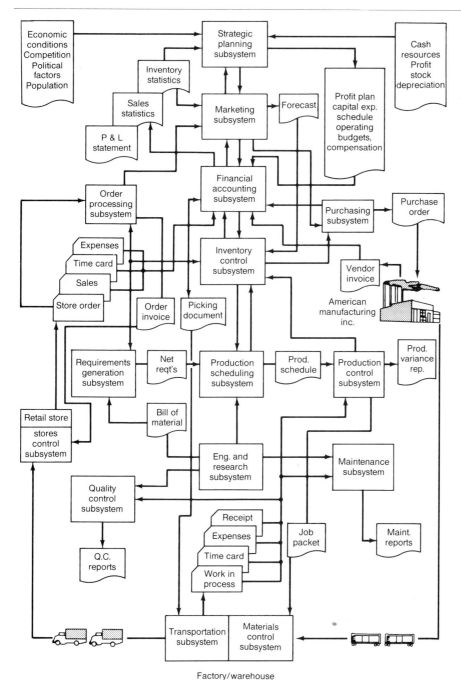

EXHIBIT 3.14
An information system model for a manufacturing company. (*Source:* Jerome Kanter, *Management Oriented Management Information Systems,* 2nd ed., Englewood Cliffs, NJ: Prentice-Hall, 1977.)

might have standing instructions to deliver a list of past-due customer accounts from the accounts receivable system to the credit department, where the list would serve as input to the customer credit system. Within this system the list would be combined with other information to assist in determining whether a customer should receive additional credit.

Information is also integrated when managers communicate information to one another. Managers are able to "pool" information from a number of information systems and to synthesize it for a variety of managerial purposes. Previous discussions of human information processing have demonstrated the efficiency of this form of interaction as well as its shortcomings.

In computer systems, integration can be accomplished by automated responses to internal conditions in certain situations. The programmed economic order quantity (EOQ) formula is an example. When inventory of a sales item becomes low, as indicated by programs that monitor the inventory computer files, computer programs automatically calculate a quantity to reorder and have a reorder request printed for the purchasing department. As part of this process, the computer may access and retrieve data from several systems; for example, it may first access a purchase order system to determine whether any purchase orders are already outstanding, then access a sales history system to establish the level and pattern of past sales for the item, then perform calculations to find the optimum quantity to order, and finally access the purchasing system to obtain names, addresses, item prices, and other pertinent information about vendors of the item in question. On the basis of this information, the computer prepares a request for a purchase order.

Formal data bases, which are a technically complex computer development, provide further opportunities for integration. Organizations with data bases can update records in several information systems simultaneously by entering one transaction, which serves as input to all the systems. Equally important, data bases greatly enhance the computer's ability to transfer data from one system to another automatically as needed. Finally, data bases enable information to be simultaneously extracted from multiple systems by one computer program. Two chapters of this text are devoted to data base technology and its implications for management.

Integration of information systems is a matter of degree. No MIS has all its computerized systems completely integrated, in part because doing so would not be cost-effective. Integration can increase the complexity of the entire information system in many ways; for example, more complex computer programs are required when systems are integrated than when they are not. Complexity, in turn, usually makes systems design more difficult and requires more computer equipment. Greater automated integration may increase the total computer processing costs in many organizations.

The major benefit of integration is better flows of information within an organization. Reports are likely to be more timely, and more information relevant to a managerial activity should be available whenever needed. This benefit is a powerful argument in favor of an integrated information system, since the very purpose of an information system is to provide the right information at the right time.

Another benefit of integrating systems is that it forces managers to share the information generated by their departments because the information routinely flows to other systems that need it. Information is then utilized more widely to help the entire organization achieve its goals. Without such enforced sharing, managers are often inclined to view information generated by their organization unit as their exclusive property and may make it available to others only at a price—such as in return for a favor from the other department—or not at all. Both withholding information from other departments and negotiating about its use generally harm the organization.

A careful tradeoff between the costs and benefits of integration should be made to achieve an optimum level of systems integration. However, because the methods and mechanisms of information systems integration are still being developed, most organizations' information systems appear to be less integrated than they should be. Increasing the degree of integration of the information systems of organizations is one of the important trends in information systems.

THE MANAGER/MACHINE INTERFACE

The data of an organization does not become information until it is communicated in a useful form to the organization's personnel who need it. This communication takes place at what is usually termed the "man/machine interface," but here will be called the "manager/machine interface." The manager/machine interface is the contact point at which the computer system provides information to managers or at which managers provide data to the computer system.

There are many examples of excellent *data processing systems* that are unsuccessful as *management information systems* because the manager/machine interface is not well developed—the machine and the manager do not communicate with each other effectively. Computer programs that are not designed to interact with managers are largely to blame for this. These programs communicate on the computer system's terms without accommodating managers' different styles and varying degrees of computer experience. This general problem area—the lack of user-friendly information systems—is one of the several reasons why information systems for managers typically are underdeveloped.

Most experts believe that there are two primary causes of this lack of user friendliness. The first is that systems analysts and data processing specialists do not have an intimate understanding of the management processes of organizations and hence are unable to tailor information systems to an organization's needs. The second cause is an inability to fully understand the way the human mind processes information, with the result that computer programs do not "think" (process data) as managers do and therefore are unable to communicate effectively with managers.

The several modes of communication between managers and computers are summarized in Exhibit 3.15. In one mode, the manager provides data input to the information system. An army of clerical personnel accomplishes the vast majority of this data entry task, but managers at all levels are called upon to provide a great deal of the information for the system; for example, managers make pay-rate changes, specify the number of hours worked by the employees they supervise, approve vacation pay, prepare budget and long-range planning data, correct errors in the data files, and specify credit limits for customers. Ultimately this data originated by managers enters the computer system for processing, generally by being passed either to subordinate clerical personnel or directly to the data processing department for input. In many instances, however, if systems were more user-friendly, managers could increase their own and the organization's efficiency by themselves entering the data directly into the computer system.

Information accessing is another mode of manager/machine interaction. While it is usual for both clerical and technical and professional personnel to routinely retrieve data from computer systems via computer terminals, it is unusual for managers to do this. Yet managers often need additional details about a particular problem, such as details about a labor budget variance within a plant. In many cases the potentially most efficient way for managers to acquire needed data is by directly asking the computer for it, and they would do so more often if the organization's information systems were more user-friendly.

A more advanced mode of manager/machine communication is continuous interaction by a manager with computer files. For example, a manager might initiate a multipart dialogue with the computer system by informing it that a general type of data is sought, such as data about products' life cycles. The computer may respond with a series of questions that pinpoint more precisely what data about which product's life cycle is desired, or the computer may provide product life-cycle information that

---

Modes of Direct Managerial Interaction with Computer Systyems   EXHIBIT 3.15

Developing computer programs
Dialogue, or "browsing through the files"
Accessing data
Providing input

is available within the system, such as lists and descriptions of the products about which life-cycle information is available.

A series of sequential interrogations by the computer follows (with the computer perhaps providing information each time about data that is available), and the manager responds to the computer each time. Ultimately the computer might offer the manager several related data sets, some of which the manager did not know existed.

The preceding is a sophisticated form of what is sometimes called "browsing through the files," which involves a manager's accessing and reviewing data in files and using this review to select other data that the manager would like to browse through. Several organizations now provide such a sophisticated browsing capability for their managers. Rokart and Treacy believe there is a trend toward having even very senior managers keep terminals in their offices so that they can retrieve multiple data sets in sophisticated ways for analysis.

A final mode of manager/machine interaction involves managers designing information systems for their own use by writing simple computer programs at their terminals. For example, if sales in a region are plummeting for no known reason, a sales manager might wish to use a computer terminal to write a few program instructions that will retrieve sales data and organize and analyze it according to salesperson, type of product, or customer type, for instance, in an attempt to find the cause of the problem. There are software systems in the nature of "query languages" that can be added to most computers to permit this type of managerial activity. However, the time required by managers to develop their own programs is usually significant. More frequently, a manager to whom such a system is available will ask an assistant to develop the program.

One reason why managers feel frustrated about using computer systems is that a great deal of training is necessary for effective use of the systems. Exhibit 3.15 lists the modes of direct managerial interaction with computer systems in order of the extent of the training and experience that managers must have in order to interact in each mode. It is reasonable to predict that as today's college students who receive training in computer systems move into the managerial ranks, the level of user frustration will decrease and the extent of direct manager/machine interaction will increase.

"Social distance" between managers and computer systems is also a manager/machine interface problem. There can be a social distance between two persons whose thought patterns, experiences, or stations in life are different, and this inhibits their ability to communicate with each other. However, if they both make an effort to do so, they can adapt their modes of communication and increase their ability to communicate. When a manager and a computer system attempt to communicate, however, it is the manager who must do all the adapting—the "conversation" mode of the computer is rigidly fixed by a specific format. This decreases the flexibility of the adaptation processes and causes a frustrating social distance between the manager and the system. When the manager fails to respond properly to a computer program, the program is likely to break off communication with a statement such as INVALID COMMAND, NO SUCH FILE, or SYNTAX ERROR. Usually a computer user's manual offers the manager the technical assistance needed to understand the computer's break-off communication, but this increases the time required for managers to interact with the system; also, user's manuals are seldom written in a way that makes them readily understandable by managers who have little experience with computers.

"Tutorial" computer programs that assist and educate the manager by generating helpful suggestions about correcting communications errors can greatly reduce social distance. The number of computer systems that are user-friendly in this respect is increasing.

Another dimension of a manager's problems in attempting to communicate with computer systems is that often the manager knows what information is needed but does not know how to locate it. After several time-consuming searches for data in a computer system, the frustrated manager stops trying to interact directly with the system. Again, there is a growing number of user-friendly systems that help managers quickly locate the information they need. Nevertheless, this problem greatly discourages direct managerial interaction with computer systems.

A major trend in systems development that seems destined to greatly facilitate managers' communiction with computer systems is the use of "productivity languages," which are sometimes called "nonprocedural languages" or, when used by managers, "managerial decision support languages." Productivity languages are specially developed computer languages that enable programmers to increase their programming productivity. These languages are easy to learn and are being adopted by user-managers for their own use. Using such a language, managers can efficiently interact with the computer system in all four of the modes listed in Exhibit 3.15.

Productivity languages are ushering in an entire new era. Traditionally, programs for routine data processing of payroll, cost accounting, and so on, have been prepared and modified by programmers within the data processing department. Currently, however, in most medium-sized and large organizations the typical waiting period for new programs and program modifications requested by users is about 3 years; this is due largely to an acute shortage of qualified programmers. Dissatisfied users who need new or modified systems, as well as data processing departments that are frustrated because of their inability to provide adequate service, are looking for alternatives to the development of programs by professional data processing personnel. The alternative that most are choosing is to have the user group's own personnel develop the needed applications programs by mastering easy-to-learn productivity languages. Often the data processing department establishes an Information Center which has special user service representativies who train personnel to use these productivity languages and who provide ongoing consulting services.

SUMMARY

The information system of an organization can never be fully automated or totally comprehensive. However, a very sophisticated MIS is possible and practical if it is based on a good overall plan and is developed by skilled systems personnel; adequate management participation and sufficient financial resources are also necessary.

An intelligence information system systematically gather data about the external environment from both internal and external sources. Most of the information gathered is usually directed to strategic planning. Subscriptions to data bank services may be of great help. Manager profiles determine to whom the intelligence information is distributed.

Information systems that serve key tasks must often be cross-functional and should be subject to constant revision to ensure their continued effectiveness. Key tasks are sometimes served by a decision support system, which includes a model, a data base, and a manager who directly intereacts with the model.

Integration of an information system is the linking of quasi-independent information systems. Most organizations would benefit from increasing the degree of intergration of their information systems.

The manager/machine interface is the linkage between the computer and the manager—the point at which they "talk to each other." Traditionally, computer systems have not been user-friendly, but new developments, such as productivity languages, are helping solve this problem.

KEY TERMS

data: facts, estimates, or opinions without significance or utility.

information: the result of the processing of data; information has utility.

purging: the systematic removal of outdated data from intelligence files.

integration: the interlocking of information systems, usually to permit data to flow easily among them.

cross-functional integration: the integration of information systems of different functional areas.

manager/machine interface: the contact point at which the computer system and the manager interact.

user-friendly information system: an information system designed to accommodate the different styles and degrees of computer experience of the nontechnical personnel who will use it.

productivity languages: easy-to-learn computer languages that increase the speed of program preparation and the user friendliness of a computer system. When used by managers, they may be termed "managerial support languages."

key task: a task that must be managed extremely well in order for an organization to succeed in accomplishing its overall goals.

REFERENCES

Ackoff, Russell L., "Towards a System of Systems Concepts," *Management Science,* July 1971.

Alter, S., "A Taxonomy of Decision Support Systems," *Sloan Management Review,* Fall 1977.

Darrow, J. W., and Belilowe, "The Growth of Databank Sharing," *Harvard Business Review,* November–December 1978, p. 180.

Hershey, Robert, "Commercial Intelligence on a 'Shoestring,' " *Harvard Business Review,* September–October 1980, p. 22.

Huff, Anne S., "Strategic Intelligence Systems," *Information and Management,* 1979.

Keen, P., and S. Morton, *Decision Support Systems: An Organizational Perspective,* Lexington, MA: Addison-Wesley, 1978.

Keen, P., and G. Wagner, "DSS: An Executive Mind-Support System," *Datamation,* November 1975.

Riley, M. J., "An Introduction to Systems Management," in M. J. Riley (ed.), *Management Information Systems,* 2d ed., San Francisco: Holden-Day, 1981, pp. 15–25.

Rokart, John F., "Chief Executives Define Their Own Data Needs," *Harvard Business Review,* March–April 1979

Rokart, John F., and Michael E. Treacy, "The CEO Goes On-Line," *Harvard Business Review,* January–February 1982, p. 82.

Sprague, R., and H. Watson, "Bit by Bit: Toward Decision Support Systems," *California Management Review,* Fall 1979.

Unlocking the Computer's Profit Potential, McKinsey & Company, 1968.

Wagner, G. R., "Decision Support Systems: Computerized Mind Support for Executive Problems," *Managerial Planning,* September–October 1970.

REVIEW QUESTIONS

1. Assume that you are attempting to write a user-friendly program for use by your organization's managers; what features would you try to incorporate into the program so that it would communicate effectively with the managers?

2. What are intermediate results? What is their effect on report timeliness? What is their effect on errors in reports?

3. Describe the processing of a computerized budgeting system.

4. Describe the relationship between external reporting and internal reporting with respect to information sources and the differences in data processing activities.

5. Could a university benefit from an intelligence information system? Explain.

6. What are the key tasks of a professional football team? Are any of these cross-functional in nature?

7. What sets a decision support system apart from most other types of information systems?

8. What are the advantages of increased integration in an MIS?

9. How can computer systems be made more user-friendly?

10. Do you think that in 20 years most senior managers will utilize desktop computers or computer terminals extensively? Why or why not?

Chapter 4

MANAGEMENT
INFORMATION SYSTEMS

PAYOFF THOUGHT

A management information system, in the full meaning of the term, is an obtainable goal. Enlightened long-range planning, which is the key to achieving this goal, is possible only if there is a full appreciation of the many dimensions of the concept of management information systems discussed in this chapter.

CHAPTER OBJECTIVES

1. To define management information systems

2. To present the concept of information as a resource that requires managing

3. To establish a framework for the reporting systems component of management information systems

4. To explain the sources of managers' dissatisfaction with their organization's information systems

WHAT IS A MANAGEMENT INFORMATION SYSTEM?

This textbook is about management information systems, but the meaning of this term has proved elusive. There are so many dimensions of management information systems that no simple definition is adequate. A background in systems studies is necessary to fully appreciate the meaning of the term "management information system," or MIS.

The preceding chapters have supplied this background. The following is a brief, formal definition of an MIS:

> An MIS is a *comprehensive* and *coordinated* set of *information subsystems* which are *rationally integrated* and which *transform data into information in a variety of ways* to *enhance productivity* in *conformance with managers' styles and characteristics* on the basis of *established quality criteria.*

The italicized key words and phrases in this definition are discussed below.

A Management Information System Is Comprehensive

The word "management" in "management information system" is all-encompassing. A management information system includes transactions processing systems and information systems designed primarily for managers at all levels. A management information system embraces formal and informal information systems as well as manual and computer systems; it also includes project information systems, office information systems, forecasting information systems, intelligence information systems, decision support systems and other computer models that process business data, and numerous other specialized or structurally distinctive information systems. On balance, perhaps the most important component of the management information system is the manager, whose mind processes and disseminates information and interacts with all other elements of the management information system.

A Management Information System Is Coordinated

The components of a management information system usually are not administered from one central point in the organization; various user departments, the data processing department, possibly a separate data administration function, and others may have jurisdiction over individual parts of the management information system. However, a management information system is centrally coordinated to ensure that its data processing, office automation, intelligence, and decision support systems, as well as other components, are developed and operated in a planned and coordinated way; to ensure that information is passed back and forth among the subsystems as needed; and to ensure that the information system operates efficiently. This coordination typically is accomplished by a separate steering committee or by the data processing or data administration manager.

A Management Information System Has Information Subsystems

A management information system is composed of subsystems, or quasi-separate component systems that are a part of the overall, unified system. Each of these systems shares the goals of the management information system and of the organization. Some of the systems serve just one activity or level in the organization, while others serve multiple levels or multiple activities. The overall structure of the multiple systems should be carefully established as a part of long-range systems planning.

A Management Information System Is Rationally Integrated

Subsystems (the collection of quasi-separate systems) are integrated so that the activities of each are interrelated with those of the others; this integration is accomplished primarily by passing data between these systems. Computer programs and files can be designed to facilitate data flows among the systems, and manual procedures also are used to accomplish this integration.

While integration makes information processing more efficient by reducing both intermediate processing and the incidence of independent generation of the same data by multiple departments, an even more important benefit is that it provides more timely, complete, and relevant information. Senior managers, particularly, benefit from integrated systems because they need cross-functional information. Although total integration of subsystems is neither achievable nor desirable, a substantial degree of integration is required for an effective management information system.

A Management Information System Transforms Data into Information in a Variety of Ways

When data is processed and is useful to a particular manager for a particular purpose, it becomes information. There are many different ways in which data must be transformed within an information system. For example, cost data for a particular organization may be summarized on a full-cost, variable-cost, and standard-cost basis for each organization unit, as well as by each cost type, customer type, and product line.

The numerous ways in which a management information system should transform data into information are determined by the characteristics of the organization's personnel, the characteristics of the task for which the information is intended, and the expectations of external recipients of the information.

A Management Information System Enhances Productivity

A management information system enhances productivity in several ways. It enables routine tasks such as document preparation to be carried out more efficiently, it provides higher levels of service to external organizations and individuals, it supplies the organization with early warnings about internal problems and external threats, it gives early notice of opportunities, it facilitates the organization's normal management processes and it enhances managers' ability to deal with unanticipated problems.

A Management Information System Conforms with Managers' Styles and Characteristics

A management information system is developed in recognition of the unique managerial styles and behavioral patterns of the personnel who will use it, as well as the contributions made by managers. At the organization's more senior levels, the management information system is likely to be carefully tailored to each individual manager's personal tastes; it will be retailored to each new senior manager who takes over. At the organization's lowest levels, the management information system is more likely to be tailored to the usual way in which clerical and operations personnel use information and interact with the information system.

For middle managers, the information system is tailored to the general characteristics of managers discussed in the preceding chapter. For professional and technical personnel, the information system is tailored to the nature of the specialized task, but with attention also given to the way the minds of these specialists process information.

Systems designers must carefully consider the human factor when developing a management information system. Otherwise, the resulting system will be ineffective and probably will be discarded by its users.

A Management Information System Uses Established Quality Criteria

A management information system must be designed to the required tolerances for timeliness, relevance, and accuracy of information. These tolerances vary from task to task and from level to level within an organization. With respect to timeliness, for some tasks data may be gathered over long periods of time and transformed into information for managers only periodically or at irregular intervals; for other tasks information may be needed at regular intervals, but a lengthy grace period may be allowed before it is reported after the end of the period. For still other tasks information is needed as quickly as possible after the close of the period, and for many tasks information must be available during the period when it is generated or even as a transaction occurs.

A management information system should provide only relevant information. Determining what information is relevant may be difficult in situations in which analyses vary for different managers or according to particular circumstances, such as in the case of special problems. The management information system must be flexibly structured to quickly supply whatever information appears to be needed for special problems.

Relevance may also be unclear with respect to the amount of detail required by a manager. For example, a manager who receives summary cost variances may decide that one of the several variances requires detailed study. Routinely providing full detail about all summary variances would mean that most of the detail provided would be extraneous and irrelevant.

The resolution of this dilemma is to design the management information system so that the usually unneeded detail is not routinely provided but is readily available if the manager later deems it relevant. If the data files are properly structured to anticipate the possible need for additional detail, it can be quickly retrieved if requested by a manager.

The information accuracy requirement is a matter of degree. Complete accuracy is sought for some purposes, such as transactions processing; reasonable accuracy is required for other purposes, such as forecasting near-term materials requirements; and rough estimates may suffice in certain circumstances, such as for long-range planning. The information system should differentiate between these types of circumstances and provide information with the required degree of accuracy. Often there is a tradeoff between accuracy and timeliness of information; for example, a manager may be forced to choose between receiving an estimate of the day's sales at the close of the day and receiving accurate sales statistics for the day by 5 p.m. the following day.

An information system must be accurate with respect to the consistency of information provided by its different parts. If its different systems provide conflicting information, users' confidence in the system may be adversely affected. Conflict can result, for example, when the same transaction is processed by two systems and reports are generated by both systems after the first processing but before the second, as well as when processing errors are not corrected (even if they are already detected) before reports are prepared. In general, a greater degree of integration of the systems protects against the first situation. The second situation can be alleviated by a careful error-detection program and an error-correction schedule that ensures that errors that might result in conflicting reports are corrected before the reports are prepared.

Other quality characteristics are also important. A management information system should provide feedback about its own efficiency and effectiveness. The reporting of computer malfunctions and transactions processing error rates is a simple example of this feedback. Statistics prepared by the system about who uses each system facility and how much they use each one are more sophisticated forms of feedback. Computer programs can record and report how much computer time is used by each user, how many pages are printed for each user, and how much internal data file space is utilized by each user's data, as examples; these and other usage statistics can be used for managerial analysis or as a basis for charging each user for computer usage if desired.

Feedback must be still more sophisticated, however, in that it should indicate how well the management information system is accomplishing its intended purpose. To a great extent, feedback about effectiveness must come from the participants in the management information system. This entails assessments of how well the management information system has identified trends, monitored the environment, and accomplished its other tasks. This feedback should be systematized and made a routine aspect of the management information systems control and management activities.

The management information system must also be able to adapt in response to feedback about its performance. That is, it must be designed to be easily modified if, for example, different information is needed because the environment changes or if the organization undertakes new activities (such as introducing new products) which require new modes of processing. The information system should be capable of being easily expanded to accommodate growth or new types of processing activities and also easily contracted, for example, in response to the elimination of a product line. One of the important requisites in terms of a management information system's adaptability is modularity—the management information system should be composed of many modules, or subsystems, rather than be designed as one or only a few very large systems.

Another desirable quality of an MIS is selective sharing of data. Two or more managers often need to utilize the same information; the system should have features which allow ready access to information by multiple managers. An advanced feature that promotes this sharing is data bases.

On the other hand, it is often important to reserve certain information for the exclusive use of only selected managers. Sometimes this need extends down to the record or field level, in which case some parts of a record are available to all managers, but only certain managers are permitted to examine other parts. For example, an employee's current address or marital status may be needed by employee benefits or other personnel, but access to information about pay rate, hours worked, gross pay, and other details of payments may be restricted to certain payroll managers. This selective sharing quality can be established by controls that are a part of the computer programs.

A MANAGEMENT INFORMATION SYSTEM: A MATTER OF DEGREE

As has been suggested in the preceding pages, an MIS is the result of careful attention to planning and design. Furthermore, it is created over a period of several years and is never finished because there are always systems to add or modify.

The preceding description of a management information system is idealized in the sense that the abstract concept is described as if it were reality; in fact, it is a view of the real world as seen through rose-colored glasses. In reality, the MISs of even many advanced organizations fall short of this ideal in some respects. The extent to which organizations have all the described ingredients of an MIS is a matter of degree. Indeed, some organizations' information systems are well developed in certain areas but are lacking in others.

Often it is impossible to say that an organization does or does not have a management information system in the many senses in which an MIS is described in this text. There is no one attribute or set of absolutely determinating attributes that an information system must have in order to qualify as a management information system. This inability to establish definitively whether a management information system exists in an organization tends to make the entire concept of a management information system somewhat fuzzy to students, but a person with experience in information systems does not find this frustrating.

An organization's particular circumstances influence the extent to which its information systems have the characteristics of a management information system. Size is perhaps the major determinant; an MIS is expensive, and large organizations are usually able to afford more sophisticated information systems than small ones.

The organization's traditions and pattern of evolution are also important. For example, in an organization in which the accounting group controls the computer systems, the management information system is sometimes less broadly developed than would otherwise be the case. This is due to the fact that accounting applications usually have first priority and the computer group supplies less service to other areas of the organization than to accounting.

The organization's management style is also a factor which influences the sophistication of the information systems. The style in some organizations is to make decisions on the basis of very little information, whereas other organizations make extensive analyses which require a great deal of information from their information systems. Also, management processes that are fluid and highly adaptive seem to be more conducive to encouraging a management information system than highly bureaucratic management processes.

Whether an organization has centralized, decentralized, or coordinative management also influences the nature of the management information system needed; another determinant is whether the organization is organized on a product line, functional, or matrix structure basis. The most sophisticated management information systems are likely to be associated with the coordinative, matrix form of organization, especially if the organization is in a dynamic environment. Less sophisticated information systems often are found in a functional decentralized organization.

The nature of the product line also greatly influences the nature of the information system. High technology and complex products (e.g., those with many components), a large number of different products, a diversity of general types of products, several different end markets for products, and differing production processes for product groups all contribute to the need for a more sophisticated information system.

A management information system is an achievable goal, even though it is not possible to determine at precisely what point an organization has achieved it. At present, several hundred companies, at least, have an information system that clearly qualifies as an MIS, and thousands that are striving toward this goal will achieve it within the next several years.

It should not be assumed that a management information system is an unmixed blessing. Developing and operating a management information system consumes a large quantity of resources, and conscious trade-offs between using resources for this purpose and using them for other purposes must be made. Most smaller organizations, for which a full-fledged management information system is not practical, should carefully select the management information system ingredients that are cost-effective for their needs. Additionally, in many or even most instances in which organizations are seeking a management information system, defective systems planning, design, or implementation means that although sufficient resources are expended, neither a management information system nor its benefits are attained.

A management information system should not be confused with a "total system," which the popular literature of a few years ago presented as an information system that captures and processess all the organization's data with computers. Total systems are a myth. A great deal of the information of an organization, and much of its most important information, does not flow from a computer system. Personnel at all levels must rely heavily on informally gathered information and on information provided by manual information systems—the manager will always have to rely to an extent on paper, pencil, and a pocket calculator. This is true, and always will be, no matter how well developed an organization's MIS becomes.

A management information system will never be complete. Some parts of it will always be under revision in a way that will cause inconvenience. Furthermore, some parts of an MIS will become obsolete as new technology appears or as organizational changes occur, and some parts will remain obsolete for long periods of time while higher-priority projects are completed.

A management information system can assist managers only by offering information and performing certain analyses; it cannot think for them. A management information system can make only the more straightforward, quantitatively based decisions by itself, and even these must be carefully reviewed by managers. Further, the direct value of the formal management information system to top management has so far been somewhat limited; this shortcoming will probably be overcome only gradually and partially.

The development of a management information system is limited by the extent of the participation of the managers who will use it. Organizations whose managers participate only superficially will have low-quality information systems.

CAPABILITIES OF A MANAGEMENT INFORMATION SYSTEM

A solid understanding of what the organization's information systems are able to accomplish is essential. Knowledge of the potential capabilities of a computerized information system enables managers to systematically analyze each of the organization's tasks and match them with computer capabilities.

A particular management information system may have several technical capabilities designed into it. Collectively these capabilities entirely disprove the often-heard assertion that "a computer is only a high-capacity adding machine or calculator: it can't do anything different; it can only do it faster." Computer information systems can have a number of capabilities far beyond those of noncomputer systems. These capabilities have revolutinized the nature of information systems and are revolutionizing the management processes which utilize the information that these systems provide. Already, significant changes in the way organizations are structured and managed have been traced to the existence of computer information systems. Micro- or mini-computers make these same capabilities available to small organizations. However, usually the smaller the organization and the smaller its computer system, the fewer of these capabilities are simultaneously present to the fullest extent.

Several of the most important technical capabilities of computer systems are listed in Exhibit 4.1. Each of these is discussed below.

Batch Transactions Processing

Most organizations handle a large number and variety of transactions. For example, the marketing activity alone may generate cash sales, credit sales, sales returns, sales backorders, sales commissions, customer credit or adjustments, and consignment sales transactions, as well as a variety of other sales-related transactions, each for hundreds or even thousands of different products. Additionally, many types of processing that are only indirectly related to the selling activity are also carried out, such as ad-

---

Capabilities of Computer Systems　　　　　　EXHIBIT 4.1

Batch transactions processing
Single-transaction processing
On-line, real-time transactions processing
Data communications and message switching
Remote data entry and file update
Record search and analysis
File inquiry
Decision algorithms and models
Office automation

vertising effectiveness analyses, product life-cycle studies, and market survey analyses based on questionnaire responses, to name but a few. Other functional activities likewise involve numerous types of computer-processed transactions.

An efficient way to process these transactions is to collect all transactions of the same type for a period of time and process them as one "batch" of transactions. For example, the sales transactions for a particular product may be processed once a day as one batch, with all entered at one time into the computer for processing. This approach enables data processing personnel to better control the entire processing cycle for that type of transaction, and it makes possible efficient scheduling of computer processing. Payroll transactions are an example of a transaction type that is almost always processed in batches.

Single-Transaction Processing

An alternative to batch processing is single-transaction processing, whereby each transaction is entered by itself into the computer system. While the efficiencies of batch processing are lost, there is usually no delay while waiting to accumulate a batch of transactions for processing, and therefore the records are updated on a more timely basis. Single-transaction processing is usually used where accelerating the speed of processing provides significant advantages, such as earlier delivery of merchandise sold.

On-Line, Real-Time Transactions Processing

If the transaction is processed not only singly but also as it occurs, it is said to be processed in an "on-line, real-time" (OLRT) mode. OLRT means that the record files for the transaction type are kept on-line; that is, they are electronically connected to the computer, and the transaction is processed quickly enough (in real-time) to affect the activity that generates the transactions.

Airline reservations systems are an example of OLRT data processing. A request for a flight reservation is entered, and the computer responds immediately with a reservation or with a notification that the flight is fully booked for the class of ticket sought. In the latter case, the real-time response permits the person to choose a different flight or perhaps agree to purchase another class of ticket.

Data Communications and Message Switching

Two or more computer systems can be linked by telephone lines or other data transmission methods so that transactions data, record files, and computer programs can be transmitted between them. Elaborate computer-controlled communications systems route the data to wherever within the computer systems the data is "addressed." In this manner, data pertaining to management reports, payroll, and so on, can be sent from one location to another to update files or to be printed as reports, payroll checks, or other documents.

Message switching uses this computer communications network. Message switching involves an "electronic mail" system, whereby an organization's managers send "letters," or messages, to managers at other locations instead of using the postal system. The electronic letters are received by a computer at their destination and are printed by that computer for subsequent delivery, or they may even be routed to the display terminal in the addressee's office. In either case, delivery is much faster than with the postal system.

Large multilocation companies are increasingly turning to message switching, and it is now commonly encountered in industry. An IBM executive has estimated that an IBM letter sent from one branch to another costs about $0.06.

Remote Data Entry and File Update

Utilizing the data communications systems enables transactions to be entered at the location where they occur and transmitted to another location for processing. The processed transactions can then update the records held at the second location, they can be returned to the originating location, or they can even be sent to some other location for reporting or for updating other records. If this is done using the batch method, it is referred to as "remote job entry" (RJE). It can also be done on a single-transaction entry basis in an OLRT mode. An airline reservations system is an example of an OLRT, remote data entry and file update system.

Record Search and Analysis

Often a computerized system makes particular types of records continuously available for reveiw. Parts inventory and customer accounts receivable are among the record types most often kept on-line. Typically, by means of a simple instruction to the computer which includes a record identification number, a clerk can request that a particular record or group of records be displayed on a cathode ray tube (CRT), which is sometimes called a "visual display station" (VDS), or a "visual display device" (VDD), a "visual display terminal" (VDT), or a "monitor." Many universities, for example, can have a student's complete academic record displayed within moments of a request so that the record can be used during a session with the student's adviser, for determining whether graduation requirements have been fulfilled, or for other purposes.

Less frequently, the computer performs routine analysis on these records and displays both the results and the record on the CRT, or the analysis is displayed instead of the record. For example, when the detailed record of a customer's purchases of many different products is displayed, the clerk may input a one- or two-word code that produces a summarization of purchases by type of product. The total dollar sales of each product as well as its average price might appear below the display of the entire record. Alternatively, the record detail might be omitted, and only the summarized sales would be shown.

File Inquiry

A manager often needs to inquire into a data file's records in order to get information needed for a management problem. For example, a manager might wish to see the records of all persons paid for more than 10 hours of overtime during the preceding week, to review the records of all employees who have filed more than one worker's compensation claim during the past year, or to see which items in inventory that cost more than $100 are in stock in a quantity that will last more than 3 months, judging from the average usage rate for the proceding 6 months. Many information systems are designed in such a way that a manager can easily formulate simple inquiries such as these and the computer can provide the answers almost instantly. "Query" languages are especially designed for this purpose.

File "browsing" is a variation of this simple inquiry approach. In browsing, a manager accesses a record within a file and uses information within that record to determine which record to access next. For example, a manager may be interested in tracing the probable cause of a product failure due to high temperature conditions. The product record, accessed from a remote terminal, shows the general characteristics of the product's several components, each of which is also used in several other products. The record also contains the computer addresses of the records depicting each component more fully. The manager chooses for follow-up the component that, from its general description, seems most likely to be damaged by high temperatures and keys in the address given for that record; that record is then shown on the video display. The record describes the various parts of the component and gives the computer address of each part's record. The manager selects a likely part, retrieves its record, and discovers that the part's detailed specifications show that it is made of a plastic which loses strength under excessive heat. By browsing through several records, the manager has located the probable source of the product's trouble when it is exposed to high temperatures.

This browsing ability depends upon records that are integrated by having information about one record contained in another record. This is sometimes referred to as an "associative capability"; that is, one record is associated with another by a relationship or by an attribute that they have in common. In the preceding example, the component is a part of the associated product.

Some information systems are designed so that even very complex requests can be programmed in a matter of a few days to produce complex, unscheduled reports. Without specialized design features, these same reports might require several months of programming. For severe management problems, the rapidity with which special reports can be produced may mean the difference between solvency and bankruptcy.

Decision Algorithms and Models

Computer programs may contain mathematical formulas that are used when certain conditions prevail within the computer files or when a particular event occurs. When triggered, the algorithm performs calculations that result in an action by the computer system, such as a a warning report; such a report is sometimes referred to as a "triggered report."

The best-known example of a programmed algorithm is the economic order quantity (EOQ) formula for inventory reordering. When the quantity of an item in inventory drops below a specified level, the EOQ formula calculates a recommended reorder quantity for that item. This recommendation is based on the actual quantity of the item remaining in inventory, the expected demand for the item, its cost per unit, quantity discounts that are available, and a variety of other considerations that are incorporated into the mathematical equation of the EOQ formula. Most systems have specific provisions to ensure that the "decision" made by the computer is reviewed for reasonableness and can be altered by a responsible manager.

More elaborate mathematical models, such as linear programming models, transportation models, mathematical programming models, and other management science optimizing models, also can be incorporated into the management information system. For example, a transportation model may determine the most efficient routes for delivery vehicles, or a linear programming model may determine the lowest-cost mix of different grain types that will enable a flour milling operation to achieve certain specifications for each batch of flour.

These elaborate decision models are routinely used as a part of the management information system in some organizations. Usually data from one or more information subsystems serves as input to the models, and often the models generate information that is input to another subsystem. The grain-mix linear programming model mentioned above, for example, would use information from the purchasing information system about the cost and quantities of each type of grain and would generate information about the average cost and characteristics of each batch of flour. In turn, the marketing information system would use the cost information to assist in establishing prices.

Office Automation

Office automation involves using computer power to automate clerical activities in the office, including the routine "pencil-pushing" clerical activities of managers. Office automation is one of the major trends in American industry. Many persons believe that it will eventually dramatically increase the productivity of white-collar workers. While office automation has made giant strides in the last 5 years, this technology is still in its infancy; although some companies would testify that office automation has increased their clerical efficiency, fewer could demonstrate that it has yet reduced their overall costs.

The trend toward sharply reduced costs of computers and related equipment has made office automation an alternative to traditional clerical approaches that should be evaluated. As computer power becomes less expensive, more and more activities can be economically computerized.

Often, computer power is combined with office machines to automate the office. For example, typewriter technology has made possible an electronic typewriter with a "memory" that serves the triple functions of traditional typing, data entry to a computer via its keyboard, and low-speed but also low-cost and high-quality computer printing. The typewriter's memory permits temporary storage of short documents, rapid correction of errors by erasing and replacing them electronically rather than correcting them manually, and convenient printing of multiple "clean" original copies when the document is edited and corrected. Such an electronic typewriter has some of the characteristics of word processing.

Word Processing

A word processing office automation capability can be effective in any office typing environment and is especially useful where information in narrative form must be reproduced frequently with only minor changes each time.

The typical office application involves producing a series of personalized letters in standard form, each of which contains identical or very similar information but each of which is addressed to a different person and perhaps contains a few phrases or unique entries, such as different order quantities or a personal greeting. To accomplish this, a standard letter or series of standard paragraphs is stored in computer memory. By means of instructions to the computer, the specific paragraphs can be selected in a desired sequence, and words, phrases, or sentences can be changed or deleted. Unique information, such as the name and address of the addressee, is then entered, and the computer types all letters at a high rate of speed. The result is a rapidly produced, usually error-free letter that is individualized in some respects but is in most respects a standard letter. When dozens or hundreds of such letters are prepared, the cost savings are significant.

Word processing is also quite useful for saving both time and expense in manuscript editing. For example, a student might first handwrite a term paper and then type it into a word processing system, making editorial changes as it is entered. The system stores the manuscript in its memory and prints a copy for the student. Prespecified margins, spacing, and caption types are automatically inserted. The manuscript can then be further edited and reorganized, and only the changes are then keyed in. The computer makes the requested changes and prints out the altered manuscript. This process of changing, or editing, the manuscript is repeated as often as necessary. One or more complete retypings may thereby be avoided, and the final copy is not disfigured by changes.

Some authors prefer to automate the process further by composing the manuscript at a word processing keyboard, which makes it unnecessary to handwrite it initially. Also, by using the CRT to display the manuscript, an author can enter changes directly into the computer without first editing a printed copy.

While there is a class of small computers that are dedicated to word processing and perform few or no other computing chores, word processing also can be accomplished on inexpensive microcomputers; through terminals used on large-scale, million-dollar-plus computers; or on systems of any size in between. Which computer system is used may depend in part on the complexity of the word processing required or on which system is already available for other data processing tasks and has excess capacity.

Clerical and Managerial Workstations

Exclusively word processing systems are beginning to lose ground to multifunction "workstations" that are actually general-purpose microcomputers. The microcomputers are good at word processing and also provide a broad range of other capabilities. For example, if the workstations are connected to a central computer system, they can serve as a direct entry data input station, and electronic mail can be routed anywhere in the system.

Additionally, the microcomputer workstation can be independently programmed and used directly for special managerial analyses and for storing and accessing a variety of data files needed only by that office. The workstation's functional capabilities can be tailored closely to the tasks of the office or of the manager who operates the workstation. Some managers are finding that such a workstation increases their own efficiency at office and data management so much that they no longer require the services of a secretary.

REPORTING CAPABILITIES

All information systems have reporting capabilities. There is a variety of types of reports, and these reports should have certain characteristics; that is, the reports should be designed to conform to certain reporting principles, as discussed below.

Principles of Reporting

Some managers passively accept the recommendations of systems analysts with respect to the characteristics of the reports they receive, and others simply continue to receive the reports that were provided when they assumed their position. However, managers can and should take an active role in determining the type and information content of the reports they receive. Several general principles should be followed when selecting reports:

• *Reports should highlight the important information.* Managers should not have to waste time searching through a voluminous report to find the few pieces of information they need.

• *Reports should be as simple as possible.* Reports should communicate information quickly; reports that are simple in format and simple in the sense that only a few key items are included and highlighted achieve this best. Extraneous detail should be deleted; for example, amounts in a balance sheet report usually should be reported to the nearest round figure, which may be $1,000 or even $1 million. Simplicity of reports does not imply that the information system is ineffective.

• *Backup detail should be available.* Generally backup detail should be readily available but not provided, or it may be provided as a separate supplementary report. For example, the full detail of specific categories, such as current assets, should not be shown on the balance sheet; a separate schedule for each specific category is preferable if full detail must accompany the balance sheet.

• *It should be recognized that managerial reporting systems are usually in transition.* Dynamic environments, changes in the organizational structure, evolving perspectives of managers, and new managers in the job mean that the system of reports is seldom stable. This seemingly chaotic condition is normal and is a sign of a healthy organization; a stablized reporting system may indicate a stagnant organization.

• *Some reports should be decision-formatted.* To the extent that the decision analysis can be programmed, the analysis should be done prior to report preparation, and the results should be prominently displayed. For example, if a manager uses contribution margin analysis for pricing decisions, the contribution margins of each product at each of several prices might be calculated by the computer programs and provided in the report.

• *The information system should be structured to report the causes of performance.* Usually this means that the information system is tailored to assign the results of each manager's activities to that manager. A responsibility accounting system is often used to accomplish this.

Summarization of Information

At the operations and supervisory levels managerial reports often must contain extensive details, such as a listing of the products produced or a listing of customer account balances. Above the supervisory level, however, most reports contain summarized information.

There are several types of summarization. The one most frequently used in business reporting is aggregation—the simple combining of the same categories of information within departments and across departments. Exhibit 4.2 illustrates a simple three-level aggregation system for one day's sales of products 1 and 2. The total day's sales figures at the

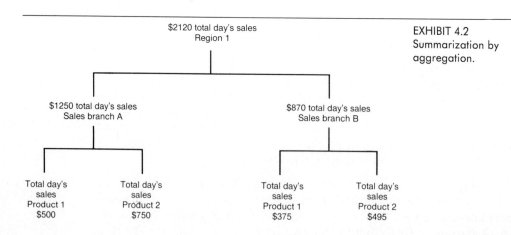

EXHIBIT 4.2
Summarization by aggregation.

bottom of the exhibit are already aggregations of many sales. At the second level, product 1 and product 2 sales for the day are combined at each sale branch, and at the third level, the total day's sales at each sales branch are aggregated for the region. A further degree of aggregation is possible in the exhibit: the total day's sales might be aggregated at the regional level only on a weekly basis.

In this example, aggregation has caused loss of information at the regional level in that the regional manager receives no information that shows total regional sales for each product. However, this information is available at each branch, and the manager who so desires can request that the aggregation process be altered to provide more detailed information to the region on a routine basis. Alternatively, this backup detail may be kept available and provided only when requested.

Compaction is another form of summarization. With compaction, data that is not considered important for a particular purpose is deleted. For example, a verbal report stating that "I visited the supervisor, who said that production will resume at 8 a.m. tomorrow morning," might be compacted to the terse statement: "Production resumes at 8 a.m." Compaction may be viewed as similar to shorthand. Its use in formal business data reporting is usually restricted to a few specialized circumstances.

Statistics provide an important form of summarization that is frequently useful in preparing business reports. Averages, medians, percentages or percentile distributions, ratios, and standard deviations are all statistical indicators that provide information about a set of transactions or other detailed data. Summary statistical indicators such as these can be presented either along with or without the detail on which they are based. A statistical sample can also be used as a summary of large amounts of data.

Written or verbal narrative descriptions can also summarize information. Verbal reports can be an efficient way to communicate, as has been noted in an earlier chapter, but they often suffer from a lack of precision and completeness with respect to the information communicated. Often, for example, narrative descriptions include only the highlights of more detailed information or the conclusions that were derived from deliberations. Both are forms of information summarization. An example of a summarization that highlights more detailed information is the summary that appears at the end of each chapter in this book. Uncertainty absorption, discussed in an earlier chapter, is an example of summarizing a situation by providing opinions that were inferred from the details rather than providing the details themselves.

Report Presentation Modes

The most common forms of nonverbal reports are written narrative form, tabular form, financial statement form, picture form, and graphic form.

Tabular Report of Units of Production   EXHIBIT 4.3

Product	This Month Last Year	Last Month	This Month	Last Year to Date	This Year to Date
Product 1	510	445	480	4452	3964 (−)
Product 2	428	410	440	3008	2892
Product 3	421	327	370	2410	2215
Product 4	803	701	722	5771	5117 (−)
Product 5	1097	844	1051	9304	8894

Each of these can be manually prepared in hard-copy (paper) form or can be computer-generated in either video display or hard-copy form. Narrative description is often used where the information is subjective and qualitative, at least to an extent. Term papers, theses, and the President's State of the Union address are examples of narrative reports. The managers of decentralized divisions typically send corporate headquarters monthly written reports discussing their division's problems, opportunities, progress, and goals. Usually these descriptions are accompanied by financial statements.

Financial statements are tabular summaries of financial activities. Most financial statements follow an organization's standard format, which the recipients understand and can readily interpret. This standardization also permits meaningful comparison of the financial statements of different periods and different organizational entities. Often the finanacial statements of one company are similar to those of other companies, and thus useful comparisons of the companies can be made. Financial statements can include operating and financial ratios or percentages that highlight the relationships between the various categories of financial data; if they do not, the ratios usually can be calculated. For instance, gross profit as a percent of sales and return on assets is considered useful information and can be readily calculated from a balance sheet and income statement.

Other forms of tabular reports are also frequently used, such as the one shown in Exhibit 4.3, which tabulates the production figures of one department. A review of this report quickly indicates that this month's production is greater than last month's but is somewhat less than that of the same month last year (except for product 2). Further, it can be seen that for all products, production figures were higher for the year to date last year than this year. It is often important for managers to be aware of large changes from a preceding period, and these may be highlighted in reports. For the report shown in Exhibit 4.3, for example, the computer was programmed to highlight changes from the preceding period (month and year) that exceeded a 10 percent increase or decrease by underlining the related current-period figure; decreases from the preceding period are further highlighted by the (−). If the data tabulations are not extensive or if key figures are highlighted, tabular reports can communicate information quickly and efficiently.

When the information is not quantitative or if only a general impression or an overview is needed, pictures can be used effectively. For example, a picture of a roly-poly, jovial person may be used to portray good financial health, and a picture of a thin, scowling person in tattered clothes may be used to portray the opposite. While pictures are often used in advertising to communicate a general impression to consumers, they are seldom used to report information to managers about an organization's activities.

Graphs are one form of pictures that managers do use. Graphs are numeric data converted to picture form. They usually portray relationships or comparisons between quantitative information elements, such as the relationship between fixed costs and variable costs, or a comparison of the profits of two or more divisions.

Graphic reporting is becoming recognized as more efficient than either descriptive or numeric reporting for some purposes. Graphics can communicate an entire pattern of information quickly, increasing a manager's ability to absorb the information presented. Placing numeric data in graph form is itself a process of data interpretation; thus data in graphic form is in effect preinterpreted before the manager receives it. Managers therefore usually grasp the meaning of information presented in graphic form more quickly than they do that of information presented in numeric or descriptive form. However, if too much information is presented in a graph, the graph becomes cluttered, and the result is information overload.

Presentation graphics is the form of graphics that is roughly comparable in purpose to printouts and other forms of managerial reports; prep-

The HP 150 personal computer, with HPTouch, supports a full range of peripherals, including the new HP 7475 plotter. The HP 150 is shown with on-screen graphics and with hard-copy graphics output from the plotter. (Courtesy of Hewlett-Packard Company.)

aration of presentation graphics is usually done by graphics specialists and may be a time-consuming activity, especially if subsequent modification is required. Interactive graphics is a form of graphics for which computer programs are especially developed to facilitate flexible and easy alteration of input data. Using interactive graphics, managers modify the displays on a video display device. For example, with interactive graphics a manager can alter one of the variables in the graph—such as the proportion of fixed costs to variable costs—and immediately see the graphs reconfigured; in this situation a new profit break-even point would be calculated, and graphs which portray the new cost and break-even configuration would immediately appear on the display device.

Computer graphics for business management is one of the strongest growth areas in computing. Inexpensive computers and graphics software, coupled with studies showing that managers absorb information better when it is presented in graphic form, account for this strong trend. All major computer manufacturers now offer business graphics systems, most of which will present the graphics on a CRT or print out the graphs. Additionally, several microcomputers now have good business graphics CRT capabilities.

Exhibit 4.4 shows typical computer-prepared business graphs. These graphs can be prepared easily by inputting the quantitative data and selecting the graphics mode (e.g., a line or bar graph) with a key entry or

(a)

EXHIBIT 4.4
Typical computer-prepared business graphs.
[*Sources:* (a) Courtesy of Digital Equipment Corporation. (b) © Data General Corporation. (c) Courtesy of Hewlett-Packard Company. Used with permission.]

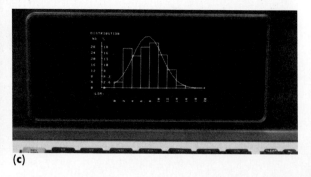

(b)   **(c)**

a simple keyboard-typed command. Usually the variety of graphics modes that can be selected or constructed is limited more by the imagination of the manager than by the capabilities of the graphics system. Typically used are time-series graphics, with time on one axis and events or financial amounts on the other axis to shown the pattern variables over time; bar charts; area graphs (such as sales for each territory shown in a map graph); pie charts; histograms; and correlations of two or more variables to display the relationship between them. Color graphics systems are available from many vendors.

Exhibit 4.5 gives the student the opportunity to perform an experiment relating to the efficiency of communicating financial information

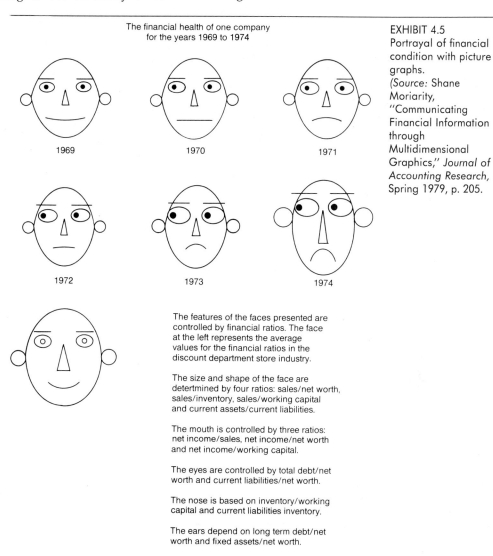

The financial health of one company
for the years 1969 to 1974

1969   1970   1971

1972   1973   1974

EXHIBIT 4.5
Portrayal of financial condition with picture graphs.
(Source: Shane Moriarity, "Communicating Financial Information through Multidimensional Graphics," *Journal of Accounting Research,* Spring 1979, p. 205.

The features of the faces presented are controlled by financial ratios. The face at the left represents the average values for the financial ratios in the discount department store industry.

The size and shape of the face are detertmined by four ratios: sales/net worth, sales/inventory, sales/working capital and current assets/current liabilities.

The mouth is controlled by three ratios: net income/sales, net income/net worth and net income/working capital.

The eyes are controlled by total debt/net worth and current liabilities/net worth.

The nose is based on inventory/working capital and current liabilities inventory.

The ears depend on long term debt/net worth and fixed assets/net worth.

using graphs. Before reading further, and knowing only that the cartoon faces in the Exhibit are carefully constructed to portray overall financial trends in a company, give yourself exactly 30 seconds to scan the two rows of faces from left to right. Then cover the exhibit. Judging from the last face, on the right in the second row, what is your opinion of the financial trends of the company and its financial health?

In Exhibit 4.5, specific financial relationships determine the expressions on the faces. Experiments indicate that financial information about the health of an organization can be quickly communicated by facial features; in the exhibit, a broad smile is interpreted as robust profits; a frown, as slight losses; and a scowl, as large losses. Each of the facial characteristics, such as the size of the eyes and the shape of the nose, is also designed to communicate financial relationships.

Most students correctly conclude from their 30-second view of Exhibit 4.5 that the company was in moderately good health in 1969 but that its health deteriorated more each year until in 1974, it was either bankrupt or on the verge of bankruptcy. Consider how much time would be required to reach these same conclusions by analyzing balance sheets and income statements for the period 1969–1974!

The way in which information should be summarized depends on the purpose for which it is needed. Often, the same information is summarized in more than one way. For example, the same information may be first aggregated and reported on a budget classification basis for cost control purposes and then on a contribution margin basis by product line to evaluate the performance of each product line; finally, it may be aggregated by type of expenditure for preparation of accounting financial statements. Some of the same data may then be summarized and reported in graphs or in statistics. Computer programs can transform the same data by a series of data processing steps to provide these and other types of summary reports.

As can be seen, different reports can be based on the same data but serve a different purpose. In general, the more levels that exist in the hierarchy, the more manual intervention in the system by data processing personnel is required to summarize information for the entire organization. However, a high degree of integration of the MIS serves to reduce the direct attention of data processing personnel during processing and to increase the speed with which all summary reporting is completed.

Types of Reports

Periodic Reports

What is most commonly expected of information systems is that they will provide routine reports on a scheduled time-period basis. Typically these reports are issued weekly, monthly, quarterly, or annually. These periodic reports cover a broad range, from standard accounting financial statements and reports for public relations use to reports about the status of chemical or other processes monitored by engineers or laboratory technicians.

Computerization has extended and enhanced the periodic reporting capability considerably. It has dramatically decreased the time lag between the end of the period and the completion of the reports; for accounting financial statements, this lag might decrease from 2 or 3 weeks to a week or less after the end of a quarter or from 3 or 4 months to as little as 1 month after the end of a year. A major reason for this is the sheer speed of computer processing and report printing. Additionally, certain end-of-period data processing activities can be programmed and automated.

The frequency of periodic reports often increases because of computerization. Elaborate reports that might be provided only monthly if prepared manually might be prepared weekly if a computer is used.

The decreased cost of computer processing often increases the scope of periodic reports. Reports which previously were not considered cost-effective to prepare at all or which were completed and delivered so late that their decreased utility robbed them of cost effectiveness may become worthwhile when they can be produced less expensively and more quickly by computer. Thus, computerization usually increases substantially the total number of periodic reports that an information system produces; indeed, the increase is sometimes so great that managers do not have time to review all the periodic reports they receive.

The computer also makes it easier for periodic reports to include information generated by several different information systems. This is due to the fact that data can be more readily retrieved by computer from several separate files for combination into one report. For example, the computer can retrieve sales information about each product from the sales file and information about full and marginal costs of production for each product from its respective file and can combine these three types of information to produce periodic gross profit and contribution margin reports. However, a contribution margin system such as this is very complex, and even with a computer the data processing required is extensive.

The preceding discussion begins to explain why even small organizations are becoming computerized. Better periodic reporting may make a computer system worthwhile even if it does not reduce total costs. The other reporting options noted below are also available to small organizations and can be used to justify computerization.

Key-Indicator Reports

Key-indicator reports are an important variation on periodic reports. These reports typically provide a few of the critical statistics from the preceding day's operating activities to managers on a daily basis. For example, by 8 a.m. the sales manager of each district in a large, geographically decentralized company might receive a report on the total district sales for the preceding day, and the national sales manager may have a report on all

Typical Key Indicators That Are Reported Daily   EXHIBIT 4.6

Marketing	Accounting	Manufacturing
Cash Sales	Collections on account	Units of product started
Credit sales	Total cash receipts	Units of product completed
Credit rejections	Total cash payments	Units of product scrapped
Gross profit	8 a.m. balance in the bank	

sales nationwide before noon that day. Also, the production department supervisors might receive a report of total production and a product scrap count for their departments for the preceding day at the time they start their morning work.

As other examples, the average profit margin for sales of products in a particular product line might be provided for the preceding day, or inventory levels in units or in dollars might be provided daily for as many or as few inventory items as desired An early-morning report each day on the quantities of those inventory items which are critical to the production processes can help ensure that shortages of these items never cause production to stop. Exhibit 4.6 lists typical key indicators that the computer in a small manufacturing company could report each day.

Key-indicator systems are used when a manager wishes to monitor certain critical aspects of operations at frequent intervals in order to react rapidly to trends or problems in these areas. Key indicators are chosen because they are basic indicators of the health of the part of the organization that the manager controls or because they are in especially dynamic parts of the organization where operations can go awry very quickly. Often, key indicators are tied in with an exception reporting system so that the manager will receive reports only of the indicators which are outside the range of acceptability. Usually the key-indicator system is designed so that the manager can receive the full detail related to a reported exception if the key indicator itself is not adequately informative.

The major benefit of a key-indicator system is its timeliness, which enables managers to keep their finger on the pulse of the most important activities within their jurisdiction on a daily basis. A computer system can provide the key-indicator operating results at very frequent intervals.

On-Call Reports

On-call reports are periodic reports that a manager decides are needed before the end of the period, perhaps because of an unexpected operations problem or a threat from, or an opportunity in, the environment. For example, a manager may want to see a report of a product's production costs for the month to date, even though only a monthly report is scheduled. Perhaps at the beginning of the month a new supervisor was assigned to the department producing the product and the manager wants to be able to advise and counsel the supervisor by mid-month, but periodic reports would not be available for about 3 more weeks.

Computer systems can be organized to make this type of report, known as an "on-call report," available on short notice. This capability usually involves keeping the files that provide the reports updated at frequent intervals so that whenever a report is requested, the file that provides it is already up to date. Because doing this can be expensive, usually only certain periodic reports can be provided on an on-call basis. Often, too, this capability is only partial; only certain parts of a periodic report may be on call, and these sections may be available only through a terminal, rather than being prepared and distributed by data processing personnel.

Special Reports

Special reports, sometimes referred to as ad hoc reports, are another type of unscheduled report that may be requested by managers. Special reports are requested because the organization has encountered unexpected problems or has unanticipated information needs.

In most organizations, managment involves a stream of problems; some of these are unusual and unanticipated and will arise only once. Examples are inventory buildups or shortages, sudden slumps in the sales of products in a particular product line or in the sales of a particular major product, and uncertainlty about the effects of a proposed merger on the organization. Many of these special problems cross functional lines, transcend a single geographic area, or involve information from outside the organization or from several levels within it. Further, many of these problems are critical to the organization's continued prosperity.

Acquiring the information needed to analyze these unexpected problems is often difficult; for example, the information may be stored in geographically dispersed files or scattered throughout a series of differently structured files and be capable of being retrieved only by specially written programs. When the data processing schedule is busy, several weeks or even several months may elapse before a manager receives a special report that has been requested. In the case of most operating problems this is not fast enough, and in the case of serious problems it may be disastrous.

Information systems designed to facilitate the rapid gathering of information needed for resolving unanticipated management problems are said to have an "ad hoc reporting capability." This capability is especially important if information is needed from several different functions, for example, from sales activities, from inventory, and from production activities. An ad hoc reporting capability requires establishing and maintaining a comprehensive directory of the data file contents that can be quickly referenced to find the needed data's location in the file. This capability also requires an efficient means of retrieving this data. Specialized data retrieval software programs that are commercially available, such as Easytrieve, provide efficient accessing but lack adequate directory capabilities. A formal data base provides both attributes.

Exception Reports

Reporting in many organizations incorporates the exception reporting principle: Only those information items which will be of particular interest to a manager are reported. Usually, these items indicate that normal operations have gone awry. Exceptions may be highlighted within reports that also contain nonexception data, or only the exceptions may be reported. In the latter case, for example, a periodic inventory status report may list only inventory items for which the quantity on hand is either too high or too low, deleting the vast majority of items for which quantity levels are about right.

Exception reporting can be incorporated into normal periodic reporting. For example, rather than printing out a report of an entire aged accounts receivable list each month, the computer may be programmed to list exceptions that include only all accounts receivable balances of more than $100 that are more than 2 months old. Similar periodic exception reports can report production variances, out-of-stock or excess inventory conditions, and a variety of other unusual circumstances, as illustrated in Exhibit 4.7.

Key-indicator reports can also use the exception reporting principle to flag for management's attention the exceptional items among a series of key indicators. On-call reports can also highlight exceptions.

Unusual or suspicious circumstances can also be reported as exceptions. For example, an unusually large money transfer to or from a financial institution might provoke an automatic notification to a senior executive, as might also an unusually large number of unsuccessful attempts to enter the computer files from a remote terminal. Similarly, a large materials usage variance in producing a batch of a product could trigger an exception notification so that a manager would know of the variance long before it appeared on a periodic report.

Typical Conditions Reported as Exceptions   EXHIBIT 4.7

Merchandise orders received with more than 5 percent defective items
Sales back orders not filled for 30 days
Sales with discounts over 10 percent
Regional sales levels that are 5 percent less than quota, by sales item
Production scrap levels over 2 percent
Installment loans for which the period's payment was not received
Inventory items that were used or sold 20 percent faster or slower this period than last period
Cost variances over 10 percent of budget

Summary of Report Types	EXHIBIT 4.8

Periodic reports
Key-indicator reports
On-call reports
Special reports
Exception reports

Exhibit 4.8 summarizes the several types of reports discussed. Computerization has affected each category, as explained in the preceding pages. Key-indicator and on-call reporting capabilities, where they exist, have done much to eliminate managers' dependence on the weekly or monthly reporting cycle. Managers with sophisticated information systems can now receive information when they need it, rather than having to wait for the next periodic report.

INFORMATION RESOURCES MANAGEMENT (IRM)

What is IRM?

IRM is a concept, an idea, and a perspective, rather than an entity. In its most fundamental form, IRM is an attempt to focus attention on the information that is produced by a system rather than on the system itself or on the hardware and software components of the system. With IRM, information and its availability and usage have primacy; computer systems are viewed as important only because they are necessary to generate and manage information. The emphasis of IRM is managerial, not technical.

In a real sense, IRM is a reaction of managers to technicians' dominance of information systems—traditionally, the data processing group has been in charge of the information function within the organization, and all information personnel reported to the manager of data processing. However, data processing groups have tended to be preoccupied with the short-term technical and transactions processing aspects of their activities and have historically focused on the development of individual systems or even individual programs that are designed for a specific and limited purpose. This has resulted in specialized files and applications programs dedicated to those files.

However, these files, each devoted to its own task, often do not share information readily with other files and are not designed in recognition of the long-run relationship of the file/program set to the entire information system of the organization. Further, different data format standards and record coding systems have proliferated within each organization. Communication and integration of data across organizational boundaries have suffered.

The computer programs written in this milieu are often technically elegant and utilize the computer efficiently. However, data processing usually has not focused on how effectively information systems serve managers and specialist users, other than those involved with transactions processing. The temptation—often not resisted—has been to offer managers information that is a by-product of the numerous transactions processing systems rather than to develop the integrated systems that serve managers' purposes best.

Equally important, the preoccupation of the data processing group with the computer and the technical aspects of computer applications has meant that emerging new capabilities such as word processing and office automation have not been properly woven into the fabric of overall information systems development. The consequence is that these capabilities have not been given proper guidance or been incorporated into a cohesive plan for systems development.

To continue, typically relatively little effort has been devoted to ensuring that all information of the organization is made available to whoever in the organization needs it. Often one department, unaware that the information it needs already exists for another department, either does without the information or duplicates effort by independently generating the information for its own use. Often, too, managers of the information-generating department feel proprietary about their information and withhold it from other units or use it as a bargaining lever.

These problems and others have been so serious that traditional approaches to providing information within organizations have been rethought. The concept of information as a resource of the entire organization has emerged and is now beginning to alter attitudes toward information systems. There are three distinct elements of this change of perspective:

1. Information is viewed as a *resource,* not as a by-product of transactions processing.

2. Information is seen as a resource of the *entire organization,* not of just the department that generates or receives it.

3. Information comes from many sources, not just from traditional data processing activities.

When information is viewed as a resource of the organization, it is seen to be conceptually separate from the computer or other system that contains the data, and the necessity of managing information using the same management techniques that are used for other resources, such as cash and inventory, becomes apparent. Applying management principles to the resource of information demonstrates that the marginal cost of making particular information widely available within the organization is usually low, whereas the benefits of doing so are often great. Further, the principle of "global optimization," derived primarily from mathematics, indicates that in many circumstances any value lost to an information-originating department because it shares its information (such as a decreased ability to compete with other subunits of the organization) generally is more than offset by the increase in the shared information's value to the entire organization.

IRM is, as noted, a perspective. It is also an approach to organizing and integrating the diverse elements that constitute an information system. Finally, IRM is the *management* of these ingredients and of the information of the organization in a coordinated manner. In managing information, IRM takes the perspective that what is most important is that information, as a resource of the organization, has value and should be managed in much the same way in which other resources are managed. IRM attempts to apply normal resource management methods to information.

With respect to this management of information, there are both similarities and differences between information and most other resources, such as inventory and equipment. The similarities are:

1. Information has a cost. Its total value should exceed its total cost; if it does not, the information should not be acquired.

2. Information has a return on investment, although this is more difficult to measure than that of many other resources.

3. There is an opportunity cost of not having information. Like many opportunity costs, it is often overlooked.

4. Combinations of data elements can provide value added that is greater than the sum of the parts of the data elements.

5. The effective use of information requires good organization for its use; this is what IRM is all about.

Information differs from other resources in the following respects:

1. Most other resources are consumed in production (e.g., inventory) or are worn out (e.g., equipment), but information can be reused indefinitely at a low marginal cost per additional usage. This makes information a particularly valuable resource.

2. Information is intangible. This makes it more difficult to see how it should be used and to measure how effectively it has been used, which accounts partly for the fact that information management concepts have emerged only slowly.

The management of information takes into account all the similarities and differences discussed above. It requires cost and value analyses and estimates of the return on investments in information. It identifies information opportunity costs, which might be overlooked because information is an intangible commodity. It combines data elements in a variety of ways to enhance the value of information. It sees to it that information acquired is reused to the point where, in economic parlance, its marginal cost equals its marginal utility. It establishes a specific organization to ensure that all this is done.

The Ingredients of IRM

All the information resources of an organization should be within the purview of an IRM activity. These include:

- Business data processing
- Systems and applications development within an MIS context
- Data management
- Networking
- Office automation and word processing
- End-user computing
- Information centers

The task of IRM is to integrate and coordinate the above activities for the entire organization. The last five of these require a brief word of explanation.

Data management consists of managing data in the organization's data bases in such a way as to make it widely available throughout the organization; in many organizations a data base administrator is appointed to accomplish this task.

Networking is the task of developing and managing the organization's communications networks so that they provide efficient data flows throughout the organization. This activity is critical to integration of the information resource flows.

Office automation and word processing activities consist of automating the clerical processes so that they are accomplished efficiently and so that the information resulting from them can be disseminated via the communications networks.

End-user computing is a related but broader concept that takes account of the current strong trend toward user departments' doing a major portion of their own data processing and data analysis. For end-user computing, user groups must be given controlled access to data in the data bases of the organization, and the results of end-user processing must be made available for distribution to wherever they are needed by the communications networks.

Many organizations now have an information center. Because this is a new type of information activity, there is as yet little agreement about its activities and purposes. Most information centers, however, are created primarily to assist end users acquire and develop their own computing systems.

It is the task of the IRM function to integrate and coordinate each of these activities. It can be seen that IRM is an all-encompassing, information-focused concept that involves no less than organizing all aspects of the information activities and flows.

Organizing for IRM

Because the concept of IRM is new, organizations have so far attempted to implement it in a variety of ways. In different organizations one or more of the following persons may be given significant responsibilities for IRM:

- The data base administrator

- The information center director

- The director of user services

Increasingly, organizations are realizing that no one of the above persons' responsibilities are so encompassing that that person can properly coordinate the entire IRM activity. To achieve this overall development and coordination, many organizations are appointing what has come to be known as an "information czar," whose formal title is "vice president of information" and to whom the persons listed above, as well as the director of computing, report.

The consequence of the movement toward IRM is that organizations are beginning to look at the totality of their information systems when planning and designing subsystems. Organizations that do this are more likely to establish information systems that encompass all the important information flows; in short, their information systems are being molded into an MIS.

An organization that lacks IRM may pay a heavy price. A study by A. T. Kearney, an international consulting firm, of companies in a variety of industries indicated that only 8 percent of these companies were successful in managing their information as a resource. This 8 percent had formal plans to organize, control, and monitor the information resources and "out performed the rest of the sample by 300% in terms of average return on equity, return on total capital and net profit margins over a five-year period." This suggests two conclusions: First, at present few companies are managing their information resources well; and second, those few companies are able to utilize their information resources to enhance their productivity dramatically. Top management's deep involvement to managing information as a resource was identified as the critical ingredient in successful information management programs.

THE NEED FOR A MANAGEMENT INFORMATION SYSTEM

The design, implementation, and opertion of an MIS are both expensive and difficult. This effort and expense must be justified. Several factors make such a system more necessary than it was just two or three decades ago.

One factor is that managers must deal with a much more complex business environment than has existed before. One of the major reasons for this complexity is increased government regulation, which requires organizations to undertake many activities that were previously unnecessary; usually these involve filing a variety of regulatory reports. Another reason for this complexity is the wider variety of products and services that organizations offer their customers; managing this greater variety requires more sophisticated information systems.

The business environment is not only more complex but also more dynamic. Managers have to make more decisions quickly, and typically less time must elapse between the emergence of a management problem and its satisfactory solution. This is true partly because competitors have learned to adapt more rapidly to their environment. An MIS that provides both sophisticated and timely information is a necessary part of the required adaptation. Indeed, a major trend in information systems is toward developing capabilities intended to facilitate the organization's rapid adaptation to change. On-call reports, ad hoc reports, and key-indicator reports are examples of these capabilities.

Another factor in the need for more sophisticated information systems cannot be overlooked: Schools of business and management have upgraded the quality of managers. Managers now understand and utilize more sophisticated management techniques than their predecessors did. Managers of today routinely use marginal analysis, standard costs, and direct costing as well as traditional full costing, sensitivity analysis techniques, and a variety of other management methods not widely used two decades ago. Applying these techniques requires more sophisticated information than was previously needed, and this in turn requires a more sophisticated information system. This consideration will become even more important in the years ahead.

WHY MANAGERS ARE OFTEN FRUSTRATED WITH THEIR MANAGEMENT INFORMATION SYSTEM

Despite the razzle-dazzle computer technology that is available and is in widespread use and despite the widespread implementations of advanced capabilities of computer systems, many managers are not happy with their computerized information systems. In many cases, this is due to the fact that the information systems have not lived up to expectations and managers believe they still do not receive the information they need. Several of the many possible reasons for these frustrations were mentioned or were implicit in previous discussions, and they will be summarized here, along with others. The discussion is most applicable to senior managers, who are usually the most critical of their information systems, but most of the discussion also applies to a lesser degree to managers at other levels.

The reasons why managers are often not satisfied with their information systems are:

1. Much of the information needed by senior managers is future-oriented or comes from outside the organization. It is difficult to integrate this information into a structured or systematized management information system. Planning and intelligence information systems help overcome this problem, but even with these systems the problem remains.

2. Much of the information needed by senior managers is for one-of-a-kind problems, which are difficult to anticipate. Since such problems will not recur, constructing an elaborate information system for them is usually not cost-effective, nor would this provide the information as quickly as it is needed. Managers may see as a shortcoming the inability of a management information system to provide information quickly for special problems.

3. Managers receive much of their information from discussions with people rather than from the computer system. Managers usually do not view people as a part of the management information system, or often they do not realize the extent to which the information received from discussions with people was originally provided by a computer system, and therefore they consider the management information system to be deficient.

4. Managers may attempt to rely too much on the formal management information system, which can never fulfill all their information needs. They must consciously cultivate informal information sources.

5. Managers' responsibilities often change, necessitating substantial revision of the management information system. This often means that the management information system is always in transition and is never completed, and this is a source of managerial frustration.

6. Managers and computer technicians usually have different types of minds and speak different jargons. This means that channels of communication are often blocked by misconceptions and misunderstandings.

7. Many managers do not understand information systems technology well enough to appreciate its potential or limitations. This lack of systems knowledge contributes to a lack of trust in the computerized management information system.

8. Systems analysts do not understand management processes or how managers' minds process data; thus the systems they build for managers are often unsatisfactory.

9. Managers are action-oriented and prefer to spend small amounts of time on a large number of projects and problems. They are not inclined to devote large blocks of time to assisting relatively passively in the development of a management information system. However, it is precisely their extensive participation that is the most vital ingredient in the development of a management information system.

10. Many organizations still hold the perspective that information systems for managers merely provide summaries of information from the operations level, when, in fact, managerial information systems must be carefully designed to integrate information from many sources and may be coupled only loosely or not at all with operations information systems. Managers who have this narrow and erroneous perspective are unable to recognize the capabilities that their information system could have and therefore do not ask for extended capabilities.

There are no simple solutions to these problems. Managers should be encouraged to participate fully in the MIS development processes. A great advantage of asking young managers to play an important role in management information systems development is that they can be expected to continue their participation as they move up in the organization. Thus the quality of the entire management information system will gradually be upgraded by upwardly mobile young managers.

Another area that requires extensive attention is systems planning. The nature and sophistication of a management information system are closely related to the quality of the planning that brought it about. Indeed, the quality of its planning is the most important factor determining the character and quality of the management information system. Lack of planning will result in a hodgepodge of poorly functioning information systems that are not synchronized with the organization's needs. Careful long-range planning should result in a cohesive, articulated set of systems that are both efficient and effective.

SUMMARY

An MIS is a comprehensive and coordinated set of information subsystems which are rationally integrated and which transform data into information in a variety of ways to enhance productivity in conformance with managers' styles and characteristics. This transformation is made on the basis of established quality criteria for timeliness, relevance, accuracy, feedback, and selective availability of data.

A computer system, which forms the basis of most management information systems, can possess many different technical capabilities.

These include OLRT operation, message switching, remote data entry, file inquiry, decision modeling, and word processing.

Information may be summarized by means of aggregation, compaction, statistics, written or verbal narrative descriptions, or graphics. Business computer graphics is one of the strongest growth areas in computing. Information reports should be brief and as simple as possible, and they should highlight the important information. Types of reports include periodic reports, key-indicator reports, on-call reports, special (ad hoc) reports, and exception reports.

Information resources management (IRM) is an emerging concept that treats information as a valuable organizational resource. Information is similar to other resources in that it has a cost and a return on investment, and failure to acquire it or to use it properly involves an opportunity cost. Information differs from other resources in that it is intangible and can be reused at little additional cost. Management of information takes into account these similarities and differences.

KEY TERMS

batch transactions processing: processing transactions of the same type together as one batch; this is an efficient way to process transactions.

on-line, real-time (OLRT) processing: processing in which the record files for the type of transaction are kept electronically connected to the computer and in which the transaction is processed quickly enough for it to affect the outcome of the activity that generated it. Airline reservations systems are an example of OLRT processing.

message switching: a computer capability that involves two or more computer systems that are linked within a communications system so that an organization's managers can send "letters" (electronic mail) to other locations of the organization without using the postal system.

remote data entry: the process of entering transactions at the location where they occur and then transmitting them to another location for processing.

remote job entry (RJE): batch data entry from a remote location, usually processed in batch mode at the central site.

aggregation: The summarization of information by numerically combining like items.

information resources management (IRM): a concept that encourages managing information by utilizing resource management techniques.

REFERENCES

Diebold, John, "Information Resources Management—The New Challenge," *Infosystems*, June 1979.

Kearney, A. T., *Infosystems*, October 1981.

Martin, James, *Application Development without Programmers*, Englewood Cliffs, NJ: Prentice-Hall, 1982.

REVIEW QUESTIONS

1. Does the word "management" in the term "management information system" mean the same thing as "management" in the sense of the activities of managers?

2. Compare a management information system with at least one other type of system, noting the similarities and differences. (Consider biological systems, communications systems, systems of higher education, the solar system, and so on.)

3. What characteristics of an information system make it a management information system? Concentrate on what distinguishes an MIS from other business information systems.

4. Can a particular item be only data to one manager but information to another? Explain.

5. Can you tell defintively whether a particular organization has a management information system? Why or why not?

6. In what kinds of circumstances would an OLRT system probably be useful?

7. Which of the technical capabilities of a computer, as discussed in the chapter, would be most useful for the following?
   (a) Preparing dividend checks for stockholders
   (b) Determining whether a customer can receive more credit
   (c) Responding to a customer who asks about an account balance
   (d) Processing a one-of-a-kind transaction
   (e) Updating a file at one location with a transaction from another location

8. In what ways can information be summarized? What information summarization techniques do you use when you study for an examination?

9. What are the formats in which reports can be presented?

10. In each of the following circumstances, what type of report would you recommend, and why?
    (a) Manager X is beginning next year's planning and wants to review last year's product costs.
    (b) Manager Y has just returned from a 3-week management training seminar; it's now the middle of the month, and manager Y wants to catch up on developments.
    (c) Manager C's company is in a dynamic industry in which circumstances change rapidly and managers have to keep on top of things.
    (d) Manager F does not like to review operations and wants only to be told what's wrong.

11. Discuss the difficulties that might be encountered in providing each of the following types of reports if a computer system were not used:
    (a) Periodic reports
    (b) On-call reports

(c) Key-indicator reports

(d) Special reports

(e) Exception reports

12. Why are information systems for managers difficult to design and build?

13. What is a key-indicator reporting system?

14. Assume that you are the production manager of a small manufacturing company that produces about 15 products "for inventory"; that is, the items are produced and are placed in inventory for later sale to customers. What key indicators would you like to have reported each day?

15. Assume that you are the marketing manager of this company. What key indicators would you like to have reported each day?

16. Assume that you are the executive vice president of this company. What key indicators would you like to have reported each day?

17. Why is an ad hoc reporting system difficult to establish?

18. When information begins to be viewed as a corporate resource rather than just as an output of the computer system, what changes in attitudes, organization, data usage, and so on, are likely to follow?

PROBLEM

"The reader who has been even vaguely aware of data processing developments within the past several years will probably surmise what the fundamental premise must be—data as a resource. Much has been said about the data resource; it is created, it does cost money, it is assembled, reassembled, inventoried and it does provide the 'raw material' for that valuable product, information. Whether one wishes to look at data as a resource or not is a matter of choice, but to deny all of the essential facts about data as an entity is both illogical and inaccurate.

"Some organizations feel that the data resource concept is too fancy, too intricate, overly sophisticated. We disagree. When one considers that in most medium and large companies cash managers concern themselves with literally day-by-day and even hour-by-hour deposits and withdrawals of cash, all for the purpose of extracting the ultimate value from this obvious resource, then one should be able to understand that data is also a resource which must be properly managed."

Source: Peter C. Townsend, ". . . And There Was Data," *Infosystems,* September 1980, pp. 74, 76.

Problem Question

1. Analyze each of the statements made about data in this excerpt from Townsend's article with respect to the ways in which data is similar to cash and other resources. In what ways is data different from other resources?

CASE 1

The Hanes MIS

by Myles L. Mace

Robert E. Elberson, president and CEO of the Hanes Corporation, uses a monthly report to communicate corporate operational results, status, and problems to members of the board. Hanes consists of five autonomous, profit-and-loss measurable operating units: Hanes Hosiery, Knitwear, L'Eggs, Bali, and Pine State. Each unit is headed by a president and several functional vice presidents.

Here, Elberson describes how basic data are collected for the preparation of the president's letter.

Elberson: Several years ago, we instituted a management assistance program, which is designed to improve control of all operations. Every department in each of the five operating units has key indicators that can be quantified and that reflect measures of its performance. For example, production control has measures of late deliveries (number and length of time), cost of machine changes, inventory-in-process, and so forth—indicators that are operational measures and not exclusively financial.

Some key indicators are tracked daily, others weekly, and still others monthly. At the end of each accounting period (four weeks), there is a full-scale review of results. The first step is that the vice president of manufacturing, say of Hanes Hosiery, has a group meeting of his supervisors. Each supervisor reports on his department's performance (as measured by his key indicators) against (a) his operating plan (budget), and (b) what he said he would do last month. He attempts to explain any significant deviations to both his peers and his superior. This process is repeated at a monthly meeting of the functional vice presidents with their operating unit president. Then, the corporate vice president of finance and I hold an all-day meeting—referred to internally as our monthly "barrel" session—with each of the presidents of the five operating units. It is from this upward distillation process that the vice president of finance and I draw the subject matter for the monthly president's letter to our directors.

I think that this method of keeping directors aware of what is going on has a number of values:

• Reviewing actual performance against plan and latest estimate and getting all this done in 30 days has been good discipline—not only for me but for the rest of the organization.

• In order to distill information for the letter, I must sort out the most important from the less important. This procedure and putting it down in black and white force me to step back and look at the business as a complex entity.

• In my opinion, verbal presentations can be shaded and slanted more than written ones. Also, past letters can be a valuable reference for the discerning director. For example, a past letter might contain a glowing report on some activity that has since gone sour and has not recently been mentioned.

• The letter is an efficient method of imparting information. People can read facts faster than they can speak about them. And, most important, the letter enables us to devote most of our board meeting time to a give-and-take discussion of the key issues involved in running the business rather than to reporting facts about what has happened since the last meeting.

Source: "Management Information Systems for Directors," *Harvard Business Review,* November–December 1975, p. 24.

Case Questions

1. Discuss the Hanes approach to reporting in terms of the theory of reporting presented in the chapter.

2. Choose one of the following functional areas, name six to ten key indicators in that area that might be usefully reported each day, give the source of the information about each indicator, and suggest any special characteristics that the information system would need to report each key indicator on a daily basis.

(a) Marketing
(b) Production
(c) Personnel

(d) Accounting
(e) Inventory

CASE 2

by George J. Feeney

And finally, I see a pressing need for balance among three groups within most organizations— the users, the data processing organization, and the corporate management. There is a conflict of interest among these three groups that supersedes simply misunderstanding each other's functions.

End users want functionality and capability. They don't care about costs, architecture, standards, tomorrow, or any of a dozen other concerns that consume us in dp. These users want things done, and done now. Management, on the other hand, cares a great deal about costs, but usually has very little idea of the practicalities involved in meeting user needs and even less idea of just what those user needs are. This group wants only to lower the budget. Then we get to the dp organization with its factory mentality. The dp group only

wants to get the work out; never mind what the work's for. They tend to respond rather than to initiate.

That is perhaps the biggest challenge to the data processing professional in the next 10 years— to establish the leadership that strikes some reasonable balance between the budget-mindedness of management, the production-mindedness of data processing, and the function-mindedness of users.

Source: "Calling a Spade a Spade . . . A Chat with MIS Executives," *Datamation,* 1979, p. 60.

Case Question

1. Discuss Feeney's remarks in the context of IRM.

CASE 3

MacVeagh's Example Company

Charles MacVeagh watched the development of the information reporting system in a company that he cites an example. He describes the company and its reporting system as follows:

"The company is a multi-division, multi-plant, geographically-dispersed, vertically-integrated food industry producer. Additional hyphenated adjectives could be provided, but these seem sufficient to complete the sketch.

"The company is typical of many companies today in that the resources of a number of organizations are directed to a variety of markets for the benefit of a common group of stockholders.

"It is not typical of many such companies in that it possesses, and uses profitably, an advanced information system that processes the transactions of more than 20 different organizations by a common accounting system and presents to corporate

management in a timely and accurate manner profit and control information determined on comparable bases for all component organizations, summarized and compared to plan. . . .

"Top corporate management receives a summary report showing profit by each organization, by division, and in total for the period and year to date, compared to plan.

"Each line on the top management summary report is supported by a P&L for the divisions and/ or organization, which is also given to the division and/or component organization managers.

"Each P&L is organized on a similar basis, being divided into a sales responsibility section, a manufacturing responsibility section, and an administrative responsibility section. The use of responsibility accounting concepts on the face of the P&L is made possible by the use of standard costs, divided into volume-related and time-related elements, as noted above, and described somewhat more fully below.

"The sales responsibility section shows revenue data less standard direct costs equalling contribution. As far as the sales people are concerned, the standard direct costs are constant. Thus, they can be held responsible for maximizing contribution by varying the items under the control—volume, price, customer, and product mixes.

"To assist them, they are provided with extensive analytical reports—children of the marriage of the order entry and standard cost systems. These detailed analyses provide progressively greater detail regarding where the contribution came from and where the plan was or was not fulfilled, traceable down to the individual salesman, customer, product, and transaction.

"Manufacturing has the responsibility to produce the volume ordered at, or more efficiently than, the standards prescribed by the standard cost system.

"To show at a glance how the manufacturing people met their responsibility, the total manufacturing cost is shown on the face of the P&L, perhaps sub-totalled by major responsibility summary and showing plan, variance, and actual.

"This total is, in turn, supported by progressively more detailed reports down to the first line supervisor where details of plan, variance, and actual are shown by natural expense classification. As with the sales analyses, the top management or indeed anyone else can go from the top summary report to the basic transaction to determine what happened and why—and therefore what should be done about it.

"Total manufacturing cost appears on the P&L to give a total that can clearly be analyzed into subordinate parts. For profit computation, of course, this total must be adjusted for the inventory value of goods manufactured in the period.

"To describe the situation in accounting language, the credit to inventory is the amount shown in the sales responsibility section as 'standard cost of goods sold.' The debit to inventory is the amount shown in the manufacturing responsibility section, deducted from total manufacturing costs, and labelled 'standard cost of goods manufactured.' The net change in the inventory balance sheet accounts is, of course, the difference between these two figures.

"For monthly management reporting purposes, our example company deducts only standard direct costs from total manufacturing costs to compile the monthly statements. The balance, by definition period costs and variances, is then deducted from the sales contribution to provide operating profit.

"For financial information released to the public, an adjustment for period costs in inventory is made. The adjustment is usually minor—a small price for even the most ardent direct-coster to pay for freedom from quibbles about consistency.

"Like the manufacturing responsibility section, the administrative responsibility section shows plan, variance, and actual by major responsibility groups, supported by detailed cost center reports.

"Administrative costs deducted from operating profit equals taxable profit. This amount must then, of course, be severely reduced to reflect the company's continuing commitment to the policies of the government. For monthly management reports, the provision is applied on a consistent percentage basis to the taxable profit figure for each organization. The resulting net profit figure is the one that shows up on the component organization's line on the top management summary report.

"A simple enough report hierarchy. The president can go from the top summary report to the totals for each division to the profit detail for each component organization down to, if he wishes, the salesman or the foreman at the firing line. He has thus a clear, coordinated picture of the results, in financial terms, of the multiple activities of the resources under his command. He has an information system."

Source: Charles MacVeagh, "MIS: Building a Structure That Works," *Price Waterhouse Review,* vol. 22, no. 2, 1977, p. 42.

Case Questions

1. What benefits might MacVeagh's example company's management derive from the information system described?

2. Which of the capabilities described in Chapters 2, 3, and 4 does this information system have and not have? Of those it does not have, which might be especially useful?

SECTION TWO

FUNDAMENTALS OF COMPUTER SYSTEMS

The chapters in this section present computer systems technology from a manager's perspective in enough breadth to provide a general understanding of computing technology. Three topics of particular importance to managers are among those covered: telecommunications, data bases, and microcomputers.

This section accomplishes two primary objectives. First, it presents concepts and "jargon" that managers must understand in order to communicate with computer technicians in computer language. Second, it provides the background of technical knowledge needed by managers who will participate in systems development activities, as most managers will, at least to some degree.

Chapter 5

GENERAL CHARACTERISTICS
OF COMPUTER
INFORMATION SYSTEMS

PAYOFF THOUGHT

Entry-level positions and careers in information systems are readily available, challenging, and lucrative for qualified business school graduates. As you read this chapter, pay special attention to aspects of the industry in which you might want to seek an entry-level position.

CHAPTER OBJECTIVES

1. To examine the role of computers in society and management

2. To distinguish between the categories of computers on the basis of size and usage

3. To present an overview of the information technology industry

4. To explain the types of careers and entry-level positions available in the information technology industry

THE RISE OF COMPUTERS

Until the twentieth century almost all data processing was done manually. Clerical personnel used paper, pen, and pencil to maintain records. Such data processing was the ultimate in labor intensiveness. Frequent clerical errors caused transactions to be misrecorded and company records to be misrepresented. Information was often received too late to serve any but historical and custodial purposes.

During the first half of the twentieth century electromechanical data processing equipment became widely employed. These machines are both electrical and mechanical—they employ electricity for their functioning, and mechanical movement within the machines processes the data. Punched-card machines are examples of electromechanical devices that were used throughout this period and are still in use. Electromechanical data processing equipment represented a great advance over manual data processing because it was faster and more accurate. Also, unlike humans, these machines never grew tired, although they did have frequent mechanical failures. Electromechanical equipment still required a substantial amount of labor and still allowed tremendous opportunity for clerical mistakes.

Electronic computer data processing began after World War II. A landmark in its development was the Eniac, a 20-ton vacuum tube computer completed in 1946 by Mauchley and Eckert, professors of electrical engineering at the University of Pennsylvania. The Eniac now reposes in the Smithsonian Institution. In 1981, a party was held to celebrate the thirty-fifth birthday of the Eniac and the computer age. The Eniac was dusted off, plugged in, and assigned a set of calculations to perform. The same request was made of a Radio Shack TRS-80 microcomputer. The 30-lb microcomputer completed the task about 5 times as fast as the 20-ton behemoth Eniac, a startling indication of the tremendous advances made in computing technology in just 35 years.

Electronic computers now pervade business data processing as well as other areas in our society. The entire computer revolution has come about during the lifetime of today's middle- and senior-level managers, almost none of whom studied computers as part of their formal education because computer technology either did not exist or was not widely used for business data processing. Business data processing has been extensively taught in colleges and universities only since about 1970.

Electronic computers accomplish all data manipulation and file updating electronically rather than mechanically. However, certain components of computer systems are still electromechanical; for example, the typical printer contains electronic components, but must also have mechanical movement, which makes it susceptible to mechanical wear and breakdown.

The electronic nature of computers gives them several important attributes. First, computers are extremely fast at processing instructions, that is, at performing calculations and at making logical comparisons. Second, computers are extremely accurate in their processing; rarely does a computer make an electronic mistake that it does not catch itself and signal to the computer operator. Almost all errors in computer data processing are caused by faulty programs prepared by humans or by faulty input data provided by humans. Third, computers are extremely reliable; being primarily electronic and without moving parts, they seldom have failures.

The combination of these attributes has tremendously increased data processing's productivity and reduced its cost. An advertisement in *Computerworld* claimed that if the automobile industry had done what the computer industry has done in the last 30 years, a Rolls Royce would cost $2.50 and get 2 million miles per gallon. This greatly increased productivity has led to the development of entirely new products and services that were unaffordable before the advent of computers because the data processing involved was too costly. For instance, the entire space age would be impossible without computers because they control the launching of missiles and the placement of satellites in orbit; without computers, spaceships such as *Columbia* would be impossible. As a more down-to-earth example, credit cards also could not exist without computers because of the tremendous amount of data processing they require.

The speed, accuracy, and reliability of computers serve other management needs beyond just data processing. Computers also affect the way managers manage, the way companies conduct operations, and the functional alignment of organizations—who reports to whom and who does what.

Computers find wide use in virtually every industry both for data processing purposes and for management purposes. Their use is especially heavy in manufacturing, banking, insurance, communications, and government (IBM Corporation's largest single customer for its computers is the United States government).

WHAT MANAGERS SHOULD KNOW ABOUT COMPUTER SYSTEMS

1. The implications of computers for society.

2. The general principles of how computer systems operate.

3. The components of computer information systems and how each component functions.

4. The various configurational alternatives of computer systems—that is, what components can be combined to constitute a computer system.

5. The special characteristics that enable computers to accomplish tasks that are impractical for manual or electromechanical systems.

6. Computer terminology, or "jargon." Knowledge of "computerese" is essential for the following purposes: (*a*) understanding the structure of the information system of a given organization, (*b*) communicating with an organization's data processing personnel to foster further development of the computer information system, and (*c*) enabling managers to participate directly in systems development in ways that will be discussed later in this text.

Understanding these six aspects of computer technology will enable managers to ask intelligent questions and interpret the answers given by their organization's data processing specialists and to participate deeply in the development of their organization's information systems.

Computers are so complex that no one individual fully understands even a medium-sized computer-based information system. Indeed, only the composite knowledge of several systems professionals enables complex computer systems to be developed. Therefore, managers cannot hope or expect to fully understand computer technology or even their own organization's computer systems. However, managers can expect to master the general principles of computers and, through these, achieve an understanding of the capabilities, limitations, and operating costs of their organization's computer systems.

Further, managers studying a text such as this can develop an overall knowledge of, and perspective on, information systems which even many technical specialists lack. Computer professionals are often trained in great depth in a narrow specialization; for example, persons trained primarily in programming have only a limited perspective on how to consider the management processes and how the computer affects customers' perceptions of the organization when developing information systems. Thus broad, but not deep, understanding of computer-based management information systems nevertheless may give a manager a superior overall background in information systems and an advantage in discussing with data processing professionals the topic of the development of computer-based information systems for management.

THE IMPORTANCE OF COMPUTERS

Managers should be aware of the implications of computers that affect all society. One of these is the social question of privacy and the depersonalization of individuals. Many people feel that computer systems allow personal data kept in computer files to be made widely available and that this is an abuse of personal privacy. In recent years almost every state in the United States has enacted privacy legislation; this has been brought about by the ability of computers to gather extensive information about individuals and make it available for improper or illegal purposes. Federal legislation has also been enacted, and European countries too have passed privacy legislation. The Scandinavian legislation is considered to be particularly comprehensive. Efforts continue around the world to establish rational schemes to prevent individuals' privacy from being threatened by the availability of personal data through computer systems. One of the tasks of a manager is to ensure that the computers in that manager's organization are managed so that the individual privacy of customers, employees, and other persons is respected fully.

Beyond the privacy issue there is also the feeling that computers depersonalize relations between organizations and individuals, as expressed in statements such as, "Whenever I communicate with that organization, I get an answer from a computer, and the computer doesn't understand my problem. It's difficult to get through to people to explain my problem to them." Most of us have had this experience, and it certainly is true that computers are being used to communicate with individuals, in many cases beyond the computers' capabilities of doing so.

Everyone finds this depersonalization frustrating, and it is a problem that the managers of an organization are in a position to control. The organization can solve this problem by being sensitive to it and by insisting that the technical personnel who design the computer systems take the necessary steps to ensure that it is people rather than computers that deal with problems related to employees, customers, and the general public. In fact, computers in general permit people to be *more* individualistic by taking over tedious, low-level clerical work so that people can concentrate on more creative and interesting activities.

Another major implication for society is that computers lower the cost of products. They do this primarily by drastically reducing clerical and data processing costs, but also through their efficiency in controlling manufacturing activities and assisting in product design. It is reasonable to state that, without computers, the cost of most consumer products would be at least 10 percent greater and that for some products the cost would be more than 50 percent greater. The trend toward cost reduction through computer use can be expected to continue in the future, and one role of managers is to see that computer systems are used in every way possible to reduce the cost of providing the organization's products and services to consumers.

Computers also dramatically affect the well-being of consumers by enabling them to own a great variety of products that simply would not exist otherwise. For example, it is computers that enable consumers to have such a wide selection of options on automobiles. Without computers, the massive logistics activities involved in offering a nearly limitless combination of options would be almost literally impossible. Computers also make possible direct dialing in long-distance telephone service, automobile engines that maximize efficiency through computerized metering of fuel, and hundreds of other new products.

Computers also affect employment in ways that can be directly controlled by managers. While on the one hand computer programmers and systems analysts are needed to develop computer systems, on the other hand computer-related technology reduces the number of jobs in other spheres of activity. For example, computer-aided manufacturing (CAM) equipment and computerized robots decrease the number of factory workers needed. In the long run these and other computer technologies will reduce production costs and the number of hours per week that workers in general will have to spend at their jobs. However, in the short run, for a period of at least a decade, specific individuals will be losing their *entire* jobs rather than simply having reduced hours of work per week. It is little comfort to someone who has been replaced by a robot and is out of work to know that the robot will make products available to other persons at a lower cost.

It is managers who decide how quickly computerization proceeds in an organization and which people lose their jobs as a consequence. If they wish to, managers also can develop retraining programs so that displaced employees can assume other positions in the organization; they can arrange, for at least a lengthy transition period, for all employees to work fewer hours rather than for some not to work at all; and they can take innumerable other steps to ease the transition of displaced employees to other, usually more skilled and productive, positions. Computerization is necessary and inevitable, but the hardships it causes for displaced employees can often be eliminated.

WHAT IS A COMPUTER SYSTEM?

The following types of components make up a computer system:

1. Electronic components (circuitry) that perform calculations and logic checks, store data in memory, and provide a pathway for data movement throughout the computer system.

2. Electromechanical components that have mechanical movement, such as data input-output equipment. As previously noted, these are failure-prone.

3. Data items consisting of individual elements of data, such as words. Examples are names and addresses of employees, hourly wage rates, and number of hours worked.

4. Data files, which are storehouses for data items. A payroll file, for example, would contain the names and addresses of employees, their hourly wage rates, and their hours worked, each of which constitutes one data item for each employee.

5. Programs, which are sets of instructions written by people (programmers) to tell the computer what to do and how to "process" (manipulate or calculate with) the data.

Programs are written over a long period of time by many people to accomplish a wide variety of tasks. Programs usually contain errors ("bugs") when first developed and must be "debugged"; that is, the errors in the programs must be found and corrected. Also, as the organization's needs for information change, existing programs must be rewritten and debugged again; this is called "program enhancement," "program maintenance," or simply "maintenance." Maintenance consumes about 50 to 70 percent of programmers' time in long-established and mature data processing centers.

Computer systems have built-in "controls." Some of these controls are part of the computer hardware, and some are part of the computer's programs. Certain controls are intended to detect machine malfunctions, whether mechanical or electronic, and signal these to the operators of the computer system. Other controls are intended to detect errors in the input data provided by users and to detect program errors. However, it is impossible for either hardware or program controls to detect all input and programming errors.

Programming errors sometimes cause a computer system to "crash" (stop processing the program or stop all computer processing) until the error is located and corrected. Programming errors can also cause computer systems to lose data or erase files. The complexity of programs means that errors may not surface for months or years, at which time they may cause major problems, perhaps when processing a never-before-encountered variant of a transaction type.

Electronic components and electromechanical components that fail and incorrect procedures or procedures that are incorrectly followed by computer personnel can also cause computer systems to crash. Typically, a large, complex computer system is able to run and process data for somewhere between 95 and 99 percent of the scheduled processing time; this is called "uptime." The total amount of computer uptime can be greatly influenced by the steps that data processing personnel take to maintain the computer system and to minimize disruptions in computer processing.

TYPES OF COMPUTER SYSTEMS

Almost all business data processing computers are stored-program, general-purpose computers. "Stored-program" means that the programs directing the computer's operations are kept within the computer system during the actual processing. A general-purpose computer is one that can be programmed to perform a wide variety of tasks, such as business, scientific, production control, and process control tasks.

Exhibit 5.1 lists six major categories of computer systems that most authorities agree on, although they disagree on the dividing lines between the categories. In the past, certain of these categories employed distinctive

Computer Categories and Size   EXHIBIT 5.1

Type	Cost	Space Requirements
Supercomputers	$4,000,000–$10,000,000	Large room
Mainframes	$300,000–$4,000,000	Room
Superminicomputers	$75,000–$400,000	Small room
Minicomputers	$15,000–$75,000	Office
Supermicrocomputers	To $30,000	Closet or office
Microcomputers	To $10,000	Desk top

technology, but today large computers incorporate ingredients of microcomputer technology, micros utilize technology developed for other classes of computers, and so on. Thus computer systems must now be classified according to characteristics other than type of technology.

An important characteristic of computers is cost. As shown in the exhibit, micros are the least costly, typically ranging up to about $10,000 for a complete computer system, including input-output capability. At the upper end of the list, supercomputers may cost as much as $10 million per computer system. In terms of physical size, computers range from desktop microcomputers to computer systems that would fill a classroom with the CPU and peripheral components. All computer systems, even the microcomputers, have very fast processing speeds; however, the processing speed of supercomputers is by far the fastest.

Exhibit 5.2 illustrates the capacity of different computer categories in terms of the number of terminals that can be attached, although terminals are but one indicator of computer capacity. The typical microcomputer has one terminal, or workstation, and this can be occupied by only one operator. On the other hand, mainframe computers will support hundreds of computer terminals, enabling hundreds of persons to use the computer at the same time. Because supercomputers are at present used for scientific rather than business processing, they may have few terminals, even though they could support a great many. Exhibit 5.2 also illustrates the kinds of business tasks that each type of computer typically handles.

The extent of support services offered by vendors who supply the computer system can also differ. Because of the low cost of microcomputers, vendors cannot afford to offer extensive support such as problem-solving assistance and repair and maintenance for each machine. However, the larger and more costly the computer system, the more assistance the vendor is willing to provide. For example, large mainframe computer systems are usually served by vendor engineers, who may remain on the site 24 hours a day to ensure that any computer system malfunction will receive immediate attention.

Computer Capacities and Tasks   EXHIBIT 5.2

Type	Input-Output Capacity (Terminals)	Typical Business Tasks
Supercomputers	Large number possible	None
Mainframes	Large number of terminals, often hundreds	Large-scale business processing—all tasks
Superminicomputers	Many terminals	Medium-scale business processing—all tasks
Minicomputers	Multiple terminals	Small-scale business processing with small- and medium-scale applications
Supermicrocomputers	Multiple terminals	Data entry and small- and medium-scale business applications
Microcomputers	One terminal	Small- and medium-scale business applications—often dedicated to one or a few specialized tasks

Exhibit 5.3 shows that microcomputers are used for the tasks typical of a small company, usually transactions processing tasks. Micros are also used in large organizations for managerial analysis tasks. Minicomputers have more capabilities and may be used at small companies or at branches of large companies for a wide variety of business data processing tasks. Superminicomputers perform a full range of business data processing tasks. Large companies are likely to need one or even several large mainframe computers. Recently, superminicomputers have begun to replace small- and medium-scale mainframe computers because superminis can perform the same amount of business data processing at a lower cost. Many experts believe this is due to the fact that superminicomputers embody a more advanced technology than small- and medium-scale mainframe computers.

Who is likely to directly use and manage the computer system? As shown in Exhibit 5.3, microcomputers are often used by managers and clerical personnel because micros are frequently more "user-friendly"; that is, both their hardware and their programs are less complex and permit unsophisticated users to learn the system easily. Supermicrocomputers and minicomputers overlap greatly in functions, and both are likely to be used by business personnel who have some, but not extensive, special

Usage and Operation of Computer Systems   EXHIBIT 5.3

Type	Typical Use	Typical Operators
Supercomputers	For large-scale scientific research	Professional data processing personnel
Mainframes	In medium-sized and large organizations	Professional data processing personnel
Superminicomputers	In medium-sized organizations	Professional data processing personnel
Minicomputers	In small organizations and branches of medium-sized and large organizations	Specially trained business personnel
Supermicrocomputers	In small organizations and for data collection in large organizations	Specially trained business personnel
Microcomputers	For personal and hobby use, in small organizations, and for special analyses in large organizations	Managers and clerical personnel

training in computer systems; some students now reading this text will be managers in charge of supermicrocomputer data processing installations within months of their graduation.

On the other hand, both superminicomputers and mainframe computers usually are run by professional data processing personnel with years of computer experience. Supercomputers, of which there are fewer than 50 in existence, are usually operated by professional data processing personnel.

THE INFORMATION TECHNOLOGY INDUSTRY

Computers have spawned and become the driving force of an industry that embraces far more than just the production, sale, and operation of the computers themselves. This industry, here called the "information technology industry," is based on electronics and is defined broadly to include many subindustries, such as computer manufacturing, the manufacturing of other devices used with computer systems, data communications activities, robotics, factory automation equipment, computer graphics, computer-aided design and computer-aided manufacturing (CAD/CAM), electronic office equipment, and the design, development, and sale of computer programs by software houses, to mention only a few.

The information technology industry is not only the largest industry in the world, but also the fastest-growing, with a 15 to 20 percent compounded annual growth rate worldwide. Furthermore, this growth rate is expected to continue until at least 1990. Part of the reason for such rapid growth is the common belief that information technology developments will dramatically increase industrial and clerical productivity.

If for no other reason, students should be knowledgeable about the information technology industry because of its economic clout. No business manager can afford to be unaware of what is happening in a major economic sector of the United States and the world, especially a sector that is so dynamic. Furthermore, a manager in any organization who must participate in allocating resources to information systems will find it useful to know the structure of the information technology industry. Probably 10 to 20 percent of the students reading this text will have careers in the industry, and many will eventually become managers of a computer center or bosses of managers of a computer center. These managers will be expected to understand the industry and pass judgment on the acquisition of computer and other information systems technology. The last section of this chapter discusses several types of career possibilities within the information technology industry.

The Development of the Industry

From the development of the first computers in the late 1940s until the middle of the 1950s, Univac Corporation dominated the computer industry. In the mid-1950s the boards of directors of Univac and IBM implemented distinctly different strategic policies. The board of directors of Univac, which held about 60 percent of the world computer market at that time, decided that the most important future market for computer systems would continue to be in scientific data processing and that business data processing, at that time an almost totally undeveloped field, would remain a minor market for computer systems. The board of directors of IBM, however, which held about 10 percent of the computer market but was an important force in the office products industry, reached the opposite conclusion, deciding that the future growth of the computer industry would be primarily in the area of business data processing.

Since then, both scientific data processing and business data processing have thrived, but the overwhelming majority of the growth has been in the area of business data processing. IBM's "general-purpose" computers, designed in recognition of business data processing, quickly took over the marketplace, and by the mid-1960s IBM held about 70 percent of the world market for computer information systems. This has since eroded somewhat to perhaps 60 percent of the total world market, but IBM remains the dominant computer company. Many other companies, however, have been nibbling at IBM's empire by competing head-on, by finding special niches within the large mainframe computer industry, or by helping to create and develop entirely new but related industries in which they, rather than IBM dominate. For example, minicomputers, microcomputers, robotics, graphics, office automation, CAD/CAM, and a series of other industries all have a multitude of competitors, although each has its three or four leaders.

The several signal events in the brief history of the computer industry have been much written about and will not be mentioned here, aside from noting that at least three distinct computer "generations" have marked the development of mainframe computer systems. The first generation of computers, extending until about 1956, was characterized by vacuum tubes, which many of today's students may have seen only in picutres or in museums. Vacuum tubes look like electric light bulbs, and data was transmitted and stored by turning thousands of these tubes on and off in complex patterns. The vacuum tubes visibly lit up and blinked as this took place, making an impressive visual show while the computer was running. Vacuum tube technology, while much faster than the electromechanical technology which preceded it, nevertheless consumed a great deal of energy, was unreliable, and gave great bulk and weight to computer systems.

IBM introduced a computer system in the mid-1950s that used transistors rather than vacuum tubes. This extremely important development made these second-generation computers several times faster, much smaller, more energy-efficient, and more dependable. In the mid-1960s IBM introduced a third generation of computers which used large-scale integration and printed circuits. This resulted in still faster computing speeds, still smaller size, and still greater dependability, as well as greater energy efficiency. The cost per transaction processed decreased dramatically with each new generation of computers because each one cost no more but was far faster and more dependable. Other manufacturers also introduced the new technologies in their own new-generation computer systems.

Since about the mid-1960s it has been difficult to judge that a particular technological breakthrough has resulted in an entirely new computer generation. Instead, a series of relatively minor technological developments introduced piecemeal have accumulated; thus in the 1980s computer systems are clearly far more technologically advanced than they were in the 1960s. However, whether computers are now in their fourth, fifth, sixth, or seventh generation is not easy to determine, and experts do not agree. The entire computer industry now uses large-scale integration consisting of magnetic-oxide semiconductor (MOS) technology, known as "chip" technology because each MOS unit looks like a small wafer or chip.

The late 1960s saw the introduction of minicomputers using an advanced and somewhat different technology from that used by the mainframe computer systems. The companies producing minicomputers were also by and large different companies from those which made the large-scale computer systems, although most originated as producers of components of large-scale computers. In this way a semi-independent minicomputer industry emerged. In the mid-1970s a similar process occurred with microcomputers, which use a technology that is slightly different from, and is less expensive and somewhat slower than, the technology used for either minicomputers or large-scale computers. Microcomputers are based on MOS chips, and the computer logic and memory are inexpensively mass-produced. The microcomputer industry also has remained somewhat independent of both the minicomputer industry and the mainframe industry, with a substantially different but overlapping group of companies participating in it.

In the mid-1970s the technology of mainframe computer systems and that of minicomputer systems began to merge. Today the technologies of microcomputers, minicomputers, and mainframes are so intermixed that it is difficult to say that they have distinctive characteristics. Although a particular computer can still be clearly classified as a microcomputer because it uses microcomputer technology, it is not the case that a mainframe uses only mainframe technology or that a minicomputer uses only minicomputer technology. Much of the technology now incorporated into mainframes originated in minicomputer technology and microcomputer technology, and a great deal of the present minicomputer technology originated with microcomputers.

The Economics of Change in the Computer Industry

What causes change in the computer industry? A major factor is the rapid advances in electronics technology of all types, from telecommunications to data transmission to robotics to microminiaturization and chip circuitry. Two economic considerations have also been very important, the first being the dramatic decrease in the cost of the most advanced technology. The cost per transaction processed by computers is now hundreds of times lower than it was when computers were first developed. Second, paralleling this decrease has been an increase in the cost of labor. Given these economic conditions, it is only natural that technologically advanced, low-cost equipment is being substituted wherever possible for labor-intensive activities such as the manual operations involved in data processing. The computerization of activities which previously were done manually has become cost-effective and is taking place across a wide front in industry, beginning right on the factory floor, where microcomputers are being utilized for control and where robots are replacing factory labor. It continues through each level of the organization, and now middle- and higher-level managers have begun to utilize low-cost microcomputers in their analyses. Relatively more expensive typists and secretaries are being replaced at least in part by word processing and other types of electronic office equipment.

The Computer Marketplace

The Large Computer Systems Market

Large computers—mainframes and supercomputers as well as super-minis—still make up about 60 to 70 percent of the total computer market in terms of dollars invested in both the computer and the related equipment, although microcomputers are now overwhelmingly dominant in terms of numbers. This suggests that the market for large computer systems is of greatest interest to large computer companies because of the greater number of dollars involved, and to an extent this is true. However, small computer systems are much more important, even to manufacturers of large computers, than the lower amount of dollars invested in them would indicate. One reason is the very rapid rate of growth in the micro-computer market. Another is that many companies that initially purchase small computers such as micros for data processing quickly find their needs for computer power escalating, as the company grows or as it places more applications on the computer system. Therefore, these customers must acquire a larger computer system. To do this they need a natural migration path, known as "upward compatibility," to larger computer systems. This is necessary so that the applications programs and data files in which they have invested thousands of dollars and many years of effort can be used on the larger replacement computer system with little or no change.

Usually upward compatibility is best provided by a larger computer from the manufacturer of a company's present computer system. Studies indicate that about four out of every five small computer users who trade up to a large computer system purchase a larger system offered by their present vendor in order to maintain this upward compatibility. Personal friendships with the present vendor's personnel and fear of the unknown with respect to another vendor's products and services are other reasons why an organization is strongly biased toward purchasing its next computer from the same vendor. Thus, a major reason why manufacturers of large computers also produce and sell minicomputers and microcomputers is to secure the future business of companies when they later acquire a larger computer.

The manufacturers of large computer systems either sell or rent their computers. These manufacturers provide service contracts for maintenance of the equipment and employ thousands of service personnel to ensure that the systems they have provided continue to function properly.

IBM, the dominant manufacturer of computers, also produces a wide variety of related equipment. IBM has a reputation for having an outstanding marketing organization, very strong management processes, and good research capabilities for developing technically advanced equipment. IBM's service organization is also considered excellent; its broad customer base makes it likely that any medium-sized or large city will have a number of IBM service personnel available at all times to respond rapidly to customer needs.

In the United States, Univac, Honeywell, Burroughs, and Control Data Corporation (CDC) are other long-established companies that manufacture large computer systems and computer-related equipment. These companies each hold a share of the market that varies from about 4 to 8 percent. Amdahl, a relatively new company, specializes in producing very large computer systems to compete directly with the largest IBM computers. Each of these five companies that compete directly with IBM is considered to be advanced technically and to have strong research and development programs. Because of IBM's commanding market position and very strong marketing capability, ech of these companies attempts to supply about 1.3 to 1.5 times the power of a comparable IBM machine for the same price; that is, these companies attempt to offer equipment with about 1.3 to 1.5 times the price/performance ratio of IBM equipment.

A number of non-American companies also compete in the large computer market. Japanese companies and companies in the major European nations are the most advanced. In the Soviet bloc countries the only computer in this class is the RYAD, which bears a very striking resemblance to IBM computer systems. Most observers believe that the Japanese firms are the most aggressive of these foreign competitors and that they can be expected to gain a significant market share in the years ahead. One reason appears to be that the Japanese companies devote a larger proportion of their revenues to research and development than United States computer companies do.

The Peripherals Market

The manufacturers of peripheral equipment are another important factor in the computer marketplace. Peripheral equipment includes printers, tape decks, disk drives, and a variety of other types of equipment that attaches to computers. While all the major computer manufacturers also manufacture peripherals, hundreds of companies manufacture only peripheral equipment. These companies are called "plug-compatible manufacturers," or PCMs. "Plug-compatible" means that the equipment produced is so compatible with a particular computer and the related equipment provided by another company that it can be plugged directly into that equipment and operate without modification. Plug-compatible equipment can therefore replace or supplement the peripheral equipment available from computer manufacturers. Usually PCMs provide higher price/performance ratios with their periphral equipment than the large computer manufacturing companies; the increase in the price/performance ratio is typically in the range of 1.5 to 4.0. In many cases the plug compatibility of these peripheral devices is only with the computer equipment of one computer manufacturer (usually IBM).

Attempting to interface computer equipment with other equipment with which it is not plug-compatible can lead to complicated technical problems, and the cost of solving these problems often outweighs the benefits of doing so. Indeed, even the old and the new versions of a similar computer model produced by one manufacturer may require a year of engineering time before the two computers can share data files and processing with each other through an effective interface.

The Minicomputer Market

There are several minicomputer manufacturers, of which DEC (Digital Equipment Company), Wang, Data General, and Prime are perhaps the best known. Historically, the minicomputers of DEC, one of the largest of these companies, have held their resale value best in the used-minicomputer market. This suggests, and independent studies have borne out, that DEC equipment and service are highly regarded by users. A host of PCMs now produce peripheral equipment that is plug-compatible with the most popular minicomputers.

The Microcomputer Market

About 150 microcomputer manufacturers exist at this writing, but new ones enter the marketplace and existing ones drop out each month. Within a few years it is probable that the number of microcomputer manufacturers will be less than 50. At the present time, most mainframe and minicomputers also offer a family of microcomputers. Prices have been dropping steadily in this market, and portable microcomputers are becoming popular. Japanese manufacturers have been attempting to acquire a significant portion of the microcomputer market, but have had only limited success.

The Software Market

Software—both systems and applications—is another very large segment of the marketplace. Thousands of software producers and vendors offer tens of thousands of computer programs for sale. The problems of potential purchasers are twofold: (1) locating prewritten software programs that are potentially suitable for their particular application and (2) evaluating these software programs to determine which is the most satisfactory for a particular application. Often, trade journals, industry publications, and clubs and associations of users of a particular computer system are useful sources of information for dealing with these problems.

CAREERS IN THE INFORMATION TECHNOLOGY INDUSTRY

Information technology, as a very fast growing industry, conforms to growth-industry dynamics. These dynamics are that where a shortage of personnel exists, promotions are usually faster, employees are given more responsibility sooner, starting salaries and subsequent increments are greater, and industry personnel have greater mobility than in industries with lower growth rates.

As Daniel J. Hiltz (*Datamation*, April 1981, p. 219) has noted:

> The number of job openings for programmers and systems analysts will grow much faster than the rest of the labor force (U.S. Bureau of the Census, 1980). As a result, salaries of dp (data processing) workers are escalating more quickly than other occupations. Although traditional theories of market economics would predict that these high salaries will rapidly attract additional workers into the field until demand and supply are once again synchronized, analysis of demographic trends and changes in labor force participation suggest that the current situation may not be alleviated for some time.

Equally important is the fact that graduates with a background in business studies are in even greater demand. Al Strong states in *Software News* (June 7, 1982):

> While the shortage of trained data processing professionals multiplies, universities continue to give students the wrong kind of data processing training. . . . Almost every student they graduate comes to us ready to begin work on scientific programs—moon shots, research in the physical sciences—when what we need are business applications programmers. . . . For want of a better solution, our biggest dp users hire these people anyway and promptly send them back to school for retraining in business principles as well as business programming.

This growth-industry environment has tremendous appeal for new college graduates, and a significant proportion of them enter the information technology industry. Between 1980 and 1990 the number of programmers in the United States is expected to double, the number of systems analysts to more than double, and the number of employees in all other computer occupations to nearly double. Yet the demand is expected to exceed even this high rate of supply.

Many students erroneously assume that the essence of systems work is that it is highly technical. In fact, the value of technical expertise varies widely, depending upon the position held. However, it is fair to say that in most systems positions for which business graduates are sought, job success is more dependent upon people and management skills, such as the ability to relate to other people and understand their business problems, the ability to communicate effectively, and the ability to understand the management processes. Business graduates who enter systems work can expect that it will involve extensive work with people. Those systems personnel whose jobs require that they be superb technicians will be mainly engineering and computer science graduates.

Types of Positions Available

Careers in information systems can be divided into three general categories: (1) careers with companies that are providers of information technology, (2) careers in data processing within organizations, and (3) information systems careers within user areas. In the first category many positions are available in the marketing groups and service organizations of the manufacturers of all types of computer systems and peripheral equipment; there are also positions within such related industries as data communications and software. In the software industry, for example, there are many opportunities not only to market computer software but also to originate and develop new software packages.

One aspect of career opportunities with companies that sell information technology merits special mention. Each of these companies employs functional specialists such as accountants, marketing analysts, and finance specialists. As with any industry, the functional specialists who not only know their areas of specialization but also have a solid understanding of the industry's products (in this case, computer-related products) will enjoy a distinct advantage. The hiring policies in the information technology industry will naturally favor functional specialists who have completed advanced course work in information systems.

Consulting also provides opportunities within the information technology industry. Consultants may be systems consultants, software consultants, or hardware consultants, to name only a few. While it would be unusual for students just completing their undergraduate education to become consultants immediately, since consultants generally require significant experience in their field, it is not unusual for M.B.A.s to find employment with systems consulting firms. Many information systems graduates will discover opportunities awaiting them with consulting firms after 2 to 5 years in information systems positions that provide solid experience in a specialized aspect of information technology.

In the second of the three general categories, numerous opportunities for employment exist within organization's data processing departments for computer programmers, computer systems analysts, equipment operators, and liaisons with users. An entry-level position in programming is typically that of a programmer trainee or junior programmer, with well-defined career positions above this for senior programmers and for systems programmers (programmers who write and modify programs that run the computer) as well as for programming and systems development managers. A similar well-defined progression exists for systems analysts who are concerned with the broader aspects of relating computer systems to the organization's information needs. Systems analysts must be familiar not only with computer systems but also with the organization's structure and management processes. More than in the case of most other systems positions, systems analysts interact extensively with users and other persons and must have strong interpersonal skills. Programmers, on the other hand, are expected to be specialists in program development techniques.

Many organizations offer a natural evolution from programming to systems analysis; thus experienced and qualified programmers who wish to do so can become systems analysts. It is usually the systems analysts and systems designers who must translate each user department's needs into specific records, files, and overall program design; programmers then develop and debug the programs specified by the analysts. Some organizations offer entry-level positions as programmer-analyst trainees, combining these two functions at this level as well as at higher levels.

Various other types of positions also exist within the data processing department. These include membership in a systems control group and positions in data base administration, technology monitoring, hardware configuration analysis, and scheduling or operating the computer systems. In thousands of smaller organizations a new or recent college graduate with advanced course work in business systems may become the manager of small computer center; such a position may involve significant responsibilities, including managing the personnel who operate the computer system.

In the last of the three general categories, that of data processing specialists within user areas, the tremendous backlog of uncompleted applications programs—an average of a 3-year backlog of programming in American companies—is providing opportunities. This situation is frustrating for users, who are seeking ways to develop applications programs more rapidly. Because of these efforts, user areas are increasingly employing persons who have the specialized skills that qualify them for the user's tasks and who also have information systems development skills such as those acquired through systems course work at a school of business. These employees become (at least for a period within their careers) systems specialists within the user departments that develop information systems for their user area. Thus, accountants are employed within accounting departments to develop accounting applications programs that the data processing department lacks time to write. Similarly, marketing specialists produce marketing applications programs. Increasingly, the programs are developed for microcomputers within the user areas.

Present estimates are that by 1986 such functional-area specialists will account for 50 percent of all computer utilization for business purposes. This is one of the most important trends in business data processing. These nonprofessional data processing personnel often use the services of "information centers"—centers that are staffed by data processing professionals who provide consultation and advice about such matters as which language to choose for an application or the idiosyncrasies of a language that is being used. In this way the more specialized skills of data processing professionals are being leveraged to help decrease the backlog of applications programs.

To sum up, the information technology industry, as broadly defined, offers a wide variety of career opportunities. Because this is a rapidly expanding and extraordinarily dynamic industry, opportunities within it for high salaries, advancement, and career mobility are far greater than in almost any other industry. To take advantage of these opportunities, students should seek additional systems courses beyond the introductory information systems course typically required by business schools.

Certification Programs

Several professional associations offer professional certification programs. Candidates take examinations in specialized subjects that include computer-related topics; certain of these programs also require experience in the specialized activity. Successful candidates receive a certificate indicating that they have become certified in their specialization. One of these professional associations is the American Institute of CPAs, which twice annually gives examinations for certification as a CPA (certified public accountant). One of the four sections of this exam, the auditing section, requires substantial knowledge of computer information systems. It is often useful for students who are preparing for this portion of the CPA exam to complete an advanced course in computer auditing and controls.

The National Association of Accountants (NAA) administers the certified management accountant (CMA) examination for candidates who seek managerial accounting careers. This examination also covers material related to computer data processing, computer controls, and computer auditing. The Institute of Internal Auditors provides a certification process for persons wishing to become internal auditors. This examination, the certified internal auditor (CIA) exam, covers a substantial amount of subject matter relating to computer accounting and information systems. The computer-area emphasis is on systems design, computer controls, and computer auditing.

In 1980 the EDP Auditors Association began giving examinations for persons intending to become certified in computer auditing, a challenging and financially rewarding professional field. The examination for the certified EDP auditor, which is composed mainly of questions relating to all aspects of computer information systems, strongly emphasizes computer technology, computer controls, and computer auditing.

An important certification program is that for becoming a certified data processor (CDP); the examination is typically taken by persons who either are or wish to become professional data processors. For the business student seeking a career in information systems, the CDP examination and certification are particularly important because they place the individual's computer technology credentials beyond question. Pursuing additional systems course work within schools of business, such as completing a major in information systems, puts a passing grade on the CDP examination well within the reach of business school graduates.

The examination for the CDP tests the areas of (1) data processing equipment, (2) computer programming, (3) software concepts, (4) systems analysis and design; (5) quantitative methods, and (6) principles of management. On-the-job experience is also required; while this varies depending on the circumstances, the typical college graduate in business information systems would require at least 1 year of experience.

SUMMARY

The information technology industry is the largest and fastest-growing industry in the world. The computer revolution, which is the driving force behind this industry, began right after World War II and has evolved from the vacuum tube Eniac computer through transistors to present-day integrated-chip technology. From the exploration of space to the use of credit cards, electronic data processing has permeated our society, creating new opportunities and new problems.

Managers need not understand computer systems in full technical detail, but they must comprehend the general principles of these systems in order to communicate effectively with data processing personnel and gain an overall perspective on their organization's information systems. Managers must also be able to participate as members of systems development teams.

Computer systems consist of electronic components (circuitry), electromechanical components (such as data input-output equipment), data items, data files, and programs. Computers fall into six categories: supercomputers, mainframes, superminicomputers, minicomputers, supermicrocomputers, and microcomputers. These differ in physical size, cost, ability to support multiple terminals, extent of vendor support offered, and typical usage. Large computers still dominate the market in terms of total invested dollars, but microcomputers have taken over in terms of numbers. Large markets in peripherals and software have emerged.

Career opportunities in the information technology industry abound in the general categories of (1) providers of information technology, (2) data processing personnel within organizations, and (3) information systems specialists within user areas. Several professional certification programs are available to interested candidates.

KEY TERMS

electromechanical data processing: data processing using machines that run by electricity and process data through mechanical movement within the machines.
electronic data processing: data processing using computers that manipulate data through electronic circuitry rather than mechanically.

computerese: computer terminology; computer jargon; "computer speak."

program: a set of instructions that tells a computer what task to perform and how to perform it, such as how to manipulate data.

program maintenance: the modification of computer programs to serve an organization's changing needs for information; also known as "program enhancement."

crash: a computer or peripheral shutdown caused by a procedural input or program error or by a machine failure.

downtime: time during which a computer or a part of a computer system is not functioning.

uptime: time during which a computer system is functioning.

stored-program computer: a computer that processes data by using programs that are stored within it.

general-purpose computer: a computer that can be programmed to perform a wide variety of tasks.

supercomputer: a multimillion-dollar computer used for scientific purposes; fewer than 50 new exist.

mainframe: a type of large computer that can often support hundreds of terminals.

superminicomputer: a type of computer that can support many terminals; superminicomputers are used for medium-scale business processing.

minicomputer: a type of computer that can support multiple terminals.

supermicrocomputer: a multiworkstation computer used for data entry and small-business applications.

microcomputer: a desktop computer that usually has only one terminal.

upward compatibility: the compatibility of a smaller and a larger computer system making it possible for the same software and peripherals that are being used on the smaller computer to be used on the larger computer also.

peripherals: the equipment that attaches to computers; printers and disk drives are examples of peripherals.

plug compatibility: the ability of one manufacturer's peripheral equipment to operate without modification when plugged into another manufacturer's equipment.

REFERENCE

Weil, Ulric, *Information Systems in the 80's: Products, Markets, and Vendors,* Englewood Cliffs, NJ: Prentice Hall, 1983.

REVIEW QUESTIONS

1. Briefly outline the history of the computer age.

2. In what ways is electronic data processing superior to manual and electromechanical data processing?

3. Discuss the issue of privacy in an age of computers.

4. Discuss the impact of computerization on the availability of consumer products.

5. What six aspects of computer technology should a manager understand?

6. How is a manager's knowledge of computer technology likely to differ from that of a data processing specialist?

7. What are the five types of components that make up a computer system?

8. Discuss the ability of the six types of computers to support multiple terminals.

9. Discuss the typical uses of each of the six types of computers.

10. What type of computer are managers and clerical personnel most apt to use personally? Why?

11. Name some of the subindustries within the information technology industry.

12. Outline the historical development of the information technology industry.

13. What factors have contributed to the spectacular growth of the information technology industry?

14. What is the meaning of "plug compatibility"?

15. Name and discuss the three general categories of careers based on expertise in information systems.

Chapter 6

COMPUTER SYSTEMS

PAYOFF THOUGHT

Don't let computer experts dazzle you with "computerese." Learn the fundamentals of computer terminology thoroughly so that you can follow a computer conversation; when a term is used that you do not understand, ask its meaning in a way that clearly indicates you understood what was said to that point. From then on, the experts will be more respectful and more reluctant to try to "snow" you with computer jargon.

CHAPTER OBJECTIVE

To provide a background in the fundamentals of computer technology and related data input and output technology.

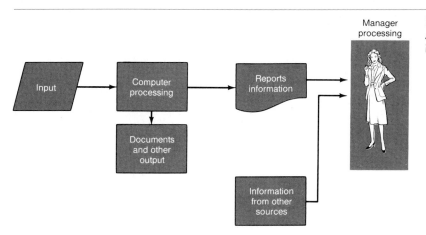

Manager
processing

EXHIBIT 6.1
A computer-based
information system.

A COMPUTER-BASED INFORMATION SYSTEM

Exhibit 6.1 shows a computer-based information system that includes more than just computer-prepared information. This exhibit is a reminder that managers are part of an information system and that they receive information from sources other than just the computer. For the most part, however, the chapters in this section focus on the technology of computer systems and not on the managers who use the systems.

THE CENTRAL PROCESSING UNIT

The central processing unit (CPU) is the heart of the computer system. The CPU, shown at the center of Exhibit 6.2, consists of three major sections: (1) main memory (also known as "primary memory"), (2) the control section, and (3) the arithmetic logic unit (ALU). The entire CPU is composed of electronic circuitry; included in this circuitry are registers that are used to hold data and instructions to the computer in a manner similar to the way data is held in the registers of a calculator.

The primary purpose of the ALU is to perform all calculations and logical comparisons for the entire computer system. It calculates (adds, subtracts, multiplies, and divides) and performs logic comparisons ("equal to," "greater than," and "less than") on data held in its registers, according to instructions held in other registers. Although the ALU can process only one instruction at a time (that is, follow one instruction to make one calculation or comparison), its speed at following one instruction is measured in microseconds (millionths of a second) or even nanoseconds (billionths of a second).

The control section of the CPU shown in Exhibit 6.2 has several functions. It contains a master clock that precisely allocates and keeps track of tiny time slices devoted to each of the CPU's activities. The control

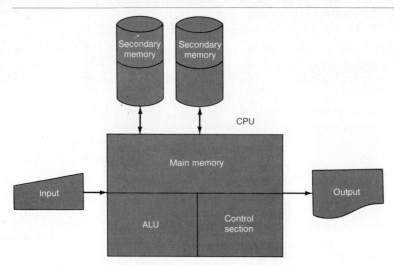

EXHIBIT 6.2
The elements of a
computer system.

section receives and decodes computer program instructions, interpreting and placing the operator portion (the part of the instructions that tells the ALU what to do) in an ALU register. It also directs data traffic within the CPU; for example, it controls the movement of data into the ALU for processing.

To the computer, all machine-readable material is data. Applications programs, systems programs (for the moment, think of systems programs only as programs that enable the computer to run itself), and data elements such as pay rates and number of hours worked are each a different type of data, and all are stored in main memory and processed in turn within the ALU as data. The processing of systems programs consumes ALU time and therefore decreases the amount of time that can be devoted to processing user jobs. CPU processing of systems programs is often referred to as "overhead processing."

Main memory stores data that is waiting to be processed by the ALU and also data that has just been processed. Main memory must be very fast (that is, data must be transferred to and from main memory at a very fast rate) because the ALU can process data extremely quickly, and the ALU must operate at close to top speed to maximize the productivity of the entire computer system. Because main memory must be the fastest memory available in the computer system, it must use the most advanced technology possible. This technology is also the most costly. Accordingly, main memory is the most expensive data storage in the computer system per unit of storage capacity.

Main memory storage capacity is measured in terms of "bytes"; a byte is usually one character of information, such as an "A" or a "B" or a single-digit number. Some computer systems have as little as 5 kilobytes

(5000 bytes) of main memory, and some have several million bytes (megabytes) of main memory. The typical microcomputer has in the range of from 32 to 64 kilobytes, usually referred to, respectively, as "32K" and "64K."

Secondary memory (also termed "auxiliary memory," or "auxiliary storage," or "mass memory," or "mass storage" is additional memory that is electronically connected to the CPU but is not an integral part of it. (This is illustrated in Exhibit 6.2.) Secondary memory is necessary because of the high cost and consequent limited capacity of main memory. Being slower, secondary memory is less costly than main memory, and much larger amounts of it can be economically justified in a computer system.

The purpose of secondary memory is to economically store data that must be quickly transferred into main memory so that main memory always contains data available for instant transfer to the ALU. Secondary memory may contain any type of data, including systems programs. Secondary memory devices can also serve as data input devices. For example, a secondary memory device can be loaded with data off-line (while it is not connected to the computer) or at another computer center and later placed on-line. Data can then be "read" into the computer by this means rather than through the regular input devices shown in Exhibit 6.2. As suggested in the exhibit, multiple secondary memory devices can be attached to a computer's CPU, and a large computer system may have dozens of them.

Many computer systems, especially large ones, have "memory partitions" that divide main memory into several sections. Data for a particular task is stored in a particular memory partition. For example, the applications program and data of a task (often referred to as a "job") may be stored in one main memory partition, another applications program and set of related data may be stored in a second partition, and so on. In this way, several or perhaps even dozens of separate tasks may be stored in separate partitions of a CPU's main memory. Since the ALU operates very quickly, it can often process an instruction and related data several times faster than the next instruction and its related data from that same task can be located and brought into the ALU. Accordingly, multiple partitions make possible multiple data paths into the ALU; thus as soon as the ALU finishes processing one instruction and related data from one task, an instruction and data from another job can enter and be processed immediately, thereby saving the ALU from idly awaiting another instruction and data from the first program. If the ALU had to complete one entire job before beginning another, it could be idle as much as 90 percent of the time.

This ability of some computers to process two or more jobs concurrently maximizes ALU utilization and is referred to as "multiprogramming." When multiple partitions are used, the computer system may "poll" each partition, sending the ALU a data stream from each partition in turn and allowing each job equal priority. Alternatively, many computer systems can assign individual jobs a priority (often on the basis of how much the user is willing to pay for fast processing of a job), and the highest-priority jobs are finished more quickly than the others. With such a priority system the ALU processes instructions of lower-priority jobs only if it would be idle while waiting for the next instruction or data set of a higher-priority job. Jobs performed on a low-priority basis are said to be "done in the background" and often require a long time for completion.

With multiprogramming, the processing of the data of different jobs is controlled by the control section's master clock, which allocates a tiny slice of time for each instruction and data set processed. Not surprisingly, the term "timeslicing" is used to describe the time allocated.

Timesharing is a related concept. With timeslicing and multiprogramming, the ALU can process the programs of several or perhaps hundreds of users so quickly that to each user the computer appears dedicated to that user's program only. The term "timesharing" can describe either the computing arrangement that serves a single organization's users or an arrangement whereby a "timesharing company" sells it clients time on its computer system so that several clients can use the timesharing company's computer at the same time.

SYSTEMS PROGRAMS

The computer hardware must be managed by computer software known as "systems programs." Systems programs also allocate the resources of the computer system to each user job; for example, they assign a secondary storage location to a program. Without systems programs, the hardware could not function. The most important set of systems programs, and indeed one of the most important elements of the entire computer system, is the operating system. The primary purpose of this set of programs is job management—the operating system initiates, schedules, monitors, and controls various user jobs within the computer system. As part of this task the operating system allocates the computer system resources. For example, it locates and places jobs (programs and data) in main storage, determines which input-output devices will be used for a job, and manages the data files in secondary memory.

DATA FILE AND RECORD SYSTEMS

Manual versus Computer Files

Integral to the understanding of computer systems are the concepts of data files and how data is stored inside a computer system. This section provides elementary concepts about these two topics that will help dispel the "mystique" of computer systems.

In a computer system, data files are hardware media (physical devices) that store data in electronic form. A useful way to view computer data files is to compare them with manual files, such as the standard filing cabinet found in almost every office of a university or company. A manual file system is shown in Exhibit 6.3. At the top of the exhibit is a "physical file," which is the filing cabinet. The physical file shown contains three sets of records: accounts payable, accounts receivable, and sales. The data in each one of these sets is regarded as one "logical file," logical in the sense that the records within each logical file are closely related in some logical way. In the accounts payable file, for example, the records are logically related because they all involve individuals or companies to whom money is owed. The logical relationship between the records in the sales file is that they all involve customers to whom merchandise or services have been sold.

The physical file of the filing cabinet shown in Exhibit 6.3 contains

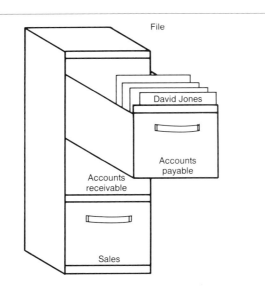

EXHIBIT 6.3
A manual data storage system.

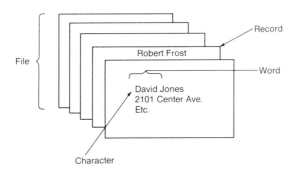

three logical files, but this is not a necessary relationship. It is possible for an accounts payable logical file to be so large that it requires two or more physical files (filing cabinets). Conversely, if there were few records in each logical file, more than three logical files might be stored in one physical device. The distinction between logical and physical files also occurs in computer systems, and understanding this distinction is important.

Exhibit 6.3 shown that the accounts payable file contains several different accounts. Each of these is considered to be one record; David Jones, for example, is the record for one account payable. The analogy with computer files is exact; each logical computer file contains multiple related records. The bottom of the exhibit shows that each record in a manual file contains "words" (such as "David" and "Jones" in the first record) and "characters" (such as the "D," the "A," and so on, in the word "David"). Again, computer systems are exactly analogous; each record in a computer file contains words and characters.

Thus in both computer files and manual files there is a hierarchy going from character to word to record and then to an entire logical file. The logical file in each is conceptually separate from the physical file or files in which the logical file is contained.

Internal Representation of Data

Continuing the comparison between manual and computer file systems, Exhibit 6.4 shows a type of computer main memory called "core memory." Although for the most part core is no longer used in new computer systems, its characteristics help explain the way data is stored internally in the computer CPU and data files. In core storage a series of wires crisscross to form a grid, as shown. At each junction of wires in this grid a magnetizable donut-shaped device known as a "core" encircles the

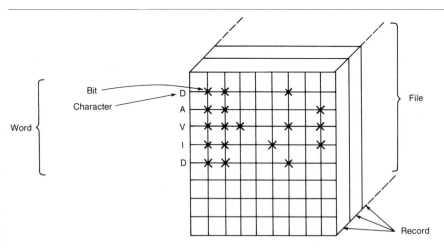

EXHIBIT 6.4
Internal data representation in core main memory (EBCDIC-coded).

junction. (A core position is also called a "bit position.") The control unit of the CPU passes an electric current through selected wires of the grid in a carefully controlled pattern. When electric current is passed simultaneously through two crossing wires encircled by a magnetizable donut (core), that core unit becomes magnetized, or "on." If a current is passed through only one wire, the core unit is not magnetized and is left "off." In this manner each core unit can be magnetized or not (turned on or left off) to form a pattern of bits that represents data.

Specific computer codes establish specific combinations of magnetized and unmagnetized cores. As shown, each combination of these on-and-off bit patterns represents a character. Because each core is a bit position, each character can be seen to be a combination of bits. In turn, a combination of characters makes a word, which is stored in one entire segment or face of core storage. Multiple segments of core storage constitute a record, and multiple records constitute a logical file.

Codes commonly employed to organize these bit positions into characters are ASCII, binary-coded decimal (BCD), and extended binary-coded decimal interchange code (EBCDIC); the exhibit shows EBCDIC. Each computer system uses one of these codes as the basis for organizing its internal memory systems and recording data in a form that can be electronically read and interpreted.

All computer memory systems use a method similar to that described above to store data. While the physical device on which data is stored in memory (including secondary memory file systems) is not usually core, the general principles of data storage are the same: a coding system such as EBCDIC or BCD is used, and data is represented by combinations of electronic bits that are magnetized or not, by electronic switches that are on or off, or by electronic "gates" that are open or closed. It is this characteristic that makes computers binary (two-state) electronic devices; all data in a digital electronic computer is represented by combinations of these two states.

Exhibit 6.5 makes the correspondence between computer and manual data processing characteristics explicit. The computer concept of a bit (an abbreviation of "binary digit") has no corresponding analogy in the manual system; it is the basic electronic building block within a computer. The

Manual and Computer Systems Memory Correspondence　　　　　　　　　　EXHIBIT 6.5

Computer		Manual
Bit	=	—
Byte	=	—
Character	=	Character
Word	=	Word
Record	=	Record
Logical file	=	Logical file

computer concept of a byte also has no direct and unequivocal correspondence in a manual system. A computer byte is a combination of bits, typically 8, although the number varies among computers. In many computer systems a byte is equivalent to a character; that is, the number of bits per byte is also the number of bits per character. The concepts of "character," "word," "record," and "logical file" are the same in computer and manual systems.

Data fed to the computer through input devices is not always in the same code as the internal code utilized by the computer. If the codes differ, the data must be converted from the external input code to the internal storage code before the computer can process the data. An example of this is encountered with punched cards, which are frequently used as data input media. The Hollerith code, the most common code for punched-card systems, consists of 12 data bit positions (punched-card hole positions) which are punched in a particular combination to represent a particular character. This data representation code is a vestige from punched-card data processing systems, which originated in the late 1880s. To represent data inside a computer using a 12-bit character code would be extremely inefficient. Therefore, machines that read data into the computer from punched cards convert this Hollerith code to whatever internal code the computer uses.

MAIN MEMORY: MOS CHIPS

Main (primary) memory devices include core memory (already discussed) and semiconductor devices known as "magnetic-oxide semiconductor chips," or MOS chips. Exhibit 6.6 illustrates the complex circuitry of an MOS chip. Chips are tiny wafers of silicon on which are chemically etched complex circuitry which can serve either for data storage or for any logic, calculation, or control task. The particular chip shown is a data storage chip; in the exhibit the complexity of the circuitry can be seen clearly. Chips are increasingly being used as main memory because their price is decreasing and the data storage capacity per chip is increasing. Rapid advances in chip technology during the past few years now enable chips no bigger than a thumbnail to contain 512K bits of data storage capacity. Usually several chips are grouped together when a computer system uses chips as main memory.

Microcomputers are based on MOS chips. A small microcomputer may contain just one high-performance MOS chip which includes main memory, the control unit functions, and the entire ALU. However, most microcomputers contain several chips, each specialized to a particular function. Chips also have a host of other applications: they are under the hoods of automobiles to monitor engine performance, they control the actions of robots, and they act as the brains of "smart" terminals, to give a few examples. They are also widely used in communications devices. The heart of most electronic toys is an inexpensive chip.

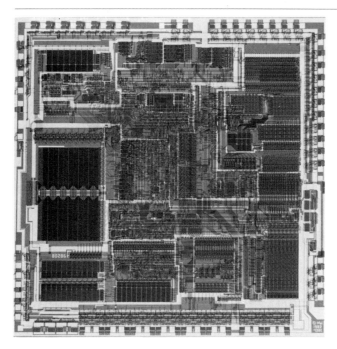

EXHIBIT 6.6
This 8748 microchip illustrates the complexity of the circuitry of microcomputer chips. *(Courtesy of Intel Corporation.)*

An entire industry is based on the design and manufacture of data storage and logic chips. While chip technology is complex, the essentials of the process of chip development are easily understood. The chip's logic or memory structure is first developed by designers on a large-scale medium, such as paper placed on a large drafting table. Next this circuitry design is photoreduced, usually to less than ½ in. square. A chemical process etches this design on a magnetic-oxide semiconducting coated silicon wafer in a production process that may involve the manufacture of thousands of chips in a batch. The completed chips permit bits to be moved rapidly along their circuit paths or to be stored in data storage areas within the chip.

SECONDARY MEMORY

Secondary memory is less expensive than main memory, and secondary memory can be accessed, read, and updated less quickly than main memory. Secondary memory technologies involves data stored in the form of magnetic spots (bits) on a magnetizable surface; in concept, secondary memory technologies operate similarly to the way sound or data is stored on the tape of an ordinary tape recorder.

Among the technologies used for secondary memory the foremost are bubble, magnetic tape, and disk. Magnetic-tape memory is of two types: reels of tape, which are commonly used with larger computer systems, and cassettes, which are often used with microcomputers. Disk technology is also of two types; "hard disks" are used extensively with large computer systems (and increasingly with microcomputer systems), and "floppy disks" are used primarily with mini- and microcomputer systems.

Magnetic Reel Tape

Magnetic reel tape is a commonly used secondary memory medium, particularly in medium- and large-scale computer systems. Secondary memory systems for microcomputers can be ordinary home-use tape cassettes; the cassettes are placed in an ordinary cassette tape recorder, which is plugged into the microcomputer for data transfer. While most microcomputers have this cassette-tape secondary memory capability, the trend in microcomputing is away from this technology and toward disk technologies.

Secondary memory magnetic-tape systems for mainframe computers are much more sophisticated, using a large tape drive/reader, as illustrated in Exhibit 6.7. The tape is ½ in. wide and several hundred feet long and is wound on a tape reel; in the exhibit, one reel contains the tape initially, and the tape is transferred to the other reel as it is read. The tape has either seven or nine magnetizable lengthwise tracks and uses a magnetic-oxide technology almost identical to that of standard tape-recorder systems. Bits are implanted crosswise on the tracks in code form. Although these systems are more complex, the operating characteristics of a computer tape system are similar to those of an ordinary voice tape recorder, except that the data on computer tapes is not converted to sound but instead is read into the computer in bit form.

Tape as a secondary memory medium can store large amounts of data

EXHIBIT 6.7
Magnetic tape.
(Control Data.)

in compact form, can transfer data to main memory very rapidly, and is inexpensive. Furthermore, tapes are a convenient way to store users' data and programs; the tapes are easily removed from the tape drive and stored in racks in a "tape library" room adjacent to the computer system. When needed again for more processing, the tapes must be found and re-mounted on the tape drive. Most medium-sized and large companies that use tape technology have several thousand tapes stored in their tape library.

The major disadvantage of magnetic tape is that data must be read and processed in sequential order; that is, each record on the tape must be processed in sequence, one record after another, regardless of whether the data of that particular record needs to be read or changed. In Exhibit 6.8, for instance, if a record stored near the far end of the tape (such as record 511) must be processed using data contained in another record at an earlier position on the tape (such as record 2), to extract the data from the earlier record means starting over and reprocessing the entire tape form the beginning until that record (record 2) is reached a second time. Likewise, if data from one record needs to be retrieved for processing by some other computer program, the entire tape must be placed on a tape reader and read up to that record's position before the data can be retrieved and processed. To read the typical tape from beginning to end requires several minutes; on average, it takes 5 minutes to retrieve one record from a tape that requires 10 minutes for reading. Many data processing situations require data from only one specific record or just a few of the thousands of records on the tape, and the time wasted finding specific records on a tape cannot be tolerated.

The most common use of magnetic tape as a secondary storage medium is for files that are always or nearly always processed in sequence. In these situations the records are maintained on tape in a specific sequence, and all records are processed in that same sequence; this type of processing is known as "sequential processing" and is very efficient, once the data to be processed has been sorted into the same sequence. When

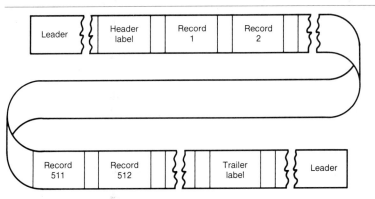

EXHIBIT 6.8
Half-inch magnetic tape.

records need to be processed in a sequence different from the sequence in which they appear on the tape or when multiple records on a tape must be processed but in no preestablished order, the entire contents of the tape is read into main memory, where the records can be sorted into any desired sequence or where any particular record can be accessed directly without sequentially processing all records if the programs exist to accomplish this.

In Exhibit 6.8, the "leader" sections of tapes are blank and are used to initiate winding the tapes on the reels. The "header" and "trailer" sections are specialized records that identify the contents of a tape and provide other information about the data on the tape.

Hard Disk Storage Devices

Exhibit 6.9 illustrates a hard disk drive cabinet with two disk "packs"; each pack contains several disks shaped like platters that resemble phonograph records. Hard disk technology is about two decades old and has been continuously improved upon; thus the density of data on disks is now much greater, data retrieval speed is much faster, and the cost per unit of data stored is much lower than previously. Disk technology remains very competitive with other secondary memory technologies, and disks are the most commonly used form of secondary memory.

Exhibit 6.10 illustrates a disk pack containing 11 disks. Many disk packs can be removed from their cabinet and stored separately, and these disks act as an off-line data storage medium; others are permanently fixed in their cabinet. With removable disks, a different disk can be placed in the cabinet for another processing task. Many hard disks are of the Winchester variety; these disks are completely sealed to prevent dust, finger smudges, and other elements from invading the disk unit and causing errors or physical damage.

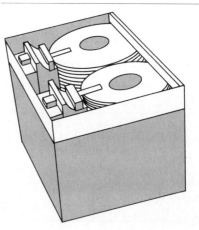

EXHIBIT 6.9
A hard disk drive cabinet with two disk packs.

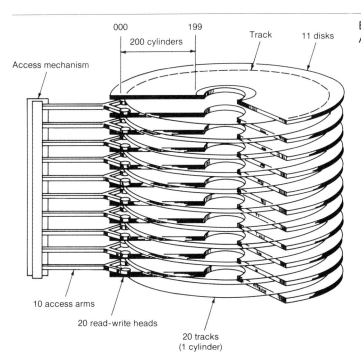

EXHIBIT 6.10
A hard disk system.

Disk systems involve two types of mechanical movement: the high-speed continuous circular rotation of the disks and the movement of the access mechanism containing the access arms and the attached read-write heads. The access mechanism shown in Exhibit 6.10 moves the read-write heads in and out between the rotating disks on the disk packs so that the read-write heads can read data from different parts ("tracks") of the disks or write data onto them. Both the rotation and the in-and-out movements must be precise because the read-write heads must be very close to the disks but cannot touch them. If the read-write heads do touch the disks (a phenomenon called a "disk crash"), the result is damaged disks and destroyed data. Disk crashes occur infrequently but nevertheless often enough for most data processing personnel to have had personal experience with them.

Exhibit 6.10 shows one track on each disk surface. Tracks are positions on the disk that can be magnetized so that data can be represented on the disks on a standard code such as BCD. When a read-write head moves in or out, it repositions itself directly above or below a track. As the exhibit shows, usually there are no tracks on the top of the top disk or on the bottom of the bottom disk of a disk pack.

Although Exhibit 6.10 shows only one track per disk surface, in reality there are many. Exhibit 6.11 illustrates 100 tracks and also shows a magnification of one portion of one track to illustrate how data is stored; each

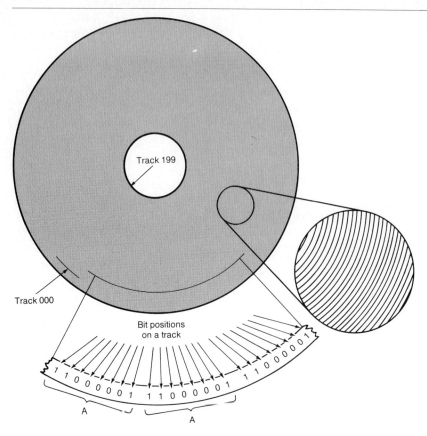

EXHIBIT 6.11
A disk surface and a
section of one track.

Track 199

Track 000

Bit positions
on a track

"A" in EBDIC code

"1" mark in the display represents one magnetized spot, or bit. Each arrow points to a possible bit position; note that many of the bit positions are vacant (do not contain magnetized spots). As stated previously, data is represented by bit patterns in coded form. The illustrated bit pattern represents an "A" in the EBCDIC code.

Exhibit 6.12 magnifies one entire track from one surface of one disk. Assume that the record at address 5555 on this track is needed for processing. The operating system of the computer keeps track of which disk pack contains each data set (such as a set of data for a payroll job). The operating system then processes an index contained on the disk pack (usually on the first track) which indicates the physical address on a particular track of the data needed. The operating system then directs read-write heads to a position over this track (all read-write heads move together). As the disk rotates, the read-write heads read the addresses of records on the track (by sensing the magnetized bit patterns that represent these addresses) until address 5555 is read. The operating system recognizes that the record which follows is the record that must be retrieved, placed in main memory, and then processed by the ALU. Accordingly, the operating system directs the read-write heads to read (copy) that record, and the computer circuitry places a copy of that record in main memory to await processing. This type of record access is known as "direct access" because the computer operating system can go directly to the record (or, rather, to the track that contains the record) without first processing all records in the file that are on the preceding tracks of the disk and without processing other disk packs that may be part of the computer system. High-speed disks have direct access times in the range of from 5 to 100 milliseconds (thousandths of a second).

Direct accessing is efficient when only one record or a few records from a file are needed. However, a great deal of relatively slow mechanical movement is required to retrieve many records from the same disk pack; thus in this case, sequential processing becomes more efficient. For example, because all or almost all employees will be paid during a given pay period and because most payroll records must be accessed and processed, sequential processing is more efficient for payroll preparation, which, accordingly, often uses magnetic tape. Employee files, however,

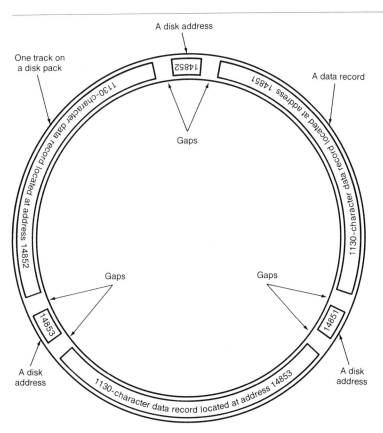

EXHIBIT 6.12
A single disk track containing three records. (*Source: SRA 1978.*)

and many other record files that can be efficiently processed sequentially for routine reports often must be accessed for one record at other times for other reasons, so these file records need both sequential and direct access. Disks can accommodate this dual need.

Exhibit 6.10 shows 11 disks in the disk pack and 20 tracks, each on a different disk surface, directly over and under each other. Count them; remember that the top surface of the top disk and the bottom surface of the bottom disk do not have tracks. The collection of tracks above and below each other is known as a disk "cylinder," as shown. If there are 100 tracks per disk surface (as in Exhibit 6.10), there will be 100 cylinders on the disk pack.

Because the read-write heads are attached to the access arms and because all access arms move together, the read-write heads will be simultaneously posed at every track of one cylinder. Records can be stored in sequential order from the top to the bottom of the cylinder; thus the first record is on the first cylinder track, the second is on the second cylinder track (which is on the disk surface immediately below the first cylinder track), and so on. For sequential processing (of employees' records for paycheck preparation, for example), the records in sequence at the same position in a cylinder can be retrieved simultaneously and processed sequentially within the CPU, then the next set of records at the next rotation point on the same cylinder can be retrieved and processed, and so on, until the read-write heads move to the next cylinder in sequence to process the next records in sequence. Because the records are on disks rather than tape, each record can also be accessed directly for other processing needs.

Hard disk units are being increasingly used with microcomputers. Typically, the hard disk is one platter with data on the top surface and the underside and is a 5¼-in. Winchester (fully enclosed) disk of about 10 megabytes capacity, selling in the range of from $1500 to $2000. While this is extensive memory, many mainframe hard disk systems contain in excess of 100,000 megabytes of data. The trend is toward hard disks for microcomputers with more capacity, and several are in the 30-megabyte range. One 5¼-in. microcomputer disk system by Qume Corporation is illustrated in Exhibit 6.13.

Bubble Memory

Bubble memory consists of small wafers within which are embedded metal-alloy "bubbles" which can receive an electric charge. As a current is passed close to these bubbles, usually by a circuitry wafer adjacent to the bubble wafer, the polarization of these metal-alloy bubbles can be reversed, thereby moving bits (charges of electricity) through the bubble system and storing data or retrieving it from the bubble memory.

Bubble memory has high potential because of its low production costs

EXHIBIT 6.13
A high-capacity
microcomputer disk
system. (*Courtesy of
Qume Corporation, a
subsidiary of ITT
Corporation.*)

and its direct access capabilities; thus it may become widely employed as a main memory technology in the future. At present, however, it is used primarily as secondary memory and as memory within such devices as printers.

Floppy Disks

Floppy disks (also known as "flexible disks") are a low-cost and widely used data storage medium for microcomputers. They are inexpensive, typically costing about $2 to $5 each, and a floppy disk drive is in the $200 to $500 range. Floppy disks can be directly accessed, but their access times are not nearly as fast as those of hard disks. Each disk drive contains only one floppy disk, which can be removed and replaced by another disk in seconds by the operator. Floppy disks provide convenient off-line data storage. Storage capacity on a floppy disk is usually in the range of from 100 to 500 kilobytes of data, just a small fraction of the amount of data that a single disk in a disk pack system can store.

Exhibit 6.14 shows a floppy disk. Unlike the read-write heads of a hard disk system, those of a floppy disk system are in direct contact with the surface of the rotating floppy disk. The direct contact causes a minute amount of abrasion, so floppy disks eventually wear out. Some companies replace their floppy disks at regular intervals by copying the old disk onto a new disk. Note the "write protect notch" near the lower lefthand corner of the floppy disk. When this notch is not covered, the disk can be written on. When an adhesive sticker covers the notch, the disk is "write-protected," and no data can be written on it. This write protection prevents a disk from being inadvertently erased by data written on top of the existing data.

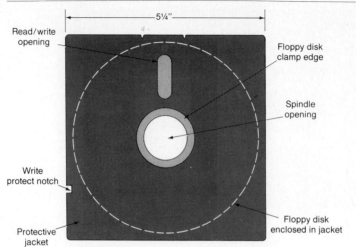

EXHIBIT 6.14
A floppy disk.

A COMPUTER INFORMATION SYSTEM

Exhibit 6.15, which is an elaboration of Exhibit 6.2, shows a computer system of moderate complexity. The two side wings illustrate secondary memory in the form of banks of magnetic-tape reel units and disk packs. Exhibit 6.2's "input" and "output" are shown in Exhibit 6.15 as different types of input-output (I/O) devices, which are examined later in this chapter. By the conclusion of this chapter the student will understand the nature and operation of the computer system components shown in Exhibit 6.15 and will possess an overall knowledge of the hardware dimension of computer information systems.

Channel Devices and Controllers

All input to the computer system enters main memory through data entryways known as "ports." In a large-scale computer system each computer port is attached by a high-speed data transmission cable to a channel device, which is a hardware component that regulates data traffic to and from a port. A channel device receives data from input devices, accumulates this data in its own "buffer" memory (small and temporary memory), and forwards the data to main memory at high speeds as directed by the operating system. In turn, the operating system directs the flow of data from main memory to a channel device, which then distributes this data to output devices.

There are two general classes of channel devices. One is high-speed disk or tape channels, which are especially designed to receive data from high-speed input devices (or from main memory) and forward this data to main memory (or to output devices). The other is slow-speed multiplexor channels, which receive data from low-speed input devices, merge

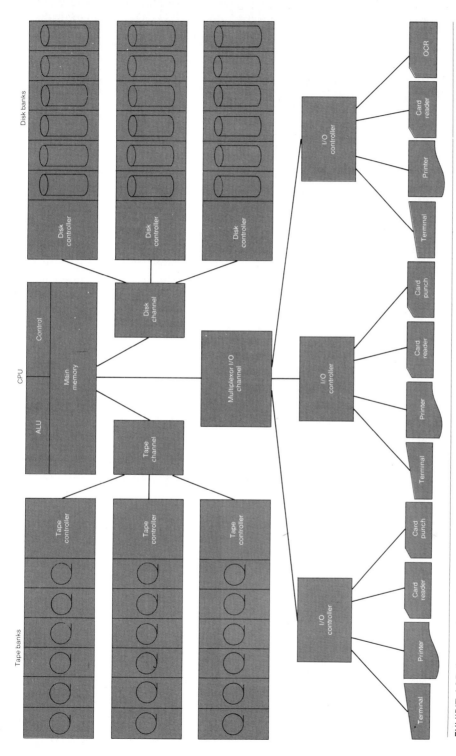

EXHIBIT 6.15 A computer system.

(multiplex) the data so that it utilizes the full capacity of the high-capacity input port, and then forward the data to main memory. The multiplexor also separates a high-speed data flow from main memory into multiple low-speed data flows for data output by slow-speed devices.

A channel device is similar to a small computer system in that it has some logic capabilities and some ability to manipulate data. It usually is not directly connected to input-output devices, but rather is connected to I/O control units; in Exhibit 6.15 these are high-speed disk and tape controllers and low-speed I/O controllers. Control units control the data flows by directing the flows to and from the I/O devices that are attached to them. Exhibit 6.15 shows that each channel device can have many associated control units, each attached by a cable. Control units also may have some limited computer capabilities in the form of a modest amount of logic capabilities and a small amount of internal buffer data storage.

The linkage between the CPU, channel devices, controllers, and I/O devices illustrates a major principle of computer systems operations: delegation of control tasks within the computer system. The operating system initiates the inflow of data from the channel devices and the outflow of data from main memory to the channel devices. Then the operating system delegates monitoring these flows to the channel devices. If the operating system monitored the flows itself, the ALU (which must process each operating system instruction) would be fully occupied with controlling an individual channel device during the entire period the channel device was activated and would be unable to undertake other processing. Therefore, when the operating system has data for output through a channel device, it sends a command to that device activating it to receive data and directing it to notify the operating system upon completion of the assigned task. The operating system and the ALU then turn to other tasks, such as processing transactions internally, until the CPU is interrupted by a signal from the channel device indicating that the assigned task is completed. The operating system acknowledges this message and may then assign another task to the channel device.

The reverse occurs when the channel device has data to be input to main memory—it notifies the operating system of its readiness to transmit data. The operating system then sends one instruction directing it to transmit data and returns to its other duties. When the transmission is completed, the channel device notifies the CPU and is assigned another task. In this way the operating system and the ALU are able to control multiple channel devices while using only a small fraction of the ALU's total time.

This same general sequence of activities occurs in the interaction between channel devices and disk controllers, tape controllers, and low-speed I/O controllers. Each channel device can control several of these controllers and delegates to each the control of the data flows between the channel device and the I/O devices.

INDICATORS OF COMPUTER POWER

Computer power is the rating of the amount of work a computer system can complete in a given period of time. Computer power is tied to a number of different indicators of processing speed and efficiency, no one of which by itself accurately measures computer power.

One important indicator of computer power is the number of CPUs a computer system possesses. Some computer systems have one CPU, and others have two, three, or four. A multiple-CPU computer is said to be a "multiprocessor" computer system in that it can process multiple instructions *simultaneously,* rather than *concurrently,* like a *multiprogramming* single-CPU computer. In some computer systems CPUs can be routinely added to upgrade the computer system's capabilities and increase its processing speed (an additional CPU may be referred to as an "attached processor"). However, some single-CPU computer systems can process data faster than other computer systems having multiple CPUs; about all that can be said is that a computer system with two CPUs is usually nearly twice as powerful as that same computer system configured with only one CPU.

Another important indicator of a computer's power is the CPU's speed in processing each instruction. Sometimes this characteristic is referred to as "MIPS"—millions of instructions per second. Some faster CPUs take just hundreds of nanoseconds to process an instruction.

Still another important indicator is the size of a computer's instruction set. An instruction set may number well over 100 separate instructions, each of which can direct the ALU to perform a unique, individual task as one ALU processing step. For example, if a computer had no DIVIDE instruction, it would have to accomplish arithmetic division by repeatedly processing the SUBTRACT instruction. If the instruction set is small, the CPU must process multiple instructions (or one instruction several times) to accomplish the same task that could be accomplished with a single instruction in another computer system. Accordingly, in general the more instructions there are in the computer's instruction set, the more powerful the computer system is because it can perform the same amount of processing with fewer steps than it could if it had a smaller instruction set.

Main memory size is an additional indicator of a computer system's ability to accomplish data processing. All else being equal, the larger the main memory, the more capable the computer system because it can contain and process larger programs and data sets. Many microcomputers have main memories that are too small for even one medium-scale business program, let alone the several large-scale programs that a large computer can process at one time. Also, the number of separate ports of main memory and each port's data transmission speed are important determinants of a computer system's efficiency and speed.

Several types of "cycle time" also influence computer power. One is the amount of time it takes for data to move from main memory to the

ALU and back to main memory. Another important cycle time is the amount of time needed to transfer data from channel devices to main memory. A third cycle time is the amount of time it takes to transfer data from secondary memory to main memory and return it to secondary memory. Medium- and large-scale computer systems now widely employ "virtual memory," a software technique that greatly accelerates data transfer from a disk unit to main memory by enabling large blocks of data to be moved at one time. Increasingly, the more sophisticated microcomputers are also using virtual memory systems.

One of the most important indicators of computer power is "word size," or the number of bits that are manipulated together during processing by the CPU. The larger the word size, the faster the rate of processing, all else being equal. Most computers systems' word sizes are 8, 16, 32, or 64 bits.

The speed of I/O devices also influences the power of the computer system. For example, all else being equal, a computer system with high-speed printers is considered more powerful than a computer system that is identical except that it has only low-speed printers. A final indicator meriting mention is the processing efficiency of the operating system and the other major systems programs. Operating systems vary widely in their efficiency, which is primarily a function of how well they are designed and programmed.

There are other indicators of the speed and efficiency—the power—of computer systems as well. No one is definitive; all must be taken together in estimating the computer system's power. The ultimate test, however, is the amount of "throughput"—the actual number of work units accomplished (such as transactions processed) in a given period of time. But even this indicator is ambiguous, for throughput is a function of the type of processing that is taking place. For example, one computer system may be able to process accounts payable very rapidly but may be slow at processing scientific data, while another may be just the opposite. Also, throughput depends upon the particular configuration of the computer system. In comparing the throughput of two systems for a certain type of processing, adjusting the configuration of the slower system, such as by adding another channel device at a modest additional cost, may make the slower computer much the faster of the two.

Microcomputers, much ballyhooed because of their great speed in internal processing, are often termed "very powerful." Indeed, the internal processing speed of a large microcomputer (as measured, for example, by the amount of time the CPU takes to process each instruction) may be fairly close to the speed of a large computer system but may cost a tiny fraction of the price. To conclude that such a microcomputer is nearly as powerful as a large computer is tempting but erroneous. The many other indicators of computer power suggest that a microcomputer has only a small fraction of a large computer system's overall power. For example, as noted above, limited main memory size restricts the size of programs that can be used on a microcomputer. Even more important, most microcomputers are limited to one user at a time performing only one task at a time, whereas most large mainframe computers are multiuser and multitasking: dozens or even hundreds of tasks can be run concurrently in online, real-time, and timesharing modes, and hundreds of individual workstations may be attached to the computer system. Viewed in this perspective, microcomputers are very powerful for their cost and hence are very cost-effective, but they are in no position to compete one-on-one with large computer systems in terms of throughput. Consequently, where data processing tasks are large, a mainframe computer system is usually most cost-effective. A later chapter will show, however, that because microcomputers are cost-effective in many circumstances, large numbers of them will be used within organizational subunits to accomplish data processing tasks on a decentralized basis.

DATA COLLECTION AND INPUT-OUTPUT SYSTEMS

An old adage in data processing is "garbage in, garbage out" (GIGO), which means that the computer system's output can be no better than its input: if "garbage" such as misleading, improper, irrelevant, or erroneous data is input to the computer system, the output will be at least as misleading, improper, irrelevant, or erroneous. In fact, the greatest opportunities for errors in computer systems occur during data input because the input activity—converting data to machine-readable form—is to a great extent a manual operation. In large organizations, transactions may be manually handled through more than 30 steps before entering the computer as input, providing ample opportunity for errors.

More than 90 percent of all data processing errors occur during data input. Most of these are typographical errors such as transpositions of data, clerical errors such as misreading data, or lost transactions. In a complex data processing system, misplacing transactions, at least temporarily, is surprisingly easy, especially if the transactions are corrections of previous errors and thus have been taken out of the "mainstream" of other transactions. It is a wise data processing group that establishes very careful control over the input of its data. Often this is done by a separate data I/O control group that oversees the procedures for data preparation and entry and for error correction.

Many different technologies are available for data input and output, and many organizations use several of these technologies simultaneously. This increases the possibility of undetected errors because it increases the overall complexity of the information system.

To minimize input errors, careful scheduling of data input activities is essential, and it is important to develop detailed procedures for all aspects of the input activity; this includes carefully designing input forms

EXHIBIT 6A
Hard disk drive with
multiple disks.
(*Courtesy of Sperry
Corporation.*)

EXHIBIT 6B
A 5¼-inch floppy, or flexible, diskette being removed from its dust jacket for
insertion into a microcomputer system. Through technology similar to that for
recording music on hi-fi records, a 5¼-inch diskette typically holds about
320 kilobytes (320,000) bytes of data, or about 80 typed pages. (*NCR Corporation.*)

EXHIBIT 6C
A data center based on
Honeywell's large-scale
DPS 88 computer
system. (*Courtesy of
Honeywell, Inc.*)

EXHIBIT 6D
Storage of magnetic tapes in a tape library. (*Courtesy 3M.*)

EXHIBIT 6E
Data entry from Burroughs CRT workstations. Dual CRTs provide enhanced data entry capabilities and added workstation flexibility. (*Burroughs Corporation.*)

to help ensure that all required data is input with each transaction. Typically, for each different type of transaction, input personnel must complete a form having its own unique format. Usually transactions of like kind are gathered and processed together by specialized input personnel; such a set of transactions is known as a "batch," as previously discussed. Batch processing promotes efficiency and reduces data errors during input, in part because "batch controls" can be employed that effectively manage and control the entire set of transactions as one batch.

Data can be input at the computer site itself or at a remote site. In the latter case, known as "remote data entry" or "remote job entry," communications facilities are required to transmit the data from the remote site to the computer center. Remote entry can be done transaction by transaction or by entering batches of transactions at one time. A remote batch system uses special types of high-speed equipment.

INPUT DEVICES AND MEDIA

Most of the input-output devices discussed in this section and the next, and the technology associated with them, are used for both on-site and remote-site data input and output. While input devices are discussed in this section, and output devices are covered in the next, in some cases input media are also output media, as will be seen.

Punched Paper Cards

Punched cards are small cards made of heavy paper that can be used for both data input and data output. Data is encoded on each card in the form of small holes punched as a pattern that conforms to one of the standard data codes. The card is then "read" by a card-reader machine that senses the location of the holes, converts the data to electronic bits, and forwards the data to main memory.

The two common types of punched paper cards use the Hollerith code, which has 80 columns, and the BCD code, which utilizes 96 columns on a much smaller card. Both types of cards are illustrated and discussed extensively in many computer data processing reference books. About a decade ago, 90 percent of the world's computer-processed business transactions were input to computer systems by punched paper cards, but the use of newer technologies has cut this to about 10 percent today.

It is quite common for data to be punched out as output on paper cards by card-punch machines under the control of the computer, especially if the ouput is intermediate processing that must be further processed against additional computer files. In some smaller accounting computer systems, often called "unit record systems," paper cards are used not only as transaction input-output media but also as master files to record all transactions for, say, a particular customer or vendor. This use of cards is also decreasing.

As a data input mechanism, cards are used in three ways. The first is in batches; many like-type transactions are first punched into cards (usually one transaction per card) by a clerk using a keypunch machine. Then each batch is placed in a card-reading machine, and the data from the cards is read directly into the computer system at a moderate rate of speed.

Second, cards are often used for small jobs. In most data processing centers, even those which have converted from cards to other types of I/O media, one or more card punches and readers are kept available for small jobs because these devices are convenient and easy to use. Clerical personnel and managers can have a few (or even a few hundred) coded instructions of small programs keypunched and entered into the computer along with related data for processing without either having to learn a more advanced technology or having to ask professional data processing personnel for assistance.

The third common use of punched cards is in educational environments, where many college and university students still use card systems as input to the computer. Even here, however, the use of punched cards is on the wane.

Terminal Entry Systems

Various combinations of a cathode ray tube (CRT), an input keyboard terminal (which resembles a typewriter but which has many additional keys, usually including a special numeric key pad), and a low-speed printer are often used for computer input and output. A CRT is also called a "video display terminal" (VDT) or a "monitor."

A keyboard terminal may be used by itself or in conjunction with a CRT as an input device, a CRT may be used by itself as an input device or as an output device that does not provide "hard copy" (a permanent form of output), or a small printer may be combined with a keyboard or a keyboard and a CRT to permit input, screen output, and hard-copy output.

As suggested above, one type of CRT is for output only, and another can also accept input. The first type uses basically the same technology as a television set and can display textual material, financial and other types of alphabetic and numeric data, and graphics. The more sophisticated type of CRT can accept data entered directly onto the CRT screen by a light pen held to the screen. The information on the screen is identical to that within a sector of the computer system's memory; thus by maneuvering the light pen, data can be erased from the screen and simultaneously from memory, or lines can be drawn on the screen and thereby be entered into memory. This type of CRT input is the basis of CAD (computer-aided design), which is widely used for engineering design activities.

More common than a stand-alone CRT is a combination of a CRT and a keyboard, as illustrated in Exhibit 6.16. This combination is often used

EXHIBIT 6.16
A transactions entry
terminal.

for direct transaction entry to the computer system. Transactions may consist of inquiries from managers or clerical personnel about a customer account or records of another type that are on-line within the computer system.

Transactions also may be data input transactions, such as sales to customers or the receipt of inventory items. There is a trend toward utilizing a CRT-and-keyboard terminal for input of these and other types of routine, high-volume transactions. Clerical personnel usually key in the transaction, which appears on the CRT in the format in which it was keyed in. The terminal operator reads and reviews the transaction; uses the keyboard to correct it, if necessary; and then enters the transaction directly into the computer system by pressing an ENTER key. Often the format in which the transaction should be entered appears as a template on the screen, and as data is input, the CRT cursor (a blip of light that shows where data being entered will appear on the screen) automatically moves to the space on the template where data must be entered next.

A CRT, a keyboard, and a printer are often used in conjunction as one complete data processing workstation. Adding the printer enables the operator to input data at the terminal, view it on the CRT, and get data printed out all at the same site. Such a combination may be used for a transactions entry, for instance, to record a sale initially, with the sales invoice being computer-calculated and printed out immediately for mailing. This combination is also commonly used for word processing as well as when managers or clerical personnel enter inquiries into the system. In the latter case, various data or records are requested and are displayed on the CRT screen by the operator, who then enters a command that prints the information on the adjacent printer.

CRT-and-keyboard terminals can be "dumb" or "smart." Dumb terminals can enter data to the computer system and can display data on the CRT. Smart, or "intelligent," terminals are more expensive and can be programmed to perform some of the functions of a computer system; increasingly they are actually modestly configured microcomputers being utilized as terminals. Quite commonly a smart terminal is used to perform certain tests on, and analyses of, the input data. For example, a smart terminal may be programmed to verify that all information required for a particular transaction has been entered, that data which should be alphabetic is alphabetic, and that numeric data is indeed numeric, among other "editing" (error-checking) activities. Additionally, a smart terminal often is used in mixed mode to enter transactions or programs to the large computer when the power of a large computer is required or to independently process a small job that is within its own capabilities. Smart terminals are usually priced from about $1000 upward.

Magnetic-Ink Character Recognition

Magnetic-ink character recognition, commonly referred to a "MICR," is a data input technology that utilizes a machine to read data written in standardized "fonts" (character styles). By far the dominant form of data input in the banking industry, MICR is capable of being applied in many other areas. It is very effective and inexpensive, and managers should constantly be alert to situations in which MICR can replace more costly or more error-prone types of input technologies.

The check shown in Exhibit 6.17 illustrates the use of MICR in the banking industry. The American Banking Association has developed a standard MICR code, which appears along the bottom of this check. All MICR characters at the bottom and to the left of the check amount are prerecorded on the check and consist of routine symbols that route the check to the bank of issue through the Federal Reserve banking system from whatever bank first receives it. The check number recorded at the bottom of the check is identical to the check number at the upper righthand corner. The account number is the number of the issuer's account at the bank in which the account is held.

A check may be processed at many points in the banking system. The first step is for an input clerk at a keyboard terminal in the first bank that receives the check to record the check's amount in MICR font at the bottom of the check (see the figures at the bottom right in the exhibit). The font characters consist of magnetizable ink, and these characters are then magnetized so that they can be read and interpreted. When the check has completed its travels through the Federal Reserve system and is received at the issuer's bank, it is placed in a batch with other checks received

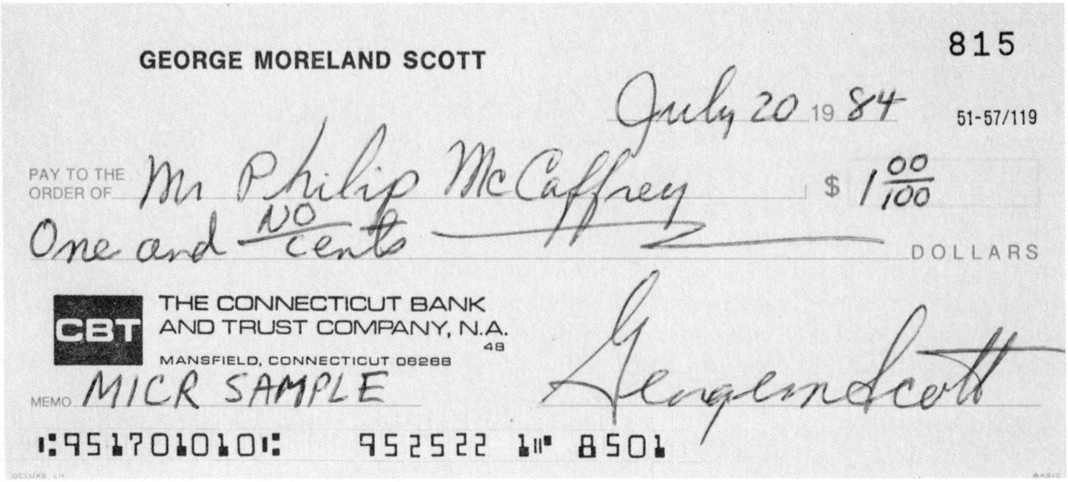

EXHIBIT 6.17
MICR used for checks.

during that time period and is processed rapidly by an MICR reader, which reads the check number, the amount, and the issuer's account number from the font at the bottom of the check. The computer then enters the amount in the issuer's account. Later processing of customer accounts enables the computer system to prepare customer bank statements automatically.

Optical Character Recognition

Optical character recognition (OCR) is a technique for optically rather than magnetically recognizing data patterns encoded on a source document. The data is in the form of special font characters or slash marks. An OCR machine reads the data by using either electric-eye or laser-optics technology to convert the data to digital form and enter it into the computer system. Most students have taken examinations that involve placing heavy slash marks between designated lines on a preprinted form to respond to multiple-choice questions; this is one of the most frequently encountered uses of an OCR system.

OCR technology is based on programming the OCR machine to recognize patterns of slash marks or numbers, letters, or other characters printed in a specialized font. The patterns of data on the OCR forms can be complex, requiring sophisticated computer programs to interpret them. An example of the use of OCR in conjunction with a moderately sophisticated program is a business game developed by the author. Students were asked to make basic business decisions each fiscal period (one month) about prices, production rates, inventory levels, the number of production machines to be purchased or sold, and other matters that determined the fictional company's short- and long-term profitability. Each decision was entered in slash-mark form in a designated sector of an OCR preprinted form. (For example, two slash marks in the equipment purchases section of the form indicated that the student wished to purchase two new production machines, thereby increasing production capacity.) The forms were read and interpreted by an OCR reader, and the game's programs then processed the data to produce a balance sheet and an income statement for each student for each fiscal period.

OCR can be used to advantage where input is provided directly by the user on an OCR preprinted input form. This makes the input process simple and fast and eliminates the need for converting data to machine-readable form after it has already been recorded on a separate source document. The disadvantage is that OCR machines are quite costly. In many applications where OCR technology could be potentially beneficial, another technology such as MICR may be more cost-effective.

Point-of-Sale Data Entry

Point-of-sale (POS) data entry devices capture the data from a sale or other retail transaction as it occurs, making this a real-time activity. The great advantage is clerical savings that accrue because transactions do not have to be first recorded manually and later converted to computer-readable form; POS data entry immediately inputs data to the computer system as each transaction occurs. Another advantage is that many POS systems are integrated into inventory and other systems to provide up-to-date information for operations control and management purposes. Some experts estimate that from 60 to 80 percent of all data needed for operations and management control in retail stores (exclusive of planning needs) can be captured by POS devices at the time transactions occur.

POS data input is in common use. Sears, Montgomery Ward, J. C. Penney, and other major retail chain stores have thousands of POS devices operated by sales clerks. Supermarkets have also adopted POS technology. Many banks now issue a special bank card so that customers can conduct business with the bank via an electronic teller. A customer can insert this special card into an electronic teller machine at, say, 3 a.m.; key in a personal code number; press additional keys to indicate the type of transaction (for example, cash withdrawal from a checking account) and the amount; and in less than 30 seconds receive the cash. During those few seconds the electronic teller has verified that the customer's account balance is sufficient to cover the cash requested, has posted the transaction for later entry in that account, and has activated the machinery that mechanically counts the cash and passes it through a slot to the customer. Exhibit 6.18 illustrates this sequence of activities. As part of a promotional campaign for its electronic teller, one bank programmed its machine to occasionally provide a "bonus" by passing out more money than the customer requested.

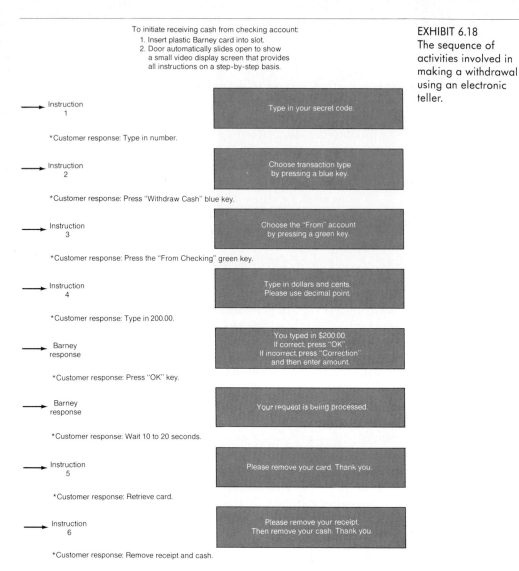

To initiate receiving cash from checking account:
1. Insert plastic Barney card into slot.
2. Door automatically slides open to show a small video display screen that provides all instructions on a step-by-step basis.

Instruction 1 — Type in your secret code.

*Customer response: Type in number.

Instruction 2 — Choose transaction type by pressing a blue key.

*Customer response: Press "Withdraw Cash" blue key.

Instruction 3 — Choose the "From" account by pressing a green key.

*Customer response: Press the "From Checking" green key.

Instruction 4 — Type in dollars and cents. Please use decimal point.

*Customer response: Type in 200.00.

Barney response — You typed in $200.00. If correct, press "OK". If incorrect, press "Correction" and then enter amount.

*Customer response: Press "OK" key.

Barney response — Your request is being processed.

*Customer response: Wait 10 to 20 seconds.

Instruction 5 — Please remove your card. Thank you.

*Customer response: Retrieve card.

Instruction 6 — Please remove your receipt. Then remove your cash. Thank you.

*Customer response: Remove receipt and cash.

EXHIBIT 6.18
The sequence of activities involved in making a withdrawal using an electronic teller.

The typical transaction processing sequence with POS systems is as follows: (1) As the transaction occurs, it is recorded for the first and only time by a POS device; (2) the POS device enters the transaction into the computer; and (3) the computer updates records in its files on the basis of the transaction data entered. Some POS systems also perform other tasks.

Electronic Cash Registers

Of the several types of POS machines, the one generally encountered in retail stores is the electronic cash register (ECR). ECRs can handle cash transactions, credit transactions, and inquiries into the system, such as determining a customer's credit status or the inventory level for a particular item.

Tag Readers

A second type of POS device is the tag reader, often used along with an electronic cash register. Many retail clothing stores use tag-reader systems. Clothes have price tags coded with circular punched holes that give the inventory item number and price information. The tag is similar to a punched card in that a reading device must read and interpret it. When the tag-reading device is clamped onto the tag, it interprets the data contained in the pattern of holes and reads this data into the computer system, which uses it to prepare the sales slip and update inventory records.

A different kind of tag-reader system is similar in function but has data implanted on a strip of magnetizable material on the tag. Magnetic-strip tags must be placed in a special type of code-reading device.

Bar Codes

There are a number of bar-code scanning systems. Bar codes consist of a series of printed bars of different widths, but of the same length, that are placed directly on a merchandise item; they are usually printed on the carton in which the merchandise is packaged. The code is passed over an optical scanning machine, which reads and interprets the pattern of different bar widths. Alternatively, a hand-held light pen can be passed over the bar code so that the pen rather than the coded item is moved. The light pen contains an optical scanning mechanism that reads the code.

By far the most common bar code is the Universal Product Code (UPC), used on grocery items. This code is standardized and appears on approximately 80 percent of prepackaged grocery items. The UPC consists of 10 pairs of vertical bars that identify the manufacturer and the product for inventory control purposes. On the basis of the UPC, the computer files can also be searched to retrieve the price of the item and record it automatically on the sales slip at the checkout register. However, many systems have not activated this feature of the UPC because consumers insist on seeing the price marked on each item individually in a form they can read. Without the cost savings that accrue from eliminating the marking of prices on each individual item, automated pricing at the retail counter often is not advantageous.

Key-to-Tape and Key-to-Disk Systems

Key-to-tape technology and key-to-disk technology, which together have become the dominant input methodology during the last decade, are different but related technologies. The choice between the two is based largely on cost (key-to-tape systems are less expensive) or on a need for the additional capabilities which key-to-disk systems can provide.

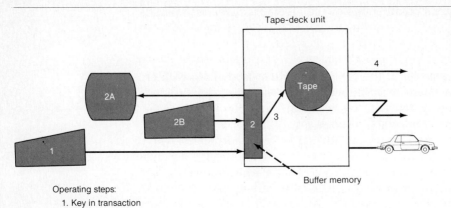

EXHIBIT 6.19
A key-to-tape system.

Operating steps:
1. Key in transaction
2. Verify transaction
3. Place transaction on tape
4. Input to computer

Key-to-Tape Systems

A key-to-tape system is illustrated in Exhibit 6.19, in which the numbers denote the steps in the data entry process; the two sets of numbers in the exhibit are coordinated. Step 1 is to key in the transaction from a workstation terminal. This can be done on the basis of batches of source documents, such as sales slips or notices of payroll hours worked, or on a real-time basis, such as when a transaction is received over the telephone or over the counter and is immediately keyed into the terminal without any manual preparation of a source document. The transaction enters a magnetic reel tape deck that also contains buffer memory, as shown. One of two transaction verification activities now takes place (step 2); which one depends upon the type of system. With one method (shown as 2*a*) the transaction in buffer memory is displayed automatically on a CRT which is located at the input terminal or which is a part of this terminal; the transaction then is scanned and reviewed by the terminal operator. If the operator verifies that the transaction is correct, an ENTRY key is activated (step 3), which transfers the transaction from buffer memory to magnetic tape, where it becomes the next in a sequence of transactions written on the tape. If an error has been made, the operator corrects it by using the terminal and again verifies the transaction. Because many such input terminals are connected to one tape-deck console, it is unlikely that two transactions from the same terminal will be placed on the tape in sequence one after the the other; rather, transactions from all terminals will be interspersed throughout the tape.

    If the system uses the other verification method (2*b*), the transaction is retained in buffer memory, and the source document is forwarded to an operator at a second terminal. This operator keys in the same transaction a second time, and the two transactions, which should be identical, are compared by a program within the buffer memory. If the transactions are identical, the transaction is transferred from the buffer memory and is placed next in sequence on the tape (as step 3). If the comparison indicates that the transactions are not identical, either the input operator or the verification operator has made an error; the verification operator then keys in the transaction again, and it is again compared. If the comparison shows that the error was in verification rather than in original entry, the transaction is entered onto the tape; if it does not, the transaction is deleted from buffer memory, and the source document is returned to the original input operator or to another operator for reentry and reverification. This form of verification, because it employs double input and computer-based comparison, offers greater assurance than errors will not occur during data input, but it is more time-consuming.

The choice between the two validation methods depends upon the seriousness of the consequences of introducing errors into the system. Where entry speed is more important than absolute accuracy, the first validation approach is more suitable, but where strict accuracy is a major concern, the second verification approach is preferred.

Periodically, or when the tape is full, the transactions on the tape are transferred to a central computer system (step 4), which may be in close proximity or located a few miles or even thousands of miles away. Three likely means of transmitting this data are shown in Exhibit 6.20. The first, at the top, is by direct coaxial-cable connection and may be utilized if the computer is nearby. The second, shown in the middle, is by data communications lines such as local or long-distance telephone lines. The third is by physical conveyance, such as by automobile, truck, or airplane.

A key-to-tape system is more economical than a key-to-disk system. However, it offers no means of sorting the transactions of the tape without using additional equipment. Transactions often need to be sorted by numeric sequence; by time periods, such as by day; or by specific customers. Where a key-to-tape system is used without additional equipment, the taped transactions must be sorted internally by the main computer system, which consumes valuable CPU time. In addition to this problem, a key-to-tape system lacks certain capabilities of a key-to-disk system that are described below.

Key-to-Disk Systems

Exhibit 6.20 shows a key-to-disk system. The input and verification processes are similar to those of a key-to-tape system, with the important differences that disk rather than tape technology is used and the transactions are entered onto a disk in a disk-drive unit. A major advantage of a key-to-disk system is the ability to sort transactions on disk. Different types of transactions either can be entered directly to separate sectors of the disk and kept separate initially or can be placed in sequence on the disk. Sequenced transactions can at a later time be sorted by type on the disk within the disk drive with little effort (shown as step 5 in Exhibit 6.20). Even if the transactions are initially placed in separate sections of the disk according to type, it may be necessary later to sort them numer-

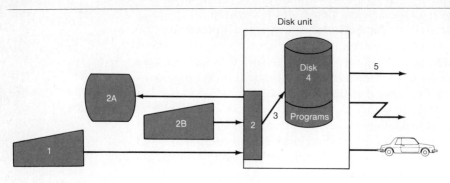

Disk unit

EXHIBIT 6.20
A key-to-disk system.

Operating steps:
1. Key in transaction
2. Verify transaction
3. Place on disk
4. Sort (and merge two or more disks)
5. Input to computer

ically or alphabetically or in some other manner, such as by individual customer.

Another type of sorting can merge two or more disks from different key-to-disk systems before entry to the computer system. This is typically done where multiple key-to-disk systems in the same room or building are connected to one another by cable. The data from one disk can be transferred to another disk and merged with that disk's data by sorting the data of both disks together into the prescribed sequence.

Key-to-disk systems also permit convenient alteration of a transaction already entered on the disk. For example, if a telephone sales transaction has been received by a terminal operator and entered onto the disk and a few minutes later the customer calls back to change or cancel the order, a key-to-tape system must treat the second call as a separate transaction. With a key-to-disk system, it is possible without undue effort to key in the customer number and locate the original transaction on the disk and then alter the transaction in accordance with the customer's new wishes. This transaction revision capability offers unusual benefits in some highly fluid data entry circumstances.

A key-to-disk system is also capable of reserving a sector of the disk for editing routines, for a "menu," or for training programs. For example, editing routines may be invoked to review all transactions on the disk before they are transferred to the computer system to ensure that all data fields contain the proper type of data and to check that customer and other types of identification numbers entered as parts of transactions are valid. Errors found can then be corrected by entries through the terminals.

The menu capability permits each CRT to display, at the operator's request, a menu, or list, of possible actions that can be taken or choices that can be made by the operator in a given set of circumstances. A similar capability is that the CRT can display a format for the type of transaction being processed to assist the operator in filling the proper spaces with data, as discussed previously with reference to direct input transaction terminals.

Training programs can be placed on a separate sector of the disk and used to prompt operators on the sequence of steps to take in entering and verifying each type of transaction. Fully trained operators can also make use of them for dealing with transactions of a type they seldom encounter or tend to forget how to process.

While the key-to-tape and key-to-disk systems described above use standard tape and hard disk technology, less expensive systems using key to cassette tape and key to floppy disk are also available. Appropriate for low-volume data input, these low-budget systems are inefficient for an environment in which multiple terminals are inputting data to the key-to-tape or key-to-disk system and in which transactions entry is a continuous daily activity. Whereas cassette-tape and floppy disk systems would be likely to have few workstations or only one, standard tape and hard disk systems usually would have several, and perhaps dozens, within a single system.

An advantage of key-to-disk and key-to-tape systems over many other types of data entry systems is that much of the data handling is electronic rather than mechanical. This results in less downtime for the entire system and for each data input station within the system. It also increases the speed with which data can be input, and it usually results in a quieter, more work-conducive environment. In most high-activity work situations key-to-disk and key-to-tape systems are believed to offer 20 to 40 percent faster data entry than electromechanical systems such as punched-card systems.

OUTPUT DEVICES AND MEDIA

Printers

Computer printout, one of the most prevalent forms of output for computer data, is produced by a wide variety of printer technologies for two general types of activities. The first, data processsing production activities that range from document preparation to report generation, requires high-speed printers. The second is printing associated with the I/O systems of individual managers or clerical personnel or with personal computers and hobby computers; for these tasks, low-speed printers are usually sufficient.

Prices for printers range from around $200 for a simple printer for a microcomputer to more than $100,000 for a very-high-speed printer. Low-cost, low-speed printers are character printers; that is, they usually print back and forth (bidirectionally) across a page, printing one character at a time. Typically, character printer speeds are from 10 to 200 characters per second. High-speed, high-cost printers are line printers that print an entire line at a time. Most printers print up to either 80 or 132 characters per line.

Printers fall into two general classes. Impact printers have characters or "pins", that are physically struck by strike bars in the fashion of a typewriter. Impact printers may be "letter-quality" (designed to provide output of very high quality) or "dot-matrix," which produces output that is usually recognizable as having been printed by a computer. Dot-matrix printers are usually faster and less expensive than letter-quality printers. Some dot-matrix printers can also be used to provide graphics output. Both letter-quality and dot-matrix printers are frequently used on micro-computer systems.

The other general class of printers is nonimpact printers, which are faster than impact printers because the character is not mechanically placed against the paper. One type of nonimpact printer is the ink jet printer, which sprays an inklike material in tiny jets onto the paper at a high rate of speed. With this process the printed paper requires a few seconds for drying, which can be accomplished by passing it through a heating com-partment in the printer. Printers of this type can achieve speeds in excess of 2000 lines per minute.

Another type of nonimpact printer is the laser printer, which can print in the range of from 20,000 to 30,000 lines per minute. Laser printers are the most expensive printers available. The laser works by burning char-acters into the paper with laser beams.

Printer technology continues to improve at a rapid rate. In particular, printers for microcomputers are improving in terms of their versatility and reliability and the numbers of different models available, each of which has its own characteristics. Additionally, competition among vendors as well as technological improvements point toward reduced prices for mi-crocomputer printers. At present, high-quality dot-matrix printers with a speed of about 150 characters per second can be purchased for around $600, and letter-quality printers with a speed of 10 to 20 characters per second are in the same price range.

Plotters

A plotter is a specialized output device for preparing computer-drawn graphs and charts. With an electrostatic process or a series of ink pens, plotters can provide a large output format in multiple colors. Plotted output is often used in engineering and scientific applications and some-times for managerial purposes such as group presentations. Increasingly, however, graphics for managerial purposes is being done using ordinary dot-matrix printers, which are associated with microcomputers, rather than the much slower special-purpose plotters.

Microfilm and Microfiche

Microfilm and microfiche are data output media based on a photography technology. The medium used is a film that is technically similar to ordi-nary camera film. Microfilm consists of long filmstrips and looks like rolled-up camera film. Microfiche is the same film medium cut into small, flat rectangles, typically from 2 by 4 in. to about 4 by 6 in.

The advantages of microfilm and microfiche are their compactness and low cost. Photoreduced data can be entered on them in such small size that the entire St. James version of the Bible has been recorded on one microfiche measuring about 2½ by 3½ in. This diminutive size is important when the quantity of data stored is massive and storage space is at a premium. The great disadvantage is that microfiche cannot be directly read by a computer or by the human eye. To be read by a computer, the microfiche must be output in a stylized font compatible with MICR or OCR devices; then a special microfiche copying device must convert the microfiche to paper copy, which an MICR and OCR machine finally reads. This arrangement is awkward at best and is seldom encountered in practice.

For human perusal, microfilm and microfiche retrieved from storage must be placed on a special reader and magnified hundreds of times. If copies in human-readable form are desired, some readers can produce printed copies from the magnified image on the reader. Because of the limitations of microfilm and microfiche, their primary use is for encoding information that either is for archival purposes or must be referenced only occasionally and for which it seems unlikely that hard copy will ever be desired. Libraries often record certain infrequently used journals and books on microfilm so that these bulky items need not take up library shelf space.

SUMMARY

Because computers are so important a part—although by no means the only part—of most information systems, a basic understanding of how they work is essential for a manager. This chapter described the nature and operation of the hardware components of a computer system and also dealt briefly with systems software concepts.

The CPU is the heart of a computer system. Its major sections are main memory, the control section, and the ALU, each of which performs a different vital function. Secondary memory is an external and slower type of memory that is directly connected to main memory. Timeslicing and timesharing help maximize the utilization of the ALU.

Systems programs include the operating system (which initiates, schedules, monitors, and controls various applications jobs), systems utility programs (such as sort programs and report generation programs), and special-function systems programs (such as file managment programs). The analogy between manual systems and computer file systems is a close one, and comparing the two is a good approach to understanding computer file systems. A computer stores data internally by using a coding system that represents data through combinations of electronic charges or on-off switches.

The technology of MOS chips has advanced rapidly in the past few years. MOS chips can serve as computer memory or as logic circuitry and have a host of applications. Hard disks and magnetic tape reels are the most frequently used secondary memory media for large computer systems; bubble memory has a high potential for future use. Microcomputers usually use less expensive tape cassettes or floppy disks for secondary memory.

Channel devices regulate traffic to and from imput-output devices. The linkages between them, the CPU, controllers, and input-output devices illustrate the principle of delegation of control tasks within the computer system.

General indicators of the power of a particular computer are the number and processing speed of its CPU, the size of its main memory, its "cycle times," the speed of its input-output devices, its word size, and its efficiency in processing systems programs. The ultimate test, however, is the amount of "throughput."

Careful control over data preparation and input is crucial, since more than 90 percent of all data processing errors occur prior to entry into the computer. Data can be input or output at the computer site itself or from a remote location. The two common types of punched paper cards, now used for only a small proportion of all computer input, are the 80-column Hollerith card and a smaller 96-column card which uses the BCD code. A CRT, an input terminal, and a low-speed printer are often used in various combinations for computer input and output. Examples of data input technology are MICR, OCR, and point-of-sale terminals, which include electronic cash registers, tag readers, and bar-code scanning systems. Key-to-tape and key-to-disk systems together are today's dominant data input methodology. Key-to-tape systems are less expensive, but key-to-disk systems have more capabilities.

The most prevalent form of hard-copy output for computer data is printout; several types of printers are available to provide it. Microfilm and microfiche are data output media that offer compactness and low cost but must be read by specialized devices.

KEY TERMS

central processing unit (CPU): the heart of the computer system, consisting of main memory, the control section, and the ALU (arithmetic logic unit).

main memory: the part of the CPU that stores data; main memory has the fastest data transfer speed of all types of memory in a computer system and is the most costly per unit of storage capacity.

control section: the part of the CPU that sequences the computer's activities, decodes program instructions, and directs data traffic within the CPU.

arithmetic logic unit (ALU): the part of the CPU that performs arithmetic calculations and logic comparisons according to instructions held in instruction registers.

secondary memory (secondary storage, auxiliary memory, auxiliary storage, mass

memory, mass storage): additional memory which is electronically connected to the CPU by coaxial cable and which transfers data to main memory; it is not as fast or costly as main memory.

multiprogramming capability: the ability of some computers to process programs for two or more jobs concurrently, maximizing the utilization of the ALU.

polling: the process by which one computer system calls another via telecommunications and instructs the second computer to transmit a stream of data, which it does automatically; often the second computer is unattended.

timeslicing: the process of allocating small "slices" of time to different computing tasks of the ALU.

timesharing: the concurrent processing of instructions from each of multiple users' programs by using timeslicing in a multiprogramming environment.

systems programs: computer programs that enable the computer system to run and manage itself and to perform specialized tasks for the computer system or for users' programs.

operating system: a set of systems programs with the primary purpose of managing the processing of users' programs, including managing the data files and allocating systems resources to users' jobs.

bit (binary digit): the computer's most basic unit of data storage; it is based on the two-state nature of computers.

byte: a unit of data formed by a combination of bits.

magnetic-oxide semiconductor (MOS) chip: a silicon wafer that singly or in combination with other MOS chips can serve as computer memory, as computer circuitry, or in either capacity as a component in other electronic devices.

magnetic tape: a secondary memory medium using a technology similar to that of an ordinary tape recorder; two types are reel tape (for larger computers) and cassette tape (for microcomputers).

sequential processing: processing file records in the same sequence in which they are maintained in the file.

disk: a data storage medium shaped like a phonograph record; large computer systems use disk packs, which are stacks of disks that form one unit. An inexpensive version for small computers is the floppy, or flexible, disk.

channel device: a computer hardware component, connected to the computer at a port by a coaxial cable, which regulates traffic from data input-output devices.

controller: a computer hardware component to which a channel device delegates control of the input-output devices.

dumb terminal: a terminal which can enter data to the computer system and receive data back but which cannot be programmed.

smart (intelligent) terminal: a terminal that can be programmed to perform editing and certain other functions of a computer system.

magnetic-ink character recognition (MICR): a data input technology utilizing highly stylized fonts; MICR is widely used in the banking industry.

optical character recognition (OCR): a technique for recognizing patterns encoded on a source document through use of an electric eye or laser optics.

point-of-sale (POS) data entry: the entry of transaction data to the computer system without first recording it in non-computer-readable form.

key-to-tape system: data input system that places a transaction on magnetic tape after it has been entered by keyboard and verified.

key-to-disk system: a data input system that places a transaction on a disk after it has been entered by keyboard and verified.

REFERENCES

Kroenke, David M. *Business Computer Systems: An Introduction*, Santa Cruz, CA: Mitchell, 1981.

Spencer, Donald D., *Introduction to Information Processing*, 3d ed., Merrill, Columbus, OH: 1981.

Walsh, Miles E., *Understanding Computers*, New York: Interscience-Wiley, 1981.

REVIEW QUESTIONS

1. Why is it useful for business school students to understand the rudiments of computer systems technology?

2. What are the functions of the control section of the CPU? Of the ALU?

3. Why must main memory have a high data transfer rate?

4. Why are memory partitions useful?

5. What is the difference between multiprogramming and multiprocessing?

6. What are the tasks of an operating system?

7. What is the difference between a logical and a physical file? Give an example.

8. Explain how data is represented electronically inside a computer system.

9. Why is a coding system needed to help represent data within a computer?

10. What are MOS chips used for?

11. Why is the limitation to sequential processing of magnetic-tape systems a serious disadvantage in some circumstances?

12. Explain how a hard disk unit operates.

13. What is a disk cylinder, and why is a cylinder important for sequential processing on a disk pack?

14. What is the difference in the functions between channels and controllers?

15. How can the "power" of a computer be measured?

16. Is a microcomputer nearly as powerful as a large computer? Why or why not?

17. Why does a key-to-tape system input transactions to a computer faster than a punched-card system?

18. Would a grocery store be likely to use a tag-reader POS system? Why or why not?

19. Explain the relative advantages and disadvantages of magentic-tape and disk data storage technologies.

CASE

An Integrated POS System for ZIM

Some nationwide retail chains integrate their POS systems nationally. While these systems have marked similarities, they also differ significantly. This case presents a composite POS system for

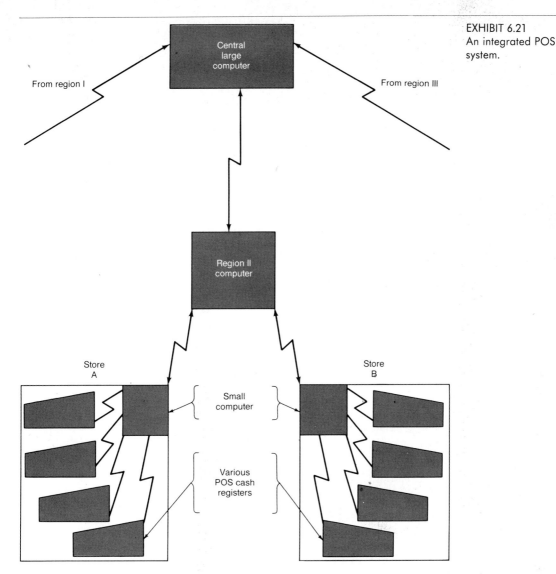

EXHIBIT 6.21
An integrated POS
system.

Zilog International Merchandising Co. (ZIM), a fictional chain of department stores with operations throughout the United States and Canada. ZIM's system is illustrated in Exhibit 6.21, which shows four levels in the system's hierarchy. The first (see the bottom of the exhibit) is the department level in the individual stores, where electronic cash registers (ECR) serve as the basic data entry unit in the system. Sales personnel enter transactions at these ECRs, which have certain error-checking features of smart terminals, although they do not have independent processing capabilities.

The second level is that of the entire store, where a microcomputer receives transactions from the ECR as they occur and updates the store's data files. The third level is regional, where a larger computer integrates data from all stores in the region. The fourth is the headquarters level, which includes all United States and Canadian ZIM stores; at this level a still larger computer system integrates data provided by all regions.

ZIM has its own credit card, the ZIMCARD. When a credit sale occurs, the customer presents the merchandise to the salesperson, along with a

ZIMCARD. The salesperson inserts the card into the ECR, which reads the customer ZIMCARD number and asks the store's microcomputer to verify the customer's creditworthiness. This computer contains credit and other account data for the individual customers who applied for their ZIMCARDs at this particular store. The computer checks whether the customer has remaining credit and also whether this might be a stolen ZIMCARD or one reported lost; lists of lost and stolen cards for the entire system are prepared weekly. The computer has an up-to-the minute record of all credit sales, since these are recorded as they occur, but cash receipts are processed at a regional center in batches based on each store, and recording of these receipts usually lags several days behind the actual receipt of the cash. Customer bills are also mailed from the regional computer system.

In any case, the customer's credit status is reported back to the ECR at the sales department, and the sale proceeds if credit is approved. The salesperson then records the sale in the ECR by using a light pen to read the data on the item's sales sticker; this automatically records the item's manufacturer, identification number, and price. Alternatively, the salesperson may key in this data if the sticker has been mutilated and cannot be read. In the case of sale items, the price is provided by the store's computer, and therefore sale prices need not be marked on each individual item. The salesperson's identification number is also keyed in. As can be seen, in large part this is an on-line, real-time system.

If the credit sale is for a customer whose ZIMCARD was issued by another store in the region (ZIM has 12 sales regions), the embossed coding on the card indicates this, and the store's computer automatically telephones the regional computer, which performs a credit check of the accounts in the issuing store's computer and reports the credit status back to the salesperson; this causes about a 3-minute delay on average. However, if the card is from outside the region, computer-to-computer credit checking can be done only from midnight to 6 a.m. each day or on weekends, so that the customer must wait until the next day to complete the purchase. If the purchase is greater than $50, however, one of the managers will telephone the regional computer center of the issuing store, ask for a credit check, and wait about 2 minutes to receive the credit check. Customers who have moved out of their region are asked to apply for a new ZIMCARD at a store in their new region within 30 days. Fewer than 5 percent of each ZIM store's credit sales are to customers of a different store in that region, and fewer than ½ percent are to customers from a different region.

From this point, all processing of the sales transaction is automated. The item sold is deleted from the inventory records contained in the inventory file of the store's computer system, and the ECR calculates the amount of the sale and the sales tax and prepares a sales slip. The credit sale is recorded and is automatically processed against the customer's account in the customer's account file; however, if the customer then cancels the sale, the sale cannot be immediately deleted from the customer's account but deletion must be approved later by a manager, and the customer account then updated in batch mode.

Each sale is also recorded in the sales file to update the master sales account for that sales department. From the salesperson's identification number the sale is recorded in the salesperson's record for calculation of sales commissions and for sales analysis purposes.

The store's computer is able to provide information useful for managerial purposes. The system monitors the day's sales and other types of activities (such as items returned) to give managers the most recent information for making such decisions as determining storewide and departmental staffing levels and what items should be placed on discount. At the end of each day the computer system prepares daily peformance indicators and makes them available in report form early the next morning for the store's managers. These performance indicators provide statistics about the preceding day's sales both storewide and by department and are broken down into cash sales and credit sales. Inventory status information is included by citing the inventory levels of critical items in each department. Performance indicators take into account additional inventory received by the store during the day or overnight to give an up-to-the-minute picture of the store's inventory position.

Weekly and monthly reports are prepared on the basis of the store's computer files. These reports include sales reports by store, by department, and by product class, as well as employee time reports and salary reports. The computer also prepares monthly financial statements and operates independently from the POS part of the integrated system to prepare payroll at the store level. On-call and exception reports can also be provided.

The computers of all the stores within each region transmit data via communications lines to a regional computer located at a regional warehouse, as shown in the exhibit. For ZIM, inventory control is a key task for two reasons. First, stores cannot let inventories become depleted because customers will be lost to competing retail outlets. The second reason is the high cost of having too much inventory throughout the ZIM network. Inventory stocks are maintained at the individual store level, the regional level, and the national level. Without careful inventory control, any or all of these reservoirs could overflow, and the resulting high carrying costs could become the single most influential factor affecting ZIM's profitability.

The inventory system associated with ZIM's POS system keeps inventory records up to date in the stores throughout the system, permitting drastic reductions in the quantities of merchandise that the stores must reorder and also reducing the amount of time in advance when this merchandise must be ordered and received. The ZIM POS merchandise reorder system "polls" the inventory files at the store level at night, when data communications charges are lowest, by having each regional computer automatically dial each of the store computers in its region for inventory information. Each store has EOQ formulas as part of its inventory system, and so it transmits orders for additional inventory to the regional computer; for some items, the store's computer transmits inventory levels, and the regional computer system's EOQ formulas make the merchandise ordering decisions.

After all stores in a region have been polled and replenishment decisions have been made, the regional computer searches its own files to determine which ordered merchandise items the regional warehouse can ship and which will be back-ordered or sought from another source. The computer then prepares merchandise order printouts for each store. In the morning, inventory personnel will fill these orders for possible shipment that day. If too little merchandise is ordered for a particular store for a given day to make shipping economical, a regional manager may defer the shipment for 1 or 2 days until more orders accumulate.

Similarly, the computer at the central warehouse polls the regional computers for those items which are purchased by the central purchasing group and are distributed to regional warehouses from a central location. This polling is also for items purchased by this central group but shipped directly to each regional warehouse from the manufacturers. However, some regional specialty items are purchased within the region by regional managers, and the inventory status of these items is not polled by the central computer.

CASE QUESTIONS

1. In what ways is the ZIM POS system similar to, and in what ways is it different from, the system of a national retail chain with which you have had experience?

2. How would lists of lost or stolen ZIMCARDs be distributed? What would probably happen if a customer attempted to use a stolen card for purchases?

3. What are the consequences of the several-day delay in recording cash receipts? How could cash receipts recording be accelerated, and what would be the costs and benefits of this acceleration?

4. Why is the billing and cash receipts activity handled at the regional rather than the store level? How would the billing and cash receipts system operate for customers from outside the region?

5. What are the advantages of having the computer system provide the prices of items that are on sale rather than placing "sale" price stickers on them?

6. What purposes does the entry of the salespersons's identification number serve besides that of calculation of commissions?

7. Should the system be changed so that if a customer cancels a sale, the salesperson can void the sale on-line? Why or why not? Do these reasons also apply to a later return for credit of items purchased?

8. If you were a ZIM store manager, what daily performance indicators would you like to have? Which of these could the system, as described, probably provide?

9. Explain the advantages of ZIM's inventory control system.

Case prepared by George M. Scott.

Chapter 7

COMPUTER SOFTWARE

PAYOFF THOUGHT

The general strategy for acquiring computer software should be first to decide whether processing efficiency is important for the program in question. If it is, search for commercially vended programs and compare these with the alternative of using a procedural language for program development. If it is not, consider using a productivity language to develop the program.

CHAPTER OBJECTIVES

1. To explain the nature of computer software and its relationship to hardware

2. To explore the different types of programming languages and suggest situations in which each is most appropriately used

WHAT IS SOFTWARE?

At most mature data processing centers the cost of software exceeds the cost of hardware. This simple fact is one reason why software is so important a part of computer systems.

Software consists of the computer programs that direct the processing activities of the computer. Computer programs, in turn, consist of instructions to the computer, or "program statements," that are precisely stated and organized in conformance to the syntax and other rules of program construction of a particular computer language. Several programs which are focused on a particular task or which manipulate a particular set of data are called an "application."

Programs are said to be "written" by programmers, who are professional persons who "do programming." Programs are "read" (placed) into the computer and "run" (processed) by the computer as one type of data. Programs can be and frequently are revised or extended, an activity termed "program maintenance."

The difference between software and hardware is ambiguous in one area. The computer's operating system is a software system, and yet operating system program instructions can be placed in the computer as circuitry rather than programmed as software; the operating systems of microcomputers are often partly circuitry. These "firmware" components are in a gray area since they are neither hardware nor software in all respects; they perform the function of software (they are programs that direct the computer), but they exist as hardware. Because firmware is in chip form, it cannot be easily changed, as software can.

Computer hardware is tangible, can be seen and touched, and is more easily explained and described than computer software. In many ways, however, understanding computer software is more important for users and managers than understanding computer hardware. One reason is that not only is software expensive to purchase, but also in most computer centers software maintenance constitutes about 50 to 70 percent of all personnel activity. Another reason is that software is often the weak link in systems development; acquiring computer equipment that is capable of accomplishing a given set of processing tasks is usually less difficult than developing the computer software that will actually accomplish the tasks. Accordingly, managers involved in systems development must often devote a substantial portion of their attention to studying and analyzing software needs.

A final reason for the importance of software is that it is the interface between the user and the computer system. Often the manager must understand some aspects of the software in order to utilize and further develop the information system.

TYPES OF SOFTWARE

There are two generic types of software: systems programs and applications programs. Systems programs fit into three classifications: (1) operating systems, (2) utility programs, and (3) special-purpose programs. Operating systems were discussed briefly in the preceding chapter; that discussion is extended here.

Operating Systems

A computer can have one or multiple operating systems. An operating system for a computer can be unique to that computer model or family (a "proprietary" operating system), or it can be an operating system that is employed on different computer models produced by different computer companies. Apple DOS is a proprietary system, for example, because it is used only on Apple computers. CP/M, MS DOS, and UNIX are examples of operating systems that are widely employed on a variety of computers produced by different manufacturers; the first two are used only on microcomputers, whereas UNIX is used on both minicomputers and microcomputers. Programs written for Apple computers with Apple DOS can run only on Apple computers, but programs written, for example, for a computer with a standard CP/M operating system can usually be run with no changes or only minor changes on other brands of computers that use CP/M. However, the operating system itself must be tailored to the unique circuitry of a particular computer system; thus a CP/M operating system designed for one computer cannot be run on another computer, even though user programs written for a CP/M operating system may be run on both of those computers if each has a CP/M operating system.

An operating system is software rather than circuitry, so it can be more easily modified; these modifications may be made by the using organization or by the vendor. Operating systems, as well as other vendor-provided software, often have "versions"; for example, version 1.0 may be the first version of an operating system released, and when significant changes are made by the vendor, these might be released as version 2.0. Usually, new versions implement improvements or provide new capabilities to an operating system, and the new version may be made available to purchasers of the old version at a very low price.

While not directly a part of an operating system, job control language (JCL) is closely associated with mainframe operating systems. JCL is a language that enables the programmer to communicate information to the operating system about how to process a particular program and job submitted by the programmer or user. Mainframe users must, for example, tell the computer system the specific language in which the program is written, what file the data is in, what the user wants the program to accomplish, and the type of output wanted. This is done by writing instructions to the operating system in JCL which tell how the job should be processed and which permit the correct computer system resources to be assigned to the job.

For many programs the JCL instructions are simple and straightforward, but for complex data processing tasks the communications between the user or programmer and the computer system are complicated, and JCL languages must be sophisticated and complex to provide this communication. Experienced professional programmers usually have taken a JCL course that is as demanding as a college course.

Utility Programs

Utility programs include sort-and-merge programs, which sort data into alphabetic, numeric, or other sequence or which merge data sets or computer data files. Transfer utility programs are used to transfer data or programs from one type of medium to another, for example, from magnetic tape to disk, from cards to tape, from seven-track tape to nine-track tape, or from floppy disk to hard disk.

A third variety of utility is a diagnostics utility, which provides messages to users explaining syntax and logic errors as an aid in debugging programs; while operating systems typically include some diagnostic aid routines, specialized diagnostics utility programs are often much more specific in describing the nature of the problem to the user. For example, an operating system might report "Line 301; illegal instruction," whereas a diagnostics routine might report "Line 301; no PRENT command exists in COBOL." A related type of utility is a memory dump. Memory dumps are often used where the program developer has been unable to isolate and correct a particular program error. The dump utility will print out the entire contents of the data file (which may be a "working" or temporary file rather than a permanent file) so that the user can attempt to ascertain the error through detailed analysis of the file contents. Memory dumps may also be used when a complete copy of a file's contents is needed, perhaps as a backup in case the file is inadvertently destroyed or lost.

Code conversion utilities convert data from one code to another, perhaps from BCD to EBCDIC or from Hollerith to EBCDIC. Text editors are utilities that permit a terminal operator to modify data in an internal program. Text editors are widely employed by professional programmers who write programs on-line via a terminal. Report generation programs facilitate the rapid development of reports without extensive programming.

Job accounting programs keep track of the systems resources used by each job (such as the amount of CPU time used) and provide this information to the user as well as to the computer center management for billing, analysis, and computer control purposes. These are only a few of the types of systems utility programs.

Special-Purpose Programs

The third category of systems programs includes those intended to extend the capabilities of operating systems and to provide specialized services to applications programs. These programs are exemplified by file management programs, which relieve the operating system of certain tasks of data file management and usually add capabilities that the operating system does not have. File management programs vary greatly; the most sophisticated are known as "data base management systems," which are designed to manage entire sets of computer files that have a specialized file design.

Another type of systems software often used in conjunction with a data base management system is the data dictionary. A data dictionary defines the characteristics of all the data contained in the data file system.

APPLICATIONS PROGRAMS AND THEIR OPERATION

Applications programs are programs written to accomplish a user's specific task. Payroll programs, accounts receivable programs, market analysis programs, portifolio management programs, and personnel programs are all examples of applications programs. Applications programs establish the precise nature of the processing that must be done, the data files that must be processed to accomplish the job, how the results of the processing are to be reported, and numerous other details relating to a specific job, or "application."

The general procedure for developing and operating applications programs is as follows:

1. The programs are written (programmed) by systems or user department personnel or are purchased from an outside organization.

2. The programs are tested on the computer to find errors, and the errors are corrected. This is known as "program debugging."

3. The programs are input to the computer for the purpose of processing data.

4. The data that the programs will process may be input to the computer system either along with the programs or later, or the data may already be in internal files, from which it is extracted for processing.

5. When both the data and the program are available, the program is processed by the CPU, which reads and interprets its instructions; the data is placed in the ALU and manipulated arithmetically or logically as commanded by the program instructions, all as described in the preceding chapter.

During steps 2 to 5, computer operators (the persons who manage the computer) play an important role; their exact role varies from one system to another. They might, for example (1) receive the programs from the programmers or from a program library, (2) place the programs in the computer, (3) place the data file on-line if it is not already, (4) monitor the computer system during processing to ensure that the programs process correctly and stop the processing or take other steps if they do not, and (5) activate the printer and monitor its operation while the results of processing are printed. Operators also perform many other tasks that pertain to the operation of the computer rather than to the processing of a particular program. With a microcomputer system, the programmer and the operator are likely to be the same person.

The debugging of programs is critical to their successful operation. All communications with the computer system must be absolutely accurate. Therefore, computer programs must be written with great precision, and pains must be taken during debugging to ensure that all errors are eliminated. Two types of errors are language syntax errors and logic errors. Language syntax errors occur when the procedures of the programming language are not adhered to strictly during the writing of the program, causing the program instructions to be incorrect. For example, misspelling program instructions (e.g., spelling a PRINT instruction as PRENT), failing to leave a space after a period in an instruction when a space is required, or simply omitting a comma or a special character in the program will create syntax errors. In most cases, syntax errors result in a program that the computer cannot process. Often the computer system will provide diagnostics that inform the programmer about the nature and location of the syntax error.

Logic errors involve an incorrect combination or sequence of correct instructions or an instruction to the computer to process data in an illogical way. For example, instructing the computer to multiply the sales price per item by the sales tax rate and then multiply the result by the number of that item sold would be a logic error; the sales price per unit should be multiplied by the number of units sold, and the result then multiplied by the sales tax rate. Often programs with logic errors can be processed by the computer but will give the wrong results; this would usually be the case with the example given.

PROGRAMMING LANGUAGES

Computer programs are "written" using a language known as a "computer programming language." The purpose of a programming language is to enable programmers to develop structured solutions to data processing problems and to communicate the exact nature of these solutions to the computer system. Most of the 200 or so computer languages now in use were developed to have certain characteristics that make them especially suitable for a particular type of data processing problem. FORTRAN, for example, was designed for scientific data processing.

Types of Programming Languages	EXHIBIT 7.1

1. Machine languages	5. File and data base query languages
2. Assembly languages	6. Productivity languages
3. Procedural languages	7. Specialty languages
4. Interactive languages	

Exhibit 7.1 lists several general categories of programming languages; each of the several categories contains numerous specific languages.

Machine Languages

Machine languages, termed the "lowest" languages because they are the most closely related to the actual circuitry of the computer, are binary codes that communicate directly with the circuitry; they are programmed in combinations of 0s and 1s. A machine language instruction is illustrated in Exhibit 7.2. Machine languages are the only languages that the circuitry can directly interpret without translation. Since the circuitry of each model of computer differs from that of all others, each computer must have its unique machine language. No machine language program written for one computer can be processed by another unless the computers are identical in their circuitry. Even the machine languages of two different models of computers in the same computer family are not compatible.

In the early days of computing, all programs were written in machine language. Now, however, because of advances in languages, almost no programs are written in machine language. As suggested by Exhibit 7.2, writing lengthy programs in machine language would be extremely difficult. A programmer would have to know the meaning of specific combinations of 0s and 1s for each instruction coded. Locating errors in a string of thousands of 0s and 1s would be difficult. Nonetheless, programs in machine language process much more efficiently (consume less ALU time) than programs written in other languages that must first be translated to machine language; the translation process itself consumes ALU time.

Assembly Languages

Assembly languages are sometimes referred to as "symbolic languages" because they were the first languages to use symbols rather than 0s and 1s. The symbols consist of letters and characters, which can be combined for each instruction and are easier to remember than 0s and 1s. Assembly languages are at a level above machine languages in that since they use letters and characters, some of which are combined into understandable words and abbreviations, and are more English-like than machine languages. An assembly language must be translated (assembled) into ma-

```
11001000100011111010101010101011101010111010001111101001010100010101
01010010101011100101010101010100000010111101111000110111011111011100
01010101110010010010001011111010011100101010100010101010111111101010
01000101010100101111100010101011000011100101001110010011100100010011
01010111001010101010100100101010101111101011010001011101101001111101 01
```

EXHIBIT 7.2
A machine language
instruction.

chine language; thus it uses the ALU less efficiently than machine language.

Each computer uses a unique assembly language, and programs written in one assembly language cannot be run on a different computer. Assembly languages are therefore "machine-dependent," or "machine-specific." However, they are usually similar for different computer systems in the same family of computers; thus an assembly program for one member of the family sometimes can be modified to run on another computer in the same family. The result of translating an assembly language program is "object code," which is equivalent to machine language. The object code can be retained for reuse to eliminate the need to reassemble the program each time it is used. Whenever the program is changed, it must be reassembled.

Usually one assembly language statement directly represents one machine instruction, but in symbols rather than in 0s and 1s. This "one-to-one" relationship of assembly instructions to machine instructions is altered with "macro instructions," however, whereby one assembly command represents many machine language instructions that are stored in a "macro library" within the computer system and are automatically inserted in the program whenever the macro command is encountered. For example, GET 5 as a macro command might result in several machine instructions, being retrieved from the macro library and inserted in the program to carry out a printing activity.

A decade ago most systems programs, including operating systems, were written in assembly language because of the processing efficiency of this type of language. Assembly language was preferred for systems programs because systems programs were frequently used and had to process efficiently to conserve expensive ALU time.

However, as the cost of computer power has decreased and as that of talented programmers has increased, processing efficiently has become relatively less important than programming efficiently, and now a high proportion of systems programs are written in languages that are easier to use such as PL/1 or PASCAL. This shift in the relative costs of computer power and programming continues to affect the organization of computer systems in a variety of ways.

Procedural Languages

Procedural languages are one type of high-level language. Procedural languages are so called because the programmer has to describe in great detail the procedures that the computer system must follow to process the data. Procedural languages are used to develop programming applications that solve particular problems for user groups. These languages are "high-level" because they are written more as a person thinks (in mathematical equations and English) rather than as a computer processes (in binary form of 0s and 1s).

A characteristic of procedural languages is that they must be translated to machine language using a compiler for that language. Compilation is similar to assembly activity for assembly language programs in that they both produce machine language in the form of object code after translation. With compilation (and assembly), the entire program must be written and debugged, and then all instructions of the program are translated at one time.

High-level languages are machine-independent in that a high-level language program can be processed by any computer system with a compiler (translation program) for that language if the compiler conforms to the same standards for that language. For example, a program written in FORTRAN can be processed by any computer that has a FORTRAN compiler. It must be kept in mind, however, that most compilers (which are machine-specific) have slight variations even if they embrace the same standards; thus a program usually must be modified in minor ways before it can be run using a different compiler for that same language.

Some high-level language compilers are "subset" compilers; that is, they can translate only some of the instructions that can be written in that language. Microcomputer systems usually use subset compilers because the full-size compiler is a large set of programs that would consume too much of the microcomputer's limited main memory; there might be none remaining for the data and programs that are to be processed. With subset compilers, programs written for one computer system may require substantial revision or complete rewriting before they can be compiled on another computer system. Some subset compilers, however, have been standardized so that a program for one computer may process with no (or minor) changes on another computer system that uses the same standards for its subset compiler.

High-level programs are easier to write than assembly language programs, and most programmers learn programming by using procedural languages. Examples of these languages are FORTRAN, COBOL, ALGOL, PASCAL, ADA, and PL/1. Each of these languages has its own special characteristics. FORTRAN, for example, is particularly adept at scientific programming, which utilizes mathematical symbols and equations extensively. COBOL was designed to have excellent file management and input-output capabilities. An acronym for "common business oriented language," COBOL is intended as a language for business programming, which involves extensive input and output and large data file processing activities.

COBOL is the dominant language for business data processing, but most procedural languages can be satisfactorily used for most data processing jobs, although their processing efficiency and ease of programming may differ. In smaller organizations the language used for a particular application may depend on what language the programmer is proficient in.

The general types of programs for which high-level languages are used include programs designed for file maintenance (that is, updating records in a file such as by processing transactions), report generation (which consists of establishing the format of a report), printing out or displaying a report, data retrieval, statistical manipulation, and simulation. Numerous other types of tasks can also be accomplished by high-level language programs.

Interactive Languages

Interactive languages are another type of high-level language used to develop applications programs. The languages are called "interactive" because they allow an on-line, real-time dialogue between the user and the computer. Typically, programming errors are reported to the programmer immediately by the computer, and when the user asks a question, the computer responds, or when the computer asks a question, the user responds. These languages are designed to be used through a terminal rather than on a batch basis.

A characteristic of interactive languages is that they use an interpreter rather than a compiler for translation to object code. An interpreter is a set of programs that translates (interprets) each instruction as it is entered at a terminal; if the instruction is incorrect, the translation will not occur, and the interpreter notifies the programmer of the error and its nature. With the real-time feedback, the programmer can make program corrections at each step of the program, whereas with a compiler language, the errors are not known until the program is completed and compilation is attempted. The instant feedback provided by an interpretive language significantly increases the speed of program development, but interpreters consume more ALU time for translation than compilers do.

BASIC is an interactive language that is similar to FORTRAN but cannot perform some of the arithmetic functions as efficiently as FORTRAN can. APL is another language developed for interactive computing. Additionally, many of the procedural languages have been modified so that a newer version uses an interpreter rather than a compiler; in these cases, two versions coexist, and both may be in widespread usage. COBOL and FORTRAN, among others, exist in both a procedural version that requires a compiler and an interactive version that uses an interpreter.

File and Data Base Query Languages

File and data base query languages are intended to permit programs to be quickly written to access information and retrieve it from computer file systems. Usually, these languages will also place the retrieved data in a report format specified by the user. Most query and retrieval languages are able to access a variety of different types of computer file structures. Many have a "user exit," which enables the user to incorporate procedural language programs within the query programs in order to accomplish more complex retrieval tasks; usually the procedural language used is COBOL.

EASYTRIEVE is a popular query and retrieval language. Computer auditing packages also possess this query and retrieval capability, but they go far beyond this by also including various sampling and statistical routines oriented to auditing tasks.

The capabilities of the languages in this class often overlap those of productivity languages, discussed next. FOCUS, for example, is a query and retrieval language that is also considered to be a productivity language and, in addition, is a part of a data base system.

Productivity Languages

Productivity, or "nonprocedural," languages are interactive languages refined for faster, easier program development; some are quite easily learned. They are nonprocedural in that they require the user to specify only the data needed instead of also specifying the processing procedures. The rapid evolution which productivity languages are now undergoing is one of the most important trends in computing. These languages address the problems of the shortage of qualified programmers and the backlog of computer applications.

Productivity languages are being used more and more by nonprofessional data processing personnel housed within user departments. With applications backlogs in the range of 3 years, user groups are looking for alternative ways to accomplish their data analysis tasks. Because many productivity languages are easily used, user departments are designating their own personnel to develop applications programs. Often these programs are developed for use on a microcomputer within the user department.

Professional data processing personnel have not overlooked the increased productivity provided by productivity languages. Increasingly, programmers who are proficient in much more powerful and difficult languages are nevertheless turning to productivity languages to decrease program development time. Sometimes, however, professional programmers disdain productivity languages as beneath them because the languages are simple and are unable to produce "elegant" problem solutions.

One reason these languages increase productivity is that one command translates into a greater number of machine language commands; hence, fewer instructions are required per program, and the programs are shorter and more quickly developed. This is illustrated in a simple way in Exhibit 7.3, which compares four types of language. Another reason is

| Language Types Compared with Driving an Automobile, Based on a Drive to the Local Grocery Store | EXHIBIT 7.3 |

Language	Analogy with Driving
Productivity	You are providing instructions about how to go to the store. With a "productivity language" for automobiles you say, "Go to the store," and the car drives to the store.
Procedural	"Drive two blocks straight ahead, turn left, and enter the first driveway on the right."
Assembly (with macro instructions)	"Shift to first gear, accelerate to 15 mph, shift to second gear, accelerate to 25 mph, shift to third gear, accelerate to 30 mph, decelerate in advance of second corner. . . ."
Machine	"Lift hand 10 in., move right 16 in., open fist, drop hand onto gearshift lever, grip lever, depress clutch (assuming a foot is already on it). . . ."

Note: The computer must be provided totally detailed instructions for accomplishing each task, and this is done only by machine language. Assembly, procedural, and productivity languages must be translated into machine language.

that users of a productivity language do not need to write extensive instructions to communicate with the computer system; the language itself handles much of this "procedural" communication. Additionally, productivity languages often "prompt" users; for example, the language system may present a "menu" that lets the user select the next activity, which it then accomplishes without programmed instructions from the user.

Many productivity languages are part of software packages that accomplish other tasks; for example, several of the most common productivity programs are enhanced inquiry or "query" systems associated with formal data base management systems. Other productivity languages are associated with statistical programming languages such as SAS.

Using a productivity language at least doubles program development speed and in some cases may increase it by 5 to 10 times. Productivity languages run very inefficiently on a computer system, however, because their translation consumes more of the ALU's time and other computer resources than other languages require. Because the CPU and other computer hardware components are decreasing dramatically in price, the efficiency with which programs run is not as important as it once was. Additionally, the shortage of professional programmers and the related increasing labor cost of programming encourage data processing managers to utilize their professional programmers as productively as possible. The trend toward use of productivity languages is expected to continue and even accelerate.

Current predictions are that within 5 years productivity language programs will utilize approximately 50 percent of all CPU processing time in organizations, up from about 10 percent at present. In terms of the number of programs processed, probably the overwhelming majority—70 to 80 percent—will be productivity language programs, perhaps half of which will be developed by user groups. The explanation of how productivity languages will consume only 50 percent of CPU time but numerically will be used for 70 to 80 percent of the programs processed lies in two offsetting phenomena. The dominant one is that most productivity language programs will be the smaller programs and those which are processed less frequently; the large programs and those which are frequently processed will continue to be written with more complex languages that can represent more complex problem situations and process more efficiently—these will be the 10 percent of the programs that now utilize 90 percent of CPU time. Partially offsetting this is the fact that the more numerous smaller productivity language programs will run less efficiently, using a disproportionate amount of CPU time.

A perspective on this is illustrated in Exhibit 7.4, in which the percentages are the author's estimates for 1984 and 1989. In a field as dynamic as computer information systems, new trends and events not now contemplated seem likely to alter, perhaps dramatically, the actual 1989 outcomes. (One possibility is that as microcomputers grow ever larger, the clear-cut distinction that now exists between them and mainframe computers will disappear.) Nevertheless, the exhibit provides several interesting insights:

1. User groups are expected to be writing more than half the total number of programs by 1989 (A, B, E, and F).

2. A dramatic trend will be the increase in the number of user-written microcomputer programs—from about 5 percent now to around 35 percent in 1989 (A). Data processing departments will set up groups (now known as "information centers") that will specialize in assisting user groups in these activities.

3. Another dramatic trend is that data processing professionals will be developing far fewer "traditional" programs for use on mainframe computers—only the large, frequently run programs that must have maximum processing efficiency will continue to be developed in this way.

4. There will be a significant increase in the number of productivity language programs developed by user groups for mainframe computers (B). Many of these will be the larger user-developed programs and those developed for routine transactions processing rather than for managerial analysis.

5. Data processing professionals will significantly increase their use of productivity languages (C and D).

6. The use of microcomputers by data processing professionals will increase (C and G), but will not be a major factor.

7. The number of programs developed for processing by microcom-

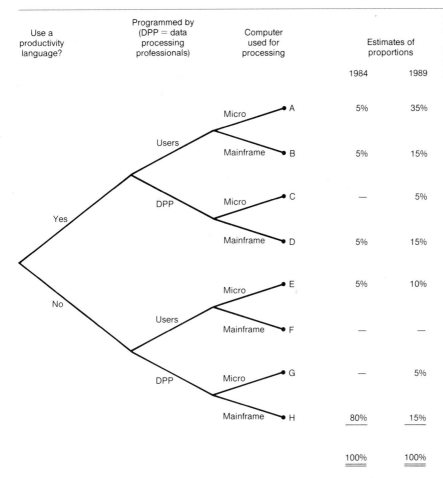

Use a productivity language?	Programmed by (DPP = data processing professionals)	Computer used for processing	Estimates of proportions	
			1984	1989
		A	5%	35%
		B	5%	15%
		C	—	5%
		D	5%	15%
		E	5%	10%
		F	—	—
		G	—	5%
		H	80%	15%
			100%	100%

EXHIBIT 7.4
The percentage of new programs developed in medium-sized and large organizations.

puters will increase to more than half, including those developed by users and professionals using both productivity and nonproductivity languages (A, C, E, and G).

The preceding points carry great implications for present-day students. A large proportion of the students reading this text will be writing computer programs using a productivity language. Graduates with majors in accounting, marketing, finance, and management can all expect to do this either full-time or as only one of their responsibilities. Of course, graduates with a major in business information systems are the most likely to become deeply involved in these systems development activities. In some cases the programs will be written on large-scale mainframe computers, but more often they will be written on microcomputers controlled and run by the user groups.

Before this section ends, a further trend should be mentioned which is in many respects an extension of the productivity language concept but which is not so much a new language type as it is a new approach to the development of programs. So-called "application generators" are specialized programs that aid programmers in developing applications programs. Programmers feed the specifications for the needed programs into an application generator package, which automatically writes the code for the program. While the programs written by application generators often process less efficiently than other programs, this efficiency is no longer a major concern; additionally, the next generation of application generators can be expected to have improved processing efficiency.

Specialty Languages

Many languages cannot be readily classified among the types discussed above. For the most part these are high-level languages that have a special purpose and also possess the user friendliness of productivity languages. Many also enhance the ability of users to instruct the computer in one way or another. A number of these can be characterized as decision support system (DSS) languages, many of which are oriented to financial mangement. IFPS (Interactive Financial Planning Systems) and SIMPLAN are examples of mainframe decision support systems for financial management; microcomputer DSS programs (including IFPS for micros) also exist. Numerous DSS languages exist for the marketing, accounting, and other administrative functions. Most DSS languages have the following in common: (1) They are easily learned and used by managers, (2) they are oriented to financial analysis, and (3) they are equipped with program modules that provide financial analysis functions ranging from automatic footing and cross-footing to sophisticated time-value discounting features, any of which can be invoked with one or a few commands.

A report generator language is designed to facilitate formatting and outputting reports. While other higher-level languages, such as FORTRAN, can accomplish this, it is often easier with a report generator language that is based on specifying parameters rather than writing detailed program statements.

Statistical and simulation languages are two classes of languages often used for research purposes. Statistical language packages have integrated statistical algorithms that process data to prepare regression analyses, standard deviations, and so on. Examples are MINITAB, SAS, and SPSS for mainframe computers and STAT-PRO and MICRO-STAT for microcomputers.

Simulation languages permit programmers to develop program statements that simulate an event or a condition. While other languages, such as FORTRAN, can be used, simulation languages may be more efficient because they are specialized to this class of applications. GPSS-II (General-Purpose Systems Simulator-II) and SIMSCRIPT are two well-known simulation languages for large-scale computers.

Of the several other specialized languages in existence, only one will be mentioned: the audit software package. Audit software packages, sometimes called "generalized audit software packages," are intended to test the controls used with transactions processing in computer systems. Audit software packages use statistical techniques to select and analyze data samples from the computer files, perform a number of statistical tests, and test for data attributes such as credit balances in accounts receivable. Each audit software package has a language associated with it that enables an auditor to design and program audit tests, and each language has its own unique syntax and logic characteristics. Several audit software packages exist, inlcuding one for each major CPA firm.

COMPARISON OF THE GENERAL TYPES OF LANGUAGES

Exhibit 7.5 compares the attributes of the types of languages discussed; specialty languages are excluded because they do not follow the pattern of other languages. As the exhibit indicates, the higher the level of the language, the more user-friendly it is likely to be in terms of helping the user develop a program, the fewer the instructions that are probably needed to develop a program, the less the programmer must know about the specific nature of the particular computer (the machine is more "transparent" to the programmer), and the easier the language is to learn and to use. The lower the level of the language, the greater the processing efficiency of the program.

These characteristics are used to evaluate the tradeoffs in the choice of which language to use for writing a particular program. These tradeoffs are summarized in Exhibit 7.6. In general, lower-level languages are more expensive to program but run more efficiently. High-level language programs require less labor to write and therefore are less expensive to pro-

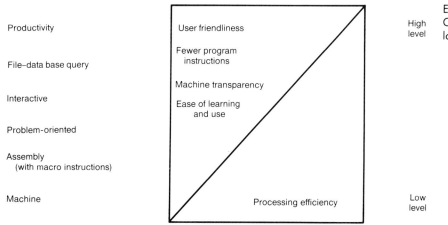

EXHIBIT 7.5
Characteristics of language types.

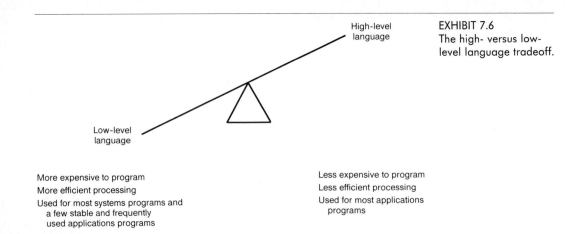

EXHIBIT 7.6
The high- versus low-
level language tradeoff.

High-level
language

Low-level
language

More expensive to program
More efficient processing
Used for most systems programs and
  a few stable and frequently
  used applications programs

Less expensive to program
Less efficient processing
Used for most applications
  programs

gram; they are used for most applications programs. As programming becomes more expensive because of increasing labor costs and as hardware becomes less expensive, the balance point in Exhibit 7.6 will shift toward using higher- and higher-level programming languages; even now, many programs which previously would have been written in an assembly language are instead being written in a procedural language, and programs that previously would have been written in a procedural language are being written in a productivity language.

LANGUAGE TRANSLATION

The translation of computer programs written in one language into machine language is done by translation programs. Assembly languages and all high-level languages must be translated into machine language (object code), as previously noted. Three types of translation programs, also noted previously, are assembler programs, which translate programs written in assembly language; compiler programs, which translate high-level procedural language programs; and interpreter programs, which translate interactive language programs.

Exhibit 7.7 illustrates program translation and is applicable to all languages that must be translated. (There are minor variations among assemblers, compilers, and interpreters that the exhibit does not show.) This "high-level-to-low-level" translation involves first inputting a program to the computer system, along with any JCL commands needed. The operating system then activates the appropriate assembler, compiler, or interpreter to process the input program. If there are errors in the input program, the program will not assemble, compile, or interpret, and diagnostics are provided to the user as shown.

If the program is written in assembly language, each instruction translates into one machine language instruction, unless it is a macroassembler that translates one instruction into multiple instructions. In contrast, each

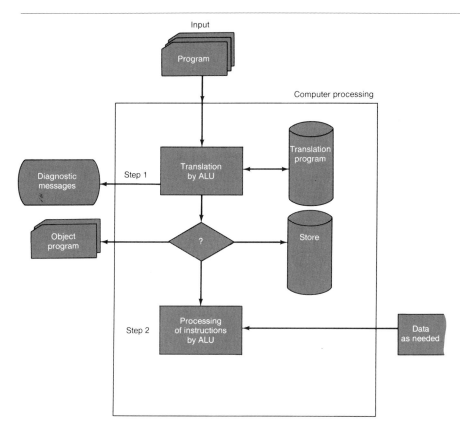

EXHIBIT 7.7
A high-level-to-low-
translation.

higher-level language instruction translates into multiple object code instructions. This "one-to-many" translation accounts in good part for the lesser translating efficiency of compilers and interpreters.

CHOOSING A PROGRAMMING LANGUAGE

Exhibit 7.8 shows the comparative attributes of seven high-level languages. The student must be cautioned that when the topic is computer languages, discussions are long and intense, tempers flare, and seldom is one expert convinced by the arguments of another. All programmers have a favorite language (or languages), to which they are emotionally attached; thus few people can argue objectively about the relative merits of languages. Given these conditions, any comparison of programming languages based on any criteria whatsoever is likely to be disputed by a large number of experts on programming languages. Nevertheless, Exhibit 7.8 and the following discussion attempt to compare computer languages in order to provide an elementary understanding of the attributes of several of the most important ones.

Exhibit 7.8 compares languages in terms of several characteristics. The

Programming languages: comparative characteristics

EXHIBIT 7.8
Characteristics of
programming
languages.

	COBOL	FORTRAN	BASIC	PL/1	FOCUS	RPG-II	ADA
Friendliness English—like	Yes	No	Yes	Mixed	Yes	Yes	Mixed
Ease of Learning	Hard	Medium	Easy	Hard	Easy	Easy	Medium
Program length	Long	Short	Medium Long	Medium	Short	N.A.	Medium
Power (in terms of capabilities)	High	Medium	Medium	High	Low	Low	High
Program structure	Fair	Poor	Poor	Good	Poor	Poor	Good
Processing efficiency	Medium	High	Low	High	Low	Low	High
Portability (ANSI)	High	High	Medium High	Low	Low	Medium	Medium
Orientation	Business	Science	G.P. and interactive processing	G.P.	Analysis	Small business	G.P.
Special characteristics	Business orientation		Easily learned, all-purpose language for beginners		A productivity language		A good first language
		Scientific orientation		Broad range of capabilities		Specifications rather than code instructions	

(G.P. = general purpose)

first, user friendliness, is an overall assessment of how easily the language is used and learned; if a program is English-like, for example, it is easier to trace through and understand its logic. Ease of learning is a composite of several aspects of the language, such as the strictness of the procedural rules used (some languages are less "forgiving" of minor syntax errors than others); in general, this criterion relates to the length of time required to become an expert programmer with the language.

Program length in the exhibit pertains to the number of instructions that must be coded to accomplish a user task. In general, programs in languages that require fewer instructions can be written more quickly, using the programmer's time more efficiently.

The power of a language as cited in the exhibit relates to how well it can accomplish the full range of business data processing activities without resorting to awkward and time-consuming unconventional programming techniques. Power would be evaluated quite differently if the criterion were the full range of scientific rather than business processing activities; for example, COBOL (rated high in the exhibit) would be rated low, and FORTRAN (rated medium) would be rated high.

The program structure characteristic of Exhibit 7.8 refers to each language's ability to produce programs that conform to the principles of structured programming, which is a systematic approach to program design that makes program development easier, makes the program more comprehensible to someone trying to understand its logic, and greatly enhances the ability to modify a program quickly. Of the languages shown, only two—ADA and PL/1—provides good program structure, and COBOL may be considered fair with respect to this characteristic.

Processing efficiency is measured in terms of the amount of CPU time required to translate and process a business program using each of the languages; while the assessment of this characteristic here is in terms of efficiency of the language, in practice the way the particular compiler or interpreter used was designed and implemented can be at least as important a determinant of processing efficiency.

Portability is assessed primarily in terms of how many computer systems have a translator program (compiler or interpreter) for that language; since each of these languages is high-level and conforms to ANSI (American National Standards Institute) standards, any computer system having the translation program for the language could translate it. In general, portability of programming languages among microcomputers is low, except among those which use the same operating system.

COBOL

The most important characteristic of COBOL is its strong orientation toward business usage. Exhibit 7.8 shows it as having a high degree of portability because most business data processing establishments have a COBOL compiler that conforms to ANSI standards; most COBOL programs can be run with only minor modifications on other computer systems except microcomputers. COBOL appears to be the most English-like of the procedural languages because most of its instructions are written in English. However, COBOL is considered difficult to learn; it generally takes a year or more of programming for a programmer to become expert in the language. Programs written in COBOL are typically quite lengthy and process with only a medium level of efficiency; compilation is rather time-consuming.

In past years, estimates of the proportion of business programming done using COBOL have ranged as high as 90 percent of all business data processing in medium-sized and large companies. With the emergence of productivity languages, this percentage has dropped. A limitation of COBOL is that it was not designed to be an interactive language and therefore has no special commands to enhance its on-line program development capablity. Many COBOL compilers have been modified to include at least a limited repertoire of such commands.

FORTRAN

FORTRAN, the oldest language included in the exhibit, has a strong scientific orientation. Its instructions are coded in equation form rather than being very English-like. FORTRAN is considered easier to learn than COBOL and is a powerful language for scientific purposes, but not nearly as powerful for business purposes. It compiles and processes efficiently. FORTRAN is seldom used for business data processing.

BASIC

BASIC was the first popular language developed for interactive processing. It is intended to be a general-purpose language with FORTRAN-like characteristics for scientific data processing and also to have a capability for business data processing. BASIC is the primary language that microcomputers use for all purposes, and virtually all microcomputer systems have a BASIC compiler. This gives BASIC programs a high level of portability among microcomputers with the same operating system. Additionally, a fairly high proportion of mainframe computers also have a BASIC compiler.

BASIC is an English-like language; its major characteristic is that it is simple and easy to learn. However, programs written in BASIC are long, making compilation time lengthy and processing efficiency low. BASIC is not considered a powerful language. Its major disadvantage is that it is awkward to use for complex programming tasks. If the student has very little time to devote to learning a computer language, BASIC can reasonably be the language of choice. However, BASIC is generally held in low esteem by professional programmers, and few business applications programs are written in BASIC in medium-sized and large companies.

PL/1

PL/1 was developed by IBM as a general-purpose language with a broad range of capabilities. The intention was that PL/1 would replace both FORTRAN and COBOL. This has not happened, however, in part because other major computer manufacturers have been slow to develop PL/1 compilers for their machines, restricting the use of PL/1 largely to IBM equipment. Additionally, PL/1 is somewhat similar to COBOL, which was already being used in many installations; therefore, to replace COBOL, PL/1 would have had to provide superior characteristics. While PL/1 may be marginally perferable to COBOL in some respects, the difference is not enough to have made data processing departments switch to PL/1. PL/1 is considered a difficult language to learn.

FOCUS

FOCUS, the only productivity language in Exhibit 7.8, is a part of a data base system of the same name. The general orientation of FOCUS is toward data analysis rather than applications programming. While other languages can also be used for data analysis, FOCUS is easy to learn and is easily used for writing programs that extract selected categories of data from the files for anlaysis purposes. Because relatively few companies have FOCUS compilers, the portability of a FOCUS program is low, although among those systems with FOCUS its portability is high. FOCUS programs typically are written for data analysis circumstances that are unique to a particular situation within a company; thus the need would seldom arise to transport FOCUS programs to another computer.

RPG-II

Many experts class RPG-II as a nonlanguage in that program code instructions are not written. Rather, with RPG-II the programmer defines the input file format by providing field names and specifications about the field, such as its length. Then the programmer defines simple operations that will be done to the field, such as multiplying the contents of field A by the contents of field B. Facilities are also provided to specify report formats for report generation purposes.

RPG-II is not well suited to the development of programs involving complicated formulas or complex logical operations. It can, however, be used for the straightforward business data processing tasks typically found in small companies. Few medium-sized or large companies use RPG-II, but many smaller companies do.

ADA

ADA, which was first used in 1980, is the newest language among those in the exhibit. It has strong scientific programming capabilities and also has good input-output features, which are needed for business. The use of ADA is advocated by the U.S. Department of Defense. Some programmers expect that ADA will become popular as a replacement for FORTRAN, PL/1, and COBOL. It is commonly considered an excellent first language for programmers to learn because it assists them by providing structure to programs and instills a programming discipline of structured thinking that is believed ot be important for programmers to learn at an early point. Additionally, since ADA has many of the features of a variety of other languages, a knowledge of ADA facilitates the learning of other languages.

Choosing a Language

When deciding which language to use for a particular application, several questions should be considered. First, an obvious one: Does the computer have a compiler for a particular language? A second question is: Are programmers readily available who are skilled in the language? Third: Will the program that will be developed need to be processed on more than one computer? If so, the computers must have compatible compilers for that language.

Another question: How efficiently must the program process on the computer system? A related consideration here is how often the program will be used between modifications; if it will be used frequently, it is important to choose a language that processes efficiently and to be certain that the compiler that will be used is inherently efficient at translation. On the other hand, if modifications will be frequent, the major criterion for choosing a language is ease of programming rather than efficiency of processing.

In some situations, managers within or outside data processing must review or understand the program. For this purpose an English-like language with a simple structure and automated documentation may be preferable.

Last but far from least: What is the nature of the problem? If resolving the problem requires a program that performs extensive calculations, a language such as FORTRAN, PASCAL, PL/1, or ADA is appropriate. On the other hand, if the major requirement of the program is extensive input and output, with only a modest amount of internal calculations and file updating, COBOL or BASIC might be the best choice. In the case of a simulation problem, a simulation language or one of the science-oriented languages, such as FORTRAN, would be suitable. If the problem involves data manipulation, such as retrieving and organizing data for managerial analysis, FOCUS or another productivity language could be profitably used.

Students' Perspective on Language Portability

The portability concept has another dimension not yet noted: the extent to which the experience a programmer gains in a particular language is transportable to another environment, either within that organization or in another organization. Programmers naturally want to learn and work with a language that has utility beyond their particular organization or their particular computer system within the organization. Working with a language that is not widely accepted would restrict programmers' mobility.

From this perspective, business students should want to learn COBOL because at the present time most business programming is in COBOL and the COBOL compiler is the compiler most frequently encountered in medium-sized and large business organizations. On the other hand, students seeking employment in small companies may be equally well served by learning BASIC or RPG-II. Virtually all experts agree, however, that neither BASIC nor RPG-II does much to help students learn other, more powerful languages. A student who chooses to learn ADA now could have an advantage if ADA becomes popular for business data processing in the future, as it well may.

PROGRAMMING IN CONTEXT

To some instructors of information systems as well as to some programmers in industry, programming is synonymous with information systems. Indeed, the student may easily become totally engrossed in programming while taking information systems courses. One reason is that the problem-solving challenge involved in programming appeals to many people. Another reason is that programming consumes a large amount of time outside the formal classroom, leading the student to believe that if programming takes up so much more time than information systems topics, it must be commensurately more important.

A better perspective is that programming is but one of many important topics in information systems. Management information systems concepts, business data processing techniques, computer hardware and software, systems development techniques beyond programming, project management, and control and management of information systems are only a few of these. The person who takes a job as a programmer in industry will become a much better programmer by paying careful attention to the full range of information systems topics. Employees who focus primarily on the technical aspects of programming are unlikely to be viewed by their managers as having good potential for subsequent careers as managers within data processing or elsewhere in the organization. Most managers state that their organization needs programmers but is in even greater need of managers within data processing; managers lament the fact that so few programmers have the breadth of background and interests that provides the potential to move quickly into the managerial ranks.

SUMMARY

Understanding computer software is in many ways more important for users and managers than understanding computer hardware. A computer system's software costs usually exceed its hardware costs, and often software is the weak link in systems development.

Systems programs enable the computer to run itself, and they perform tasks for the computer or auxillary services for applications programs; applications programs seek to accomplish specific user tasks. All programs must be debugged by eliminating syntax and logic errors.

Programming languages fall into several categories. Machine language communicates directly with the computer; assembly language, which is one step "up," must be translated into machine language. Both are machine-specific. Assembly language is easier to use than machine language;

easier still are the higher-level programming languages, which are machine-independent. Compilers or interpreters are needed to translate them into machine language. Each high-level language has its own special characteristics which make it particularly suited for certain types of applications. Using high-level languages makes programming easier, and productivity languages, which are very high-level, are being used more and more as programming costs increase and as hardware costs decrease.

Many factors influence the decision concerning whether to purchase or to develop a program: the availability of qualified programmers, the increasing cost of programming, the programming backlog, and the availability of a satisfactory commercially vended program. In general, microcomputer users should buy rather than develop their business applications programs.

Choosing which language to use in writing a program requires familiarity with the different characteristics of each language, since some suit certain applications much better than others. COBOL still dominates mainframe business data processing, but its dominance is being diminished.

KEY TERMS

software: instructions or "statements" embodied in all types of computer programs that define for the computer the tasks to be accomplished and direct the computer to perform these tasks.

syntax error: a programming error that occurs when the procedures of the programming language are violated, causing the program instructions to be incorrect.

logic error: a programming error that involves an incorrect combination or sequence of instructions or an instruction to the computer to process data in an illogical way.

machine language: a binary code that communicates directly with the computer's circuitry; machine language is unique to each model of computer.

assembly language: a computer language using symbols rather than 0s and 1s; it is one step up from machine language and is unique to each model of computer.

high-level programming language: a language written the way a person thinks (in mathematical equations and English) rather than as a computer processes (in binary form of 0s and 1s).

procedural language: a high-level language that requires the programmer to specify carefully the procedures that the computer must follow for processing.

interactive language: a type of high-level programming language that allows an on-line, real-time dialogue between the programmer and the computer.

file and data base query language: a language that specialized in accessing and retrieving selected data from computer files.

productivity language: a nonprocedural interactive language that provides fast and easy program development.

object code: the result of translating assembly language or a high-level language; it is equivalent to machine language.

job control language (JCL): a language that enables the programmer to communicate instructions to the computer about how to process a program.

assembler program: a program that translates programs written in assembly language into machine language.

compiler: a translator program that translates a high-level programming language into machine language.

subset compiler: a translator program for a subset language that is less comprehensive in its capabilities than the high-level language.

interpreter: a translator program that translates one instruction of a program at a time into machine language.

one-to-one translation: the translation of each program instruction into one machine language instruction.

one-to-many translation: the translation of each program instruction into multiple machine language instructions.

application generator: a specialized program that aids programmers in developing applications programs.

REFERENCES

Long, Larry E., *Manager's Guide to Computers and Information Systems,* Englewood Cliffs, NJ: Prentice-Hall, 1983.

Nash, John F. and Martin B. Roberts, *Accounting Information Systems,* New York: Macmillan, 1984.

REVIEW QUESTIONS

1. Why is it important for users and managers to understand software?

2. Describe the general procedure for the operation of programs.

3. Distinguish between syntax errors and logic errors and give an example of each.

4. Discuss several types of systems utility programs.

5. Discuss the characteristics of machine language.

6. Discuss machine dependency in relation to programming languages.

7. In what circumstances might it be preferable to write a program in assembly language rather than a high-level language?

8. Why is assembly language used less now than it was a decade ago?

9. What are the differences between assemblers, compilers, and interpreters?

10. What are subset compilers, where are they usually found, and why are they necessary?

11. Discuss the dominance of COBOL in business data processing. Is COBOL becoming less dominant now? What languages may be competing strongly with COBOL?

12. What are the five general types of tasks for which high-level languages are used?

13. Give some advantages, disadvantages, and examples of interactive languages.

14. What are some reasons why productivity languages are able to increase productivity? Why aren't they used for all applications?

15. Discuss the predictions for the future of productivity languages. What implications do these predictions have for you and your classmates?

16. Discuss several types of specialty languages.

17. How will the use of different types of programming languages be affected as programming costs rise and as hardware costs fall?

18. What is the function of JCL?

19. What can a macro instruction do?

20. Discuss some of the factors that affect the decision concerning whether to purchase or develop a computer program.

21. Why might ADA be a good language to learn?

22. What are some criteria to consider when deciding which programming language to use for a particular application?

23. How important is a technical knowledge of computer programming in the overall picture of information systems?

CASE

Computer Companies Develop Devices to Ease Programming

By Susan Chance
Staff Reporter for The Wall Street Journal

If you believe the old hands in the business, a crisis in information processing is fast approaching. There simply aren't enough programmers—people who write instructions telling computers how to handle information—to meet the demand.

A Labor Department study says that by 1985, the computer industry will need 640,000 programmers, but only 476,000 are expected to be available. Surveys conducted by computer giants like International Business Machines Corp. indicate that most large corporations already have a big backlog of "to-be-developed" programs for their large computers. This is partly because today's programmer spends 70% of his time reworking old programs to enable them to handle new requirements or to make them work with new equipment.

Faced with this problem, computer companies are working on ways to streamline and simplify the programming process. One fairly new tool they've developed is called an "application generator." This is a standard program module, or program unit, that can be used when putting together the software, or instructions, for a complex business computer system.

The principle behind application generators is this: Most business data processing systems—from computerized airline reservation systems to automated bank debit systems—have elements in common. Computers are required to move information from remote terminals to a main computer base, or to send information to and from many files, or to check information against a file or to update and change a file.

Normally all the coding and testing of these elements is done each time a program is written. That's an error-prone and time-consuming process, requiring thousands of lines of new code (complex and specific sets of commands) and a considerable amount of routine work.

If the common elements of business-computer applications are precoded and stored, the programmer can, in effect, "paint by number." He can plug the common elements into the particulars of the software he's writing for, enabling him to skip many steps.

The advantage of application generators, says Aaron Goodman, an IBM engineer, is that the code is pretested, and if problems occur, they can be corrected by the vendor. Also, because hundreds of customers are running the same common modules in their programs, those parts of the programs tend to be thoroughly debugged, or error-free.

Almost every major computer maker has or is working on application generator products that permit this modular approach to programming.

Hamilton Brothers Oil Co., however, gives application generators a mixed review. The Denver company recently found itself under pressure to computerize its accounting and finance system within a 20-month period. It used an application generator from American Management Systems Inc. called Generation Five to help with the design and development of the system.

The project was finished on time, thanks to Generation Five, which was used to develop many of the 300 programs the system required. But, says James H. Waldrop, Hamilton's data processing chief, the standard modules that were used may reduce processing efficiencies later because Hamilton's own programmers didn't incorporate their own shortcuts along the way.

For microcomputers, shortcuts to writing programs are just beginning to proliferate. But computer owners should be wary of claims about how easy they are to use. The inexperienced user may want to buy ready-made programs off the shelf for his routine needs.

A product for the experienced programmer that probably does take a lot of the scratch work out of writing programs is Pearl, from Computer Pathways Inc. in Salem, Ore. Pearl is designed to help write business-application programs, such as for accounting functions and for mailing-list files.

Pearl helps the user to design his own program by asking him a series of questions. Then Pearl automatically writes the code for basic tasks such as moving information to and from files. The result, say its authors, is that the programmer is spared routine work and can reduce the time he takes to write a program by as much as 70%.

Another product for microcomputers being touted at computer fairs is called The Last One. It is designed by D.J. "Al" Systems of England and is distributed in the U.S. by Southwest Microcomputer Systems, Santa Monica, Calif.

The Last One produces ready-to-use programs tailored to the individual's requirements for anything from a personalized library catalog to "what-if" cost analyses. The product displays on a video screen a list of computer selections in menu form. As the user chooses each menu item, The Last One, like the Pearl, asks questions to help it create a program. If the user doesn't know the answers, however, he's in trouble because the instruction booklet is hard to understand.

Moreover, though The Last One uses many English words when asking questions, the words have special meaning and require a bit of study. Even with special hand-holding, which is available by telephone and at computer shows, the uninitiated may decide after trying to use The Last One to give up computers altogether.

Source: The Wall Street Journal, June 15, 1982, p. 21.

Case Questions

1. Is an application generator a productivity language?

2. Why would "standard modules" of an application generator "reduce processing efficiencies later," and what kinds of shortcuts could Hamilton's programmers have implemented if they had done the programming themselves and not used an application generator?

3. On the one hand, computer scheduling often is not as big a problem for microcomputers as it is for mainframes; why is this? On the other hand, however persons who develop and operate programs for microcomputers often are not as knowledgeable about computers as persons who do this for mainframes. How do these considerations influence whether programs for microcomputers should be developed using an application generator or bought ready-made off the shelf? How does the cost of microcomputer programs also influence this decision?

Chapter 8

MICROCOMPUTERS

PAYOFF THOUGHT

Microcomputers are bringing about a revolution in computing and in managers' work styles. To gain a competitive edge, every manager and future manager should start now to understand and use microcomputers.

CHAPTER OBJECTIVES

1. To communicate the excitement about microcomputers that now exists in the hobbyist and business worlds

2. To provide an overall understanding of microcomputer technology within the framework of the fundamentals of computer systems established in previous chapters

3. To emphasize the potential of microcomputers for extending the range of managers' thought processes and for altering the ways managers manage

THE EXCITEMENT OF MICROCOMPUTERS

Computer experts and novices alike often find microcomputers exciting and become devotees. Microcomputers can become an absorbing interest; to a true devotee, few experiences in life are comparable. Learning about and using microcomputers provide the same degree of emotional release to some persons that athletics offers to many others. To some people, microcomputing resembles the gradual unfolding of the subtleties of a complex activity, such as becoming an expert downhill skier. For most devotees, it's a quiet form of exhilaration—an internal and personal feeling.

Not everyone who is exposed to microcomputers experiences this feeling. To some, microcomputers represent frustration. The technology is complex (compared with, for example, that of a television set); there are too many opportunities to go astray and too few experts to show the right way; and, until experience is gained, hours and hours can be unproductively spent trying to make a system or a software package function. Nevertheless, millions of people are now interested in microcomputers, and many more millions will be in the next few years, at least to a degree. Some of the reasons for this are discussed below:

1. From playing games to programming, microcomputers can be fun. They give a pleasing sense of "being in control." People who own them spend less time watching television and sometimes start to ignore their families and their jobs—but often as much with a sense of accomplishment as with a sense of guilt.

Interestingly, for most users games are one of the least appealing aspects of microcomputers. Yes, the games are fun, but serious microcomputer users have a mild disdain for video games, even though they acknowledge that their own programming activities are often just a fun way to play with the computer. Certainly the saying, "The difference between men and boys is the cost of their toys," has some relevance to the microcomputer world.

2. Microcomputers are relatively easy to use. Large computers must be operated by highly trained professionals, but micros can be used by novices. Part of the fun is that micros are easy to learn about and understand—despite the fact that they are sometimes frustrating. Micros are "user-friendly" in that the instructions usually are easy to follow, "help" routines and "menus" (programs which present a list of activities that the user may carry out next and which ask the user to choose from this menu) are plentiful, keyboards have numerous built-in "special-function" keys that accomplish entire subtasks with one keystroke, and no computer expertise is needed to get started (although expert assistance is often very helpful).

3. Microcomputers are useful. Unlike most things that are fun and easy to use, micros accomplish work. They are much more useful than pocket calculators because they have large memories and branch logic capabilities, and because an abundance of programs is available, and yet in some ways micros are easier to use than pocket calculators. With certain applications programs it is literally true that all a user must do is insert a disk containing the program, turn on the microcomputer, and follow simple directions that appear in English on the screen. Furthermore, experiments with new applications or new ways of doing existing applications can be carried out quickly at little cost and, if successful, can be implemented immediately.

4. Microcomputers offer the rare opportunity to participate in a technological revolution, most of which will have taken place during the years 1982 to 1987. Using microcomputers is fun and exciting, and so is following the progress of this revolution on a week-by-week basis in microcomputer journals.

5. Microcomputers let you become an expert. After 2 months of working with a microcomputer, you know your way around and can talk knowledgeably with microcomputer experts. After 6 months, you are an expert on microcomputers and their software and are the owner of an acute sense of accomplishment. Professional programmers of large computers may become expert programmers, but even after a decade they may not thoroughly know the complexities of the computers they program.

One fascinating aspect of microcomputers is that for the first time in computing, persons with degrees in computer science and engineering or with long years of experience with large computers—the high priests of Computerdom do not have a hammerlock on a major computer technology. Speaking metaphorically, hundreds of thousands (and soon millions) of basically self-taught micro users can go at it in the arena with the best of the computer specialists and stay the course rather than lose in the first round under a flurry of "computerspeak."

Managers who are learning to use microcomputers are delighted with this turn of events. Many have long chaffed under the almost complete domination of technical persons over the computer information systems that are so vital to organizations' and managers' work activities. One effect of microcomputers is to make more employees computer-literate and better able to work with—or second-guess—computer professionals.

6. Microcomputers are reliable. The user usually knows what a microcomputer is doing, and microcomputers seldom fail because the environment and the systems are much less complex than those of large computers. However, microcomputers can bring frustrations aplenty when new components are added or new software packages are acquired—not all additions work properly unless the microcomputer is first adjusted.

If microcomputers or peripheral devices do fail, often the user can run diagnostics programs to identify the problem and can order and install the needed parts. More frequently, the unit is brought to a repair center that operates and charges much the way a television repair center does, perhaps even offering a "loaner" or rental replacement unit until the repairs are completed.

7. Microcomputers provide a study in industry growth dynamics. Business students should be aware of industry growth patterns from the inception to the maturity of the typical industry. The microcomputer industry gives signs of following the classic pattern, except that it is highly compressed in time. While the automobile industry required half a century to reach maturity, the large computer industry took about three decades, and the minicomputer industry required about a decade, the microcomputer industry may accelerate this process and mature in 6 or 7 years.

Typically, a few pioneer companies start an industry and are joined by large numbers of underfinanced, poorly managed companies. The industry then enters a shakeout stage precipitated by increased competition or a weakened economy, and only the financially sound and managerially strong companies survive intact. Even during this period a central tendency in technology emerges, and products in the industry increasingly have similar characteristics. Finally, at maturity, there is intense and long-term competition between large, well-organized companies that are run by professional managers rather than entrepreneurs and up-from-the-ranks technical personnel.

The microcomputer industry is still early in this cycle; there are large numbers of microcomputer manufacturers, few have been forced out, and more are entering the industry. The consensus is that a shakeout period will come soon. As the industry develops during the next 3 to 5 years, it will be a fascinating case study.

DEFINITIONS OF MICROCOMPUTERS

Microcomputers can be defined in a number of ways: in terms of their function, their cost, their size, or various technological considerations. Perhaps the simplest definition, one that has captured the fancy of many persons, is that a microcomputer is "a computer on a chip." In fact, this defines a microprocessor, not necessarily a microcomputer. A microprocessor—a single MOS chip—contains the logic of a CPU, and one-chip microcomputers do exist, but individual MOS chips are used primarily for control of microwave ovens and other household appliances as well as for a variety of other purposes, such as for performance control under the hoods of automobiles. Microcomputers, on the other hand, usually contain many chips, one of which is a microprocessor and others that serve control, storage, and other functions. A microprocessor chip is shown in Exhibit 8.1.

Microcomputers are sometimes defined in terms of their cost, which ranges from less than $100 up to about $15,000. The upper figure includes not just a microcomptuer but also an entire system with extensive periph-

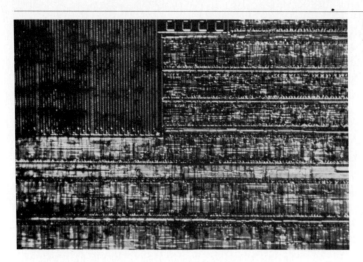

EXHIBIT 8.1
A microprocessor as a
one-chip computer.

eral equipment. The cost of business microcomputers is still decreasing, at a rate of about 25 percent per year; however, at the lowest end of the market—microcomputers that are used only in the home—prices have stabilized.

Microcomputers may also be defined by size. A microcomputer exclusive of peripherals weighs from about 1 to 40 lb, with 25 lb being typical. Almost all business microcomputers are compact enough to sit on a desk top, several are small enough to be called "transportable" (they can be easily carried), and a few are true portables that fit into an attaché case.

Micros can also be defined in terms of their functional characteristics. For example, micros are often said to be small computers that can be used for small jobs. In the next few years microcomputers will be limited less and less to small jobs.

Microcomputers are often described as "personal computers." Micros are "personal" in that most are used by only one person, making them a personal workstation. Typically, they are also personally managed because a single user determines how each will be used.

Micros are also described as "plug-in-and-run" computer systems, implying that they can be lifted out of their packing box and plugged into a standard wall socket to become operational immediately. This, in turn, implies that micros are user-friendly.

Another way to define microcomputers is in terms of some of their more important technical characteristics. Thus, a microcomputer is a collection of MOS chips, usually with the ALU on one microprocessor chip unit consisting of a single integrated silicon circuitry system and with the control unit on another chip. Additonal individual chips are for random access memory (RAM), read-only memory (ROM), and other special functions. This collection of chips is mounted on a plastic circuit board which also contains a pattern of conductors that interconnect the chips and supply the power. Typically, each chip is about ¼ in square and may contain 60,000 to 250,000 "gates," or logic functions. Main memory is volatile (data disappears if the power is turned off). The ROM chip is a program in the form of circuitry rather than software, and it contains permanent instructions that are part of the operating system. The operating system includes file creation, file editing, and file-copy capabilities, as well as a number of other, more specialized capabilities. Microcomputers may be 4-bit, 8-bit, or (increasingly) 16-bit word-size computers (word size indicates the number of bits that are processed together and stored in one storage location). In general, computers with larger word sizes process faster because they process more bits per processing cycle. Mainframe computers typically have 64-bit words, which accounts partly for their greater power.

Perhaps the best definition of a microcomputer is a composite of all the preceding ones. No adequate succinct definition exists.

A MICROCOMPUTER SYSTEM

Exhibit 8.2 shows a microcomputer system. The microprocessor, which includes the entire CPU, is shown at the center left. The bus shown in

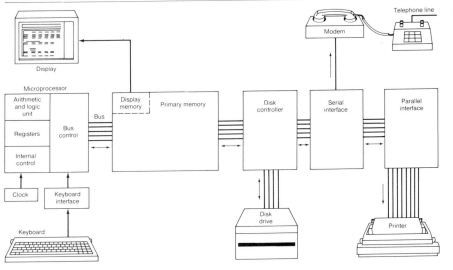

EXHIBIT 8.2
A microcomputer system.

HARDWARE OF A PERSONAL COMPUTER includes devices for processing and storing information and for communicating with the user and with other electronic devices. A set of parallel conductors called a bus connects the main components. The processing unit, which generally includes not only the microprocessor chip itself but also various auxiliary chips, carries out essentially all calculations and controls the entire system. Information can be entered into the system through a keyboard. Pressing a key generates a coded signal unique to that key; the code is stored in the display memory and so appears on the cathode-ray-tube display. The primary memory, which consists of semiconductor memory chips, holds programs and data currently in use; it is a random-access memory, meaning that the content of any cell can be examined or changed independently of all the other cells. Disk storage generally has a larger capacity than the primary memory, but it is slower and its information is recovered in larger blocks. The interfaces connect the computer to other devices, such as a printer or a modem (which gives access to other computers through the telephone system). In a serial interface information is transferred one bit at a time; in a parallel interface multiple conductors carry several bits (in most instances eight) at a time.

Source: "Personal Computers", *Scientific American*, December, 1982 the exhibit is a pathway for data transfers between the components of the microcomputer. A bus permits the simultaneous transmission of large amounts of data back and forth within the microcomputer system.

The primary memory shown in the exhibit is a series of chips, with typically 16,000, or 16K, memory positions on each RAM chip; some chips, however, have 64K or 256K memory positions. The data on the monitor at the upper lefthand corner has been moved to the display memory section of primary memory and remains there while being displayed. The monitor displays data in the form of a series of light dots, known as "pixels," which are combined in patterns to represent characters or graphs; a "high-resolution" monitor has a large number of pixels per character.

The disk drive shown could be either a floppy or a hard disk. Most microcomputers have a controller for each disk drive, as shown in the exhibit, but one controller might control multiple disk drives.

The serial interface passes 1 bit of data at the time into a "modem" for transmission over a telephone line, a shown. The type of modem pictured is an acoustic coupling modem, into which a standard telephone is inserted to accomplish data transmission. Some modems are direct-wired to the telephone system without connecting to a telephone instrument.

The parallel interface shown transmits data along several parallel conductors to another microcomputer system component—in this illustration, a printer. Some printers connect to a serial interface rather than a parallel interface.

The software packages that are part of a microcomputer system cannot readily be shown in an exhibit. Each microcomputer system has at least one operating system. Some are unique to that microcomputer, while others are used by other microcomputers also. CP/M and MS DOS, for example, each serve as the operating system of several different brands of microcomputers; a variation of the latter, known as "PC DOS," is used by the IBM PC microcomputer.

The microcomputer's ROM contains the operating system's "boot-strap" program, which is used to "boot" (load) the operating system into primary memory by sending the ALU a simple set of instructions upon request from the operator. These instructions direct the disk controller to look for information on a specific disk drive; this information is the software portion of the operating system, which is then booted into the CPU's primary RAM memory.

The operating system then assumes control of the computer system. One part of the operating system, the basic input-output system (BIOS), communicates with the peripheral devices. Because these are not the same on all microcomputers of the same model, the BIOS may need modification to enable it to "handshake" (communicate) with a peripheral device.

Through its BIOS the operating system instructs the CPU to send information to an I/O controller, which in turn activates the peripheral device that it controls. In this way the operating system loads into primary memory the applications program and related data, controls the program's processing of the data, and directs output to peripheral devices.

Other software packages typical of a microcomputer configuration like that shown in Exhibit 8.1 include a spreadsheet package, video games, a word processing program such as WordStar, decision support system packages such as DSS/F, compilers such as COBOL and PASCAL, and a BASIC interpreter. BASIC is the most common microcomputer programming language, and almost all microcomputer systems have a BASIC interpreter. Of course, the system will also have applications programs that use the compiler or interpreter; for example, if there is a COBOL compiler, COBOL applications programs are probably used to process transactions in business data files. Various utility programs may also be present.

A microcomputer system need not be nearly as elaborate as that shown in Exhibit 8.2. Some, for example, weigh less than 1 lb, have CPUs that cost less than $100, and are not configured with a disk system, but instead rely on standard cassette-tape recorder tapes for both storing and loading programs and data. Although an entire microcomputer system configured might cost less than $400, including a television set used as a monitor, its ability to perform business data processing is almost nil. It can, however, provide instruction in the rudiments of the BASIC language and can run a variety of programs.

For most 8-bit-word microcomputers, 64K of main memory positions is the maximum available. Sixteen-bit-word microcomputers typically allow chips to be added to raise the total main memory to 512K, or in some instances even higher. Microcomputers with 512K of memory capacity and 16-bit word sizes are equivalent in some respects to mainframe computers of the early 1960s but cost less than $6000, whereas the mainframes carried a price tag in the million-dollar range.

A wide range of enhancements are available to upgrade a microcomputer system, including memory enhancements and an awesome variety of peripheral equipment. Some business situations might demand two or more disk drives, multiple printers (each with a different type of capability), or even a "dual-processing" (two-CPU) capability. In dual processing each CPU has a specialized function; for example, one CPU may be configured for a CP/M operating system, and the other may support the MS DOS operating system to allow processing of programs written for each of these. Alternatively, one microprocessor may be the standard microprocessor, and a second may be a specialized math processor which enables the system to process mathematical formulas and numeric data as much as 10 times faster than with just the standard CPU.

Another upgraded version of microcomputers is the multiworkstation microcomputer, previously described as a supermicrocomputer. One approach to this is a multiprogramming operating system that permits attaching multiple workstations (keyboards) to a single microcomputer. Such

EXHIBIT 8A
IBM Personal
Computer. (*Courtesy of
IBM Corporation.*)

a system typically would have a large amount of primary memory and a
hard disk; each workstation might or might not have its own floppy disk.

One such multiworkstation microcomputer, available from the Molecular Computer Co., accommodates up to 62 separate keyboard stations.
The molecular system adds 64K of RAM as each terminal is added; thus
the speed and other capabilities of each terminal remain constant. The
operating system coordinates all terminal activities, and a hard disk unit
accompanies the entire system.

The variety of peripheral equipment that can be added to a microcomputer is astounding. While mentioning all these peripherals is impossible,
a sampling will provide a perspective on what a microcomputer system
can be made to do. First, managers can use numerous graphics packages
to rapidly develop pie charts, line graphs, bar graphs, and other graphs.
Some of these graphics packages are integrated with other packages, such
as a spreadsheet, decision support systems data bases, or a combination
of these.

Two types of output devices can provide copies of the graphs that
appear on the display monitors: (1) printers with a special graphing capability that can print in as many as eight colors and (2) specialized plotters
that use a series of multicolored ink pens to plot graphs. While specialized
plotters and printers cost more than ordinary printers, most are under
$3000.

Speech synthesizers enable the computer to create voicelike sounds
and broadcast them over a speaker system. Unlike a microcomputer that
controls a tape recorder, a speech synthesizer uses no tape recorder—the

EXHIBIT 8B
Apple Macintosh.
(Courtesy of Apple
Computer, Inc.)

sound is not prerecorded, but instead is constructed directly by the computer system in response to instructions. Speech synthesizers formulate complex oral responses in real-time modes in reaction to a variety of conditions presented to them by programs and input data.

A "semidisk" or RAM disk permits a section of main memory to act as if it were a floppy disk. Then, any activities that would normally be done with the floppy disk are done instead in much faster RAM. This can dramatically accelerate activities that must wait for the floppy disk to be accessed and changed, such as word processing activities. However, RAM disk is "volatile" in that if power is lost, the data disappears; thus all the results of processing could be lost, for example, if the computer system was inadvertently turned off.

With RAM disk the processing speed of disk read-write operations is increased by a factor of about 10. After the data is processed or at intermediate points, the RAM disk contents can be read back out to a floppy disk for permanent storage.

MICROCOMPUTER USERS

Microcomputer users fall into six general groups:

1. *Hobbyists.* Relatively few in number, hobbyists are interested in programming and in the technical aspects of microcomputers.

2. *Home computer users.* In the home, micros are used for video games, as electronic mail devices that communicate with information systems or other computers, for maintaining personal records, and for letter and other textual data generation. Home use of microcomputers is expected to increase substantially over the next several years, to several million units. Consumers view the microcomputer much as they view a television set— as an appliance. For home computer users, instructions must be particularly clearly written.

3. *Educators.* Microcomputers now pervade school systems at all levels and are employed to teach programming, to teach computer systems, and as learning aids using educational programs in a variety of academic disciplines.

4. *Professional persons.* Managers, engineers, scientists, and other professional people look to the microcomputer to solve specific business problems and increase their personal productivity. Often they purchase a microcomputer to use at their office with their own funds. Professional persons prefer not to become too deeply involved; usually they learn a word processing system and the BASIC language and use a spreadsheet program to help them solve their problems. For many professionals, the compelling reason for purchasing a microcomputer is their frustration over the perceived unresponsiveness of their organization's data processing department.

5. *Small businesses.* Most small companies have never had computers. By some estimates, more than 80 percent of the small companies that could profitably use a computer do not have one. For many of those which do, however, the microcomputer is revolutionizing the way they are run. In the future literally millions of microcomputers will be put to use in small companies. For this reason alone it is important for the students of business to understand microcomputer systems and their capabilities. The majority of business graduates find positions with relatively small companies, many of which will have just one computer system, and that will be a microcomputer system.

6. *Large organizations.* Large companies and other large organizations are purchasing great numbers of microcomputers—often hundreds at a time—for use by managers and clerical personnel as well as for process control and quality control tasks. While the data processing organizations of companies do use microcomputers, the major users are in functional departments. Micros are employed for decision support systems and other forms of managerial analysis, as well as for relatively simple and straightforward transactions processsing activities that either cannot be developed on the mainframe computer or for other reasons (such as proximity and availability to users) are better developed on microcomputers.

The data processing departments of many organizations are coordinating functional departments' microcomputer acquisition to ensure that the microcomputers can interface with the mainframe and with one another. To an extent, microcomputers are changing the complexion of or-

EXHIBIT 8C
Microsoft Windows, a software extension to Microsoft Corporation's operating system, MS-DOS, version 2.0, is shown here running on Honeywell's microprocessor-based business system, the microSystem 6/10. MS-Windows provides a common operating environment for applications programs and consists of two parts—a window manager (bit-mapped display) and a mouse cursor control device. The window and mouse features allow users to view unrelated applications simultaneously and easily exchange data between the different programs integrated under MS-Windows. (Courtesy of Honeywell, Inc.)

ganizations' data processing departments. Previously preoccupied with large programs and data processing tasks accomplished on the mainframe computer, these groups are becoming increasingly user- and service-oriented and are providing both the acquisition assistance and the continuing "hand-holding" needed by users who want to develop systems but do not possess the required expertise.

MICROCOMPUTERS IN THE OFFICE

The greatest usage of microcomputers at present is in the office, and this will continue to be the case in the future. The potential of microcomputers to increase the productivity of office personnel is considered to be great. Office costs exceed 50 percent of total costs in many types of organizations and have been rising 7 percent per year on average. Naturally concerned about controlling these costs, organizations view the microcomputer as a tool for increasing clerical and managerial productivity. Microcomputer uses in the office environment fit into seven general categories, as discussed below:

1. *Word processing.* One of the largest uses of microcomputers in the office is for word processing. Microcomputer-based word processing systems are of two general types. First are the stand-alone word processing systems, such as those produced by Wang and the IBM Displaywriter. These are dedicated to word processing and are not intended to perform a variety of data processing tasks, but supplemental software permits many of these systems to do other types of data processing as well.

The second type of word processing micro is one which is designed and distributed as a general-purpose computer system but which also has been configured with a word processing software package. The numerous packages available range in price from less than $50 to about $400. Almost every general-purpose microcomputer is used partly for word processing. Acquiring a microcomputer can often be justified entirely on the basis of its word processing capabilities.

Whereas many dedicated word processing systems support multiple terminals, most general-purpose microcomputers are single-workstation systems and permit only one individual at a time to perform word processing or other tasks. Dedicated word processing systems typically have editing and formatting features that are not available with most of the word processing programs used in general-purpose microcomputers.

2. *General accounting.* Numerous accounting programs are available for general ledger, accounts receivable, inventory, payroll, order entry, accounts payable, purchasing, and other accounting applications. Most are in the range of from $300 to $1000 per application.

Most 8-bit-word microcomputers are limited for accounting purposes when the size of main memory is 64K or less. While the type of operations the organization conducts greatly influences how severe a limitation this is, in general main memory of 8-bit-word microcomputers can contain an applications program and a data file with a capacity for only about 500 customer accounts, fewer than 10,000 inventory items, and $5 million in sales revenues. For 16-bit-word microcomputers, data capacities for accounting usage are generally several times as great.

3. *Other transactions applications.* Many areas of organizations other than accounting have transactions that must be processed, and in many instances these areas are placing their applications on their own microcomputers. Some groups may be discouraged by the backlog of work in the computer center. Others believe they need operational control over the system, perhaps because they need to control the data processing schedule. Whatever the reason, the effect is the same; the microcomputer is causing many departments to establish their own microcomputer-based data processing centers.

4. *Information management.* Microcomputers are used for accessing, manipulating, and retrieving data in report form. Often this is data from accounting files, but often it is data from files established for this purpose. A typical usage is the preparation of lists, such as lists of employees who have a particular attribute (e.g., more than three medical insurance claims filed in the previous year), mailing lists, and lists of customers whose purchases of a particular product exceeded $1000.

More sophisticated data management software permits data to be manipulated in complex ways to provide managerial reports. Such a program is known as a "data base management system" (DBMS). A well-known DBMS for microcomputers is dBase-II.

5. *Financial analysis.* In the past, virtually all organizations have used "spreadsheet analysis" extensively for the development of budget forecasts, for profitability analyses of possible new products, for historical summaries of financial data for past periods, for forecasting, and for many other purposes. Data was usually placed manually on a wide, column-ruled piece of paper known as a "spreadsheet," and an adding machine was used for the calculations required. Electronic spreadsheets display data in the same way—in rows and columns.

Electronic spreadsheets on microcomputers have taken the place of traditional paper spreadsheets. Financial assumptions, if any, are first input to the machine (sales revenue per unit = $1, cost of sales per unit = $0.51, and so on), then a mathematical formula is established (such as revenues − expenses = income), and finally data (such as the number of units expected to be sold) is entered in tabular form at a keyboard or retrieved from an internal file and placed in the spreadsheet. The microcomputer performs the calculations, following the formula established. Changes in assumptions or data (such as a different quantity of sales) are easy to make, and recalculations are almost instantaneous. Often output can be in either spreadsheet or graphic form. VisiCalc, SuperCalc, and MultiPlan are three popular spreadsheet programs. A typical spreadsheet has 63 columns and 254 rows, for a total of 16,000 cells for data.

6. *Financial modeling and DSS programs.* Another common use of microcomputers in the business world is for decision support system (DSS) modeling. Financial modeling programs for microcomputers are similar to financial analysis programs using electronic spreadsheets. There are important differences, however. The spreadsheets began on microcomputers and have a strong orientation to on-screen data manipulation, whereas DSSs have a tradition of mainframe usage without screens; they have only recently been adapted to microcomputers and do not have a screen orientation to the same degree as the spreadsheets. However, DSSs on micros have greater power for model building and analysis. DSS programs include prewritten modules—algorithms—that solve specialized financial problems. Typical of these are modules for discounted present-value analysis, interest calculations, time-series analysis, risk analysis, and various statistical routines such as for averaging and determining standard deviations. A few keystrokes on the keyboard can place these routines within a financial model to thereafter perform automatically their specialized calculations whenever data is entered.

DSSs usually also have their own programming language, which permits them to deal with very complex problems. A final advantage of DSSs is that they have more compatibility with mainframe files and programs, having been developed for the mainframe environment in the first place. Thus, a microcomputer DSS version and a mainframe version of the same DSS can be used with a high level of compatibility between the two. This also facilitates using microcomputers to extract data from the mainframe computer system, to receive data from data services such as Dow-Jones, and to perform managerial analyses that would be impractical without a computer. The convenience of a microcomputer frees a manager who needs to use the DSS from dependence upon the schedules or other vicissitudes of data processing centers.

7. *Communications.* Office microcomputers may be linked to a local network of micros that share resources such as printers and Winchester disks. In this mode, microcomputers can also serve as a local electronic mail system. The network can be interfaced with the mainframe computer, allowing each microcomputer to extract data from the mainframe computer files and use mainframe software packages as if the microcomputer were a dumb terminal.

Either linked to a local area network or independently, a microcomputer can transmit data over common-carrier telephone lines, becoming part of a telecommunications system. Microcomputers can be vital parts of distributed data processing systems.

INFORMATION SERVICES FOR MICROCOMPUTERS

A number of personal and professional services are available through microcomputer systems that communicate with remote data bases. One information service is The Source, a Reader's Digest subsidiary that provides stock-market quotes, commodities prices, access to financial forecasts, and news stories that might affect the financial markets. The Source also offers electronic mail, enabling a user to send instant messages to anyone across the country for the price of a long-distance telephone call. The Source also makes available information about airline schedules and restaurant reviews; through The Source a plane ticket can be purchased, or a hotel room reserved. The microcomputer accesses The Source's data files through telecommunications systems. The Dow-Jones News Retrieval Service also offers stock-market quotes every few minutes on stocks, bonds, and options, as well as news items related to the stock market.

CompuServe is another extensive information service available to microcomputer users with a modem. It offers electronic magazines, national news wires, worldwide weather reports, current movie reviews, electronic banking, and information on financial markets. It also provides electronic mail service, electronic games, and other services.

Consumer shopping services are also available through microcomputer systems. The computer of Telephone Software Connections in Torrence, California, receives orders for computer products 24 hours a day from microcomputers or terminals all over the country. If the order is for a software program, the company's computer will transmit that program over telecommunications lines directly to the computer system that ordered it.

MICROCOMPUTER "FRIENDLINESS"

Microcomputer systems are often said to be "user-friendly." What does this mean?

There are two dimensions of user friendliness, the first being how the microcomputer appears to the user. Microcomputers are handsome, are appliance-sized, and convey an air of "what you see is what you get." Their appearance is not awe-inspiring or intimidating. These features make managers much more willing to try microcomputers and even make them expect that the experience will be fun.

The other dimension is that microcomputers are much easier to use than mainframe computers. Micros are designed for novices; mainframes are designed for professional data processors. Micros are friendly enough to be used by tens of millions of Americans, including those properly termed "managers." While a relative few highly skilled professional data processors, scientists, and engineers and a smattering of other professional persons use large computers, microcomputers are being adopted by multitudes of professional persons and managers who have purposely steered clear of large computer systems.

Instruction manuals for microcomputers are usually more understandable than those for mainframes. Error diagnostics often provide not only an explicit statement of the nature of the error made but also instructions on how to correct it. The languages used are less complex, and some (such as BASIC) are interactive, giving the user instant on-line feedback about what the computer is doing. Microcomputer instructions have been simplified to the point where usually only a few codes need to be memorized, and HELP routines are immediatley available on-screen if the user forgets a code, makes an error, or cannot recall the next procedure to follow.

Most authorities believe that during the next few years microcomputers will become even easier to use than they are at present. Many hail Apple's Lisa computer as the first of the "new generation" of computers in terms of user friendliness. Lisa uses "mouse graphics"; a user need not enter instructions through the keyboard but rather uses a cursor directed by a "mouse" to "point" to an instruction on the screen, which the computer then executes.

INCOMPATIBILITY PROBLEMS OF MICROCOMPUTERS

A major problem in the microcomputer marketplace is incompatibility of peripheral equipment and programs between different manufacturers' microcomputers and between microcomputers and mainframe computers. For example, not all printers are plug-compatible with all microcomputers. Many printers and other pieces of equipment are made only for Apple computers, other peripherals can be used only with Radio Shack computers, and still others can be used only with the IBM Personal Computer. Interfacing more than one type of microcomputer system within one local area network may be so costly as to be economically unjustifiable.

If different kinds of microcomputers are intended to share data, programs, or peripheral equipment, compatibility problems must be carefully considered in advance, including the fact that 8-bit-word and 16-bit-word microcomputers cannot exchange data and programs. While the trend is toward greater use of 16-bit-word microcomputers, for many purposes 8-bit-word systems will continue to dominate the marketplace. The expectation that 32-bit-word microcomputers will be commonplace in the near future further compounds the problem.

Different operating systems also cause lack of compatibility between microcomputers, as was noted earlier in the chapter. One attempt to overcome this incompatibility is a circuit board for the IBM 16-bit-word PC that permits processing of 8-bit-word CP/M programs.

Incompatibility problems are not unique to microcomputers. They have always plagued mainframe computer systems. However, the professional data processors who use mainframe computers can cope with interfacing problems better than the relatively unsophisticated users of microcomputers.

Incompatibility between micros and mainframes is also a problem on at least four levels, each successively more difficult. The first is where data files need to be up-loaded or down-loaded (transferred to or from the mainframe system by the microcomputer system). If the two computer systems both accept a common computer code such as ASCII, these file exchanges usually can be accomplished by connecting the two computers through a modem and a telephone line.

A second level of difficulty occurs when the microcomputer operator asks the mainframe to do special processing tasks, for example, when the operator desires to access a mainframe file, transfer it to another data file within the mainframe, and then print the file on the mainframe's printer, all through instructions input through the microcomputer.

A third level of difficulty occurs when a microcomputer system is intended not only to process data by itself but also to act as a dumb terminal connected to a mainframe computer. For the microcomputer to use all the resources of the mainframe, such as directing the mainframe's processing of programs and utilizing its high-speed printers, a high degree of compatibility between the two computer systems is necessary. Not only do technical differences between the two computer systems create difficulties here, but also such considerations as the compatibility of the micro's keyboard commands with the commands understood by the mainframe are important.

A final level of difficulty is encountered if the microcomputer has a specialized program to transfer to the mainframe for processing of data within the mainframe; alternatively, the problem could be the transfer of a program from the mainframe for processing with data in the microcomputer. The former circumstances might arise when the data files are too large to be processed in the microcomputer. The latter circumstances might arise when, for example, it is desirable to use mainframe programs within the microprocessor because of high user charges for mainframe processing or because the mainframe computer is too busy to provide a fast response.

LIMITATIONS OF MICROCOMPUTERS

Microcomputers place a great deal of low-cost computer power at the fingertips and under the complete control of managers and clerical personnel. Although microcomputers have limitations, microcomputer research and development continues to reduce many of these.

Perhaps the most basic limitation of microcomputers is their small word size. Although cycle times are fast—in the range of 5 to 10 million cycles per second—the total amount of data processed within a cycle time is considerably less than with larger-word-size computers. The larger word sizes of the 16-bit and 32-bit microcomputers, expected to be prevalent in the near future, will help reduce this limitation.

Smaller-word-size computers have less extensive instruction sets, and simple operations may require repeated cycles for certain types of data processing that are not necessary with larger-word-size computer sytems; this further reduces the amount of work that a microcomputer completes in a given period of time. Microcomputers may have as few as 20 or as many as 100 separate instructions, but large computers often have more than 150.

Most microcomputers are single-task machines; that is, they can accomplish only one user task at a time. For example, when printing is in process, the CPU can control the printing operation only, and the operator cannot simultaneously be entering data to the system. This limitation is being reduced by designing operating systems—and even programs such as word processing programs—that permit multitasking. For example, in the near future some microcomputers are expected to be able to transmit data via a telecommunications system, receive data on a separate telecommunications system, print data, and allow the operator to enter or edit data on-line, all simultaneously.

Another limitation of microcomputers is that first-time users often have difficulty finding reliable sources of help and information. Salespersons may or may not have the expertise needed; if they do, they may or may not take sufficient time to help a user. Many software companies have "hot lines" that purchasers of their software can call toll-free for assistance—but many do not.

Maintenance of a microcomputer can also be a problem. Large computers receive maintenance on a regular schedule, in some cases for 2 hours each night. This approach is not necessary with simpler microcomputers, however, and typically they go for months with no attention devoted to their well-being. When a problem does emerge, it is not discovered and corrected during a routine service check; instead, it causes the microcomputer system to fail. It may be a day or a week or longer before repairs can be made; to an organization that relies heavily on its microcomputer for activities vital to the organization, even a day's downtime can be serious. To sum up, microcomputer systems are very reliable, but this reliability makes their users vulnerable because they are not prepared to detect an imminent failure and they are unable to effect repairs quickly when their microcomputer does fail.

Software reliability is a problem in the microcomputer industry. Thousands of vendors, many quite small, develop and sell programs, and some are not thoroughly tested and debugged. The inexperienced user's best policy is to rely on well-established software houses.

MICROCOMPUTERS AND DATA SECURITY

Microcomputers introduce new dimensions to an organization's data and equipment security problems. A micro that has access to the mainframe's files can quickly and easily transfer data to a floppy disk. The disk then can be removed easily from the premises and put to a use that was neither intended nor endorsed by the organization. In effect, highly portable copies of data files are conveniently available to members of the organization who have access to the microcomputers. Even if the mainframe data files are protected from access by unauthorized individuals or equipment, microcomputer programs can be written that systematically probe and attempt to circumvent the mainframe's data security system.

Additional data security concerns are that floppy disks are small and fragile and therefore are easily lost or damaged. The lack of big-system data security discipline increases the likelihood that no backup duplicate disk will be made. The proliferation of microcomputers in organizations also means the proliferation of all other security problems that have always accompanied small systems—lack of adequate separation of duties, fewer processing controls, a casual operating environment with loose controls over program development and program changes, and so on.

In some circumstances microcomputers can enhance data security. Particularly sensitive data files can be developed and processed exclusively on a microcomputer by the one person who must know the file contents. The files can then be placed on a floppy disk, main memory erased, and the floppy disk locked in the manager's safe when not in use. No data processing personnel are involved, the data is never on a large system with multiple users and therefore is absolutely unavailable for unauthorized retrieval, and reports can be printed at the microcomputer workstation, eliminating the possibility that they will be read or copied by output personnel, that more copies will be printed than were authorized, and that there will be erroneous distribution to the wrong location. Not only are virtually all data security problems eliminated in this way, but also the manager who is responsible for the files has total control and need have no lingering concerns that a security breach might go undetected.

Microcomputer equipment itself presents security problems. Microcomputers can be carried off easily or even misplaced or permanently "borrowed." The problems here are similar to the problems encountered with other small units of equipment, such as typewriters, except that microcomputers are more appealing and are therefore a more likely target of thieves.

TRENDS IN MICROCOMPUTERS

Several emerging trends already mentioned will be further emphasized here. One of the most important is that many microcomputer manufacturers are designing their systems to be compatible with the IBM PC. IBM has become the industry leader.

Another trend is software "bundling," which means including, at no extra charge, multiple software programs with a computer system that is purchased; typically these programs include an operating system, a BASIC compiler, an electronic spreadsheet, a word processing program, and perhaps a file management program. Keyboards that are physically detached from the CPU are increasingly favored; with a long cord they can be moved about to enhance comfort and convenience of use.

Memory is being increased. Whereas 64K of main memory is now more or less the minimum in a business microcomputer, and a few micros reach 512K, 2 megabytes (2000 kilobytes) of main memory probably will be commonplace in the future. Also, greater data density on floppy disks is a clear trend; 320 kilobytes is common at the present time, but over 2 million kilobytes per 5¼-in. floppy disk is expected in the near future.

A related trend is toward even smaller disks; 3½-in. disks with very high density may become prominent. Sony Corporation has developed a 3½-in. floppy disk that is enclosed within a plastic cartridge and has high data density. These Sony disks are now included as a part of several microcomputers and are highly regarded.

The market for easily transportable computers is growing, since many users find easy transportability of a microcomputer a great convenience. For example, managers often wish to take a computer home for the weekend, and microcomputer hobbyists take them along on vacation. Transportables are barely small enough to fit under an airplane seat. Portable microcomputers—a new breed—are also now popular. A portable has about 64K of main memory and a several-line liquid crystal display in place of a monitor, and fits into an attaché case.

Decreasing costs are also affecting trends. Lower-cost printers and other peripheral devices mean that the typical microcomputer system will include more peripheral units with greater capabilities. As ROM prices drop, a greater proportion of microcomputer operating systems will be on ROM chips rather than offered as software programs. Bubble memory also should find its way into the microcomputer market in the form of mass (secondary) memory.

"Windows" are now on microcomputers. Windows permit one monitor screen to contain multiple screens, or windows, each of which displays data from different parts of a file or from entirely different files. Data can be transferred back and forth between windows. Windows are a convenient way of moving blocks of data, such as graphs, or a paragraph of a manuscript or letter. The user can also use each window as a work space to edit or enter data. As many as seven windows are a part of some window packages. Windows are thought to make microcomputers more user-friendly.

Integration of different types of software programs is also a clear trend. "Integration," as used here, means that software packages that perform different functions can be conveniently used together and, indeed, are purchased as one multifunction package. Most integrated packages are built around one central application that is more highly developed than the others. This central application may be a word processing function, a data base function, or an electronic spreadsheet. Graphing is a function that is frequently a part of an integrated package. To illustrate, by using the same integrated package, both data and text material can be retrieved from a file, placed in the cells of a spreadsheet, processed, and graphed.

Software development tools for microcomputers are becoming numerous and more sophisticated. These include microcomputer-based productivity languages and program generator software packages. Respectively, these are (1) languages that are easily learned and easily used by managers to develop applications and (2) software packages which are provided with vital information about what a needed computer program should accomplish and which then automatically write the code for the needed program.

One trend is the involvement of Japanese manufacturers in microcomputer markets. In the past, these manufacturers have had difficulty understanding the United States market and have lagged behind in developing microcomputer software. This is expected to change, however, and the competitive advantages of the Japanese in hardware reliability and low prices will make themselves felt. The Japanese are expected to become increasingly competitive with their microcomputers but probably will be even more competitive in the peripheral markets, which constitute 50 percent or more of the entire microcomputer hardware marketplace. Already, Japanese companies command a high proportion of the American market for microcomputer printers.

WHY ARE MICROCOMPUTER SYSTEMS IMPORTANT?

Microcomputers have great importance to today's business students primarily for one monumental reason—microcomputers are already widely used by managers in business, and the extent of their use is increasing at a phenomenal rate. Companies that in 1981 had no microcomputers for managerial use now may have hundreds or, in a few cases, thousands. All business students of today should study and gain experience with microcomputers for the simple but compelling reason that they will be using microcomputers for managerial analysis.

Microcomputers help managers extend their thinking; to an extent, they become an extension of managers' minds. At a microcomputer the manager's thoughts often can be quickly translated and placed in the computer system via the keyboard, and they are then processed almost as if the manager were mentally processing them. While this may be an exaggeration, nevertheless managers with extensive microcomputer experience report that they do think of the microcomputer as an extension of their own thinking capabilities.

There is little doubt at this time that the microcomputer revolution's effect on society and on business will be roughly comparable in magnitude to that of many major technological developments of the past, such as the steam engine and the airplane. Some observers believe that the microcomputer is bringing about an information systems equivalent of the industrial revolution.

Two analogies dramatize the microcomputer's importance to our society. The first involves the telegraph and the telephone. For the first time, the telegraph enabled people to communicate almost instantly over long distances. The telegraph was somewhat specialized and isolated, though, in that sending a telegram required traveling to a telegraph station to give the message to the operator for transmission. At the receiving end, the telegram had to be delivered or picked up. The telephone, a later invention, uses a similar technology consisting of lines across the country, but it allows an individual to use a telephone at home to directly dial another person with a home telephone. The telegraph is still in service and is still useful. However, the telephone popularized personal telecommunications, and hundreds of millions of telephones now exist, whereas telegraph stations are rather restricted in number. In information systems, the mainframe computer is analogous to the telegraph, and the microcomputer is analogous to the telephone.

The second analogy uses trains as the mainframe computer equivalent and automobiles as the microcomputer equivalent. Both trains and automobiles transport people over long distances on wheels using a mechanical apparatus combined with a power system. But individuals do not own trains; they only ride on them, and relatively few trains have come into existence. Automobiles, however, popularized the mechanical mode of transportation, and hundreds of millions of them now travel the world's roads.

The situation in the case of mainframe computers and microcomputers is similar. These technologies are not in conflict. Rather, mainframe computers handle specialized jobs, and relatively few of them exist, probably under 100,000. Microcomputers, on the other hand, have popularized computing. Microcomputers now number in the millions; soon they will number in the tens of millions, and one day perhaps in the hundreds of millions. It is expected that by 1990 microcomputers will easily dominate the entire computer industry in terms of dollar revenues to computer companies. The microcomputer can be expected to give individuals the same convenience in the realm of computing that automobiles and telephones offer in their spheres.

In the world of commerce, the impact of microcomputers may be profound. Some predictions are that by 1986 microcomputers will have the same speed as the largest mainframe computers of 1975, will be only one-fiftieth the size, and will cost only about one-hundredth as much. If the price declines and power increases are even half these amounts, the impact on business will be profound. Microcomputers can be expected to be used by functional-area personnel to perform a high proportion of the organization's transactions data processing, as well as for managerial analysis. Most micros will be dedicated to specific tasks, and most will be integrated via a distributed local area network system.

For example, in accounting departments, microcomputers probably will be dedicated to specialized accounting tasks—one may be dedicated to hourly payroll transactions processing, another to salaried payroll, another to accounts receivable transactions processing, another to maintaining stockholder records and preparing dividend checks, and so on. The typical accounting data processing workstation arrangement will involve multiple keyboards for each microcomputer, and this is also likely to be true in other functional areas.

These developments are occurring for several reasons. One is that most central data processing groups have large backlogs of applications for the mainframe computer, but users cannot wait and are turning to microcomputers on a "do-it-yourself" basis. The existence of systems development aids for microcomputers, such as application generators and productivity languages, facilitates this. Another reason for these developments is that in some instances (although by no means all), users prefer to control their own systems development and data processing schedules. This control is not possible when the applications are developed by professionals and run on mainframe computers, but it is possible when this is done by users themselves on their own microcomputers.

The computer revolution is, in some senses, bringing business data processing full circle. For three decades the dominant business data processing trend has been toward removing data processing responsibilities from the functional areas and centralizing them in ever-larger computer centers that have increasing returns to scale in terms of data processing efficiency. Now, however, microcomputers are also very cost-effective, and organizations are finding that with micros, data processing tasks can often be nearly as efficiently and much more effectively performed within the functional areas. To a substantial degree, data processing is being returned to the functional departments.

TWO FAMILIES OF MICROCOMPUTERS: APPLE AND IBM

An estimated 150 manufacturers produce microcomputers at the present time. Two manufacturers' product lines are examined briefly below.

Apple, one of the most successful companies in the microcomputer industry, holds a major share of the market and has played a large role in popularizing microcomputers. Apple has encouraged other software and hardware vendors to develop products designed to be used with Apple microcomputers. One estimate of the number of applications programs now available for Apple computers tops 11,000, of which Apple directly provides only a small proportion. In the past, Apple has used its own operating system, so Apple computers have not been compatible with other microcomputers; future Apple computers will probably have a degree of compatibility with IBM microcomputers. Experts generally agree that Apple computers are easy to use and reliable.

The overwhelming majority of Apple computer systems now in existence are 8-bit-word computers; however, in 1983 Apple introduced Lisa, a 16-bit-word microcomputer. The Apple product line includes the Apple II, Apple IIe, Apple Plus, Apple III, Apple III Plus, and Lisa computers.

The Macintosh Apple microcomputer, introduced in 1984, is intended to serve the home computer market, the low-end business market, and the university education market. The basic machine has 128K of main memory and a 9-in. high resolution display screen. Using advanced technology based on the much more costly Lisa, Macintosh has achieved unusual user friendliness; the retail price is in the $2000 range.

IBM has taken the microcomputer industry by storm, introducing its first microcomputer, the IBM Personal Computer (PC), in late 1981, several years after the microcomputer market emerged. Since then the IBM PC has captured a large part of the market, and many observers now consider it the dominant microcomputer. The PC is a 16-bit-word system. Exhibit 8.3 shows the PC's main circuit board, the actual size of which is 8½ by 12-in. Exhibit 8.4, a schematic of that same board, explains the location of the various components, such as the Intel micrcprocessor and the ROM and RAM chips. Note the slots for expansion modules; these can be used for a variety of purposes, one of the most common being to add random

EXHIBIT 8.3
The IBM PC's main
circuit board. (*Source:*
"Personal Computers,"
Scientific American,
December 1982.)

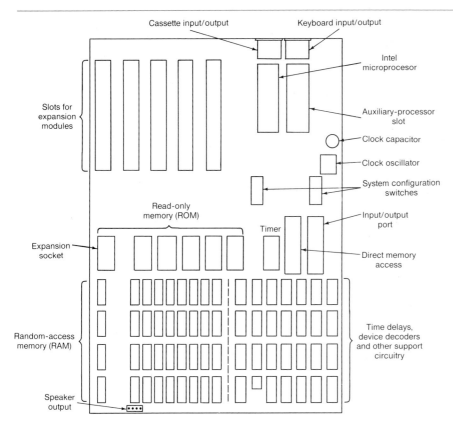

Cassette input/output

Keyboard input/output

Intel microprocesor

Slots for expansion modules

Auxiliary-processor slot

Clock capacitor

Clock oscillator

System configuration switches

Read-only memory (ROM)

Timer

Input/output port

Expansion socket

Direct memory access

Random-access memory (RAM)

Time delays, device decoders and other support circuitry

Speaker output

EXHIBIT 8.4
A schematic of the IBM PC's main circuit board.

MAIN CIRCUIT BOARD of the IBM Personal Computer is shown in the photograph on page 260 and its major elements are identified in the drawing above. The size of the board is 8½ by 12 inches. To it are attached a large number of silicon chips carrying integrated circuits; each chip is about a quarter of an inch square and is encased in a rectangular plastic package fitted with electrodes. The chips and elements such as resistors and capacitors are interconnected by conductors printed on the board. The microprocessor, the 16-bit 8088 made by the Intel Corporation, has 20,000 transistors and operates at a frequency of almost five million cycles per second. "System programs" are stored permanently in the read-only memory (ROM); random-access memory (RAM) stores programs and data that change from time to time.

Source: "Personal Computers", *Scientific American*, December, 1982

access memory board. The expansion slots can also be used for semidisk memory; for boards that serve as interfaces for external peripheral equipment such as printers, plotters, and telecommunications equipment; or for other purposes.

Vendors other than IBM already offer several thousand programs and additional peripheral equipment for the IBM PC, and the number is increasing rapidly—a cottage industry has emerged, with literally thousands of companies, both small and large, producing software or hardware products for the PC. One of the major reasons for the PC's success is its popularity with large companies.

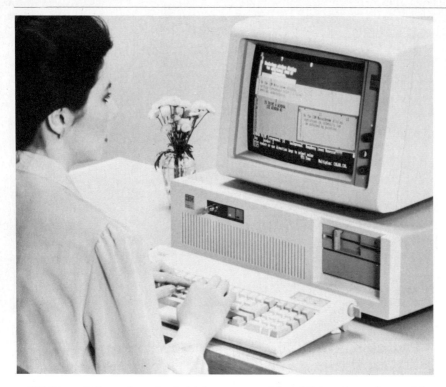

EXHIBIT 8.5
The IBM Personal
Computer AT. (*Courtesy
of IBM Corporation.*)

IBM has followed up its initial success with additional products. The IBM PC XT is an "extended" PC that includes a hard disk unit and runs all programs that can be run on the PC.

The IBM PC XT/370 is an upgraded IBM PC XT that permits the unit to function in "emulation mode" as an IBM 370 series mainframe computer so that IBM 370 programs can be run and developed on the PC XT/370; this gives this microcomputer extreme compatibility with IBM mainframe computers and also makes available to it a large number of IBM 370 software packages. This microcomputer can also run all IBM PC programs.

The IBM 3270 Personal Computer can display up to seven windows. It can serve not only as a microcomputer compatible with the IBM PC but also as an IBM 3270 terminal connected to the mainframe.

The IBM PC JR is the low-end product and comes in two versions. The entry version has 128K of main memory and is in the $1000-plus range with an inexpensive monitor and printer; it uses software cartridges similar to video-game cartridges rather than floppy disks. An enhanced model has 256K of main memory, a floppy disk, and other enhancements. The PC JR has only limited compatibility with the PC.

In August 1984, IBM introduced the IBM Personal Computer AT (for Advanced Technology). Based on the Intel 80286 microprocessor chip that is about three to five times as fast and powerful as the Intel 8088 chip used in the IBM PC and XT, the AT is hailed by some as a next-generation microcomputer and the first "desktop mainframe." Illustrated in Exhibit 8.5, the AT is available in a base model and an enhanced model, the former with a 1.2M floppy disk drive (compared with a 360K floppy disk in the PC and XT) and the latter with a 1.2M floppy and a 20M hard disk within the cabinet. Both models can be beefed up to have as much as 3M of main memory (compared to 640K for the IBM PC and XT) and to include two 20M hard disks; the maximum memory (including main memory, a floppy disk, and two hard disks) is 41.2M, an amount that dwarfs the maximum of the IBM PC and XT. Multiuser operating systems will be available for the AT.

The AT is able to run the IBM software for the PC and XT. Estimates are that 80–90 percent of the non-IBM software for the PC and XT can also be run on the AT. The base price for the enhanced AT model is less than $6000.

Other vendors are certain to introduce similarly powerful desktop microcomputers. With this development, inexpensive, very powerful microcomputers that are fully capable of medium-scale transactions and other data processing tasks become a practical reality.

GETTING STARTED WITH MICROCOMPUTERS

The payoff thought at the beginning of this chapter advises that it is wise to start learning about micros as soon as possible. But how does the student begin? Assuming that there is no specific deadline, a simple, inexpensive strategy is to purchase either a very low cost micro or a more sophisticated but used one. In general, a used micro is a better value for this purpose because its price is often 40 to 60 percent of the cost of a comparable new computer; yet it retains its original functional utility, and extra components and extensive software may be thrown in free. An 8-bit-word computer with a CP/M operating system, or a used Apple computer are likely selections in terms of a blend of economy, capabilities, and program availability.

For an organization, one possible approach is to choose an employee volunteer to begin using a microcomputer (perhaps even at home). This opportunity to become the organization's microcomputer expert should appeal to employees who are trying to find a competitive edge. The organization should allocate to this person a sum of money (perhaps around $1000) to find and purchase a microcomputer system, which the person then is able to keep permanently. After a few months, this new "expert"—who by then may actually *be* an expert—assumes the responsibility for analyzing the organization's needs for microcomputers, recommending a microcomputer, and developing a plan for using the microcomputer productively.

The person selected should have managerial instincts rather than be primarily a technical person. A managerial orientation provides greater assurance that the organization's needs with respect to how microcomputers should be used will be properly identified. Additionally, a technical person is too likely to overestimate the ability of nontechnical personnel to adapt to, accept, and productively use a microcomputer system; as a result, the microcomputer selected may have technical superiority but not be sufficiently user-friendly. There are, of course, endless variations on the scenario outlined here. For example, selecting two persons rather than one to begin using micros introduces a competitive element and increases the chance that one, at least, will be successful.

Persons interested in exploring microcomputers should review the journals in the field. These include *BYTE, Mini-Micro Systems, InfoWorld, Personal Computing, Microcomputing,* and *Creative Computing* to name but a few.

SUMMARY

Microcomputers are an exciting new world. They are revolutionizing computing because managers no longer must depend on specialized technical personnel to gain convenient access to computer power. The outstanding characteristics of microcomputers are their small size (due to chip technology), low cost, and user friendliness. Microcomputer systems can include monitors, disk drives, printers, and modems, as well as software packages, and micros can even be configured for dual-processing and multiworkstation capabilities. Specialized plotters and printers, speech synthesizers, and semidisks are other types of peripheral equipment that is available.

The major business users of microcomputers are clerical personnel and managers in functional departments, and word processing personnel. Extensive software is available for general accounting, financial analysis and modeling, decision support systems, and most often types of data processing. Microcomputers can be linked to information services such as The Source and CompuServe and to consumer shopping services such as Telephone Software Connections.

A major problem in the microcomputer marketplace is software and equipment incompatibility, not only between microcomputers but also between them and mainframes. Progress is being made toward reducing this limitation and others.

Microcomputer industry trends include a growing market, software bundling, decreasing hardware prices, more communications and networking use of micros, an increased involvement of Japanese manufacturers, the growing availability of turnkey systems, portable micros, integration within software programs, windows, and program development aids. Because microcomputers can in effect become an extension of mangers' minds, they have the potential to revolutionize management.

Microcomputers have a social significance that can be likened to that of telephones and automobiles. For business data processing, microcomputers are returning the direct management and control of much of organizations' data processing to the functional areas, where microcomputers are located.

KEY TERMS

modem: a piece of peripheral equipment that allows the transmission of data over telephone lines.

speech synthesizer: a device that enables a microcomputer to create voicelike sounds and broadcast them over a speaker system.

semidisk: an MOS RAM chip on a board added to a microcomputer, with accompanying software that makes the RAM of the chip act as if it were a floppy disk.

compatibility: the ability of pieces of peripheral equipment or software components to be used together as a part of the same computer system.

MS DOS: an operating system that is compatible with most programs used by the IBM PC.

software bundling: including multiple software programs at no extra cost when a microcomputer system is purchased.

BIOS: a microcomputer's basic input-output system, which is part of the operating system and controls input-output data flows.

turnkey system: a set of hardware and software components sold as a complete computer system and intended to accomplish specific data processing tasks.

REFERENCES

McWilliams, Peter A., *The Personal Computer Book,* Los Angeles: Prelude Press, 1982.

Microcomputers: Their Use and Misuse in Your Business, New York: Price Waterhouse, 1983.

Toong, Hoo-min D., and Amar. Gupta, "Personal Computers," *Scientific American,* December 1982, p. 86.

REVIEW QUESTIONS

1. Discuss some of the reasons for the excitment about microcomputers. How do you, personally, feel about microcomputers? How do you feel about mainframe computers?

2. In what senses are micros "personal" computers?

3. Describe a typical microcomputer system.

4. Define a microcomputer.

5. What is a dual-processing microcomputer? How is this different from a multi-processing computer system?

6. What components, parts, and peripherals are required for a microcomputer?

7. Can you think of ways that speech synthesizers might be used?

8. Is each of the groups of microcomputer users mutually exclusive? Explain.

9. Discuss the different attitudes of professional data processing personnel toward the use of microcomputers.

10. What are the general categories of microcomputer use in the office environment?

11. If you have used both a large computer system and a microcomputer, compare the user friendliness of each.

12. Discuss the microcomputer incompatibility problem, including incompatibility with mainframes.

13. What are the limitations of microcomputers?

14. If you have used a microcomputer, did you experience any frustration? If so, explain.

15. How do microcomputers both enhance and inhibit information security?

16. What are several of the emerging trends in the microcomputer industry?

17. What is software bundling?

18. How can an individual break into the world of microcomputers? How can an organization become involved with microcomputers?

19. Why should an organization's microcomputer expert be a manager rather than a technical person?

20. What is there about microcomputers that encourages their use for traditional data processing tasks by functional departments?

CASE 1

California Insurance Company of Hartford

Bob Santana is the director of MIS for a medium-sized insurance company in Hartford, Connecticut, "the insurance capital of the world." He has called in a consultant (you) and poured forth the following story.

"I've been in this computing business for more than two decades—I've almost grown up with computers—and I've been the director or the assistant director of information systems for 10 years. During that time, and before, I've been involved in continuous fire fights with user groups. On the one hand, of course, they are our customers, and I recognize that we must given them what they need. On the other hand, I do not believe that what they want is always what they need or should have. For example, we went through a period when every major division wanted its own data processing center and mainframe computer, with each center staffed by its own data processing personnel. We managed to beat them back and have retained a fully centralized data processing organization, but it was a tough battle. Now we have hundreds of terminals throughout the company that connect directly to our two large IBM 3081 computers.

"Then there was the data base question, which caused another ruckus about 5 years ago. That's not fully settled even yet, at least not to my satisfaction. There were demands from most user groups that they have their own data bases so that they could control their contents and usage. A few users went in the other direction, saying that there should be only a limited number of data bases within the entire company, and some even said that there should be only one large data base for the entire company. My own data processing people had their own ideas, particularly about which DBMS we should have. With this question, we have let the will of the majority rule. We now have many different data bases and use two generalized DBMSs—IMS and ADABAS, both of which are large-scale, sophisticated DBMSs. We also have several limited-purpose DBMSs. Most of the data bases break down along departmental lines; for example, the payroll department has three separate data bases up: two on ADABAS and one on IMS. Of course, having so many data bases makes each one easier to maintain, but it does cause some problems too, and I'm not certain that it's good for the organization.

"There have been two long-term problems that we've never been able to deal with satisfactorily, and they are still very much with us. The first is that we have never been able to hire enough highly qualified professional personnel. This has been a problem with all companies, and we have probably done as well as the others, but we often employ lower-quality programmers than we would like, for example, and then they often stay only a couple of years before they leave for a better job.

"In the meantime, because we don't have enough good people to do the jobs that must be done, I have to take special precautions with all my people to see that they don't waste too much time letting users cry on their shoulders about trivial systems problems or new applications that we simply do not have time to bring up on the computer. In effect, I must insulate my group from the users; I recognize that this causes high user frustration levels, but users must realize the necessity for this— with limited staff we have to do things in an orderly, sequential way and cannot charge off in all directions.

"The other problem, which is related, is the backlog problem. One would expect that after all these years we would start running out of demand for new applications, but just the opposite is true.

Most of my systems development budget goes for program maintenance—about 60 percent—and the combined backlog for maintenance and new applications is about 3 years. Even beyond this, there are jobs that users don't even formally put on our backlog list because the list is already so long; some I probably don't even get told about.

"A final problem is a relatively new one, and so far I'm losing this battle. During the past 2 years, end users have started to purchase hordes of microcomputers. They are being used by everyone for everything, it seems, but especially for Lotus 1-2-3 spreadsheet kinds of applications and for fairly small jobs using BASIC, although a few users are also running PASCAL, COBOL, and even data base programs. The majority of these applications are developed by the users themselves, although some are purchased applications programs such as accounts receivables or accounts payable that are used for specialized jobs. I'm amazed at the variety of applications.

"I have been unsuccessful in getting a policy established that lets me control this proliferation of microcomputers. There are questions of organizational jurisdiction, duplication of software purchases, and standardization of hardware and software, to name but a few. Also, there is the fact that, collectively, microcomputers total to a whole bunch of money. Further, I am not certain that micros even have a major role to play in an organization as big as we are. But even our top-level systems steering committee is ambivalent about the problem and has taken no action; I know that at least three of its eleven members have a microcomputer in their office or their assistant's office, and I found this out just by chance.

"How can I combat the microcomputer problem? What's it going to lead to? I need to know, if for no other reason than because I can't do coherent planning without some idea of what will happen with microcomputers in our organization in the future."

Instructions

1. As the consultant, address in a general way all the points other than the microcomputer question.

2. As the consultant, address all aspects of the microcomputer issue in detail. As a part of your answer, be certain to address the two questions raised by Bob Santana. *Hint:* Think of the interrelatedness of the circumstances and problems of the case.

Case prepared by George M. Scott.

CASE 2

Microcomputers Gaining Primacy, Forcing Changes in the Industry

By Willian M. Bulkeley
Staff Reporter for The Wall Street Journal

Personal computers and other microcomputers are well on their way to becoming the biggest part of the computer industry.

Just as automobiles surpassed trains as the biggest sector of the transportation industry after the turn of the century, microcomputer sales will surpass mainframes during this decade, experts predict. So fast are sales soaring that, according to some estimates, sales of microcomputers will exceed to $6 billion this year, topping the 20-year-old minicomputer industry. Companies in every part of the computer industry are rushing to tap the vast market for micros in big and small business.

The change is profound, because the predominance of mainframes, the giant computers often costing millions of dollars, has long been taken for granted. Through the 1970s, minicomputers—which are smaller and more accessible than mainframes and often bear prices in the $20,000 to $100,000 range—were the fastest-growing sector of the industry. The most powerful minis became as capable, and almost as expensive, as the smallest mainframes.

Squeezing Out Minicomputers

Now, however, most industry observers think microcomputers will squeeze all but the most powerful minicomputers out of the marketplace. Microcomputers are built around microprocessors—computers on a single chip of silicon the size of a fingernail. They include: personal computers for home use and costing from $80 to $1,000; personal computers for individual use in offices and costing as much as $5,000; and the most sophisticated small-business and engineering computers, which may cost as much as $30,000—for more than the cheapest minicomputers. . . .

Howard Anderson, president of Yankee Group, a Boston-based consulting firm, estimates that 150 computer makers are selling microcomputers. They range from International Business Machines, which joined the rush in 1981, to brand-new "start-up" companies.

Most of these outfits buy microprocessors from semiconductor companies such as Intel Corp. or Motorola Inc. and license the necessary software. Since the development work is largely done elsewhere, costs are low, and a company can produce a working model within a year. Says Mr. Anderson, exaggerating somewhat: "There are companies entering the business that 90 days ago thought a Z-80 was the top-of-the-line Datsun." (A Z-80 is a microprocessor designed by Exxon Corp.'s Zilog subsidiary.)

Clearly part of the motivation here is all the money to be made. Companies that have been profitable selling big computers one at a time are trying to figure out how to sell thousands of little ones. Software producers that make money selling a big insurance company a $50,000 package to manage computer data are trying to write software that will do the same thing on an Apple for an insurance agency. Such a package might sell for only $1,500, but the potential volume makes it worthwhile. International Data Corp. estimates there are 56,000 mainframe computers in the U.S. and 570,000 minicomputers. It says 2.4 million microcomputers were sold last year alone—and they all need software.

Here is a look at how three different types of companies—a microcomputer company, a software company and a computer distributor—see the market and their place in it. . .

McCormack & Dodge Corp.

Finance and accounting software written by this Needham, Mass., concern runs on mainframe computers at dozens of the biggest U.S. companies. But by the time McCormack & Dodge looked into converting the software to microcomputers, it concluded "that market is already saturated," says Robert K. Weiler, vice president for marketing.

Instead, the company is developing for its corporate customers software that will make it easier for a microcomputer user to extract information from corporate data bases stored on mainframes. "We're looking at the marriage of micro and mainframe," Mr. Weiler says. "That big machine in the basement will function as a library," storing and finding information for microcomputer users, he predicts.

Microcomputers are more economical than mainframes for many corporate jobs. McCormack & Dodge experimented with drawing graphs of financial projections. On a mainframe, one graph cost $36 in computer time. On the microcomputer the cost was six cents. "With the mainframe, you're

moving a dinosaur. You have to match the function to the task," Mr. Weiler says.

Plans such as Mr. Weiler's could mean larger sales of mainframe computers. Mayford Roark, executive director of systems management for Ford Motor Co., says, "People using microcomputers have increased demands on mainframes in our experience." Ford recently chose Victor Technologies Corp.'s Victor 9000 as its microcomputer, and Mr. Roark says Ford will probably buy 1,500 such computers this year, triple the number installed now.

Source: Abridged from *The Wall Street Journal,* Jan. 13, 1983, p. 33.

Case Questions

1. What are the implications for mainframe computers of the surge in sales of microcomputers?

2. What is involved in having microcomputers communicate with mainframes? Of what use is this to managers?

3. How many microcomputer manufacturers do you expect will exist in 1990? What are the implications of your conclusion for a company's decision now about which microcomputer system to purchase?

CASE 3

Imitators Are Starting to Go After Market for the Popular IBM Personal Computer

By Richard A. Shaffer
Staff Reporter for The Wall Street Journal

The clones are beginning to attack what eventually could become the largest part of the personal-computer market.

Because International Business Machines Corp. dwarfs the rest of the other computer makers combined, its powerful mainframe computers long have tempted imitators. In recent years, they have captured a tenth of the sales of such data processors. Now that IBM's year-old Personal Computer is proving so popular, the copiers—or IBM-compatible manufacturers, as they call themselves—are going after its market as well.

Today, Compaq Computer Corp. of Houston is

planning to announce the fifth, and by some accounts the most interesting, of the IBM imitations. The Compaq computer is to be priced at $2,995, or about $800 less than the IBM product. It is quite portable, weighing only 28 pounds. It provides two built-in disk data-storage units, together with a keyboard and a nine-inch display screen. It runs all major IBM programs without modification.

"We think the Compaq will appeal primarily to companies who already have a large investment in IBM personal computers and the software and training for them, and who want a few portable machines for employees to take home nights or weekends or on field assignments," says Compaq President Rod Canion.

Compaq plans to sell the portable model through dealers who already carry the IBM line. "I see it as a valuable companion product to my IBMs, not as competition," says Ed Ramos, president of Futuredata, a New York retailer.

The importance, however, of machines that work like IBM's Personal Computer but aren't made by IBM goes beyond the fortunes of their manufacturers. These imitations could help would-be IBM customers save money or obtain features, such as portability, that IBM doesn't offer.

The imitations also could allow retailers who can't get the IBM product to profit from the demand for it. And, most significantly, the clones' success or failure may provide some guide to the prospects of the widely feared Japanese manufacturers, who faltered in their first venture into the U.S. personal-computer market but are preparing another foray, this time with IBM-like manchines.

The market in Japan for personal computers is growing so rapidly that most Japanese manufacturers aren't able to meet local demand and don't plan to seriously go after the American market until well into next year. But they are developing computers that will run at least some IBM programs hoping to avoid the inadequate software and confusing instruction manuals that have been such a handicap to date.

"IBM compatibility is absolutely necessary for companies getting into the personal-computer market," says Ed Faber, president of ComputerLand, the nation's largest group of franchised computer retailers. "There's no doubt that the Japanese machines will take this route. The only question is how far they'll go beyond it."

Several U.S. companies already are prospering with imitations of such well-known personal computers as those made by Apple Computer Inc. and Tandy Corp. Only a year ago, for example, Franklin Computer Corp. of Pennsauken, N.J., introduced an Apple clone, the Ace. Today the company is selling about 1,500 Aces a month. That's less than 1% of what Apple itself sells, but it amounts to about $27 million in annual retail sales. "The market has really been a lot better than we expected," says Jan Wright, Franklin's advertising manager.

Columbia Data Products Inc., of Columbia,

Md., expects to do equally well with its IBM imitation, the Multi-Personal Computer. "IBM cannot meet the demand for its Personal Computer and people aren't going to wait," says Jack Horner, a company manager.

IBM clones could be even more significant than Apple or Tandy copies because most of the independent software companies, which develop the bulk of the preferred personal-computer programs, are concentrating on writing IBM programs. That emphasis practically guarantees that major new software will first become available for the IBM. To have any hope of offering it, other brands of computer will need some IBM compatibility.

But compatibility is a complex issue, and one that seems certain to confuse personal-computer buyers.

Many of the new personal computers, particularly those from Japan, are being built around the microprocessor used in the IBM product, the Intel Corp. 8088, and the closely related 8086. In addition, several dozen companies have licensed the principal language and operating system, or housekeeping program, that IBM uses, Microsoft Basic and MS-DOS by Microsoft of Bellevue, Wash.

Few of those computers, however, can run IBM programs without modification because of what might seem to be minor differences in the data-storage attachments, keyboards, video circuits of BIOS. The BIOS, or Basic Input-Output System, is a program that adapts a standard operating system, such as MS-DOS, to the electronic idiosyncrasies of a given brand of machine.

No practical machine could be completely IBM-compatible without duplicating the IBM computer, an action that would violate copyright and patent laws.

Thus, the term "fully compatible" usually refers to a computer that attachments and improvements designed for the IBM will fit. Such a computer also would enable a user to buy an IBM program and run it on the look-alike machine merely by following the instructions and video-screen diagrams in the manual.

Few of the new computers that are often described as IBM-compatible fully meet such a test. For example, the recently announced DOT computer from Computer Devices Inc. of Burlington, Mass., stores its programs and data on magnetic disks that are only three inches in diameter. Thus the DOT cannot directly use IBM programs, which are on five-inch disks. Dynalogic Info-Tech Corp. of Ottawa, Canada, has used a different keyboard and video-display system for its IBM clone, the Hyperion. Datamac Computer Systems Inc. of Sunnyvale, Calif., relies on a different microprocessor for its series 1600.

At the Japan elecronics show in Tokyo, which ended on Monday, six major Japanese companies displayed IBM-compatible personal computers. However, the Intel 8088 microprocessor isn't used in three of them—the Hitachi Ltd., Mitsubishi Electric Corp. and Nippon Electric Co. computers—and that reduces their compatibility. Matsushita Electric Industrial Co., Sanyo Electric Co. and Toshiba Corp. all use the 8088 as well as the IBM languages and operating system.

Sanyo, however, which plans to sell its MBC-55 in the U.S. starting next summer for about $1,000, says the computer won't run such important programs as IBM VisiCalc, a popular program for financial modeling. Matsushita, which plans to begin selling its JB-3000 in the U.S. under the Panasonic brand next spring, says it will give buyers a special utility program for converting IBM programs to run on its computer. Toshiba says it intends to rely primarily on programs of its own for the Pansopia 16.

Even compatibility isn't enough, however, retailers and computer makers agree. Datamac, for example, believes its look-alike is far superior to the original, but doesn't plan to compete directly with IBM, concentrating instead on large customers, such as companies that already own many personal computers. "We make a better machine," says Sam Goodman, Datamac's executive vice president, "but even that's not enough to compete at the retail level with IBM."

Adds Mr. Faber of Computerland, "The new machines will have to run IBM software, and then offer some considerable advantage just to offset the halo effect of the IBM name. You cannot just come out with an IBM copy and expect to get a major market share.

Source: The Wall Street Journal, Nov. 4, 1982.

Case Questions

1. What trends discussed in the chapter does this case illustrate?

2. Explore the concept of "IBM compatibility." In what ways may the term "fully compatible" be accurately applied, and in what ways may this compatibility be lacking, even if a computer, program, or peripheral device is advertised as fully compatible?

Chapter 9

DATA COMMUNICATIONS AND DISTRIBUTED PROCESSING SYSTEMS

PAYOFF THOUGHT

Major technological breakthroughs in the communications arena are now occurring. Students should pay particular attention to these developments because they will have a dramatic impact on the information systems of companies in the next few years.

CHAPTER OBJECTIVES

1. To explore the technology of data communications and distributed data processing and to show their importance to information systems

2. To give students a managerial understanding of distributed data processing, which rests on data communications technology

DATA COMMUNICATIONS

Why must data be transported from one physical location to another? There are several answers to this question. Perhaps the most important are these:

1. Transactions often occur at a place different from the place where the data resulting from those transactions will be processed or used. Therefore, the transactions data must be transported to the processing location and then perhaps transported again to another location for use.

2. It is often economical to send messages such as letters through the organization's own communications systems rather than through external systems, such as the United States mail. Using its own communications systems for "electronic mail," an organization can send messages that arrive within seconds of the time of departure and at a fraction of the cost of alternative methods.

3. An organization with multiple processing centers may find it worthwhile to balance its work loads by moving data to be processed from one center where the computer system is overloaded to another where the work load is light.

4. When data can be sent to another site to be processed or reported, expensvie equipment, such as specialized graphics or plotting equipment or ultra-high-speed printers, is needed at only one location, reducing overall costs to the organization. Software packages that are kept at only one location can also be shared in this manner.

Data can be transported from one place to another in many ways. One possibility is by foot messenger. Probably the most famous foot messenger is the Greek runner who ran 26 miles with news of a great war victory and died as soon as he delivered it; this is the likely origin of the modern-day marathon run.

Data delivery by foot messenger is still common in today's business world, although the distances are shorter. In every organization data and reports of all types are delivered to managers by messengers from other parts of the organization. Any visitor to a large office building is likely to see many clerical personnel in the elevators carrying portfolios of data or reports to managers on another floor. Automated office information systems have the potential to substantially reduce such personal data delivery within organizations.

Many companies use automobiles to carry data and reports from their data center to other corporate locations. Mail and various commercial parcel delivery services, such as United Parcel Service, regularly deliver data and reports. It is an unusual airline flight that does not carry magnetic-tape data files to a destination in another city.

Electronic transmission has long been one form of data transportation; this mode originated with the telegraph system, which has existed for well over a century. Recent developments in electronic data transmission have greatly increased the data traffic over electronic transmission systems, which are usually termed "telecommunications systems." Many large organizations already have extensive telecommunications systems. Technological advances will continue to make this mode of data transportation even more popular in the future. Some of these advances will be examined in this chapter.

TELECOMMUNICATIONS SYSTEMS

A Simple Data Transmission System

Exhibit 9.1 illustrates three simple types of telecommunications systems. All three are "off-line" in that none are connected to a data processing system. The first two types, those shown in Exhibit 9.1a, b, existed long

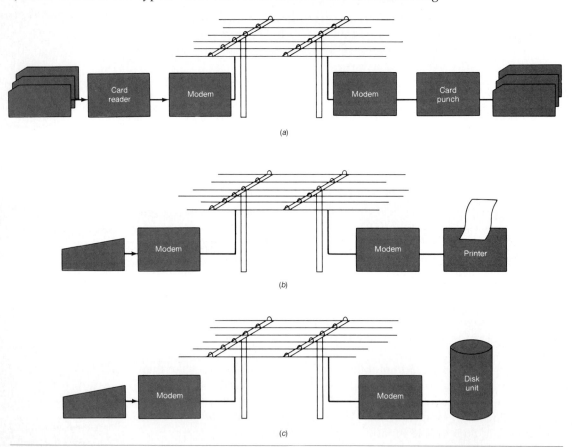

EXHIBIT 9.1
Off-line data communications.

before computers were invented. Exhibit 9.1*a* illustrates a punched-card system, whereby data is punched into cards which are read by a card reader and is then converted to electronic impulses by a machine. The data is then transmitted over telephone lines to the receiving station, where the electronic impulses enter a card-punch machine, which creates a deck of cards identical to that at the sending end. These cards at the receiving station can then be read into the computer system. This card-to-card approach is relatively slow and labor-intensive because the cards must be punched and then loaded to the card reader and at the other end the new cards must be removed from the card-punch machine. Punched-card telecommunications systems also have low data transmissions rates.

Exhibit 9.1*b* illustrates a remote terminal through which data is entered to the telecommunications system, being printed out at the receiving station. News services such as United Press International (UPI) and Associated Press (AP) have used variations of this technology to transmit news stories to newspapers around the country.

Exhibit 9.1*c* shows a system that resembles what a preceding chapter discussed as a key-to-disk system. The difference, however, is that the terminal that inputs data to the disk unit is at a distant location; thus the data is telecommunicated to the disk unit.

Each of the examples in Exhibit 9.1 utilizes common-carrier telecommunications lines, a high proportion of which are various types and grades of ordinary telephone lines. However, the data generated at the source is in digital form, whereas most existing telecommunications lines transmit only analog data.

Digital and analog transmission are of the forms illustrated in Exhibit 9.2. To interface digital data with an analog system requires converting the digital data to analog data. This is accomplished by a modulator-demodulator device, a term commonly shortened to "modem," as in the exhibit. Before being entered to the telecommunications lines, data is "modulated," that is, converted to analog form by a modem; when transmission is complete, the data must be converted back to digital form, or "demodulated," also by a modem. The modulation and demodulation functions are different and could be accomplished by separate devices. In practice, most stations both receive and transmit data, using a dual-purpose modulation-demodulation device. All three examples shown in Exhibit 9.1 use modems.

Modems are relatively inexpensive devices; their cost is a function of the speed of the data transmission they are required to handle and of any

Digital   Analog   Digital

Conversion: digital–analog–digital

EXHIBIT 9.2
Digital and analog transmission forms.

special characteristics they might have. For microcomputers, a low-speed modem of 300 characters per second can be purchased for under $200. A higher-speed microcomputer modem of 1200 characters per second may cost about $600. Some microcomputer modems are "smart," such as the Hayes Smartmodem. Smartmodems may, for example, automatically receive data without human intervention that is transmitted from a remote computer.

TELECOMMUNICATIONS LINES

Telecommunications lines can be classified according to data flow characteristics, speed, and whether they are switched or private lines.

Data Flow Characteristics

Data transmission lines may be simplex, half-duplex, or full-duplex. Simplex lines, which permit data transmission in just one direction, are used only in specialized circumstances where data flows only one way, for example, where the computer transmits sales orders to the warehouse so that warehouse personnel can prepare the shipment. Normally the warehouse personnel would have no reason to use the line that brings them order information; if they have questions, they are more likely to use the telephone rather than query the computer system.

A half-duplex line permits data transmission in both directions, but not at the same time. Half-duplex lines are more expensive than simplex lines but less costly than full-duplex lines. Full-duplex lines permit data transmission in both directions simultaneously.

Exhibit 9.3 illustrates different line grades. Narrowband lines, sometimes referred to as "subvoice-grade lines," have the lowest bits-per-second transmission rate and can be used with slow-speed devices such as remote terminals. Voiceband lines are capable of supporting the human voice; all telephone lines are of at least this grade. Most data transmitted by microcomputers would utilize voiceband lines. Broadband lines, which

Types of Data Communications Lines

EXHIBIT 9.3

Line Type	Speed	Total Cost	Average Cost per Bit	Error Rate
Narrow Band (subvoice grade)	50–300 bits per second	Low	High	High
Voiceband	300–500 bits per second	Medium	Medium	Medium
Broadband	To 1 million bits per second	High	Low	Low

have transmission speeds up to about 1 million bits per second, are used for remote job entry (RJE) when transactions are batched together for rapid transmission and in situations where two high-speed computers are communicating directly with each other over telecommunications lines. Undersea cables are one example of broadband lines.

Exhibit 9.3 indicates two characteristics typically associated with increased speed and capacity of the transmission lines. The first is that as speed and capacity increase, total cost for data elements transmitted over a heavily utilized broadband line will be substantially lower than the average cost for data elements communicated over a heavily used narrowband line. The second characteristic is that, in general, as line capacity increases, the data transmission error rate decreases; however, the error rate is also a function of the individual line characteristics.

Switched versus Private Lines

A switched-line system involves data transmission through a series of switching stations which reroute the data so that it does not travel on just one line from its origin to its destination, but rather is switched from line to line. This is typically the case with telephone system lines, for example. Switched lines are sometimes termed "dial-up lines" because they normally involve dialing an ordinary telephone or telephonelike device and paying on a per-call basis. Dialing destinations within the range of a local telephone call does not cost extra; for destinations outside the local call zone, long-distance rates take effect.

The telephone company computers switch the data transmissions, whether they are telephone conversations or computer data transmissions, according to criteria such as the shortest route, the route with the least traffic, and the lines least likely to cause data errors. This means, for example, that on one occasion data sent by a company from New York to Los Angeles might take a route from New York to Philadelphia and then to Pittsburgh, to Detroit, to Chicago, to Salt Lake City, and finally to Los Angeles, while on the next occasion data might go from New York, to Atlanta, to Dallas, to Phoenix, and finally to Los Angeles.

Which route data will take in a switched-line system cannot be known in advance. Most switched-line systems use ordinary telephone lines, which were developed to support the human voice. These lines vary in quality with respect to line noise, attenuation, and echoes. Such variations are not a major problem with voice communication, but they cause errors in data transmission. Conditions such as electric storms in one region may also cause data loss or errors. Accordingly, one transmission by an organization from point A to point B may be almost error-free, while the very next transmission from point A to point B may contain numerous data transmission errors. Telecommunications systems have elaborate means of detecting the occurrence of errors; transmission errors usually require retransmission of the data.

Private lines are one approach to reducing the error rate. The first of the two types of private lines is a dedicated line leased from a common-carrier company such as American Telephone and Telegraph. An organization pays for the exclusive use of the dedicated line, which can be "conditioned." Conditioning is a process of testing and "insulating" the line against the occurrence of errors. Conditioned dedicated lines can minimize data transmission error rates.

Another type of private line is a line that the organization owns for the purpose of transmitting its own data. Although this situation is unusual, it may occur when a company owns a large tract of land that gives it the right-of-way for its own telecommunications system.

Wide Area Telephone Service (WATS) is a type of semiprivate line on which an organization leases a certain amount of time monthly; other organizations may also be leasing time on that same line. A rate is set for the time contracted for on the basis of the distance the data travels. There is an extra charge for time used beyond the contracted amount.

American Telephone and Telegraph and other organizations are developing digital telecommunications services. The AT&T service, known as Digital Data Service (DDS), is intended to encompass 96 cities eventually. This system, however, is not fully installed at the present time. Digital data transmission does not require conversion of data from digital to analog form, and consequently modems are unnecessary. Digital Data Service also has a greatly reduced error rate during transmission, which by itself makes digital transmission more desirable than analog transmission. Several European countries already have extensive digital line service.

COMPUTER-CONTROLLED DATA TRANSMISSION

Data transmission can be on-line, with a computer directly receiving the transmitted data. Exhibit 9.4 illustrates this. Exhibit 9.4a shows a remote typewriter terminal transmitting data directly to a computer at a distant location. Exhibit 9.4b illustrates several terminals doing this; the computer must control the input of each, which is a simple but time-consuming activity for the CPU. To relieve the CPU of this chore, a "communications front-end device," variously called a "communications controller," a "front-end processor," or simply a "front-end device," is typically used to control the remote terminals and other remote data input devices. This communications device, which may be a microcomputer or minicomputer configured for this purpose, edits data received to determine whether there are errors or whether the data needs to be forwarded to another destination. The front-end device maintains a message log assigning each incoming message a serial number, date, and time, and it forwards data intended for another destination within the communications network after adding that destination code. When receiving data from low-speed devices

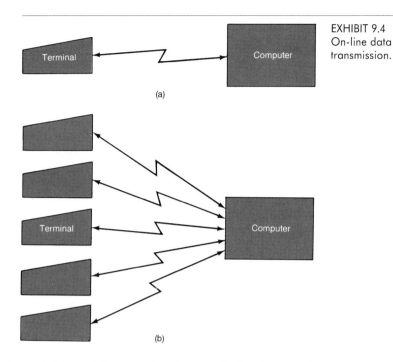

EXHIBIT 9.4
On-line data
transmission.

(a)

(b)

that are transmitting in serial form (character by character), the front-end device will also convert the data into parallel form, which permits multiple characters to enter the CPU simultaneously; this is another way in which the front-end device enables the CPU to utilize its time much more efficiently.

If the sending terminals are within a few miles of the computer system, data transmission costs can be low. However, if the terminals (which are low-speed devices) are far from the computer system, as in Exhibit 9.5a, data transmission costs may be very high because long-distance rates are paid for each of the multiple lines. To reduce such costs, a multiplexor is often used, as shown in Exhibit 9.5b. The purpose of the multiplexor is to merge ("multiplex") the data streams from multiple low-speed input devices so that the full capacity of the transmission line to the computer system is utilized. At their destination the multiplexed data streams must be demultiplexed and reassembled into their individual messages, another task that the front-end processor accomplishes. Accommodating the data stream from multiple terminals served by a multiplexor will require a line with higher capacity, and consequently the cost will be greater; nevertheless, the cost of this and the added multiplexor may total only a fraction of what several separate lines used regularly on a long-distance basis would cost.

Exhibit 9.5b shows that a system of communications lines may be mixed, with narrowband lines feeding data to the multiplexor and with a

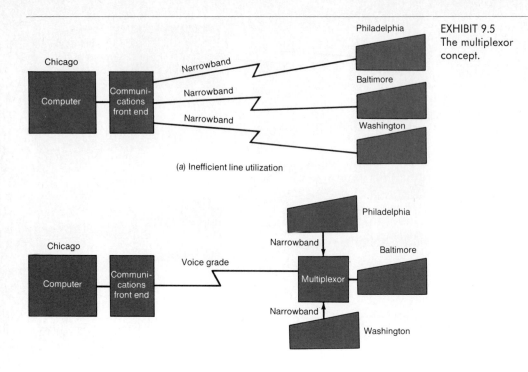

EXHIBIT 9.5
The multiplexor concept.

(a) Inefficient line utilization

(b) Efficient line usage

voiceband or broadband line leaving the multiplexor to transmit high volumes of data to the CPU. The number of possible configurations of such a system is almost infinite; a major task of an organization's communications experts is determining the least costly alternatives by making assumptions about the placement of terminals and multiplexors as well as about the expected level of transmission from each transmitting device. With the split-up of AT&T, the largest provider of communications lines, into multiple operating companies, the telecommunications arena is in turmoil, and increasingly a new specialization is found in organizations—that of a telecommunications specialist.

A data concentrator is a device similar to a multiplexor, but it performs additional functions. Concentrators can establish priorities for lines, allocating the line time as particular data flows require; using sophisticated techniques, they can also compress data to remove unnecessary characters and blank spaces in messages, which are replaced at the terminus. This compression function reduces the total amount of data transmitted, thereby reducing the total line capacity required for transmission.

The fastest way to transmit data is from one computer directly to another computer, as illustrated in Exhibit 9.6. This mode is likely to be used, for example, when one computer is overloaded; it transmits data to

EXHIBIT 9.6
"Two computers talking to each other." A simple distributed data processing system.

another, lightly loaded computer for processing, balancing out the total work load between the computer systems. Two computer systems communicating directly with each other in this manner form a distributed data processing system, which can be simply defined as "two computers talking to each other." Exhibit 9.7 shows a more complex distributed data processing system involving multiple computers communicating to one another, several of which also have terminals that input data directly to them.

HIGH-SPEED DATA TRANSMISSION

Microwave Data Transmission

Several types of high-speed data transmission are now under development or in use. Three of these are microwave, satellite, and laser systems. None of these three are line transmission technologies.

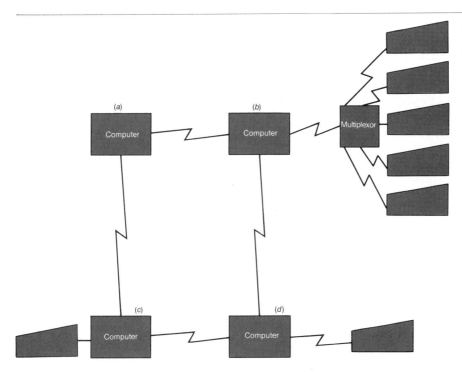

EXHIBIT 9.7
A complex distributed data processing system.

Microwave is a radio broadcasting technology. Microwave radio beams are line-of-sight (they travel in a straight line only), requiring that microwaves be transmitted by one station and received by another station without any obstructions between them. Because of hills and mountains, the curvature of the earth, and obstructions such as tall buildings, microwave stations are typically placed about 25 to 50 miles apart, on the highest points in the region. In large cities, microwave transmission and receiving towers may be placed atop some of the tallest buildings.

Microwave technology has a very high transmission speed, in the range of about 1 million bits per second. Microwave channels may be leased or privately owned. Oil companies in Houston own microwave towers atop oil-drilling platforms in the Gulf of Mexico that pass large volumes of data back and forth between their Houston offices and the drilling platforms. Microwave stations are found in all parts of the United States. A microwave station is shown in Exhibit 9.8.

Satellite Data Transmission

Satellites also utilize microwaves. An earth microwave station broadcasts a microwave signal aimed at an orbiting satellite, which receives the signal and retransmits it to another microwave station on earth, as shown in

EXHIBIT 9.8
A microwave tower.
(Courtesy of Western
Union Corporation.)

EXHIBIT 9A
Communication
satellite. *(Reproduced
with permission of
AT&T.)*

Exhibit 9.9*a*. Whereas for all previously discussed transmission systems the cost of transmission is a function of distance, it costs no more to transmit data by satellite from point A on the earth to point B than it does to transmit data from point A to point C in Exhibit 9.9*a*. Thus, the longer the distance the data must be transmitted, the more likely that satellite transmission will prove to be the most economical mode.

Satellite transmission is also advantageous where the sending and receiving stations are separated by a large body of water and where no undersea data cable exists. This situation allows only radio transmission of data, and satellites are the only radio technology capable of sending high volumes of data long distances with few errors.

Exhibit 9.9*b* illustrates a situation in which data transmitted to a satellite is rebroadcast by that satellite to another satellite, which then retransmits the data to an earth microwave station. This is necessary when the position of a satellite relative to the receiving microwave station on earth is not direct line-of-sight, such as when the earth itself is an obstruction to the line-of-sight data flow, as illustrated in Exhibit 9.9*b*. Communications satellites are placed in orbit at about 23,000 mi above the earth so that their speed is synchronized with the earth's rotation speed and they appear to remain stationary above one spot on the earth.

Laser Data Transmission

A laser is a concentrated beam of light capable of carrying tens of thousands of times as much data as a microwave signal. Laser communications

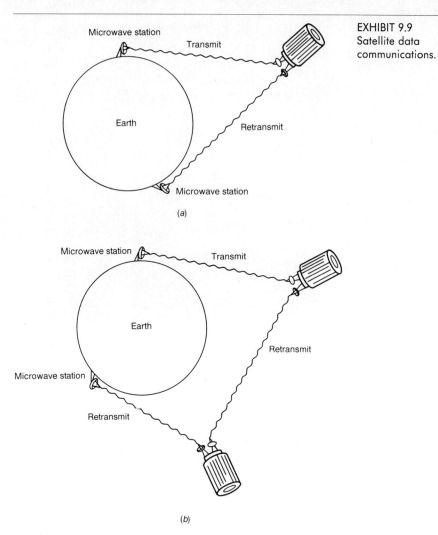

EXHIBIT 9.9
Satellite data communications.

technology is on the leading edge of research and development, and so far it has been used only for short-distance transmission of data. Communications experts predict that in the future laser technology will be widely employed over longer distances and will dramatically reduce data transmission costs.

COMMERCIAL COMMUNICATIONS NETWORKS

Many companies have developed their own in-house communications systems that rely on common-carrier, or commercial, telecommunications. Numerous commercial data networks provide such services as data transmission, remote processing by their computers, and access to many specialized programs for special-purpose data processing tasks. Perhaps the largest of these commercial services is the General Electric Mark II network, which originates in southeastern Europe, spans North America, crosses the northern Pacific Ocean to Japan, and continues down to southeast Asia and Australia, spanning 17 time zones. It is said that 90 percent of the world's telephones are within local calling distance of this network. The GE system is controlled at a supercenter in Cincinnati that has several large computer systems. The entire system embraces over 100 computers. A major feature of the GE system is that subscribers, wherever they are located, have immediate access to thousands of programs for such special data processing tasks as statistical and engineering analyses.

Companies that cannot justify developing their own extended networks can use a system such as the GE network to move data around the world to and from their own computers or to have it processed by the GE computers. At the other extreme, individuals using microcomputers can also interface with this system (although subscriber rates for individual use are high) in order to input data to GE's large-scale computers, where sophisticated programs that cannot be run on a microcomputer can process the data.

NETWORK CONCEPTS

Individual companies can establish their own networks. In general, these are of two types: external networks, which transmit data via common-carrier communications systems such as the public telephone network, and local area networks, which transfer data among computers that are physically separated but remain in close proximity to one another.

External Networks

An external network may be organized by a company for its own use and may serve many purposes, a common one being transmission of unprocessed data to a central location for processing. For example, all transactions of a particular type may be processed at a central computer, where the data files are kept. Or, as already mentioned, data can be transmitted to another location for processing because the computer at the first location is too busy to process it. Sometimes data is transmitted to one location for processing because that location has the required specialized software or output equipment or because only the computer at that location can process the needed programs.

Programs instead of data can be telecommunicated. For instance, when a program used at multiple locations has been revised at one location (perhaps the host computer location, where most of the programmers are), it can be transmitted as data to the other locations, where it replaces the previous version of the same program.

Entire data files may be transmitted rather than programs or unprocessed transactions. It is common, for example, to establish and update a computer file at one location where the transactions occur, but then transmit the file to another location where detailed managerial reports are prepared or where the file might be needed for managerial inquiry purposes. (If the purpose is to have reports at another location, in many situations it is preferable to prepare them at the first location and transmit them.) Such a file transfer might occur monthly, weekly, or even daily, depending on need.

Organizations that routinely transfer large amounts of data usually have sophisticated network equipment and software. The following step-by-step example illustrates a few of the capabilities of such a networking system:

1. A system user needs a specialized financial analysis program that is "on the network"; that is, it's on a computer system at another location of the organization.

2. The user signs on at a terminal (which may be a microcomputer) and requests the program. The user need not know the program's physical location.

3. A network communications control program routes the user's request to a central computer known as the "host computer."

4. At the host computer another network program acknowledges the request and checks a directory in the host computer that gives the locations of all programs available through the network.

5. If the directory indicates that the program sought is at another computer center, the host computer routes the request to that other location.

6. A network communications program at the site of the program needed verifies the user's authorization to use the program and checks whether the program is available for use at that time.

7. If the program is available, the data (which is still at the originating site) is routed directly to the program site by the network programs and is input to the program.

8. The data is processed and returned to the user's site.

This entire process takes place almost instantaneously and is "transparent" to the user: the user may not know that the request has gone to another location and that the data has been processed on another computer system.

The following is a step-by-step example of using a network for "electronic mail":

1. Manager X wishes to send a message to selected other managers in the organization's far-flung locations. The manager or an assistant keys the message into a terminal, along with the identifying code and the electronic address of each addressee (or the system may provide the addresses from a directory file).

2. The networking control programs instantaneously send the message to computer centers at the various locations of the addresses.

3. At each site the message may appear instantly on a video display at the manager's office, or it may be printed at the computer center or another location and delivered within minutes of being sent. The transmission cost is a small fraction of the postage for a first-class letter, which would not be delivered for perhaps several days.

A third scenario is this: LMN Company has major data processing centers in New York and San Francisco, which are busiest during the morning. Much of the data processing consists of on-line transactions that must be processed in real time. In New York the morning transactions processing load is so heavy that it exceeds the computer system's capacity; customer service deteriorates, and other LMN priority processing cannot be done at all. Therefore, LMN Company forwards some of the processing load to its San Francisco computer. Because of the time difference between the two cities, the New York morning peak period coincides with the 6 a.m. to 9 a.m. slack period in San Francisco. The San Francisco computer is able to process data rapidly and return the results to New York. The New York computer, whose work load is reduced, is able to give users faster turnaround on their jobs.

From nine o'clock until noon San Francisco time is the San Francisco computer's heavy data processing period. During this period the New York computer has excess capacity (perhaps), so data is sent from San Francisco to New York for processing and is returned to San Francisco in a timely fashion, thereby permitting a rapid response time for the data processing jobs that remain in San Francisco. There are many variations on this general approach. Assuming that the company has a leased line with adequate excess capacity during these periods, the marginal cost of this data transmission might be zero.

If data flows within a network are heavy, use of dedicated lines is likely. Since these carry a large monthly charge, network configuration becomes critical. One commonly employed configuration is the star configuration, in which a host computer at the center of the star has the communications programs that control the entire network. Exhibit 9.10 shows a star network. The devices that interface along the points of the star to the host may be keyboard terminals, microcomputers, large-scale computers, or even other types of data input devices. When a unit at point A transmits data to a unit at point C, the transmission is routed to the host computer, where it is switched to point C.

Exhibit 9.11 illustrates a ring network, whereby data is forwarded from one device in the ring to the next device in the ring. For example,

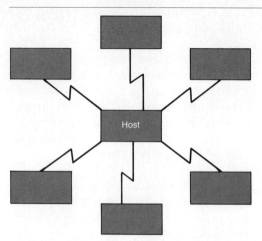

EXHIBIT 9.10
A star network.

(Nodes may be any data transmitting or receiving devices)

data sent from device A destined for device E would go from device A to device B to device C to device D and finally to device E.

Another type of network is the complex network illustrated in Exhibit 9.12. Here the communications packages that control the data flows permit any computer in the network to transmit data to, and receive data from, any other device within the network. Because of the additional line charges and the more extensive and sophisticated communications control software required, such a complex network costs more than either the star or the ring network. A complex network is likely to use both switched and dedicated lines.

The complex network has an advantage over the star and ring networks in terms of reliability. If the host system of a star network is down, the entire network is incapacitated. If one of the computers of a ring network is not functioning, it may be difficult to transmit data to certain other computers in the ring. In a complex network, however, if one computer system malfunctions, all the other systems can still transmit data to one another.

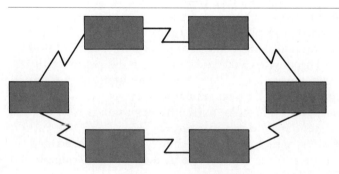

EXHIBIT 9.11
A ring network.

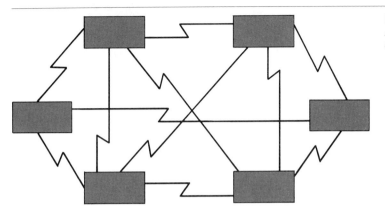

EXHIBIT 9.12
A complex network (not all nodes connected).

Various combinations of network types are possible. Exhibit 9.13 illustrates a combination of star and ring networks; four star networks are interrelated with a ring network. To transmit data from node B of star 1 to node C of star 3 requires that data from star 1B first be routed through the star 1A node, which directs the data to the star 4A node, which in turn routes the data to the star 3A node. Now within star 3, the destination network, the data is routed by the star 3A node to node C.

In such a configuration each star network would have its own set of network control programs to direct data flows within its network, and each data flow would pass through the host computer en route to another point of the star. Each star network would also contain programs capable of directing data flows to its two adjacent stars' host computer systems.

The network control programs of each star network in the exhibit, while complex, are not nearly as complex as the program required to direct traffic within a complex network that permits as many destinations from each star as there are destinations within the entire communications network. Also, while the number of dedicated lines in the star-and-ring combination network is large, the number of lines (both dedicated and switched) necessary for a complex network to make the same number of connections would be much larger. A combination network can achieve economies over a complex network in terms of communications line charges and network program control costs, but these economies may be offset by the inconvenience of less direct data flows in the star-and-ring combination structure.

In networks such as those described, several types of computer equipment must be interfaced, but some may not be compatible with others. To interface technically incompatible equipment units may require additional, extra-cost software and hardware. Some attempts have been made to establish standards to permit interfacing diverse types of equipment and software. A notable attempt is by IBM's Systems Network Architecture (SNA), which sets standards for external networks. SNA standards are

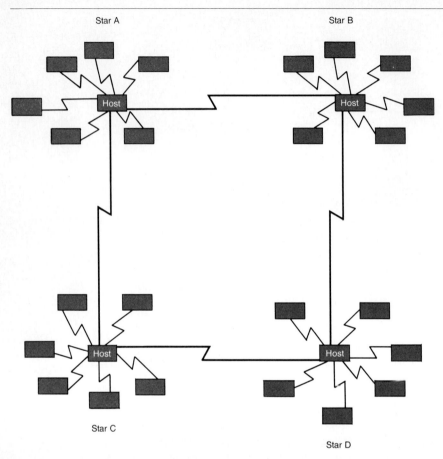

Star A

Star B

EXHIBIT 9.13
A combination of star
and ring networks.

Star C

Star D

not universally accepted within the industry and are most usefully employed in networks consisting primarily of IBM equipment. There remain
many differences in the computer hardware, software programs, and communications control packages of different manufacturers, and these often
prevent computer systems of different manufacturers from being easily
interfaced.

Local Area Networks

Local area networks are becoming increasingly important in organizations.
A local area network links a variety of data processing equipment that is
physically contained within a local area, such as one building or a complex
of buildings. In concept it is similar to an external network, except that
for the most part external networks use common-carrier communications
systems and must employ modems to convert data to analog form and
multiplexors to merge data streams. In local area networks, computing
devices are hard-wired into the network, and no multiplexing is normally
used. Also, local area networks are more likely to include data flows from

a wider variety of types of equipment. For example, a local area network might include not only mainframe computers, minicomputers, and micro-computers but also dedicated word processing systems, badge readers for the factory floor employees, facsimile machines, and graphics equipment and plotters. While all these could be part of an external network, some would not be cost-effective if used in an external network system. A major purpose of local area networks is to improve an organization's internal communications. Developers of local area networking systems hope that data and reports will no longer be walked from office to office within a company but, rather, that the network will accommodate all data com-munications.

ETHERNET represents the major attempt to establish standards for local area networks. Several microcomputer and several communications systems component manufacturers adhere to ETHERNET, which is spon-sored by Xerox Corporation. One example of ETHERNET's importance is that the Apple-Net, although designed primarily for local networking of Apple microcomputer systems, is also ETHERNET-compatible, enabling Apple computer systems, using Apple-Net to interface with devices of other manufacturers of ETHERNET. Apple-Net permits attachment of up to 128 devices on a cable up to ⅓ mi long.

DISTRIBUTED DATA PROCESSING

Three developments of the last decade have largely shaped present-day data processing and information systems: (1) the development of mini- and microcomputers; (2) data base technology; and (3) the emergence of distributed data processing (DDP) systems. These three phenomena are interrelated in that mini- and microcomputers account for a good measure of the economic feasibility of DDP, and data bases can be "distributed" along with the computer systems to enhance the effectiveness of DDP systems.

A Definition

Few experts agree on the precise definition of DDP. Most, however, would accept at least the major elements of the following definition:

> A distributed data processing system is an interactive system of computers that are geographically dispersed and connected by telecommunications, with each computer able to process data independently and forward it to other computers within the system.

Most DDP systems have a host computer that performs certain func-tions for the entire network and a centrally imposed discipline that im-poses hardware and software standards. A host computer is usually larger than the other computers in the system and may hold files that are not present at other locations; it may be the central repository for programs that are utilized at other locations. Also, the majority (and sometimes all) of the professional systems personnel are stationed at the host computer site. However, there is no reason why a DDP system must have a host computer, as long as there is another system of promoting cooperation between the computers of the DDP system.

A DDP system often has certain specialized-function locations, such as a location where specialized computers do only word processing, only process control, or only specialized scientific data processing. A DDP system usually has load-sharing capabilities, allowing an unusually heavy data processing burden at one location to be partially shifted to another computer at a different location, as discussed in the preceding LMN Company example. A DDP system also usually has within-system backup capabilities, at least to an extent, so that if one of the computers in the system is unable to function, another computer in the system can take over its tasks. Most distributed processing systems include a wide variety of computing equipment, such as intelligent terminals, dumb terminals, minicomputers, and microcomputers, which could be from a variety of manufacturers.

DDP is as much a new way of organizing computer systems as it is a new computer technology. While new technology has played an important role in the emergence of DDP systems, DDP has long been technically feasible and in some cases economically practical; only during the last 5 years, however, have significant numbers of computer systems been reorganized into DDP systems. The increasing use of DDP systems has resulted as much from a recognition of the shortcomings of highly centralized computer systems as from technological developments.

DDP and networking are related but different concepts. Networking is the electronic linking of multiple computer sites and encompasses the software necessary to enable data to be transmitted among the sites. DDP is the interaction of computers at those multiple sites. Networks may involve only one computer system, with terminals rather than computers at other locations. DDP by definition involves two or more computer systems. Networks are an essential ingredient in DDP and a technical underpinning for DDP systems. The network is, in effect, a "traffic cop" for data passed between different locations, and the economics of DDP are closely tied to the efficiency of the network.

Tailoring the Information System to the Organization

An axiom of information systems design is that the information system should be tailored to the organization. An earlier chapter noted that some organizations are decentralized, having few interactions and information flows between the divisions and headquarters and between divisions. Additionally, the managers in charge of the decentralized units are delegated the authority and responsibility over the critical aspects of operations, such as investment decisions and marketing strategies. For a decentralized organization, a decentralized information system is appropriate; local managers need control over their information systems in order to organize their operations according to their own perceived needs.

In a managerially centralized organization, managers at headquarters make the major decisions for all parts of the organization and therefore need information from all its parts. This environment makes a centralized data processing system important, for it requires a system that has most of the computer resources at a central location, usually the headquarters location.

The earlier chapter also noted that a new mix of the organization's responsibilities and tasks is developing in many companies. This form of management is termed "coordinated management" and may also be described as "mixed-mode management." Coordinated management involves extensive interaction between managers at the various levels; thus a great deal of information must flow back and forth between headquarters and the major divisions. Division managers are responsible chiefly for organizing their divisions and participating in or making the major decisions affecting the profitability of those divisions. Yet corporate management must have much of the same information that the division managers use because corporate management is deeply involved in the decision-making processes throughout the organization. In an organization with coordinated management, the data flows are complex and heavy both within and between the organizational units; a decentralized data processing system cannot effectively serve the needs of headquarters managers, and a centralized information system cannot serve the needs of the division managers. What this environment demands is a complex arrangement of computer information systems at the local sites as well as at headquarters, with heavy flows of information throughout the organization. The DDP concept adapts to this environment almost perfectly, allowing local division managers to be influential in developing an information system that serves the needs of their local operations. The communications linkages give headquarters managers access to the information that is generated and processed at the local level, and headquarters can also have its own information systems tailored to its needs.

The three types of managerial orientations outlined above are obviously best served by three different general types of information systems. Until the emergence of DDP in the last few years, however, the argument in favor of centralized data processing centers was very persuasive. This argument was grounded in the economies of scale. Most experts agree that throughout the history of computing, larger computers have been more cost-effective than smaller ones. Information systems therefore have tended to be based upon ever-larger computer systems. Thus, to a great extent the larger computer systems' lower cost per transaction processed is the reason for highly centralized computer systems, even where centralized systems are not compatible with an existing decentralized or coordinated management philosophy. It is probably true that less centralized computer systems would have encouraged more companies to become managerially more decentralized or coordinated.

A school of thought has developed to the effect that DDP is preferable to centralized computing where the nature of the organization demands decentralized or coordinated management of its major tasks. It is also held that a DDP system offers the information system a greater ability to evolve and that DDP is better able to provide solutions tailored to specialized tasks. Indeed, the belief is that the more critical the computer is to a specialized data processing task, the more the group in charge of that task must be able to exercise significant control over the development of the computer system.

New Technology

During the past decade new developments have made DDP systems both technically and economically more feasible. One area of technical advances is in communications technology. The increasing efficiency and capabilities of communications front-end devices, along with the development of communications controllers and multiplexors, are significant advances in DDP. Equally important is the development of sophisticated network control software. This software can now easily and efficiently perform a number of tasks—such as data routing, data transmission priority establishment, polling, and data access security—that previously were difficult to perform or inefficiently accomplished.

Data communications cost reductions have also played a significant role in the emergence of DDP. Microwave systems, satellites, and other advanced forms of communications have dramatically reduced transmission costs per message transmitted.

Another relevant technological development is the emergence of inexpensive small computers. A decade ago, when minicomputers achieved widespread use because of their low cost, DDP systems using minicomputers at most locations became economically feasible. Since then, microcomputers have been brought to a high state of development. The price/performance ratio of microcomputers is so low, and their convenience so great, that they are supplanting small- and medium-scale minicomputers in organizations and are becoming important parts of DDP systems.

Thus, low-cost computing power is available for placement in multiple locations throughout an organization. The economies of scale of large data centers using large computing systems are no longer as valid, and the optimum size of a data processing center is now smaller than previously. This is illustrated in Exhibit 9.14, which indicates that in 1973 the range within which a computer system was considered to be most cost-effective

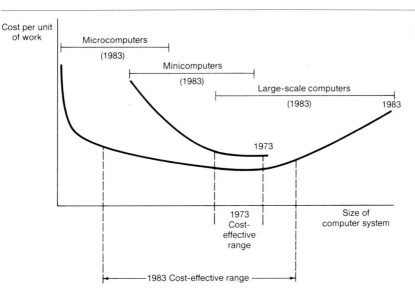

EXHIBIT 9.14
The role of computer size in promoting DDP.

was narrow, and only large computers were within it. In 1983 not only was the dollar cost per unit of work lower for systems of all sizes, but also the range of sizes of computer systems that could process at a low cost per work unit had broadened considerably; while large computer systems remain within this range, now much smaller computer systems, including the larger microcomputers, can be as efficient, or nearly as efficient, as large computer systems. This by itself does not necessarily mean that multiplication of computer sites is preferable, but it does mean that factors other than computer size will be decisive in determining how information systems are organized, and these factors dictate a distributed data processing system for many organizations.

The Distribution Options

Which functions are distributed to local computers in a distributed system depends upon the particular set of circumstances. Some of the functions that may or may not be distributed are shown in Exhibit 9.15.

Functions That May Be Distributed   EXHIBIT 9.15

1. Data collection and entry

2. Data editing and error correction

3. File design and program maintenance

4. Large file location

5. Transactions processing

Item 1 of Exhibit 9.15 groups data collection and data entry together because it is often more efficient to enter data at the point of collection, which is usually a regional or local site. The development of point-of-sale and other advanced data entry and transaction recording devices favors distributed data entry. In regard to item 2, it is usually considered to be most efficient to do editing and error correction at the point at which the transaction enters the system because errors can often be caught and corrected more readily at the time that they occur; delay (which may occur if errors are corrected at a central location) will often result in forgetting details of the transaction or losing supporting documents.

Different DDP systems may handle file design and program maintenance differently. In many DDP systems these activities are centralized, with the data processing staff placed primarily at the central host location. In other DDP systems professional staff members are at local sites, and these activities are distributed. In the latter case, personnel at the distributed location may report to either the central data processing manager or the local managers. Large files may be retained either at the central site location or at distributed locations. In either case, the DDP system network enables these files to be accessed from any part of the system. Small files are most likley to be retained at their originating location in a DDP system.

Transactions relating exclusively or primarily to local operations are likely to be processed locally even if they could be done about as efficiently at a central data processing center. For example, it is quite common to prepare payroll for local employees entirely at the distributed location.

Advantages and Disadvantages of DDP

Although a DDP system may have many advantages, disadvantages can usually be cited as well. Both are summarized in Exhibit 9.16.

One advantage that some observers perceive is that DDP reduces the

---

Possible Advantages and Disadvantages of DDP   EXHIBIT 9.16

Possible Advantages	Possible Disadvantages
Increased manageability of the computer system	Possible disintegration of control over the computer system
Decreased communications costs in some circumstances	Utilizes complex, ill-understood new technologies (network analysis and telecommunications)
Greater adaptability to the organizational structure	Greater communications costs in some circumstances
Improved local morale through local participation	

complexity of mammoth centralized data processing centers, which (according to these observers) makes them impossible to manage effectively. These experts also believe that the systems overhead costs of a larger system rise faster than its benefits. When there are many large computer systems in the same room, interacting in complex ways and sharing common resources such as dozens or hundreds of disks and tape units, it is impossible for any single person to understand the entire system thoroughly. Programs alone constitute a significant element of overhead of such a system because they must be so complex. Distributing computer power makes each computer center in the system relatively less complex and therefore inherently more manageable. Offsetting this to some degree, however, is the fact that DDP requires complex networks, which must also be managed.

Decreased communications costs are also cited as an advantage of DDP. In some circumstances this may be the case. For example, if the organization is managerially decentralized, requiring relatively few interactions between the divisions and headquarters, local processing can keep communications costs low. Many decentralized organizations need a large proportion of their data only locally; in some organizations 70 to 80 percent of all data generated at local centers can be processed locally and need never be transmitted through the communications network. However, in many DDP systems, communications costs constitute more than half of the total costs; it is probable that in many circumstances DDP increases communications costs, requiring DDP to be justified on other bases, if it can be.

A clear advantage of DDP is its adaptability to the structure of the organization; DDP can be configured to any organization because each location's equipment and data processing activities can be structured to that location's needs. Another advantage that DDP advocates cite is that a DDP system can be more responsive to the end user. For example, data processing schedules can be tailored to the needs of end users rather than being established at a central location, which perhaps may not properly understand the scheduling needs of remote locations. Freed from central scheduling, local managers can complete financial closings faster, get faster identification of operating problems, and more quickly get special runs that they need for unusual problems. Also, because end users can more easily bring about changes at a local DDP site than at a centralized data processing center, the local system is more likely to adapt and continue to be responsive to the users' needs.

The local control and participation that a DDP system can offer may also bring about happier relationships. At least a degree of local control lets the line managers play a more active role in systems development and control. A happier environment results partly because local managers believe they now have greater control over their own destiny; managers want to assume responsibility for operations which influence their performance, which computer information systems clearly do. A greater degree of local control and participation makes managers more likely to view the computer system as "ours" rather than "theirs."

Not to be overlooked is the fact that if one computer center of a DDP system fails, the entire system does not fail. Other centers can often take over the failed computer's work load.

A major potential disadvantage of DDP systems is the possiblity that the overall control of the information system will disintegrate. If this does happen, the advantages of DDP will be forsaken. It can happen if the local computer centers are given complete independence. A central authority must retain final say over the purchase of equipment throughout the system and must ensure that all the system's software is compatible so that it can be exchanged and used in more than one location. These considerations suggest that the entire DDP system must be centrally planned and controlled. This can usually be best accomplished by information systems managers at a host computer location. Also, by maintaining the programming, systems analysis, and other technical staff members at the host site, it is easier to establish and enforce the discipline that a DDP system needs throughout.

Finally, the art and science of networking is just emerging, and organizations usually have too few persons who are experts in determining the most cost-effective short-run configuration of planning an effective distributed system for the long run. Telecommunications is also an emerging field in which there are too few specialists within organizations. These considerations mean that organizations must often proceed more slowly than they would like, since to make haste in this arena may be to invite costly mistakes.

SUMMARY

The ability to transport data electronically serves many purposes. The telecommunications systems that accomplish this vary from off-line punched-card systems to sophisticated on-line real-time distributed data processing systems. The telecommunications lines that these systems employ may vary greatly in terms of data volume, speed, and other characteristics. Lines may be switched or private; private lines may be "dedicated" or owned by the organization. Modems convert data from digital form (used by computers) to analog form (used by most telecommunications lines) and back again.

On-line data transmission uses a communications front-end device to perform important functions. Multiplexors can reduce transmission costs of several clustered terminals. A data concentrator performs additional functions. Three types of high-speed data transmission systems are microwave, satellite, and laser systems.

Companies may use commercial data networks, such as the General

Electric Mark II, or develop their own networks—either external networks (which transmit data via common-carrier communications systems) or local area networks (which link a variety of data processing equipment that is physically contained within a local area). The major attempt to establish standards for local area networks, which are becoming increasingly important in organizations, is ETHERNET.

The emergence of distributed data processing systems interrelates with two other important developments: data base technology and the rise of mini- and microcomputers. DDP and networking are related but different concepts. Most DDP systems include specialized-function computers at certain locations, and most have both load-sharing and within-system backup capabilities. The DDP concept is well suited to a coordinated style of management. The once persuasive argument for centralized data processing, grounded in economies of scale, has weakened as new advances have made DDP systems both technically and economically more feasible and as diseconomies associated with the complexity of large-scale systems have become better recognized. DDP systems may distribute many different functions, such as data collection and entry, error correction, and local payroll preparation. DDP has many possible advantages, including increased system manageability and improvement of local morale, but safeguards must be taken to prevent disintegration of control over the computer systems; some central discipline must remain.

KEY TERMS

modem: a modulator-demodulator device that converts digital data to analog form for transmission and reconverts it after transmission.

switched lines (dial-up lines): telecommunications lines which transfer transmitted data from one telecommunications line to another so that the route of the data to its destination cannot be predicted in advance.

communications front-end device: a piece of equipment that manages the data transmission to and from a computer system; it may be a specially configured microcomputer or minicomputer. Among its tasks are error detection and correction, and message forwarding to other computer systems.

multiplexor: a device that merges ("multiplexes") data streams from multiple low-speed devices so that the full capacity of the transmission line is utilized.

data concentrator: a device similar to a multiplexor which performs the additional functions of establishing priorities for lines, allocating line time, and compressing data.

distributed data processing system: an interactive system of computers that are geographically dispersed and connected by telecommunications, each of which can process data independently and forward data to another computer within the system.

external network: a telecommunications network that transmits data via common-carrier communications systems, such as the public telephone network.

local area network (LAN): a network that links a variety of types of data processing equipment that is physically contained within a local area, such as one building or a complex of buildings.

electronic mail: a system of electronically transmitting messages within a computer communications network.

star network: a network configured like a star, in which a host computer is at the center.

ring network: a network configured to forward data from one device in the ring to the next.

complex network: a network which permits any computer within it to transmit data to, and receive data from, any other device within the network.

ETHERNET: a set of network standards for local networks; it is sponsored by Xerox Corporation.

SNA: a set of network standards for external networks; it is sponsored by IBM.

REFERENCES

Enslow, Philip H., Jr., "What Is a 'Distributed' Data Processing System?" *Computer,* January 1978.

Kaufman, Felix, "Distributed Processing," *Data Base,* Summer 1978.

Patrick, Robert L., "Decentralizing Hardware and Dispersing Responsibility," *Datamation,* May 1976.

REVIEW QUESTIONS

1. Discuss several situations in which data may need to be transported.

2. Explain several ways in which data can be transported.

3. When did electronic transmission of data originate?

4. Describe three types of simple telecommunications systems.

5. Explain what modems do and why they are necessary.

6. Explain the differences between simplex, half-duplex, and full-duplex data transmission lines.

7. Name two situations in which broadband lines would be used.

8. What is a switched-line system?

9. What is a conditioned, dedicated line?

10. What is WATS?

11. Cite two advantages of digital data transmission.

12. Explain the several functions of a communications front-end device.

13. How do serial and parallel transmission differ?

14. What does a multiplexor do, and why is it used?

15. What functions does a data concentrator perform?

16. Discuss the characteristics of microwave data transmission.

17. Why is it true that the farther data must be transmitted, the more likely it is that satellite transmission will prove to be the most economical mode?

18. When is transmission of data from one satellite to another necessary?

19. Discuss the General Electric Mark II network. In what situations would it be advantageous for a company to use this network?

20. How can a networking system balance the work load among its computers?

21. Describe a star network, a ring network, and a complex network.

22. Name the major advantages and the major disadvantage of a complex network, as compared with the ring and star networks.

23. How do local area networks differ from external networks?

24. What is ETHERNET, and why is it important?

25. Why is it only in the last 5 years that significant numbers of computer systems have been structured as DDP systems?

26. Explain how the concepts of DDP and networking differ.

27. Discuss the impact of an organization's form of management (centralized, decentralized, or coordinated) on its information system.

28. Discuss four developments that have made DDP systems technically or economically more feasible.

29. Which functions are often distributed in a DDP system, and why?

30. Name five possible advantages of a DDP system.

31. What kind of discipline does a DDP system need, and why is it needed?

Chapter 10

CONVENTIONAL AND DATA
BASE FILE ORGANIZATIONS

PAYOFF THOUGHT

Managers should understand the nature of both conventional and data base file organizations to ensure that data base systems, if justified, are implemented so that they provide benefits directly to managers as well as to data processing personnel.

CHAPTER OBJECTIVES

1. To portray data access and retrieval as the culmination of data processing activity

2. To represent file organization as the key to data access and retrieval

3. To explore the fundamentals of conventional and data base file systems

DATA FILES: THE KEY TO INFORMATION AVAILABILITY AND PROCESSING EFFICIENCY

The primary purpose of information systems is to provide information for a variety of managerial purposes as well as for needs at the operations levels of organizations. Supplying this information requires that:

1. Data can be easily accessed and retrieved from the computer system.

2. After retrieval, the data can be quickly processed; a correlary to this is that data should also be efficiently processed.

In a very real sense, the focus of all the data processing activities and resources is on enhancing the ability to access and retrieve data and to process data quickly and efficiently when it is retrieved. The way the data processing function is organized, the human resources devoted to data processing, the computing equipment acquired, and the software programs written and purchased are all intended to accomplish this end. This is portrayed in Exhibit 10.1.

The most important factor influencing record accessing, retrieval, and processing is data file organization, the subject of this chapter. "File organization" refers to the structure of the files that contain data and the addressing systems that facilitate data access and the retrieval of data from these data files. The importance of the topic of data file organization to the student is that study of this topic provides an understanding of how information is made available by the computer system and of the changes that sometimes must be made to the data files to permit data to be made available quickly. An appreciation of this topic also facilitates an understanding of why revision of data file structures can be difficult and should not be undertaken lightly.

Two generic classes of data file organizations exist, and within each general class are several specific types of file structures. The first generic type is here termed "conventional file organizations," and the second is "data base file organizations." The specific types of organization within these will be examined in this chapter and are noted in Exhibit 10.2.

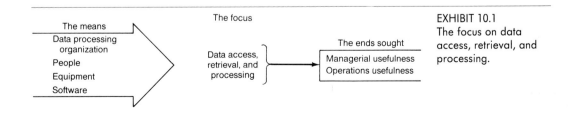

EXHIBIT 10.1
The focus on data access, retrieval, and processing.

Conventional and Data Base File Organizations   EXHIBIT 10.2

Conventional File Organizations	Data Base File Organizations
Sequential	Inverted list
Direct access	Hierarchical (tree)
Indexed sequential	Network
	Relational

CONVENTIONAL FILE ORGANIZATIONS

Both conventional and data base file organizations are in widespread use. Conventional file organizations are so called only because they existed before data base structures were developed and thus, for two decades, were the conventional way in which files were organized. With conventional files, typically there is one file or a few files per "system," and each file is processed by its own set of applications programs. For example, there might be one data file for the payroll system and several payroll programs that process the data in that payroll file. However, nonpayroll programs would not be able to access data in the payroll file.

Sequential File Organization

In sequentially organized files, each record is stored in a particular sequence, usually in either numeric or alphabetic sequence. Normally the first data field in the record contains the type of data on which the sequence is based; this field is called the "primary key," which is associated with a chart of account numbers or with another input coding system to permit input data to update the internal files. For instance, if the first field of a record contains the customer number, the sequence is numeric by customer number, and the primary key is customer number; transactions about customers that are entered into the files will be organized with the customer number as the first field of the record.

Processing of a sequential file is accomplished in recognition of the established sequence of records. New data file records must be inserted at the proper sequential location in the file, and transactions that will be processed against the records of the file must first be sorted to the same sequence as the records in the file. Of course, computer programs automatically place the new records in sequence, and other programs sort transactions into the proper sequence.

The records in a sequential file are processed in sequence by reading and updating as necessary the first record in sequence, then the second record, and so on. For example, if the first record is a customer account for Aaron, Abraham, with a balance of $10, and a credit sale transaction is being processed for $5, the computer reads Mr. Aaron's record, notes the balance of $10, adds the new transaction detail to the record, adds $5 to the balance, and changes Mr. Aaron's balance from $10 to $15. Then the next record in sequence is read and updated to reflect any credit sales transactions.

If there is only one transaction to be processed, say, a credit sale to Malinowski, Zelda, the computer must read the entire sequential file by reading the first record in the file, then the next, and so on, until Ms. Malinowski's record is located so that the sale can update her record. The task of locating one record may require substantial processing and be quite time-consuming in some circumstances. Such is the case when searching, a magnetic-tape file; magnetic-tape files are always sequential, and the search for a particular record on magnetic tape may require several minutes of computer processing. Sequential files may also be placed on disks or other physical file media.

Sequential file organization is used with batch processing. Batch processing exists where transactions of one type are accumulated, then gathered into a batch, sorted into the same sequence as the file they will be processed against, and then "batch-processed." Batch processing uses the computer system efficiently, once the transactions have been sorted to the same sequence as the file, because transactions can be processed very rapidly against a sequential master file. Numerous sorting programs exist, and sorting can be done by the computer, or it can be done off-line, such as with a key-to-disk system.

Sequential data processing is inefficient where just one or a few records need to be accessed frequently and where there is seldom a need to sequentially process most of the records in the file. Sequential processing is also inefficient when a condition within one record indicates that a preceding record should be accessed next, for example, when the customer account record that is 900th in sequence indicates that the quantity discount terms for that customer are based on the quantities purchased by that customer as well as by that customer's parent and when the quantities purchased by the parent are recorded in the parent's customer record in, say, the 300th position.

Sequential files are sometimes described as "flat files," because they do not permit a hierarchy of record relationships such that one record can conveniently reference another record to secure additional data needed for processing, as was needed in the preceding example. Indexed sequential and direct access files are also flat files in this sense.

Direct Access File Organization

Direct access file organization permits a record inquiry or update to be taken directly to the location of the disk track of the desired record without reading any of the records on other disk packs or other tracks on the disk that contains the record. This file organization is likely to be used when it is frequently the case that only one record at a time is accessed and read or updated on a "real-time" basis, that is, when the record must be accessed while the business transaction is in process because the contents of the record will affect the outcome of the transaction.

Airlines reservations systems are an example of one type of direct access systems that relates the record key to its physical address. The computer record of a flight must be accessed while the transaction with the customer is in process because whether the passenger purchases a ticket for a flight depends on the availability of seats, as indicated by the computerized flight record. Direct access files are usually kept on-line (electronically connected to the computer) for significant portions of each day, and some may be kept on-line at all times.

With the airlines type of direct accessing, an algorithm is applied to the record key, such as a customer number, to transform it into a "random address"; the record is then stored at that physical address. This is often called the "hashing" or "randomizing" technique. While there are many different hashing routines, typically they involve multiplication and division of the primary key in a consistent way for all input transactions. Thus, when a file record must be direct-accessed, its primary key is manipulated with an algorithm that is always used, the key is always transformed into the same address, and the record is direct-accessed at this address.

As a simple example to illustrate hashing, if customer number 12345 is multiplied by 9 and divided by 4, in conformance with an algorithm, the result is 27776.25; the algorithm may reveal that the four leftmost digits are the physical address and that the record is stored in disk location 2777, or the record already at that address is updated with the transaction. When that record must be accessed again, the application of the same algorithm gives the same physical address of the record. In reality, of course, hashing algorithms are more complex than this illustration and are mathematically determined in order to conserve disk space and prevent duplication of transformed addresses.

Exhibit 10.3 illustrates another type of direct access organization of files; with this approach a sequential index of record keys is used. Assume that a sales transaction is processed to update John Smith's record. The transaction, including the primary key identifier of "Smith," is entered at the remote terminal, and the index is searched sequentially. A two-part reference is contained in the index file for each record in the customer files. The first part corresponds to the primary key identifier of records in the files, and the second part provides a unique physical address on the disk that contains Smith's record. The computer's operating system, which keeps track of all record locations, then directs the read-write heads to the disk track on which the record is located and updates the record on the basis of the sales transaction.

With direct accessing, the records may be stored in sequence (this facilitates the processing of batches of transactions sorted to that sequence), or the records may be stored in random order. In the simplified

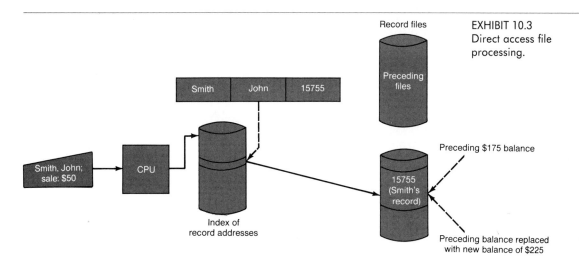

EXHIBIT 10.3
Direct access file
processing.

example given above, an address for every record is entered into the index; in practice, additional techniques are used so that not every address must be placed in the index. As individual records are added to, and deleted from, the file, they must also be added to, and deleted from, the index; different direct accessing systems vary with respect to how such "housekeeping" matters are handled.

If the records are stored randomly, they may nevertheless be processed sequentially by an indirect approach. To process sequentially, the index keys (which are in sequence) are read one by one, and as each is read, the related record is direct-accessed and processed in sequence. Obviously, this indirect approach is not as efficient as processing records that are already maintained in sequence.

A degree of processing overhead is present with the direct accessing approach illustrated in Exhibit 10.3 because a lengthy index must be processed to locate the address of the desired record and because maintaining an up-to-date index also requires computer processing. However, each index record is short, and an entire index can be read quickly. On the other hand, the records in a data file are often quite lengthy; thus it usually is much faster for the computer to read the index to find the record address and then proceed directly to the disk track containing the record than to read even a few records in sequence in the record file. The advantage of direct accessing is the speed of access for a specific record.

Indexed Sequential File Organization

Indexed sequential file organization is a combination of both direct access and sequential file accessing; records are stored so that both direct and sequential processing can be done. Indexed sequential files are often referred to as "ISAM files" (indexed sequential access method files).

With indexed sequential file organization, records are placed in the sequence desired for sequential processing, such as alphabetically or numerically, according to their primary key. A separate index gives the direct access address of a block (a group) of these sequential records. When sequential processing programs are used, the records are processed in sequence as a sequential file. When only one or a few records need to be accessed, the index is consulted by the operating system to locate the address (the disk face, track, and record number) of the first record in the block that contains the record needed. The disk read-write heads move to that block, locate that record, and then read all the records in the block sequentially until the desired record is located. This permits bypassing the early records in a large file when searching for a specific record. As a result, not all the records must be read that precede in sequence the one sought, and the access time for a specific record is greatly decreased. While permitting direct access to a block of records (rather than to a specific record, as direct accessing does), indexed sequential organization retains the efficiencies of sequential processing when all or a high proportion of the records in a file can be processed in sequence, such as for periodic updating of customers' accounts on the basis of batched transactions.

Exhibit 10.4 illustrates an indexed sequential system. Customer accounts are maintained sequentially by groups (in fact, there would be many more than just the four blocks shown). John Thomas, whose customer number is 12345, calls to inquire about his account balance. Several thousand or tens of thousands of customer records may be stored on one or more disk packs. A clerk might key in Mr. Thomas's request at a remote terminal by entering a command similar to: CUST NO 12345: DISPLAY ACCOUNT BALANCE. Using the primary key of customer number, the operating system first accesses an index placed on a disk. This index contains only a minimum of information—in this illustration, only infor-

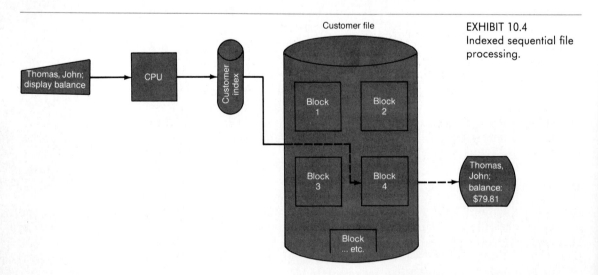

EXHIBIT 10.4
Indexed sequential file processing.

mation about the physical address of each record block and the customer number of the last record in each block. The operating system reads the index in sequence until it finds the first block with a customer number higher than 12345; it then knows tht the John Thomas record is in that block of records. The operating system direct-accesses that block and reads its records sequentially until John Thomas's record (12345) is located. Mr. Thomas's account balance is then displayed on a CRT. Of course, the actual chain of events is more complex than in this illustration, and there is a wide range of variation with respect to how systems function. For example, many systems use a hierarchy of indexes rather than just one index in order to accelerate the index search process.

In the above simplified example, the indexed sequential organization has saved the time required by the CPU to read all the customer records in all the blocks that precede the one containing the record sought. The cost of saving this time is the establishment and reading of an index file that is very small relative to the record file.

THE CONVENTIONAL DATA PROCESSING APPROACH

Conventional data file organizations have inherent problems that inhibit data access in some circumstances. Exhibit 10.5 shows a traditional system of data files and their associated applications programs; these files could have any of the types of file organization discussed in the last section. Typically, a file (or more than one file) is established for each functional application, such as payroll, accounts receivable, or accounts payable. A systems designer creates a new data file format layout that defines the contents of the file and the length and sequence of the fields for the record's data. A programmer then writes (creates) a program to process the data in the records of the file. Because no, or little, attempt usually is made to use the same standards for the file formats or the names of the data elements in all the organization's files and programs, the programs for a file can be processed only with that file. (For example, for one data file an employee's social security number may be defined as SS#, and for

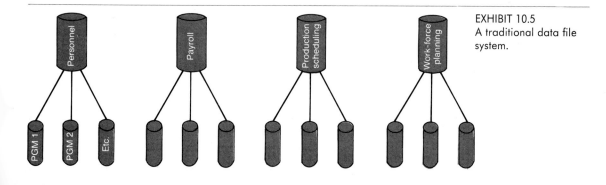

EXHIBIT 10.5
A traditional data file system.

another it may be SOCSEC.) Data thus becomes identified with specific programs and a specific file; this close relationship is known as "program/file dependence."

Typically, each file has several programs written for it, as suggested by the exhibit. The payroll file, for example, will have programs which alter pay rates as raises are given, which revise the file by adding new employees, and which delete terminated employees. Additionally, there will be programs to prepare payroll checks for salaried personnel, other programs for hourly personnel, and perhaps a different set of programs for each division of the organization because each has different payroll procedures as a result of different union contracts or different management decisions. For example, one division may pay employees weekly, and another may pay them twice monthly. Also, variations in payroll tax legislation among the states and cities necessitate different payroll programs for different geographic areas.

Much of the data contained in any one of the files shown in Exhibit 10.5 is also contained in other files. For example, both the personnel file and the payroll file will contain each employee's name and address, the names of dependents, employee pay rates, and other information about each employee. Similarly, the personnel file and the work-force planning file also contain employee names and pay rates, and both also may contain duplicate information about employee skills. However, the same information is likely to be defined and formatted differently in different files. As just a few examples, field lengths for the same data elements (such as for employee names) may be of different lengths in the different files; in one file the employee names may be formatted with first names first, and in another with surnames first; and the program of one file may define the employee-name variable as EMPNAME, and that of another file may define it as EMPLOYEE. Thus, duplicate data elements exist within the files, although usually the data is defined and formatted inconsistently.

This traditional data processing approach results in several problems that reduce the effectiveness and efficiency of data processing. First, as suggested above, a great many identical data elements are stored in two or more files, causing higher storage costs as a result of "data redundancy." Because the cost of large-scale memory has been dramatically reduced in recent years, the direct cost of data redundancy is not a major concern. A more serious but indirect cost of data redundancy is the greater chance that inconsistent data will be provided in reports from different files. Inconsistent data usually is the consequence of updating one file correctly and another erroneously or of processing transactions or making error corrections on different schedules. Thus, if the payroll file is updated prior to the personnel file for pay-rate changes, reports from the files when one has been updated and the other has not will mean that all information from the files based on pay rates will be inconsistent. As indicated in an earlier chapter, managers are irritated by inconsistent data, and too many inconsistencies encourage managers to question the credibility of the information system; no explanation by data processing personnel may convince the managers that valid reasons exist for these discrepancies.

Another major problem associated with conventional file systems is the amount of labor-intensive data processing activity that is required. For example, credit sales transactions must be processed with the accounts receivable master file to update customer accounts and must also be processed with the sales master file to update sales records. This multifile processing activity causes additional complexity that increases the probability of data processing errors, and it requires time-consuming labor that delays period-end reports.

Error correction can also be a problem with conventional files. Data processing schedules must be carefully adhered to, with the consequence that batches of transactions may be accumulated for several days or weeks before being processed. If a transaction then cannot be processed properly because of the previously undetected error, the transaction situation that existed several days or even weeks before may need to be reconstructed. During the interim period the memories of the people involved may have faded, or backup paperwork may have been removed or misplaced.

Preparation of special-purpose reports is difficult with the conventional data processing approach. If these reports require that data from several different data files be integrated, special programs must be written to access each file because each file's data definitions and format are unique. Then the data must be reformatted and placed in a new file created for this purpose. Finally, a separate program must be written to process the data in this special new file. In some cases the preparation of special reports requires several worker-months of effort.

The preparation of special reports by means of traditional data processing is illustrated in Exhibit 10.6. The reformatting indicated in the exhibit may be as simple as sorting the data to a different sequence, based on different processing keys. However, the reformatting could be as laborious as changing record formats and redefining variable names of identical data elements so that the specially written programs are accessing the same data in fields of the same length and in the same position for all records.

For routine data processing too, the data from one file often must be integrated into a different file for processing by the programs of the other file. This requires some mechanism to routinely enable the integration of data in different files. The integration approach usually used is as follows: The data in one applications file is extracted by a program written for this purpose and is placed in a "transfer file" that holds the data until it is passed along to another applications file by processing the transfer and applications file together; the data can then be processed by the programs of this second applications file if these programs have been written to accommodate the data received for the transfer file.

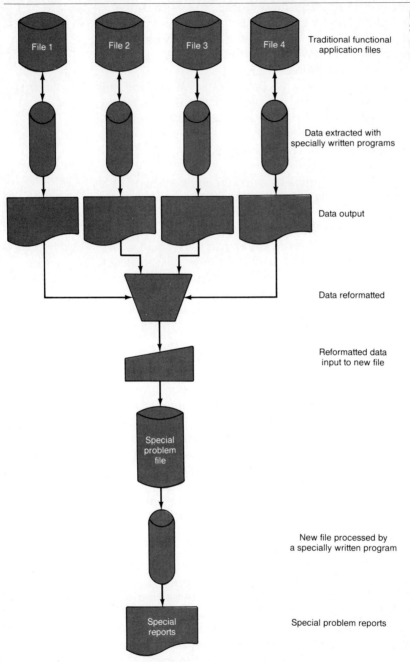

EXHIBIT 10.6
Special report
preparation from
multiple traditional files.

Traditional functional
application files

Data extracted with
specially written programs

Data output

Data reformatted

Reformatted data
input to new file

Special
problem
file

New file processed by
a specially written program

Special
reports

Special problem reports

The creation and use of transfer files is an awkward and time-consuming approach to file integration. For example, any modifications to the file from which the data is transferred must be communicated to the programmer associated with the other file so that the data transfer programs and the programs of the second applications file can be appropriately altered. As the number of transfer files increases, correct sequentialization among the records of the sending file, the transfer programs, and the applications programs of the receiving file becomes tricky; precise updating according to a schedule is necessary, but it becomes increasingly difficult to manage.

In some data processing centers more resources are devoted to file maintenance of this and other types than to the primary data processing activities of the organization. The effects of all these considerations are increasing costs of data processing, a decreasing ability to meet data processing production schedules, and a greater incidence of incorrect information and delayed reports.

DATA BASES: A PREVIEW

Because of the problems with conventional data file processing noted in the preceding sections, data processing personnel have attempted to streamline the integration of data files and data processing activities. Many of the efforts to automate the integration of functional files helped create the file organization and other technologies that have merged to bring about data bases, and the data bases that emerged were technological phenomena with the purpose of improving data processing. Now, however, data bases have moved beyond the primarily technological phase and should be justified because of their utility for management purposes. Indeed, the major advantage of data bases relates to their managerial usage.

Improved data access has been presented as the key to information usefulness for both managerial and operations activities. Data access can be greatly improved by the implementation of data base technology. This improved access provides benefits to managers, the clerical personnel who conduct the operations activities, and the data processing personnel who must access data for their own purposes or as a part of their services to managers and the administrative functions. The major ways in which improved data access helps these groups are diagramed in Exhibit 10.7. As shown in the exhibit, improved data access inproves routine reporting and file inquiry activities (an inquiry is an interrogation of a file to find specific information, such as a customer's balance) as well as nonroutine (special-purpose) reporting and inquiries. Further, these reporting and inquiry activities are improved for situations requiring data from within one functional area as well as from multiple functional areas (such as

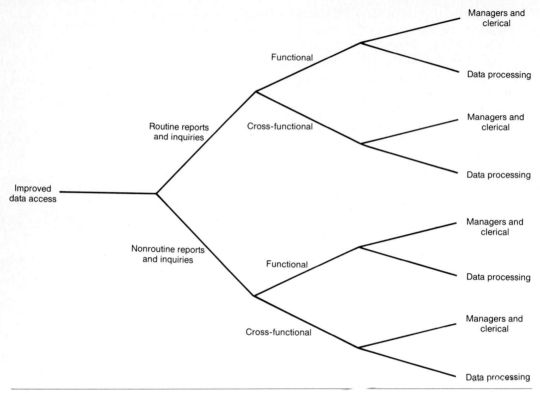

EXHIBIT 10.7
The impact of data access on information usefulness.

personnel, production, and payroll), and this benefits managers, clerical personnel, and data processing personnel, as illustrated in the exhibit.

The specific ways in which data base technology improves data access and therefore benefits the types of activities mentioned will gradually unfold in the remainder of this chapter and the next. While studying this material, the student is urged to focus attention on trying to perceive how data bases provide these benefits, rather than becoming totally absorbed by the intricacies of data base technology. As will be seen, one of the key attributes of data bases is the integration of the data files by establishing bases of association between records both within a file and in different files.

DATA BASE FILE ORGANIZATIONS

This section describes four types of data base file organizations. First, however, a discussion of file pointers is presented; file pointers are used with what is often called a "list file organization." File pointers establish linkages between records and are a basic part of the file organization of all the data base systems discussed here except the relational system. However, pointer systems are, strictly speaking, not a data base technology, since they were used with conventional file organizations for many years before data bases came into existence.

With pointer systems, a "pointer" usually is placed in the last field of a record or, if more than one pointer is used, in the last fields. A pointer is the address of another, related record that is "pointed to," and the pointer directs the computer system to that related record. Exhibit 10.8 shows a system of pointers embedded in records. In the exhibit each pointer occupies a field of a record. Applications programs instruct the computer to recognize the pointer and to proceed to the pointer address to retrieve the data sought for processing by the program. For all but the last data base system that will be discussed, it is the pointers that serve to integrate data files and permit records from what otherwise would be separate files to be processed together without the need for transfer files or other forms of intermediate processing.

The records shown in Exhibit 10.8 are in a sequential payroll file. For illustration purposes, each record has two appended fields that can contain pointers; in one pointer field, the pointer points to records of other employees in the organization who hold jobs with the same title (in practice,

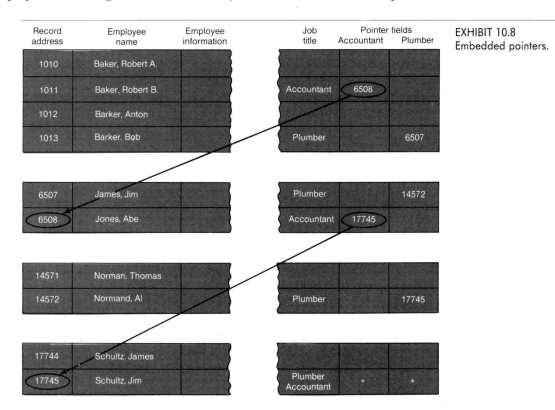

EXHIBIT 10.8
Embedded pointers.

one pointer field in each record could serve the same functions as the two that are used in this example). If, for instance, a listing of the records of accountants is needed, the processing of several thousand employee records to locate the records of accountants can be avoided by having the applications program instruct the computer to retrieve all records chained together by the pointers in the appropriate field of the accountants' records.

In the exhibit, the file can be read sequentially from the start until the first accountant's record is found. This record, at address 1011 (which represents a physical address in secondary memory), belongs to Robert B. Baker and is read; its pointer field indicates that the next record belonging to an accountant is at address 6508. The computer system proceeds directly to that address without processing the intervening records (which may number in the thousands) and reads that record and the address in its pointer field for accountants. The next accountant's record is shown in the pointer field to be at address 17745, and the computer goes directly to that record, retrieves it, and also reads and interprets the pointer field for accountants in that record; the symbol there indicates that 17745 is the last accountant's record in the file. By this process the records of all accountants can be quickly identified, read, and printed in list form. The records listed are those of Robert B. Baker, Abe Jones, and Jim Schultz.

A similar inquiry about plumbers results in a list of the payroll records of Bob Baker, Jim James, Al Normand, and Jim Schultz. As can be seen, Jim Schultz has the distinction of being both a plumber and an accountant, and for this reason his record is included on both lists.

Inverted List File Organization

An inverted list file is shown in Exhibit 10.9. At the top of the exhibit is a personnel file of employee records in alphabetic sequence; an actual personnel file would contain many more fields of data for each record than are shown. The address in the leftmost field represents the physical address of the record on a direct access storage device such as a disk. The next field is the primary key, and in this example it consists of the names of employees.

With inverted list file organization, a sequential file is maintained, and in addition several smaller files called "lists" are established. The lists at the bottom of the exhibit are constructed from information contained in the records of the sequential file shown at the top of the exhibit. For example, it can be seen that list 1 is an "inversion" of the position field in the sequential file in that instead of a primary key based on employee names that identifies the entire employee record (including the employee's position), the primary key in list 1 is based on position; employee names are not included in list 1.

Note that in list 1, each type of position is a separate record at a separate address and that each record in the list consists only of pointers

Sequential personnel file

Address	Name	Present position	Other experience	Marital status	Languages spoken	Pointer: Payroll Record address
111	Baker	Plumber	Supervisor, accountant	M	French, Spanish	1907
112	Carson	Carpenter	Plumber, supervisor	S	Spanish	1908
113	Jones	Supervisor	Janitor	S	Brooklynese	1909
114	Robbins	Janitor	Plumber	M	French, German	1910
115	Smith	Plumber	Cook, supervisor	S	None	1911
116	West	Plumber	Clerk, supervisor	S	French	1912

Inversion process

To prepare an inverted list file, "invert" the records so that the file consists of "attribute lists", i.e., several lists, each showing which employees have one particular attribute. The attribute is then linked by pointers to the record of each employee having the attribute.

Inverted lists

List 1: Position

Address	Position	Pointers		
500	Plumber	111	115	116
501	Carpenter	112		
502	Supervisor	113		
503	Janitor	114		

List 2: Experience

Address	Experience	Pointers			
504	Accountant	111			
505	Supervisor	111	112	115	116
506	Plumber	112	114		
507	Janitor	113			
508	Cook	115			
509	Clerk	116			

List 3: Marital status

Address	Status	Pointers			
510	Married	111	114		
511	Single	112	113	115	116

List 4: Languages spoken

Address	Language	Pointers		
512	French	111	114	116
513	Spanish	111	112	
514	German	114		
515	Brooklynese	113		

EXHIBIT 10.9
An inverted list file organization system.

to related complete records (to employees with that position) in the sequential file. By reading the "plumber" position record in list 1, the addresses of the sequential records of all plumbers can be found. For example, in list 1 the employees at the sequential file addresses 111, 115, and 116 are currently employed as plumbers, and if an inquiry or an applications program seeks information about plumbers, the computer system first reads list 1 and then follows its pointers to read the complete records of Baker, Smith, and West. Similarly, in list 3, it can be seen that the pointers for "married" permit the immediate determination of the addresses of the records of the two employees in the sequential file who are married and that they enable the computer system to access these employees' full records in the sequential personnel files.

As noted, the inverted list file system includes a sequential file in addition to the attributes lists. The sequential file enables efficient data processing of batch transactions and also provides a convenient single source for all the information about a particular employee. For instance, if it is necessary to review the complete records of the employees who speak German, the pointer in list 4 points toward the sequential file address 114, which provides Mr. Robbins's full personnel record.

An inverted list data base structure accelerates file search and report preparation. If several thousand employee records exist in a sequential file, searching the file to find, for example, the three employees who have experience as translators of Russian would involve extensive data processing, since each record would contain the complete personnel history of each employee and would be lengthy. This task would also require that a special program be written by a programmer.

The data processing involved in examining a list file containing only the addresses of records of persons with experience in Russian translation and then retrieving the records of these three employees would be slight by comparison. This task could easily be accomplished in a couple of minutes by a clerk or manager at a remote terminal, which would eliminate the inconvenience and delay involved in requesting the assistance of the data processing group.

The benefits of an inverted list file structure for this type of inquiry can be seen readily. Of course, as employees are added and deleted or as record items are added, deleted, or changed, a great deal or "overhead" data processing is incurred because the system must change the pointers in each list.

Hierarchical (Tree) File Organization

This file organization is based on natural hierarchical relationships between records; related records in the hierarchy are chained together with pointers. Hierarchical relationships between records may be thought of as similar to a family tree, in that a "child" record is related to a "parent" or "father" record in a definite way. For example, a customer account may be the parent to which that customer's invoices are related and chained by pointers. Similar hierarchical (family-tree) relationships serve as the reason to chain parts or component records to a product record in a

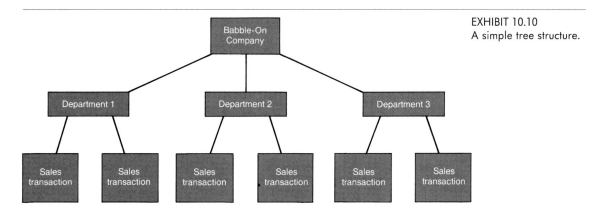

EXHIBIT 10.10
A simple tree structure.

manufacturing inventory system, to chain book and topic records to an author record in a library system, to chain debit and credit records to an accounting entry, or to chain subsidiary account records to a general ledger account. In most types of record sets, a hierarchical relationship between records can be discerned. Hierarchical organization is often described as a "tree structure" because the branches of the tree portray the hierarchy.

A tree structure is illustrated in Exhibits 10.10 and 10.11. In Exhibit 10.10 the natural hierarchical relationship of the records is evident. A vendor's customer, Babble-On Company, has three departments, each of which purchases products from the vendor company. The vendor's tree data base is structured to accommodate the hierarchical relationships between the customer, the customer's departments, and the detailed list of products associated with each sales transaction. This structure can accommodate a great many departments and a great many sales transactions within each department for each period. From this hierarchy an invoice can be prepared by the vendor for each transaction, and a report of the total sales to each department for each period can be produced readily. Additionally, even if Babble-On has many accounts with this vendor, it may

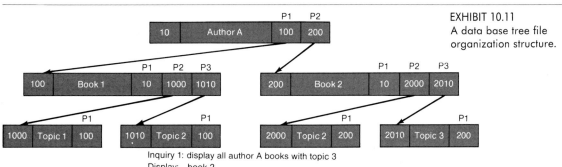

EXHIBIT 10.11
A data base tree file organization structure.

want one integrated monthly statement. This statement can be easily produced for all purchases of Babble-On's departments for mailing to that company's central accounts payable department. Finally, immediate responses concerning the purchases of any department of Babble-On can be obtained at any time by means of an inquiry to the data base. Of course, all the vendor's customer accounts would be organized in the same way that Babble-On Company's is.

The tree structure is portrayed in more detail in Exhibit 10.11. The author records are the parent records for the book records, and the book records are the parent records for the topic records. It can be seen that author A has written books 1 and 2; the first pointer field (P1) of author A's record points to book 1 at address 100, and the second pointer field (P2) points to book 2 at address 200. Similarly, it can be seen that two topics are chained to book 1 by pointer fields 2 and 3, indicating that book 1 contains information on these two topics. Book 2 also has within it information on two topics, as indicated by pointer fields 2 and 3. Thus, if an inquiry is made about what topics author A has written books on, the record of author A can be accessed, and its tree branches (pointers) followed from author to books to topics; the reply is then made that author A has written books on topics 1, 2, and 3.

In some circumstances there will be a need to traverse (follow pointers) not only from the top of the tree to the bottom but also from the bottom of the tree to the top, that is, from topic 1, for example, to book 1 to author A in order to identify author A as the author of a book containing information on topic 1 and to retrieve author A's record. For this it is necessary also to have a pointer from the child (topic) to its parent (book) and one from the book to its parent (author A). This is illustrated in Exhibit 10.11 by the pointer field P1 for topic 1, which points to its parent at address 100, and by the pointer field P1 for book 1, which points to its parent at address 10.

Additionally, it is typical in a tree file structure to provide for traversing laterally between records. While not shown in the exhibits, this can be accommodated by a tree structure.

Inquiry 1 in Exhibit 10.11 illustrates the accessing and retrieval processes in a tree structure system. The request to display all author A books that include information on topic 3 prompts the computer first to locate author A, which may be accomplished by reading a list of the authors (or by direct access). When the author A record is located, the pointer fields indicate the location in another part of the data base of the book records (perhaps even on a different disk). Similarly, when the book records are read, their pointers indicate the physical location of the topic records. The system then ascertains that only book 2 deals with topic 3, and this information is displayed as the answer to the inquiry.

The computer follows a similar routine for inquiry 2. In this example, the computer will first process the topic records in their section of the data base to identify all records dealing with topic 1. Each pointer in the topic 1 records will be followed back to its parent until the record of the author of the book containing information on topic 1 is located and displayed.

In Exhibits 10.10 and 10.11, it is the logical relationships rather than the physical storage arrangements for the records that are shown. The records could be physically stored randomly or in some organized sequence. Typically, records of each type are stored together. In Exhibit 10.11, for example, all author records would probably be stored together in author-number sequence so that these records could be efficiently processed to prepare royalty checks.

Network File Organization

The natural relationships between the records in Exhibit 10.12 are identical to those in Exhibit 10.11. Note that in Exhibit 10.11, topic 2 is associated with both book 1 and book 2; this necessitates storing two records for topic 2 and causes a duplication of these records in the data base. Often, duplicating records or fields within records is preferable to eliminating this redundancy completely. The complete elimination of redundancy, while theoretically possible, could result in a data base so complex that in practice it would be too difficult to implement and too costly to operate.

The duplication of records in Exhibit 10.11 can be eliminated by the network structure shown in Exhibit 10.12, whereby the child record, topic 2, is given the two parents of book 1 and book 2, as indicated by the pointers from both book 1 and book 2 to topic 2. With the inquiry in Exhibit 10.12, the computer will search until it finds topic 2 in the topics region of the data base. Because there is only one topic 2 record, the pointers will be followed from that record to its two parents of book 1 and book 2, and both will be identified as containing information on topic 2. Unlike a tree structure, which permits each record to have only one relationship, a network structure allows each record to have multiple parents. Using the tree structure of Exhibit 10.11, the reply to the inquiry would have been processed to find all topic 2 records.

As suggested by the example, a network structure permits more complex associations among records than a tree structure does; in theory,

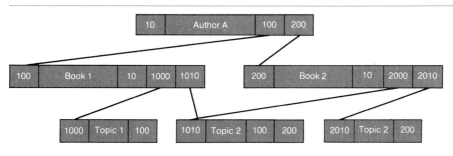

EXHIBIT 10.12
A data base network file organization structure.

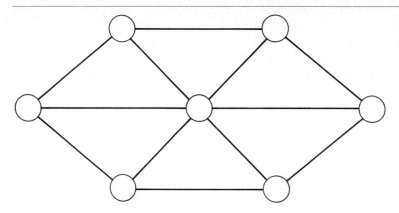

EXHIBIT 10.13
A generalized network
file organization
structure.

every possible relationship between records in the data base can be accounted for. Exhibit 10.13 portrays a generalized network file organization structure, with each circle representing a record and each line representing a linkage with another record, as indicated. The record in the center is associated via pointers with the six records surrounding it, and each of those six records is associated with three records. Although not shown, each of those six records could also have pointers to all six other records. As the number of the records increases arithmetically, the number of possible relationships increases geometrically; thus, as a practical matter, network structures become cumbersome beyond a limited number of pointers.

Relational Data Base Systems

A relational data base structure differs from the inverted list, tree, and network structures in that there are no predefined data access pathways in the nature of pointers; the relational structure does not use pointers.

The two essential characteristics of a relational structure are:

1. The file is in table form (similar in this respect to a sequential file).
2. Associations between records are made on the basis of the *values* in a field of records rather than on the basis of *addresses* (pointers) within records; thus there are no predefined data retrieval pathways.

Consider the two table files of records shown in Exhibit 10.14; the files can be processed separately or together. For example, if a request were directed to file A to list all accountants, the program would locate the title value field and read all title records, and only the records with the value "accountant" would be reported:

| Jones | 1234 | Accountant |
| Able | 4123 | Accountant |

A Relational File Structure

EXHIBIT 10.14

File A: Payroll Records

Employee Name	Department	Title
Jones	1234	Accountant
Smith	2341	Plumber
Baker	1234	Manager
Able	4123	Accountant
Dexter	4321	Manager

File B: Personnel Records

Employee Name	Department	Title
Dexter	4321	Manager
Brown	5421	Supervisor
Saunders	1234	Secretary
Jones	1234	Accountant
Reuben	5275	Accountant

This is known as the "selection" operation of a relational data base system. If the same selection request were directed to both files, the list selected would be:

Jones	1234	Accountant
Able	4123	Accountant
Reuben	5275	Accountant

The Jones record appears identically in both files, but the relational system would eliminate duplicate records.

Similar selection operations could be conducted for other values. For example, the request directed to both files to list all employees in department 1234 would produce:

Jones	1234	Accountant
Baker	1234	Manager
Saunders	1234	Secretary

Two files of records can be merged on the basis of one attribute field that both tables share; the shared field need not be in the same relative position within the records of each file. For example, the relational data base system could use a "join" operation for the two files shown in Exhibit 10.15 that would operate on the title field that the two files have in common.

Specific, programmed join rules are used. The first value in the title field of the first file (manager) is compared with each title value in the

---

Merging Files to Produce a Table   EXHIBIT 10.15

Employee	Department	Title
Dexter	4321	Manager
Brown	5421	Supervisor
Saunders	1234	Secretary
Jones	1234	Accountant
Reuben	5275	Accountant

Title	Pay Grade	Vacation Allowance
Accountant	Professional	3 weeks
Manager	Bonus	4 weeks
Secretary	Hourly	2 weeks
Supervisor	Salary	3 weeks

second field; each "match" (identical value) brings about a join of the matched records. Then the second value in the title field of the first file (supervisor) is compared with each title value in the second file, and so on. The result of all join operations is the table below.

Every relational operation is performed on a table of records and produces a new table. It can be seen that the relational structure is clean and conceptually simple, although the examples are overly simplified. The relational structure differs from an ordinary sequential structure in that:

1. Records in a relational system may be in any order (however, placing them in sequential order may in some situations make routine batch processing more efficient).

2. Records may be added to, and deleted from, a relational system with a minimum of processing overhead because there are no pointers that need to be added, deleted, or reorganized.

3. In a relational system the result of every processing operation is a new table of records; thus new files are easily created for new purposes.

While relational data bases seem simple, in fact they are based on strict mathematical constructs that are the result of several years of re-

Employee	Department	Title	Pay Grade	Vacation Allowance
Dexter	4321	Manager	Bonus	4 weeks
Brown	5421	Supervisor	Salary	3 weeks
Saunders	1234	Secretary	Hourly	2 weeks
Jones	1234	Accountant	Professional	3 weeks
Reuben	5275	Accountant	Professional	3 weeks

search by computer companies and universities. The advantages of a relational data base over other types are:

1. Relationships between records do not have to be established when the data base is created; users can dynamically establish associations between records to suit their own purposes by selecting fields from files and building new files.

2. Data can be added to files without affecting existing data.

3. Programmers can become familiar with relational systems in less than half the time required for other types of data bases.

The disadvantages of a relational data base are:

1. Duplication of field definitions in different files causes a high level of data redundancy and increases the chance of eventual inconsistent data in duplicated fields.

2. Relational data bases require extensive computer processing because every search for data necessitates searching the entire data base (reading all records) rather than only following pointers.

With respect to ease of formulating queries to access data, relational data systems may be preferable in situations where the need for data probably could not have been anticipated, whereas other data base systems are likely to permit easier formulation of queries where the needed internal data paths among records are already in place as pointers. Overall, deciding whether a relational or another data base system is preferable requires a careful analysis of each situation because the virtues of each depend on the nature of the data processing that will be done.

DATA BASES: SOME CHARACTERISTICS AND BENEFITS

A data base file organization has many advantages. A series of previously separate conventional files are managed together as one large, integrated system of files. With a data base, associations between records enable the programs of applications from several functional areas to process all data that is contained in the data base.

Exhibit 10.16 summarizes much of the material presented in the chapter to this point by comparing the characteristics of data base systems with those of conventional systems. (However, the exhibit was originally published before relational data bases were in existence.) To emphasize the distinctions between the two types of systems, they are portrayed as if they were entirely mutually exclusive, although the dividing line between data base systems and conventional file systems in not entirely clear-cut.

The characteristics of data bases summarized in Exhibit 10.16 provide benefits for data processing, and some also have important implications for managers, as described in the following chapter. One benefit for data

	Data base system	Conventional files
Logical files	Records related to several applications (data processing tasks or jobs) are a part of the same file or data base, in that they are in the same "logical file." In concept this is as if the data base consisted of one gigantic pool of data, which is equivalent to a merging of several or many conventional files.	Each application is separate from every other application, and data for each is located in a different logical file.
File structures	File structures are complex and are generally tree, network, or inverted list structures.[4]	File structure is likely to be relatively simple, primarily a "flat" or linear file structure similar to that typically found on magnetic tape.
Intra-file linkages	Linkages exist among the different records of the data base related to a common task (which may be an updating, processing, or report writing task) so that related data can be accessed simultaneously by following the linkages from one record to others. Examples of linkages embedded in records are chains and pointers; the traversing of these linkages may be directed by either systems software or applications programs.	Record linkages do not exist; related data are not extracted by following linkages from one record to another.
Systems software	A "data base management system" (DBMS) is used to "manage" the data in the data base, as examples, to simultaneously update records, allocate storage space and provide data security. The DBMS consists of several systems programs and normally takes up about as much storage space as the computer's operating system. The DBMS is required in addition to the operating system (which usually must be modified to accommodate the DBMS), and the DBMS and the operating system interact in complex ways.	Only the operating system and other normal systems software is used.
Applications programs	The data base approach emphasizes the independence of applications programs and data. Data names and other descriptions of content and data format are purged from the programs and placed within the data files. The data, neutral with respect to any specific applications programs, are readily available to all programs with access rights to the data base. The neutrality of the data base also enables it to be more efficiently updated and accessed.	Applications programs are written for a specific purpose to serve a particular file of data. Only the few applications programs developed specifically for a particular file can access that file, and these programs can access no other file. Data elements are tied to specific computer applications programs by embedding unique data names and other descriptive or data definitional characteristics into these programs. One consequence is that a large proportion of corporate data is "locked up" by existing computer programs because entirely new programs have to be written to access data for other than routine reports.
File and program standards	Almost all file design characteristics must be standardized, and applications program syntax, data definitions, and so on must be scrupulously maintained according to common standards to permit multiple applications programs to access the data base.	Typically, each separate file and its associated programs share common standards not shared by other file/program sets. Thus an applications program not only cannot update multiple files simultaneously, it cannot be processed at all against files other than the one it was written for.

EXHIBIT 10.16
Conventional files compared with data base files. (*Source: George M. Scott, "Auditing the Data Base," CA Magazine, October 1978.*)

processing is reduced data redundancy, except for relational data bases. Even large organizations have discovered after implementation of a data base that they have somewhere in the range of from only 400 to 700 unique types of data items; often these have been distilled from several thousand in the conventional file system, many of which had identical meanings but were differently defined in different files and programs. Reduced data redundancy increases data processing efficiency and reduces the possibility of conflicting information in the data base.

Data bases have other advantages. Program/file independence, which means that the programs contain no references to data location and no data descriptions, reduces the amount of programming effort required to write the applications programs. Programs can be written more quickly, and each program can access the entire data base, with the result that often fewer programs must be writen. In turn, these programming advantages help decrease the time required to develop programs for critical management problems, often by severalfold.

A related data processing advantage of data bases is that applications programs need not be altered when the format of records is altered because the applications programs merely identify to the data base management system (DBMS) the data that is needed; it is the responsibility of the DBMS to know where within the file and within the record the data is located. In conventional files, whenever a record format is altered, several applications programs usually must be revised.

A data base can increase the possibility that information will evolve, rather than become obsolete as new information needs emerge, because multiple avenues are provided for acessing data, such as by means of applications programs, query language, and the use of any of multiple access keys. For example, if sales data is stored in a conventional system according to the primary key of product serial number and if information about product serial numbers of sales to a particular customer is needed, the data cannot be easily accessed. However, an inverted list system with an inverted list consisting of customers may resolve the problem. In this example, if an inverted list with customer as the key does not exist, but changing information needs indicate that it will be required in the future, the data base could be made to evolve gracefully by adding a customer list file without altering the data base structure or the existing programs.

Other benefits of data bases are that data base integration results in less intermediate processing where cross-functional data is needed (there should be no transfer files needed within the data base environment) and that less data input activity is required where one transaction updates multiple records simultaneously. The reduction of these activities, in turn, reduces the incidence of data processing errors and inconsistent records; as a result, data processing operates within a more controlled environment. Also of importance is the fact that with a data base, current operations data is readily available. Finally, more timely correction of errors such as invalid codes is possible because typically in a data base environment, transactions are processed sooner after they occur than in a conventional file environment.

As has been indicated, data bases represent a significant development in data processing technology. The implications of data base file organization extend beyond technical considerations and embrace the dimensions of better information services for managers. Data bases can serve as one of the cornerstones of information systems for management purposes and can significantly influence the management processes in organizations by reducing the constraints of information availability and timeliness.

Unfortunately, in practice data processing personnel frequently lose sight of the purpose of data bases as being to increase access to data so that better information can be provided faster and instead devote most of their attention to installing and improving data bases as a convenience for data processing, for example, to make program revision easier. One consequence is that many data bases are unifunctional rather than cross-functional; that is, they contain data from only one functional area, rather than from multiple functional areas. Unifunctional data bases provide most of the benefits for data processors, whereas cross-functional data bases are much more difficult and time-consuming to design and implement. Cross-functional data base development requires much more extensive participation of managers, which is difficult to get. The author knows of one medium-sized company with five data bases that are entirely within payroll and with no data bases that cross functional boundaries.

In most cases data bases cannot be justified on the basis of data processing convenience, cost savings, or other data processing considerations, and data bases should not be implemented primarily for data processing personnel. Data bases are expensive to design and implement, require extensive processing capacity and communications capability, and also may require additional data processing personnel. The additional costs of a data base system are usually greater—and sometimes much greater—than the cost savings and usually cannot be justified on the basis of convenience value to data processors.

SUMMARY

This chapter examined sequential, indexed sequential, and direct access conventional file data structures and inverted list, hierarchical (tree), network, and relational data base structures. Sequential files require processing every record in sequence, but with an indexed sequential structure an index provides a starting point partway through the file where sequential processing can begin. Direct accessing involves an index containing the addresses of specific records sought; thus no sequential processing is required.

Data processing using conventional file organizations has several shortcomings. These include a great amount of intermediate processing caused by the frequent need to create transfer files; the existence of inconsistencies in related files, as some files are updated but others are not (or are not updated without errors); and the convoluted activity required for preparation of special reports that must utilize data from multiple separate files. Most data base file organizations can reduce or eliminate these problems.

The essential characteristic of the inverted list data base file organization is that a table file (flat file) of records is first established (usually in sequential form), and then separate "lists" are made for particular attributes of the flat file. The original flat file is retained. Pointers in each list predefine a path back to a record in the original table file. A tree data structure is a hierarchical rather than a table structure. A "parent" record is linked via a pointer to a "child" record at the next level in the hierarchy to define data access paths, with no child record having two parents.

A network file structure is conceptually similar to a hierarchical file structure; both have parent-to-child (and usually child-to-parent) data access pathways. However, with a network structure, each child may have multiple parents, permitting very complex record associations. A relational structure involves flat files that are manipulated according to a set of rules that establish associations between records on the basis of field values that the records have in common.

Data bases have many advantages for data processing. However, they are expensive to design and maintain, so in most cases they should be justified on the basis of their utility to managers rather than their utility to data processing personnel.

KEY TERMS

data file: any storage location for data records.

electronic data file: a data file that stores data in electronic and computer-readable form.

file organization: the structure of the data files with respect to their format (such as position and size of each data field), record sequence, and relationships among records.

sequential file organization: a data file structure that involves storing records in a definite physical sequence, such as alphabetically.

direct file organization: a data file structure that permits any record to be accessed immediately without first accessing all earlier records in the file.

indexed sequential file organization: a data file structure that permits access directly to an intermediate point in a data file and uses sequential processing thereafter to locate a particular record.

data redundancy: the existence in the data files of duplicate data items.

pointer: the physical address of a record that is placed in another record to enable a program to proceed from the other record to the record pointed to by the address.

inverted list file organization: a data base file structure that consists of lists of pointers that point to specific records in a sequential file that possess certain attributes.

hierarchical (tree) file: a data base file structure that is based on a hierarchical relationship among records so that related records are linked by pointers.

network file organization: a data base file organization that permits any record in a data base to be associated with any other records through the use of multiple pointers.

relational file organization: a data base file structure that establishes associations among records on the basis of identical data fields rather than pointers.

REFERENCES

Davis, Gordon B., *Computers and Information Processing,* New York: McGraw-Hill, 1978.

Barley, Kathryn S., and James R. Driscoll, "A Survey of Data-Base Management Systems for Microcomputers," *BYTE,* November 1981, p. 208.

McFadden, Fred R., and James D. Suver, "Costs and Benefits of a Data Base System," *Harvard Business Review,* January–February 1978.

Martin, James, *Principles of Data Base Administration,* Englewood Cliffs, NJ: Prentice-Hall, 1976.

Sandberg, G., "A Primer on Relational Data Base Concepts," *IBM Systems Journal,* vol. 20, no. 1, 1981.

Scott, George M., "A Data Base for Your Company?" *California Management Review,* Fall 1976.

Scott, George M., "Auditing the Data Base," *CA Magazine,* October 1978.

Weiss, Harvey M., "Which DBMS Is Right for You?" *Mini-Micro Systems,* October 1981, pp. 157–160.

Wiorkowski, Gabrielle K., and John J. Wiorkowski, "Does a Data Base Management System Pay Off?" *Datamation,* April 1978.

REVIEW QUESTIONS

1. How are special reports prepared with a conventional file system? How is this different with a data base system?

2. What are the characteristics of each of the following file structures?

(*a*) Sequential
(*b*) Indexed sequential
(*c*) Direct accessing
(*d*) Inverted list
(*e*) Hierarchical
(*f*) Network
(*g*) Relational

3. What are the similarities and differences between the following?

(a) Sequential and relational file organizations
(b) Hierarchical and network file organizations

4. How do pointers make data bases "integrated"? What mechanism integrates relational data bases?

PROBLEMS

1. Prepare a generalized network file organization schematic similar to that of Exhibit 10.13 for the records shown in Exhibit 10.8.

2. Assume that the file in Exhibit 10.8 is an indexed sequential file that contains no pointers but does have a record index containing the address of the first record of each letter of the alphabet.
(a) How would payroll pay-rate changes probably be processed?
(b) How would processing be done to prepare a list of all employees whose last names begin with "Sc"?
(c) How would processing be done to prepare a list of all plumbers? How could the record of the first plumber in the file be located?

3. Answer the questions below using the pointers in the file.
(a) Crocker is located in the northern region. What other customers are also in the northern region?
(b) Jackson is in the western region. What other customers are also in the western region?
(c) Garner, Howe, Ish, and Brown are all wholesalers. Establish a pointer structure in the pointer field provided which links these wholesaler customers.

Computer Address	Customer Number	Customer Name	Data	Pointer Field	
				Region	Wholesalers
10	4	Deaker	xxx...	12	
11	2	Brown	xxx...	18	
12	9	Jackson	xxx...	17	
13	7	Howe	xxx...	15	
14	3	Crocker	xxx...	16	
15	5	Fibers	xxx...	13	
16	8	Ish	xxx...	19	
17	6	Garner	xxx...	10	
18	10	Tamer	xxx...	11	
19	1	Allen	xxx...	14	

4. In recent years one of the largest United States cities was thought to be in financial distress, but the extent of this distress could not be known because the city's data processing department was unable to provide reliable information about the debts of the city to its vendors. In many instances, a single vendor sold a multiplicity of goods and services to several of the city's departments. A data base was installed and soon enabled the city to receive a full accounting of its debts, which indicated that it was on the verge of bankruptcy. How would a data base accomplish this, and how was the data base probably organized?

5. What data base or bases could a university use? Consider first the various functions at a university (registration, student records, fund-raising, student activities, and so on) and the information needs of each. Then consider what should be in the data base and how it would be used. Finally, consider the cross-functional information flows that do or could exist, and suggest cross-functional data bases, specifying their information content and how they would be used. (This problem may be done in enough detail to qualify as a class project.)

CASE

Watergate Plumbing

Watergate Plumbing has acquired a small plumbing subsidiary in France and wishes to send an employee from the United States to manage this new subsidiary for a few weeks and to train the French employees in the use of the American parent's management system. This employee must possess certain qualities; it is preferable that the employee be single because it is costly to send a married employee's family abroad for so brief a period, and yet it is unreasonable to expect a married employee to be separated from a family for several weeks or months.

Watergate Plumbing uses an inverted list data base for its personnel files. (This data base is identical to that shown in Exhibit 10.9, which the student should refer to for the remainder of this case.) To determine whom to send to France, Mr. Watergate interrogated the data base. An inquiry command was typed in at a terminal using the query language commands illustrated in Exhibit 10.17; no applications programs needed to be written. When the inquiry was made, the computer performed the steps shown. Processing of list 4 found the addresses of the employees who spoke French (the addresses of Baker, Robbins, and West) and placed these in a section of memory used for temporary storage of data being processed. The computer system continued to find and store the record addresses of the employees possessing the other required attributes by processing the other lists, none of which were lengthy since they contained only the sequential file addresses of employee records. The computer then performed an internal compare-and-select function, as shown in step 9. In this case it was found that only the employee whose record address was 116 possessed all the

required attributes. Because the inquiry command requested that the records of all employees with these attributes be displayed on a video display device (a PRINT command would produce a printout), record 116 was displayed as in step 10.

If the original inquiry had elicited too many responses, further requirements might have been imposed. For example, if the inquiry had shown that more than 100 employees possessed the attributes specified and if the temporary manager of the new French subsidiary would have had to visit and consult with the German manager of the German subsidiary, it would have been possible to further specify in a subsequent inquiry that candidates also had to speak German.

Assume that the inquiry command also requested that the employees' addresses and pay rates be displayed. If neither of these pieces of information had been included in the sequential personnel file, this command could have been accommodated by following the payroll address pointer shown as 1912 in West's personnel record in Exhibit 10.9. In that file, the program would have found additional data about West for display, including his address and pay rate.

It can be seen that the necessity to read and process every lengthy record in the personnel file during an inquiry was eliminated by instead reading one or several much shorter inverted lists. Additionally, the program required to make inquiries into a data base system can be quite simple and consist of only a few instructions in a query language. This inquiry capability can be, in effect, a modest special-report preparation capability that enables managers to prepare more timely special reports; if the manager had to submit a request to

EXHIBIT 10.17

Situation

A company has acquired a small plumbing subsidiary in France and wants to send an employee to there for a short period of time to manage it. The person to be sent should have supervisory and plumbing experience, should speak French, and should be single.

Inquiry command at a Terminal:

DISPLAY EMPLOYEE RECORDS WHERE EXPERIENCE = PLUMBING & SUPERVISORY AND MARITAL STATUS = SINGLE AND LANGUAGE = FRENCH

Processing Procedure by the Computer

1. ACCESS LIST 4 (FRENCH)
2. STORE ADDRESSES 111, 114, 116
3. ACCESS LISTS 1 AND 2 (PLUMBING)
4. STORE ADDRESSES 111, 115, 116, 112, 114
5. ACCESS LISTS 1 AND 2 (SUPERVISOR)
6. STORE ADDRESSES 113, 111, 112, 115, 116
7. ACCESS LIST 3 (SINGLE)
8. STORE ADDRESSES 112, 113, 115, 116
9. PERFORM AN INTERNAL COMPARE-AND-SELECT FUNCTION:
   FROM STEP 2: 111   114   116
   FROM STEP 4: 111   112   114   115   116
   FROM STEP 6: 111   112   113   115   116
   FROM STEP 8:   112   113   115   116
10. DISPLAY ALL RECORDS MEETING THE SPECIFIED CONDITIONS:
    116   WEST   PLUMBER   CLERK/SUPERVISOR   S   FRENCH

data processing for the information sought, it might be a matter of hours, days, or even weeks before a special report could be provided. This delay might be caused in part by scheduling problems and in part by a possible need to write programs for each of several independent files. In a data base system, inquiries that produce special reports are able to transcend the boundaries of individual applications files.

Note: This case is intended to demonstrate some of the advantages of an inverted list file organization over conventional file organizations. The query language used is unique with each data base system; the query commands used in this case are illustrative only.

Case Questions

1. The chapter notes that pointer systems existed before data bases: could a pointer system have been established in a conventional file to accomplish the inquiry of the case as well as similar inquiries? Explain.

2. Referring to Exhibit 10.5, explain the processing activities that would be the result of the inquiry: DISPLAY ALL EMPLOYEE RECORDS WHERE MARITAL STATUS = SINGLE AND EXPERIENCE = ACCOUNTANT OR SUPERVISOR

Case prepared by George M. Scott.

Chapter 11

DATA BASE SYSTEMS

PAYOFF THOUGHT

Managers should view data bases as a managerial development, with technical underpinnings, that has the major purpose of benefiting management and thereby enhancing the effectiveness of the entire organization. The greatest payoff from data bases, and the primary way in which they can be justified, is better information for managing the organization.

CHAPTER OBJECTIVES

1. To explore the relationship between data bases and the concept of data as a resource

2. To explain the components and elements of a data base system

3. To examine the nature of operations-level data bases

4. To portray data bases as an important tool for managers at all levels, with particular attention to data bases organized for key managerial tasks

5. To present data base design considerations that are especially important for designing managerially oriented data bases

6. To consider how data bases can alter management practices

INFORMATION AS A RESOURCE

The concept of information as a resource to be managed was carefully developed in an earlier chapter. There the information resource management (IRM) idea was explored, and the similarity of management of information to management of other resources was discussed. The concept of information as a resource of the organization provides a major impetus to the development of data bases. A thorough understanding of the information resource management concept assists managers and data processing personnel alike to appreciate the need for a strong managerial orientation of the organization's data bases. This understanding also reinforces the need to plan the data base initially within the context of the organization's full range of activities, its organization structure, and its management processes.

In a conventional data processing environment, individual data files are for one functional activity, and the data files and applications programs tend to be "owned" by the functional departments for which they were created; departments are proprietary about the data originated in their area and about the files and programs created for this data. The originating department usually exercises a degree of jurisdiction over the data, normally controlling the format of the data input to the computer and determining what data is computerized. Other departments may find that even if the computerized data is available to them, it is not in the form they need. Data is not widely shared within the organization, and its use is suboptimized.

One of the most important concepts behind data bases is that of a "data pool." This involves automating the transfer of data from the files of different functions to applications programs in a way that enables data to be processed by the other files' programs without any program modifications. With this concept, data is no longer associated with a particular functional file's programs exclusively or with the department that provided the data, but instead is a part of a larger pool of data that is readily available to all programs. The data files involved then constitute one large logical data file, or data pool, even though as a practical matter the data pool concept often involves multiple files, each of which stores functionally related records.

However, when data is placed in a data base that encompasses data from several functional areas, each organizational unit is forced to share the data. Because data bases are usually kept on-line, the data is accessible at any time to the programs of any application and to queries from managers, assuming that they have access rights. Managers begin to view the data base as a pool of data that is an entity unto itself, conceptually separate from the computer system that processes the data.

When this atmosphere is fully developed, the perspective becomes one of seeing information as the desired output of an information production process which has the dual purpose of manufacturing information for operations and manufacturing information for management use, with about equal emphasis on each. This perspective on the part of middle and senior managers is an important element in establishing the organizational climate within which an MIS can be fully developed.

Their view of data as a resource alters managers' expectations of the information system and, in sometimes subtle ways, begins to alter the management processes through a chain reaction. An information resource perspective affects the extent to which data bases are designed to serve management purposes. This in turn reduces the constraints imposed by information availability. With reduced constraints, the management processes are gradually altered in a variety of ways, discussed in the last section of this chapter.

The greater sharing of data also alleviates constraints on the organization's structure. With terminals accessing the data base, information is readily available for centralized management purposes or, with equal facility, for decentralized management purposes. Information need not be "locked up" in the files of headquarters or those of the divisions, but instead can be available to managers at all locations.

Data sharing also has implications for the information systems strategies of individual organization units. With conventional file systems, often one department routinely gathers the same information as another in order to reduce dependence on the other department. With a data base system, the need for this duplication of data gathering is eliminated. Also, with a low marginal cost of data, managers are more likely to be innovative in using it for new purposes. The entire information function tends to become more "usage-oriented" and less preoccupied with data collection and storage and transactions processing.

Finally, viewing information as a resource ultimately causes managers to see it as a part of an interrelated system of financial, physical, human, and information resources. They see that all these resource types must be managed in concert to achieve the goals of the organization.

WHAT IS A DATA BASE?

Regardless of its file organization, a data base system includes several components that collectively give it certain distinct, specific characteristics. The following is a succinct definition of data base:

> A data base is a computer file system that uses a particular *file organization* to facilitate *rapid updating of individual records, simultaneous updating of related records, easy access to all records by all applications programs,* and *rapid access* to all stored data which must be brought together for a particular *routine report or inquiry* or a *special-purpose report or inquiry.*

A data base *system* includes the data base files as well as several other components. These components are described later in this chapter.

Each of the italicized phrases in the preceding definition has a special meaning that helps define a data base. "File organization" indicates that the data base has one of the four file structures examined in the last chapter that enable programs to establish associations between the records in the data base.

A data base facilitates "rapid updating of individual records" and "simultaneous updating of related records"; that is, a data base permits the entry of an individual transaction to update all records affected by that transaction simultaneously. For example, consider a $100 credit sale. In a data base system, the following accounts, along with others, could be updated simultaneously with the input of the one transaction:

- Sales record

- Salesperson's commissions record

- Division sales record

- Accounts receivable customer record

- Inventory item record

- Cost of sales of individual item record

Although most data bases are organized so that only certain of the preceding records are updated simultaneously, it is possible to have all records updated simultaneously if a data base exists that includes sales, accounts receivable, inventory, and cost of sales records.

If transactions are entered as they occur, records that are simultaneously updated are continuously up to date for managerial inquiry purposes. Simultaneous updating also means that the records have consistent contents. For example, the total of the sales record would be consistent with the salespersons's commissions record because the latter is based on the former and both are updated at the same time.

"Easy access to all records by all applications programs" means that the standard data definitions and record formats permit, for example, a payroll applications program to access the social security numbers of, and data about, dependents from the personnel section of the data base and that work-force planning programs can access pay rates from the payroll section and employee skills from the personnel section of the data base. Without a data base, each applications program would be able to access only data from its own file.

With respect to "rapid access" to all stored data needed for a "routine report or inquiry," routine reports can be provided quickly after the end of the accounting period and often whenever requested during the period if the processing of transactions is kept up to date. This is possible because transfer file processing is not required at the end of the period and because data summarization for reports can be fully automated within a data base; in sum, little period-end processing is required. Similarly, inquiries can be routinely made into the files, for example, to see whether a particular product is available for immediate shipment.

Rapid access with respect to a "special-purpose report or inquiry" means that records are kept continuously up to date for unanticipated inquiries into the files by managers and that the structure of the data base files facilitates the rapid development of special programs to prepare reports about unanticipated problems; this feature will be considered later in the chapter.

COMPONENTS OF A DATA BASE

Exhibit 11.1 provides a conceptual view of a data base as several traditional files placed in a common "pool" so that all the data elements in the files of this pool are readily available to all programs that are authorized to access the data base. A description of the logical structure (data relationships) and a complete listing and description of the names and attributes of all data elements of a data base are known as its "schema." The schema is the overall view of the entire data base.

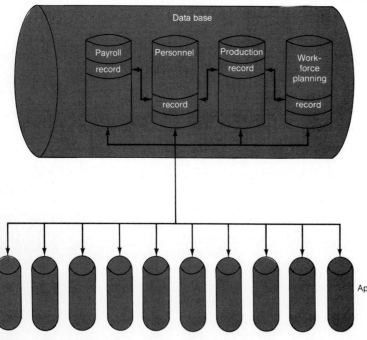

EXHIBIT 11.1
A conceptual view of the data base.

Application programs from multiple functions

As indicated in the exhibit, a large number of applications programs can access the entire data base system of files. These programs can be associated with any of the functional activities of the organization. It is usually the case that only the applications programs of those functional files which are included in the data base (or in another data base) will conform to the standards required for access to the data base.

Each applications program will actually access only a small proportion of the data elements in the data base—those data elements which the program needs for its processing. This subset of the schema needed by an applications program is called a "subschema." A subschema is the view of the data base that consists of only a certain part of the data base, and for a particular applications program the subschema consists of the data elements that it will use.

The arrows connecting the records in Exhibit 11.1 indicate that specific records within each of the previously independent files are now linked to other records by pointers, as is done with three of the four types of data base file structures. When pointers are used, the records are said to be "chained"; a record pointed to—the next record in the chain—may be physically located in another section of the data base and may be logically an integral part of another set of records in another functional area, but the effect of the linkage established by the pointer is to include the record pointed to as a part of the same logic set of records that includes the record containing the pointer.

The system of pointers serves to integrate the data base; that is, the pointers establish relationships between the records so that records can be logically related in complex patterns, thereby providing a flexibility and utility unique to data bases.

Exhibit 11.1 is an oversimplification of the interaction of programs with the data base. Exhibit 11.2 extends this view by portraying the major components of the data base system; not all systems have all the following components:

1. *The data base files.* These files have data elements (individual items of data) stored in one of the four data base file organization formats.

2. *A data base management system (DBMS).* The DBMS is a set of software programs that manages the data base, controls access to the data base, provides data base security, and performs other tasks. The DBMS will be examined further later in this chapter.

3. *A host language interface system.* This is the part of the DBMS that communicates with the applications programs. The host language interface interprets instructions in high-level language applications programs, such as COBOL and FORTRAN programs, that request data from the files so that the data needed can be retrieved. During this process the computer's operating system interacts with the DBMS in complex ways that vary with the particular DBMS. With this arrangement the applications programs do

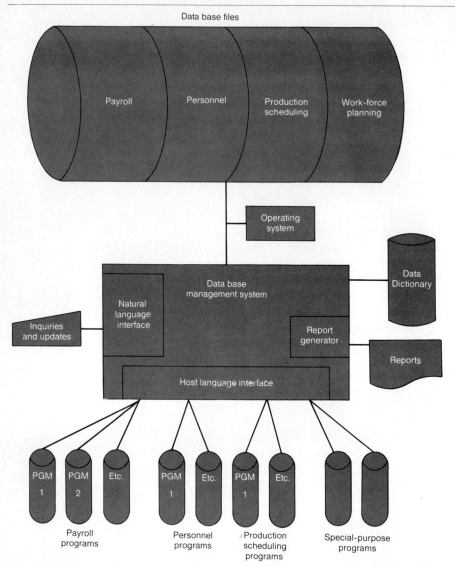

EXHIBIT 11.2
The data base
components.

not contain information about the file, which accounts in part for the program/file independence of a data base system; that is, there is nothing in the program that restricts its use to a particular data file.

4. *The application programs.* These programs perform much the same functions that they do in conventional systems, but are independent of the data files and use standard data definitions, as will be further explained at a later point. This independence and standardization make rapid special-purpose program development easier and faster. Applications programs using the host language interface usually are developed by professional programmers.

5. *A natural language interface system.* This query language permits on-line update and inquiry by users who are relatively unsophisticated about computer systems. This language is often termed "English-like" because instructions input using it are usually in the form of a simple command in English, rather than consisting of symbols and equations. While most of the commands of query languages are preprogrammed and are activated when the user keys in combinations of English words to accomplish an inquiry task, as illustrated in the last chapter, query languages also permit on-line programming of simple routines by managers who wish to interact with the data base. For example, managers may be able to develop "what if . . .?" models or investigate the status of projects in process by writing short programs rather than using existing query language commands. The natural language interface system may also facilitate the development of elementary special reports by managers or their assistants. However, professional programmers utilize the normal programming languages for more complex special-purpose report development. In general, query languages differ from applications program languages in that they are not designed for problem solving but instead are designed primarily to access the data base and retrieve information about record status and content.

6. *The data dictionary.* This is a centralized depository of information in computerized form about the data in the data base. The data dictionary contains the schema of the data base—the name of each item in the data base and a description and definition of its attributes—and these descriptions and definitions are referred to as the "data standards." The data dictionary includes information about locations of data in the data base files and many also contain data access rules and security and privacy information about the data. With most data base systems, the DBMS receives a request from a program for data and then accesses the data base dictionary to determine whether the program has the right to receive the data sought and to ascertain the location of the data in the data base.

7. *On-line access and update terminals.* These may be adjacent to the computer or even thousands of miles away. They may be dumb terminals, smart terminals, or microcomputers.

8. *The output system, or report generator.* This provides routine job reports, documents (such as invoices), and special reports.

THE DATA BASE MANAGEMENT SYSTEM

As has been mentioned, the DBMS is a set of systems software programs that manages the data base files. The DBMS accesses the files, updates the records in either batch or single-transaction mode, and retrieves data as requested. The DBMS also has the responsibility for adding and deleting records, reorganizing the data base by reassigning storage space to make processing more efficient, and performing other housekeeping chores.

Additionally, the DBMS has the responsibility for data security. In a data base environment, data security is a vitally important consideration.

One reason is that the data base is accessed by many users. The DBMS grants or withholds clearance to the applications programs and terminal users for accessing the data base files. Many of these programs and users are permitted to access certain records (or fields within records) in the data base but not others, and the DBMS ensures that only those areas are accessed for which clearance has been granted.

Another reason for the importance of data base security is that the centralization of so much data in one logical file makes the organization vulnerable to damage to, or destruction of, the file. The DBMS must ensure that the data base, if destroyed in whole or in part, can be accurately and quickly reconstructed. To accomplish this, the DMBS contains programmed routines that enable it to determine which records were affected by a malfunction or error and to reconstruct those records.

IMS, a DBMS of IBM, can be used to illustrate the operation of a DBMS. With IMS an applications program contains data specification information that indicates the nature of the data needed by the program. This information is passed as a data request to the program specification block (PSB) of IMS. The PSB determines the access rights of that program. IMS then accesses the data base descriptions file (a data dictionary) to find the data descriptions. This information is given to data management routines of IMS that retrieve the data from the files for use by the applications program.

Numerous DBMSs are in existence, ranging in price from less than $500 to around $200,000. Many of these are for minicomputer and microcomputer systems, and they often have quite restricted DBMS capabilities. It is common, for example, for minicomputer and microcomputer DBMSs to have only limited file access security and file reconstruction capabilities, and many also have limited or nonexistent query language capabilities. Over 40 DBMSs exist for microcomputers.

Exhibit 11.3 lists several well-known data base systems that vary widely in terms of type, capabilities, and cost. IMS, for example, is in the $100,000 range, but lacks a sophisticated query language capability. Several of those listed in the exhibit can operate on any of several manufacturers' computers. At present dBASE-II appears to be the best-known data base system for microcomputers. FOCUS and ORACLE are relational data bases which were developed for mainframe computers but which also now operate on IBM and IBM-compatible microcomputers. The cost of ORACLE for mainframe computers is around $90,000, and for microcomputers it is in the $1000 range. Not all available relational data bases possess all the characteristics of pure relational data base systems.

In choosing a DBMS, several considerations other than cost are important. Four of the most important are:

1. *The query language.* A DBMS without a query language capability is satisfactory for data processing but is limited for managerial usage. In

Several Well-Known Data Base Systems	EXHIBIT 11.3

Computer Type	Primary File Type
Mainframe:	
IMS	Hierarchical
ADABAS	Inverted list
TOTAL	Mixed
IDMS	Relational
QUERY-BY-EXAMPLE	Relational
SQL	Relational
Microcomputer:	
dBASE-II	Relational
DATA BASE PLUS	Relational
Mainframe and Microcomputer:	
FOCUS	Relational
ORACLE	Relational

particular, rapid preparation of simple special management reports is inhibited by the lack of an adequate query language.

2. *Security considerations.* Certain DBMSs do not have adequate data security provisions; for example, some lack user passwords that permit only authorized users to access the data base, and others have file recovery systems that are awkward or nonexistent.

3. *Processing "overhead" costs.* A DBMS is the same as other software programs in that its programs must be processed by the CPU, which decreases the amount of time the CPU has available for its primary task of processing data rather than programs. This overhead cost varies widely among DBMSs, but if it is significant relative to total computing capacity, it seriously limits the ability of a computer system to complete its data processing tasks.

4. *Suitability for type of application.* Each DBMS is relatively better for certain types of accessing, inquiry, or report preparation activities than for others. A relational data base, for example, is especially well suited to situations in which large new files must be created by extracting data from existing files; this would be the case in some circumstances when separate files must be built for a decision support system. The inverted list file organization is excellent where a high proportion of the retrieval needs cannot be specified in advance but where combinations of attributes from different records are often needed. This is due to the fact that each attribute that is likely to be needed in combination with others can be placed in its separate list. Full flexibility can be achieved with the inverted list structure by placing every attribute of records in a separate list; however, for records with many attributes fields, the maintenance of the system of pointers as records are added, deleted, or changed in location consumes a great deal of processing time.

Prior to selection of a DBMS, the expected mix of types of tasks that it will be required to perform should be identified and compared with the relative advantages of available DBMSs. Independent testing agencies rank DBMSs according to several criteria. Often their reports are published in data processing journals.

THE GEOGRAPHY OF DATA BASES

Each organization may have several data bases; they may be all at one location, or they may be geographically distributed. The following discussion examines three general geographic configurations of data bases in the context of an organization with operations at a headquarters location and at two divisional locations.

The first arrangement is that of one centralized data base, as shown in the first example in Exhibit 11.4. The entire data base is physically at one location—in this case, at headquarters. For many such centralized systems, the local divisions can access the data base via telecommunications.

The second configuration shown in Exhibit 11.4 is that of independent data bases. With this configuration, headquarters has its own data base, and each division also has a separate data base. This type of configuration is logical for those circumstances in which the three different locations perform essentially different functions and seldom need direct access to data at another location, for example, when headquarters is the administrative center of a decentralized organization and when each division is a self-contained profit center.

The third data base structure illustrated in the exhibit is that of a distributed data base, which is associated with a distributed processing information system. Data in the same logical data base is physically distributed among all three locations. The data base linkages are established between data elements and records as if all the data were at the same location. Any data that is available in the data base at one location can be automatically accessed by programs from either of the other locations. While the technical problems involved with implementing and managing a physically distributed data base are severe, they are not insurmountable.

DATA BASE TECHNOLOGY: A SUMMARY

Most data base systems have most of the following characteristics:

   1. A file structure that facilitates the association of one internal record with other internal records

   2. Cross-functional integration of files so that records which previously would have been in entirely independent files can now be associated and processed together automatically

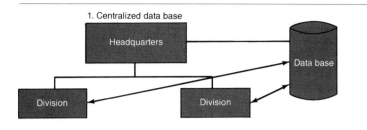

1. Centralized data base

EXHIBIT 11.4
Alternative data base
organizations for
multiple locations.

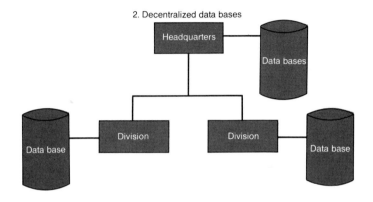

2. Decentralized data bases

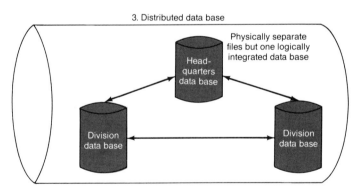

3. Distributed data base

Physically separate files but one logically integrated data base

3. Program/data file independence, which eases the updating and maintenance of the data base and enhances special-report capabilities

4. Common standards throughout with respect to data definitions, record formats, and other types of data descriptions

5. A DBMS to manage the data files

6. A data dictionary that contains information about the data and the data base

7. Large-scale direct access memory to contain the data and the DBMS

8. Sophisticated communications equipment and programs that permit multiple users to access the data base simultaneously

9. Sophisticated backup, recovery, and restart techniques to permit reconstruction of the data base files if data is lost or destroyed

10. A query language that permits easy on-line inquiry as well as records update on a transaction-by-transaction basis

Each of these characteristics existed to a degree before data bases emerged. It is the combination and further refinement of them in recent years that has led to data base systems.

Data bases are primarily the consequence of the evolution and continued refinement of existing technologies. Equally important, data bases reflect the concept of viewing data as a resource of the organization; this perspective has helped bring about the merging of technologies and the era of data bases.

OPERATIONS DATA BASES

There are two general classes of data base usage: operations activities usage and managerial activities usage. In this section the advantages of operations data bases for operations activities are explored.

Generally, operations activities require full detail about the transactions involved. At this operations level, the key attributes of data bases, many of which also have relevance to managerial activities, are as described below:

1. *Consistency of related information elements.* A mark of operating personnel (as well as of managers) is that they are continuously alert for information that is inconsistent with information they already possess. If information from different sources about the same transaction is consistent (one source tends to confirm and support the other), this information, as well as the information system, has greater validity. On the other hand, inconsistency of information acquired from different sources provides ample reason to wonder about the quality of the information system. If these inconsistencies are pervasive, operations personnel may develop time-consuming supplemental information systems of their own.

A major source of inconsistent data is the lack of file synchronization in a traditional file system, which is caused by updating related records in different files at different points in time, for example, when a newly married employee's name is changed in different files at different times, causing reports taken from each file on one date to show the employee as having two different names. Additionally, a schedule usually exists for the correction of data processing errors that are deemed noncritical; thus information extracted from the files before corrections are made is inconsistent with information extracted after they are made. A great advantage of data bases is that all related records are maintained synchronously.

2. *Timeliness of transactions information and of management reports.* The more closely that information pertaining to operations in process, as well as information for managers, can be provided on a real-time basis, the more useful the information is. Because of simultaneous updating of all records affected by a transaction and the frequent use of on-line transaction entry, data base records are more likely than conventional files to be up to date, and data base information for all purposes is more apt to be the most current. Also, because with data bases, multiple files do not have to be processed sequentially for the preparation of a report, reporting can be provided on a more timely basis.

3. *Backup detail provided by inquiry capability.* Operations personnel often must reference backup details, such as transactions with a vendor in a preceding period, that are needed to answer customer questions about account status. Also, all managers can cite many instances when they have received highly summarized routine reports and then found that greater detail was needed to follow up on an unexplained circumstance, such as a production cost variance. Frequently the data needed exists in the computer system but is not quickly available.

If the detailed backup data is retained within an on-line data base that has a query language, the details needed can usually be accessed rapidly through the "window" provided by the data base query language.

4. *Data sharing.* The sharing of a large pool of operations data among multiple user departments is possible with a data base. For example, production engineering and inventory personnel may need information related to one another's current activities that can be made available as needed. Without a data base, information about other departments' activities probably would be available only several days after the end of each accounting period, if at all.

MANAGERIAL DATA BASES

The second general class of data base usage is for managerial activities. This is potentially by far the most important usage, but in most organizations with data bases, it is the least developed data base usage area.

1. *Intelligence systems.* The importance of intelligence information systems has been noted in an earlier chapter. Intelligence information needed from outside the organization for strategic planning purposes is both substantial in quantity and critical to top-management activities.

The combination of intelligence systems and data bases constitutes one of the most important ingredients in a MIS. DBMSs are especially capable of managing large masses of detailed data, such as are found with intelligence systems. Perhaps of even greater importance to the MIS is the associative capability provided by data base systems—the ability to integrate data using structured but flexible automated procedures. Indeed, one of the most difficult intelligence tasks is the integration and synthesis of information into one or more coherent perspectives that "tell a story." It is precisely here that a data base is potentially very useful.

2. *Special management problems.* As was previously noted, data bases improve managers' ability to respond rapidly to special management problems, thus providing an enhanced ad hoc reporting capability.

Unlike the information needed for management control and planning activities, however, the information needed for special problems cannot be reasonably anticipated. Data for special-problem usage cannot be placed in a data base with the assurance that it will be needed in a particular form or format, or even needed at all. The questions of how to anticipate the approximate probable needs for data for special problems, of how to organize data flexibly in one or more data bases so that the organization can provide a rapid response to a wide variety of special-problem data requests, and of whether separate data bases designed especially for special-problem usage should be attempted are intriguing ones that do not have pat, ready answers. The choice of data file organization and the choice of the DBMS and query language are closely related to the rapidity with which data bases can provide information bearing on special problems.

Data bases created and maintained especially to deal with special problems may not be realistic for most organizations. Instead, existing management control data bases in conjunction with intelligence data bases are likely to be used for special problems. Each data base file should be established to facilitate easy development of special-problem reports, such as by attempting to anticipate possible future data needs and making provision for pointers in the data base so that the anticipated data associations can be established if needed. It can be seen that for this to be accomplished satisfactorily, the data base designer should have an intimate knowledge of the management processes and the general types of special problems that may arise, or the designer should consult extensively with managers who do have this intimate knowledge.

Because of program/file independence, common standards, and other data base characteristics, a data base system can accelerate the preparation of reports for unanticipated problems by a magnitude of several times; for example, the acceleration might be from several weeks to several days. Thus, although "unanticipated problems" cannot be anticipated, nevertheless it may be possible to provide the information needed for these problems more rapidly with a data base.

3. *Management models.* A third way that data bases can serve senior managers is by enhancing the ability to develop computer models for management use. Although extensive modeling has been done for managers over the past decade, modeling may be said to be still in its infancy. At present, most DSS and other computer models do not draw their data from, or contribute their data to, a data base, and a separate data base is usually desirable for each DSS for a variety of reasons, not the least of

which is that direct manipulation of data in an operations data base creates a high risk of introducing errors into that data base. However, data can be extracted from an operations data base for inclusion in the DSS data base. This data does not have to be reformatted and placed in a separate file for accessing by the model, which is the common practice for modeling with non-data base systems. The ability of relational data base systems to quickly generate entire new files (which could become the DSS data base) appears to recommend them for companies that expect to develop decision support systems.

A microcomputer can extract data from the data base of the mainframe and use it to build a specialized data base in the microcomputer system. The data in the micro's data base is then fed to a spreadsheet model for routine managerial analysis, for "what if . . .?" modeling, or for dealing with special managerial problems. Managers of the future will be intimately familiar with this type of activity.

4. *Key-task information systems.* Data bases can serve managers by helping to organize the information system around key management tasks. Data bases should be structured around key tasks at each level, usually with one data base for each key task. Successful accomplishment of key tasks often requires coordinating information from multiple functional areas, which argues in favor of cross-functional data base systems for key tasks.

Exhibit 11.5 illustrates the types of conventional files that might be integrated into a data base to serve each of the key tasks listed in the lefthand column. The exhibit is based on the assumption that each of the tasks listed is a key task, which would be unlikely to be true for any single company, although each of the tasks listed will be key to some companies.

The marketing key-task data base of Exhibit 11.5 can be discussed as an example. A data base created in an organization in which marketing is a key task might enable a sales manager to routinely receive the following kinds of information on a daily, weekly, monthly, or "on-call" basis:

1. Customer service levels, such as the number of salesperson's calls to each customer for the period.

2. The proportion of orders backlogged. Details about each backlogged order could be available on call.

3. Total sales and gross margin by product, product line, customer group, and territory.

4. Credit sales by customer group, territory, product, and product line.

5. Credit sales by customer, along with associated analyses of the creditworthiness of each customer.

6. Full detail or summaries by category of advertising costs.

7. Analyses of distribution costs.

8. Breakdown of sales by territory, salespersons, and product class.

Data Bases Structured on Key Tasks   EXHIBIT 11.5

Key Task	Environment	Data Base
Cost control (grocery chains and automobile manufacturers)	A highly competitive, price-sensitive industry with low margins.	Inventory, accounting, production, and distribution.
Maintaining product quality (aircraft and computer manufacturers)	A high-technology industry in which products must conform to exacting quality standards.	Engineering, production, R&D, product inspection and customer complaints.
Inventory management (hardware and grocery chains and automobile parts companies)	Stock outages damage marketing efforts, but inventory carrying costs are very important	Production, inventory purchasing, back orders, and vendor information.
Customer product service (office and medical equipment service companies)	Customers expect a great deal of attention because the product is highly technical or requires frequent maintenance and repair.	Customer information, maintenance and repair, and back orders.
Customer account service (retailers and wholesalers)	Customer inquiries and complaints are frequent, customers expect personal service, billings are complex, merchandise returns and allowances are common, and maintaining collections from customers is important.	Accounts receivable, customer information, customer credit, product inventory, back orders, and customer returns.
Marketing (processed food and pharmaceutical companies)	A highly competitive environment in which carefully orchestrated and controlled sales efforts are essential.	Advertising, promotion, sales, credit, inventory, back orders, cost of sales, customer information, and intelligence.
Technological innovation (electronics and aerospace firms)	A high rate of technological change.	R&D, engineering, and production.
Planning (high-fashion companies, multinational companies, and military organizations)	Strategy development is all-important and must be coordinated throughout the organization.	Accounting, intelligence, marketing, capital expenditures, and others.

These kinds of information would assist marketing and corporate-level managers to detect the sources and causes of poor service or shifts in consumer preferences, would help these managers allocate advertising and promotional resources, and perhaps would also be useful for sales personnel training programs.

The marketing example can be extended. With cross-functional integrated files it is possible to establish associations within the data base between sales price and cost of sales for a given product on a transaction-by-transaction basis, for a certain time period, or by class of product. Each permits gross profit calculations to be made automatically under the direction of applications programs. In many organizations, continuous careful monitoring of gross profits, known as "margin management," is a key task.

Because key tasks seldom coincide with functional areas, a key-task data base design approach is quite different from a functional-area approach to data base design. With a key-task data base approach, all data items are included in the data base if they help provide information needed for the key task, regardless of the functional-area origins of data items.

It is one thing to suggest that data bases should be designed according to key tasks; it is another to accomplish this. The concept of key management tasks is not widespread in management circles. Consequently, organizations do not always explicitly focus on key tasks. For this reason the first job of data base designers may be to ensure that the key tasks at each management level are identified. Key tasks can be identified only by the organization's managers, and often this must be a collective effort by the managers.

Data bases cross functional boundaries to support critical managerial activities. Accordingly, data bases are a major factor in accomplishing the integration of the MIS. As noted by John Diebold: "Data integration has long been an operational problem child; in the past, because of the lack of cost-effective technology; now, because we lack organization and methodology to structure the data for integration." Data base technology is the cost-effective technology needed for data integration, and the key-task concept provides a useful basis on which to structure the data for integration.

COMPARISON OF DATA BASE MANAGEMENT SYSTEMS

Several operations and managerial benefits of data bases have been noted. No single type of data base organization is best for achieving all these benefits. However, one must be chosen for each collection of files that will be integrated into a single data base. Further, it is preferable that as few different DBMSs as possible be utilized in the entire organization; ideally, only one should be used, since there are training and other advantages to this. The major choice criteria for DBMS selection are listed in Exhibit 11.6. The first, the preference of data processing personnel (because of convenience for programmers, the elegance of the system, or whatever reason), usually is not a wise basis for choice. In many situations, the second criterion may be the most important. How well the data base accomplishes routine reporting for operations or managerial purposes (or for both) is especially likely to be decisive where the nature of the data in the data base is such that inquiry and special reporting capabilities are not consid-

---

DBMS Choice Criteria   EXHIBIT 11.6

Preference of data processing personnel

Routine reporting:
 Operations
 Managerial

Inquiries

Special-report development

Managerial modeling/DSS

---

ered important. Where some combination of routine reporting, inquiry, and special reporting capabilities will be needed, each must be given weight in the deliberations. In a few situations the data base will exist for the primary purpose of answering inquiries, and in others the purpose will be for managerial modeling; in these situations the data base system should be chosen on the basis of the primary intended use of the data base.

There are many DBMSs to choose from. One general guideline is to determine whether a DBMS with a data base inquiry capability is needed and, if so, whether the DBMS will be used by managerial and clerical personnel. If a data base inquiry capability is necessary, several DBMSs without a significant query language capability (natural language interface) can be eliminated from consideration. If managerial and clerical personnel will be using the DBMS, several others can be eliminated that have query systems that are so complex or specialized (not user-friendly) that they must be used by computer experts.

Exhibit 11.7 outlines the general advantages offered by each of the four data base system organizations. Each type of data base system has certain basic features that give it technical advantages for certain managerial needs. However, the usage listed in the exhibit should be considered indicative only; even specific DBMSs within a category vary widely in their features, and many combine features of more than one data base file organization.

DESIGN PRINCIPLES FOR DATA BASES

So far data bases have been portrayed as providing great benefits to managers. The reality is that although this is potentially true, as yet these benefits have not been realized in most organizations. Thousands of data bases have been implemented, but relatively few of them are designed to serve middle and higher levels of management. In part this is due to the fact that managers do not fully understand the managerial potential of data bases. Managers who attempt to remedy their condition of data base

Comparison of Data Base Organizations for Managerial Purposes

EXHIBIT 11.7

Data Base System	Technical Advantages	Managerial Usage Suited for
Inverted list	Instant retrieval of records with particular attributes that are already included in existing lists. Lists can be added for additional attributes, but creating new lists causes delays.	Routine reporting; routine managerial queries; development of ad hoc reports.
Hierarchical	Natural relationships are predefined and provide easy access paths.	Routine reporting; can be designed to serve key tasks; development of ad hoc reports.
Network	Natural relationships or any other combination of records can be linked with preestablished pointers.	Key tasks; ad hoc reporting; specialized circumstances in which unusual data associations are needed.
Relational	New tables and files can be quickly constructed.	Routine reporting; creation of new data bases for DSS systems and "what if . . .?" models.

ignorance are likely to consult with their data processing personnel. These data processing personnel naturally provide a technical description of data bases that emphasizes the advantages that technical persons understand best—which are advantages related to data processing rather than to managerial usage. If managers turn to the data base literature to learn about data bases, they will be further treated to discussions of the technical aspects of data bases because almost none of the data base articles and books are concerned with managerial usage of data bases.

A closely related problem is that data processing personnel usually do not give proper attention to the possibility of utilization of data bases by middle and senior managers. Nevertheless, managers must attempt to control the development of data bases in an organization. Five systems development principles that are especially relevant to developing data bases that serve management purposes are discussed below:

1. *Take a global perspective.* Whenever a new application is contemplated, it should be viewed in light of the entire scheme of the information system. Too often, new applications are developed in a helter-skelter manner as the need becomes apparent, and thus the resulting overall system of applications is an unplanned mosaic without a coherent pattern.

While the cost of this unplanned development is high with a conventional system, it is intolerable with a data base system because each conventional application is a separate, stand-alone system, whereas each data base should be a composite of what previously were several applications

systems. Without a "big-picture perspective" of the organization's operations and data base needs and without the overall plan that this implies,
the risk is high that applications will be united in the wrong combination
to form a data base, that the wrong type of DBMS will be chosen for each
situation, that data base priorities will be misspecified, or that other serious
mistakes will be made. Of course, if mistakes occur with the first data
base, the subsequent data bases that are developed are likely to compound
the consequences of the initial mistakes. An effective data base system
cannot be established one application at a time—an entirely new orientation and a coherent data base master plan are required.

2. *Use a "top-down" design.* There is a danger that a data base project
begun by first focusing on information needs at the bottom of the organization—a "bottom-up" approach—will never lose its operations-level
orientation and therefore that management's data base needs will never
receive adequate attention. J. Muenz describes a data base development
in which this appears to have happened; existing operations data bases
were developed, modified, and extended, and several new operations data
bases were added over a period of several years, but there is no indication
that any attention was given to how data bases could serve senior-
management needs.

The top-down approach to designing data bases explicitly recognizes
management needs. This approach focuses first on senior- and middle-
management information needs and then on operations needs. Data bases
intended to serve high-level managers should not provide information as
a by-product of existing operations-level data bases.

3. *Provide for selective information reporting.* The data base should be
designed, as far as possible, so that one primary report can be provided
for each major management activity, with backup detail available on request. This primary report should contain all the relevant information
required for the managerial task for which the report is generated and
should not contain extraneous information. Managers should not be forced
to go through several data base reports simultaneously to sort the relevant
information from their relevant information. While this selectivity principle
should be obvious, it is not easily put into practice and is too often
overlooked, in part because the focus in data base design often is not on
serving management needs.

4. *Provide for different and multiple data bases for different levels of management.* The difference in the types of information needed for managerial
activities at different levels and the differences between control and planning activities lead to the data base design principle that data bases should
be designed by type of managerial activity (such as key tasks) for a particular level of management. In many situations at least two types of data
bases at each level will be most useful; one or more data bases may be
needed for management control, and one or more may also be needed for
planning activities.

An analysis of management needs for data bases suggests that several data bases that are at least semiautonomous appear to be required for management usage. For example, in most instances a large manufacturing company would need, say, a personnel, payroll, and production scheduling data base at the operations level that might also provide summary reports to higher-level managers for management control purposes, and it would also need a separate work-force planning and recruiting-strategy data base for planning purposes for the exclusive use of higher levels of management. The data items in these separate data bases would not necessarily be entirely mutually exclusive, however. For example, details in an operations data base about job skills of present employees might be included in summarized form in a planning data base for use by senior managers.

5. *Do not convert existing files.* If data base personnel intend to develop a data base by converting existing conventional files, this should be viewed as evidence that they probably (1) are not aware of information resource management concepts (or at least do not practice them), (2) are not practicing the first two principles of global perspective and top-down design, (3) are intending to develop data bases that are not cross-functional, and (4) will end up with a more expensive and probably no more effective file system, in terms of managerial utility, than existed before conversion. Probably the overwhelming majority of existing data bases consist primarily of a conventional file system converted to a data base system, with the consequence that they provide little more assistance to managers than the conventional files did.

THE IMPACT OF DATA BASES ON MANAGEMENT PROCESSES

Management processes—the ways in which managers conduct their activities—evolve over time in response to changes in the social, cultural, regulatory, and economic environments. Two other major factors that promote changes in the management processes are the general levels of education in management methods and new technological developments aimed at helping management. In the latter category must be included such technological developments as nationwide telephone systems and commercial aviation, both of which have helped managers better govern far-flung enterprises. Computers themselves are a technological development with a similar effect.

Data base technology is an enhancement to computer technology that will have a dramatic effect on the way managers manage. The overall effect of data bases is the integration of the information system, which in turn serves to integrate as well as to alter the management processes by increasing data accessibility and transforming management into more of a real-time process.

As the technology to organize data bases for management purposes is developed and as data bases becomes widely used, managers' modes of operations will change. The general effect will be the consequence of the reduction of information constraints on management activities; increasingly, the information needed by managers will be readily available in the form needed and at the time needed. Managers' activity cycles will be less controlled by accounting periods and data processing schedules and will be more influenced by the natural cycle and rhythm of the organization's operations. Managers' control and planning decisions need not be deferred until the period-end reports are received and analyzed, but instead can be scheduled more evenly throughout the period because the most important reports will be available on call. Managers will be able to respond to critical events with actions based on full information almost as soon as the events occur, and they will be able to detect and react to changing trends or other conditions more rapidly.

However, these changes in management processes will be only a matter of degree, and to the extent that they do take place they will happen only gradually. The technology needed to organize data bases for management purposes is still in the process of development. Even after the technology is fully developed, several years will pass before its use becomes widespread, and another several years will elapse before most managers learn to take full advantage of it. It may well be today's students who will finally understand and reap most of the benefits of data base technology.

DATA BASE ADMINISTRATION

Whether data base technology is successfully developed and implemented in a particular organization is determined to a great extent by a function usually termed "data base administration," headed by a data base administrator (DBA). When data for multiple applications is integrated into the files of a data base, no segment of the data can be controlled by any one group, and the efficient distribution of the data to all users who can benefit from it cannot be inhibited by parochial interests. Also, explicit procedures for changing the data base, such as for changing record formats or adding or deleting records, must be established because the changes affect many users of the data base.

These considerations mean that the data base development and control function must be centralized under the control of the DBA. The DBA should be granted wide-ranging authority with respect to data base policies, content, and control and should apply normal resources management principles to maximize the utilization of data as a resource. In these senses the DBA is comparable to any other resource manager with corporatewide responsibilities, such as the cash manager who must gain maximum value from the cash available and who must do this at a minimum cost. But the role of the DBA is also a much broader one, for the DBA is also a change agent whose responsibilities include demonstrating the benefits of data base technology to the other managers of the organization and educating them in the use of this technology.

The DBA is the key to a successful data base. The DBA ensures that the data is available for sharing by the entire organization. The DBA is also in the best position to ensure that the data base is developed for management purposes; for this reason it is essential that the DBA have a management perspective and a depth of knowledge about the organization. In most circumstances this means that the DBA should be primarily a manager and only secondarily a data base technician. Since these attributes of a DBA are important, today's graduates from business schools—accountants, management majors, information systems majors, and others—probably have as good a chance of becoming DBAs in companies of all sizes as computer science and data processing graduates, or perhaps even a better chance. The position of DBA is one of the most promising ones for managers who are en-route to higher-level general management positions.

The most important responsibilities of the DBA are those which relate to being a change agent—the responsibility for introducing a new technology, demonstrating its benefits, and persuading members of the organization to accept it. The DBA also has several other specific responsibilities, including those listed below:

1. Guiding the initial design of the data base and further developing and extending the data base as this becomes necessary.

2. Establishing and policing data base standards.

3. Deciding on the content of the data base, making certain that data that should be included is initially collected in the form needed and becomes a part of the data base, and ensuring that data that is not cost-effective in the data base is excluded. These tasks require that the DBA have good negotiating skills and a good perspective on the entire organization's information needs.

4. Establishing and monitoring data base control and security policies and procedures designed to ensure that (a) data base updating is controlled and accurate, (b) data is available to users with a bona-fide need and is not available to others, and (c) lost or destroyed data can be recovered. An increasingly important part of this responsibility is establishing and monitoring conformance to policies about access of microcomputers to the organization's data base.

5. Servicing data base users. This activity entails showing users how to use and gain maximum benefits from the data base. Much of this function is an education and training activity.

The DBA position usually has been placed within the EDP department; thus the DBA reports to the manager of computer services. In this position the DBA may lack the influence within the organization that is required to be an effective change agent, to enforce data base discipline and common standards, to establish priorities of development, and to control the data base. There is no clear-cut solution to the organizational problems involved, but in the next several years it may be the case that in information-intensive companies with successful data bases, the data base administration function will gradually drift away from the data processing function and percolate upward in the organization. A logical position for the DBA may be one in which this person reports to the vice president of information, placing the DBA at the same level in the organization as the manager of computer systems.

DISADVANTAGES OF DATA BASES

This chapter and the preceding one have been properly optimistic about the promise and prospects of data bases. It is appropriate, however, to close this chapter by noting that data bases are not an unmixed blessing. Indeed, data bases have many disadvantages, particularly large-scale data bases. Some of these are discussed below:

1. *Insufficient data base expertise.* Perhaps the most serious disadvantage is that data base technology is complex, and too few organizations have personnel with the necessary expertise to implement and manage data bases properly. This increases the probability of unsuccessful or partially successful data base implementation. Indeed, few data bases appear to be unqualified successes.

2. *Higher data processing costs.* Data bases are usually responsible for a significant increase in the data processing of an organization and for a commensurate increase in the cost of data processing. In large measure this is due to the fact that the DBMS programs, which are large, must be processed to access, retrieve, and update the data, and in part it is due to the overhead associated with managing and reorganizing the complex file systems.

3. *Increased hardware and software needs.* Direct access memory capacity, greater communications capability (including communications software packages), and additional processor capacity are required with most data base systems. Of course, this substantially increases the hardware costs.

4. *Data security and integrity.* Data security and integrity remain major problems with a data base. Most of the security and integrity problems are related to the fact that many users have access rights to the data base and that the associative capabilities of a data base make all data in the data base potentially available to every user. Elaborate security systems must be implemented to prevent access to sections of the data base by unauthorized personnel.

A related serious problem is that microcomputer users now regularly seek access to data bases to retrieve data for manipulation by their micro-computers. There is the danger here that these users will "pollute" the data base by inadvertently altering the files, and there is also concern that a microcomputer can quickly copy the data onto a floppy disk, which can then be removed undetected from the premises.

Controls must also be implemented so that the data base files can be reconstructed from other data sources established especially for this contingency, such as transactions listings placed on magnetic tape. These data base "restart" systems are often complex and have high continuing costs of maintenance, but they are essential. In many situations a lost or destroyed data base file that cannot be reconstructed would force an organization into bankruptcy.

SUMMARY

Data base systems include the files and a data base management system (DBMS). A DBMS usually includes a host language interface, a query language, a data dictionary, and a report generator. Numerous DBMSs exist, ranging in price from nearly $200,000 for DBMSs for mainframe computers to less than $500 for DBMSs for microcomputers.

The technical explanations of data bases presented in the last chapter serve as a background for this chapter. Data bases have great potential for assisting operations activities and the planning and control activities of managers, and there is a need to structure data bases to key management tasks. The technical advantages of the four types of data base structures are related to types of managerial information needs.

There are several general principles for the design of data bases. Data bases can alter the management processes in various ways. Data bases also have several disadvantages.

Data base administration is a complex and demanding task. A data base administrator (DBA) is usually appointed to monitor, manage, enhance, and police the data base. The primary mission of the DBA is to manage data as a resource so that maximum value is gained from the data base.

KEY TERMS

data base management system (DBMS): an extensive software package that manages data base files.

host language interface system: a part of the DBMS that enables programs written in professional programming languages (e.g., COBOL) to communicate their data needs to the DBMS.

natural language interface system: A Englishlike, easily learned programming language within the DBMS that facilitates inquiries into the data base; this language may also permit elementary programs to be written to process data in the data base.

data dictionary: a description in electronic form of the precise nature and format of every data item in the data base.

REFERENCES

Diebold, John, "Information Resource Management—The New Challenge," *Infosystems,* June 1979.

Muenz, J., "The Corporate Data Base—Growth and Major Applications," *Proceedings of the Tenth Annual Conference of the Society for Management Information Systems,* Chicago, 1978.

Nolan, R., "Computer Data Bases: The Future Is Now," *Harvard Business Review,* September–October 1973.

Rockart, John F., "Chief Executives Define Their Own Data Needs," *Harvard Business Review,* March–April 1979.

Scott, George M., "A Data Base for Your Company?" *California Management Review,* Fall 1976.

Scott, George M., "Auditing the Data Base," *CA Magazine,* October 1978.

Scott, George M., *Research Study on Current-Value Accounting Measurements and Utility,* New York: Touche-Ross Foundation, 1978.

Sobszak, J., "A Data Base Story," *Datamation,* September 1977.

Townsend, Peter C., ". . . And There Was Data Base," *Infosystems,* September 1980.

Tsichritzis, D. C., and F. H. Lochovsky, "Designing the Data Base," *Datamation,* August 1978, p. 147.

Vaneck, Michael, and George M. Scott, "Data Bases: The Auditor's Dilemma," *The CPA Journal,* January 1980.

REVIEW QUESTIONS

1. Explain the role that the concept of data as a resource should play in data base development. To what extent do you believe that the typical manager thinks in these terms?

2. What are the functions of a DBMS?

3. Why is a data base entirely within one function likely to be suboptimizing in terms of using data as a resource?

4. What makes a data base integrated?

5. Describe the ways in which data bases differ from conventional file systems. (Answering this question requires a review of this chapter and the preceding chapter.)

6. What is program/file independence?

7. What kind of education and training do you think that computer systems technicians should have to enable them to develop data bases for managers?

8. Outline the computer technology that a manager must understand in order to guide the development of data bases.

9. What are the advantages to operations personnel, and to managers, of a highly developed inquiry capability?

10. Data bases are often described as providing multiple data access paths and retrieval sequences. Explain what these are.

11. What are the benefits of data bases for managerial activities? For data processing activities?

12. Should the DBA have primarily a technical background or primarily a managerial background, or should the DBA be expected to have expertise in both areas?

13. What are the major functions performed by the DBA?

14. Explain the major disadvantages of data bases. Do you expect that all these disadvantages will persist over a long period of time? If not, which will be reduced or eliminated, and why?

PROBLEMS

1. From Exhibit 11.5 select the key-task area other than marketing with which you are most familiar; then (a) describe the kinds of decisions that a manager must make related to that key task and (b) specify the kinds of information that a manager would need from a data base to make those decisions.

2. On the basis of your study of this chapter and the preceding one, explain some specific ways in which data bases may alter the way managers conduct their activities.

3. In ". . . And There Was Data Base," Peter C. Townsend states: "The reader who has been even vaguely aware of data processing developments within the past several years will probably surmise what the fundamental premise must be—data as a resource. Much has been said about the data resource; it is created, it does cost money, it is assembled, reassembled, inventoried and it does provide the 'raw material' for the valuable product, information. Whether one wishes to look at data as a resource or not is a matter of choice, but to deny all of the essential facts about data as an entity is both illogical and inaccurate.

"Some organizations feel that the data resource concept is too fancy, to intricate, overly sophisticated. We disagree. When one considers that in most medium and large companies cash managers concern themselves with literally day-by-day and even hour-by-hour deposits and withdrawals of cash, all for the purpose of extracting the ultimate value from this obvious resource, then one should be able to understand that data is also a resource which must be properly managed."

Analyze each of the statements made about data in this section of Townsend's article with respect to the ways in which data is similar to other resources. In what ways, if any, is data different from other resources?

CASE 1

A Data Base Story
By J. J. Sobczak

Proving Once Again That What Goes Around Comes Around

One day several years ago, in the data processing department of a large eastern manufacturing firm, the v.p. of dp decided that many of his people had been in the same job for too long. He and his managers decided to have a number of employees make nonpromotional moves to broaden their experience.

Included in these job assignment transfers were two senior systems analyst/project leader types we'll call Charlie and Joe. Both Charlie and Joe had similar backgrounds. Though neither was rated as exceptional, both were quite competent and had distinguished themselves through the years. Charlie had been associated with the accounts payable system for seven years, including the last three as project leader. He fully understood the system and there was not a question about accounts payable that Charlie could not answer. Joe had had similar experience with the inventory control system, and was recognized in the department as the only one who really understood the entire system. They approached their new assignments with great apprehension. Each was being asked to leave a world where he had full control and complete job knowledge, and enter a world where he knew very little.

A month or so after the transfers, Charlie and Joe were having a cup of coffee together.

"You know Charlie," Joe said, "the other day I spent some time going through the accounts payable master file and I was amazed how many fields the two systems have in common. It's not always obvious because the terminology is different, but I found that not only were many fields the same, many come from the same source document. Fields such as part number, vendor, vendor address, the three digit vendor code, plants shipped from, plants shipped to, price, and at least twenty others."

Charlie said, "I've noticed the same thing. In fact, I was wondering whether we should write a little program to compare the common data between the two systems to make sure there aren't any discrepancies. I've got a programmer I can spare for a few days, and if you can have one of your guys create an input file for him, I'll have him write a comparison program. What do you think?"

"Well," Joe said, "I think that's a good idea. If there are discrepancies it's better we find out before someone else does. I'll have an input file in a few days. Have your guy call Sam and tell him the data he wants and the format he wants it in."

About two weeks later Charlie and Joe met again to discuss the results of the comparison program. Murphy had struck again, and there were countless discrepancies.

"Boy," Joe said, "this is worse than I thought possible. We better find out why the files don't match." Within a few days a number of problems were discovered. In many cases field sizes and edit standards were different. Often, when errors with noncritical data were detected, the using department didn't bother entering the correction. Many times discrepancies existed only because of the timing differences in update cycles. The corrections were made and Charlie and Joe slept easier.

Then one day, three months later, Charlie and Joe decided to run the comparison program again. A few days later Joe stopped into Charlie's office to review the program results.

"How does it look?" Joe asked.

"Well," Charlie replied, "it's not as bad as last time, but there are still a number of discrepancies."

"What should we do?"

"I don't know," said Charlie, "but we better do something. Let's take the same type of corrective action we did last time, but at the same time I think you and I should think about a more lasting solution. Let's sleep on it for a few days and meet again Friday to discuss it."

Friday came along and Charlie was anxious to discuss some of his ideas with Joe. He had been doing quite a bit of thinking and had arrived at what seemed to him an ideal solution.

As Joe walked in his office Charlie blurted out. "Sit down Joe, I think I have an answer but I want to bounce it off you."

"Great, go ahead," said Joe, somewhat relieved because to him the problem was still as perplexing as it had been three days before.

"Well," Charlie said, "my idea is to combine the accounts payable master file and the inventory control master file into a single master file. Then there will be only one entry for each field, and discrepancies will be impossible. If the vendor's address is wrong at least it will be consistently wrong wherever it appears."

Joe interrupted, "That doesn't really seem like much of a solution. It would make our lives more comfortable because our bosses are less likely to find out about our current problem. But the basic problem as far as the company is concerned would still be there—we'd still have bad data."

"Wait a minute Joe, you're jumping the gun. There's more," retorted Charlie, "I think we could improve our data accuracy by having the department most interested in an element of data be responsible for updating it. For example, the accounts payable department would be responsible for updating the price field. If you remember, that was one of the fields where our investigation of discrepancies showed that the inventory control file was usually the one that was wrong."

"Right," Joe inserted, "that's because the material people use that field more as a memo item." Joe bagan to show more interest.

Charlie went on. "There is another advantage that I think will help sell the idea to management. Think of all the duplication of effort that will be eliminated. For each duplicated field, the using departments have to mark up the input documents, submit data for keypunching, and process the error corrections. The data must be keypunched and the cards handled. Computer resources are used to edit and update the data, and storage resources store it. That's a lot of extra work. Well, what do you think?"

"Great," Joe said, "and I just thought of another advantage. The accounts payable department manager asked just last week for some special reports that included information we don't have, but I know is in the inventory file. For example, he wants the company part classification code on his report. If we had a consolidated master file, I could easily give him reports like that."

"Hmmm, I never thought of that," said Charlie, "this is sounding better all the time. What do you think our next step should be?"

"Well," Joe said. "I think we should run this by Gardner. He's in systems programming now, but he's still the sharpest guy around here. If there are any holes in it, he'll find them."

"Good idea, Joe" agreed Charlie, "I'll give him a call and ask him to meet with us as soon as possible."

Gardner was the most respected member of the data processing department. He had been a programming hotshot and then an outstanding systems analyst. He eventually was transferred to head up the systems programming department because he knew more about systems programming than anyone else, even though his career had been mainly in the applications area. The next day Gardner agreed to sit down with Charlie and Joe to discuss their problem and proposed solution.

They explained the history of the discrepancies and the concept of eliminating them by having only one master file. They described their theory on why they believed accuracy would be improved, how duplication of people and machine resources would be eliminated, and the advantages to each department of being able to receive special reports containing data from the other's master file.

When they finished, Gardner, who was not the type who jumped to conclusions, said, "You guys have an intriguing idea. There may be a few implementation problems, but let me spend a few days analyzing your idea. I'll get back to you in about a week."

"Fine," said Charlie. "Let's set up a meeting now for a week from Monday. We can all benefit from spending a little more time thinking about this."

When the time for the meeting came around, Charlie and Joe were anxiously awaiting Gardner's opinion.

"Well Gardner, what do you think?" blurted Joe.

"First of all," Gardner started "I think implementation of your idea is more complicated than you imagined. In fact, I've concluded that special software would have to be written to manage the data." A look of dejection came over Joe's face. "Don't look so forlorn," Gardner continued. "I know that sounds like bad news but on the other side of the coin, I think it may be worthwhile to develop that software. In fact, I've discussed it with some of my people and they're raring to go. All we need is management approval. You see, I think you have an idea that could actually revolutionize systems in our company.

"One of my people found that many of the data fields your two systems have in common can also be found in the customer service files and the engineering master files. And the same problem you found exists with other systems, too. You've uncovered the tip of the iceberg, so to speak.

"For example, the employee skill file and the payroll file have all kinds of duplicated information, not to mention the redundancy in many of the manually maintained files departments need because our data processing systems don't serve their needs. "You really started me thinking when you mentioned the accounts payable department manager requested a special report that required information from the inventory master file. I suddenly realized that many others in the company might be able to use information contained in somebody else's master file. That information itself could be considered valuable. Our problem is that we think of data as belonging to a using department and computer application. Instead, we should think of information as a corporate resource."

"That sounds great," said Charlie, not really understanding, or caring to understand what Gardner meant when he said information should be a corporate resource, "but tell us about the special software that has to be developed."

"Okay," Gardner continued. "You see, if you just combined the data into one large master file with the idea of sorting it into the appropriate sequence, you're going to run into a number of problems. First of all, you both are planning to eventually change your systems to an on-line operation, right?" Charlie and Joe both nodded. "Well the first thing a software package must do is store the data so both of your systems can access it at the same time and obtain the information it needs in the proper form. Even if you didn't go on-line, you would have a problem organizing your master file, because although duplication exists, a one-to-one

record correspondence between the files does not exist.

"You will have another problem preventing changes in one system from affecting the other. For example, you don't want to have to change all the programs in one system just because the size of the other's master file has increased.

"Security will be another problem. The accounts payable department won't be happy about having its data so readily accessible to other people. What I would propose to do is have my people write a software package for handling these problems and others I foresee. It would allow for storing information in what I'll call a data bank." Charlie and Joe didn't fully appreciate all the points Gardner was making, but now they understood that the problem was more complicated than merely creating a single consolidated master file.

"Well, what's our next step?", asked Joe.

Garnder replied, "I think we should present this to Morley. He has the authority to let us proceed and will have some ideas on how to sell it to management. He's pretty forward thinking, and I'm sure he'll support us." Morley was the department manager with responsibility for both applications development and systems programming. Gardner enjoyed working for him and considered Morley the only really competent data processing manager in the firm. Though Charlie and Joe had difficulty grasping the concept of centralized data banks, Gardner was confident Morley would understand the potential.

They met with Morley the following day. Charlie and Joe explained the background carefully, omitting the data discrepancy part of the story. Gardner then explained his ideas, the potential he saw for revolutionizing systems in the company, the need for a software system to manage the data, and his manpower estimates for developing the software.

Gardner was right. Morley's eyes lit up and he understood what Gardner was getting at almost immediately. One of his major concerns was that top management viewed data processing as simply a method for reducing "general and administrative" expenses. Computers did not help them make the critical decisions that are vital to the company's success. Top management's general view was that if the computers weren't here, the only real effect on the company would be that there would be a lot more clerks with eyeshades running around. One of Morley's concerns was that before long, there wouldn't be any more clerks with eye-shades to replace. If that happened, the status of dp in the organization could drop even further.

Now Gardner, with Charlie and Joe, was proposing a whole new way of looking at data processing. If the vital information in the company somehow could be stored in centralized data banks, all kinds of possibilities opened up for inserting data processing into the firm's decision-making process.

Morley recalled his own ill-fated attempt to develop a corporate financial model that suffered from the inability to obtain accurate and timely data. The one thing that experience did teach him was that management was amenable to such applications. If someone could develop a better way of helping them run the business, they would be willing to spend the money required to develop that capability, even though the benefits could not be quantified in dollars and cents.

Morley gave Gardner, Charlie, and Joe the go-ahead. He proceeded to sell his management and the using departments that initially would be affected. An early decision was to concentrate first on the original idea of combining the accounts payable and inventory control systems. Gardner and his people, however, set out to develop a generalized software package that could be used for combining other applications.

Shortly thereafter, Gardner received a promotion to a position outside data processing. A few years later he was transferred to the company's European subsidiary for a two-year tour of duty. During that time he wasn't able to stay abreast of the corporate data bank project, but he did read the various articles that could be found in management-oriented publications on what was being called data base instead of data bank. These articles made him proud that he had been instrumental in what appeared to be a significant advancement in data processing. Occasionally, he received miscellaneous reports and letters from his old dp department that made it clear that the data base philosophy had taken over.

When his European assignment was over and Gardner was transferred back to corporate head-

quarters, he made it a point to visit the data processing department. He wanted to discover first hand the progress they were making toward developing a corporate data base.

As he walked into the department he first ran into Joe.

"Hi Joe," Gardner greeted him. "How are things going?"

"Fine Gardner, it's nice to see you," replied Joe.

"How is your data base coming along?"

"Well overall pretty well, except for a few software problems we've had converting to a new version of our data base management package. About three years ago we found it was too costly to maintain the software package your department developed because equivalent packages were commercially available at a reasonable price. The only mistake we made, I think, was that we haven't standardized on one package. For example, Charlie, who is now the data base administrator for the inventory control data base, uses different software than we do with the accounts payable data base."

Gardner was startled. "Are you saying that the inventory control data base and the accounts payable data base are separate?" he asked. Joe nodded affirmatively. "How can that be? The whole idea in the first place was to combine them into a single data base. If they're separate you're right back to where you were years ago. What happened?"

"Oh, we gave up on the idea years ago," Joe replied. "We had too much trouble with the users. Soon after we launched the system the accounts payable department wanted to expand the vendor classification code to include a credit rating. There were a lot of good reasons for doing it, but the material control people wouldn't agree. Their people were used to the old code, and they'd have to change their forms. They just weren't going to go along with it. I was the data base administrator but I didn't have the power to control either user. We ended up putting in two codes, one for each department. We continually had similar problems until we just gave up. Well, I'd like to talk to you longer but I have a meeting to attend." With that Joe rushed off leaving Gardner visibly shaken. Gardner headed for Morley's office.

He found Morley in his office and after exchanging greetings mentioned the conversation he had had with Joe. "What happened, Morley?" It sounds like you're right back where you were years ago except that you're using more exotic and expensive software to access the data."

"Well Gardner, that's not quite true," replied Morley. "The new data base software packages have on-line query facilities that give us a capability we didn't have before, but other than that, you're right. We haven't progressed much. In fact when you consider the added machine overhead and cost of the data base software, we may have regressed."

"Joe described a problem you had with the vendor classification code. Was that typical?" asked Gardner.

"Gardner, that was just one of many, many problems. We had cases where the accounts payable department was pressured by their management for reports that required data that was controlled by the material control department. The material control manager refused to work the extra overtime required because they were already over their overtime budget and had their own priorities to worry about. Well, you can imagine the frustration that created in the accounts payable department. Instances like that forced us to split the data bases."

"Where did we go wrong?" Gardner asked, though he almost knew the answer.

Morley replied. "We completely underestimated the people problems involved in establishing a data base. Users think of the data associated with their application as their data. You don't just appoint a data base administrator and eliminate those feelings. The psychological ties are too strong. Instead of being concerned with these problems, we got all wrapped up in the technical detail associated with setting up a data base. We concentrated on things like network vs. hierarchical structure, inverted lists, and audit trails. We should have concentrated on the organizational aspect of the problem."

What about all the other data bases you have around? Did they have the same problem?" queried Gardner.

"No," answered Morley, "because none of them are integrated data bases in the way you and I think. You have to understand that data base has become the 'in thing.' People are using data base

management software where they used to use sequential or direct access methods. Otherwise the applications are no different than they used to be. In fact, some of the so-called data bases we have don't even use data base software. They just started calling their old files data bases. One of the other managers here takes pride in the fact that he has installed thirty-seven different data bases. Sometimes it gets quite humorous to watch. I've sat in meetings where they argue about data base administrator job responsibilities. Because they don't have a true data base they don't need one. Yet they read that they do need one. They end up defining a job that sounds suspiciously like a systems programmer."

"What about other companies?" Gardner asked. "Do they have the same situation?"

"I've been attending manufacturer user group meetings for the past few years," replied Morley, "and I've made it a point to find out what others are doing. Surprisingly, many are just like us. Occasionally I run into someone who is developing an integrated data base system. Almost always they are the ones who talk about the data administration problems rather than the technical software problems. But we are definitely not alone."

"Have you given up hope?" Gardner asked.

"No, the potential of what we are trying to accomplish is too great. I still have dreams that data processing can become an essential part of the company's decision-making process. That true company-wide information system can be developed using the data base approach. But we are going to have to stop devoting 95% of our resources to the technical data base software details because that's only 10% of the problem. We have to think of data base as a systems philosophy, not a technology."

As Gardner left, he wondered whether he was part of the biggest hoax ever perpetrated on data processing, and whether there were enough Morleys in the world to turn the situation around.

Source: Datamation, September 1977, p. 139.

Case Questions

1. In "A Data Base Story," why might the company's data bases be described as "limited-scope" data bases?

2. How useful are limited-scope data bases? What are their limitations?

3. Do you believe that the data processing and other managers of this organization:

(a) Understand information systems?

(b) Participate deeply in systems investigations?

(c) View data in the fullest sense as a resource?

Justify your answers.

CASE 2

The Corporate Data Base—Growth and Major Applications

By James J. Muenz

The first IMS data bases were implemented in April of 1973. They contained information about our locations, customers, products and their prices. The data base administration function was in place, and elaborate security procedures were established to prevent unauthorized access to information. The initial data dictionary was also installed. These data bases were implemented primarily to support the order entry system and the master file update system.

The order Entry System was planned in two parts. Part 1 was implemented in 1973 and provided:

1. On-line entry of orders and credits from districts;

2. Generation of pick lists, and shipping documents, and

3. Automatic Pricing and Invoicing of Direct Shipments.

Part 2, which extended this facility to district warehouses, would be implemented later. Relationships were established between the product, price group and product group data bases to reduce the number of price update transactions and to provide an association of products to their families. Another relationship was established between customers and their sales district locations to facilitate order entry processing. The data base now contained all of the information necessary to process and price orders.

By July of 1974, some of the original data bases were expanded and new information was added. We began storing product formulas, ingredients and plant production standards. We also began creating price change history form update transactions. Another transaction file, the param-

eter hold file, was created to store sales contest information.

For the first time multiple applications were updating the same data base. This fact, coupled with some IBM software limitations, caused us to develop and install our own control data base. This data base is used to insure the integrity of the update process, and to enforce backup and recovery when updates fail.

These new data bases were installed primarily to support a new product costing system which provided more detailed ingredient and supplies cost data. It permitted individual plants to process their cost changes and it reported gross margin effects due to cost changes on an exception basis as they occurred.

The structure of the Kraft Data Base by July of 1974 had grown from the original 7 data bases to 12, and the total number of information segments were doubled to 43. Additional links were established with the product data base. We now had all of the information required to explode ingredients and formulas and calculate monthly product cost and marginal income. We could also begin tracking price changes through time.

In February of 1975, location inventory and pending shipment information was added. The location data base was also expanded to include order forecasting parameters and point of supply information. This new information was required for the consolidated finished goods inventory application.

This system replaces and improved the existing Inventory application. It:

1. Books all inventory movement transactions;

2. Maintains in-transit inventory accounts;

3. Automatically generates exception reports on inventory variances;

4. Produces comparative reports on inventory and service level performance;

5. Provides inventory status and expected changes over time, and provides for automatic reordering.

The data base structure then grew to these 14 data bases representing 59 segments of information. Relationships were established linking inventory to the product and location data bases, and the structure was beginning to become complex.

The corporate data base now contained all the data necessary to process and control inventory, to produce stock status, and to create product replenishment orders.

In October of 1975, national and division account information were added, and the new corporate accounts receivable system began using the data base. It also used existing customers and location data and obtained invoice information from files created by the order entry system.

The new accounts receivable system provides:

1. Local control of receivables;

2. Centralized processing, reporting and national account analysis;

3. Automatic aged trial balance at various levels;

4. Tighter control over high-rise accounts.

This represents the structure in October of 1975 with the addition of the two accounts receivable data bases. The number of information segments was increased from 21 to 70—more than three times its original size.

This year, employee information, sales history, and organization information were added, and ex-isting data bases once again were changed to meet the requirements of four systems.

* * *

The data base will undoubtedly change as additional information is added for future systems. New technology and changes in the business environment will also have an impact. However, with the proper performance and control tools in place, there should be no surprises. The data base will continue to provide Kraft management with the information it needs to compete effectively in the marketplace.

Source: Proceedings of the Tenth Annual Conference of the Society for Management Information Systems, Chicago 1978.

Case Questions

1. To what extent are these data bases intended to serve middle- and senior-level managers?

2. To what extent are these data bases cross-functional in nature?

3. How useful would these data bases be for solving special problems that cross the boundaries of several functional areas? What probably would be involved in developing the special reports required?

4. To what extent does each of the data bases probably:
   (a) Provide information faster than previously?
   (b) Provide information that previously was not available?
   (c) Reduce the total data processing cost?
   (d) Make it more convenient for EDP to process and maintain the data files?

Chapter 12

ACCOUNTING INFORMATION SYSTEMS

PAYOFF THOUGHT

The functional information systems of an organization are its backbone. Understanding the entire information system is impossible without understanding the functional information systems.

CHAPTER OBJECTIVES

1. To provide insight into the accounting information systems

2. To explore the structure of responsibility accounting system and sales order entry system.

FUNCTIONAL INFORMATION SYSTEMS

This chapter and the next deal with functional information systems. Students who are unfamiliar with elementary accounting should refer to the chapter glossary for the meanings of commonly used accounting terms.

A functional information system is a system that provides detailed information for a specific type of operations activity or related group of activities, as well as summarized information for management control of such activities. A functional information system may also supply data that is useful for another functional activity or for planning purposes, but this is usually incidental to its primary purposes.

The backbone of an organization's information system is its functional information systems, since these process transactions and make possible various housekeeping and administrative activities; they also provide most of the information necessary for management control as well as some information useful for planning. Nevertheless, these systems, once in place, usually do not require extensive attention from managers, although data processing personnel are continuously modifying and fine-tuning them. (Exceptions are information systems associated with key tasks of the organization.) However, those managers who rely on a particular functional information system should be full participants in its design and development.

Each function has an information system composed of multiple subsystems, all of which provide information for the tasks within the function. The major functional systems of many organizations are those listed in Exhibit 12.1; in addition, most organizations have several minor information systems for such functions as safety programs, the motor pool, and employee recreational activities. The first three systems listed in the exhibit are the most important in many organizations.

In certain types of organizations, one or more functional information systems may be particularly highly developed; these usually correspond to critical tasks in the industry. For example high-technology companies

---

The Major Functional Systems of a Manufacturer's MIS   EXHIBIT 12.1

1. The accounting information system
2. The marketing information system
3. The production information system
4. The inventory management information system
5. The personnel information system
6. The distribution information system
7. The purchasing information system
8. The treasury information system
9. The credit analysis information system
10. The research and development information system
11. The engineering information system

---

are likely to have an extensive and sophisticated information system for their research and development functions, and producers of high-fashion products may have very sophisticated inventory management information systems to provide a rapid response to changing consumer fashion preferences.

GENERAL CHARACTERISTICS OF ACCOUNTING INFORMATION SYSTEMS

In many organizations, about one-third to one-half of the total transactions processed are accounting transactions, and in the typical small organization 70 percent or more of all transactions processed may be accounting transactions. Accounting transactions are defined here as transactions under the administrative jurisdiction of the accounting department; however, a great deal of the information provided by accounting transactions processsing is used primarily by marketing or other functional groups besides accounting; thus to a certain extent "accounting systems" are not just for accounting, but also provide data directly to other groups or to the information systems of other groups.

There are two general categories of accounting information systems; the first provides reports to groups outside the organization according to strict reporting requirements imposed by accounting and governmental authorities, and the other, which is for operations and managerial usage, is designed to provide information in whatever form managers need. Both types of accounting information systems process accounting transactions and supply information for keeping track of the organization's resources and for evaluating its status and progress. Because the two types of systems utilize the same transactions, one transactions processing activity usually serves both systems, and often the two systems also share data files and other components; consequently, they are intricately interwoven and overlapping, which makes accounting information systems among the most complex of all information systems.

Accounting information systems are concerned with *financial transactions*, that is, events (transactions) that are measured in terms of money. The accounting information system uses a highly structured framework that includes several subsystems and usually utilizes "double entry accounting." Because each financial transaction exchanges something of monetary value for something else of monetary value, it has a basic duality—something is given and something is received. Each half of this transaction—what is given and what is received—is recorded separately and is processed in different ways within the accounting information system.

For example, in a cash sale transaction, merchandise is given (sold) and cash is received. The sales and the cash receipts portions of the transaction are separately recorded in different data files of the accounting information system and are processed in different ways to provide different kinds of documents and reports. Accounting transactions may be entirely within the organization, as when an inventory department supplies a production department with raw materials for manufacture into products.

The double entry nature of accounting provides a natural control over the accuracy of data processing. Each half of the transaction, equal in amount initially, must remain so throughout the steps of data processing; in accounting parlance, "the debits must always equal the credits." Accordingly, at various intermediate points in the data processing and at its conclusion, a checking procedure called "balancing" compares the sum of debits with the corresponding sum of credits. If the two sums are not equal, this "out-of-balance" condition indicates that an error had been made. Because of the complexity of transactions processing, out-of-balance conditions are common and cause a great deal of consternation among data processing personnel, who must meet tight schedules but who often cannot proceed to the next processing step until an out-of-balance condition is corrected. If not corrected, out-of-balance conditions are likely to cause inconsistent reports to managers and errors in documents (such as invoices and vendor payment checks) that are prepared by data processing personnel.

Reporting activities of accounting information systems are cyclical, although transactions processing activities are more or less continuous. Transactions are summarized at the end of each period for a series of reports measuring the organization's financial status and the results of operations during the period. The end-of-period reports usually include at least a balance sheet and an income statement; in medium-sized and large organizations, these reports also include a series of supporting schedules for each of several or even dozens of affiliated organizations.

The data processing activities of summarization and report preparation are completed in a recurring, cyclical fashion and in the same sequence after the end of each period. The reporting period for most activities is 1 month.

Many organizations superimpose an additional quarterly cycle on the monthly cycle, summarizing transactions for the 3-month period as well as for the preceding month and preparing quarterly reports in addition to reports for the month. Organizations also have an annual cycle: summarized transactions and prepared reports for an entire 12-month period. Generally, the reports prepared at year-end are more extensive and detailed than other end-of-period reports, necessitating more year-end data processing activities.

End-of-period accounting activities are time-consuming and must be carefully scheduled. Monthly reports may not be completed until several days after the end of the month, and, because of the greater work involved, 1 to 2 months may elapse after year-end before all annual reports are completed; the same activities typically take 2 to 4 times as long to complete if they are not computerized. Computer systems may require surplus capacity during the period so that they can accommodate the higher postperiod data processing activity.

Because periodic reporting is so important to the operations of many organizations, it is sometimes said that the organization is "driven by its reporting cycle." This implies that managers cannot conduct certain significant management activities until they receive the postperiod reports. The capabilities of a sophisticated computer information system, however, enable managers to receive requested reports at any time during a period. An organization whose information system provides this capability ceases to be driven by its reporting cycle, and managers are able to rethink and reorganize the way they conduct their activities.

Because they are oriented to time periods, accounting information systems use "accrual accounting." Accrual accounting establishes which expenses and revenues should be recorded in a period. First, it is determined which period a revenue is earned in; if necessary, an adjustment (termed an "adjusting entry") is made to place the revenue in the proper period. Second, it is determined which expenditures were used to generate the revenue of the period, and any necessary adjustments are made to place these expenses in the same period as the related revenues; this is an application of the "matching principle" in accounting. Third, expenditures that cannot be directly associated with a particular revenue, such as building and equipment depreciation costs, are matched to periods by using a systematic allocation method, such as a depreciation method.

The adjusting entries needed to place revenues and expenses in the proper period are dictated by an elaborate set of accounting rules that form the subject matter of a series of accounting courses. In many organizations these adjusting entries number in the thousands for each period. While most adjusting entries are performed by computer programs and account for a large part of the extra end-of-period computer processing, in all organizations at least a few of the adjustments must be made manually each period.

The rules related to accrual accounting make up only a small part of the rules for accounting information systems. A comprehensive set of "generally accepted accounting principles" guides the collection, classification, and reporting of accounting information. These rules establish asset valuation principles—that is, they determine what are and what are not assets, liabilities, and transactions for accounting purposes—and specify the timing and format of reports, among other things. For example, the accounting rules dictate that an order received does not constitute a sale or provide revenue for the period unless it is filled before the end of the period. Thus, a sales order received is not a sale for accounting purposes, despite its importance to the organization.

Accrual accounting and the use of generally accepted accounting principles are obligatory only for external reporting, such as reporting to stockholders in publicly held corporations. For planning and other managerial accounting purposes, these principles are not always relevant and may actually be misleading. Organizations may establish their own managerial accounting rules and procedures. Nevertheless, because external financial reporting requires compliance with generally accepted accounting principles, the accounting information system must be designed to provide reports that conform to them, and additional systems design costs and higher data processing costs must be incurred if different accounting rules and procedures are installed to serve managerial purposes. Some smaller organizations elect to have only one accounting information system, which gathers and processes data in conformance with accepted accounting principles. The resulting reports are used for internal management purposes, even though they may be ill suited for this use.

DATA SUMMARIZATION IN ACCOUNTING INFORMATION SYSTEMS

Exhibit 12.2 illustrates a typical procedure used in large organizations with fully developed accounting information systems. In the exhibit each subsystem is designed to summarize data for managerial purposes. Special programs then convert this information to reports in conformance with generally accepted accounting and reporting requirements. Some organizations reverse this procedure—generally accepted accounting principles are first applied, and computer programs convert the reports to the format desired for managerial purposes.

The accounting information system is concerned with accurately recording events as transactions, in conformance with whichever accounting rules are used, and with keeping track of the status of the organization's physical and financial resources. This stewardship function involves the accounting concept of internal control, which is closely related to the data processing concept of control over transactions processing. The accounting information system deals primarily with the financial aspects of past transactions and with current status, while, as noted in previous chapters, a substantial portion of managers' information needs relate to nonfinancial information and information about the future.

CODING SYSTEMS

All information systems use a coding system. A code is a data identification scheme that attaches identifying numbers (numeric code), letters (alphabetic code), or a combination of the two (alphanumeric code) to data entered into the computer. Computer programs recognize and decipher this code in order to record the data in the computer files properly. The code also enables a computer program to later locate data needed for

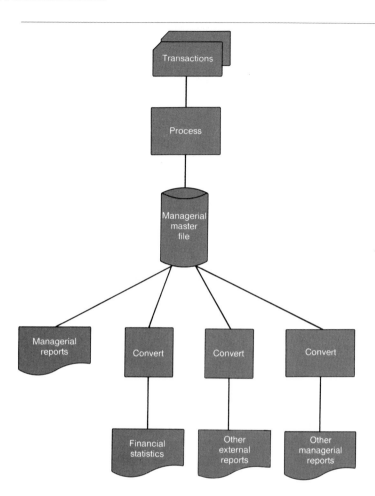

EXHIBIT 12.2
Data conversion for
report preparation.

processing because the code includes the logical address of the record containing the information needed. In a similar manner, a manager who keys in the code can access the data with the help of an internal program.

The code is often a multipart code, with each part having a particular meaning and use. For example, one part of a multipart code might indicate that the transaction is a cash sale, and another part might indicate that a particular branch office made the sale. The coding also might allow sorting the sales file and preparing reports according to geographic regions, customer types, and salespersons. Data can then be retrieved and processed in multiple ways, such as first preparing a report about all cash sales and then preparing a report showing these cash sales by branch office.

Multipart code systems also enable one transaction to be entered into multiple files easily. For example, a sales transaction might simultaneously be processed against both the sales and the customer data files. The ability

A Block-Code Chart of Accounts

EXHIBIT 12.3

1000–1999	Cash and receivables
2000–2499	Materials inventory
2500–2999	Finished goods inventory
3000–3999	Equipment
4000–4499	Plant
4500–4999	Current liabilities
5000–5499	Long-term liabilities
5500–5999	Owners' equity
6000–6999	Sales revenue
7000–7999	Production costs and cost of sales
8000–8999	General and administrative expenses
9000–9499	Selling expenses
9500–9999	Nonoperating expenses and revenues

to update multiple records simultaneously with one data input activity greatly increases the efficiency of data processing.

The coding system used for accounting information systems, called the "chart of accounts," assigns a code number to each detailed balance sheet and income statement account in the general ledger. The general ledger is a listing of all the accounts and their balances that are necessary to prepare a fully detailed balance sheet and income statement.

Exhibit 12.3 shows a simplified chart of accounts based on a block code. A block code sets aside a block of numbers for each general type of account. Note in the exhibit that each category of accounts in the balance sheet and income statement has either 500 or 1000 numbers that can be assigned to individual accounts; for example, there can be up to 1000 separate types of cash and accounts receivable in this chart of accounts. Exhibit 12.4 expands the chart of accounts of Exhibit 12.3 to show several of the individual accounts within selected blocks.

Using the chart of accounts numbers, computer programs can rapidly extract data from the computer files and prepare financial statements and accounting reports of all types. Each accounting transaction is coded with a chart of accounts number when it is originally recorded. That is, the number is attached to the transaction and is then recorded along with the transaction so that when the transaction is entered into the computer, the code number directs it to the proper file, where the transaction amount is added to ("updates") the contents of that file. For example, a transaction coded as a sale will update the sales file by recording the details of the sale in that file and adding the total amount of the sale to the total of all sales in the file. The following example illustrates the operation of a chart of accounts coding system.

Assume that Robert Smith sells one unit of product Y on credit for $175 to a wholesale customer, that Mr. Smith receives a 10 percent com-

A Chart of Accounts Including Selected Individual Accounts

EXHIBIT 12.4

1000–1499		Cash
	1010	Cash—control
	1011	Petty cash
	1012	Cash in bank—operations
	1013	Cash in bank—savings
1500–1599		Receivables
	1560	Employee advances receivable
	1570	Customer accounts receivable
	1580	Interest receivable
2000–2499		Materials inventory
2500–2999		Finished goods inventory
3000–3999		Equipment
4000–4499		Plant
4500–4999		Current liabilities
5000–5499		Long-term liabilities
5500–5999		Owners' equity
6000–6999		Sales revenue
	6010	Sales revenue—product A
	6370	Sales revenue—product X
	6380	Sales revenue—product Y
	6390	Sales revenue—product Z
7000–7499		Production costs and cost of sales
7500–7999		Payroll costs
8000–8999		General and administrative expenses
9000–9499		Selling expenses
	9010	Sales supplies
	9200	Sales transportation costs
	9210	Sales commissions
	9220	Sales taxes payable
9500–9999		Nonoperating expenses and revenues

mission for that sale, and that the sales tax rate is 5 percent. The number that uniquely identifies the customer is 1443. The designation 01 in the multipart code indicates a retail customer, and 02 indicates a wholesale customer. Robert Smith's employee number is 1234, and his sales department is number 51 of division 5. The record layout for this credit sales transaction might be as shown in Exhibit 12.5.

Each "field" in a record is a section of the record that holds a specific type of data, and the computer programs are written to recognize what is in each field and to process it properly. From Exhibit 12.4 it can be seen that only record fields 1, 2, and 3 of Exhibit 12.5 contain codes that are chart of accounts code numbers; fields 4, 5, and 6 contain additional codes

	Type of transaction	Product sold	Sales commission	Customer number and type	Selling division and department	Salesperson	Quantity sold	Sales price	Tax rate
Record	1570	6380	9210	1443-2	5-51	1234	0001	175.00	.050
Record fields	1	2	3	4	5	6	7	8	9

EXHIBIT 12.5
A credit sales input format.

that permit files to be processed in more ways than this chart of accounts makes possible, and fields 7, 8, and 9 include data about the transaction. (Typically there would be more than just three fields for transaction data.)

The record shown in Exhibit 12.5 contains extensive information about the transaction. The computer processing of this transaction might involve a transactions file for credit sales transactions and four master files (credit sales, inventory, sales commissions, and customers). While systems differ widely in their file organization and processing steps, the processing steps might be approximately as follows:

1. The credit sales transaction is entered into the computer as a part of a batch of sales transactions for that day or other time period.

2. The computer calculates the sale amount, sales tax, and total sale including tax for the transaction (sale amount = $175 × 0001 units = $175; sales tax = $175 × 0.05 = $8.75; total sale = $175 + 8.75 = 183.75) and places the transaction (including information about the sale amount, sales tax, and total sale) on magnetic tape along with information about other transactions. This creates a transactions file.

3. This transaction file is then processed together with:

(*a*) The customer master file to place the transactions information in each customer's account within this customer master file and to establish a new balance for each customer. In some systems the customer master file is updated directly by the transaction at the same time that the transactions file is prepared. Many systems would also record the salesperson's identification number and the selling division's and the department's identification numbers in the customer master file.

(*b*) The inventory master file to reduce the number of items shown in inventory records by the number of items sold.

(*c*) The sales commissions master file to enter Mr. Smith's sale ($175) as well as other sales for Mr. Smith and other salespersons in their accounts. This file will serve as the basis for determining sales commissions for all salespersons.

(*d*) The sales master file to establish new sales balances for each class of sales and in total. This file will serve as the basis of sales reports.

Subsequent processing of the credit sales file would result in sales analysis reports, and later processing of the inventory master file would produce inventory-level and turnover reports on an item-by-item, product line, and total inventory basis. Processing of the sales commissions master file would produce sales commission payment checks for each salesperson. Reports and documents later prepared from the customer master file would include invoices, customer statements, aged accounts receivable and other receivables reports and analyses, and a variety of analyses of customers such as by dollar amounts purchased for each of several classes of products and by profitability of each customer; further processing of customer accounts could also provide reports useful for analyzing the effectiveness of salespersons' efforts.

Some computer systems would perform all the preceding steps automatically after the transaction was entered (see Exhibit 12.15 and the accompanying discussion), but in the case of systems that have their files on magnetic tape, each step requires intervention and assistance by a computer operator.

Later processing of the various files could also provide analyses to show how much of each product was sold by each division and department and to indicate the pattern of sales to each type of customer (e.g., consumers and wholesalers) as well as to individual large customers. Additional information could be recorded to permit other analyses as well; for example, the record could include information about sales discounts and the geographic locations of customers.

The preceding simple example of a coding system for one type of transaction is intended for illustrative purposes only. Actual coding systems often become much more complex. It is not uncommon for a code for a particular transaction to contain more than 50 digits.

Each organization attempts to establish a record format that enables it to gather all data about a transaction that may be needed at a future time. Data not captured initially often is impossible to generate later. However, if the data is gathered initially and is contained anywhere in the record, programs developed to satisfy a later need can classify and process it in ways not envisioned when the coding system was established.

An organization's coding system may be structured in one of several ways. In many codes, each digit has "place significance"; that is, each digit has a meaning which is determined by its place in the code. This approach allows little room for expanding the code, but it increases processing efficiency because there are no extraneous code positions and the code can be compressed into as few digits as possible.

In most organizations, the preprinted forms used for each type of transaction already include some of the code. For example, all customer sales transactions may be recorded on a form already bearing the general ledger account number for customer sales, thereby saving the effort involved in entering this part of the code number.

RESPONSIBILITY ACCOUNTING INFORMATION SYSTEMS

There are several types of internally oriented accounting information systems. These information systems provide information for the two interrelated purposes of control and planning. Control consists of control over operations, management control, and performance evaluation of activities. The transactions processing and internal operations information systems provide detailed information about operations to supervisory-level managers for operations control and summarized information to higher-level managers for management control. Performance evaluation is based in large part on this same information.

The second purpose of internally oriented accounting information systems is to provide information for planning. One dimension of this is information about how successfully the organization has been pursuing its goals. The fact that such information is essentially the same as that used for performance evaluations illustrates the interrelationship between management control and management planning. Information that indicates the success of past operations is critical to planning future courses of action and flows indirectly from the operations control activities, in that it is the formal evaluation of these activities that provides the insights needed for planning. This suggests that a prerequisite for good planning is analyzing the success of past activities, and for this reason the organization's cyclical planning activities are usually begun immediately after performance reviews.

The information needed for management control purposes usually is information that permits comparing actual accomplishments with ideal or expected accomplishments during a period of time. The expectations are generally stated in the form of a plan that includes expense and revenue standards, or goals. Comparing actual expenses and revenues to the standards results in a variance, sometimes known as a "budget variance." Variances are analyzed to determine how operations can be improved as well as to evaluate the performance of both the operations activities and the managers.

The managerial accounting information system that tracks production variances is the cost accounting system, discussed later in this chapter. The responsibility accounting information system is more broadly based and encompasses the entire organization; it is usually referred to as the "budget," the "profit plan," or the "responsibility accounting system."

The responsibility accounting information system often is the major ingredient in a management control system. Generally this information system provides reports each month.

The three key elements of responsibility accounting are:

1. Short-term activity goals established in advance as performance standards

2. The accumulation of costs and revenues and their comparison with standards on the basis of organization units that are "responsibility centers"

3. The separation of costs and revenues into controllable and uncontrollable categories for each organization unit, usually according to which unit incurs the costs or generates the revenues, that is, according to which unit is responsible for the costs or revenues.

The responsibility accounting information system does not attempt to allocate costs and revenues to evaluate the efficiency of production for each product, to assign costs to products for cost of sales and inventory valuation purposes, or to assign responsibility for costs caused by underutilization of productive capacity; these tasks are accomplished by the cost accounting system, which aggregates costs horizontally through production processes. The responsibility accounting information system is instead the primary information system for aggregating costs and revenues on a hierarchical basis.

An example will illustrate how the responsibility accounting information system aggregates information. Assume that the Spidey Company's Ridge Oak plant produces automobile components and has five departments. These departments are milling, grinding, assembly, rustproofing, and machine and plant maintenance. The Ridge Oak plant and two other production plants are under the jurisdiction of the vice president of production. The other functions of the company are marketing, accounting, and engineering.

Exhibit 12.6 illustrates the hierarchical aggregation of information within a responsibility accounting information system. In this example, only four levels of hierarchy exist (excluding employees). Also, this example cites only controllable and uncontrollable costs, whereas many companies use three categories: "controllable" for costs that are fully the responsibility of the responsibility center manager, "semicontrollable" for costs over which the manager has some influence but not full control, and "uncontrollable" for those costs over which the manager has no control.

The following points should be made about Exhibit 12.6:

1. Each level is a responsibility center for which responsibility accounting reports are prepared.

2. Each report separates costs controllable by the responsibility center from costs not controllable by the responsibility center.

3. Each report shows the variances in a format that allows the important ones to be clearly identified. In the case of the milling department, for example, it can be clearly seen that for September, the raw materials and equipment repairs unfavorable variances are significant; these excessive costs should receive the attention of the supervisor and the plant superintendent. At the plant superintendent's level, where costs are ac-

A Responsibility Accounting System EXHIBIT 12.6

*President's Responsibility
Accounting Summary*

Controllable Costs and Revenues	September			Year-to-Date		
	Budget	Actual	Variance	Budget	Actual	Variance
Marketing revenues	$910,000	$842,610	$ 67,390	$8,000,000	$7,642,890	$357,310
Senior executives' salaries	35,000	35,000	– 0 –	315,000	315,000	– 0 –
Marketing costs	191,840	197,860	(6,020)	1,655,800	1,815,080	(159,280)
Production costs	290,760	293,650	(2,890)	2,546,860	2,559,590	(12,730)
Engineering costs	33,040	36,400	(3,360)	277,930	290,820	(12,890)
Accounting costs	27,700	28,100	(400)	254,380	263,710	(9,330)
Depreciation	120,000	120,000	– 0 –	1,080,000	1,080,000	– 0 –
President's office	22,200	22,320	(120)	184,760	186,740	(1,980)
Total controllable costs	$720,540	$733,330	$(12,790)	$6,314,730	$6,510,940	$(196,210)

Uncontrollable costs

President's salary	$ 8,000	$ 8,000	$ – 0 –	$ 72,000	$ 72,000	$ – 0 –

( ) = unfavorable variance

*Vice President of Production's
Responsibility Accounting Cost Summary*

Controllable Costs	September			Year-to-Date		
	Budget	Actual	Variance	Budget	Actual	Variance
Superintendents' salaries	$ 9,500	$ 9,800	$ – 0 –	$ 85,500	$ 85,500	$ – 0 –
Ridge Oak plant	86,490	89,630	(3,140)	773,940	787,240	(13,300)
Ridge Maple plant	93,700	94,770	(1,070)	811,560	814,440	(2,880)
Ridge Hickory plant	78,370	76,800	1,570	676,880	670,540	6,340
Vice president's office	8,900	9,150	(250)	74,780	77,670	(2,890)
Property taxes and insurance	13,800	13,500	– 0 –	124,200	124,200	– 0 –
Total controllable costs	$290,760	$293,650	$ (2,890)	$2,546,860	$2,559,590	$ (12,730)

Uncontrollable costs

Depreciation	$74,000	$74,000	$ – 0 –	$666,000	$666,000	$ – 0 –
Vice president's salary	5,500	5,500	– 0 –	49,500	49,500	– 0 –

( ) = unfavorable variance

EXHIBIT 12.6
(continued)

Ridge Oak Plant
Superintendent's Responsibility
Accounting Cost Summary

Controllable Costs	September			Year-to-Date		
	Budget	Actual	Variance	Budget	Actual	Variance
Supervisors' salaries	$ 8,400	$ 8,400	$ – 0 –	$ 75,600	$ 75,600	$ – 0 –
Milling department	25,240	26,020	(780)	243,960	243,780	180
Grinding department	13,710	16,040	(2,330)	111,760	117,720	(5,960)
Assembly department	22,000	20,800	1,200	194,400	195,700	(1,300)
Rust-proofing department	6,440	6,340	100	53,210	54,010	(800)
Maintenance department	6,300	7,240	(940)	54,410	59,860	(5,450)
Plant office	4,400	4,790	(390)	40,600	40,570	30
Total controllable costs	$ 86,490	$ 89,630	$ (3,140)	$ 773,940	$ 787,240	(13,300)

Uncontrollable costs

Depreciation	$ 26,000	$ 26,000	$ – 0 –	$234,000	$234,000	$ – 0 –
Superintendent's salary	3,000	3,000	– 0 –	27,000	27,000	– 0 –
Property taxes and insurance	4,600	4,600	– 0 –	41,400	41,400	– 0 –

( ) = unfavorable variance

Ridge Oak Plant
Milling Department Supervisor's
Responsibility Accounting Cost Summary

Controllable Costs	September			Year-to-Date		
	Budget	Actual	Variance	Budget	Actual	Variance
Raw materials	$ 4,340	$ 4,720	$ (380)	$ 42,500	$ 43,900	$ (1,400)
Direct labor	14,700	14,570	130	144,600	142,700	1,900
Operating supplies	1,080	1,090	(10)	9,460	9,740	(280)
Equipment repairs	2,100	2,700	(600)	19,400	19,510	(110)
Energy costs	3,020	2,940	80	28,000	27,930	70
Total controllable costs	$ 25,240	$ 26,020	$ (780)	$ 243,960	$ 243,780	$ 180

Uncontrollable costs

Depreciation	6,000	6,000	$ – 0 –	54,000	54,000	$ – 0 –
Allocated maintenance	2,100	2,450	350	19,000	21,900	2,900
Supervisor's salary	2,200	2,200	– 0 –	19,800	19,800	– 0 –
Property taxes and insurance	1,130	1,130	– 0 –	10,170	10,170	– 0 –

( ) = unfavorable variance

cumulated for all departments, it can be seen that for September, the grinding department and maintenance department total costs are much higher than was expected and that these same departments are also problem areas for the entire year-to-date.

4. All costs that are the responsibility of (that is, controllable by) one level are also considered to be the responsibility of each higher level; thus each manager in the hierarchy is motivated to be concerned about the performance of subordinates.

5. The arrows in the exhibit indicate that the costs at each level are aggregated to each higher level. As shown, the supervisor's total controllable costs of $243,780 actual year-to-date costs are included in the total controllable costs of the superintendent, which in turn are a part of the total controllable costs of the vice president, which in turn are included in the president's total controllable costs.

6. As costs are aggregated to each higher level, more and more costs become controllable by the manager. For example, the supervisor's salary is not controllable by the supervisor, but it is controllable by the plant superintendent. The president is responsible for all costs except the president's salary.

7. Certain "programmed" costs, such as depreciation and managers' salaries, do not have variances because the exact amounts of these costs for the following period are often known in advance; depreciation, for example, is usually an allocation of costs incurred in the past.

8. No attempt is made at any point in the responsibility accounting information system to determine income; although based on much the same information, income determination is accomplished by the financial reporting information system.

The responsibility accounting information system should be designed according to "flexible budgeting" concepts so that budgeted amounts are based on actual levels of production activity. For example, referring again to Exhibit 12.6, in the milling department the raw materials costs would be much higher for 80,000 units milled than for 40,000. Even if the hoped-for activity level was 80,000 and only 40,000 units were milled, the raw materials budget standard (the flexible budget) is based on the expected raw materials for 40,000 units. The low level of milling activity (40,000 units rather than 80,000) would be detected and reported by the cost accounting system.

Although not shown in Exhibit 12.6, responsibility accounting information systems frequently report the variance not only in monetary terms but also as a percentage of the budgeted amount. In the superintendent's report in Exhibit 12.6, for example, including these percentages would show that while for the year-to-date the maintenance department does not have the highest variance in monetary terms, its variance percentage is 10 percent, which is nearly double the next highest percentage. Often the budget variance percentage is given not only for the month and year to date but also for the same month and the year-to-date for the preceding year, to allow comparing the preceding period's results.

Responsibility accounting is the single most important information system in many organizations. A preceding chapter noted that the basic information system's structure follows the organization's hierarchy and that data is aggregated according to this hierarchy. This basic information system in most major and many smaller organizations is the responsibility accounting information system. The aggregation processes within this basic system can now be understood on the basis of cost and revenue responsibility.

In organizations that do not use responsibility accounting information systems, the most common form of basic aggregation is according to natural cost classifications. For instance, payroll costs are aggregated at each level, supplies costs are aggregated at each level, and so on.

COST ACCOUNTING INFORMATION SYSTEMS

Another type of internally oriented accounting information system is that of cost accounting. While the responsibility accounting information system aggregates costs hierarchically, in a manufacturing company costs of product manufacturing are also accumulated horizontally. Exhibit 12.7 illustrates the flow of information about production costs within a "process" cost accounting system. In a process system, units of product move from process to process (perhaps on an assembly line), and at each station a production process takes place. For example, a metal product may be cast in two parts in a mold at the first production process, then grinding or

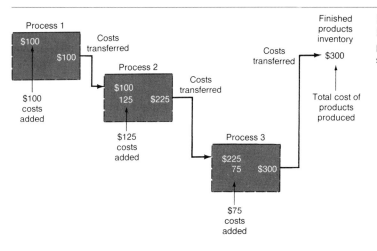

EXHIBIT 12.7
Information flows in a process cost accounting system.

machining takes place in the next department, then holes are drilled for bolts to connect the two halves of the castings in a third department, then in a fourth department the casting is assembled by bolting the halves, and finally in a fifth department the assembled product is polished, painted, chromed, or otherwise finished before it is placed in inventory as a finished product ready for sale.

The cost accounting information system measures the costs of labor and materials used for a production process for a given number of products, accumulating these costs in a cost accumulation account. Exhibit 12.7 shows three accounts (records): one each for process 1, process 2, and process 3. When one process is completed and the products are transferred to the next process, the processing costs are transferred to the accumulation account for that next process.

Exhibit 12.7 indicates that $100 of costs is incurred in process 1 and then transferred into process 2. Process 2 incurs an additional $125 of costs, and this $125 plus the already transferred $100 are then transferred to process 3. Using this system allows accurate determination of the cost of each process for each unit of the product when the product is completed. Also, because the total costs of all processes are accumulated as the products finish each process, the total cost of the products transferred to inventory is known, and the average total cost of each product finished can be calculated. For example, if 150 units of the product were started and completed for the $300 of total cost shown in Exhibit 12.7, a simple calculation would show that the average cost of each unit was $2.

The cost accounting information system serves two major purposes, the first of which is cost control. Cost control is particularly effective if budgeting is used in production so that for each process expected costs, or "cost standards," are first established and the actual costs are later compared with these estimates. The resulting variances can be used as a basis for making cost-reducing improvements in production efficiency. A production budgeting system like this is termed a "standard cost accounting system."

The second purpose of the cost accounting information system is to place a value on the inventory of finished or partly finished products. Inventory value, reported to outside organizations as one indication of the company's worth, influences the public's perception of the company and affects the price of its stock on the stock market.

The cost of each type of product as indicated by the cost accounting information system is also an important ingredient in certain managerial decisions. The sales price of a product, for example, often depends in part on its production cost. Another decision strongly influenced by production cost is whether to continue producing a particular product.

The same cost data that is processed by the cost accounting information system is also processed by the responsibility accounting information system. The cost information is originally gathered as transactions in the same manner as data relating to other types of transactions. For the most part, cost accounting transactions consist of (1) instances in which raw materials and supplies are checked out of inventory and used in production (the transaction is recorded by materials transfer requisitions), (2) the cost of the labor used in production in each process (indicated by employee time cards), and (3) transferring products from one process to the next or to inventory (recorded on transfer vouchers). These transactions are entered into the computer system to update the records of both the responsibility and the cost accounting information systems.

THE ACCOUNTING PROCESS

The recording and processing of accounting transactions consists of the following steps:

1. *Recording* all details of the transactions in a *journal*, or "book of original entry"; any facts about a transaction omitted here usually cannot be recorded later. A journal is a chronological listing of transactions. Journals may be specialized; for instance, there may be a separate sales journal and a separate accounts payable journal.

2. *Posting* the transactions to an account in a *subsidiary ledger*. To "post" means to transfer or "enter" the dollar amounts of transactions. A subsidiary ledger consists of all accounts in a particular category, that is, accounts in which all transactions of the same kind are recorded. For example, it may consist of customer accounts in which all the accounts of customers are included and all transactions with a customer are recorded in that customer's account.

3. *Posting* all subsidiary ledgers to a general ledger, which in a manual system is a book, or "ledger," that lists each subsidiary ledger as one account in the book.

Usually it is the total for all accounts in each subsidiary ledger, rather than each individual transaction or each account total, that is posted to the general ledger. Thus, the amounts entered in the general ledger are already summarized.

Journals serve as a basis for controlling the organization's individual transactions by ensuring, for example, that all are originally recorded; if a transaction is later lost or not processed properly, its full details can be checked in the journal. Journals may also provide useful summary data for managers, such as the daily total in the sales journal.

The subsidiary ledger usually supplies information needed for further data processing. Additional processing of the customer ledger, for example, produces customer statements, aged accounts receivable analyses, and an analysis of the pattern of sales to different types of customers as well as to specific customers. The general ledger is the basis for the

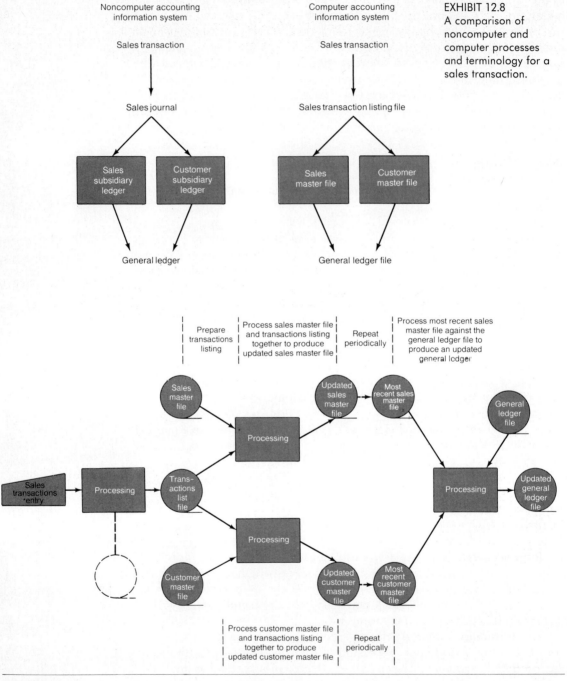

EXHIBIT 12.8
A comparison of noncomputer and computer processes and terminology for a sales transaction.

EXHIBIT 12.9
Computer processing of sales transactions.

preparation of highly summarized reports such as the income statement and balance sheet.

Exhibit 12.8 shows the correspondence between the accounting processes just described in accounting terms and these same processes described in data processing terminology. Most accounting textbooks describe the accounting process only in terminology used in noncomputerized accounting systems; yet managers must relate accounting terminology to "computerese." The example of a sales transaction is used to enhance the comparison.

Exhibit 12.8 demonstrates that the manual and the computerized processes are analogous; only the terminology differs. While different computer systems vary from that shown in the exhibit, a rough correspondence between the manual and the computerized processes remains, which will be evident to a thoughtful manager who understands Exhibit 12.8.

Exhibit 12.9 shows the data processing activities associated with the computerized sales order entry system of Exhibit 12.8. The symbols used for the files in the exhibit are the standard symbols for a system using magnetic-tape files; of course, many organizations use disk files.

Several aspects of Exhibit 12.9 merit explanation. The sales and customer master files contain data on previous sales transactions. In processing the transactions file, the computer calculates the dollar amount of the sale and the sales tax, placing this information in the appropriate master files; as this occurs, a new master file is created that contains the previous data as well as the data relating to the current transaction. These new files are shown as the updated master files. In the system shown, sales transactions might be processed in "batches," perhaps at the end of each day or perhaps only once per week; the section in the exhibit labeled "repeat periodically" indicates this. At the end of the period the "most recent" master files, (that is, those containing the transactions through the end of the period) are processed with the existing general ledger file that contains the results of transactions only through the end of the preceding period; this processing results in an updated general ledger file that is current as of the end of the period just completed.

The variations of this process are numerous. One common variation suggested by the dashed-line file is that the batches of transactions may be processed directly against the master file rather than having the master files updated by the transactions listing file. In this case, the transactions listing file usually is prepared only as a control and reference file to protect against the possibility that transactions might be lost or erroneously processed.

THE GENERAL LEDGER SYSTEM

Exhibit 12.3 showed the account coding structrue of a simplified chart of accounts. Exhibit 12.10 displays the major accounts in the general ledger

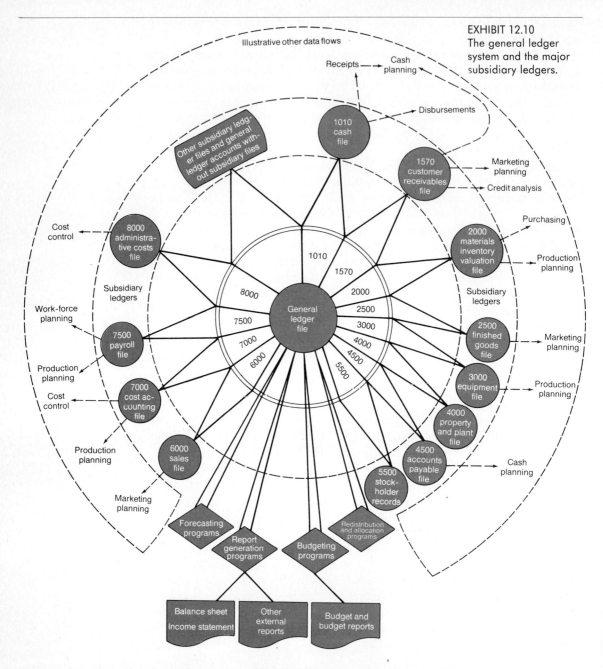

EXHIBIT 12.10
The general ledger
system and the major
subsidiary ledgers.

system based on the chart of accounts of Exhibit 12.3 (note that the account numbers of the two exhibits are coordinated).

A general ledger system consists of the general ledger file, shown at the center of Exhibit 12.10, and a series of subsidiary ledgers (master files) such as those shown within the dashed concentric circles. The subsidiary ledgers usually contain the details of the transactions and are updated frequently (often daily or weekly) from the journals or directly from the transactions, as previously discussed. Most general ledger accounts are updated periodically (often monthly) with only summary data from the subsidiary ledger accounts. General ledger accounts that have too few transactions to warrant a subsidiary ledger may be updated directly from the transactions journal.

The simple example of Exhibit 12.11 illustrates several points about the operation of a general ledger system. First, certain accounts in both the general and the subsidiary ledgers are "continuous" in nature; that is, for example, each customer account has a beginning balance and an ending balance, as the associated general ledger account does. Second, the total of the beginning balances and the total of the ending balances in the subsidiary accounts must equal the beginning balance and ending balance, respectively, in the general ledger account (for the beginning balance, $50 + $90 + $20 = $160; for the ending balance, $90 + $120 + $25 = $235). This balancing is an important technical control for ensuring the accuracy of all accounts in the system. Third, only the net amounts of the transactions for each period for each customer are transferred to the general

---

Subsidiary Ledger–General Ledger Interaction.   EXHIBIT 12.11

Accounts Receivable Subsidiary Ledger

	AREN ADAMS		
	BALANCE, BEGINNING OF PERIOD		$50
	→ CREDIT SALES, THIS PERIOD	$75	
	→ CASH RECEIPTS, THIS PERIOD	($35)	
POST	NET THIS PERIOD		40
TRANSACTIONS	BALANCE, END OF PERIOD		$90
THIS			
PERIOD	JOHN JONES		
	BALANCE, BEGINNING OF PERIOD		$90 POST
	→ CREDIT SALES, THIS PERIOD	$30	TOTAL
	→ CASH RECEIPTS, THIS PERIOD	-0-	THIS
	NET THIS PERIOD		30 PERIOD
	BALANCE, END OF PERIOD		$120
	MERIDITH MARTIN		
	BALANCE, BEGINNING OF PERIOD		$20
	→ CREDIT SALES THIS PERIOD	$25	
	→ CASH RECEIPTS, THIS PERIOD	(20)	
	NET THIS PERIOD		5
	BALANCE, END OF MONTH		$25

General Ledger Accounts Receivable

BALANCE, BEGINNING OF PERIOD	$160
TOTAL ACTIVITY FOR THE PERIOD	75
BALANCE, END OF PERIOD	$235

ledger; these may be transferred as one total for all customer activities during the period ($40 + $30 + $5 = $75).

The subsidiary ledgers (master files) are utilized extensively for managerial purposes. The nature of the information they typically provide and the purposes for which this information is used are shown in the outermost ring of Exhibit 12.10.

In most information systems the master files are processed separately to extract the information needed for a particular purpose. This is illustrated in Exhibit 12.12, where the sales master file is processed by specialized sales analysis programs to obtain information useful for sales forecasting. This information is input to a sales forecasting system along with similarly derived information from other files and from noncomputerized sources, such as from archival sales files of preceding years (needed to help establish long-term trends) and from the current market environment.

A separate sales forecasting file constructed from the data thus extracted is processed by forecasting programs that contain forecasting routines such as trend analysis, statistical algorithms, and report generating instructions. The resulting sales forecast is based in part on the subsidiary sales ledger (sales master file). Many of the subsidiary ledger files are similarly processed to provide other reports essential to management.

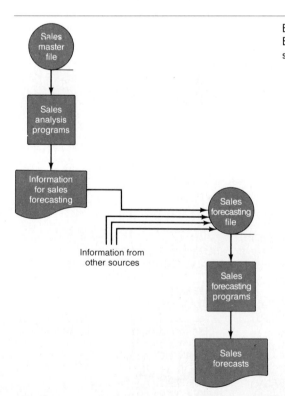

EXHIBIT 12.12
Extracting data from a sales master file.

If the organization has a budgeting system other than the responsibility accounting information system, it is usually on a type-of-cost–revenue basis and is tied directly to the general ledger system. The budget is initially constructed by placing cost and revenue expectations for every general ledger account in a separate "budget file" that has the same account codes as the general ledger file. At the end of the period, the budgeting programs extract the details of the period's actual costs and revenues from the subsidiary ledger files. These details are then placed in the budget file and are processed to prepare a budget analysis that includes variances from the budget.

Increasingly, budgeting is accomplished within the structure of a responsibility accounting information system, whereby all costs and revenues are associated with a responsibility center. Data is gathered in the subsidiary ledger files, from which it is extracted when needed for the responsibility accounting information system. Each cost and revenue must be coded with both a general ledger account number and an organization unit number. Exhibit 12.13 illustrates this process; the resulting reports were shown in Exhibit 12.6.

The redistribution and allocation programs shown at the bottom of Exhibit 12.10 access many of the general ledger and subsidiary ledger files to make the adjusting and closing entries previously mentioned. These programs also allocate the costs of utilities and service departments, such as the maintenance department, to the other departments. Many of these redistribution and allocation programs are intended to serve both the managerial and the external reporting needs of the organization. They

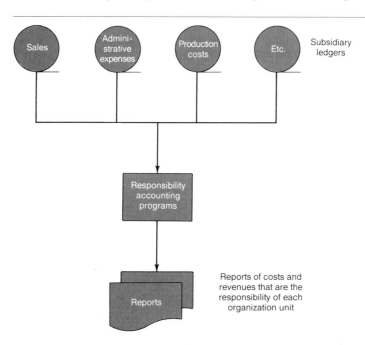

EXHIBIT 12.13
Data processing for a responsibility accounting information system.

perform housekeeping chores such as calculating depreciation for plant and equipment, establishing valuations for various types of inventory, and determining production overhead costs so that these can be allocated to each unit of product.

THE FINANCIAL REPORTING INFORMATION SYSTEM

Many of the reports provided by a company to outside agencies are financial in nature and are generated by the financial reporting information system. Among the most important external reports are "general-purpose financial statements," which include the balance sheet, the income statement, and other statements. The chart of accounts is the basis of the information system that produces these general-purpose financial reports, which satisfy the needs of stockholders and other external groups. The computer programs that assemble and prepare these reports are shown at the bottom of Exhibit 12.10. In many organizations, these programs need access only the general ledger file. Prior to this report preparation, however, any subsidiary and branch accounts that use the same general ledger chart of accounts system must be consolidated into the general ledger system; in some systems the general-purpose report generation programs carry out this consolidation activity. The allocation and redistribution data processing must also have been completed.

The financial reporting subsystem of a large company may also generate hundreds of specialized financial reports for government regulatory agencies each year. Usually, the more a regulatory financial report varies, in terms of format and content, from information utilized for the general-purpose financial statements and the more additional information that must be included, other than that which is in the general and subsidiary ledger files, the less likely it is that computer programs will exist to prepare a particular report. Financial statements for the Securities and Exchange Commission and for various city, county, state, and federal payroll tax, income tax, and property tax reports are among the most likely to be at least partially computerized.

THE SALES ORDER ENTRY SYSTEM: BATCH BASIS

The two most widely used general approaches to data processing are "batch" processing and "on-line" processing. This section uses a sales order entry system to illustrate batch processing.

In companies with a large number of customers or products, a crucial information system is the sales order entry system. A well-developed sales order entry system can reduce the costs of filling orders and enhance the company's image, drawing new customers while helping retain current ones. Faster shipment of goods ordered and fewer errors in billing, for example, promote customer goodwill, which increases sales.

Additionally, the sales order entry system can provide managers with information useful for analyzing customer acceptance of products, competitors' actions, product quality, customer characteristics, and marketing strategies. The sales order entry system directly or indirectly updates the subsidiary and general ledger files of sales, customers, and finished goods inventory, as well as the back-order file (which records sales orders received for which no merchandise is yet available for shipment). The sales order entry system also provides information to the purchasing system, the customer credit system, the sales forecasting system, and the market research system, among others.

As has been noted, the sales order entry system either encompasses or interacts with a substantial portion of the total information functions in many companies and, like many other information systems, cannot be exclusively identified with only one of the organization's functional areas. It services both marketing, which embraces all customer-related information, and accounting, which uses information about sales for account invoicing, statement preparation, account collection, and cash forecasting and control purposes.

Batch processing accumulates transactions in batches (groups of transactions) before or during processing. For certain types of data processing activities, batch processing is very efficient and inexpensive.

Exhibit 12.14 shows batch processing in a sales order entry system. Sales order entry systems vary greatly; Exhibit 12.14 is intended to illustrate only the general flow of information in such a system. For simplicity, all sales are assumed to be credit sales.

The exhibit shows a batch sales order entry system in which sales are manually prepared on sales slips. Product number; quantity ordered; customer name, number, and address; salesperson number; and all other information that will be needed for later processing must be placed on this sales slip. In some systems the product price per unit is placed on the sales slip, and in others the price is provided by the computer system.

As shown, these orders are gathered into batches at the sales location and are periodically (typically daily) approved for credit either within the sales department or by a separate credit department; in either case, a delay may occur while the transactions await credit approval.

The batch is then transferred to the data center for conversion to machine-readable form for entry into the computer. This conversion activity follows a present schedule; thus, depending on the backlog, anywhere form a few minutes to a day or two may elapse before the conversion takes place. Then the transactions are usually listed on magnetic tape, forming a computer-readable transactions batch, as shown in the exhibit. This tape is then delivered to computer operators, whose schedules may delay further processing for a day or more.

When entered into the computer, the transactions in this example are processed together with the inventory master file. During this processing each item on the sales orders is checked against the inventory master file to see whether adequate numbers of the product are in stock; if there is

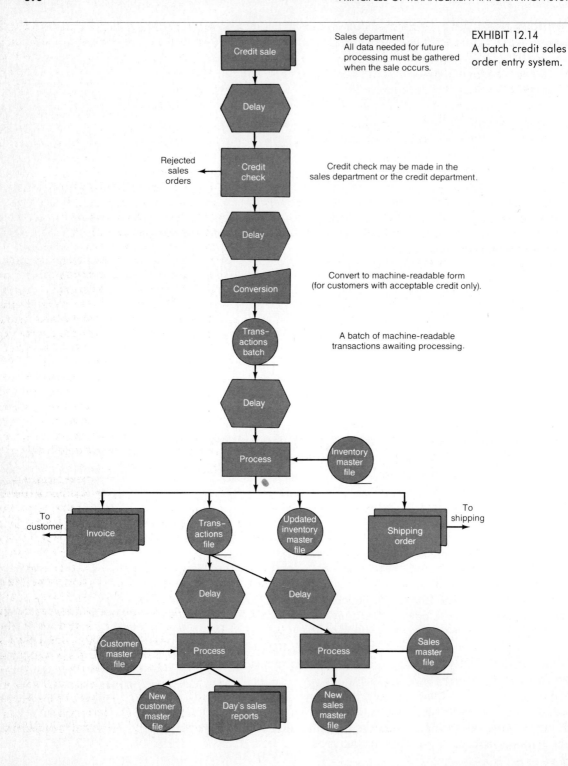

Sales department
All data needed for future processing must be gathered when the sale occurs.

Credit check may be made in the sales department or the credit department.

Convert to machine-readable form (for customers with acceptable credit only).

A batch of machine-readable transactions awaiting processing.

EXHIBIT 12.14
A batch credit sales order entry system.

not a sufficient quantity of the product, the order for that item is canceled, or the item is placed on back order (not shown). For sales items in stock, the inventory number is decreased in the inventory master file by the quantity being sold, and the computer calculates the price for the quantity ordered of each item (taking into consideration quantity discounts and similar price adjustments) and determines the total sales price and tax for each customer order. The computer programs then direct the preparation of customer invoices and shipping orders. Generally a sales transactions file containing full details of the sales transactions also is prepared, usually on magnetic tape.

During this process the customer master file may also have been placed in the computer, and each customer's account updated for the transactions, or this updating process may take place afterward, as is illustrated in the exhibit. The sales transactions file may then be used to produce summary sales reports about the transactions in the file, as shown; alternatively, these may have been produced at the same time that the file was created and the invoices were prepared.

The sales transactions file must be later processed with the sales master file to produce a new sales master file. Both the sales master file and the inventory master file will be used to provide periodic reports to managers.

While activity sequences in batch-processing sales order entry systems vary widely, all such systems include delays of varying lengths from the time the order is received to the time the shipping department is notified and the customer accounts and inventory systems are fully updated. These delays often exceed a week and in some instances are greater than 3 weeks. A delay may mean that merchandise sold is shipped later than necessary, that the customer accounts used by the credit and collection departments or used to deal with inquiries from customers are not current, or that the sales and purchasing departments will not have up-to-date information about the quantities of each item in inventory.

The delays in transactions processing and file updating described above are found in all types of batch-processing systems, such as vendor payment systems, cost accounting systems, and personnel information systems. However, batch-processing systems are less complex and less costly than on-line, real-time systems, described next. Additionally, processing transactions in batches permits the use of controls, such as record counts, that guard against inaccurate or misplaced transactions.

THE SALES ORDER ENTRY SYSTEM: ON-LINE, REAL-TIME

An on-line, real-time (OLRT) sales order entry system can fully process a transaction as soon as it is entered; thus no delays occur during computer processing. When coupled with a point-of-sale (POS) transaction recording and entry system whereby the transaction is initially recorded in machine-readable form and entered directly into the computer, the system is fully automated, and even the delay in entering the transaction is eliminated. An OLRT system with POS transaction entry is illustrated in Exhibit 12.15.

In an OLRT system, all files of the subsystem involved with a particular type of transactions processing must be electronically connected to the computer when a transaction of that type is entered into the computer. For technical reasons, the files of an OLRT system must consist of magnetic

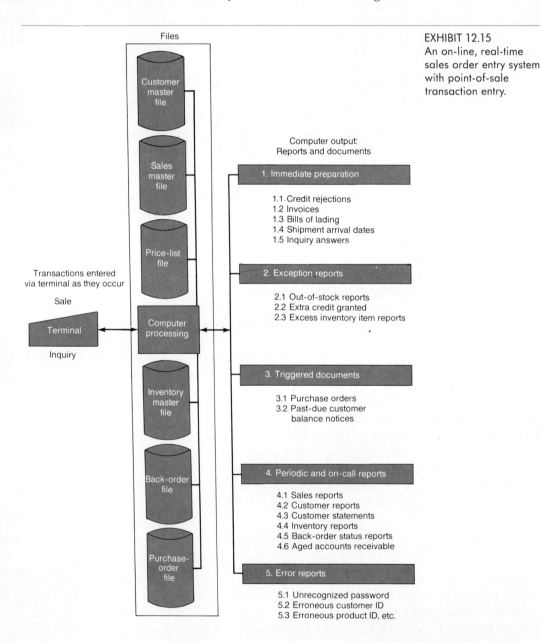

EXHIBIT 12.15
An on-line, real-time sales order entry system with point-of-sale transaction entry.

Files

Customer master file

Sales master file

Price-list file

Computer output:
Reports and documents

Transactions entered via terminal as they occur

Sale

Terminal

Inquiry

Computer processing

Inventory master file

Back-order file

Purchase-order file

1. Immediate preparation

1.1 Credit rejections
1.2 Invoices
1.3 Bills of lading
1.4 Shipment arrival dates
1.5 Inquiry answers

2. Exception reports

2.1 Out-of-stock reports
2.2 Extra credit granted
2.3 Excess inventory item reports

3. Triggered documents

3.1 Purchase orders
3.2 Past-due customer
     balance notices

4. Periodic and on-call reports

4.1 Sales reports
4.2 Customer reports
4.3 Customer statements
4.4 Inventory reports
4.5 Back-order status reports
4.6 Aged accounts receivable

5. Error reports

5.1 Unrecognized password
5.2 Erroneous customer ID
5.3 Erroneous product ID, etc.

disks rather than magnetic tapes; disk systems involve a more sophisticated technology than magnetic-tape systems. Exhibit 12.15 shows six disk files, each containing accounts or other information that the computer programs can access immediately.

The OLRT system illustrated operates in a dramatically different manner from the way batch systems do. Assume that customers order by telephone and that the salesperson who receives customers' orders immediately keys the transactions in at a terminal, as shown in the exhibit. Controlled by the sales order entry computer programs, the following occur immediately in roughly this sequence for each transaction:

1. The salesperson tells the computer the nature of the transaction by entering a transaction code identifying it as a credit sales transaction; this activates the sales order entry computer programs. The customer number and the item number and quantity are then entered.

2. The computer program checks the customer's account in the customer file to "validate" the customer number (to establish that a credit customer exists with that number) and to see how much additional credit the customer can be granted; the up-to-date credit status of the customer is contained in the customer's account. If the customer cannot be extended further credit, the salesperson is notified by the computer and the credit transaction is canceled.

3. The product number of the product ordered is checked for validity in the inventory file, and the quantity shown by the inventory file to be in stock is compared with the number of items ordered. If there is an insufficient quantity of a product, the program examines the purchasing file to establish when the next shipment is due, provides this information to the salesperson, and awaits further instructions. The system conveys the information to the terminal of the salesperson, who consults with the customer and then cancels the order for that item or changes the order to the quantity available and back-orders the additional items desired, according to the customer's wishes.

4. The computer program then seeks product pricing and quantity discount information from the price list file and special "preferred customer" discount information, if any, from the customer file. The cost to the customer, including tax, is calculated by the computer.

5. The details of the transaction, including the cost details, may appear on a display device at the salesperson's terminal so that they can be told to the customer. Changes may be made in the order by the customer and entered into the computer. The salesperson signals the computer when the customer approves the transaction.

6. An invoice is printed out for mailing, either at the salesperson's terminal or on a printer at a central location.

7. On a printer at the warehouse location of the merchandise the computer system prepares a multipart shipping document, which is the authorization for shipping personnel to select, pack, and ship the merchandise ordered. One copy of the document, known as the "bill of lading," is enclosed and shipped with the merchandise.

8. Product records in the inventory file are adjusted to reflect the decrease in inventory caused by the sale.

9. The customer's account is updated to reflect the details of the transaction, and a new customer balance is calculated and placed in the account.

10. The record for each item in the sales file is updated with details of the transaction. This updating may include all details necessary for sales analyses based on customer type and territory, as well as other factors. A separate transaction listing that records all details of the entire transaction in one transaction file (not shown) may also be made for control and backup purposes.

The transaction processing described above may occur within a matter of a minute or two after the transaction is originally entered, while the customer is still on the telephone. In an OLRT system, the records can be kept current on a minute-by-minute basis. Inquiries from customers about the details of a recent transaction, about account balances, or about quantities of a product that are available for sale can be entered through terminals and receive almost instant responses. If the price list file and the purchase order file are also maintained on a current basis, inquiries about prices and expected arrival dates of shipments can be answered promptly.

Additionally, transactions can be rejected immediately if the customer is not eligible for credit or if the item ordered is out of stock. With a batch system, neither credit eligibility nor product availability may be known for a day or more after the order is received. Common errors in batch systems, such as the entry of an incorrect customer number or an erroneous product number, may require days to detect and even more time to correct. With an OLRT system, such errors are usually detected and corrected immediately.

Each of the reports shown in Exhibit 12.15 can be produced at any location desired. Typically, the credit rejection report, the inquiry answers, and the error reports are displayed or printed at the terminal where the transaction is entered. Triggered reports occur when an internal condition automates a programmed algorithm, such as when the quantity of an item on hand drops below a reorder level. Then a computer program may calculate a recommended number to be reordered, using an economic order quantity (EOQ) formula, and a purchase recommendation along with vendors' names and recent service histories may be sent to the purchasing department.

For report category 4 of Exhibit 12.15, the periodic reports shown are likely to be prepared whether it is a batch or an OLRT system. Because the OLRT files are maintained in an up-to-date status, OLRT systems require less end-of-period processing, and periodic reports usually can be completed much more rapidly than with a batch system. The on-call reports shown in the exhibit usually have the same format and content as a periodic report but are available at any time from the OLRT system because its records are kept continuously up to date. For example, a manager may request a report of sales since the first of the month that is up to date as of the end of the preceding day, and this report can be provided immediately at any time during the month. Often the manager can enter this request through a terminal, and the system will provide the report automatically. With a batch system, a request for an unscheduled sales report would require extensive, labor-intensive file processing, and the report might not be completed for several days.

The OLRT system discussed in the preceding pages is a highly integrated system; it is apparent that one transaction input results in data flows to several different files. The most important advantages of an OLRT system obviously are processing of all aspects of the transaction immediately and the continuously current data files. Efficiency of operations is increased by the decreases in manual intervention during file processing and by the initial recording of the transaction in machine-readable form. Customer service is improved in numerous ways; for example, customers receive faster responses to inquiries, and shipments are initiated immediately. Immediate invoicing accelerates account collections from customers. Immediate identification of inventory shortages facilitates prompt reordering, thereby producing better inventory control and lowering the total inventory required; this in turn reduces capital costs invested in inventory.

Managerial information needs are also better served. Periodic reports are received earlier, and many reports are available on call. OLRT systems are a major factor in breaking the reporting cycle's grip on how organizations are managed.

However, keeping the files on-line requires larger computers with greater amounts of memory. Also, the computer programs are much more difficult to design, implement, and modify because they are more complex. For some types of computing tasks, high levels of customer service, lower inventory levels, faster information for management purposes, or the other benefits of OLRT either do not exist or are not important, and batch systems may be more cost-effective. The typical organization with sophisticated information systems has a combination of OLRT systems and batch systems.

ACCOUNTING SOFTWARE PACKAGES

Large organizations usually have such complex operations that they find it necessary to design and develop their own accounting applications programs. Some of the largest organizations employ more than 1000 professional data processing personnel to do this. Smaller organizations, however, often have simpler, more straightforward operations and cannot afford to tailor-make every applications program. To serve these organizations, computer companies and independent software vendors provide prewritten applications programs at a small fraction of what it would cost an organization to write its own programs. Typically, these programs can be modified somewhat at little or no additional cost to adapt to minor variations in an organization's accounting processes, such as variations in the length of the chart of accounts code or in the lengths of individual data fields in records. Also, smaller organizations are usually willing to modify their accounting practices somewhat in order to adopt particular computer programs if this will eliminate the high cost of developing their own programs.

Thousands of prewritten accounting applications programs are available; the number of vendors offering these software packages may exceed 1000. Most small business computer companies offer their customers a wide selection, and, for each of the better-known microcomputers, independent vendors also provide a series of accounting applications programs. The most common prewritten applications programs are for accounts receivable, payroll, sales order entry, inventory, accounts payable, and general ledger systems, as well as for financial statement preparation and income tax determination. A variety of software packages are also available for market analysis, production control, personnel management, strategic planning, budgetary control, forecasting, and other applications areas.

Smaller organizations should carefully consider the possibility of purchasing prewritten programs before trying to develop their own. Descriptions and evaluations of prewritten accounting programs, as well as advertisements for these programs, appear regularly in *Computerworld, Datamation, Byte, Software News,* and other data processing publications. A great many software packages tailored to a specific industry are also available, such as patient records and hospital accounting systems for hospitals and project management and construction cost programs for different types of construction companies. Often these software packages are advertised in the trade journals associated with the particular industry.

SUMMARY

The backbone of an organization's information system is its functional information systems. Each function has an information system composed of multiple subsystems. The accounting information system is a major functional information system in virtually every organization. It is also a feeder information system: much of its information is used by other functional information systems.

The two general classifications of accounting information systems are external and internal information systems. Certain external reports must conform to generally accepted accounting principles. Internal reports need not conform to these principles, but cost and other factors often prevent an organization from developing an additional information system that is tailored to management needs.

The chart of accounts serves as the basis of a coding system for the accounting information system. Each general ledger account is assigned a code number, and each accounting transaction is coded with its appropriate number when it is originally recorded.

The responsibility accounting information system aggregates costs and revenues on a hierarchical basis. All costs that are the responsibility of one level are also considered to be the responsibility of each higher level.

Cost accounting information systems aggregate costs horizontally—production costs accumulate in an account, record, or file as each unit of product moves through the steps of the production process. The two major purposes of cost accounting information systems are cost control and valuation of finished or partly finished product inventory.

The accounting process consists of recording all details of a transaction in a journal, posting the transactions to a subsidiary ledger, and posting the subsidiary ledger accounts to a general ledger. These processes may be manual or computerized. The budget is initially constructed by placing cost and revenue expectations for every subsidiary ledger account into a separate "budget file." At the end of the period, actual costs and revenues extracted from subsidiary ledgers are placed in this file and are processed to prepare an analysis showing budget variances.

An organization's sales order entry information system may use a batch approach, which involves delays at several points, or an on-line, real-time (OLRT) method, which provides rapid data processing but is more costly to design and modify. The purchase of commercially available software packages may reduce the cost and difficulty of implementing computerized accounting systems.

KEY TERMS

functional information system: a system whose purpose is to provide detailed information for a specific group of related operations activities, as well as summarized information for management control of that group of activities.

chart of accounts: the transaction and account coding system used by an accounting information system.

accounting cycle: a period of time at the end of which accounting transactions are summarized for the period and reports are prepared.

debit: the first part of a double entry accounting transaction.

credit: the second part of a double entry accounting transaction; debits and credits must be equal for each transaction.

double entry accounting: a system whereby each transaction is entered both as a debit and as a credit to provide a natural control over the accuracy of data processing (debits must always equal credits).

out-of-balance condition: a condition that exists when the sum of debits is not equal to the corresponding sum of credits, which indicates an error.

accrual accounting: a type of accounting that uses formal rules to determine in which period expenses and revenues are to be recorded.

adjusting entry: an accounting entry that allocates a revenue or an expense to its proper accounting period.

matching principle: an accounting rule that matches expenses to revenues and revenues and expenses to the proper accounting periods.

block code: an accounting code that sets aside a block of code numbers to assign to each type of account within a general category of accounts.

general ledger: a listing of all the accounts and their balances that are required for preparation of a detailed balance sheet and income statement.

field: a section of a record that holds a specific type of data; all records of that type will reserve that record section for that type of data.

place significance: a way of structuring a coding system so that each digit has a meaning, which is determined by its position (place) in the code.

variance: a figure resulting when an actual expense or revenue is compared with a standard (which is usually a budget estimate).

responsibility center: a unit of an organization to which the responsibility accounting information system assigns responsibility for certain costs and revenues.

journal: the "book of original entry," which is a chronological listing of accounting transactions.

subsidiary ledger: a ledger in which all transactions of a particular kind are recorded; there is usually a separate subsidiary ledger for each major type of transaction.

back-order files: files that hold sales orders received for which no merchandise is yet available for shipment.

batch processing: accumulating transactions in groups to be processed at one time, typically once per day or per week.

on-line, real-time (OLRT) processing: the complete processing of a transaction as soon as it enters the computer system.

REFERENCES

Clancy, Donald K., "The Management Control Problems of Responsibility Accounting," *Management Accounting,* March 1978.

Corr, Arthur V., "Accounting Information for Managerial Decision," *Financial Executive,* August 1977.

Horngren, Charles T., *Cost Accounting: A Managerial Emphasis,* 5th ed., Englewood Cliffs, NJ: Prentice-Hall, 1982.

Lubas, Daniel P., "Developing a Computerized General Ledger System," *Management Accounting,* May 1976, p. 53.

MacVeagh, Charles, "MIS: Building a Structure That Works,"*Price Waterhouse Review,* vol. 22, no. 2, 1977, p. 42.

REVIEW QUESTIONS

1. How would the functional activities of a wholesaler probably differ from those of a manufacturer? (See Exhibit 12.1.)

2. Explain the major differences between managerial and external reporting information systems with respect to their purposes and structure.

3. If a company has either a managerial or an external reporting information system but not both, which is it likely to have, and why? Is it likely to suffer from a lack of the other? If so, why?

4. What does "basic duality" of a transaction mean? Explain the dual nature of (a) a sales transaction and (b) a payroll transaction. What are the implications of this duality for the accounting information system?

5. Why is a coding system a necessary part of an information system?

6. What information would need to be included in a purchase record layout?

7. How is information from the past relevant to planning purposes?

8. What are the similarities and differences in terms of processes between non-computerized and computerized accounting information systems?

9. What kinds of reports are likely to be prepared directly from the general ledger system file?

10. Explain fully what happens in process 3 of Exhibit 12.7.

11. Design a record format for an inventory receipt transaction that enables the following to be accomplished:

    (a) Recording the kind of inventory that was received

    (b) Recording the warehouse that received the inventory

    (c) Establishing how many units were received, as compared with the number ordered

12. Referring to Exhibits 12.14 and 12.15, note the several ways in which a batch system is more labor-intensive than an OLRT system.

13. With reference to Exhibits 12.14 and 12.15, what are the advantages for managerial purposes of an OLRT system over a batch system?

14. With references to Exhibit 12.15, note the probable sequence of processing activities if a customer calls to inquire about an account balance.

15. In an OLRT sales order entry system with immediate transaction entry, what happens if the inventory file indicates that an insufficient number of products is on hand to fill a customer's order? How might this situation be handled in a batch sales order entry system?

DISCUSSION QUESTIONS

1. Which information systems are likely to provide what information for product pricing decisions?

2. If you were the plant superintendent of the Spidey Company (Exhibit 12.6), how would you investigate and resolve the production variances incurred?

3. Review Exhibit 12.14 carefully. Analyze the delays at each stage of data processing and note their impact on efficiency of operations, costs, cash receipts, customer service, and managerial information needs. Suggest how the delays could be minimized without using an OLRT sales order entry system.

PROBLEM

Your boss, Louisiella Larue, gives you the following assignment: "Since our chart of accounts was developed, our company has been split into nine divisions. Please develop a modification to our chart of accounts so that it will encompass all nine divisions for all assets, liabilities, expenses, and revenues; for example, the accounts payable for division 9 should have its own unique chart of accounts number." Using the chart of accounts shown in Exhibit 12.3, establish a logical numbering system and show an account number for petty cash and for accounts payable for each of the nine divisions.

CASE 1

A Responsibility Accounting Report

Given the following costs and revenues for sales departments 1 and 2, each headed by a sales supervisor, prepare a responsibility accounting report for the organization for sales supervisors and for the sales manager to whom these supervisors report. The sales manager's monthly salary is $1000 plus 1 percent of all sales of the two departments reporting to the sales manager. The sales manager employs a secretary for $1000 per month, and depreciation and maintenance allocated to this office is $400 per month.

	Department 1		Department 2	
	Actual	Budget	Actual	Budget
Depreciation	$ 225	225	$ 250	225
Supplies	205	190	195	205
Supervisor's salary	750	750	780	780
Clerical assistance	725	775	725	735
Sales revenues	11,300	12,000	10,800	11,000
Sales commissions	1,130	1,200	1,080	1,100
Salespersons' salaries	3,000	3,000	3,000	3,000

CASE 2

An OLRT Sales Order Entry System

The LMN Company installed an OLRT, sales order entry system similar to that shown in Exhibit 12.15. The major way in which LMN's system differs from that of Exhibit 12.15 is that the transactions are not received by telephone; instead, salespersons contact customers at their place of business, record the transactions on sales slips, and upon their return to the office (often that night but sometimes not for 2 or 3 days) give the transactions of several customers to the terminal operators for entry into the computer system.

Case Questions

1. In what ways does this difference affect the utility of the OLRT system?

2. What possible modifications to its sales order entry procedures do you believe LMN should consider?

CASE 3

Producto Company

On March 4, a salesman sold 400 units of a product to a customer and promised delivery on April 15. Since the order was important to the salesman, he called the order directly to order processing and later mailed an order confirmation. The clerk in order processing misplaced the phone message. The written confirmation was received on March 12 and was processed through regular channels. On March 18, it was found that there were not any units of the required product in the finished goods warehouse. The order was placed on back order and scheduled for production during the first available production time: the week of April 28.

On March 21, the salesman found out about the back-order situation and was furious. He personally convinced the production planner that the order had to be put on a rush-order basis, even if it meant overtime to be worked in the factory. The rush-order basis on production resulted in the requirement for a rush order on the raw materials. Both the purchasing agent and the production supervisor reacted immediately. They questioned the need for a rush order and balked at the extra costs involved. They were both overruled by the division manager, and the production plan proceeded. The rush order of materials arrived late in the evening of April 11, and production commenced.

Because of the rush orders the production ran very late into the evening, resulting in a high overtime charge. The workers were tired, worked slowly, and spoiled some of the production. This resulted in 363 units that passed inspection and 41 that did not (only 2 percent spoilage was normal for the process). The units were packed for shipment on April 12, but because of scheduling delays were delivered on April 21.

The production supervisor was charged with $14,200 in overtime, a labor efficiency variance of $16,200, and a material usage variance of $20,312 because of the spoiled units. The purchasing agent was charged with a $12,603 price variance on the materials. The salesman was happy that he got a commission of $36,300 for making the sale, but he complained about the loss of $3,700 due to production failure.

The division manager received an irate letter from the customer complaining about the poor quality, lateness, and inadequate quantity of the shipment. The letter began: "This is the sorriest shipment I have ever received. For $1,800 a unit, these items should be perfect." It ended with: "You will never get another order from us." The division manager severely reprimanded the production supervisor and the purchasing agent for the lateness and the poor performance (as indicated by the variances). He then congratulated the salesman for having saved the sale by his quick handling of the back-order problem.

In this unhappy situation, who should be held responsible for the extra costs? The production supervisor and the purchasing agent were held responsible, but the situation had been taken completely out of their control by the division manager. Had the division manager not stepped in, the costs would have been controlled, but the division would have lost a $653,400 sale. Thus, the responsibility accounting information system was in place and would have controlled costs if the division manager had not interfered in order to save the sale.

There were six people involved in the case: the salesman, the order processing clerk, the production planner, the production supervisor, the purchasing agent, and the division manager. Many "if only" statements could be made about the behavior of these people:

1. If only the salesman had checked with finished goods before promising the delivery date, he could have negotiated a later delivery date or forced the order immediately through production planning on March 5.

2. If only the salesman had mailed the order confirmation a week earlier, it would have arrived on March 6, instead of March 12.

3. If only the order processing clerk had not misplaced the phone order, it would have started through channels 8 days sooner.

4. If only the production planner had originally scheduled the order before the promised delivery date and had shifted other production, the variances would not have occurred.

5. If only the division manager had recognized the potential hazard in the rush order, he could have, perhaps, negotiated a later delivery date with the customer.

6. If only the units had been in finished goods in the first place, this particular problem would not have arisen.

7. If only the sales order entry systems had been faster, the production could have been started sooner.

The production supervisor and the purchasing agent are conspicuous by their absence from this list. In the circumstances, there is nothing they could have done to avoid the variances. Since actions by any one of the other four people could have avoided the problem, they were all responsible for the variances.

Source: Donald K. Clancy, "The Management Control Problems of Responsibility Accounting," *Management Accounting,* March 1978.

Case Questions

1. In what ways, if at all, might the on-line, real-time, sales order entry system described in the chapter have helped in this case?

2. This case illustrates that no matter how well designed a responsibility accounting information system is, it may assign responsibility erroneously, and variances should only be the place to start the analysis for assigning responsibility. In this case, what should have been the process for determining responsibility?

3. How should a responsibility accounting information system be adapted, and what formal or informal managerial processes might be used to encourage participants to work as a team and avoid the kind of problem encountered in this case? (*Hint:* In the article from which this case is taken, the author discusses alternative solutions.)

CASE 4

Auto Parts Wholesale Company

Auto Parts Wholesale Company is a large wholesaler of automobile parts to automobile parts retail stores. The company has about 4000 regular customers, most of whom place orders two or three times per week. Most of the company's customers are in the midwest, including the Great Plains states and the gulf coast states.

Mr. Geez Whiz graduated last year from State University as an accounting major. While he was a student there, he completed two computer courses and now prides himself on knowing more about computers than almost anyone else in the accounting department of Auto Parts. Since becoming employed by Auto Parts, he has spent most of his time in the accounts receivable department and has made good progress there. He is affectionately known as "Wonder Boy" and "Geez, the Wonder Boy."

Because of the computer courses he took at State University, Wonder Boy had believed that computer information systems for accounting purposes were the "cat's meow," and he eagerly anticipated being able to work in a computerized accounting information system. He was delighted when, shortly after his arrival at Auto Parts, he was assigned to the accounts receivable department. However, now, after several months, Wonder Boy has become disenchanted with the accounts receivable computer system. One day, during a coffee break, he was chatting with Mr. Oldtimer. "Mr. Oldtimer," he said, "I'm certainly not very pleased with the performance of our computerized accounts receivable system. In fact, I'm wondering whether we should consider going back to a manual accounts receivable system. I think a manual accounts receivable system might have benefits that we don't seem to be getting from the computerized system."

"Geez," said Mr. Oldtimer, "that's an interesting idea. I suppose we always assume that moving forward and making progress means more and more computerization. Well, let's think about that a little bit. First, Wonder Boy, tell me what kinds of problems you see with our present computer system."

"Well," said Wonder Boy, "we seem to have a great many input errors. Somehow the computer can't seem to keep the accounts right. I've done a little analysis, and about one out of five accounts has some kind of error in it over a month's time. Of course, it goes without saying that our customers aren't very happy with this. That's one problem, but it may not be the most important one.

"Another problem," continued Wonder Boy, "is that our data is locked up in the computer system. Quite often customers call and want to know what their account balance is because many of them are marginally profitable and don't have much cash. So they want to know their balance before they decide whether they can afford to order additional merchandise from us. Of course, this doesn't say much for their own accounting systems, because they should be able to determine their balance without calling us. But most of them are small businesses and don't have good accounting systems, so they do tend to rely on us. As it is now, I can't give them a balance until the end-of-period customer accounts reports are prepared by data processing, which is usually about the second week after the end of the month. Or I can ask the people in the computer department for a special run, but I have to convince them that it's an urgent matter. When I say that a particular customer wants to know an account balance, the answer is, 'Well, that's not very critical, and to attempt to determine that at this time would be almost impossible, so I'm afraid the customer will just have to wait.'

"I can see data processing's point of view," said Wonder Boy, "but it seems to me that customer service is a major part of our business, and data processing isn't very cooperative in helping us

maintain good customer relations by providing better customer service. I've noticed that on other matters, too, data processing is sometimes less than cooperative, which makes me wonder whether we should go back to a manual system so that we can control it within this department. If we had a manual system, we would be able to turn to a subsidiary ledger book and quickly open the pages to the appropriate customer account; in a matter of just a few seconds we could probably come up with a current customer balance, assuming that all the most recent transactions had been entered. That would certainly provide better customer service than we're able to give now."

"What else is wrong with the present system?" said Mr. Oldtimer.

"I'm glad you asked," continued Wonder Boy. "There are a couple of other things I should mention. First, I've already said that the monthly reports usually aren't prepared until the second week of the following month. There are a couple of problems here; one is that I think we should have reports at least every 2 weeks rather than once a month. Second, sometimes the cutoff at the end of the month isn't very smooth, so perhaps the most recent customer purchases are charged to the customer's account but the most recent cash receipts are not; or vice versa. When this happens, the customer statements that are prepared and distributed 2 weeks after the end of the month are not accurate.

"Another problem," continued Wonder Boy, "is that although we invoice for each order of each customer, because of the time delay in updating and processing a customer's order it's sometimes several days after the merchandise has actually been shipped before we put the invoice in the mail. This seems like an unusual and unnecessary delay. It's not providing the customers the service they deserve.

"I see as a major part of the problem the fact that the people in data processing have their own schedule and that we have no control over their scheduling of our accounts receivable processing. I know they have other things to do, but getting our invoices out promptly and getting the customer statements done shortly after the end of the month are important, not to mention the fact that we need management reports such as aged accounts receivable as quickly as we can get them, and preferably even twice per month. As long as data processing controls the schedule for accounts receivable processing, I don't think we can solve these problems.

"And for all these problems we're paying a bundle!" exclaimed Wonder Boy. "Data processing is charging us enough per month for processing our accounts receivable to enable us to employ seven additional clerks if we had a manual system instead."

Mr. Oldtimer responded by saying, "Well, Wonder Boy, I've been around for a long time, and perhaps telling you about what the manual accounts receivable system was like will provide a little bit of perspective on this problem. In fact, I was one of the guys who created the manual accounts receivable system at about the time the company was started, which was long before computers were used for business data processing or even existed." Mr. Oldtimer then spent more than an hour telling Wonder Boy about how the manual accounts receivable system had worked. Not only had he designed it, but also he had installed it about 40 years ago and had worked with and improved it over a 20-year period before a computerized accounts receivable system was installed.

Finally, after a great deal more discussion between Mr. Oldtimer and Wonder Boy, which took place during coffee breaks over the next several days, Mr. Oldtimer said, "Geez, it looks as if we have the following options:

1. We could keep the present computerized system.

2. We could make modifications to the present computerized system.

3. We could exert pressure through corporate management to get priority with data processing so that we could have a better schedule for accounts receivable; this might help some of the problems, but not all.

4. We could move to a hybrid system—some sort of a combination of computer data processing and a manual system. For example, we could continue the computer data processing but keep separate books for the subsidiary accounts receivable within the department on a manual basis so that we could have the inquiry capability that you think is so important.

5. We could, as you suggest, go back to an entirely manual accounts receivable system. Of course, this system would be quite a bit larger than the one we had 20 years ago, when we moved to the computerized system, because we now have about 6 times as many customers and 8 or 10 times as many kinds of products.

6. We could explore entirely new types of computerized accounts receivable systems."

"That sounds like an excellent analysis," stated Wonder Boy, "but it also sounds as if it could be quite an extensive study. I suppose that we'd better get started, since the present system seems to be tottering on its last legs."

Case Questions

1. What are the major differences between a manual accounts receivable system and a computerized accounts receivable system?

2. Consider each of the alternatives suggested by Mr. Oldtimer as well as other alternatives that come to your mind. What are the advantages and disadvantages of each? Which do you prefer, and why?

Case prepared by George M. Scott.

Note: This case may be used for class discussion or as an individual exercise. A general knowledge of accounts receivable systems is useful; students who do not have this knowledge should review the discussion of accounts receivable in a standard beginning accounting textbook.

Chapter 13

MARKETING AND MANUFACTURING INFORMATION SYSTEMS

PAYOFF THOUGHT

Each organization should examine its activities to try to identify one or more information systems which, if developed to an unusual degree, might provide a competitive advantage. The development and continuing enhancement of any information system so identified should become a key task of the organization. In many organizations, the marketing information system may provide the competitive advantage sought.

CHAPTER OBJECTIVES

1. To survey the information needs of organizations' marketing and manufacturing functions

2. To analyze the sources of information for the marketing and manufacturing functions and to explain the structure of the information systems which collect and distribute this information

THE MARKETING INFORMATION SYSTEM

In many companies with extensive marketing activities, the marketing information system is among the least developed of these companies' information systems. One reason for this is that improved information systems for marketing often do not receive priority because they cannot be justified on a cost savings basis, and the benefits of the systems may be largely intangible and not readily observable. These benefits may nevertheless be very real and may include better information for marketing decisions (such as for product pricing) as well as better customer service.

Another reason is the apparent belief of some marketing executives that marketing decision making is primarily an art and cannot be systematized to the point where decisions can be aided by information analysis. Yet, typically, a wealth of useful information exists and could be made available to marketing managers but is not provided to them. Often information with value is available within one area of the marketing organization but is not transmitted to the managers who need it.

This lack of systematization of marketing information makes marketing a "seat -of-the-pants" activity in some companies. Marketing managers often rely on hand-me-down reports supplied as by-products of other departments' activities, such as those of accounting, production, and inventory control. This information tends to emphasize the past—such as sales in the last period—whereas marketing needs information to help predict the future, including information about market trends. Often, the functional information systems should be drastically revised to accommodate marketing's needs, and marketing also should develop certain information systems for its own purposes.

In some companies with weak marketing information systems, marketing is the most critical activity. Not only is the information that marketing management receives important, but also the information that marketing generates is vital to the rest of the organization. For example, marketing provides sales forecasts that serve as the basis for production schedules, cash flow projections, and profit plans. Because of this, the impact of ineffective marketing information systems is felt throughout the organization.

Even more important is marketing's role as a company's revenue-generating branch. A well-developed information system for marketing can give a competitive advantage here by offering better service to customers and better information for market penetration efforts. While even a well-developed marketing information system may provide inadequate information, this information usually is better than no information.

Overview of the Marketing Information System

The discussion in this chapter is based on a medium-sized company that produces multiple consumer products grouped into several product lines. The company has sales branches in several locations, each with numerous

---

The Major Marketing Information Subsystems

EXHIBIT 13.1

1. The sales information system:
   Sales support
   Sales analysis
   Customer analysis
2. The market research and intelligence information system:
   Customer research
   Market research
   Competitor intelligence
3. The promotion and advertising information system
4. The new product development information system
5. The sales forecasting information system
6. The product planning information system
7. The product pricing information system
8. The expenditures control information system

---

salespersons in the field whose customers are both wholesalers and re-tailers. In this company, products are manufactured and placed in inventory to await sale. Thousands of real-life companies fit this description.

The marketing information system consists of interrelated subsystems. The principal subsystems are shown in Exhibit 13.1. Exhibit 13.2 protrays the major information flows among these systems; not all information flows are shown.

These information flows serve to integrate the several marketing systems. In general, the more automated these flows, the more efficient the entire marketing information system and the more rapid the organization's response to market trends and merchandising problems.

Certain information subsystems shown in Exhibit 13.1 are shared with other functions. For example, the sales information system is based primarily on the sales order entry information system, which is normally staffed by sales order entry personnel within marketing but which also passes large amount's of information to accounting for accounting reports. Likewise, the sales forecasting information system may be shared by marketing and accounting. The new product development information system, the product pricing information system, and the new product planning system may serve not only marketing but also other functional areas that participate in product planning, product pricing, and new product development, although these systems are likely to be dominated by the marketing group.

The overall objectives of this integrated set of marketing subsystems are to improve the organization's ability to:

1. Identify and evaluate potentially profitable sales opportunities
2. React rapidly to changes in market conditions
3. Establish profit-maximizing product prices
4. Control marketing costs

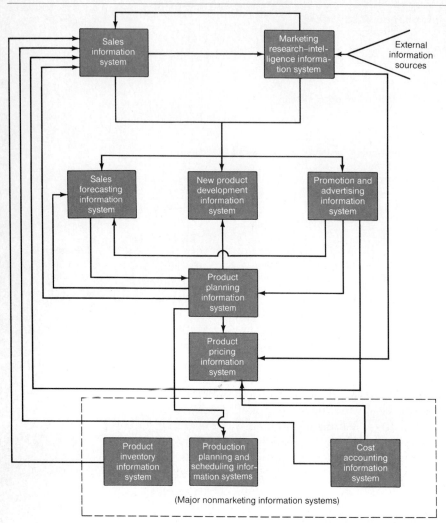

EXHIBIT 13.2
The major information
flows within the
marketing information
system.

5. Deploy sales personnel most effectively

6. Assist in allocating expenditures for advertising and other forms of promotion

The major source of information for these activities are listed in Exhibit 13.3. The following pages examine each marketing system.

The Sales Information System

Sales Support
Selling is the primary activity of most marketing groups. All the marketing information systems shown in Exhibit 13.1 and 13.2 directly or indirectly

Sources of Marketing Information	EXHIBIT 13.3

Sales invoices and other transactions information
Salespersons' customer call reports
Salespersons' debriefing by marketing managers
Sales history files
Customer account files
The cost accounting system
The profit planning (budgeting) system
Market research and intelligence-gathering activities
Sales forecasts
Production schedules
Inventory status reports

support this selling activity. However, a specialized sales support information system must provide information to sales personnel about the following:

1. Product descriptions and performance specifications
2. Product prices
3. Quantity discounts and other product discount information
4. Sales incentives for salespersons
5. Sales promotions
6. Financing plans for customers
7. The strengths and weaknesses of competitors' products
8. The histories of customers' relations with the company
9. Sales policies and procedures established by the company
10. Products that have not yet been introduced
11. Product inventory levels

This and other information comes from a variety of sources, most (but not all) of which are shown in Exhibit 13.3. Product performance specifications, for example, may come from the engineering department.

In many companies the inventory control system must provide extremely accurate and continuously up-to-date information about raw materials and finished goods inventory levels and the approximate dates when additional quantities of each material and product will be received and placed in inventory. Some companies find that the delivery dates of purchases are a critical concern of customers, who often will not place an order until they are assured that the products they are purchasing are already in inventory or will be available by a specific date.

One approach to providing this inventory information is a periodic report detailing the quantity of each product on hand as of the end of the preceding period (typically the preceding week or month). This report is usually outdated when received, however, since it generally arrives well after the end of the period. The report becomes increasingly out of date until it is replaced by the inventory status report after the end of the next period. Information from this type of system often is not sufficiently current and may cause a great deal of customer dissatisfaction; often, for example, customers are promised deliveries of their orders on a certain date because the information system indicates that adequate quantities are in inventory, but withdrawals from inventory have already been made that have not yet been recorded in the information system.

A more sophisticated information system can supply the necessary information about product availability. With the OLRT information systems shown in Exhibit 12.15, for example, the salesperson can inquire directly into the inventory file to determine the quantity of each product on hand. This provides a substantial advantage over competitors who use periodic inventory status reports.

Sales Analysis

The sales analysis information system is one of the most extensive and important systems of most companies involved in sales. Its purpose is to provide information for analyses of (1) product sales trends, (2) product profitability on a product-by-product basis, (3) the performance of each sales region and sales branch, and (4) salespersons' performance. Information for sales analysis is derived primarily from the sales order entry system; the majority is information from actual sales transactions and is contained on sales invoices. To fully support the sales analysis system, invoices should contain information about product type, product quantity, price discount terms, customer identity and type, sales region, and salesperson.

Information from other sources should also be included in the sales reports. Specifically, the sales reports must contain information about the profitability of products, product lines, sales territories, and individual salespersons. Profitability reporting requires information about product administrative and selling costs—preferably on a marginal cost basis so that contribution margins (marginal contribution to profits) can be determined. As suggested in Exhibit 13.2, much of this cost information is supplied by the cost accounting system. Without this information, sales performance may be measured by the dollar volume of sales, and the profitability (or lack of profitability) of these sales will be hidden. With margin analysis information the profit contribution of the profitable products, customers, and salesperson scan be identified; the most profitable products are not necessarily those with the highest sales volume. Similarly, unprofitable products, customers, and salespersons can also be identified. This information influences the design of incentive systems that encourage salespersons to concentrate on the more profitable products.

Reports using sales and cost information are usually prepared to emphasize trends in both sales volume and profitability. This information is directly useful to salespersons and is also supplied to the marketing research and intelligence groups for more detailed analysis.

Often, as costs edge upward because of inflation while sales prices remain stable (perhaps as a result of intense competition), these contribution margin analsyis reports show that certain products are no longer profitable, and they prompt the restyling, the reengineering, or even the elimination of certain products. Alternatively, contribution margin analysis reports may spur management to consider raising the product's price. High contribution margins also may indicate that sales promotions were successful or that certain products should be promoted more or promoted differently.

Similar contribution margin analysis reports are prepared on a sales branch and sales region basis and are used in a similar manner. Additionally, identifying strong and weak sales units enables the company to reward its most effective regional and branch managers properly.

The sales analysis system also provides most of the information used to evaluate the performance of sales personnel. By reclassifying sales by salesperson rather than by product or sales unit, sales supervisors learn whether each salesperson has met the assigned sales quota. If marginal costs are also assigned by salesperson, each salesperson's contribution margin can be established as one criterion for performance evaluation.

Each of the above reports involving sales and cost information, such as reports of product profitability, sales unit profitability, and salesperson profitability, typically would be prepared for the current week or month and the year to date, as well as on the basis of actual profit as compared with profit planned for the month and for the year to date. For example, sales units should be evaluated relative to the potential in their territory, with this potential indicated by the units' profit plans. Directly comparing units in different regions may be invalid because of differing market demand for the various products. These comparisons of planned with actual profitability make possible the calculation of variances for each product, each branch, each salesperson, and so on. Often, the information value of these variances is enhanced if they are split into a price variance (the amount of contribution margin variance caused by not selling all items at the planned price) and a volume variance (the variance due to selling a greater or lesser volume of the product than planned).

The primary types of information used for the sales analysis subsystem are (1) information about customer invoices and back orders that is provided by the sales transaction processing system (as shown in Exhibit 12.14), (2) information derived from the oral and written reports of sales personnel, and (3) product cost information obtained from the cost accounting information system. Information about sales transactions may be available from the sales files or the customer files.

The written or oral reports of sales personnel are valuable sources of information which too often are not properly organized. Sales personnel are in direct contact with customers and frequently are the first to be aware of changed market conditions, altered customer expectations, new products in the marketplace, and competitors' actions.

Marketing groups should develop a reporting activity that provides sales analysts with detailed information from salespersons. However, this "salesperson debriefing" should not unduly burden sales personnel, who often resent paperwork. Some companies accomplish this debriefing by having salespersons complete customer call reports consisting as much as possible of "yes" or "no" answers or ratings on a scale. Other companies permit their salespersons to dictate reports for later typing. These reports often supply important contextual information, which may, for example, explain why a branch's or a region's sales are lower than expected or why a particular product has succeeded or failed. Marketing departments cannot afford to ignore this source of grass-roots information.

Grass-roots information from customers is so important that often middle- and senior-level marketing managers call on customers with whom they have good rapport. Because these are clearly information-seeking visits and because the managers' orientation with respect to topics and approach often differs from that of salespersons, the managers will acquire additional information about products or competitors that was not made known to salespersons.

Sales analysis reports are among those most likely to be needed on both an on-call and a key performance indicator basis. For example, a marketing manager may not wish to wait for end-of-period reports to see the sales impact of a major advertising or promotion campaign because an ineffective campaign may need to be altered immediately. On-call or key indicator reports will permit early evaluation of a current campaign. Many OLRT marketing information systems have this capability.

Customer Analysis

The purposes of customer analysis are to establish a profile of buying habits and to determine the profitability of each customer on a contribution margin basis. Usually customers are classified into two, three, or four categories by total sales volume; for simplicity, two categories are discussed here.

One category of customers usually includes those who make the largest amount of purchases. These few customers often provide a very substantial proportion of total revenues; for example, 10 percent of the customers may provide 80 or 90 percent of total sales revenue. Frequent and detailed reports should be available about each of these major customers, and marketing managers may spend most of their time analyzing these reports to ensure that sales volume and profit margins are up to expectations, to be certain that customer service is good, and to spot trends in the buying habits of these important customers. Special pricing policies may exist for these customers, and marketing managers are quick to reward salespersons who are successful with prime customers and to remove salespersons who are not. Often, these customers demand price concessions based on the volume of their purchases, and marketing must have detailed cost information available to evaluate the reasonableness of their requests.

Information about the low-volume customers in the second category also is useful. The analysis of their purchasing activity tends to focus on determining whether each is a profitable customer so that strategies can be developed for the unprofitable customers to increase prices or reduce services or costs (such as by cutting back on the number of sales calls).

Much of the quantitative information used for customer analyses is extracted from the customer master file, as shown in Exhibits 12.14 and 12.15. Additionally, analyses of customer profitability require product cost information from the cost accounting system and information about other costs from other cost data files.

The Market Research and Intelligence Information System

Whereas the sales information system is based primarily on sales trans-actions data plus information about inventory status and product cost, the market research and intelligence information system relies on information from a wide variety of sources. While one principal source is the sales information system, other major sources are outside the organization.

Some organizations split market research and market intelligence functions into separate groups, with the former concentrating on the marketplace, and the latter concerned about only one aspect of the mar-ketplace—the organization's competitors. However, the information that each function requires overlaps, and some comes from the same sources. Additionally, both focus on analyzing the information to discern trends, sudden changes, or threats to the organization. For these reasons, both functions are examined in this section.

Customer Research

Customer research is broader and more analytic than the customer analysis associated with the sales information system. Customer analysis reporting involves reporting past customer transactions using information from the sales order entry system. Customer research utilizes this information, provides information about the market environment as a context for it, and also uses information about customers' financial and operating con-ditions and about their selling and purchasing dealings with the organi-zation's competitors. Additionally, customer research frequently analyzes potential rather than present customers.

Analyses of this information may offer insights into possible new or better ways in which the organization can serve its present customers and acquire new ones. These analyses can also affect credit terms and discounts extended to customers or can give early warnings that certain competitors pose a major threat with particular customers. Often, these analyses will lead to negotiations between the marketing managers and the senior man-agers of customers on matters (such as product specifications) that are beyond the jurisdiction of direct-contact salespersons.

Market Research

Market research is broader than customer research in that it focuses on the entire marketplace for the organization's products. One purpose of market research is to assess the overall size of the market for each product line and for each product within a product line. This usually is done on both a short- and a long-term basis. Such "market definition" can be difficult. Potential market size can change rapidly as economic conditions and technology change.

When market potential is determined and the marketplace is fully defined, the organization's market share can be established, and the roles of competitors within the market can be better evaluated. This information is useful for the product planning function shown in Exhibit 13.2 because it helps suggest sales goals and strategies that will yield the desired market penetration. This information is useful too for selecting new products. Analyses of this type also enhance the ability to forecast future sales levels of each product line and individual product. A market potential analysis is likely to result in a narrative report for input to the marketing planning activity.

The key information needs for a market potential analysis are (1) information about the economy and economic trends and the probable impact of these trends on demand for the product, (2) information about past sales and sales trends for the entire industry, and (3) information about competing "substitution" products (products that customers can substitute for the product being analyzed). Usually the market research department assumes responsibility for gathering and analyzing this information.

Salespersons often can provide information about potential new markets for products as well as about substitution products. Properly designed sales call reports can supply a wealth of information to the market research group because salespersons often find out much about the marketplace directly through their discussions with clients. Additionally, the accumulated information on sales call reports can offer important hints about shifts in the market's preferences or about the market's perception of the organization's products.

Directly questioning customers or potential customers, such as by means of a consumer survey or interview, can also provide useful information. Many companies employ independent marketing consultants to systematically gather information needed for analyzing market potential. Smaller companies often will ask consultants to undertake a complete analysis of market potential.

Competitor Intelligence

A company should gather information about its competitors. This includes information about (1) the specifications of competitors' products, (2) competitors' operating strengths and weaknesses, (3) competitors' customer service levels and customer policies, (4) competitors' financial structure and strength, and (5) competitors' new product plans, marketing goals and strategies, product promotion plans, and probable reactions to the organization's strategies. Ideally, of course, the organization would like to have a complete set of each competitor's long- and short-range plans.

Acquiring the information needed may require continuous surveillance of competitors' activities. Most of this information is not directly available to an organization. A network of sources must be developed, and information, or "intelligence," often must be inferred from independent bits of data that are processed and combined within the organization's intelligence activity.

The quantity of data that must be gathered and processed in order to gain a good perspective on competitors can be voluminous. However, extensive information is usually available from public sources and particularly from government regulatory agencies. A well-organized system of reporting by the organization's own salespersons about their observations of competitors' dealing with customers also can be useful. Marketing intelligence from commercial intelligence companies is also widely available.

Marketing intelligence information systems that gather and process information about competitors often are closely affiliated with the intelligence activity of the entire organization; at the same time, they are an integral part of the marketing information systems. Marketings intelligence information systems often provide intelligence that is extremely important in formulating the entire organization's long-range plans. Intelligence information systems were examined in Chapter 3.

The Promotion and Advertising Information System

The promotion and advertising department within marketing devotes its attention to planning and executing advertising campaigns and to carrying out various product promotions such as package coupons, contests, special sales, and trade shows. This department's activities are focused on increasing sales revenues without an equivalent increase in costs. Accordingly, information about how effective particular advertising and promotion activities are in terms of increasing revenues is sought and used in conjunction with information about possible increased costs associated with the revenue increases.

Exhibit 13.2 shows the principal information flows to the promotion and advertising information system. A major source of this information is the sales information system, which supplies information about past and present sales activity. This information indicates which products are selling well and which need promotional assistance. Product cost and profitability information, provided via the sales reports, is also important so that the more profitable products can be identified and given greater emphasis.

Sales analyses provided by the sales information system can assist the advertising and promotion group by highlighting trends that may influence the allocation of promotion and advertising expenditures. Additionally, a time-series sales analysis that correlates advertising and promotion activities with subsequent sales will indicate which are the most effective promotion campaigns for particular products.

The market research information system can supply the promotion and advertising information system with information about market size and about characteristics for each product market. This is helpful for tailoring promotion campaigns to specific market segments. The intelligence information system may be able to shed light on competitors' future promotion strategies or the probable effectiveness of competitors' past campaigns, both of which can influence the organization's promotion and advertising strategy.

The promotion and advertising information system should be a storehouse of information that helps managers build on past experience with promotion and advertising. By systematically organizing and analyzing this information, an organization can eventually establish a body of knowledge about what the marketplace is like and how it responds to each of several types of promotional activities for each product. However, the complexions of markets can change rapidly, and the information systems already described should continuously "refresh" and modify this promotion and advertising information base in light of the most recent information available.

The New Product Development Information System

New product research involves analyzing a possible opportunity for a new product and evaluating preferred specifications and probable market success. Often the market research activity initially perceives the opportunity and passes along information about it to the new product development group, as suggested in Exhibit 13.2. Alternatively, a salesperson who deals directly with customers may become aware of their need for a new product. A customer call reports system may help elicit information about new products needed in the marketplace. For example, explicit questions on the call report, such as "Do customer needs exist that our products are not filling completely?" and "Do customers need a product that is not now available?" encourage salespersons to think about new product possibilities.

During the analysis of new product feasibility, after a probable need has been identified, information from the sales analysis system about past sales of similar or related products may indicate the most desirable characteristics for the new product or the structure of the market for the product. Also, market research can be tailored to gather information about the size and structure of the marketplace for the product, and the marketing intelligence information system may help evaluate the market strength and profitability of similar products produced by competitors. These information flows are outlined in Exhibit 13.2.

The product development department uses all this information to develop specifications for a new product. These specifications may then be passed along to engineering and other groups for cost estimating. Risk profiles, which include estimated costs and revenues for the product over its life cycle, are developed as a basis for deciding whether to produce the product.

The Sales Forecasting Information System

Sales forecasting is one of the most important activities of many organizations, and for these companies the sales forecasting information system should be as well developed as possible. Of course, forecasting sales deals with the future, about which little concrete information is available; thus the range of error for sales forecasting can be wide, no matter how sophisticated the information system is. Nevertheless, in general, the better the information provided for sales forecasting, the more accurate the forecasts will be.

Sales forecasting is important for planning sales and promotion strategies and for postperiod evaluation of salespersons' performance. Additionally, other activities vital to the organization depend on reliable sales forecasts. First, sales forecasts are generally the first step in the profit planning cycle of the entire organization; for example, they initiate the short-term financial and marketing planning cycles. If forecasts for the period are seriously in error, the organization's entire budgeting activity will be based upon the wrong level of activity.

Production planning, work-force planning, and production scheduling are based on sales forecasting. Materials are ordered and personnel are employed and reassigned according to the expected sales pattern for the next period. If sales are overestimated, finished product inventory levels or materials inventory levels will be too high, and production labor costs will be excessive, or personnel will have to be laid off. Conversely, if the sales forecast is too low, sales may be lost because of inventory shortages, or higher costs will be incurred as a result of overtime work and the need to secure additional materials in a hurry.

Cash planning is also based on sales forecasts. Usually, weekly or monthly sales forecasts form the basis for estimates of cash position, which in turn form the basis for planning how much cash will have to be borrowed and how much can be invested. Obviously, sales forecasting and the systems that provide sales forecasting information are vital to market-oriented organizations.

The basic information needed for sales forecasting is the following:

1. Past sales, provided by the sales analysis information system
2. Market conditions, provided by the market research information system

3. Competitors' activities, provided by the competitor intelligence information system

4. Promotion and advertising plans, provided by the information system for this function

The general approach of medium-term sales forecasting (3 months to 1 year) is to begin with the last period's sales by product line, individual product, and geographic area and to adjust these for established trends, for newly perceived changes in the economy and the marketplace, and for competitors' new strategies. Then, expected changes that have not yet taken place are considered, such as an anticipated economic downturn or competitors' probable reactions to sales strategies that the organization plans to implement during the period.

All these types of information are merged and weighted according to their relative importance by skilled forecasting specialists. Usually this information is entered into a formal computerized forecasting system, which may accomplish the weighting, compensate for seasonal variations and other variables, and produce a forecast by product line, individual product, and sales territory. This forecast is likely to be passed along to the sales managers who do the product planning, and they may revise the sales strategies in order to modify the forecast sales levels to more acceptable ones. These new strategies, for example, may involve additional promotion and advertising expenses. The revised strategies are likely to be communicated to the sales forecasting information system to serve as the basis for revised sales forecasts.

Shorter-term sales forecasting is usually a less involved activity. A sales forecast for a week, for example, may be primarily a simple projection of the preceding week's sales forecast, adjusted slightly for strong trends and other major forces (such as holidays) that are expected to affect the following week's sales.

The Product Planning Information System

Marketing planning usually is done by product line and generally results in a long- and a short-range marketing profit plan for each product line. Developing a long-range marketing plan requires information about the organization's overall long-range plans, of which the long-range marketing plan becomes an integral part.

Similarly, the short-range marketing profit plan becomes an integral element in the entire organization's profit plan. As illustrated in Exhibit 13.2, most of the marketing information subsystems contribute information either directly or indirectly to the product planning information system. Sales history information, market research information, competitor intelligence information, sales forecasts, and information about the nature and success of promotion and advertising campaigns are all utilized as part of the product planning information system to help formulate both long-and short-range profit plans.

In turn, product planning supplies information to most marketing activities that sets their direction and focus. The most important of these information flows from the planning information system are shown in Exhibit 13.2; for example, product planning provides information to the sales activity about sales strategies, and the feedback to the sales forecasting information system has already been noted. In addition to determining pricing strategies, product planning also decides what new products will be introduced and passes along information about this to the new product development information system.

The Product Pricing Information System

Product pricing is a complex managerial activity that is affected by product costs, customer demand, market psychology, competitors' prices, and various actions taken by competitors, to mention but a few considerations. Because product cost information on a full cost or marginal cost basis is usually seen as the starting point in setting prices, pricing information systems almost always utilize information about product costs.

Cost information is most directly used when price is cost plus a percentage markup. In competitive situations, however, product costs may set a lower limit on product prices. Market research into the strength of demand for each product in the marketplace is also useful for pricing purposes. Of course, a vital ingredient in pricing is information about competitors' prices for similar products.

In many organizations pricing is done on a "margin maintenance" basis. Gross or contribution margin goals are established for products, and prices are set in accordance with what price will maintain the established margin. Past sales profitability information is useful here to help determine how much prices should be adjusted for changed costs in order to ensure that margins are maintained.

The Expenditures Control Information System

Expenditures within marketing include salaries, sales commissions, advertising and promotion costs, market research consulting fees, and the cost of purchased intelligence and market research studies. In some organizations product distribution costs are also controlled by marketing managers. Often, sales discounts, returns and allowances, and profit decreases or increases caused by a mix of sales that is different from what was anticipated are controlled in a manner similar to the way expenditures are controlled.

In most organizations, the control mechanism is the marketing profit plan, which is an integral part of the organization's profit plan, as was discussed in Chapter 12. Usually, marketing managers have the responsibility for controlling both expenditures and the other elements under their jurisdiction that influence profits. To accomplish this, they receive regular profit plan reports that show the planned level of expenditures, the actual expenditures, and the spending variances for each expenditure category, as well as additional information that helps explain the reasons for the variances. One authority, Sam Goodman, has proposed that marketing should have its own controller who would apply accounting control and quantitative methods control techniques to the marketing area.

MANUFACTURING INFORMATION SYSTEMS

The Nature of Production Activities

The role of production in organizations is to provide a product that the market demands. This means (1) producing the quantity of products needed by customers, (2) maintaining the quality of the products established by the product specifications, and (3) producing within the cost constraints imposed by the production control system. Production activities involve transforming energy, labor, raw materials, and purchased parts and components into finished products by production or assembly activities. For the purposes of this discussion, raw materials and purchased parts and components are all referred to as "materials," and no distinction is made among them.

There are four general types of production: (1) continuous-flow production, such as is used in oil refineries; (2) repetitive or mass production, which is used in automobile parts production and assembly activities; (3) project production, such as is used in ship manufacturing; and (4) discrete, job-oriented production, in which production activities may be discontinuous or in which a "batch" of a particular product is produced in a few hours, days, or weeks, after which the "production run" is terminated.

With continuous-flow and mass production, the focus of attention is on the rate of production, and the emphasis is on achieving an efficient production rate that meets production quotas and quality standards at the lowest possible cost. With project production, the focus is on one product, such as a ship. With discrete, job-oriented production, the focus is on a group of products that are produced together, and time, quality, materials, and labort usage are all controlled on a product batch basis. Discrete production often uses general-purpose equipment; thus when production of one product is terminated and a different product is started, the equipment must first be "set up," or modified, to produce the other product. Discrete production is by far the most widespread type of production and probably accounts for more than 75 percent of total production in the United States. Many companies using discrete production produce several different products, or even thousands of different products.

Discrete production processes offer the greater challenge to the information system. This section assumes that discrete production is the production mode; however, most of the discussion is relevant to all types of manufacturing processes.

Complexity is the dominant characteristic of discrete production activities, and it is the major determinant of the required sophistication of the production information systems. The product structure provides one dimension of production complexity. Exhibit 13.4 illustrates a "product structure" which, when recorded in list form rather than the hierarchical form shown, constitutes a bill of materials for the product; the relationships between the items are then indicated in each item's record. The product structure displays the relationships between the items that make up the product. By convention, level 0 in the exhibit is the completed product. At level 1, it can be seen that B and C are the major components of A and that A consists of one each of B and C (in parentheses). In turn, component B consists of D, E (four units), and F (two units), which may be parts, components, raw materials, or a combination, and C consists of G after processing. G, in turn, is composed of E (two units) and H. Note that item E is used in both components B and C.

Where the product structure is complex, production activities are correspondingly complex. An automobile or an airplane, for example, may have 10,000 or more parts in its product structure, resulting in complex production activities and complex information needs.

Another dimension of production complexity is the dynamics of the environment. A stable environment means that, all else being equal, the production activities are less complex and the production information systems can be correspondingly less sophisticated. A roller-coaster mar-

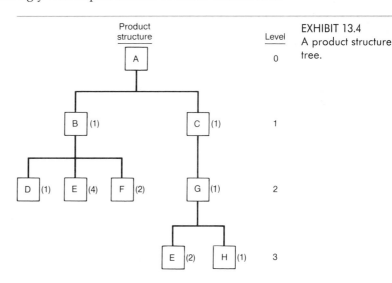

Product structure

Level

EXHIBIT 13.4
A product structure tree.

A — 0

B (1)   C (1) — 1

D (1) E (4) F (2)   G (1) — 2

E (2) H (1) — 3

ketplace in which customer demand fluctuates rapidly across a broad range means that production activities are complicated by frequent speedups and slowdowns. Rapid technological change in the industry—such as in the electronics industry—requires frequent engineering changes, which can cause continuous chaos in production activities. Dynamic environments greatly increase the amount of information required for production activities.

Large-volume production, especially where many different products are involved, also causes complexity. Thousands of American companies produce hundreds of products, and hundreds of companies produce thousands of products. A few companies produce more than 10,000 different products.

Discrete production in many companies encompasses all the above variables: complex product structures with many parts, a dynamic environment, and large production volumes, including large numbers of different parts. In these companies the production information needs are massive, and the information needs are complex.

The Present Status of Production Operations

The production problems in a complex situation may appear to be almost insurmountable. Because of the complexity, it has not always been possible to fully understand what needs to be accomplished in terms of organizing production. Production personnel also have not been provided the information tools needed for either production planning or actual production and its control. As a result, production activities have been fragmented, and production information systems have been partial, inaccurate, and not timely in providing needed information. Additionally, information flows have not been integrated.

Wight puts this in perspective:

> The typical company has hundreds or thousands of components to be scheduled. Many components go together to make assemblies. They are made from raw materials and often put into finished goods. There are branch warehouses in many companies that have to be scheduled properly.
>
> The problem is monumental, and is made insurmountable by the constant change that is part of normal manufacturing. Forecasts aren't right, machines break down, vendors deliver late, there are engineering changes, tooling doesn't work, new products are introduced, and all of this is occurring simultaneously. The only constant in manufacturing is change, and the problem is making valid schedules so that people don't have to work to shortage lists and dissipate their efforts firefighting.

Before the advent of computers, production scheduling usually was not done in a formal, systematic manner, and even today most companies use computers primarily for better materials inventory management; computers often are not used effectively for production scheduling. The typical production planning process follows the steps outlined below:

1. A tentative schedule is set, which no one expects will be maintained. Even if inventory records are reasonably accurate, little is known about the status of outstanding purchase orders or the status and completion dates of work in process. Lacking accurate information, salespersons are likely to make unrealistic delivery-date promises to customers.

2. With a wide range of uncertainty about current production activities, materials are ordered, but the quantities ordered may be too little or too great, and their arrival time often does not coincide with the date that production is to begin.

3. Inaccurate information about production status, unrealistic schedules, and frequent inventory shortages during production causes chaos. This chaos results in an inability to meet production schedules and customer delivery dates, constant delays in production while awaiting materials, and frequent rescheduling of batches, with the consequences of more machine setup time and cost and more idle personnel and equipment. This all means that production resources are used less efficiently and that production costs are higher than necessary.

Production departments attempt to control this chaos with two major forms of "expediting." The first continuously reallocates resources to try to keep critical jobs on or close to schedule. This is usually done by the production supervisor. The second uses "expenditers" to speed up receipt of materials that are not on hand but are critical to the production process. These expediters may be the supervisor, other employees, or specially hired expediters.

Materials expediting usually begins with a manual analysis of production materials requirements for a product batch already in or about to enter the manufacturing process. Usually all needed materials that are in inventory have already been requestioned for the job in order to permit an accurate assessment of what additional materials are needed. A "shortage list" is developed that shows materials that are in short supply, and expediters are assigned to secure these materials from whatever source possible.

Materials expediting may consist of, for example, pleading with the vendor to ship materials earlier than planned (perhaps at a premium price or with "special handing" costs), asking that the materials be shipped by a faster (and more costly) form of transportation such as by air express, or begging, borrowing, or (literally) stealing materials from another department or even another company. Large manufacturing companies may employ hundreds of expediters. Wight notes that 60 percent of the average production supervisor's time is spent expediting because of inadequate production scheduling.

Production Processes and Information Needs

To understand the information needs of production processes and the nature of the information systems that can fulfill those needs, it is necessary to understand the production planning, production scheduling, and resource procurement and assignment processes. Exhibit 13.5 illustrates the general nature of the production-related activities and the major information systems of a production activity. The production processes and the associated information systems are shown within the dashed lines in the exhibit. The leftmost part of the exhibit illustrates the interaction of the marketing, cash planning, and personnel information systems with production activities.

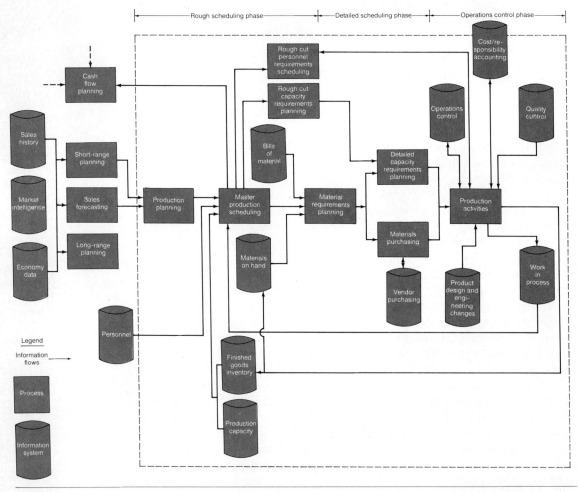

EXHIBIT 13.5
The production processes and information systems.

The cost/responsibility accounting information system at the top right-hand corner of Exhibit 13.5 is a combined production and accounting information system, as illustrated, which provides information for operations and management control by managers in manufacturing. This system also provides product cost information that is used to establish the value of inventories and the cost of sales for financial reporting purposes, as discussed in the previous chapter.

In many companies, particularly smaller ones, production is initiated in response to actual orders received. However, in Exhibit 13.5, production is shown to be initiated by a sales forecast, long-range planning information, and short-range planning information that is used for production planning. The resulting plan is developed by the organization's senior managers, including the more senior production managers, and is an aggregate plan that contains no details but establishes rough quantities of each product type to be produced and a general framework for the near- and long-term future production activities. The decisions reached are communicated to the personnel who prepare the master production schedule; the managers involved in this process are likely to be a mix of administrative staff personnel and experienced middle-and senior-level production managers. This group also needs information about current inventory levels of all finished products; if inventory levels of a product are high enough, that product may not need to be produced within the time period under consideration. Production scheduling also utilizes information from the personnel information system about the skills of available employees so that personnel can be assigned to production tasks for which they are qualified.

Part of production planning is production capacity analysis, or capacity planning. Capacity planning establishes the mix and quantities of personnel, machines, and facility resources that will be required to produce a particular batch, and it adjusts the capacity of the production department to those requirements. The information used for this purpose is found in the production capacity file of Exhibit 13.5. Production capacity analyses involve balancing production activities within the physical space available, balancing machine utilization by minimizing the amount of machine idle time and by reconciling conflicting simultaneous needs for the same machinery, and minimizing the total amount of machine setup time when different products are started into production. The production capacity file contains a variety of information relating to these matters; for example, the file may contain setup times for a machine when it is reconfigured from a particular configuration for one product to another configuration for another product, and it may contain machine speeds for each of a variety of tasks. With this information, schedulers can attempt to establish a production schedule that maximizes the usage of available equipment and personnel.

Information provided by master production scheduling is used for four major purposes, as indicated by the four arrows leaving the master production scheduling process box in Exhibit 13.5. First, an overall production schedule is provided for material requirements planning. Also, this schedule is "costed out" to gain a rough idea of the cash flows that will be required by the production processes during the following periods; this information is forwarded to the treasury department for cash planning. The master production schedule is also used as the basis for determining approximately how much capacity will be needed in various work centers to provide a rough-cut capacity requirements plan and for determining the types of personnel skills that will be needed to establish a rough-cut personnel requirements schedule.

The rough scheduling phase shown at the top of the exhibit is now completed. For the next process, information about the bill of materials for each product is combined with this master scheduling information for detailed material requirements planning. Each bill of materials contains a detailed listing of the types and quantities of materials, parts, and components required for the manufacture of one unit of the product.

The material requirements for production of a product batch can then be determined automatically from the bill of materials by multiplying the number of products in a batch by the number of each of the line items of the bill of materials that are required for the manufacture of one unit of the product. This step is often referred to as "exploding the bill of materials." The bill of materials must be continuously revised to reflect engineering changes that affect the specifications of the product.

Comparing the total requirements for each item with information from the materials-on-hand file, in terms of the quantity on hand of each type of raw material, part, or component, establishes the quantities of each that must be acquired. These can be acquired by purchase (the materials purchasing process) or by production (production activity planning). This step also establishes when each item (material, part, or component) must be ordered or fabricated to be available in time for production to start according to schedule.

The detailed capacity planning process establishes the work load by personnel skill type, machine type, and types of other detailed resources needed for production activities. In effect, this activity assigns resources to workstations. Information from the rough-cut capacity requirements planning processes is used for this activity.

The detailed scheduling and capacity planning activities are now completed in preparation for actual production activities within the operations control phase shown at the top of Exhibit 13.5. Production activities require information for physical control over operations, such as production rates and detailed instructions concerning production-step sequences and manufacturing techniques. This information is provided by the operations control information system shown in Exhibit 13.5.

A critical aspect of operations control is ensuring that production deadlines will be met. The operations control information system contains information that indicates the quantity of products that should be completed by certain times. Using this information, production personnel can determine when production is behind schedule and can take remedial actions to adjust capacity or estimated completion times. This information also enables the production department to answer customers' inquiries about the progress of their orders.

The work-in-process information system shown in Exhibit 13.5 receives information about resources committed to the production process. It contains an open order record for each product that is in production or is on order through purchasing. Each record contains materials requisitions and other related records. Information from this information system is used for the next cycle of master production scheduling as well as for operations control.

In some organizations shopworkers input data directly into a shop data collection system through terminals at their workstations. Typically, the worker inserts an employee identification card into the terminal and keys in the batch production number and the number of the task being worked on. The terminal reads the employee number from the identification card and records the start time. A similar process takes place when the employee completes the task. The operations control and work-in-process files may be combined into one information system.

Quality control information must also be gathered from the production processes to monitor the extent to which product quality indicators stay within established tolerances. Quality control checks are built into the production process at each key step in production. The quality control information system contains the product quality specifications and standards and tracks the history of conformance to these standards by, for example, gathering information about scrap levels. This information system also provides information to the purchasing function about defective materials received from vendors so that this can be considered in vendor selection.

The production design and engineering change information system records the original design specifications and production tolerances established for the product and updates this information systematically for what may be dozens or hundreds of engineering changes made to a product. These changes must be fed into the flow of production in process, and they may be made to improve the performance of products, reduce their production costs, or increase product safety. Additionally, engineering changes often result from a particular customer's request that the product be altered in a certain manner. This information system is shown in Exhibit 13.5.

The shared accounting and production information systems of cost and responsibility accounting shown in Exhibit 13.5 (these were discussed in the preceding chapter) provide information about production cost standards for labor and materials, gather information about labor and materials costs of the production batch, and supply cost variances to production managers for cost control. This information permits both determining product costs and assigning cost and quantity variances to the managers who are responsible for them.

At the conclusion of the production process, the finished products and finished parts are placed in physical inventory. At this time, the finished goods inventory and the materials-on-hand (for finished parts) records are updated, as indicated in Exhibit 13.5.

An analysis of Exhibit 13.5 indicates that even in this greatly simplified schematic, the production information flows are complex. When the complicating factors of perhaps hundreds of products with thousands of different materials required at multiple production and inventory sites are also considered, the information flows become compounded severalfold. In so complicated an environment, accurate sales forecasts, accurate materials and finished goods inventories, and accurate purchasing records are essential, but difficult to achieve. For example, if the finished goods inventory or the materials inventory records for one product are in error, purchase orders may be wrong, and a substantial materials inventory shortage may result. This shortage may cause havoc in production activities or necessitate last-minute juggling of production schedules, either of which causes inefficiences in the production processes.

With a large number of files to maintain, data processing may be unable to complete all processing on time. This delayed processing may be the cause of a large proportion of the inaccuracies in the data files. Integrating data files so that data is automatically passed from one information system to another as needed enables the files to be processed with less manual intervention and keeps them more up to date. This greatly decreases the differences between the actual status and the recorded status of production activities.

Materials Requirements Planning

How can the production activities and information systems be organized in complex manufacturing environments to avoid costly production inefficiencies? Before the advent of computers, it was impossible to avoid these inefficiencies because manual systems could not process information fast enough. Even during the first 20 years of the computers age, computer systems remained only partially effective in this area.

It is eye-opening to realize that a major cause of production inefficiency is a lack of integrated production planning, production scheduling, and production control information systems. One approach to improved production efficiency is materials requirements planning (MRP), which is a set of computer software programs. MRP integrates several production-related information systems so that MRP programs can access and extract data from these systems to accomplish production scheduling automatically. MRP's purpose is to greatly improve both inventory management and production scheduling.

Several of the MRP systems distributed by a variety of computer program vendors integrate several of the information systems shown in Exhibit 13.5 and also provide an automated inventory and production scheduling system that gives accurate and up-to-date information for production management purposes. The scope of many MRP systems is shown in Exhibit 13.6. The computer file of planned transfers, distribution requirements, etc., indicates the use by the MRP programs of information about the possible need to transfer completed parts or components to other production locations for further production activity and about the logistic arrangements for distribution of finished goods to the wholesale or other marketplace.

MRP systems probably introduce as much change to an organization as any other major type of systems implementation, and perhaps more. A primary reason for the partial success or outright failure of many MRP systems is that top management does not invest the time necessary to

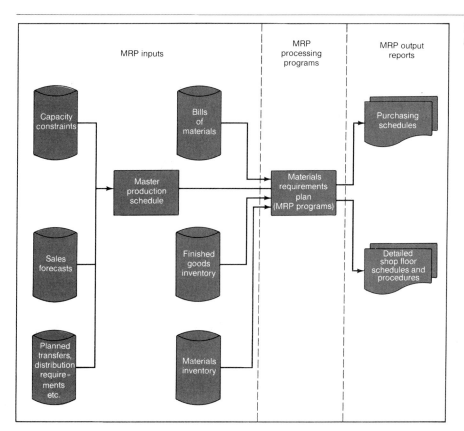

EXHIBIT 13.6
An MRP system.

learn the new MRP concepts thoroughly—top-level managers do not perceive the entire manufacturing process as an information system that requires their total commitment for successful implementation. Because MRP is also a system of management, its implementation is not primarily a data processing task; however, lacking a complete understanding of MRP, management is likely to make the error of assigning the task to the data processing department.

To achieve the efficiencies of which they are capable, MRP systems require high levels of discipline—such as not requisitioning materials long before they are needed, proper scrap reporting, and using well-defined procedures for implementing and recording engineering changes promptly. Accurate input data also is absolutely necessary; for example inventory quantity data must be accurate, and interplant transfers must be recorded accurately and promptly.

Production personnel typically do not fully understand computer systems or the need for discipline and for timely and accurate information in computer files. Also, like other personnel, production personnel resist change in general, and sometimes they resist computer systems in particular. Accordingly, the majority of implemented MRP systems have not lived up to expectations. Increasingly, however, an understanding of computer systems and the personal discipline required for successful MRP systems are arriving on the shop floor. Additionally, newer versions of MRP possess enhanced error-detection and error-tracing routines. Because of these changes, more and more MRP systems are now becoming successful.

The MRP activity shown in Exhibit 13.6 usually begins with the development of a master production schedule by family of products. The individual product members of each product line are then assigned quantities and time periods for production. This master production schedule, the bills of materials, and data about inventory levels serve as input to the MRP programs.

The MRP programs first determine the materials needs of the individual products by "exploding" each bill of materials (which describes each product in terms of its individual item components) and by multiplying the quantity of the product scheduled for production by the materials needs per unit of the product. The programs then combine the needs of all products for each type of material and determine net materials requirements by taking into account existing uncommitted materials inventory and inventory due to be received prior to production.

The MRP programs prepare two types of reports. The first type, purchase order recommendations, utilizes economic order quantity (EOQ) formulas and considers quantity discount information. Managers may revise the recommendation in light of information known to them which is not considered within the EOQ formula. The MRP programs assign a release date to each purchase order so that the materials will be received on time, but not so early as to cause a costly inventory buildup. An effective MRP system can be working several weeks ahead to help prevent shortages of materials.

The second type of report—a shop floor schedule, or "dispatch list"—is prepared for each production department. This schedule provides a day-to-day plan for shop floor activities and serves as a standard against which to evaluate each department's production activity.

MRP is also utilized when a product is manufactured only after receipt of a customer order. An order and its delivery date can be entered into the MRP system when received, and the bills of materials for the products ordered are exploded so that a materials-needed list is developed automatically. The MRP system then compares these needs with inventory records and creates a purchase order for materials not available from inventory. The MRP program determines what and how many components and products must be produced and when production must be started so that the delivery date can be met.

The benefits of a successful MRP system include:

1. Significantly decreased inventory levels (typically a 20 to 40 percent reduction) and corresponding decreases in inventory carrying costs.

2. Fewer stock shortages, which cause production interruptions and time-consuming schedule juggling by managers.

3. Less expediting by a factor of several times, with savings of labor, material costs, and premium transportation charges.

4. Increased effectiveness of production supervisors. Less production chaos and decreased expediting free them to devote more attention to the tasks in their job description, such as personnel relations and operations control.

5. Better customer service—an increased ability to meet delivery schedules and to set delivery dates earlier and more reliably.

6. Greater responsiveness to change. MRP gives manufacturing a better feel for the effects of economic swings, and changes in product demand can be translated into schedule changes quickly.

7. Closer coordination of the marketing, engineering, and finance activities with the manufacturing activities.

However, even as companies are embracing MRP, a new and more comprehensive concept is emerging. Manufacturing resources planning, or MRP-II, is a follow-on and broader information system that not only encompasses inventory management and production schuling but also includes and integrates production planning and financial planning processes. MRP-II views all manufacturing-related activities as an interactive information network; thus "factory automation," production scheduling, and materials inventory management information systems are integrated. So far, only a few companies have had extensive experience with MRP-II, but for them the benefits appear to exceed those provided by MRP.

SUMMARY

Marketing information systems may provide a competitive edge if properly developed, but marketing is still a seat-of-the-pants activity in many companies and uses hand-me-down reports from other departments. A well-developed marketing information system is a system of interrelated subsystems among which information flows.

A specialized sales support information system gives salespersons essential information, such as up-to-date inventory information. A sales analysis information system is based primarily on the sales order entry system and supplies a wealth of information about product lines, profitability, sales territories, and individual salespersons. Reports by salespersons are a valuable source of grass-roots information, and customer account analysis also yields important information.

Market research and intelligence information systems focus on analyzing information to discern trends, sudden changes, or threats to the organization. Customer research, market potential analysis, and competitor analysis information systems fall within this category.

Sales forecasting is one of the most important activities of many organizations. Sales forecasting is accomplished by merging and weighting several different types of information provided by different information systems.

The product planning information system receives information either directly or indirectly from most of the organization's marketing information systems, and in turn it supplies them with information that sets direction and focus. This system provides information about product costs, customer demand, and competitors' prices to aid managers in the complex task of product pricing.

In the manufacturing activity, discrete production processes are widespread and pose the greatest challenge to the information system. The master production schedule establishes the quantities and production timing for end products. This schedule yields priority and capacity requirements information.

Materials requirements planning (MRP) permits companies to effectively use computers to establish a detailed requirements and priority plan for materials, which in turn is used to determine detailed capacity requirements in terms of labor hours, machine hours, and so on.

KEY TERMS

price variance: the amount of variance caused by not selling all items at the planned price.

volume variance: the amount of variance caused by selling a greater or lesser volume of the product than planned.

discrete production: production which is discontinuous in nature or which is done in batches; the focus for planning and control is on the product or the batch of products.

capacity planning (production capacity analysis): establishing long-term requirements for facilities and determining the mix and quantities of personnel and materials.

bill of materials: a list of the materials, parts, and components required for the production of one unit of a product.

exploding the bill of materials: a procedure for determining how many of each of the items on the bill of materials will be required for the manufacture of one unit of a product.

margin maintenance: a technique which sets prices according to what price will maintain an established margin of profit.

expediting: continuously reallocating resources to try to keep critical jobs on or close to schedule, often by using employees as "expediters" to speed up receipt of materials.

materials requirements planning: (MRP): a computer software system that integrates several production-related information systems to accomplish production scheduling automatically.

manufacturing resources planning: a computer software system that encompasses inventory management, production scheduling, and production planning.

REFERENCES

Adler Lee, "Systems Approach to Marketing," *Harvard Business Review,* May–June 1967.

Bentz, William F., and Robert F. Lusch, "Now You Can Control Your Products' Market Performance," *Management Accounting,* January 1980.

Donaldson, William S. II, "MRP–Who Needs It?" *Datamation,* May 1979, p. 185. (A key article that discusses the fundamentals of MRP in detail from a data processing perspective.)

Doppelt, Neil, "Down to Earth Marketing Information Systems," *Management Advisor,* September–October 1981.

Goodman, Sam R., "Sales Reports That Lead to Action," *Financial Executive,* June 1973.

Hall, Robert W., and Thomas E. Vollmann, "Planning Your Materials Requirements," *Harvard Business Review,* September–October 1978, p. 105. (A discussion of the structure of MRP and the need for integration and coordination of functions when an MRP system is used. Two cases are cited.)

Wight, Oliver W., "Tools for Profit," *Datamation,* October 1980, p. 93. (An excellent article that describes the nature of MRP and stresses the people problems associated with the use of an MRP system.)

REVIEW QUESTIONS

1. Why are marketing information systems often not as highly developed as their importance to the organization indicates they should be?

2. How does the marketing information system interact with the production planning and production scheduling information system?

3. How does the marketing information system interact with the cost accounting information system?

4. Why is the sales forecasting information system important? What groups in the organization typically utilize the forecast information?

5. What role do the information systems play in product pricing?

6. What kinds of information do the information systems gather that is useful for product planning?

7. How do the marketing information systems help the organization identify potentially profitable sales opportunities?

8. Enumerate the sources of marketing information. If you had to identify one source as being more important than the others, which one would it be, and why?

9. Assume that you are a sales manager for district X and that for some unknown reason your organization's sales in the district have declined significantly during the last month. In trying to determine the cause of the sales decline, what are the sources of the information you would seek?

10. Are different information systems required to provide information for measuring product profitability, sales unit profitability, and salesperson profitability, or do all these evaluations depend on information from the same information system? Explain.

11. What is a sales call report, and how might a sales call reporting system be organized to increase the probability that sales calls will be successful?

12. What kinds of analyses are provided by the customer analysis information system?

13. Explain the activities of the marketing research and competitor intelligence groups.

14. Explain the role that information systems play in sales forecasting. What is the source of information for sales forecasting?

15. What determines the degree of complexity of production information systems?

16. How does the cost responsibility accounting information system serve both the financial and the production functions of an organization?

17. What is capacity planning?

18. How is the master production schedule prepared, and which information systems are utilized in its preparation?

19. What is meant by "exploding" a bill of materials?

20. Describe the purposes for which information in the operations control and work-in-process information systems is used.

21. How can the data processing activity be responsible for inaccuracies in the production-related information systems?

22. Why is integration of the production information systems important?

23. What problems are typically encountered during production scheduling when a traditional computer-based approach is used?

24. What are the costs of expediting? Why is expediting used?

25. How does the integration of information systems within MRP help MRP accomplish its purposes?

26. What factors make it difficult to implement a successful MRP system?

27. What is the purpose of the shop floor schedule?

PROBLEMS

1. Assume that your company manufactures small wooden tables, of which the major components are the top and four legs. Each leg has a plastic floor protector at the bottom, and each will be stained with one ounce of stain. The tabletop will be painted with three ounces of paint. There are no other components or materials. Design a product structure.

2. Referring to question 1, assume that 1000 tables will be assembled and finished. Prepare a list of materials needed for production.

3. Refer to the section in the chapter that describes the product pricing information system. Select two types of pricing methodologies, and for each one explain how a data base could facilitate establishing product prices by middle- and senior-level sales managers.

CASE

The Mead Johnson Marketing Intelligence System

Lee Adler describes the marketing intelligence system of Mead Johnson Nutritionals (a division of Mead Johnson & Company) in his article entitled "Systems Approach to Marketing." The following is excerpted from this article:

A practical instance of the use of such an intelligence system is supplied by Mead Johnson Nutritionals (division of Mead Johnson & Company), manufacturers of Metrecal, Pablum, Bib, Nutrament, and other nutritional specialties. As [Exhibit 13.7] shows, the company's Marketing Intelligence Department has provided information from these sources:

• A continuing large-scale consumer market study covering attitudinal and behavioral data dealing with weight control.

• Nielsen store audit data, dealing with weight control.

• A monthly sales audit conducted among a panel of 100 high-volume food stores in 20 markets to provide advance indications of brand share shifts.

• Supermarket warehouse withdrawal figures from Time, Inc.'s new service, Selling Areas-Marketing, Inc.

• Salesmen's weekly reports (which, in addition to serving the purposes of sales management control, call for reconnaissance on competitive promotions, new products launches, price changes, and so forth).

• Advertising expenditure data, by media class, from the company's accounting department.

• Figures on sales and related topics from company factories.

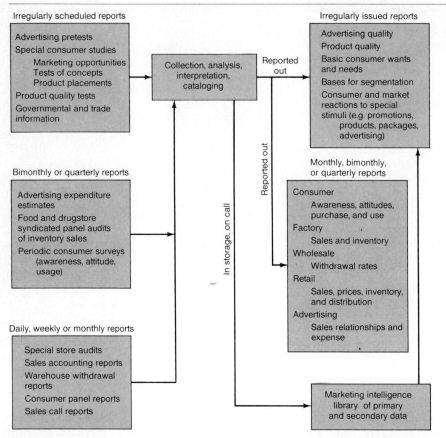

EXHIBIT 13.7
Mead Johnson's
marketing intelligence
system.

- Competitive advertising expenditure and exposure data, supplied by the division's advertising agencies at periodic intervals.

- A panel of weight-conscious women.

To exemplify the type of outputs possible from this system, Mead Johnson will be able, with the help of analyses of factory sales data, warehouse withdrawal information, and consumer purchases from Nielsen, to monitor transactions at each stage of the flow of goods through the distribution channel and to detect accumulations or developing shortages. Management will also be able to spot sources of potential problems in time to deal with them effectively. For example, if factory sales exceed consumer purchases, more promotional pressure is required. By contrast, if factory sales lag

behind consumer purchases, sales effort must be further stimulated.

Similarly, the company has been able to devise a practical measurement of advertising's effectiveness in stimulating sales—a measurement that is particularly appropriate to fast-moving packaged goods. By relating advertising outlays and exposure data to the number of prospects trying out a product during a campaign (the number is obtained from the continuing consumer survey), it is possible to calculate the advertising cost of recruiting such a prospect. By persisting in such analyses during several campaigns, the relative value of alternative advertising approaches can be weighed. Since measurement of the sales, as opposed to the communications, effects of promotion is a horrendously difficult, costly, and chancy process, the full significance of this achievement is difficult to exaggerate.

Benefits Realized

Mead Johnson's marketing intelligence system has been helpful to management in a number of ways. In addition to giving executives early warning of new trends and problems, and valuable insights into future conditions, it is leading to a systematic *body* of knowledge about company markets rather than to isolated scraps of information. This knowledge in turn should lead ultimately to a theory of marketing in each field that will explain the mysteries that baffle marketers today. What is more, the company expects that the system will help to free its marketing intelligence people from fire-fighting projects so that they can concentrate on long-term factors and eventually be more consistently creative.

Source: Lee Adler, "Systems Approach to Marketing," *Harvard Business Review,* May–June 1967, pp. 105–118.

Case Questions

1. Provide at least six examples of the kinds of trends that information provided by such a marketing intelligence system might help managers spot.

2. Provide at least six examples of the kinds of problems that information from such a system might help managers spot.

3. Would this intelligence information system probably be effective in helping management analyze its competition? If so, why? If not, how can the system be altered to accomplish this?

SECTION THREE

DEVELOPING INFORMATION SYSTEMS

A definite body of knowledge is associated with analyzing information systems needs and then designing and implementing the needed systems. This body of knowledge is presented in this final section of the book. Particular emphasis is placed on the roles that managers play in systems development activities.

Computer systems acquisition methodology is discussed in this section. A separate chapter deals with acquiring microcomputer systems.

Chapter 14

INTRODUCTION TO SYSTEMS INVESTIGATIONS

PAYOFF THOUGHT

A thorough understanding of systems investigations can enable you to participate in systems projects as soon as you join an organization, where your contribution may quickly attract the attention of senior managers.

CHAPTER OBJECTIVES

1. To outline the "life cycle" of an information system

2. To introduce the people involved and explain the various ways in which "people problems" influence systems investigations

3. To present several general principles to guide systems investigations

4. To explain how management controls a system investigation

WHAT IS A SYSTEMS INVESTIGATION?

The terms "systems analysis" and "systems design" are often encountered; "systems investigation" includes these as well as other activities. A systems investigation is a *project* undertaken to improve a specific aspect of the information system; its essence is working with *people* to devise systems that help *people* work better. A systems investigation, sometimes called a "systems development project," relies on an extensive body of methodology and a well-defined set of tools and techniques in order to analyze, design, and implement an information system or a portion of an information system.

WHY STUDY SYSTEMS INVESTIGATIONS?

The student who takes a position in a small or medium-sized company may be one of the most qualified managers in the company in the information systems area and, for this reason, is likely to be asked to participate deeply in a systems investigation. Even in large companies, the opportunity to participate in a systems investigation often is presented to junior managers whose formal education has been recently completed and who have studied systems development and implementation. The new manager should seek such an opportunity because participation is likely to provide invaluable experience. With the information systems knowledge acquired to this point in the text, the student is in a position to participate knowledgeably in systems investigations; the major ingredient lacking is a knowledge of the processes, tools, and techniques involved in systems investigations.

How can junior managers become involved in systems investigations? There are at least five ways, as shown in Exhibit 14.1 and discussed below.

1. *As a systems user.* All positions inside an organization utilize information, much of which is provided by a formal information system. Users of information systems can become actively involved in specifying their information needs—they need not wait for invitations. A user should

Ways of Participating in Systems Investigation	EXHIBIT 14.1

As a systems user
As a user representative
As a systems investigation participant
In a supervisory or advisory position
As a trained systems analyst

understand the nature of information systems in order to recognize possible improvements to these systems.

2. *As a user representative.* Often, a department of an organization formally designates one member to serve as the liaison with the organization's information systems department. Liaison activity includes meeting with user representatives of other departments, communicating the department's information needs to systems analysts, and explaining changes proposed by the analysts to other members of the department. Serving as a liaison provides a young manager an opportunity to gain insight into the organization's information systems and the structure of systems projects.

3. *As a systems investigation participant.* A new manager may be assigned temporarily to a particular systems investigation project, perhaps on a task force that utilizes the manager's specialized expertise. This temporary assignment can provide valuable experience.

4. *In a supervisory or advisory position.* As a manager acquires experience with the organization, the manager may be given a supervisory assignment in a systems investigation. For example, the manager could be made a member or an alternate member of a systems steering committee or the team leader of a systems task force.

5. *As a trained systems analyst.* A young manager may choose to spend a period of time in systems development work. The unusual opportunities available in systems work were discussed in an earlier chapter. A career path may include 1 to 3 years spent as a systems analyst, perhaps as part of a management training program. Positions as systems analysts or other systems specialists may be within the central computer group or a part of a user department. Because of the proliferation of microcomputer data centers within operating departments, an increased number of systems positions have become available with user groups.

Even if participation is restricted to communication with the organization's systems analyst, a young manager's knowledge of information systems and systems investigations provides an understanding of the analyst's activities. This knowledge also aids in understanding the entire organization's activities.

A note of caution should be sounded at this time: A systems investigation is a complex activity with many variables, and there is ample scope to permit a wide variety of serious blunders. Only a few of these can be mentioned in an elementary text; usually an information systems major completes about two specialized systems investigation courses. However, if the student applies the principles and follows the steps outlined in this chapter and the following ones, many of the more common and more serious mistakes may be avoided; the text also notes several areas of systems investigations in which caution is warranted.

THE LIFE CYCLE OF AN INFORMATION SYSTEM

The Concept

The concept of the life cycle of a system is central to systems investigations. Every system moves through several phases of a life cycle during its development, after which it functions with only minor maintenance for a period of years. The system gradually deteriorates to the point where it ceases to function effectively, and a new life cycle begins with the development of a new system.

Exhibit 14.2 illustrates a system's life cycle. The exhibit shows five phases. (Other authors illustrate the life cycle with different numbers of phases.) These are the preliminary study phase, the systems analysis phase, the systems design phase, the implementation phase, and the systems maturity and maintenance phase, which includes a separate activity called a "postaudit." The life cycles of systems vary greatly in terms of length, but typically the life cycle of an information system ranges from 3 to 8 years. The first four phases of this life cycle may properly be termed the "systems investigation phases."

The life-cycle concept is related to another important concept, that of professional information systems development teams. Large and medium-

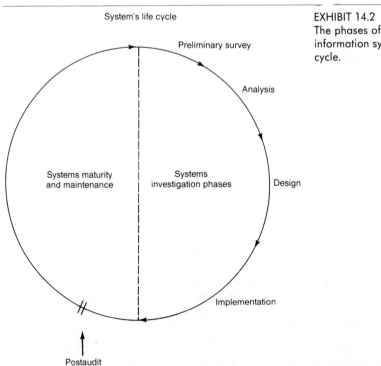

System's life cycle

Preliminary survey

Analysis

Systems maturity and maintenance

Systems investigation phases

Design

Implementation

Postaudit

EXHIBIT 14.2
The phases of an information system's life cycle.

sized organizations usually have full-time systems investigation specialists, including programmers and analysts. Typically, for all but minor systems investigations, a team will be formed at the time the preliminary study phase begins. The team is likely to be expanded for the systems analysis phase and to be altered in composition somewhat for the systems design phase. Then the team, probably again altered in its composition, implements the newly designed system. As each team member completes assigned responsibilities, that member either is assigned additional responsibilities for the project or is assigned to another systems investigation. Thus the project teams are dynamic—they are continuously forming and re-forming to participate in different aspects of the systems investigation or in other systems investigations. There is a continuous cycling of professional systems personnel through a series of systems investigations.

It is useful to outline briefly each of the phases of the systems investigation:

1. *The preliminary study phase.* During this phase, a problem with an existing information system or an opportunity to usefully develop a new system is discovered, and a limited amount of initial investigation takes place to see whether a systems project is warranted.

2. *The systems analysis phase.* During the analysis phase, a problem or opportunity associated with the system is identified, the strengths and weaknesses of the old system are examined, and what a new system should accomplish is determined.

3. *The systems design phase.* During the design phase, a new system or computer application is designed to satisfy the needs that have been determined during the analysis phase. During this phase, both hardware studies and software systems design are completed.

4. *The implementation phase.* This phase involves the programming, equipment installation, and other activities related to implementing a newly designed system.

5. *The systems maturity and maintenance phase.* This phase involves the continuous operation of the system after installation. Usually, the system achieves peak performance, and then its cost effectiveness gradually declines as its environment changes, as its operating costs change, or as its equipment becomes worn or obsolete. Near the end of this phase, the system is deemed to be no longer performing satisfactorily and is replaced.

A brief postaudit is part of the systems maturity and maintenance phase. To determine whether the investigation was conducted efficiently and to establish the extent to which the organization has received the expected benefits, a postaudit team reviews the systems investigation processes and as well as the functioning of the new system.

Because the activities of the various phases typically overlap, they may not be readily distinguishable from one another during a systems investigation. Personnel training, for example, is a part of the implementation phase, but the lead time for training personnel to accept and use certain types of systems is lengthy, and this activity often begins long before the systems design is complete. Despite this intermixing of phases, it is useful to distinguish between them; these distinctions facilitate a better understanding of the systems investigation processes. Additionally, most systems project planning and control activities are formally associated with phases, and thus it is necessary to understand these phases in order to participate usefully in the planning and control of systems investigations.

The general principles of systems investigations are similar for all types and sizes of systems projects, although the application of these principles may require different procedures, analysis, and other methods for different projects. The systems investigation activities are scaled down considerably for small projects, and for a small project the process may be quite informal.

To simplify the discussion, the assumption is made throughout that the systems investigation involves the development of a new system rather than the revision of an existing one, although the general principles are equally applicable in both situations. The chapters of this section will be concerned with formal systems investigations dealing with computer information systems. However, the student should keep in mind that the principles as well as many of the tools and techniques discussed are equally relevant to noncomputerized information systems.

Economics of the Life Cycle

The costs and benefits associated with a typical system's life cycle are shown in Exhibit 14.3. In economic terms, if the system is to be worthwhile, the total implementation and continuing operating costs discounted to the present value must be less than the total present value of the benefits of the system for the entire life of the system, and the difference between these discounted costs and benefits as a proportion of the total cost must

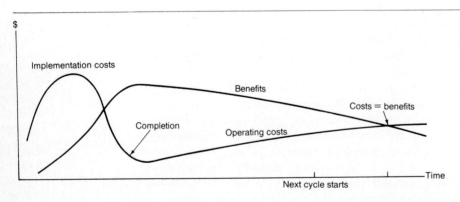

EXHIBIT 14.3
Costs and benefits of typical system's life cycle.

be greater than it would be for alternative possible new systems elsewhere in the organization.

In the exhibit, the total costs are equal to the total area under the implementation costs line, and the total benefits are equal to the total area under the benefits line. The cost curve indicates an initial high outlay during the first four phases of the life cycle. The operating costs commence after implementation of the system. Typically, operating costs decrease as the organization learns to operate the system efficiently; then costs gradually increase over time. Although costs increase for a variety of reasons, two are notable. First, as inefficiencies creep into the system, continuous minor changes become necessary. Second, as the equipment is used, repair costs increase.

The benefits from a new system may begin before the entire system is complete, as indicated in the exhibit. This occurs because certain modules of the system usually are completed and placed in operation in advance of completion of the entire system. After the system is in operation, the benefits are likely to continue to increase for a period of time until the system stabilizes; during this period, the organization learns how to utilize the system to its full potential. At the highest point of the benefits curve, changes in the way the organization conducts its business begin to decrease the effectiveness of the system. Typically, a period of gradual decline in the level of services provided by the system continues for several years.

As indicated in Exhibit 14.3, unless the system is replaced or is modified to either increase the benefits or reduce the costs, the benefits and costs curves will eventually cross, and the costs at that point in time will equal the benefits at the same point. The next systems investigation cycle should start well before the point of crossover, as is shown on the horizontal axis of the exhibit. The next system should be in place before the costs of the old system equal its benefits.

Users, management, and systems personnel must anticipate approximately when the benefits and the costs will be equal. A new systems investigation should be started months, or perhaps even years, in advance to ensure that the new system is completed in time. A commonly encountered problem in systems work is the failure of the organization to anticipate the need to replace (or overhaul) an existing system. For example, many companies fail to realize that their present computer will reach capacity in the near future, so they begin too late to acquire a new computer system. This tardiness can cause chaos and may be costly in terms of lack of effectiveness of the organization. Proper systems planning can greatly reduce the risk of this mistake.

Exhibit 14.4 demonstrates a common situation in which the life of an existing system is extended by a major systems modification that reduces the operating costs of the system. Operating costs include the labor, utilities, supplies, and "maintenance" costs required by continuous minor

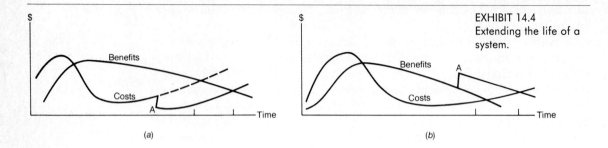

EXHIBIT 14.4
Extending the life of a system.

(a)   (b)

systems revisions. The completion of this overhaul is shown in Exhibit 14.4*a* at point A. (For simplicity, the cost of this systems overhaul is not shown in the exhibit.)

Exhibit 14.4*b* illustrates a situation in which a systems modification has extended the life of the existing system by increasing its benefits. Point A represents the point at which the benefits are increased by revision of the existing system. Many projects involving major modifications of a system achieve the dual objectives of increasing the benefits and reducing the operating costs.

THE PEOPLE INVOLVED IN A SYSTEM INVESTIGATION

Systems investigations involve people interacting with people. While technical tools are important, the most critical ingredient in systems investigations is the ability of people to work with other people. People in several categories become involved in systems investigations. These are listed in Exhibit 14.5 and described below.

• *Systems analysts.* Systems analysts are professional systems personnel who work with users to analyze existing systems and design new ones. Analysts determine what information the new or revised system must provide; how the information should be captured, processed, and

Participants in Systems Investigations   EXHIBIT 14.5

Systems analysts
Programmers
Computer systems managers
Users of information systems
User representatives
Systems consultants
Vendor representatives
Managers of the organization
Internal auditors

reported; and what programs and equipment will be needed to satisfy the requirements of the organization. Because systems analysts bear a major responsibility for the design of the information system, they possess a wide variety of systems investigation expertise. Many analysts have specialized experience and training in programming, accounting systems, telecommunications and networking, or equipment selection methods. Some systems analysts understand the computer aspects of operations thoroughly, but lack an adequate understanding of the activities of middle- and senior-level managers and have difficulty designing systems for higher-level management purposes. Some analysts also view systems development as requiring primarily technical expertise rather than an ability to work well with people, which severely limits their effectiveness. Business school graduates are less likely than more technically trained analysts to have these two deficiencies. Systems analysts often have been programmers, but many also have had experience and training in specialized functional areas, such as accounting, engineering, marketing, and finance.

• *Programmers.* If systems investigations involve the development of computer programs, programmers are used. There are two general types of programmers: applications programmers and systems programmers. Applications programmers prepare computer programs to satisfy user departments' requirements for information. They write detailed programs to accomplish the data processing specified by the analysts' flowcharts and narrative descriptions. In many organizations, the programmers also serve as systems analysts, and the distinction between the two is not maintained.

Systems programmers, the second type of programmers, often have more technical knowledge of computer systems than any of the other computer systems personnel. Systems programmers write or modify the programs that enable the computer system to control itself and to process applications programs. For example, systems programmers may modify the computer's operating systems, modify a data base management system, or develop various utility programs for the computer, such as sort routines, and edit (error-detection and error-correction) routines. Systems programmers usually do not interact extensively in their work with users, systems analysts, or applications programmers.

• *Computer systems managers.* A variety of kinds of managers exist within the computer area. In a medium-scale data processing department there usually is at least a programming manager, an input-output and data entry control manager, a hardware selection manager, a computer operations manager, a project manager, and a data base administrator if there is a data base, as well as other types of managers and a bevy of assistant managers. Most of these managers have previously served as technical personnel in the areas they manage.

• *Users of information systems.* "End users" are the personnel of the organization units for which the information systems and applications programs are designed and implemented. Users provide data to the data processing system and utilize the information provided by the system. Users may include blue-collar workers on the shop floor, clerical employees of all kinds, group leaders and supervisors, middle-level managers, technical and professional specialists, and senior managers. Working with systems analysts during the investigation, users ascertain what data must be made available for processing, and they determine their own information needs; this interaction is necessary to design a system that will satisfy the organization's needs.

• *User representatives.* User representatives, as managers within a user department who officially represent user groups, work closely with systems analysts, help define users' needs, and represent the interest of users in other ways. Their tasks include bringing systems problems to the attention of systems analysts and working with analysts to ensure that existing systems function effectively. The appointment is usually part-time, although user representatives may work full-time on a particular project for a limited period. Junior managers who are knowledgeable about information systems are likely to assume this role.

• *Systems consultants.* In many systems investigations, the participants include one or more outside consultants with specialized expertise. Sometimes an external consultant can operate effectively as a systems analyst for the organization; however, consultants generally should not design and install a system without the cooperation and extensive participation of the concerned user group. If user groups are not adequately involved, systems installed by a consultant probably will not satisfy their needs and perhaps will not be used at all.

In small organizations, without an extensive systems staff, consultants are often asked to play a broad role that may encompass organizing and managing the systems project and helping select equipment. In larger organizations, consultants are likely to be employed for more specialized tasks, such as evaluating the relative technical merits of alternative computer or software systems. Even large organizations with highly sophisticated systems personnel frequently employ outside consultants.

• *Vendor representatives.* Employed by hardware and software sales companies, vendor representatives sell their companies' products and offer advice to clients about the selection of hardware or software. As a general rule, vendor representatives can be relied upon to reflect the perspective of their employers and do not provide an unbiased analysis of an organization's needs. Vendor representatives may be called "customer service representatives" or have a similar title, and vendor technical personnel are often called "customer engineers."

• *Managers of the organization.* Whether the systems are intended to provide information directly to the managers or not, the organization's managers should be deeply involved in systems investigations. This involvement includes providing leadership, motivating users to cooperate, facilitating the required resource allocations, ensuring that systems investigations are well controlled and produce effective information systems, and formally accepting the systems developed.

• *Internal auditors.* The internal auditors of the organization should participate at numerous points in systems investigations. Their major contribution is to ensure that the completed system embodies adequate internal controls and that the system and its output can be audited. Internal auditors may also participate as members of the postaudit team after the conclusion of the systems investigation.

PEOPLE PROBLEMS IN SYSTEMS INVESTIGATIONS

When a systems investigation fails to produce a useful system, the failure is usually due to problems involving the people related to the new system; these are called "people problems." All the groups and all the individuals involved with the systems investigation have vested personal interests and psychological needs that affect their acceptance and use of a new system. Individuals may desire to contribute to the organization or to feel wanted by, or important to, the organization; they have feelings about replacing the existing system, as well as perspectives on the problems and the advantages of both the old and the new systems. Frequently they experience fears about job security and concern about the impact of a new system on their jobs.

A systems investigation is a project that involves people working together toward the common goal of improving the information system. While technical expertise is, of course, important, even more important to a systems investigation are diplomacy, tact, persuasiveness, sensitivity to people's needs and concerns, and training in interviewing techniques. Some of the people problems most likely to be encountered are listed in Exhibit 14.6 and discussed below; these problems are due to personality traits that to some degree prevent a system from being properly developed or properly used after development.

• *Commitment to the old information system.* Users of the existing information system who do not wish to learn to use a new system may oppose it because they are committed to the old system. Sometimes these users are external to the organization, such as customers who are billed by the system or who interact with it in other ways and resist its being changed. Other such users are people in a department who were instrumental in designing and implementing the old system and who feel loyal to it.

• *Resistance to change.* Everyone resists change; to an extent, we are all

People Problems in Systems Investigations   EXHIBIT 14.6

Commitment to the old system
Resistance to change
Embarrassment
Fear of being a scapegoat
Fear of job loss
Lack of interest of key personnel
Analysts' lack of personnel skills
Conflicting interests
Territorial instincts
Expressing a position too early

creatures of habit. Because the usual purpose of a systems investigation is to bring about change, it is not surprising that many people are unwilling to cooperate wholeheartedly with it. This resistance to change must be overcome by using diplomacy. Everyone, including managers who make decisions about the new system, must be shown the advantages of the new system. Often resistance to change erodes only over a fairly long period of time.

• *Embarrassment.* Because people are embarrassed by a lack of knowledge about computer systems or by an inability to specify their information needs fully, the may avoid participation in the systems investigation. This reluctance can be reduced in diplomatic ways. For example, senior managers whose participation is needed but who could be embarrassed by their lack of systems knowledge often can participate as members of the systems steering committee in ways that permit them to conceal their ignorance while learning about systems.

• *Fear of being a scapegoat.* Many systems investigation participants believe that the organization will seek a scapegoat for problems associated with the existing system or for the possible inability to initiate a satisfactory new system. These persons desire to avoid the systems investigation entirely so that they cannot be blamed for anything. Ironically, if they refuse to become involved, a measure of any blame for an inadequate new system can be assigned to them. The advantages of cooperating with the systems investigation msut be shown to them.

• *Fear of job loss.* An employees are well aware, new systems frequently eliminate jobs or substantially alter a job's content. Concern about the possibility of losing a job is one of the strongest possible motivations for not cooperating with a systems investigation or not accepting a new system after its installation. Here, the organization's track record is decisive; if in the past when jobs were eliminated, the employees who held them were given training that qualified them for equally good or (preferably) better jobs elsewhere in the organization, most employees' fears of job loss will be eliminated.

• *Lack of interest among key personnel.* Often it is difficult to capture the interest of key personnel. Many managers are quite busy and are disinclined to give their attention to a systems project, even if the new system will serve them. In particular, managers at the higher levels of organizations have schedules that seldom permit more than a few minutes for a discussion with a systems analyst, and their lofty positions give them the ability to remain aloof from a systems investigation if they choose to. To appreciate the position of senior managers, reflect for a moment on the difficulty of getting students involved in student political clubs and student business associations. Many worthy activities compete for students' time and attention, and getting them deeply involved is difficult; the same is true in the business world. Senior managers usually are already the busiest people in the organization, and yet their active assistance is necessary. They can directly contribute to the systems investigation, they allocate the resources, and they motivate subordinates to cooperate with the systems investigation. These managers may cooperate as members of a systems steering committee.

• *Analysts' lack of personnel skills.* The education of systems analysts, programmers, and designers often concentrates on technical subjects; little or no attention may be given to psychology, personnel relations, or interview techniques. As a result, in their dealings with other participants in the systems investigation, these systems specialists often are insensitive to people problems. This insensitivity is itself a people problem, which is compounded by another problem; because the mental processes of technicians tend to be different from those of managers, as explained in an earlier chapter, communication between analysts and managers is a serious problem, even if the systems specialists try to be sensitive to other people. Systems specialists should be given special human relations training.

• *Conflicting interests.* Animosity between individuals, groups, or departments often prevents cooperation on a systems problem. Individuals or groups may prefer different solutions to a particular systems problem. One very large company, for example, had acquired a medium-sized company and had imposed upon it the corporate chart of accounts. However, the personnel of the acquired company preferred the chart previously used. Discontent led to a systems investigation that was intended to establish a new chart of accounts. Five years later, the two groups finally compromised, although neither group was entirely satisfied with the new chart of accounts. In this case, as often happens with such conflicts, the systems analysts' negotiating skills were more important than their technical expertise.

• *Territorial instincts.* Often, a group within an organization that generates data may believe that this data "belongs" to it. The data provides the group with power and influence in the organization, and group members do not wish to share the information, even if that would be in the best interests of the entire organization. Such territorial instincts are not easily overcome, but good personnel skills of systems personnel are useful. Also, including a representative of the dissident group on the systems steering committee may convince the group to share "their" information. If the organization has a data base, the data base administrator is given the authority to resolve this people problem by fiat, if necessary.

• *Expressing a position too early.* Frequently, participants (including systems specialists) take initial positions for or against the existing system or a possible new system. Someone who has publicly expressed a position becomes reluctant to change that position at a later time. Participants then find themselves "locked in" to positions that are undesirable in the light of subsequent developments. Systems investigation participants should be asked to take a noncommital, "wait-and-see" stance during the early stages of a project.

Avoiding People Problems

Many people problems can be avoided. One good practice is for analysts to consult with everyone who should be involved in the systems investigation. If someone who should participate at some point is excluded initially, even as a matter of convenience or expediency, that person will be less inclined to cooperate later. Another good practice is to pay careful attention to any objections to a new system; systems personnel should undertake sincere discussions with the persons voicing the objections.

Systems personnel often err in not recognizing the participants' vested interests in the old system. For example, a new system usually requires that managers discard old work routines or techniques. If systems analysts consider the perspectives of participants, many vested interests can be identified and accommodated. Often a new system can be designed to permit personnel to continue their old work routines, with no reduction in the efficiency of the new system.

A common error of a systems specialist is that of claiming the major share of credit for the new system. However, many people participate in the systems investigation, and each deserves an appropriate share of the credit. When appreciation is expressed and proper credit is given, participants accept the new system and cooperate in other systems investigations at a later time.

Another common error is not assuring personnel that their futures are secure even if jobs are eliminated. Few systems investigations result in employees' being terminated, and most displaced personnel are assigned better positions than they had before. Inadequate training of employees for the new system positions can also cause problems. If users understand the advantages of the new system and are properly trained in its use, the system usually will be effectively implemented.

A final problem is improper interviewing techniques, which often cause the alienation of participants in the systems investigation process. Interviewing is the most important systems analysis technique. Interviewing is also useful for many activities other than systems investigations, and students should accept any opportunity to learn the principles of good interviewing. For example, a knowledge of interviewing is useful when seeking employment, and it is useful for public accountants who must interview clients to gain information during an audit.

GENERAL PRINCIPLES OF SYSTEMS INVESTIGATIONS

Several general principles of systems investigation are of paramount importance to the successful completion of a project and are examined briefly below. Others are discussed in relation to other topics in subsequent chapters.

• *Involve managers in the project.* In all systems projects, managers of the user organization should be involved, and in major systems projects, senior managers as well as managers at other levels in multiple areas of the organization should be involved. Senior managers must understand the systems projects in order to allocate resources, make decisions about the overall direction of the information systems, and motivate subordinates to develop and utilize new systems. Lower-level managers are often in a good position to urge that their subordinates cooperate with systems projects. Whenever a systems project has the potential to influence multiple areas of the organization, representatives from all areas should participate, even during the project planning stages.

• *Involve users in the project.* The necessity to involve users in systems projects appears self-evident, and yet systems specialists often attempt to develop new systems with no or with minimal user participation. The perspective of systems users is absolutely essential to the decision concerning whether to keep the existing system or design a new one. Users who provide information to, or receive information from, the system are in the best position to know about the availability of information and to know the required capabilities of a new system.

A system that is designed without extensive interaction with users usually becomes an unpleasant surprise to them and is not likely to be utilized. Users generally react negatively to any system that has been designed without their involvement. Additionally, systems developed in isolation from users usually are not adequately designed.

• *Plan the project within the context of long-range systems planning.* Without adequate long-range planning for the entire information system, individual projects are unlikely to serve the overall interests of the organization satisfactorily. Each proposed project must be evaluated in terms of the goals of the entire organization.

• *Maintain a balanced systems project portfolio.* A systems development group in a company of even moderate size generally has several systems investigation projects in process simultaneously. These projects make up its "portifolio," which is much like an investment portfolio. An investment portfolio achieves an optimum balance between high- and low-risk investments; in like manner, a systems project portfolio attempts to balance high- and low-risk projects. This balance is achieved by including both state-of-the-art and routine, easily accomplished projects, as well as projects of both short and long duration. Only a limited number of highly risky projects should be included in the portfolio at any one time. Risky projects are those with a low probability of being completed on schedule, within budget, and with the hoped-for benefits. Too many risky projects in a systems portfolio can result in a high rate of unsuccessful projects. The consequence is a reduction of confidence in the systems group on the part of management and users, low morale in the systems group, and, frequently, the termination of systems analysts or EDP managers who are blamed for the rash of unsuccessful projects.

• *Take into account the evolution of systems.* The scale and complexity of projects should be suitable to the level of sophistication of the organization. During the early stages of the evolution of an organization's information systems, systems personnel rarely have the expertise to design and successfully implement sophisticated systems. Even if ultrasophisticated systems could be successfully designed and implemented, management and clerical personnel probably could not accept the radical changes in operations and gain full benefit from the sophisticated systems. For example, an organization that does not have most major data processing applications computerized would be unwise to attempt to incorporate all its applications into a computerized data base.

• *Establish a project management system.* Formal project management systems that provide regular progress reports can be adapted to fit even small systems projects; project management systems enable projects to be managed in a systematic, controlled manner. The probability of successful implementation of a new system increases dramatically if a project management system is utilized. However, the degree of organization for project management should be tailored to the cost and value of the project. Overorganization of a small project is not cost-effective.

• *Establish the objectives and scope of a proposed system early.* If the objectives and scope of a new system are formally established at about the time the project is begun, all effort is focused explicitly on achieving the objectives. Unfocused effort is likely to be frittered away on tangential activities of little value to the organization. By some estimates, as much as 40 percent of the systems development efforts in many organizations are wasted on false starts and unnecessary tasks; this can be reduced by means of a proper and timely definition of the objectives and scope of systems projects. When a systems steering committee exists, it should play a decisive role in establishing the objectives and scope of a proposed system.

• *Identify the proper problem.* Failure to identify the most important problem is one of the most common mistakes in systems investigations. Often, for example, the problem is not a systems problem but instead is a people problem. Perhaps the users do not understand how to use the existing system and require more training, or perhaps they are resisting the system for some reason. Small organizations often identify the problem as the lack of a computer, when in fact a computer would not improve operations at all; the real problem often is that the existing manual systems are not properly designed or have degenerated over time. Another common mistake is made when an existing computer is unable to complete the data processing chores; the problem is defined as a lack of adequate computer capacity, when, in reality, the problem is the inefficient utilization of the existing computer.

Several other types of problems often are not diagnosed properly. Political problems, for example, can be caused by feuding factions. Each faction may have different expectations of the information system, or one group in the organization may refuse to make its information available to another group, with the consequence that the second group requests that a new (and redundant) system be developed to provide information that already exists. In these cases negotiation, rather than a new system, is the preferred solution.

Another type of problem may be vendor-related. Often more cost-effective hardware and software or better service is available from another vendor, but misplaced loyalty, an unwarranted reluctance to deal with more than one vendor, or other reasons prevent an organization from seeking another vendor even if the present one does not provide fully satisfactory products or services.

Typical Undiagnosed Problems   EXHIBIT 14.7

1. Inadequate understanding of the present system
2. Resistance to the existing system
3. Inefficient utilization of the computer
4. Internal political problems
5. Problems with a vendor
6. Employee turnover and absenteeism
7. Improper organization of the information system
8. Inadequate scheduling of data processing

Particularly in small organizations, the quality of data processing service may be low because of high rates of employee turnover or absenteeism. Although the difficulty may be diagnosed as a systems problem, such as inadequate computer capacity, it is a personnel problem. Another frequently misdiagnosed problem relates to the way the information systems are organized. Frequent delays in receiving reports, for example, may be interpreted as the consequence of inadequate systems capacity. In fact, the problem could be as simple as improper scheduling, a need for a night shift in data processing, or a need for a decentralized or distributed system to replace one that has adequate capacity but is too centralized.

• *Establish a reasonable completion schedule.* Systems personnel are notorious for proposing schedules that are wildly optimistic. Often this is an indication of their eagerness to please, or their optimism may be a simple matter of underestimation of the effort involved. Frequently, too, an optimistic schedule is a consequence of overzealousness in seeking the approval for a new project. Systems development personnel must be apprised of the consequences to the organization and to themselves of setting unreasonable completion estimates for projects. On the other hand, open-ended projects without deadlines also should be avoided. All projects should have a project schedule stated in hours, days, or weeks, along with a completion date. Proper scheduling allocates a specific amount of personnel resources to each project. Without careful control, projects sometimes continue indefinitely and consume inordinate amounts of resources.

• *Use a performance evaluation system.* Before the project begins, systems and management personnel should determine the criteria that will measure the success of the new system after its implementation, and these criteria should be embodied in a performance evaluation system. Performance evaluation also should encompass evaluation of the efficiency of the systems project. Additionally, the postaudit procedures should be established in advance. When the project personnel understand that the ultimate success of the system will be measured by preestablished criteria, they will commit themselves to meeting these criteria.

• *Make creeping commitments.* All decisions made during a systems investigation should remain tentative as long as possible so that they can be gracefully altered if necessary. The organization should "creep" toward a final commitment to the project and toward each resource commitment to it. When a creeping commitment approach is used, if new information is uncovered or if subsequent analyses challenge previous decisions, as is often the case, the previous decisions can be reviewed and altered with a minimum expenditure of resources. Also, there are psychological considerations. First, when decisions that are later altered are initially stated as being tentative rather than final, personnel are not as likely to lose face, feel defeated or demoralized, or believe that the organization is wishy-washy in its commitment to a project. Additionally, if a decision appears final, personnel may not remain alert for alternatives that may be preferable, with the consequence that the organization is less likely to finally receive the system it needs.

• *Start with a broad investigation and then become increasingly detailed.* Systems investigations should begin with the "big picture" of how the activity relates to the entire organization and with a consideration of broad alternatives; this may be termed "macro" analysis and design and is called "successive refinement" or "iterative refinement" by some experts. Successive analyses and designs become increasingly focused and detailed, each operating within the context established by the preceding decisions and activities; this is referred to as "micro" analysis and design. In the design phase, especially, several iterations of design, each more detailed than the preceding one, may be required before the final, fully detailed micro design is established.

• *Ensure conformance to standards.* Every systems investigation initiated should conform to the organization's preestablished information systems standards. If a standards program is not in existence, an initial investment of resources should be made to develop common programming, data definition, documentation procedure, and other systems standards. Increasingly, the development of a data dictionary is the approach adopted to establish many of the information systems standards; this approach can be usefully adopted even if a data base is not intended. Requiring that all new or revised systems conform to these standards will pay high dividends. Conformity promotes efficiency in systems maintenance and development, and it facilitates the subsequent introduction of distributed data processing systems, the integration of existing applications (such as by a data base), and the implementation of computer models and decision support systems. The development of a standards program is itself an important systems project.

• *Use a structured approach.* Systems investigations should use a structured methodology, consisting of a series of steps within each phase, each done more or less in sequence. This provides a discernible structure to the project. This structure also serves to increase the systematic nature of the activity and thereby reduces the extent of wasted effort. In general, the more structured the systems investigation, the lower the proportion of wasted effort. A large proportion of wasted effort occurs when tasks are done out of sequence and when prior completion of the preceding task in sequence would have demonstrated that the task done was not needed or should have been completed differently.

• *Establish priorities for projects.* There often appears to be an infinite number of possible systems projects. In the typical organization there is a formal backlog of about 3 years; that is, there is a list of projects requested which have not yet been initiated and which, because of resource shortages, are not expected to be initiated for 3 years. Additionally, many projects which are needed now but which may not be needed in 3 or 4 years, when they can be completed, are not on the list. In this environment, a system of prioritization should be used to ensure that the most critical systems projects are undertaken first. Typically, priorities are established by systems steering committee; after each project is given a "hearing" to determine its merits, it is assigned a priority level.

A Final Word on Systems Investigation Principles

From the preceding discussion of principles it can be seen that systems investigations are complex and that systems work is both an art and a science. Dealing with people is in good measure an art, and the science is represented by an extensive body of systems development theory and a series of principles for the application of that theory. To be a proficient analyst requires both study and experience in the application of the art and science aspects of systems investigations.

AUDITORS' ROLES IN SYSTEMS INVESTIGATIONS

During the systems analysis phase, internal auditors may be able to help ensure that the most important systems problem has been identified; the auditor's assistance can be valuable if the auditor understands the existing system as a consequence of previous audits. Additionally, near the conclusion of this phase, the auditor may make certain that any new system will provide data needed during subsequent audits of the system. Beyond this somewhat limited participation, the internal auditor is not deeply involved in the systems analysis phase.

Auditors should become deeply involved during the design phase. First, auditors should be concerned that newly designed systems will be auditable; that is, "audit trails" must exist. Audit trails are a means of tracing transactions through the system. Without audit trails, the system could not be audited after implementation; even more important, without audit trails, managers who must monitor the data processing or check on transactions would be unable to know how a specific transaction was processed, or even whether it was processed. Maintaining a listing of all transactions processed and a separate listing of all processing errors is an important ingredient in maintaining an audit trail.

Auditors are concerned about the controls in the system being designed. Controls ensure that data processing is complete and accurate; they also protect the resources of the organization from data processing errors and protect the systems from abuse by people. During systems design, systems personnel often emphasize computer operating efficiency rather than protection against losses of the organization's resources. Auditors, on the other hand, are concerned about the organization's resources and the efficient use of these resources. Because of this perspective, auditors make a substantial contribution to the design of controls for new systems.

Auditors are concerned not only about specific controls but also about whether a cohesive framework of internal controls is present and whether the specific controls planned for a new system fit properly into the overall scheme of internal controls. As a part of this concern, auditors attempt to specify the nature of risks to be guarded against in all systems; they then evaluate the controls of a new system in terms of how these controls help protect against the perceived risks.

Although auditors' exact roles in systems design vary in different organizations, many organizations prefer that the auditors recommend what risks should be controlled against and that the systems designers recommend appropriate controls. In these organizations auditors do not recommend specific controls or participate directly in the design of the new system. However, auditors review the systems design to ensure that the specific controls selected are adequate, given the risks, and that the entire interlocking system of controls is satisfactory. In so doing, auditors must consider tradeoffs between the cost and the value of controls in the light of the risks involved.

During the implementation phase, the auditors' primary responsibility is ensuring that controls designed into the new system are actually implemented. An internal auditor may also be part of the postaudit task team. A major advantage of having auditors participate throughout the investigation is that this gives them the opportunity to study the new system from the inside during its development; this study assists them in later audits of the system during its operation.

Auditors play another, more general role in systems projects. When systems changes are in process, there are unusual risks because existing controls may be ignored as a matter of convenience, because procedures are in transition, and because shortcuts are likely to be attempted. The old system may be partially dismantled, but the new one is not yet fully implemented. The subsequent switch to the new system may mean that any errors or transgressions that occurred during the transition can never be detected. Throughout a systems investigation, internal auditors should be alert to improper activities and errors that are caused by the systems project or are masked by the project.

Unfortunately, many internal auditors lack a technical understanding of computer systems and cannot contribute to systems investigations in the ways described. Furthermore, systems development groups may not encourage participation by auditors. Nevertheless, their participation is often critical to the succcess of a new system, and they should acquire the necessary expertise.

CONTROL OF SYSTEMS INVESTIGATIONS

There are two major types of control of systems investigations. The first consists of the general management control over all systems development processes, and the second relates to the control of a specific systems investigation by means of a project control system. The systems steering committee, to be discussed, is a combination of these two types of control.

Management Control of Systems Development Processes

Activities of all kinds must be controlled by the senior managers of the organization to ensure that the activities serve the organization's needs. This control by senior managers is known as "management control."

Continuous management control over the information systems, as well as over systems development, is exercised by the senior information systems manager, who may be the manager, director, or vice president of computer services, data processing, or information systems. In the past, information systems managers have often been well versed in computer technology but not in management and control methods. However, as computer information systems become more complex and as all areas of organizations become affected by them, a manager with general management and management control expertise is needed as the information systems manager. Indeed, the systems manager should have all the attributes of any good general manager, and these managerial attributes are more important than the manager's technical expertise.

Systems planning also provides important controls over information systems. Long-range planning controls the direction of systems development by establishing the framework within which information systems are developed. Budgeting provides periodic performance goals and a performance evaluation mechanism, which serve as forms of control. Capital budgets, which are an integral part of the overall computer plan, as well as of a particular systems investigation, serve as a control over capital expenditures for equipment.

Another major dimension of management control is the system which provides reports containing information about computer utilization to the computer manager, to that manager's superior, and perhaps to the systems steering committee. Typically, these reports include the usual control and performance information provided by budget reports, personnel expenditure reports, and training reports. Additionally, specialized reports are likely to contain performance statistics relating to the status of systems projects in process, the percentage of utilization of various computer equipment components, and the percentage of downtime (the percentage of time when the computer system is not operative).

Allocations of the data processing costs to the users on the basis of the extent to which they use the information systems also constitute an important management control. These cost allocation systems are known as "cost charge-out systems." Finally, both internal and external auditing serve management as a general control over information systems. Both types of auditors examine the information systems, evaluate the internal controls of these systems, and conduct detailed audits of specific information systems applications.

The Systems Steering Committee

One of the most important forms of management control is provided by the systems steering committee. In some organizations, this may be called the "computer steering committee" or the "EDP steering committee"; in others, it is called the "EDP planning committee" or the "computer planning committee." The committee is given the authority to establish the overall direction of the organization's information systems, or, alternatively, its authority may be limited to a specific systems project.

The rationale for the committee is the fact that since information systems affect the entire organization, all major users and potential users should help direct the information systems and participate in the resource allocations required for systems development. Systems steering committees ensure that the needs of various users of the information systems dictate the organization and use of the computer system; computer personnel should not make these determinations alone.

Systems steering committees may be organized initially for a particular major systems project. Then, as their utility for that project is recognized, they often become permanent, and their jurisdiction is extended to all data processing activities and future systems projects.

The systems steering committee approach is widely used in industry, and experience suggests that it tends to be the successful organizations which utilize it most often. The concept is roughly analogous to that of an organization's management committee, which is usually composed of the most senior executives and which determines the overall policy of a corporation, reviews long-range plans, and makes the major investment decisions; however, the purview of the systems steering committee is limited to information systems matters.

Purposes of the Systems Steering Committee

The purposes of the systems steering committee are:

1. To assist the computer systems manager in the development of long-range plans for the computer information systems
2. To ensure that the computer department's goals and objectives are compatible with those of the entire organization
3. To review proposals for new systems projects and for major revisions to existing systems
4. To make the major decisions with respect to the allocation of

resources to computer systems development, including decisions to ter-minate projects in process

5. To establish the development priorities of systems projects

6. To monitor and control the development of information systems in general, as well as the major systems projects, and to undertake reviews and evaluations as needed

Structure of the Systems Steering Committee

The lines of authority and responsibility within the computer department and between the computer department manager and superior managers remain unchanged for day-to-day management and control processes; the systems steering committee does not participate in routine operations or their control. However, the overall direction and policies of the computer department are established by the systems steering committee, which also exercises overall management control and evaluates the progress of sys-tems development.

Membership

The systems steering committee usually has from 6 to 15 members. Each major organizational subunit that is, or is potentially, a significant user of the computer is represented on the committee by a senior manager. The manager of the computer department is a member, and that manager's superior usually is a member and often chairs the committee. The com-puter department typically is also represented by one or two other per-sons, perhaps a specialist in computer technology and the department's assistant manager. The organization's internal auditing manager often is a member of the systems steering committee.

When no major projects are in process, brief meetings of the systems steering committee are normally held monthly or bimonthly. When major projects are in process, meetings are held as often as necessary to evaluate project progress and provide direction.

Project Task Forces

Each major systems investigation is undertaken by a group that is often known as a "project task force"; its members each have specialized skills needed to develop the new system. The project task force is usually composed of personnel who spend all or most of their time on that systems project until the project is completed or they are reassigned. A project task force frequently includes managers of user organizations who are on loan for the project, but typically most members are professional systems personnel. Project task forces are under the daily direction of the manager of the computer department, but the ultimate responsibility for their ac-tivities rests with the systems steering committee.

Benefits of a Systems Steering Committee

The systems steering committee approach to managing systems development keeps top management attuned to the many requirements of information systems and educates senior managers about the complexities and importance of information systems. Additionally, the overview judgment possessed only by senior managers is brought to a systems project. These managers help set the direction of the computer systems, assign priorities to projects, and monitor the progress of projects. A systems steering committee composed of senior managers also has the "clout" needed to provide support for the systems personnel working on each project.

PLANNING FOR INFORMATION SYSTEMS

Perhaps the management dimension that, more than any other, distinguishes successful organizations from unsuccessful ones is the quality of planning conducted by the organizations' managers. In computer departments, planning is too often a sorely neglected activity. One reason for this is the fact that computer managers usually have not been trained in planning processes. Another reason is that the computer area has been an especially dynamic part of most organizations, with almost continuous crises and major new projects at frequent intervals. The latter reason often leads computer managers to say, "We don't have time to plan!" or "Our environment is too complex and dynamic for plans to be useful—they'd be out of date in 6 weeks." In fact, the frequency of data processing crises, of technological changes, and of major systems investigations is a reason why it is even more important that planning be done for computer systems; planning helps managers anticipate the effects of these factors and enables resources to be allocated in a way that moderates their effects.

Other reasons also exist for the importance of planning by information systems groups. One is that the organization often must gain background and do other groundwork for several months or years in order to understand the possible implications for it of new technology, and this usually means an allocation of personnel resources far in advance of a payoff from the new technology. Another reason is that some major systems projects are long-term in nature and must be initiated 2 to 5 years before they are expected to be fully completed. For example, data base development in an organization should take place over about a 5-year period; a critical aspect of this development is the initial planning that establishes which applications areas will be encompassed by each of several data bases. Without this advance planning, which may take place 2 or more years before the first data base is completed, the entire project is likely to be a misadventure for the organization.

Three types of computer systems plans are needed: a long-range plan, a short-range plan, and a project plan for each systems investigation of any consequence. The long-range plan should be based on, and derived from, the long-range goals and strategies of the organization. As a simple example, assume that a company is attempting to double its sales volume within 5 years (a goal) and expects to accomplish this primarily by establishing its first retail product stores (a strategy). The computer department should be aware of this goal and this strategy so that it can plan to increase its processing capacity and can develop strategies for collecting and processing transactions data from the new retailing activity. Of course, an organization's set of goals and strategies is actually far more complex than this example, and the goals and strategies of the computer area that are derived from those of the organization are correspondingly more complex. The members of the systems steering committee usually have participated deeply in the organization's long-range planning and are able to interpret these plans properly to guide the computer group's long-range planning activities.

The purpose of the long-range computer systems plan is to establish how the computer department should maneuver itself into a long-run position that enables its computer systems most effectively to help the entire organization achieve its long-range goals. Typically, the long-range systems plan is from 3 to 5 years and is more detailed for the early years than for the later ones. The plan usually "rolls forward" to add 1 year each year, but the computer department should revise the entire plan each year, rather than simply developing a new plan for the year added.

Exhibit 14.8, although incomplete, lists many of the matters that should be dealt with in a long-range computer department plan. The technology analysis should explain how present and expected future computer, communications, and other technologies can be used to increase the effectiveness of the computer information systems.

Personnel and their recruitment, retention, and development are the

---

Partial Contents of a Systems Long-Range Plan   EXHIBIT 14.8

1. Technology analysis

2. Personnel:
   Present profile
   Future staffing levels and expertise needs
   Expected training and development programs

3. User service levels:
   Present types and levels of service
   Expected types and levels of service

4. Systems configuration:
   Present configuration
   Expected future configuration

5. Analysis of systems projects in process and scheduled

key to successful computer information systems, and this section of the long-range plan should be given particularly careful attention. With respect to user service, the computer systems serve the organization by giving service to users; thus planners should focus on how well and in what ways users are now being served as well as on how present service can be improved. In many computer departments, too little attention is focused on how to serve users better, even though providing service to users is the reason for the existence of the computer systems.

The systems configuration planning includes an analysis of the present equipment and its advantages and limitations. It also includes consideration of what equipment changes are expected during the period of the plan, given the technology expected and the goals for service to users.

An analysis of the status of major projects should also be provided in the plan. Proposed major new projects are often first formally presented to the systems steering committee as a part of the long-range plan, where they can be seen in the context of the entire information system, both present and future. It is in the long-range plan that the organization's "portfolio" of systems projects is made explicit in terms of a combination of projects that balances high- and low-risk and short- and long-term projects. Approval of the long-range plan then represents approval in principle of the proposed individual projects and of the entire portfolio within the plan. Of course, circumstances change, and a detailed proposal for each project must be prepared and approved at the appropriate time so that some projects that are approved in principle as a part of the overall plan are later rejected. However, if a major project is proposed entirely outside the framework of the long-range plan, the presumption of the systems steering committee must be either that the plan was inadequate or that the project does not have great merit.

The purposes of the short-range plan, which may be termed a "budget plan" or a "profit plan," are to establish the resource allocations that will be needed during the next period (usually a year) and to serve as a means of management control over expenditures. This budget usually is a fully detailed version of the first year of the EDP department's long-range plan. However, circumstances and planning philosophies differ, and in some instances a short-range plan is somewhat independent of the first year of the long-range plan; thus the strategies and expenditures shown in the two may differ. The short-range plan usually is prepared on the basis of months and quarters, and often a new quarter is added as each quarter is completed so that the budget is always for a full year ahead.

The third kind of plan needed, the project plan, differs significantly from the other two types. First, while a separate detailed plan exists for each project and is known as the "project plan," nevertheless both the long-range and the short-range plans also include each project in outline form. A project plan also differs from long-range and short-range in that it is not for a period of time, such as a month, a quarter, or a year, as the other plans are, but instead is for the time expected to be required for completion of the project. The project plan remains in effect even if the project is not completed when expected, but it terminates as soon as the project is completed, whether early, on time, or late.

PROJECT MANAGEMENT SYSTEMS

Project plans are usually developed around a project management system, which is a specialized combination of project planning system, project control system, and project information system. Several project management systems are in existence. All can be useful, whether a systems steering committee is also utilized or not. When a systems steering committee is used in conjunction with a project management system, the reports provided by the project management system are used by the committee to assess the progress of the project. Two common types of project management systems are bar charts and PERT (program evaluation review technique).

Bar Charts

Exhibit 14.9 shows a bar chart, which is perhaps the simplest form of formal project management. The bar chart (also known as a "Gantt chart") is used almost exclusively for scheduling purposes and therefore controls only the time dimension of projects. In the exhibit, task 1 (a part of a particular systems project) is scheduled to begin in mid-January and continue to the end of February. Task 2 commences at the end of January, before task 1 is completed, and continues until mid-March. After task 2 is completed, task 3 begins about the first of April and continues through July. Tasks 4 and 5 are undertaken simultaneously; task 4 is expected to be completed on about December 1, and task 5 on about December 15.

When a bar chart is used as a project control method, "milestones" or "checkpoints" usually are placed at the completion of each task (they may also be placed within tasks). They indicate the completion of a particular task and are the basis for determining whether the task and the

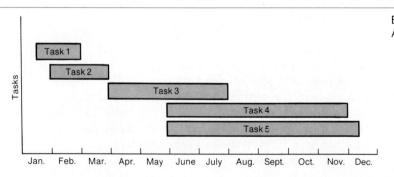

EXHIBIT 14.9
A bar chart.

project are on schedule; when a checkpoint is reached, the task just completed and the entire project are reviewed and evaluated. Reviewers ask whether resources allocated have been properly utilized and whether the task has been satisfactorily completed. However, because the bar chart incorporates only the scheduling dimension of a project, it gives little indication of which tasks must be completed before others are begun, and project costs must be accumulated and evaluated using other methods.

Program Evaluation Review Technique (PERT)

Unlike bar charts, PERT can be both a cost and a time management system; PERT is organized by events and activities or tasks. PERT has several advantages over bar charts and is likely to be used with more complex projects. One advantage of PERT is that it is a scheduling device that also shows graphically which tasks must be completed before others are begun.

Also, by displaying the various task "paths," PERT enables the calculation of a "critical path." Each path consists of combinations of tasks which must be completed. The time and cost associated with each task along a path are calculated, and the path that requires the greatest amount of elapsed time is the critical path. Calculation of the critical path enables project managers to monitor this series of tasks more closely than others and to shift resources to it if it begins to fall behind schedule.

PERT controls time and costs during the project and also facilitates finding the right balance between completing a project on time and completing it within the budget. PERT recognizes that projects are complex, that some tasks must be completed before others can be started, and that the appropriate way to manage a project is to define and control each task. Because projects often fall behind schedule, PERT is designed to facilitate getting a project back on schedule. PERT is based in part on the premise that subjective estimates of the total completion time for a project are usually greatly inferior to the sum of subjective estimates for each task.

PERT is a highly developed methodology, and full descriptions of it are widely available. Many variations of PERT exist, some of which are incorporated into computer programs and are available as computerized project management systems. PERT is explained in more detail in the appendix to this chapter.

SUMMARY

This chapter examined the theory of systems investigations and the life-cycle concept and its relationship to systems investigations. All information systems must eventually be replaced, and systems development activities are therefore more or less continuous in medium-sized and large companies. Students can expect to be involved in systems investigations in several ways.

The problem of gaining the full cooperation of people is the most critical concern in systems work—users, managers, and systems analysts can all exhibit behavior that inhibits a systems project. Several general principles of systems development, if followed, will ease people problems, provide needed structure to a systems investigation, and in other ways increase the likelihood that a successful system will result from a systems investigation. These principles constitute a part of the theory of systems development.

Auditors play significant roles in systems investigations, and management control of systems investigations is also important. Systems steering committees, computer department planning activities, and project management systems provide the three most important forms of management control of systems projects. Bar charts and PERT are types of project management systems.

REFERENCES

Braun, W. F., R. E. Bibaud and G. L. Hodgkins, "Planning for the Future Computer Complex," *Computer Decisions,* January 1973.

Canavan, Edward M., "Non-technical Side of Systems," *Journal of Systems Management,* September 1979.

Faerber, Leroy G., and Richard L. Ratliff, "People Problems behind MIS Failures," *Financial Executive,* April 1980.

Michaels, Andrew J., "Establishing PERT Systems," *Management Accounting,* October 1971.

Miller, William B., "Fundamentals of Project Planning," *Journal of Systems Management,* November 1978.

Petersen, Perry, "Project Control Systems," *Datamation,* June 1979.

Walker, Michael G., and Randolf Bracey, "Independent Auditing as Project Control," *Datamation,* March 1980.

KEY TERMS

systems life cylce: the time period that begins with the systems analysis for a new system and extends through its design, implementation, and use until the system is no longer adequate and a new systems analysis is undertaken to replace it; usually the life cycle is several years in length.

systems investigation: a systems project to analyze, design, and implement a new information system or to modify an existing one.

systems steering committee: a committee of senior executives who have the overall responsibility for monitoring and controlling the organization's information systems.

REVIEW QUESTIONS

1. What is a systems investigation? Provide several examples of systems investigations.

2. Explain the concept of a system's life cycle and its meaning for systems investigations. Is a system's life cycle the same as the period of time during which the systems investigation takes place?

3. How long does the systems maturity and maintenance phase last? How can it be extended?

4. State the purpose of each phase of the systems investigation.

5. What is the difference between a systems analyst and a programmer?

6. How can recent graduates from a business school participate usefully in systems investigations? What are the major shortcomings of these recent graduates with respect to this participation?

7. In what ways can experienced managers participate in systems investigations?

8. What role or roles can consultants play in a systems investigation?

9. What are the similarities and differences between large and small systems investigations?

10. Redraw Exhibit 14.4*a* and *b* to include the cost of overhauling the system.

11. Describe each of the participants in a systems investigation.

12. What are some of the reasons why employees sometimes do not cooperate fully with a systems investigation?

13. Jimmy Jones, a systems analyst, interviewed Robert Clark about the system used by several of Mr. Clark's employees. The system had been designed several years ago by Mr. Clark. Mr. Jones stated during this discussion: "The system clearly has outlived its usefulness and needs to be replaced; I'll have to talk to one of the people using the system, too, to document the system's problems before I design a new one." Later, while talking to an employee, Mr. Jones said, "The new system I design will be very efficient—it will need only about half as many people as the present system does." What mistakes did Mr. Jones probably make?

14. What is meant by each of the following?
    (*a*) Management involvement in a systems project
    (*b*) A balanced systems project portfolio
    (*c*) Identification of the right systems problem
    (*d*) A creeping commitment
    (*e*) Macro and micro systems design

15. For each of the general principles of systems investigations discussed in the chapter, state the following:
    (*a*) Its purpose and why it is useful
    (*b*) How, if at all, it would probably be applied differently in a small organization from the way it would be applied in a large one

16. What are internal auditors' roles in a systems investigation? How do you think external auditors roles are likely to be different?

17. What is management control over the information system, and how is this control exercised?

18. Why is control within the existing old information system so critical during the period of a systems investigation?

19. What are the advantages of a systems steering committee? Do you see any disadvantages? How is a small organization likely to accomplish the purposes of a systems steering committee?

20. Outline a planning system for an information systems department.

21. Compare and contrast bar charts and PERT.

PROBLEM

Assume that you and a friend have agreed on a day's activities. Each of you will attend your separate classes in the morning starting at 8 a.m. (Each class meets for 1 hour. You have two classes, and your friend has one class.) Then you must study for 2 hours, and you also plan to get started on a speech, which you must give at 3 p.m. After class your friend must mow and edge his lawn; he estimates that this activity will take about 3 hours. Then you plan to have lunch together at noon for 1 hour; if you are late for lunch, you will not be served. After lunch you will continue to work on your speech, and your friend will attend classes for 2 more hours. At 3 p.m. he will meet you at the student union on campus and listen to your speech at the weekly meeting of the Sailing Club; the speech must be given promptly at 3 p.m. You estimate that you need 2½ hours to prepare your speech. (*Note*: You may wish to read the appendix before starting this problem.)

1. Prepare a PERT system of the combined activities of you and your friend.
2. What is the critical path?
3. Which activity on the critical path is most likely to fall behind schedule? What resources can be allocated to it?

APPENDIX

Exhibit 14.10 portrays a very simple PERT project management system. In the exhibit the numbers in the circles indicate "nodes," or completed events, and the letters indicate tasks, or activities. Shown in parentheses beside each letter is the number of days required to complete that particular task. The structure of the diagram indicates that tasks A, B, and C must be completed before event 3 occurs.

Three paths through this PERT network can be discerned. Path 1 includes tasks A and E, path 2 includes tasks B and D, and path 3 includes tasks B, C, and E. Simple calculations indicate that path 3 is the critical path because the completion of tasks B, C, and E requires a total of 20 days, that is, 2 days more than path 1 and 5 days more than path 2. In order to ensure that the entire project will be completed within the scheduled 20 days, managers should give more attention to tasks B, C, and E than to the others. The project completion is shown as event 4.

If the project managers want to complete the entire project in less than 20 days, they must allocate more resources, such as more personnel or personnel with more useful skills, to tasks B, C, and E. For example, if task B can be completed in 5 days by replacing personnel now assigned to it with personnel who have more training in this task, the entire project will be completed in 18

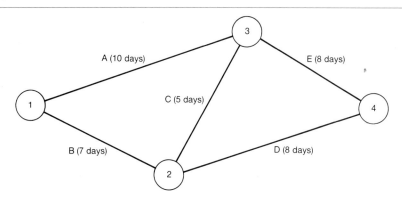

EXHIBIT 14.10
A PERT network.

Paths:
1. Tasks A and E = 18 days
2. Tasks B and D = 15 days
3. Tasks B, C, and E = 20 days

The "critical path" is path 3, consisting of tasks B, C, and E.

days. With this reassignment, both path 1 and path 3 become critical paths, and both must be monitored carefully to ensure project completion within 18 days.

PERT enables project managers to establish a schedule, monitor progress, and reallocate resources as necessary to stay on the schedule or to expedite the completion of a project. PERT has another interesting dimension; it can be used to assess performance after the project is completed. The PERT network is equivalent to a budget because days and costs are allocated (budgeted) to each task. After the completion of the project or even after the completion of each task, the actual times and costs can be compared with the PERT budgeted times and costs to determine time and cost variances. The variances can then be used to analyze performance and assign responsibility for this performance or to determine ways in which subsequent performance can be improved.

Steps in the Development of a PERT System

A PERT Project management system can be developed for a project by following the steps outlined below:

1. Separate the project into logical activities or tasks. Assign personnel to each task.

2. Identify the interdependencies among these tasks; that is, determine which tasks must be finished before others can be started.

3. Using engineering estimates, consensus opinion, or other techniques, determine the expected elapsed time for the most efficient completion of each task, for instance, an elapsed time of 5 days if two persons are assigned. Completion of a task is called an "event," which is a circle in the exhibit. This allocation of elapsed time and total personnel time becomes, in effect, two standards. Variances can be calculated if the actual elapsed or total time for completion differs from these standards.

4. Starting from the left and moving toward the right, construct a network similar to that shown in the exhibit. Construct the network so that events that must be done first are placed to the left of, and are connected to, those which follow.

5. Designate each of the completion nodes with a number and each of the activity lines with a letter; beside each letter, place the expected total elapsed time for that activity (hours, days, or weeks).

6. Calculate the critical path—that is, the earliest possible completion time—given the resource allocations made. This is important information for project control purposes.

7. Determine whether the critical path competition time makes an acceptable completion date possible. If the completion date is not acceptable, allocate more personnel, better-qualified personnel, or better or more equipment, or in other ways (such as by using air freight) plan to expedite the completion of the critical path tasks. Assess the additional costs, if any, of completing a project earlier and determine whether the time saved is worth the additional cost.

8. Monitor the activities as work progresses by completing regular reports at the milestone points, which usually coincide with the event completions, or nodes. Where possible, determine in advance of an activity's expected completion time whether the activity will be completed on schedule.

9. Reallocate resources if the critical path tasks fall behind schedule and it is essential that the entire project be completed on schedule. Again, evaluate the costs of bringing the project back on schedule.

CASE 1

The ABC Company

In response to criticism from several areas of the ABC Company, its comptroller (to whom the EDP manager reports) has appointed an EDP steering committee to "establish corporatewide priorities for information systems development and oversee this development." This committee is composed of the members as shown below and has the authority to ensure that the EDP manager makes his group conform to the priorities and directives of the EDP steering committee. The project teams are each to be headed by a systems analyst and will be appointed as projects are initiated. The EDP

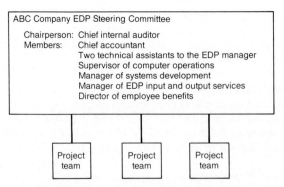

steering committee will meet every other month routinely, and more often if necessary.

Case Questions

1. Comment on the charge given the steering committee.

2. What are the purposes of a steering committee?

3. What organizational changes would you suggest?

4. What personnel changes would you suggest?

5. How should the components articulate?

6. Comment on the frequency of the meetings and how time should be spent at the meetings.

7. Should a user representative be in charge of a project team?

8. Are there any conflicts of interest in evidence?

CASE 2

The Systems Review Committee at Inland Steel

By John R. Lanahan

Guiding the Inland systems function is a steering committee which plays a key role in our activity. This committee is called the Systems Review Committee. The . . . members are:

V.P. of Finance—Chairman
V.P. Steel Manufacturing
Comptroller
V.P. Corporate Strategy
Senior V.P.
Pres. of J. T. Ryerson (A Warehouse Subsidiary)
V.P. Sales

It is our belief that the workings of this committee, representing the heads of all our users or "internal customers," has been the cornerstone of the development and installation of systems which effectively support the major operations of the business. The committee meets three times a year at a minimum.

The *first meeting* is set up to discuss current problems facing systems and data processing operations. Sample subjects have been the conflict between inter-active terminals and security, the need for an EDP audit function, and alternatives in CPU expansion.

In the first case it was explained to the Review Committee how the introduction of inter-active terminals posed a potential threat to the security of data and the integrity of fiduciary systems at the same time as they offered cost advantages and more effective systems applications. The issue was referred to the Board of Directors, which concluded

the cost and applications advantages were worth the risk. Subsequently, an EDP Audit Function was established to assure the fiduciary systems had proper controls built into them and that they were properly implemented.

The *second meeting* allows for an annual reiteration of the five-year plan, covering applications, manpower, and hardware. The *third meeting* is to finalize the annual plan and budget for next year.

It should not be assumed that the functions of the committee are nominal, stereotyped, or perfunctory. Three of the seven members are engineers who have had direct experience with computers, and all seven have had in-house and outside formal training in computers and their applications. They make real decisions about problems and engage in vigorous debate about the projects to be done and the resources required to do them. Since they represent the consortium of department heads, their approval sets a very favorable stage for development and implementation.

Source: "Information Systems at Inland Steel," *MIS Quarterly,* September 1978.

Case Questions

1. Evaluate Inland Steel's systems review committee.

2. What changes, if any, would you recommend, and why?

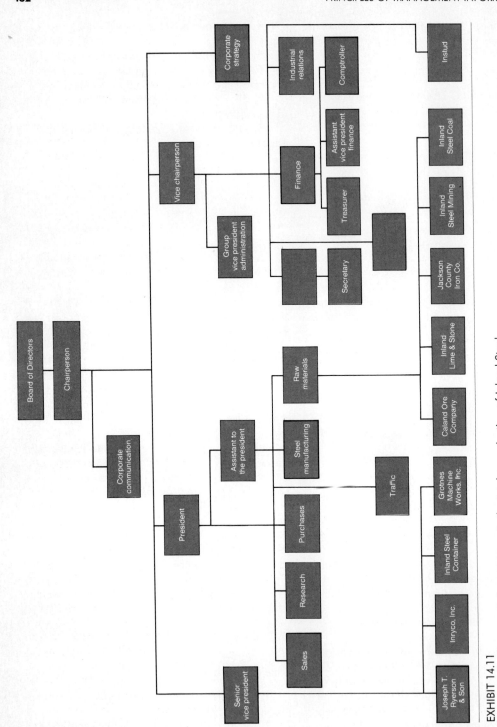

EXHIBIT 14.11
A systems review committee: positions in the total organization of Inland Steel.

CASE 3

Fruehauf Corporation

Fruehauf's standard project structure is described in their manual, which has over 200 pages. A system project is divided into the following twelve phases, and each phase in turn is divided into a number of defined tasks. . . .

Development Phases

A. Planning
  1. Initial investigation (3 tasks; 2 to 6 man-hours)
  2. Preliminary study (10 tasks; maximum of 3 man-weeks)
  3. System planning (15 tasks; 2 man-weeks to 2 man-months)
B. Development
  4. System requirements (28 tasks)
  5. System design (11 tasks)
  6. Program specifications (12 tasks, 6 repeated for each program)
  7. Conversion planning (10 tasks)
  8. Programming (12 tasks, 5 repeated for each program)
  9. User training (11 tasks)
  10. System testing (11 tasks)
C. Implementation
  11. Conversion (13 tasks)
  12. Post-implementation (10 tasks)

Several points should be noted. Each project is approached very cautiously at the outset, in terms of the amount of time expended on it. The initial investigation (phase 1) simply reviews the proposal briefly, determines if it warrants further study, and determines whether a new application system is involved or modifications to an existing system. The Director of Management Information Systems can authorize work to be performed on phase 1, and if the recommendation is to continue through phase 2, he can authorize the phase 2 work. Phase 2 is concerned with creating a general description of the proposed new system, as well as the plan and budget for the next phase.

It is at the end of phase 2 that the proposal first goes to the steering committee for review and for approval to continue. At this point, a maximum of three man-weeks of time have been expended,

and the expenditure will not have been great if the steering committee decides to terminate the project or to assign it a low priority.

Phase 3 is concerned with a thorough investigation of the existing system, if present, and a definition of that system in terms of files, inputs, outputs, and controls. The proposed system is also defined in the same terms, as much as possible. This phase really marks the beginning of the full-scale project, and user department personnel are very much involved in it. Between two man-weeks and two man-months are usually required for this phase. At the end of phase 3, the project is again reviewed by the steering committee, which must give approval for the continuation of phase 4. It is at this point that a plan and schedule for the balance of the project is presented for approval.

It should be mentioned that the Fruehauf system standards manual defines the standard documentation that must be prepared during each phase. This documentation must be completed before the project is reviewed by the steering committee. If the documentation is not completed, the phase has not been completed.

Phase 4 is concerned with a detailed definition of system requirements, primarily from the user's point of view. The project is again reviewed by the steering committee at the end of this phase. If the steering committee approves the continuation of the project, that approval covers the next three phases, up through conversion planning.

The next review point for the steering committee (after phase 7) is at the end of phase 10, when system testing has been completed. The steering committee determines whether or not conversion should begin. Finally, the steering committee performs a post-implementation review for evaluating the success of the project.

Thus the steering committee reviews each project after phases 2, 3, 4, 7, and 10, and determines whether it should be continued, terminated, or modified. The people at Touche Ross call this the "creeping commitment" concept.

In addition to this standard structure, Fruehauf uses a project control system which uses estimated man-hours for each task in each phase, and records actual versus estimated man-hours. They find that they do not need to use PERT or CPM charts, since most system projects follow a standard, rather simple pattern of activities.

When they first converted to this standard project structure, Fruehauf did not go back and create the standard documentation for all prior phases for the projects they already had under way. Instead, they had each project shift over to the standard documentation and review procedures, starting with the phase that each was then in.

Top management at Fruehauf is pleased with the management control they now have over their data processing projects. Not only are they working on more challenging projects but they also feel sure they are avoiding troubles and expenses that would have occurred under their old methods. The new methodology, as soon as it was installed, began to flag things that needed attention so that the troubles were corrected when they were still small in magnitude.

Source: EDP Analyzer, May 1973.

Questions

1. In what ways is Fruehauf's approach similar to, and different from, that suggested in the chapter?

2. What benefits accrue from Fruehauf's project structure?

3. Would Fruehauf's approach have been as effective if the steering committee had been eliminated? Why?

Chapter 15

THE PRELIMINARY STUDY
AND SYSTEMS
ANALYSIS PHASES

PAYOFF THOUGHT

The first major error that can—and often does—occur during a systems investigation is improper determination of the problem to be solved by a new system. If great care is not taken to define the problem properly, the entire systems investigation may be misdirected. Therefore, as much effort as is necessary must be devoted to this task.

CHAPTER OBJECTIVES

1. To provide a perspective on the nature of a systems investigation

2. To explain the nature of the preliminary study and systems analysis phases and the tools and techniques used during these phases

INTRODUCTION

This chapter begins the study of the activities involved in the several phases of a systems investigation. The preliminary study and systems analysis phases are similar in their objectives and methods. For the purposes of this discussion, the preliminary study phase is a separate, initial phase of the systems investigation, although it is sometimes described as a part of the systems analysis phase. During the preliminary study phase it is determined whether the systems problem discovered is serious enough to merit the expenditures of a significant amount of resources on the continuation of the systems investigation. In turn, the purpose of systems analysis is to establish in detail the specifications of a proposed new information system or a modification to an existing system. These specifications must state what the new system has to accomplish, but not how this will be accomplished. How the new system will accomplish the processing is determined during the systems design phase.

Systems investigation activities are often described as "systems analysis and design." However, the description is too limiting in that systems analysis and systems design are but two phases of the entire investigation. The term "systems development project" is equivalent to the term "systems investigation," since "systems development" describes a series of individual systems investigation projects that collectively bring about the overall development of an information system over a long period of time.

The general procedures and approach described in this chapter and subsequent ones are valid for all systems investigations. However, the formal, detailed investigation processes described here are most often utilized for large systems investigations. Smaller projects are less formal and detailed; although the same general analyses should be conducted, they usually are done in less depth and may be much less structured. The amount of resources devoted to the systems investigation should be tailored to the size of the project so that smaller investigations can be completed more economically.

A simple example involving the Abercrombie Company is presented throughout this chapter and the chapters on systems design and implementation.

THE NATURE OF SYSTEMS ANALYSIS

Systems analysis activities are quite different from the activities involved in the design and implementation of information systems. Of all the activities of systems investigation, analysis activities are by far the most people-oriented and the least structured. Analysis activities have several distinctive characteristics:

1. They involve determining what a system *should do*, which relates to the future and is partly a matter of opinion rather than fact.

2. They involve extensive *negotiation*, since each member of a community of users has an opinion, and yet during the analysis phase agreement must be reached about the nature of the problem as well as about what a new system should accomplish. A systems analyst must be extremely sensitive to people and must possess an abundance of diplomatic skills, as well as specific types of technical expertise. The interpersonal relationships in a systems analysis are complex, and hostility is frequently encountered or even created by the analyst.

3. *Compromise* is a fact of life in a systems analysis; often the compromises are so extensive that even though the analyst has done a superb job, no one is happy with the results.

4. *Estimates* rather than precise measurements are the order of the day in analysis work. Costs are estimated, computer memory requirements are estimated, future processing loads and the mixes of transaction types are estimated, and even workday requirements for project completion are estimated. Unfortunately, little of a student's course work does anything whatsoever to hone estimating skills.

5. Finally, a great deal of analysis activity is oriented to *preventing failure* rather than ensuring total success. It is not as important, for example, to find the one best set of systems specifications as it is to define the problem and develop systems specifications in ways that ensure that neither the investigation nor the resulting system will be a failure. It is more important to avoid all critical analysis phase errors than to do everything else completely right. A critical error, such as misdefining the problem, failing to consult a major systems user, or underestimating the systems capacity needed, can cause the entire project to become a disaster, no matter how well the other activities are carried out. Most major systems project failures are caused by mistakes made during the analysis phase.

It can be seen that technical training in information systems is only a part of the expertise required by analysts. Most important are an ability to deal with people (including knowing how to negotiate), a willingness to accept compromise, and a knowledge of what the critical mistakes are that must be avoided. Also important is an understanding of the organization and its industry, and especially of the functions being analyzed. While all this can be learned through course work to an extent, the best training consists of extensive experience working with other systems analysts.

STRUCTURED ANALYSIS

The interrelated concepts óf structured analysis, structured design, and structured programming are widely employed in systems investigations. For the purposes of this chapter, structured analysis is an approach to systems analysis that hinges on effectively partitioning the final product of the systems analysis phase: the systems requirements specifications.

With structured analysis, the systems requirements specifications are formulated as a series of modules rather than as one monolithic set of specifications.

The purposes of this modularization are threefold. First, each analyst of a project team can work separately and efficiently on different modules. Second, the structured modules can be more readily understood by all participants. Third, and most important, is the fact that modularization permits each aspect of the systems specifications to be separately and quickly revised. On the one hand, systems are developed in a dynamic environment, and new developments in the environment as well as new information uncovered during a systems investigation, both during and after the analysis phase, often suggest that the systems specifications should be changed. On the other hand, analysts have always believed that it is imperative to "freeze" (stop changing) the systems specifications (and later the design) at an early point, since late changes are difficult to implement in a monolithic systems specifications document and introduce additional complexity, uncertainty, and delay into the systems investigation. Structured analysis attempts to accommodate both of these conflicting needs. Only one module needs to be changed when the specifications must be changed, and this can be done more quickly because of modularization. At the same time, most of the systems specifications can remain frozen, which minimizes the chaos that is created when a change is made.

TYPES OF SYSTEMS INVESTIGATIONS

There are three general types of systems investigations:

1. Projects involving the acquisition of new hardware
2. Projects involving software for transactions processing systems
3. Projects involving the development of information systems for managers, which are also oriented toward software

Additionally, projects involving software can deal with developing new programs, modifying existing programs, or purchasing new programs. Many systems investigations involve both hardware and software. The principles of systems investigation are much the same for each of the three types of systems investigations, but the expertise required by the analysts and other participants in the systems investigations may be quite different for each type.

Hardware Projects

This type of project involves the evaluation of alternative computer hardware components and the different vendors that provide hardware. Computer hardware must be compared in terms of capability, capacity, reliability, cost, and compatibility. Capability has to do with whether the hardware can accomplish the tasks it is intended to accomplish. The capacity of hardware is often measured in terms of the number of transactions that can be processed in a given period of time.

Reliability pertains to the frequency of mechanical or electronic failure, including damage from heat, water, fire, and physical abuse. In terms of cost, original costs, maintenance costs, and operating costs must be assessed. Operating costs include labor costs and the costs of utilities; hardware components require electric power, and some require air conditioning and other special considerations.

When hardware components are evaluated, their compatibility with other existing components and software systems must be considered. Hardware compatibility means that components can be interconnected; if, after interconnection, they continue to function properly, they are compatible. Ideally, 100 percent compatibility of existing components with new components (often referred to as "plug compatibility") and of existing programs with new systems is sought. In practice, 100 percent compatibility may not be possible.

Technological obsolescence and length of life also are concerns. Often systems analysts consider the tradeoff between acquiring equipment which embodies the most advanced new technology, but which may not be fully compatible with the existing system, and acquiring equipment which uses compatible technology but which will be technologically obsolete in a shorter period of time. Although hardware may become obsolete before it is worn out, physical length of life is important. In general, entirely electronic components have an indefinite life span, but they can be damaged or destroyed inadvertently. However, mechanical or electromechanical components typically wear out within 6 to 15 years, depending on how heavily they are used. If all else is equal, the systems analyst should prefer electronic components to electromechanical or mechanical components.

Hardware must be installed, and often the site must be modified in order to accommodate the new equipment. Necessary changes may include the installation of a new floor, of a special fire-fighting system, and of sophisticated temperature and humidity control systems. Auxiliary power sources may be required to guarantee a constant power source. While some components retain data in their memory if the power source is temporarily interrupted, others do not; consequently, valuable data is lost if power is interrupted even momentarily. "Backup" and "restart" capabilities are also important; these enable the equipment to back up and reprocess the data that was being processed when a power shortage or other cause interrupted processing.

Hardware selection requires capable hardware analysts and technicians. Often, the specialists conducting this portion of a systems investigation are electrical engineers or people who have completed computer science programs. Quite often hardware selection is not a continuous system development activity, and the selection of major components takes place infrequently. For this reason, an organization may prefer to rely heavily on outside consultants rather than incur the expense of employing specialists in hardware evaluation.

Software Projects

Systems investigations involving software usually focus on one of three general activities: (1) the acquisition from vendors of prewritten software packages, (2) the development and programming of new applications or sytems programs, or (3) the "maintenance" (revision) of existing computer applications programs. Small organizations are more likely to buy their programs in ready-to-use form, and large organizations are more likely to develop their own programs, although there is now a growing trend toward the purchase of programs by large companies.

Whichever of the three types of software investigations is undertaken, it is likely that a systems analysis will be required to determine the nature of the programs needed. Generally, a systems analyst gathers the information necessary to serve as a basis for the programming effort or for determining what software package should be purchased.

The writing of new programs and the revision of old ones are continuing activities in most data processing installations of significant size. Indeed, these activities represent one of the major costs of these data processing centers; typically, programming costs easily exceed 50 percent of the total costs of data processing. These activities are worthy of the careful attention of managers to ensure that programming is done efficiently and that programming projects are carefully controlled.

The development of entirely new programs and the revision of old ones are similar activities. In the mature, large data processing organization, about 70 percent of the total programming effort is usually devoted to maintaining existing programs. For a new program, elaborate procedures are used to ensure that the program is thoroughly "debugged" and all errors in the program are located, that unauthorized program instructions are not incorporated, and that the program operates efficiently. For a program that is being revised, equally elaborate procedures should be used to ensure that the changes made were authorized and that the revised program has been properly debugged and tested. However, a formal management system such as PERT is more likely to be used for projects that involve the development of new programs than for projects involving the revision of old ones, since the former tend to be larger, more complex, and less routine than the latter.

Program maintenance is required for one of three general reasons: existing programs require correction because they do not process correctly

Incorrect Processing Situations Necessitating Program Changes (Corrective Maintenance)   EXHIBIT 15.1

1. Incomplete debugging of the new program causes it to process improperly. (It may be months or years before all bugs are discovered).

2. A prior program change introduced unexpected logic errors into the program.

3. Control weaknesses are discovered in the programs that permit unauthorized access to data files.

4. An audit trail cannot be established because a program does not record the processing it does.

(corrective maintenance), they must be modified to conform to a changed environment (adaptive maintenance), or they can provide greater benefits if improvements are made (perfective maintenance). Typical situations necessitating corrective maintenance are listed in Exhibit 15.1, and examples of reasons for performing adaptive maintenance are given in Exhibit 15.2.

Corrective maintenance and adaptive maintenance share the characteristic that usually these program changes are required and often must be made in acccordance with externally imposed deadlines. Ordinarily, no costs/benefits analysis is made to determine whether to proceed with corrective or adaptive maintenance.

The third type of maintenance, perfective maintenance, is intended to improve the efficiency of the system or enhance its benefits to users. Examples of situations leading to perfective maintenance are shown in Exhibit 15.3. Perfective maintenance is not required and can be deferred if resources are not available to make these changes. The relative costs and benefits of these proposed changes are usually evaluated. However,

Changes in the Environment Necessitating Program Changes (Adaptive Maintenance)   EXHIBIT 15.2

1. New accounting rules are employed, such as switching from LIFO to FIFO.

2. Payroll tax legislation is changed.

3. New regulatory reports are required.

4. New operating problems or changes in the management control system require new types of information.

5. A subsidiary is acquired or sold.

6. Union contract changes alter the pension fund accounting.

7. An internal reorganization changes the hierarchy of the organization, and reports must be redesigned.

Situations Involving Greater Benefits and Leading to Program Changes   EXHIBIT 15.3
(Perfective Maintenance)

---

1. An existing file structure is redesigned to increase processing efficiency.

2. Files are merged to eliminate the need for transfer files and intermediate processing.

3. Program changes will enable the program to be processed in less time.

4. A new vice president asks for changes in periodic reports.

5. Managers perceive ways to use additional information that can be incorporated into their present reports.

---

if a proposed change is not time-consuming, it may be undertaken without making any costs/benefits analysis, or after making only a limited analysis. Even in such a case, however, normal program change controls should be used, including prior approval, full debugging, and formal acceptance after completion. Many program maintenance activities also involve changes in the data files.

Consider, for example, the effect of item 2 in Exhibit 15.2 on an organization that conducts operations in a dozen states. Because each state has different payroll tax laws, the payroll files for each state will be organized differently, and the organization will have a dozen sets of slightly different payroll programs. Very likely, the payroll tax regulations of each state will change several times a year. The payroll files, and therefore the payroll programs for each file, must then be altered; each file change may require that several programs be revised. The required changes in payroll programs may number more than 100 each year and could keep one specialist payroll programmer occupied nearly full-time in perpetuity.

Consider item 5 in Exhibit 15.3. If a manager decides to include in a periodic report information about the estimated time of arrival of purchase orders that is not in the files, an analyst will first have to consult with the manager to establish precisely what information about purchase order arrival times should be reported, and in what form. Then a systems designer must revise the purchase order file or design a separate purchase order back-order file. Finally, the programs that process the purchase order file must be changed to retrieve the desired information from the existing file or from a new back-order file and to incorporate this into the report.

Management Information Systems Projects

While management information systems projects usually involve programming effort, the nonprogramming aspects become relatively more complex and critical, to the point where the entire character of these projects is different from that of transactions processing systems projects. The development of management systems focuses much more on analyzing managerial activities than on designing and developing computer programs. In comparison, the analysis of operations activities tends to consist of a straightforward study of operations and an optimization of the flow of the transactions through the system. Most programmers and systems analysts are well suited for operations analysis.

On the other hand, analysts who deal with managerial systems must understand both the managerial activities and the decision-making processes. Also, their perspective on information systems must be broad enough to include much more than just computer technology. The creation of managerial systems may require that information from several sources, including both computer and noncomputer sources, be skillfully blended into one system. Exhibit 15.4 demonstrates that an understanding of management processes is the critical ingredient in developing the MIS and that, in addition to expertise relating to computers, a more general knowledge of information systems is required. In Exhibit 15.4*b,* the pie slices with heavy outlines represent the skills that are especially critical to the analysis of managerial systems projects. Because a knowledge of management processes and management information system is so important, MIS projects often employ analysts who have been trained as managers rather than analysts whose backgrounds are in technical disciplines. As suggested in both parts of the exhibit, personnel skills, analysis tools, and some knowledge of computers are important for all analysts, no matter what type of project is being undertaken.

While different types of systems investigations require different kinds of expertise, the systems investigation principles are much the same for each. Further discussions of systems investigations will not take specific cognizance of the different kinds of expertise required for different types of investigations.

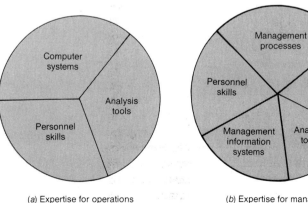

(a) Expertise for operations information systems

(b) Expertise for managerial information systems

EXHIBIT 15.4
The knowledge and skills requirements of a systems analyst.

A PERSPECTIVE ON INFORMATION SYSTEMS DEVELOPMENT

Exhibit 15.5 provides an overall perspective on systems development. Each level shapes, directly or indirectly, the nature of a particular systems investigation. This perspective is useful because it establishes a framework for all systems investigations and also shows the scope of a particular system project relative to the entire MIS.

The top part of the exhibit relates to the entire organization within which the project is undertaken. Projects are shaped by the organization structure (its specific hierarchy as well as its degree of managerial centralization), since the information system must be tailored to this structure.

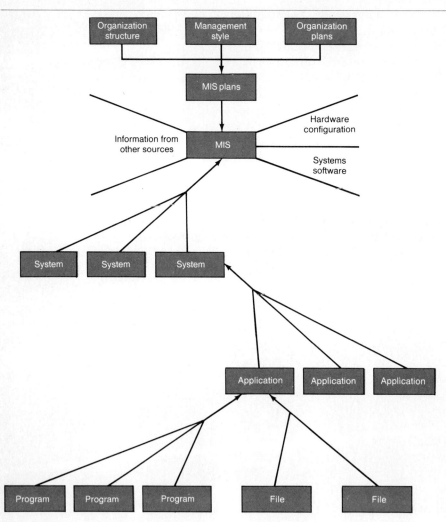

EXHIBIT 15.5
An overall perspective of systems development.

Management style also influences projects (and particularly managerial systems projects) since it determines information needs. Both of these, plus the organization's plans (and especially its long-range plans), establish the context within which MIS plans are developed. In turn, the MIS plans control the direction of the future development of the entire MIS, and the existing MIS has been shaped by past MIS plans.

As indicated at the bottom of Exhibit 15.5, individual programs are first written or purchased, and their associated files are designed. One or more programs are combined with one or more files to form an "application" that accomplishes a specific task, such as adding new employees to the payroll. Usually several applications constitute a "system," such as a payroll system. Numerous systems, including payroll, budgeting, accounts receivable, and dozens of others, together with information provided by noncomputer sources and systems software and hardware, make up the organization's MIS.

The scope and the context of a specific systems investigation are determined primarily by its level, which may be any of the following:

1. MIS
2. System
3. Application
4. Program/file

At the program/file level, the task is to develop, purchase, or maintain a particular program or to design or modify a particular file. The reference point for these tasks is the next level—the *applications* level—and the programmer/analyst needs little or no additional knowledge about the entire system. When designing or revising an entire application, an understanding of the entire *system* of which the application is a part is essential. Similarly, when designing or revising an MIS, a broad understanding of *all* its *systems* is important. Often the career of the programmer/analyst begins at the program/file level, and then progresses to the applications level and then to the systems level; finally, when a broad understanding of both operations and management systems has been acquired, the programmer/analyst has the experience needed to play a leading role in MIS development projects.

In an introductory programming class, students usually gain experience at the program/file level of systems work in that ordinarily they write a few simple programs but do not ever develop a complete application. From this vantage point, it is natural that they tend to equate systems work with programming, when in fact the higher-level activities are much richer in their variety and broader in their scope. Students who major in information systems, however, are likely to have course work at the level of systems development, and often at the MIS level.

GENERAL APPROACHES TO SYSTEMS INVESTIGATIONS

There are four general approaches to systems development:

1. Conducting a systems analysis and then seeking to purchase programs or a system from an outside vendor
2. Making a prototype of the new programs or systems
3. Having user groups develop their own programs and systems, either with or without the assistance of professional analysts, designers, or programmers
4. Developing programs and systems in the traditional manner, using professional systems personnel

The first three approaches are becoming increasingly important because of the large backlogs of undeveloped systems and the shortage of professional systems personnel. The second and third approaches have unusual aspects that are discussed separately below. Subsequent discussions have relevance to all four approaches.

Making a prototype, in essence, is an attempt to save development effort by eliminating an extensive and systematic approach to the analysis, design, and implementation phases. The process begins with a cursory rather than a thorough assessment of users' information needs conducted by systems developers, who then rapidly develop a working ("prototype") system, often within just a few days. Programs implemented in this way usually are developed with a productivity language that tells the computer what information is needed, rather than with detailed coded procedures within the program concerning how to extract the information needed by it.

The first version of the prototype system provides approximately the information sought, and users experiment with using the system. As they gain experience with the system, they use this experience to formulate additional information and system refinements needed, and the designers alter the system accordingly. After several rounds of this, the system is considered to be fully developed. This approach is sometimes used for the development of fairly simple managerial information systems (including DSS systems) but less frequently for more complex managerial systems, and it is seldom used for the development of transactions processing systems.

The prototype approach may be employed by users or professional systems personnel. When users develop managerial systems by means of this approach, the activity begins to be similar to the development of decision support systems.

The prototype approach is contrary to traditional systems development approaches, which emphasize precise definition of user needs in advance, followed by careful, systematic systems development. In contrast, prototyping emphasizes "quick and dirty" responses to loosely specified needs, with subsequent refinement and little concern about the operating efficiency of the completed systems. This approach is still in an experimental stage but has already been used in a number of companies.

User-developed systems—systems developed by persons who are not professional systems personnel—are the consequence of (1) the existence of productivity languages, (2) the shortage of qualified professional systems personnel, and, increasingly, (3) the existence in user groups of inexpensive microcomputers that are powerful enough to support one or more entire user systems. However, user-built systems are also developed using mainframe computers. The appeal of user-built systems is that they can be developed when needed, rather than when the priority position in the backlog of the system desired is reached. Also, because the systems are developed by their users, they are likely to be closely tailored to user needs and readily adaptable by users as those needs change.

A serious concern about user-developed systems, however, is that they frequently contain design errors, are not always properly debugged and tested, and often do not contain adequate data protection safeguards. Users usually do not have the systems development experience and knowledge possessed by professional systems personnel.

As noted in an earlier chapter, user-designed systems are expected to predominate in the near future. The concerns about these systems can be lessened if users follow the traditional systems development approach and use traditional analysis and design tools and techniques to the extent that they are relevant. In general, the greater the possible impact of a design flaw or data control shortcoming on the entire organization, the stronger the argument in favor of having professional systems personnel develop a system. Conversely, the more important it is for the success of the system that its designer and creator thoroughly understand the management processes that the system will serve, the stronger the argument in favor of users' conducting their own systems investigation and building their own system.

THE PRELIMINARY STUDY PHASE

The activities of the preliminary study phase of a systems investigation are summarized in Exhibit 15.6; these are problem discovery, preliminary analysis, and preparation of a preliminary study brief. The conditions that typically cause a systems investigation to be undertaken are shown in Exhibit 15.7. The systems investigation activities may begin when someone perceives that there is a problem with an existing system, when new technology or other circumstances present opportunities to improve efficiencies, when a manual information system needs to be computerized, or when new kinds of information are needed. Typical problems with an existing system include the presence of a large number of errors, late reports, inadequate processing capability, and excessive data processing

Summary of the Preliminary Study Phase   EXHIBIT 15.6

Problem or opportunity discovery: system obsolescence, system deterioration, new
  information needs, and so on

Preliminary study: a brief investigation by a systems analyst of the need for a systems
  investigation

Preparation of a preliminary analysis brief: statement of possible system problems and
  the analyst's recommendation and reasoning

Decision: to do nothing further, to defer the project, or to undertake a systems
  investigation

costs. More specific problems may also arise, such as inadequate cost
control within the organization, necessitating the implementation of a
standard costing system.

Often, a system user discovers a problem with the system or an
opportunity to improve it and requests an investigation. Sometimes it is
a systems analyst who perceives a problem or an opportunity. Many
problems with existing computer programs are first detected by programmers or other data processing personnel, who may request a program
modification. The computer operators or data processing management
personnel may detect a lack of capacity for peak periods, or they may
learn of more advanced equipment with features that would be useful.

Whoever discovers what appears to be a problem, and whatever its
nature, the problem is brought to the manager who has the authority to
authorize a preliminary study; this may be the vice president of information systems, the director of information systems, the manager of systems
development, or another manager. This manager reviews the facts and
authorizes or denies a preliminary study. The analyst assigned probably
will conduct several general interviews intended to verify the existence of
a problem, gather additional information about it, and permit an informed

Conditions Leading to a Systems Investigation   EXHIBIT 15.7

1. A problem with the existing system is discovered.

2. New technology or other opportunities can provide greater benefits or result in lower
   costs.

3. A formal system is thought to be needed where a manual or an informal one now
   exists.

4. New kinds of information are needed, for example, when a new line of business is
   added or a new regulatory report is required.

5. Resources become available for an investigation that previously was "on the back
   burner."

but tentative judgment about the problem and its seriousness. A preliminary study may require an hour, a day, or perhaps even several days, but the amount of time spent is generally quite modest relative to the total amount of time required if there is a follow-on systems investigation.

The preliminary study phase is usually a mini-analysis activity in which many of the tasks of systems analysis are accomplished, but in a superficial and quick manner. This phase is, in a sense, a "feasibility study" to determine whether a new system appears feasible; the systems analysis phase does this in full detail, and sometimes the concept of a "feasibility study" is associated with this phase. Whereas both these phases are oriented toward determining (broadly, during the first phase, and during the second in detail) whether *any* new system is feasible, during the design phase the feasibilities of several *specific* new systems are examined and compared; in this text the term "feasibility study" is reserved for the activities of the design phase.

If, after the preliminary study phase is complete, the analyst believes the problem merits further consideration, a preliminary study brief is prepared. The brief tentatively confirms the existence of a potentially important problem, estimates a range of the time and cost of a possible full-scale investigation, and speculates about the probable costs and benefits associated with revising the existing system or installing a new one. The brief is likely to recommend whether the systems investigation should continue, and it may even propose that a simple solution be considered before the investigation is continued; for example, another work shift may be suggested if computer capacity is too limited. All parties understand that the preliminary study brief is a very tentative document; at the most, it suggests only a commitment to additional investigation.

Abercrombie Company

Abercrombie Company is a medium-sized manufacturer of a broad line of sporting goods. The data processing operations manager has been studying statistics on the percentage of utilization for the computer system and has noted that this has recently edged above 80 percent.

"It's time to decide what computer will replace our present one," he concluded. "A new one could be installed in about a year if we started the analysis now. By that time, our present computer will be utilized to its maximum capacity." At the next meeting of the systems steering committee, this subject was brought up.

This brief will be reviewed by a manager within the computer systems department, and perhaps also by the systems steering committee. The problem involved will be evaluated relative to other known problems in other information systems. As a consequence of this, the problem may (1) be put aside as not deserving of additional attention, (2) be assigned a noncritical priority and set aside for future attention, or (3) be given the go-ahead for initiation of the systems analysis phase. The disposition of the problem should be consistent with long-range plans for systems development and priorities vis-à-vis other projects; the arguments of user groups should be given heavy weight in determining this disposition.

The decision to continue or not to continue the systems investigation constitutes the project's first milestone (sometimes referred to as a "checkpoint," "quick-kill point," or "go–no-go point"). A systems investigation has several milestones; at each one the project is either "killed" (canceled) or continued. The go–no-go decisions for major projects are made by the systems steering committee if one exists. The committee decides whether the findings of the study to that point merit continuation of the investigation. Without an explicit statement that the project is to continue, the project should stop. Milestones are also the points at which the project is replanned or at which more detailed planning of its remaining parts takes place. A typical project might embody 5 to 20 milestones.

Milestones impress upon systems personnel the idea of "creeping commitment," as described in the last chapter. The organization commits itself to the project only at each milestone, and the commitment is only to the next milestone, where another go–no-go decision is made. Without such a process, projects tend to acquire a life of their own because someone, often the analyst, has a vested interest in seeing them continue whether the costs/benefits ratio remains favorable or not. A significant proportion of systems projects that are started should be terminated at an early point because it can be seen that their costs or benefits will not be as originally expected.

If the decision is made to continue the systems investigation, it is communicated by a formal systems project charter, which is often called an "assignment brief." This brief consists of a set of directives that establish the overall objectives and the maximum permitted scope of the systems investigation, as well as the nature and quantities of the resources allocated to the project. The objectives describe what the systems investigation will attempt to accomplish. Any specific constraints on, or limitations of, project scope are also stated. The brief typically appoints some or all members of the task force for the project. The systems analysis phase then begins.

THE SYSTEMS ANALYSIS PHASE

There are six major components of the systems analysis phase:

1. The systems study proposal
2. The systems survey
3. Problem specification
4. The systems study proposal revision
5. Systems analysis
6. The systems requirements specifications report

Briefly, the systems study proposal is the initial planning document for the project, the systems survey is an analysis of the existing system, problem specification entails reaching agreement about the systems problem, the systems study proposal revision is the proposal altered as a consequence of the systems survey findings, and systems analysis determines what the new system should accomplish, which is specified by the systems requirements specifications report.

The Systems Study Proposal

After the assignment brief is received at the conclusion of the preliminary study phase, the project team plans the systems study activities in detail and also outlines the remainder of the systems analysis phase, as well as later parts of the systems investigation in less detail. A major part of this initial planning is the refinement of the objectives of the systems investigation if these have not been provided in adequate form. The resulting plan is here termed the "systems study proposal." Assuming that the initial proposal has been accepted, the systems survey is begun. Project planning is a vital process that continues throughout the investigation.

The Systems Survey

The purpose of the systems survey is to examine the existing information system. This examination includes the assessment and documentation of at least the following:

1. The total number of transactions of each type which are processed by the system at present and which will be processed in the foreseeable future

2. Normal-period, peak-period, and seasonal usage and variations of usage

3. The percentage of system capacity utilization

4. Trends in percentage of capacity utilization

5. Types of errors, error rates, and trends

6. The type and format of the documents and reports provided by the system, as determined by samples that are collected

7. The timeliness of the documents and reports

8. The utility of the reports provided

9. The reliability of the system, for example, its frequency of malfunction

10. How the old system could be improved

11. The nature and quality of service provided by the system

12. The responsibilities of specific employees within the system

13. The nature of any calculations performed by the system

14. Existing policies of the organization which influence the system

15. New kinds of data processing or reports that will probably be needed in the future

16. People problems that appear to be caused by the system, such as poor morale and absenteeism

17. People problems that affect the operation of the system

The systems survey should provide an understanding of the old system and knowledge useful for subsequent agreement about the nature and extent of the systems problem. During the systems survey, the focus is on three general considerations: determining the objectives of the present system, that is, the reasons for the existence of the system; establishing the general flow of transactions through the system; and gaining insights into the problems—including people problems—in the operation of the system.

No more effort than necessary should be expended on the systems survey. In particular, a study of the entire system in depth, along with full documentation of it, is not worthwhile if the old system will probably be replaced. Accordingly, the focus should be on analyzing and documenting the existing system in ways that highlight its problems and the information requirements of a new system. The study is overly thorough if the old system could be reconstructed from the documentation developed during the systems survey.

The systems survey concludes with a report that summarizes the investigative actions taken and the findings. Again, a recommendation may be made to terminate the study, temporarily suspend it, or continue the investigation. At this milestone the systems steering committee exercises its judgment and makes a decision.

Problem Specification

While the approach of "conserving resources and doing only what is clearly necessary" is appropriate for the systems survey, problem specification requires lavishing personnel resources on problem definition and examining and discussing the problem area from a variety of different perspectives. This is due to the fact that the most critical part of a systems investigation is the identification and careful specification of the problem. Even though the problem has been previously analyzed, important new information about the old system now exists as a result of the systems survey. Usually, additional resources are needed at this point to define and specify the problem properly. As an unbiased outside observer with specialized knowledge, a consultant can assist with this problem specification.

The most important issue is this: Is the perceived problem the problem that should be addressed by the investigation? Often the real problem is not a systems problem at all, or it is a quite different systems problem from the one that was originally thought to exist.

Not only must the problem be properly identified, but its proper scope and magnitude must also be specified. A common mistake is defining the problem too narrowly. The problem analysis should consider ways in which the problem is related to other possible problems in the organization.

When the systems analyst and users are confident that the problem is properly specified, the nature of the problem should be presented in full detail to the systems steering committee. The ensuing discussions should lead to a general consensus about the problem specifications and to a formalized statement of the problem. The committee should formally agree with the problem as finally specified. Consensus of the committee, composed of general managers with an overall perspective, decreases the chance that the problem will be misspecified. (Not uncommonly, the problem is restated by the committee.) Additionally, consensus ensures that no one individual or group later becomes a scapegoat if the system is designed to solve the wrong problem.

The Systems Study Proposal Revision

After the problem is fully specified and agreed to, the systems study proposal is revised by the analysts. This proposal, when approved, will (1) specify the remaining tasks in the systems analysis phase in detail and (2) outline the probable activities of the systems design and implementation phases. While the entire systems study may take several worker-months or worker-years to complete, the development of this proposal may consume only a few days. Until the systems study proposal is accepted and further work commences, the organization has committed relatively modest resources to the systems investigation.

The systems study proposal relies heavily on information gathered during the systems survey, but it also requires additional analyses and considerable project planning. A sample outline of a systems study proposal is shown in Exhibit 15.8. The first column lists the specific activities necessary to complete the remaining systems analysis phase activities, and the second column lists activities that will be involved in possible new systems.

A statement of personnel needs and a budget for the remainder of the systems analysis phase are included. These should be prepared in detail. However, the same information for the systems design and implementation phases can only be estimated, since it depends on the findings gathered during the remainder of the systems analysis phase. While a reasonably accurate schedule for the completion of the systems analysis phase can be arrived at, only a rough estimate of the schedule for the systems design and implementation phases can be provided.

Abercrombie Company

Abercrombie Company's data processing operations manager, Mr. Goldenrod, gathered operating statistics and presented them to the systems steering committee; they demonstrated that the present computer was

Outline of a Typical Systems Study Proposal EXHIBIT 15.8

The Systems Analysis Phase	The Systems Design and Implementation Phases
1. A statement of the problem	1. Alternative systems designs that should be considered
2. A statement of the objectives of the systems investigation	2. A tentative design phase budget
3. A statement of the scope of the systems investigation	3. A tentative design phase schedule
4. A summary of the expected benefits from a new system	4. A tentative implementation phase budget
5. A summary of the expected remaining costs of the systems investigation	5. A tentative implementation phase schedule
6. A statement of personnel needs for completion of the systems analysis phase	
7. The budget required for completion of the systems analysis phase	
8. A schedule for the systems analysis phase	
9. The expected format and outline of the systems requirements specifications report	

approaching its capacity. He stated the problem as "the need to replace our present computer." After a lengthy discussion, the problem was restated by the systems steering committee: "The problem isn't that we need a replacement computer—that's one possible solution to the problem. The problem appears to be that we're running out of excess computing capacity." The committee also saw a relationship between this problem and a possible need for new types of data processing capabilities. (*Question:* What are some other possible solutions to the problem?)

The final systems study proposal also includes a brief discussion of major alternatives, as indicated in the second column of Exhibit 15.8. These alternatives may be as broad as, for example, choosing a centralized system, a distributed system, or a decentralized system; this broad a perspective is especially likely to be taken at one of the higher levels shown in Exhibit 15.5, where explicit attention must be given to the overall organization of the information systems. If the focus of the systems investigation is at a lower level, the alternatives may be narrower, such as whether batch processing or single-transaction processing should be used for a particular application. Considering these alternatives can be compared roughly with considering alternatives for home entertainment equipment, such as a color television, a stereo system, or a swimming pool. Once it has been decided that a stereo system rather than a television or another "macro" alternative is preferred, for example, a number of alternatives within the broad category of stereo systems must be evaluated.

A discussion of these macro alternatives is an important part of the proposal because the systems steering committee needs information about the possible costs and benefits associated with continuing the project. Specification of alternatives permits a better-informed decision to be made about accepting the proposal for continuing the investigation. The committee cannot be well informed without at least some knowledge of the costs and benefits associated with each of several major alternatives.

The discussion of the major alternatives may include a general analysis of the probable economic, technical, and operational feasibility, as well as the general institutional desirability, of each alternative. While each of these considerations is extensively considered as a part of design phase activities, they need preliminary attention during the analysis phase. Economic feasibility asks: "Can we afford the new system, and what are its probable benefits?" Technical feasibility deals with: "Do we possess the technical expertise to implement and run the new system?" Operational feasibility inquires: "Would the new system be completed on time, and would it be accepted and used by our organization?" Institutional desirability says: "Despite the probable costs and benefits of the new system, is the project a good one to balance the risk in our systems project portfolio, has the organizational unit that will receive the new system already been much better treated than other units, and how well would the project support the entire organization's goals?" Answers to these questions cannot be definitive at this point, but they should be considered and can influence the systems steering committee's decision.

All parties involved recognize that continuing activities in the systems analysis phase may suggest additional alternatives and that subsequent analysis may discredit one or more alternatives. After possible revision and approval of the systems study proposal by the systems steering committee, the analysts begin systems analysis.

Systems Analysis

The focus of the systems survey is on the old system: its capacity, virtues, and shortcomings. In contrast, systems analysis focuses on the necessary accomplishments of a new system. The emphasis is on the type of information that the new system must provide, the required frequency and accuracy of reports, and other considerations shown in Exhibit 15.9. Systems analysis concludes with a systems requirements specifications report.

For managerial information systems projects, decision analysis (illustrated in Exhibit 15.10) is a useful approach to gathering the information.

Information Gathered during Systems Analysis   EXHIBIT 15.9

Documents and reports that must be provided by the new system

Details of the information needed for each document and report

The required frequency and distribution for each document and report

Probable sources of information for each document and report

The maximum permitted elapsed processing time for each job

The number of transactions of each type expected to be processed:
 In the immediate future
 At a specified time in the long-term future

Acceptable transaction processing accuracy levels and residual error rates

System expandability requirements

System reliability requirements

Specific circumstances for which processing controls are needed

Decision analysis focuses directly on each manager's decisions. These decisions specify the information that should be made available by the system to that manager. The first step in decision analysis is arriving at definitions of the decisions made by the managers involved. These definitions may require, first, an examination of the organization's formal position description for a manager, which should specify these decisions. Then both the manager and the manager's superior should be interviewed. Often the position description, the manager, and the manager's superior are not entirely in agreement about a manager's responsibilities. Disagreements should be reconciled before a system is designed.

The decision processes (the second step in the exhibit) must be ana-

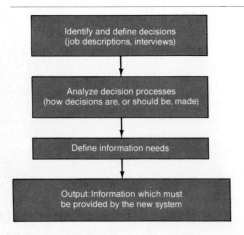

EXHIBIT 15.10
Decision analysis.

lyzed in consultation with the manager so that the systems analyst can understand the managerial activity associated with each decision. In order to have a thorough understanding, analysts often require training in management as well as in systems analysis.

Circumstances may dictate that the systems analyst accept the manager's statements about how the decisions should be made, or a skilled analyst may suggest alternative activities or analytic procedures for making the decisions. In either case, the manager and the analyst should agree about how the decisions are to be made because this determines the information that must be provided by the system. When the information needs for that system have been fully defined, they become a part of the systems requirements specifications report, which guides the design of the new system. The report becomes, in effect, the master plan for the development of the new system.

The Systems Requirements Specifications Report

The information gathered during the development of the specifications for a new system is voluminous and may represent several worker-months of effort. This information is organized into the systems requirements specifications report, which specifies what the system is required to accomplish. This report is sometimes called the "functional specifications document" or the "target document."

One of the characteristics of structured analysis is that the specifications are stated in a series of modules rather than in one monolithic document. Then, as the environment changes or as new information is uncovered that alters the specifications of the system needed, the systems requirements specifications report can be more easily altered. The contents of a typical systems requirements specifications report are shown in Exhibit 15.11, but the specifications vary widely from one systems project to another. As previously noted, they detail what the new system *must*

Contents of a Typical Systems Requirements Specifications Report   EXHIBIT 15.11

The required capacity of the system (numbers of transactions of each type, required file size, required memory size, and so on)

Special capabilities needed (such as inquiry into certain files)

Systems reliability requirements

Types, formats, and frequency of reports that must be provided

Acceptable error rates

Compatibility needs with other systems

Expandability requirements

Special security needs for sensitive data

accomplish, but they say nothing about *how* the system should accomplish this; determining the "how" is the objective of the design phase.

The systems requirements specifications report is presented to the systems steering committee. If accepted, the report serves as the guide for the ensuing systems design activities. The design alternative that is eventually accepted and implemented will be expected to meet the criteria established by the systems requirements specifications report. Additionally, these specifications represent the benchmark against which the new system is ultimately measured during the postaudit. The systems analysis phase concludes with acceptance of the systems requirements specifications report.

SYSTEMS ANALYSIS TOOLS AND TECHNIQUES

Whether the systems investigation is directed to hardware, software, or MIS considerations, many of the same systems analysis tools and techniques are used. Several of these tools and techniques are most relevant to the preliminary study and systems analysis phases, discussed earlier in this chapter; these tools and techniques are listed in Exhibit 15.12 and are briefly summarized below.

Interviewing

By far the most important systems analysis technique is interviewing. Interviewing is especially important throughout the preliminary study and systems analysis phases, but it is also useful for systems design, systems implementation, and subsequent maintenance of the system. Through interviews, analysts discover and verify facts about the old system and its problems, and they define the data input and reporting requirements of a new system. Interviewing helps get personnel involved in the systems investigation and promotes their cooperation. During interviews, personnel contribute their ideas for improvement of the existing system and their

---

Tools and Techniques Used during the Preliminary Study and Systems Analysis Phases	EXHIBIT 15.12

1. Interviewing
2. Flowcharting
3. Organization charts
4. Operating manuals
5. Position descriptions
6. Questionnaires
7. Systems documentation and forms reviews
8. Document walk-throughs
9. Direct observation
10. Work measurement
11. Examination of other systems

thoughts about additional information needs that could be satisfied by the system. Interestingly, internal and external auditors, like analysts, rely heavily on interviews for information about systems.

Information that is likely to be gathered during interviews is shown in Exhibit 15.13; this information helps define the nature of the systems investigation required from that point forward. However, various people problems are likely to be encountered during interviews. For example, interviewees may be uncooperative, or personality conflicts may develop during interviews.

Systems analysts should make an advance appointment for an interview, be prompt, and act professionally throughout the interview. Interview notes should be finalized shortly after the interview, and, to ensure mutual agreement about what happened during the interview, a copy of the notes should be approved by the person interviewed. Interviewing is discussed in more detail in the appendix to this chapter.

Flowcharting

Two general types of flowcharts are systems flowcharts, which display the general flow of transactions through the system, and program flowcharts, which portray all details of the logic of the system. A systems flowchart may provide sufficient detail about the old system for the preliminary study and systems analysis phases. Program flowcharts may be used extensively in the systems design phase to show the logic used in new systems. Flowcharts can also serve as documentation of systems. Because of the complexity of program flowcharts and the difficulty of altering them when the system is changed, many organizations use them less frequently than previously.

Organization Charts

Organization charts usually portray reporting relationships and indicate the general hierarchical flows of information. For these reasons, examining

---

Information Typically Gathered during Interviews　　　　　　　　　EXHIBIT 15.13

How the system actually works, including the handling of unusual items

What decisions are assisted by information from the system

The nature of the system problems

The location of documents describing the system

Statistics about the system, such as the number of transactions of each type processed, error rates, downtime, and percentage of late reports

What controls need to be included in the system

What manual activities are done in conjunction with the system

How noncomputerized information is used with information from the system organization charts is often an excellent way to begin examining the existing information system. However, organization charts can be misleading; few of the actual information flows are shown, and even relationships between managers may not be accurately reflected.

Operating Manuals

Manuals that describe the standard operating procedures for an existing system can provide useful information to the analyst. Manuals usually describe how a system operates, essential knowledge for an analyst. Equally important, operating manuals often describe control steps which must be taken or emphasize that particular actions must be controlled against; this helps the analyst establish the control strengths and weaknesses of an existing system, which helps define the needed controls in a new or a revised system.

Position Descriptions

Position descriptions detail the activities required of employees and the decisions that employees must make. Like organization charts, however, position descriptions should be considered indicative rather than definitive. As has been noted, a position description may state that a manager makes one set of decisions, but the manager will describe a somewhat different set, and the manager's superior will provide yet a third set. Interviews provide additional, clarifying information.

Questionnaires

Questionnaires are of two general types. One type is carefully structured to elicit specific details about an information system or about information needs. This type of questionnaire is often used when identical questions must be asked of multiple employees or when the information received must be provided anonymously. On the negative side, this type of questionnaire is impersonal, difficult to design, and misleading because even questions prepared by an expert at questionnaire construction can be misinterpreted, or answers provided may be insufficient or inadequate in other ways.

   The other questionnaire type is open-ended and general and is often used in conjunction with interviews. The questions pertain to a general subject area and are intended to initiate a discussion; it is the discussion, rather than the answers to the specific questions on the questionnaire, that provides most of the useful information. Often this type of questionnaire is sent ahead of time to an interviewee to encourage advance thought about the subjects that will be discussed during the interview.

Systems Documentation and Forms Reviews

A useful systems analysis technique is an examination of the documentation of the existing system. This documentation may include systems and program flowcharts, narrative descriptions of reports provided by the system, copies of reports and input forms, and other materials that describe the operation of the existing system. A careful study of transactions forms often provides a great deal of information about how the transactions are processed. Similarly, a careful study of the reports provided by a system will show what information the system provides.

Document Walk-Throughs

This technique consists of following (or carrying) a transaction document through the system to observe its processing at each workstation. Although a walk-through provides a good perspective on a system's operation, the technique is less useful if a significant portion of the transaction's processing is computerized; however, as noted in an earlier chapter, even in computerized systems the manual steps involved in preparing data for processing may be numerous. Document walk-throughs can verify interview information and flowcharts and are especially useful for bringing to light variations in processing caused by unapproved deviations from standard procedures or by unusual types of transactions.

Direct Observation

By walking past, or being present during, operating activities, a skilled analyst may gain insights by observing the system in operation. More formal observation may take place over a period of time or may be carried out on a sampling basis. Like document walk-throughs, direct observation indicates whether the system actually functions as it is supposed to. For example, the time required to carry out an activity is often inadvertently misrepresented to the analyst, and this can be discovered by observation. Perhaps the employee takes a coffee break during the time allotted to a particular task, or perhaps the employee not only processes documents but also transports them to another department or makes sure that the activity at a previous workstation has been carried out completely and accurately; such things may be overlooked when methods other than direct observation are used.

Work Measurement

An analysis of the present system at the operations level may include work measurement. The analyst measures the amount of work that is completed at a workstation during a given period of time or measures the efficiency with which an employee is processing transactions. Using a body of knowledge about work measurement, analysts can make careful judgments about how much processing (or other work) should be accomplished by a given employee. By extrapolation, the analyst estimates how many transactions can be processed during a given time period by a proposed new system in which several employees participate.

Examination of Other Systems

Quite often analysts are able to visit other organizations to study their systems. This provides important insights into the shortcomings of the existing system, as well as fresh ideas about designs for effective new systems.

SUMMARY

This chapter considered structured analysis concepts, explained the three types of systems investigations (hardware projects, software projects, and MIS projects), presented a perspective on several dimensions and contexts of information systems development activities, examined four general approaches to systems investigations, and discussed several systems investigation tools and techniques. The personnel involved in each of the three types of systems investigation projects need different kinds of skills. Of the several tools and techniques that systems analysts use, the most important is interviewing. Seen in context, the development of an individual computer program is only a small portion of the totality of systems investigation activities.

The purpose of the preliminary study phase of a system's life cycle is to determine, with a minimum expenditure of resources, whether a full-scale systems investigation should be undertaken. If a decision to undertake a systems investigation is made the systems analysis phase is initiated. The key tasks in this phase are (1) studying the existing system, (2) reaching agreement about the nature of the systems problem, (3) preparing a proposal for continuation of the systems investigation, (4) analyzing the information that a new system must provide, and (5) formally stating the specifications of the new system as a guide for the remainder of the systems investigation and doing this in modular, easily maintained form. Throughout the preliminary study and the systems analysis phases, milestones represent points at which progress is evaluated and go–no-go decisions are made.

REFERENCES

DeMarco, Tom, *Structured Analysis and System Specification,* Englewood Cliffs, NJ: Prentice-Hall, 1979.

Gremillion, Lee L., and Philip Pyburn, "Breaking the Systems Development Bottleneck," *Harvard Business Review,* March–April 1983, p. 130.

KEY TERMS

structured analysis: an approach to systems analysis that involves accomplishing the analysis as a series of modules rather than as one comprehensive analysis.
systems survey: the examination and evaluation of an existing information system.
systems study proposal: a formal written request to initiate a systems project.
systems requirements specifications: a fully detailed statement of what a proposed new information system must accomplish.

REVIEW QUESTIONS

1. What are the similarities and differences between the preliminary study phase and the systems analysis phase?

2. It is said that systems analysis involves extensive negotiation; why is this so?

3. What activities in systems analysis require that an analyst be sensitive to people and able to work well with people?

4. Explain how each of the following relates to systems analysis activities:
(*a*) Negotiation
(*b*) Compromise
(*c*) Estimation
(*d*) Failure prevention

5. What skills does an analyst need that typically cannot be readily learned in a classroom?

6. What advantages are students in less technical disciplines likely to have over engineering and computer science students in terms of being systems analysts?

7. What is structured analysis, and what are its characteristics?

8. Explain the nature of the three major types of systems investigations.

9. What knowledge is an analyst who is assigned to a management information systems project likely to need that is not as critical for other types of systems projects?

10. What is the nature of each of the following?
(*a*) Corrective maintenance
(*b*) Adaptive maintenance
(*c*) Perfective maintenance

11. Assume that your homework assignment is to write a program that retrieves and analyzes data from a data file made available by the instructor. Where does this type of systems project fit in the entire scheme of systems investigations?

12. Explain why a broad perspective on an organization's information systems is useful to an analyst or designer who is working at the systems level on a particular new system.

13. What is involved in the use of a prototype? In what situations is this approach especially beneficial?

14. What are the advantages and disadvantages of having users develop their own systems?

15. What steps are being taken by users because of large backlogs of systems projects?

16. What is the purpose of the preliminary study phase?

17. What is a preliminary analysis brief, and how is it used?

18. Cite several situations described in the chapter that illustrate the use of "creeping commitment."

19. Why is it necessary to conduct a survey of the existing system? How thorough should this survey be?

20. Why is proper problem specification so important in a systems investigation? How is it accomplished? Why is a consensus about the systems problem useful?

21. What is a systems study proposal?

22. What is the nature of the activities that take place during systems analysis?

23. Explain decision analysis.

24. What is the purpose of the systems requirements specifications report?

25. Review the chapter to determine the role that the systems steering committee plays during the preliminary study phase and the systems analysis phase; describe this role.

26. What is the most important systems analysis technique? Why is it so important?

27. Of what utility are organization charts in understanding data flows in an organization?

APPENDIX: Interviewing Techniques

Formal interviewing is difficult and complex; it is not a matter of dropping in to visit another employee for a casual chat. Entire courses are devoted to teaching interviewing techniques to systems analysts, and these courses are worthwhile. Some general rules are presented below:

1. During a systems investigation, interviewees are likely to be sensitive about their position with the organization, alert to implied criticism of them or their work, and busier than usual because the systems investigation may have already interrupted their schedules or caused them to alter their work activities. For these reasons a systems analyst must deal with interviewees in a professional manner and with unusual tact and courtesy.

2. Before the interviews begin, the interviewees' immediate superiors should be asked to explain to them the importance of, and need for, cooperation with the analyst. If an interviewee is aware of higher-level support for the project, cooperation is more likely.

3. The analyst should make an appointment for an interview in advance, at

the convenience of the interviewee, and should arrive promptly at the interview time. No one likes unpleasant surprises, and "dropping in" for an unscheduled interview is definitely in this category. Also, an appointment assures the analyst that the interviewee will take the necessary time for a discussion. Making an appointment also emphasizes the importance of the project and the interview.

4. The analyst should prepare for the interview by reviewing systems documentation and in other ways determining, to the greatest extent possible, what information the interviewee now receives and the structure of the system that provides it. This preinterview analysis should attempt to identify any vested interests in the present system or any other biases that might influence the interviewee's responses.

5. Each interview should have a specific purpose and should not be a "fishing expedition." This purpose should be communicated to the interviewee in advance.

6. A list of the questions to be asked should be sent in advance; this list may be in the form of an open-ended questionnaire. This procedure tends to put the interviewee at ease, it permits carefully formulated answers to be prepared in advance, it makes the interview more efficient, and it reduces the incidence of off-the-cuff answers.

7. During the interview the analyst should be straightforward, honest, forthright, and not mysterious. The analyst should appear to be someone who deserves the interviewee's cooperation. The analyst should be enthusiastic, but thoroughly professional.

8. The analyst should avoid making threatening statements that suggest replacement of the present system or significant changes in the interviewee's job. In the same vein, the analyst should sound sympathetic, supportive, and reassuring. For many employees, a major systems change can be traumatic, and they may need the analyst's moral support.

9. The analyst should avoid taking a specific and unequivocal position. For example, the analyst may say, "We are examining the present system to see whether there are any problems and to consult with everyone about what action, if any, should be taken." The analyst should not state that the system has particular problems or that it will be changed; the systems analysis process may reveal a need for changes, but no one should jump to conclusions in advance.

10. The analyst should not ask for recommendations initially and should not ask the interviewee to make a commitment either in favor of or against the present system or a possible new system. Early commitments make it more difficult later to accept any solution that is different from the one previously recommended.

11. The analyst should fulfill any promises made during the interview. For example, the analyst may agree to talk to other persons suggested by the interviewee or to forward materials requested by the interviewee. The analyst should be candid if a request cannot be honored.

12. The analyst should be brief during an interview. Many interviewees are busy and cannot devote a large amount of time to an interview.

13. The analyst should not talk about an interview with other interviewees. Each person interviewed needs assurance of confidentiality. If the analyst appears to violate the confidentiality of others, the analyst's credibility and the interviewee's cooperation will dissolve.

14. After the interview, the analyst should put the factual information provided by the interviewee into report form and send a copy to the interviewee for at least a negative evalution; that is, if the interviewee disagrees with any of the statements in the report, it should be possible to ask that they be corrected. These interview reports serve as a record of the facts gathered.

Interviewing is as much an art as a science, and sometimes a fine line must be walked. For example, it may be difficult to elicit information from an interviewee while simultaneously preventing the interviewee from making strongly negative statements about the present information system.

Chapter 16

INFORMATION SYSTEMS DESIGN AND IMPLEMENTATION

PAYOFF THOUGHT

Careful project control and management are a key to successful systems development; with careful control, several of the activities of the design and development phases can proceed simultaneously, which will shorten the total systems investigation time.

CHAPTER OBJECTIVES

1. To explain the activities and processes of the systems design and implementation phases

2. To give particular attention to the selection and evaluation of prewritten programs available for purchase

3. To discuss the purpose and objectives of the systems postaudit

INTRODUCTION

This chapter examines the final two phases of systems investigation activities as well as the postaudit and continuing systems maintenance activities. A bewildering variety of design tasks are discussed in this chapter, although not all occur in every systems investigation. The student should refer to Exhibit 16.1 frequently while reading the chapter; this exhibit is a schematic that portrays the main tasks of the systems design phase and how they interrelate.

SYSTEMS DESIGN

Systems design determines *how* a system will accomplish what it must accomplish; it involves configuring the software and hardware components of a system so that after installation the system will fully satisfy the systems specifications established at the end of the systems analysis phase. A further aspect of systems design is configuring the system so that it will be acceptable to both system users and system operators. If the system as designed cannot simultaneously meet the established specifications and be acceptable to users and operators, as is sometimes discovered, the

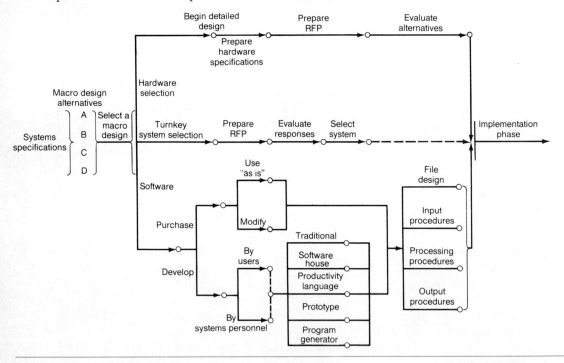

EXHIBIT 16.1
Systems design phase activities.

systems analysis activities must be renewed, and the systems specifications modified. An advantage of structured analysis is that only one or a few of the many design modules may need revision.

The Design Process

Whereas systems analysis is an unstructured, people-oriented activity that involves estimates and negotiation, systems design is more structured and technical in nature. Systems designers need a high level of technical skills, whereas systems analysts have a much greater need for interpersonal skills. However, there is extensive interaction among the members of the design team; thus the ability of designers to work with one another is a consideration. A number of specialized activities are conducted during the design phase, and a project team for a large systems design project could consist of programmers, file designers, input control specialists, hardware acquisition experts, software acquisition specialists, project management specialists, telecommunications network experts, file designers, and specialized consultants, although usually not all would be involved at the same time.

Systems consultants are most frequently used during the design and implementation phases because both these phases involve several specialized, highly technical activities, and there is a good chance that an organization does not employ personnel who collectively possess all the expertise needed. Among the most frequently employed external personnel are hardware selection consultants, contract programmers, software selection consultants, and project management consultants. Also, public accounting firms may be asked to ensure that adequate systems controls are implemented and that the final system is auditable.

Exhibit 16.1 shows the activities that may occur during systems design. All will be examined in this chapter, and the exhibit will be gradually explained as the chapter progresses. Additionally, the following two chapters will extend the discussion in this chapter relating to equipment selection.

In the exhibit, the lines represent activities or alternatives, and the circle represent events or decisions. As can be seen, the systems design is based on the systems specifications; a series of macro design alternatives are then developed and analyzed, and one is selected. Depending on which macro design is chosen, the remainder of the systems design will focus on one of the following: a hardware selection, selection of a turnkey system, or software design. Often a project combines software design and hardware selection. A turnkey selection project involves selecting a complete, ready-to-operate system consisting of a computer system and computer programs provided by a vendor; turnkey system selection is examined in the next chapter.

Structured Design

Structured design involves beginning the system design with the broadest set of alternative designs permitted by the established project scope (referred to here as the "macro design alternatives") and proceeding through a series of progressively narrower sets of alternatives until the narrowest set (the "micro design alternatives") fully defines the system in detail. This "layered" approach of beginning with a macro design and proceeding through multiple layers to a final micro design is sometimes referred to as "successive refinement" or "top-down design." With reference to Exhibit 16.1, after the macro design alternatives selection activity, structured design concepts are most relevant to the software development activities shown at the bottom of the exhibit. Using structured design, a clear, simple systems structure is sought for software that is easily maintainable, that is, readily modifiable. This is achieved in part by modular design so that each module performs one logical task and has as few linkages with other software modules as possible.

Macro Design

The initial systems macro design should be as broad as the scope of the systems investigation permits. Referring to Exhibit 15.5, if the scope was as broad as the MIS level, for example, the first macro design might consider alternatives such as (1) a decentralized system, (2) a centralized

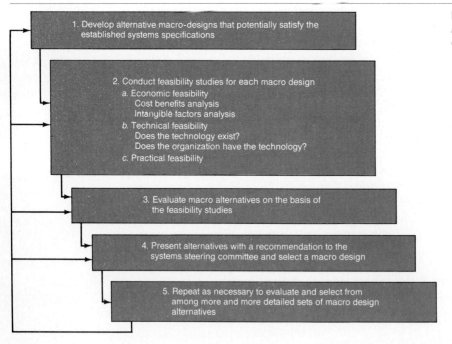

EXHIBIT 16.2
Macro systems design activities.

system, or (3) a distributed system. Or, if the systems investigation was restricted to designing one system, as portrayed in Exhibit 15.5, the macro design might consider alternatives such as whether a data base or a traditional file system should be used.

Systems design can be likened to a Chinese puzzle in which boxes are contained within other boxes. A highest-level set of macro designs is analyzed, and one alternative is chosen; then another set of macro design alternatives that exists within that alternative is evaluated; within that chosen alternative another, more detailed set is contained, this is evaluated, and one alternative is chosen; and so on. Exhibit 16.2 outlines the macro systems design phase activities and shows the approximate sequencing of these activities. The exhibit indicates that steps 1 through 4, leading to the evaluation of macro designs, are repeated as necessary. Commonly, three or more levels of macro alternatives are evaluated sequentially in a systems investigation that has a fairly broad scope.

To illustrate this process, assume that for the first macro design, three macro design alternatives are considered: (1) a centralized accounts receivable system, (2) a decentralized accounts receivable system, and (3) a distributed accounts receivable system. Each alternative is evaluated in a general way as to its economic, technical, and practical feasibility. Often, a tentative decision can be made at this highest macro level without extensive effort because corporate policy or philosophy makes one alternative obviously more appealing.

If a decentralized accounts receivable system is chosen, the next round of alternative macro designs might include the alternatives of (1) batch processing, (2) single-transaction entry, and (3) combined batch and single-transaction processing. Again, only enough design is completed to serve as a reasonable basis for evaluating the approximate costs and benefits and for making a tentative choice from among the alternatives. However, typically as successive levels of alternatives are considered, the feasibility analyses become increasingly more detailed. This is illustrated in Exhibit 16.3. Eventually, a specific configuration is chosen that is designed in detail.

Note that other macro design alternatives could also be presented in Exhibit 16.3. For example, after the choice of a decentralized system, analysts could consider the feasibilities of these macro design alternatives: decentralizing to each branch or decentralizing only to each city (so that a city containing several branch retail outlets would have only one accounts receivable system). Macro alternatives relating to hardware would be considered also.

Abercrombie Company
The steering committee considered three sets of macro alternatives.
1. Add no capabilities to the system

2. Add a data base capability
3. Add a telecommunications capability
4. Develop a distributed system

Decision: add data base and telecommunications capabilities using terminals now and design the system to accommodate later addition of computing power to convert to a distributed processing system.
1. Add a third operating shift to the computer center
2. Increase the capacity of the system by replacing or extending the computer system
3. Purchase computer time from an outside vendor (a timesharing company)

Decision: increase capacity
1. Increase capacity by adding another computer and a communications front-end device
2. Increase capacity by adding memory and an additional processor (CPU) to the present computer
3. Increase capacity by replacing the computer with a larger computer that already possesses a data base capability and a communications front-end device

Decision: replace the computer with a larger computer with the needed new capabilities

---

A Hierarchy of Nested Macro Design Alternatives*   EXHIBIT 16.3

1. Macro design alternatives, set 1:
    (a) Conduct feasibility studies for:
        A centralized accounts receivable system
        A decentralized accounts receivable system
        A distributed accounts receivable system
    (b) Evaluate alternatives and make a tentative decision: a decentralized system
2. Macro design alternatives, set 2:
    (a) Conduct feasibility studies for:
        Batch processing
        Single-transaction processing
        Combined batch and single-transaction processing
    (b) Evaluate alternatives and make a tentative decision: batch processing
3. Macro design alternatives, set 3:
    (a) Conduct feasibility studies for:
        Periodic accounts receivable report capability only
        Periodic reports and on-line inquiry capability
        Periodic and on-call reports and inquiry capability
    (b) Evaluate alternatives and make a tentative decision: periodic reports and on-line inquiry capability
4. Conduct the micro design for a decentralized, batch-processing, periodic reporting, and on-line inquiry system

---

* The systems investigation objective is to develop an efficient accounts receivable system that provides quality customer service for an organization with multiple sales branches in several cities.

Feasibility Studies

As noted in the preceding chapter, attention must be devoted at several points during the systems investigation to the feasibility of a new system, including during the systems analysis phase. Generally, however, the most thorough feasibility analyses, or feasibility studies, are completed during the systems design phase, typically during consideration of successive sets of macro and micro alternatives. Feasibility studies entail considering the technical, economic, and operational feasibility of each alternative, as well as whether or not the project is appropriate given the political and other institutional context factors as previously considered; all but this last will be considered here.

Technical Feasibility

Technical feasibility analysis evaluates whether equipment and software are available (or, in the case of software, whether it can be developed) that have the technical capabilities required by each alternative design being considered. Technical feasibility studies also consider the interfaces between the existing systems and the new system. For example, components that have different circuitry specifications cannot be interconnected, and software programs cannot pass data to other programs if they have different data formats or coding systems; such components and programs are not technically compatible. However, incompatible systems can be interfaced by emulation, which is circuitry designed to make the components compatible, or by simulation, which is a computer program that establishes compatibility, but often these approaches to technical feasibility are not readily available or are too costly.

Technical feasibility studies also deal with whether the organization has personnel who possess the technical expertise required to design, implement, operate, and maintain the proposed system. If the personnel do not have these skills, they may be trained, or new employees or consultants may be hired who have the expertise. Nevertheless, a lack of technical expertise within the organization may lead to the rejection of a particular alternative.

Economic Feasibility

Economic feasibility studies involve an analysis of the costs and benefits associated with each project alternative. With cost/benefits analysis, all costs and benefits of acquiring and operating each alternative system are identified and a two-way comparison is made. First, the expected costs of each alternative are compared with its expected benefits to ensure that benefits will exceed costs. Then the costs/benefits ratio of each alternative is compared with the costs/benefits ratios of the other alternatives to identify the alternative that is economically the most attractive. A third comparison that is usually implicit relates to ways in which the organization could spend its money other than on a systems project.

The costs of the implementation typically include the remaining cost of the systems investigation (for this purpose, already incurred, or "sunk," costs are not relevant), the costs of hardware and software, the operating costs of the system for its expected lifetime, and the costs of labor, supplies, energy, repairs, and maintenance. Throughout costs/benefits analysis, the organization should rely upon traditional financial analysis concepts and tools such as sunk-cost theory, differential cost analysis, and discounted cash flow analysis.

Some costs and benefits can be fairly easily quantified. Readily quantifiable benefits are of two general types: cost savings, such as decreased operating costs, and direct revenue increases. As an example of the latter, a customer may have contracted to provide orders of a known amount if the organization will implement an information system that provides the customer with continuous information about the in-process manufacturing status of planned merchandise shipments to that the customer's own customers can be provided with accurate estimates of when the merchandise will be available.

A major flaw in many costs/benefits analyses is inadequate attention to intangible costs and benefits. These are aspects of the new systems alternatives which do affect costs and revenues and should be evaluated but which affect them in ways that cannot be easily quantified. Intangible factors are often related to the quality of information provided by the system and to the sometimes subtle ways in which this information affects the organization, such as by altering attitudes so that information becomes viewed as a resource.

Often, systems designers feel uncomfortable basing recommendations on "vague" intangibles that must be estimated, as opposed to so-called "hard facts" of easily quantifiable costs and benefits; they prefer to be able to justify their recommendations with objectively determined data. When more emphasis is on quantifiable costs and benefits than on intangible costs and benefits, a bias against a new system is likely to exist because most costs are readily quantifiable, whereas many of the most important benefits may be intangible and so would not be properly considered.

Two major intangible benefits are better customer service and better managerial information. For example, customers may receive more timely and accurate information about shipments, more accurate statements and other reports, and new services. Electronic bank tellers which enable customers to conduct banking operations 24 hours a day and which may result in more customers and revenue for the bank are an example of a new customer service. Additionally, a new system may provide a better image of the organization to its customers, vendors, and employees that helps attract more customers or helps retain employees.

Significant intangible benefits can accrue to managers from a new information system. Indeed, the major impetus for developing a system may be the expectation of more accurate or more timely information, a better report format, or reports that are more focused on particular problem areas. For example, the reports may be received sooner after the close of the period, or the new system may make information available on an inquiry basis at all times. Additionally, in many cases a new system provides information that was not previously available at all, such as information about standard costs or incremental costs.

There may also be less obvious intangible benefits. A new system may provide better control over the operations of the organization, or it may be more readily audited or audited at a lower cost. If the computer performs more of the menial and routine aspects of employee activities, jobs may be upgraded. A final intangible benefit is that the experience gained from the systems investigation and from the use of a more advanced information system often places the organization in a better position to take advantage of future developments in computer and information systems technology. For example, the experience gained from the development of a personnel data base is likely to be invaluable if the organization decides to implement a financial data base; not only will the financial data base design be favorably affected, but also its development cost will be reduced, which is a cost saving accruing to the next systems project that should be considered as a benefit provided by the current project.

Most intangible costs and benefits of an alternative indirectly affect dollar outlays or revenues, but these are difficult to measure. One approach to quantifying intangible costs and benefits is the following:

1. Identify causes and direct effects. For example, the direct effect of computerizing repetitive tasks may be that a new system upgrades existing jobs and improves morale.

2. Identify indirect effects. For example, improved morale may result in about 5 percent less absenteeism and a 10 percent lower employee turnover rate.

3. Estimate the economic impact of indirect effects for the estimated life of the system. For example, reduced schedule delays and overtime wages due to reduced absenteeism may save about $2000 per year, and reduced new employee training costs due to reduced employee turnover may save about $3000 per year. The total benefit (cost saving) due to upgrading existing jobs would then be about $5000 per year, or $20,000 for an estimated 4-year life of the system. (The time value of money is not considered in this simple example.)

This simple approach can be used for a wide variety of intangible costs and benefits. Although arbitrary and subjective, it is preferable to ignoring intangibles. This approach might be described as "tangiblizing the intangibles."

An alternative approach is to leave the intangibles unquantified. Then, users and systems designers discuss these and reach an agreement about the relative importance of the quantified and the intangible costs and benefits. Too often, however, the intangible costs and benefits are never fully discussed, and no attempt is made to reach an agreement about their importance.

Operational Feasibility

Operational feasibility involves a determination of the probability that a new system will, in fact, be used as intended. At least four aspects of operational feasibility should be considered. First, a new system can be too complex or cumbersome for the organization's users or the operators of the system. If it is, users may ignore the new system, or they may use it in ways that cause errors or system breakdowns.

Second, a new system can elicit unusual resistance from users as a consequence of a work ethnic, fear of displacement, vested interests in the old system, or other reasons. The possibility of resistance to change to the new system must be carefully explored for each alternative. Third, a new system may introduce change too rapidly to enable personnel to adapt to it and accept it. A sudden change that has not been previously announced, explained, and "sold" to users may itself create resistance. No matter how attractive a system may be economically, if an operational feasibility assessment indicates that users probably will not accept the system or that its use will result in a large number of errors or significantly lowered morale, the system usually should not be implemented.

A final consideration is the probability of subsequent system obsolescence. Technology that has been announced but is not yet available may be preferable to the technology that is embodied in one or more of the alternatives now being compared, or anticipated changes in management practices or policies may make a new system obsolete quickly. In either case, implementation of the alternative under consideration becomes impractical.

A frequent result of negative findings about a system's operational feasibility is that the system is not eliminated but instead is simplified to enhance its usability. Other possibilities are that public relations or training programs are designed that focus on overcoming resistance to the new system, or ways are developed to phase in the new system over a long time period so that the sudden total change that would traumatize the users or operators is converted into a series of small changes.

Selection of Macro Alternatives

A macro design is chosen as a consequence of a cycle of feasibility studies, or, where a series of sets of macro design alternatives is evaluated, a selection from each set is made sequentially. As shown in step 4 of Exhibit 16.2, the alternatives within each set are presented to the systems steering committee, along with a recommendation concerning the preferred alternative. A formal report is made at this time. The report includes an analysis of each alternative, the recommendation of the study team, and the reason for the recommendation; usually, a summary is included which discusses the alternatives in less detail than the main body of the report and which includes a statement of the recommendation. If several alternatives appear to be good choices, a recommendation of one in preference to the others may not be made. During the presentation, the systems steering committee members are likely to ask questions that reflect a broad perspective on the organization and its goals. The committee may accept the recommendation of the project team, may request more information, may endorse another alternative, or may request that other alternatives be considered. This is also a milestone in the systems investigation, and the project should cease at this point unless the systems steering committee explicitly indicates that it should continue.

An evaluation of the macro design alternatives must be made in consideration of the results of the economic, technical, and operational feasibility studies. This evaluation is not based on a weighted average of these feasibility study results; an alternative that is technically or operationally infeasible must be abandoned.

After an alternative macro design has been tentatively selected, an activity that is normally associated with the implementation phase may be started: educating and "selling" user departments and system operators. At this point, the project team knows the general nature of the new system and can advocate its implementation. This education and selling must be careful and thorough in order to forestall opposition to the new system and to gain the maximum possible cooperation of users with the systems design team.

Detailed Design

The detailed, or micro, design activities are quite different for projects of different types, such as for hardware acquisition, turnkey system selection, software purchase, and software development, which are the major alternatives presented in Exhibit 16.1. Exhibit 16.4 shows these differences. In a systems investigation of broad scope, such as the development of a new accounts receivable system, the detailed design phase may also include the activities listed in Exhibit 16.5

Detailed design of a system is carried out within the boundaries of the particular combination of macro designs chosen. Design of the input-output system, design of the processing system and the sequence of activities to process data and prepare reports, and specification of the processing capacities of hardware components are among the detailed design tasks that may be associated with a major systems project.

The sequence of activities usually varies, depending on the nature of

Detailed Design Alternatives and Activities EXHIBIT 16.4

Alternative	Detailed Design Activity
Equipment acquisition	Specify the characteristics that the equipment must have
Turnkey system selection	Evaluate the characteristics that the available equipment and software have
Software purchase	Examine in detail the characteristics of the software available; design data files
Software development	Design the logic of the data flows and design data files

the project. A typical approach, however, is illustrated in Exhibit 16.6. In the exhibit, the output system that produces reports or documents is designed first: often this defines the data that must be gathered and input to the system. Usually, the focus of the analysis activities is on defining the nature of the information that must be output by the system.

Abercrombie Company

During the next 4 months, on the basis of the "grand design'" of a new, larger system with data base and telecommunications capabilities, the design team did the following:

1. Reviewed state-of-the-art technology relating to data bases, telecommunications, and most-recent-generation computer systems
2. Established a detailed design for the new system that specified the required capabilities and capacities of a new computer system, systems software, and peripheral devices
3. Developed an overall telecommunications configuration that detailed the nature of the communications network, the location of the terminals, and the eventual location of smaller computers when the system would be converted to a distributed system
4. Developed a schedule for new system implementation and a schedule and priorities for conversion of existing files and programs to the new system

---

Next the data collection system is designed; this design activity may start in a user area by specifying what data will be collected and how it will be converted to machine-readable form. The system of entering the data into the computer includes the design of an input system that delineates personnel procedures and specifies the input controls.

Often the data collection and input systems are extensive and labor-intensive, involving as many as 30 separate manual activities. A major way in which information systems efficiency and control over the information systems can be improved is by devising ways to automate these

Typical Detailed Design Activities   EXHIBIT 16.5

1. Design the data collection system

2. Design the input system

3. Design the data processing system

4. Design the file structure

5. Design the file update procedures

6. Analyze the data storage requirements

7. Design the inquiry retrieval system

8. Design the information reporting system

9. Design the applications programs

10. Design the security system

activities; point-of-sale transaction recording and entry, already discussed, is one technique that can be used to accomplish this.

Next the file system is designed. File design includes determining the type of file organization (sequential or indexed sequential organization, for example, and disk or magnetic tape), the record and field lengths for each record type, and record formats. Also included are data storage

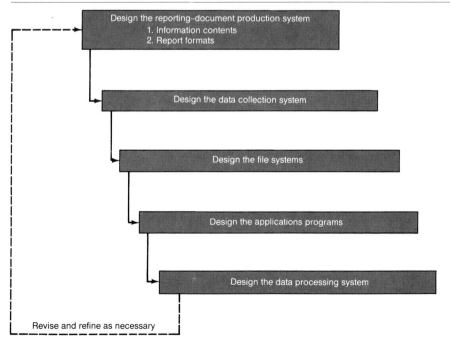

EXHIBIT 16.6
A typical detailed
design sequence.

requirements; measurements must be made of the maximum probable memory requirements of all records to be maintained in memory. The design of the file update procedures includes determining who has the authority for file updates and for establishing procedures for deleting records, adding records, and performing other file maintenance tasks. If the system is to have an inquiry capability, the design must specify how the right to retrieve information from remote terminals is determined, the input codes that will be used for information retrieval, and the type of output devices that will be utilized, along with related considerations.

When the file design has been determined, the needed structure and organization of the applications programs can be more readily perceived. Designing the applications programs is one of the major tasks in those systems investigations which involve programming. This activity includes determining the number of programs and the function of each; for example, one payroll program could simultaneously add new employees to, and delete terminated employees from, the master file, or each of these functions could be completed by a separate program. Program design also encompasses the preparation of "systems flowcharts," which show the general information flows through the system, and "program flowcharts," which portray the full logic of the new system that must be embodied in each program. In concept, this design activity is separate from the implementation activity that consists of actual program writing and debugging. In practice, however, these activities are closely related, and the programming for some programs usually is undertaken before the design of others commences, which illustrates that the activities of the systems investigation phases are not carried out entirely sequentially but instead are performed partly simultaneously. Indeed, frequently a person designated as an analyst-programmer first detail-designs an application and then immediately afterward implements it by writing its programs before detail-designing the next application in the system.

Finally, with the approach shown in Exhibit 16.6, the data processing computer system is designed. This usually includes the development of a procedures manual (often called a "run manual") for computer operators that specifies the steps operators must take to process a particular application. Where computer programs are to be written, the detailed design of the data processing system often includes the development of data flowcharts, which show how data flows through the new system. During the implementation phase, these flowcharts serve as the basis for the actual writing of computer programs.

As noted, there is no set sequence of detailed design activities—the sequence depends on the nature of the project. Often, multiple detailed design tasks are in process simultaneously. Detailed design activities are typically fluid and interactive in nature; thus, for example, as design work progresses on the file structures, feedback is provided that affects the other design activities as they proceed. Typical detailed design activities are listed in Exhibit 16.5 in no particular order.

Systems Controls

During detailed design, attention must be devoted to including controls over data input, data processing, and report and other kinds of output. These controls must be consistent with an entire preestablished information system control framework that is based on the organization's perception of its data security risks. Additionally, the controls over computer systems become a part of the organization's overall internal control scheme. If a particular control needed in a system is not included in the system initially, it usually is difficult to incorporate it after the system is installed.

General Controls

Information systems controls fall into two broad classes: general controls and technical controls. General controls are those controls which are applicable to *all* applications, and they constitute a significant part of the preexisting control framework. Provisions for the supervision of activities, administrative policies pertaining to documentation, systems development practices, error-correction policies and procedures, and internal auditing policies relating to information systems are examples of general controls.

Technical Controls

Technical controls, sometimes termed applications controls, are controls over individual applications or sets of applications. These are controls over data input, data processing, data output, and report distribution. Batch input controls are an example; they involve keeping track of batches of input transactions using such techniques as record counts and batch transmittal slips.

There is a variety of processing control types, many of which are written into programs. Programs may include instructions, for example, that ensure that data in a particular record field is numeric or alphabetic, depending on which form is correct. Limits checks are also included in programs to ensure that expected maximum or minimum quantities are not exceeded, for example, that pay for a particular class of employees is not less than the minimum wage or greater than $10 per hour, that total gross pay does not exceed $800 per week for that class of employees, or that total hours per week do not exceed 80 for any employee. Each of these processing controls should be designed in by the program designers and then translated into specific program instructions by programmers.

Other processing controls relate to ensuring that computer operators process jobs properly. The run book that details the processing steps and a requirement that an operator sign off on a job so that responsibility for processing the job can be pinpointed are examples of processing controls. There are numerous other processing controls also.

Output controls consist of techniques to ensure that all transactions that were input have been fully processed and are reflected in reports or other output produced by the system. Distribution controls consist of procedures that ensure that documents and reports are distributed in a timely manner to all persons on the distribution list and to no others.

User Controls

User controls are another type of control. User groups have a responsibility to be as certain as possible that data processing has been properly accomplished. Users often develop elaborate controls, such as calculating in advance what certain of the results of processing should be. Often, user controls are so elaborate that they amount to a partial duplication of the processing of the computer system, which can be inefficient to the extreme. Systems designers should help design controls for users that enable them to know when errors have been made during data input, processing, or output.

Error-Correction Controls

Error correction is a complex task. It is certain that errors will be made, no matter how good the new system is. Further, the probability of making a second error while correcting an existing one is much greater than the probability of making other types of errors. Therefore, error-correction procedures should be designed in advance and should be given careful attention. Often, the procedures require that errors of a particular type be accumulated for a week or longer and then be corrected all at once by skilled specialists. Sign-offs are often used when error corrections have been independently checked and found to be proper.

Systems Investigation Controls

Systems projects must themselves be controlled. Appointing a systems steering committee, using project control systems, and providing good supervision are all sound systems investigation control methods. Additional methods are also required. These include instituting a system of authorizing each task within a systems project (such as authorizing the writing of a specific program) and using controls that ensure that the new system is properly debugged and tested.

Of particular importance during a systems investigation are procedures to guarantee that existing controls in the present system will continue in effect while a new system is designed and implemented. Often, there is a temptation to disregard controls that will soon be eliminated by a new system. Yet it is when a new system is being designed, tested, and installed that the old system is most vulnerable because of the general confusion caused by these activities.

Software: Make or Buy?

A critical decision during systems design is whether programs should be purchased or should be developed by the organization. As already noted, the activities during the design phase are quite different if the software is purchased from what they are if the software is designed and programmed by the organization.

Just a few years ago organizations had little choice as to whether to purchase or develop their own programs because relatively few quality programs were available for purchase. Now, however, the marketplace has burgeoned, and thousands of high-quality programs are offered for sale. An organization seeking an accounts receivable program, for example, might be able to choose from among dozens of suitable quality programs in the marketplace, although of course not all would have been written for, or be adaptable to, that organization's particular computer system.

Each organization (and each individual who owns a microcomputer system) must decide whether to purchase a needed computer program or to develop it by designing, coding, and then debugging the program until it is fully tested. Several considerations influence that decision. One is a shortage of qualified programmers. If too few programmers are available to develop a program, the organization may be forced to purchase packages that it otherwise would develop. Other considerations are the increasing cost of programming and the extent of the organization's backlog of programs awaiting development.

In many instances the programs available for purchase are more sophisticated than the programs the organization would probably develop. For example, many of the applications programs are fully integrated with other applications programs; thus in acquiring a set of programs from a vendor, the organization is actually acquiring a fully integrated system. An example of this is MRP systems, already discussed. Also, several sets of accounting programs are available that are integrated with a general ledger system and serve as the backbone of an entire accounting system. This integration is a powerful incentive for purchasing rather than developing programs.

While each decision as to whether a program should be purchased or developed depends upon the particular circumstances, certain generalizations hold true. One is that for microcomputer systems, a program should generally be purchased rather than developed if a suitable one can be found. This is due partly to the fact that programs for microcomputers are quite inexpensive, usually in the range of from $100 to $1500, and partly to the fact that microcomputer users tend to be less able to develop their own applications programs.

With respect to decisions for programs for larger computers, two general trends are evident. First, more and more large-scale applications programs are being purchased rather than developed. Typically, a medium-sized or large organization has a data processing staff of programmers who are able to modify purchased programs so that they fit the needs of the organization more closely. Second, more and more of the smaller specialized programs are being developed using productivity languages. It is fully expected that the decreased cost of developing these programs will more than offset their inefficiency of processing.

While the presumption should be that programs for microcomputers should be purchased if possible, in the case of programs for mainframe computers a careful analysis should be made to determine whether programs should be developed or purchased. In general, the steps of this analysis are:

1. Determining what processing must be accomplished. (This is done during systems analysis.)

2. Examining the marketplace for packages that have potential for accomplishing the required processing.

3. Comparing available packages with one another and with the alternative of developing the program within the organization.

Multiple criteria should be considered as part of step 3 above. These are shown in Exhibit 16.7.

Accounting general ledger, payroll, and other more or less standard accounting packages, as well as personnel packages, are especially likely candidates for purchase. Often, an existing program that was developed by an organization many years previously continues to function, although it is no longer satisfactory and is awaiting replacement, but it is low in priority for development; it may be sensible to replace such a program with a purchased program.

Purchased programs are often more economical, even when considering the possible costs of modification and maintenance and the training costs. Purchased programs also may be more reliable than programs written by an organization for its own use, since purchased programs may have been tested in hundreds or even thousands of other organizations. Most successful programs in the marketplace also are so well written that they process efficiently and utilize a minimum of memory space, attributes that are especially important for microcomputer programs. Finally, many packages available for purchase have several "extras" which the organization may not desperately need and would not wish to pay to have programmed but which can be useful and are provided at no additional

Considerations in Software Make-or-Buy Decisions   EXHIBIT 16.7

1. The extent to which each available program satisfies the systems requirements specifications

2. The ability of the programs to be modified as needs change

3. The extent to which each program can be tailored to the organization's needs and the cost of tailoring

4. The processsing efficiency of each program

5. The security and integrity features of each program

6. The extra capabilities provided by each program that are "nice but not necessary"

7. The number and nature of the processing steps required by each program and the manual labor these require

8. The service and maintenance reputation of each software vendor

9. The user friendliness of each program

10. The provisions of the contract for each program

11. The cost of the package and of continuing vendor support

12. The training provided by each vendor

cost; examples are report generators and a wide variety of possible report types and formats.

There are disadvantages, too, of purchased programs. It is seldom the case that a program is in all ways exactly what is needed by the organization. If modifications to a purchased program are required, no one in the organization has had experience with developing the program, and the modifications may be quite difficult to make, or they may even be forbidden by the purchase contract.

Many purchased programs will require modifications to suit the needs of the organization satisfactorily. One form of modification is actual revision of the program, which may be done by the vendor for the organization or by the organization's own programmers. Often programs are provided only in object code; because object code is nearly impossible to revise, an organization that anticipates that it will want to revise such a purchased program must insist, as a part of the contract, that a source code program be provided. If modifications are to be made by the purchaser, the source code language should be one that the organization's programmers are familiar with. For most purchased programs that must be revised prior to use, the cost of revision is between 10 to 30 percent of their original cost.

Purchased programs usually have a built-in receptivity to at least minor modifications, or options can be selected within the program; the extent of these is adequate in many cases. Typical are different depreciation formula choices that can be elected, the possibility of easily adding fields to records or of changing field lengths, and the option of data fields that are numeric, alphabetic, or alphanumeric. Using these and similar types of easily implemented changes, it is usually possible to tailor purchased programs to a degree, but seldom can they be completely tailored to an organization's needs.

An alternative to modifying a purchased program is to change business practices so that they conform to the program's structure. To most organizations this is not an attractive alternative, but an incentive is provided in some circumstances by the large amount of savings that would result from using a purchased program without revision. The program might require that certain data not normally gathered by the organization be input in order for the program to function, for example. If faced with the choice between making a costly modification so that the program will operate without certain data and routinely gathering the data for input even though it is not needed by the organization, it may be preferable to choose the latter course of action.

Purchased Program Sources

Thousands of programs are available for purchase. Computer manufacturers, large and small "software houses" (companies that specialize in developing software), and computer retail stores are possible sources. Often, these are nationally advertised in weekly trade journals such as *Infoworld* and *Computerworld* and in monthly journals such as *Datamation* and *Byte*; many are available by mail order.

Another source of programs is "user groups," or associations of users of a particular computer system. User groups often recognize a need for a specific program, which may then be developed by one member organization and made available to other members. For example, utility programs and extensions of existing operating systems are typically developed by a member organization and distributed through the user group.

Buying programs is risky. Some are difficult to install, undetected bugs may exist that will later haunt the purchaser, and many have not been adequately developed and tested or may not yet be available for delivery when advertised. There is a significant "fringe element" in the software marketplace that does not subscribe to ethical marketing practices, and potential buyers must be extremely wary. The best protection is, whenever possible, to deal only with vendors who are known to be reputable and who provide after-sale support such as training, answering questions, and correcting program defects.

Purchased Program Assessment

The assessment of programs considered for purchase is difficult. Fortunately, several independent organizations objectively assess programs for sale and report their evaluations. Such assessments are available from Auerbach, Datapro, and other evaluation companies for a fee. Also, journals, such as *Datamation,* periodically publish the results of comparative analyses of several software packages of a general type. Not only are these evaluations useful with respect to comparing the particular software packages, but they also provide indications of the typical capabilities of a class of programs.

The first step in assessing a program is determining whether, on paper, it meets the requirements specifications established during systems analysis. As a minimum, the following questions should be asked:

1. Can the program provide the needed reports?

2. Does the program have adequate capacity in terms of the number of transactions it can process, the number and length of fields per record it can process, the total file size permitted, and so on? This consideration is important for all programs and is especially critical for microcomputer programs, since many programs developed for microcomputers have severely limited capacity. Typically, for example, a single transaction cannot exceed a maximum amount, such as $9,999,999.99, and the number of records permitted in a customer file may be 500 or fewer.

3. How many processing runs on the computer are required to complete each data processing job? Some programs will perform several tasks each time they are run. Others perform only one task per run; thus the program must be run several times, requiring more operator time and computer processing to complete the job.

4. How long does the program take to process? The efficiency of program processing varies dramatically among programs that perform the same task—some may require several times as much "run time" as others and use several times as much of the computer's scarce resources. With microcomputers, slow programs also usually consume equivalently more operator time, since the operator normally is idle while waiting for a program to complete its processing. Frequently the same program has been adapted to run on several different computer systems but runs more efficiently on some systems than on others.

Current users of a program are a valuable source of information about its performance. They usually candidly describe both the unanticipated problems and the unexpected benefits of a particular program. Users are also an especially rich source of information about the services provided by vendors; they know, for example, whether a vendor has lived up to promises about completion dates for modifications (if any), has been prompt in finding and correcting problems, and has provided enhancements free or at a nominal charge as they become available. They know, too, how well a program has met their performance expectations, how easily it can be tailored to meet nonstandard needs, and what provisions of the contract are too restrictive, as well as how willing the vendor is to change these provisions.

Reputable vendors are willing to provide lists of previous purchasers of a program. Since there is a natural tendency to include on the list only the names of the most satisfied customers, it is advisable to ask each purchaser contacted for the names of other purchasers. If names that are not on the vendor's list are provided, it is especially important that these purchasers be contacted.

A final way of evaluating a program is to actually process data with it on the organization's own computer. Often called a "software benchmark test," this consists of using the organization's transactions to assess the program's processing speed and user friendliness and the operation of special features such as report-writing capabilities. Preparation for a software benchmark test may be considered too demanding, or only the most promising program may be benchmarked. Often, the vendor will not make a program available for a benchmark test. While useful, program benchmark tests are merely indicative, since only experience with a program in actual operation over a long period of time provides a full test of its advantages and limitations.

Concerns about Purchased Programs

The list of factors that are of concern to a potential program purchaser is long. Many have been mentioned already. Others that are particularly important are explored here.

Perhaps the most important consideration is gaining assurance that the program is fully compatible with the computer system the organization has. Will additional peripheral equipment be needed, for example? A program may require a specific type of input equipment or specialized output equipment such as printers with graphics capabilities. Perhaps the program will work only inefficiently with the size of main memory in the computer system, or perhaps it requires a specific version of the operating system. Other system configuration concerns abound.

In what ways is the program user-friendly, and in what ways does it lack user friendliness? Does the program provide documentation of its activities (such as transactions listings) that can be used to trace errors and to provide an audit trail? Is the program portable and thus capable of being transferred more or less intact to another computer if necessary, and is this permitted by the contract?

In general, the organization should avoid newly developed programs that have not yet stood the test of acceptance by the marketplace. Similarly, the organization should be wary of programs that have been successful on other computers but have been converted only recently to the type of computer used by the organization—often conversions are poorly done, or technical differences in the equipment prevent them from being entirely successful. Also, programs are frequently developed on a contract basis for a specific company and then sold to other companies in that industry. While a contract-developed program may suit the company it was developed for to a T, it is rarely as suitable for other organizations because their business practices are different.

The purchase contract for the software can be a major concern. Vendors' contracts are written in their favor, and therefore purchasers often have little recourse, no matter what goes wrong. The purchasing organization should insist that penalty clauses for nonperformance and delayed implementation be inserted and that the contract specify in detail what the program will accomplish, what follow-up services (such as training) will be provided, and what the vendor's contractual obligations are for modifications and conversion to the organization's computer system. All software contracts should be reviewed by the organization's attorney, and especially complex software contracts, as well as those involving large amounts of money, should be reviewed by an attorney who specializes in computer systems contracts.

A final concern is comparing purchase of a for-sale program with development of the program if none is purchased. In general, it is much easier to estimate the total cost of a purchased program than to estimate the cost of one that would be developed. The effort required to develop a new program is often grossly underestimated. The organization must be particularly concerned that estimated program development costs appear reasonable. The persons who estimate the development costs of a program should be informed that they will be held accountable for any extra cost if the alternative of purchasing a program is rejected in favor of developing one and if the developed program proves to cost more than the purchased program would have.

Software Development

If the organization decides to develop the programs that will be a part of the new system, there are still alternatives to consider, as indicated at the bottom of Exhibit 16.1. The first decision is whether the programs should be developed by users or by professional systems personnel. If the decision is that users should develop them, users are most likely to do this with a productivity language. Users may instead develop program design specifications and provide these to a software company for programming, or the software company may work with users to develop the design specifications.

If it is decided that the programs will be developed by professional systems personnel, the traditional methods at which these personnel excel are more likely to be used. Increasingly, however, professional programmers are also developing programs using productivity languages or program generators. While either users or systems personnel might use prototyping for program development, this approach is most often used for the development of decision support systems by managerial personnel.

The file design, input procedures, processing procedures, and output procedures development activities shown in Exhibit 16.1 could be done by either users or professional systems personnel. User groups usually undertake these activities only if they are relatively simple, straightforward, and small in scale, which is likely to be the case with microcomputer-based systems projects.

The Request for Proposal

A request for proposal (RFP) is a request that is prepared by the organization and given to vendors, asking the vendors to prepare a bid (proposal) and submit it to the organization. As indicated in Exhibit 16.1, a RFP is likely to be prepared for projects that involve the purchase of hardware, turnkey systems, or software. Typically, a company has identified three to six vendors whose products appear to potentially meet the company's requirements, and an identical RFP is submitted to each. Government agencies normally advertise for bids, and any vendor is entitled to submit a bid. The RFP contains all details that are necessary for a vendor to prepare a fully detailed proposal.

The timing of the RFP is a function of the circumstances. In some cases, equipment selection takes place immediately after the completion of the systems requirements specifications report at the end of the systems analysis phase; if an RFP is provided to vendors at this early time, before any design work has been done, in effect each vendor is asked to decide on an appropriate design for the information system. Such a vendor-provided design is not usually the consequence of a thorough understanding of the organization's operations, and it often results in an information system that does not serve the organization's needs. However, in some circumstances, particularly when the organization does not have skilled systems designers, this approach is satisfactory. Preferably, the RFP should be prepared after one or more macro design selection cycles have been completed.

If the RFP is for acquisition of equipment and is prepared after at least some design activity, this activity produces "design specifications" for equipment. On the basis of the requirements specifications, the design specifications establish a desired configuration that might include, for example, the required minimum main memory size, the required characteristics of secondary memory, and general types and capacities of input-output equipment needed, to name but three of dozens of possibilities. Usually, design specifications should be developed without reference to any specific models of equipment or to a particular vendor's product line. Generally, an RFP for equipment is prepared and the equipment is selected prior to the most detailed design efforts, since most of the detailed design must be done in recognition of the specifications of the equipment; for example, applications programs often must be designed with a careful eye toward the nature and possible limitations of the selected computer's operating system.

After responses to an RFP have been received, they are evaluated by the organization. Usually, each vendor whose bid is competitive in terms of price and meeting the requirements of the RFP is asked to make a presentation to explain the bid and the products proposed. During the presentation, the organization's representatives inquire about all aspects of the vendor's recommendations and bid. Frequently, vendors who survive this presentation are nevertheless asked to revise their proposals in significant respects. In general, the larger the dollar amount involved, the greater the effort the vendors are willing to devote to proposals.

Abercrombie Company

An RFP was prepared that included the computer systems design specifications already established. Separate RFPs were prepared for various peripheral devices and were sent to several computer and peripherals manufacturers.

THE IMPLEMENTATION PHASE

Systems implementation is the process of installing the newly designed system, including any purchased equipment and software. While the activities of this phase can vary widely, the most commonly encountered ones are those shown in Exhibit 16.8. Similar in this respect to systems design, systems implementation relies heavily on technical skills. Systems implementation usually is a highly structured activity.

Personnel Education and Training

Extensive education and training of personnel are often required with a new system. Computer operators often must be trained to run the new system, programmers may need training to complete implementation of the system or to maintain it, input operators may need training, and users

---

Systems Implementation Phase Activities   EXHIBIT 16.8

Personnel education and training

Programming

Site preparation

Equipment installation and checkout

Purchased software installation and checkout

File conversion

Use of the new system

Final checkout and acceptance

Documentation

often must be educated about the capabilities of the system as well as about how to collect and prepare data for it.

Usually education and training extend over a long period of time and, in order to be complete by the time the system is ready for operation, must be started as soon as the general characteristics of a new system become known. Also, early education helps identify possible people problems early and ensure that users and operators will cooperate with and use the new system. During indoctrination sessions the new system is described, new technology incorporated into the new system is introduced, and its expected advantages over the previous system are discussed.

Special training of systems designers may even precede completion of the systems analysis phase. Often, designers attend training programs to acquire the technical knowledge necessary to conduct proper feasibility studies and make informed judgments. If, for example, a macro alternative considered is a data base system, but no one in the organization has expertise in data base technology, designers must receive specialized training before they can decide whether a data base is needed. Additional specialized training is then necessary so that the designers can choose a data base system and file structure and a specific vendor's DBMS. Finally, still further specialized training is required to detail-design the data base files.

Programming

Programming is an important part of many systems investigations. Program design specifications should be carefully developed using flowcharts or other techniques, and programming activities should be carefully monitored. Often, the programming effort required is much greater than was anticipated, and completed programs do not meet quality expectations. Also, improperly developed new programs can easily lead to resource losses after implementation, such as by causing errors in the computer files that in turn cause incorrect invoices.

The procedures used to control program development are similar when new programs are developed and when existing ones are modified. Exhibit 16.9 outlines a system of control procedures intended for use in both situations. The control system shown encompasses the program design activities and program implementation. Item 3 in the exhibit suggests that a separate computer, not used in routine production data processing, may be used for program development. This prevents disruption of routine data processing schedules, facilitates on-line program writing which increases programmer efficiency, and eliminates the possibility that programmers will alter or interfere with the software used for normal data processing while developing their own programs. Usually, it is large organizations that dedicate a computer system to program development activities.

A System of Procedures for Controlling Program Development of New Programs and Modified Programs

EXHIBIT 16.9

1. A request must be submitted by a user or systems analyst to the programming manager. It includes:
   A brief description of the program or program change requested
   The reason why the program or the change is needed

2. A time budget is established, and a systems analyst, a programmer, or a team is assigned to the project.

3. Program design, programming, and program debugging are completed (perhaps a separate computer is reserved for systems development).

4. The program or change is documented. Documentation usually includes at least:
   A narrative description of the program or the change flowcharts
   A copy of the program listing

5. The program is tested by a program quality control supervisor.

6. The program is formally approved by:
   The requester
   The analyst-programmer
   The quality control supervisor
   The programming manager*

7. The previous program (if any) is removed from the program library, and the new or changed program replaces it.

* The approvals constitute the only authorization required for processing all transactions that can be processed by this program; authorization of transactions for processing is a key control concern.

Programming efforts most be efficiently conducted; efficiency is promoted by a good project management system. Efficiency is also enhanced by structured programming techniques. Structured programming reduces an otherwise monolithic program to several small modules, which are then linked together for processing. Each module has just one entry point and one exit point (one interface with a preceding module and one with a following module), and there is no need to use branching, as exemplified by GO TO program instructions. The logic of structured programs is much simpler and easier to understand than the logic of other programs, and this enables them to be written, debugged, and revised more easily.

Design, documentation, and data definitions standards are also important ingredients of programming efficiency. Design standards pertain to such matters as file formats and flowcharting conventions. Documentation standards set forth the requirements for narrative, flowcharting, and other descriptions of programs. A data dictionary embodies data standards that eliminate multiple data definitions of the same data items, which otherwise may be present in different files and computer programs.

Whether a data processing installation is large or small, a standards program is necessary. Indeed, a standards program is particularly important in small installations because only one person may be involved with a system; if that person leaves, standardized documentation can enable a replacement to understand the system more rapidly. Unfortunately, maintaining standards becomes bothersome under the pressure of deadlines to complete systems. To ensure the continuation of a standards program, a manual should be prepared that details the installation's standards. Analysts and programmers must understand the standards and be policed to ensure compliance. Of course, the standards require periodic revision.

Another way to improve program development efficiency is through the use of on-line terminals to accomplish programming. For some programming groups, it is claimed that the efficiencies of on-line programming double the productivity of the programmers.

Software development or maintenance projects often causes data processing delays, high error rates, and general chaos in the organization. The ability of data processing to develop programs smoothly and make timely changes in programs is often a major basis on which higher management evaluates the performance of data processing. Unfortunately, many data processing groups have not been able to accomplish program development and maintenance efficiently.

Site Preparation

If new equipment is acquired, a computer site must be prepared. Physical security should be a major consideration when a new computer site is designed. Physical security requires attention to fireproof vault storage for critical files and programs, security locks on doors at the site, and fire detection and prevention facilities. Physical security should be considered as one part of an overall security program that includes password security and other precautions.

Large computer systems require a carefully controlled environment, including careful temperature control that includes air conditioning, humidity control and dust control systems. A critical aspect of this environment is a continuous and steady power source. Auxiliary power and power regulation systems are often required to ensure smooth power delivery.

In general, the site preparation required for microcomputers is minimal. However, a controlled power source is important for microcomputers. Minor variations from a steady power supply, known as "spikes" and "surges," are commonplace in an ordinary electric power supply and can damage the delicate electronic mechanisms of a microcomputer. Probably a majority of the repairs to microcomputers are necessitated by slightly erratic power supplies. Some protection can be provided by surge-suppressor devices, which are available for less than $100. Microcomputer electronic components are also sensitive to smoke, and smoking is generally prohibited near microcomputers.

Operating efficiency is of concern in site design, just as it is important in the design of a kitchen or other work space. The equipment must be physically located in such a way as to minimize the amount of effort required to operate and monitor the entire computer system. Attention must also be given to ergonomics, which pertains to the design of personal workstations so that they are less fatiguing and more efficient in operation. The proper placement of keyboards, the kind and intensity of light on the screens of monitors, and the height of the screen relative to eye level are all ergonomic considerations. Noise levels, too, must be given attention; in particular, many computer printers have high noise levels, and a noise-suppressing system, such as a surrounding insulated box, should be used. Too little attention is often paid to these and other human comfort factors in designing information systems.

Equipment and Program Installation and Checkout

The installation and checkout of new equipment and the more complex programs are normally supervised by the vendors. Vendor hardware engineers typically install computer equipment and perform tests to see that it functions properly. Vendor representatives usually either place purchased programs in the organization's computer system or provide detailed instructions about how to do this. Computer operating systems that are nonstandard because of changes made by the organization's systems programmers frequently complicate the introduction of vendor-provided software packages to the system; such an operating system may require modifications to a new program's control commands before the package can communicate with it.

File Conversion

If new files are designed to replace existing files, the data in the existing files must be converted to be made compatible with the new file format and structure and then must be entered into the new files. This can be a large-scale task that may occupy the time of several data input personnel for weeks or months. A conversion done manually usually entails making printouts of the contents of the existing data files and using these printouts as the basis for reentering the data in the altered form required by the new file standards. For example, record fields within the new file may be rearranged, fields may be added or deleted, or their length may be altered; the existing data that is reentered must conform to this new format. During file conversion, input errors are common.

Alternatively, computer programs can be written to convert data in the existing files to the format of the new files, and other programs can be written to transfer data from the old files to the new files electronically. This programming activity can be time-consuming, and, of course, after the conversion has been completed, the conversion programs no longer have any value. The decision as to whether file conversion is to be done manually or by preparing conversion programs is itself an important one in a large systems project.

Documentation

Documentation consists of material that explains the technical character-istics and the operation of a system. Documentation is essential to provide an understanding of a system to whoever must maintain it, to permit the system to be audited, and to teach users how to interact with the system and operators how to run it.

Several types of documentation exist. Program documentation ex-plains the reasons for, and logic of, a program and includes narrative descriptions, flowcharts, program listings, and other documents. User documentation is usually much less technical and explains to users in a general way the nature and capabilities of the system and how to use it; user documentation is usually in the form of a user's manual.

Many organizations have what is often called a "documentation pro-gram." This program consists of a formal policy stating that documentation must be prepared routinely for each new computer program, file, and system. Documentation standards that must be adhered to are also a part of the documentation program; these standards specify what documen-tation must be provided and its organization. Formal acceptance of a program, file, or system also means that the documentation has been reviewed and accepted. Without a documentation program in effect, there is a tendency for documentation to be provided only on a hit-or-miss basis and, if it is provided at all, for a variety of documentation approaches to be used.

System Conversion

When the new system (or a part of it) is ready for operation, one of four general "cutover" approaches is likely to be adopted:

1. The parallel operations approach
2. The direct cutover approach
3. The phased cutover approach
4. The pilot study approach

The least risky of these is the parallel operations approach, which is often used when a new computer system is acquired or when a new software package replaces an existing set of programs. The new system or package is run "in parallel" with the old one for a period of days, weeks, or months; that is, both the new and the old systems process the same transactions. One benefit of the parallel operations approach is that it provides assurance—before the old system is dismantled or disposed of—that the new system works properly and will accomplish the job; the discovery of an unanticipated quirk or serious defect in the new system after the old system has been dismantled can result in data processing delays or high additional expense.

Additionally, many errors may be caused by a new system, no matter how well designed and implemented it is. Running the same data through both systems in parallel permits comparing the results of processing by the new system—an unknown at its inception—with the results of processing by the old system. Despite its shortcomings, an existing system typically provides output of known dependability, and this comparison provides a means for detecting problems with the new system.

Direct cutover is the most risky approach because it entails replacing the entire old system with the new system without first being certain that the new system works. Direct cutover may be used when the conversion must be completed rapidly, when there is insufficient space or personnel to operate both the new and the old systems, or when a high level of confidence exists that the new system will function satisfactorily.

A phased cutover involves sequencing the systems investigation activities so that separate modules are designed and installed at different times; each can then begin operation as soon as it is completed. Because each module is only one part of the entire project, any operating problems with a specific module are not likely to disrupt operations seriously and usually can be corrected before the next module begins operating. A data base, for example, might be fully designed and then implemented and placed in operation in modules, with each module consisting of another data file added to the data base.

The pilot study approach is used where multiple new identical or similar systems will eventually be implemented in several departments, branches, or divisions. The system is designed, but initially it is implemented and tested in just one of the organization units. When all problems are found and corrected, the system is implemented in the other organization units.

Acceptance of the New System

When each of the functions of the new system or program has been used and found to be essentially error-free in normal data processing at least once, a thorough review should be made. This review entails a systematic determination that all previous problems with the new system have been resolved. After this review, the system can be formally accepted; it is no longer "on trial" and is now used routinely for normal operations. Acceptance often means that all affected parties, including user representatives, formally sign a document stating that the system is complete and is acceptable to them.

Formal acceptance of a system is essential to avoid future misunderstandings. It is common, for example, for a user group to say months or years later, "The system you gave us never has worked right—it's time you fixed it!" The systems personnel may reply, "You didn't tell us there was anything wrong; the time to correct any problems was when the system was finished, while everyone remembered what the project was about and before the designers moved to new projects, where they are now very busy. We're sorry, but it's too late now."

When formal acceptance is insisted on, user groups are alerted that once they accept the system, they lose the right to claim that it was not finished or was not done correctly. Systems groups are also given an incentive to solve all the problems with the system expeditiously so that it can be officially finished.

If the new system consists in part of vendor-provided hardware or software, the vendor may ask the organization to attest to the fact that the obligations have been fulfilled. The organization should respond to such a request in accordance with advice from its legal counsel. However, at the time of formal acceptance there has not been an evaluation of the performance of the new system, and in most cases the organization should not sign a statement saying that the vendor has fulfilled all obligations until after the postaudit.

Abercrombie Company

By the time the new computer arrived, about 80 percent of the file design changes and program modifications necessary to convert to the new system had been made. The new computer system was installed, and existing applications were gradually transferred to it over a 4-month period with the assistance of several vendor personnel. Each applications program was run "in parallel" on the new and the old computers at least once, and there were numerous instances of improper coding of programs during conversion, which caused errors or prevented the program from processing on the new system. After the fourth month, the old computer system was removed; it had been sold to another company that already had a computer system that was nearly identical to it, which doubled that company's computing capacity.

Conversion of the first applications to a data base system was scheduled to start about 6 months after the old system was disposed of.

THE POSTAUDIT

The postaudit is not a phase in the systems investigation; it is more of a delayed final "blip" of activity that is something of an addendum to the implementation phase. The concept of the postaudit was developed in association with capital budgeting projects and has been usefully adapted to systems investigation projects, which have many of the same characteristics as capital budgeting projects.

The postaudit is most frequently formalized for large, lengthy, and complex systems investigations, but its principles are equally suitable to even small investigations such as changes made to an existing computer application or the acquisition of a microcomputer system. The postaudit rests on two fundamental propositions: (1) that a systems investigation and the resulting new system should both be evaluated and (2) that a proper evaluation cannot be made until "the dust has settled."

The postaudit should take place when a new system reaches a "steady state" wherein all the known bugs have been eliminated, the operators and users are thoroughly trained in the operation of the system, the system is operating at a high level of efficiency, and all parties associated with the system understand its advantages and shortcomings. The postaudit should be completed before significant changes that are not a part of the original systems investigation are made and before the system begins to lose efficiency because its environment is changing. For most new systems, the steady-state condition will be achieved from 1 to 6 months after installation.

In summary, the postaudit establishes whether the system satisfies the systems specifications and how efficiently the systems investigation activities were conducted; these purposes are expanded in Exhibit 16.10. The assessment of the systems investigation is oriented toward (1) gaining insight into how to conduct future investigations more effectively and (2) establishing a track record for professional systems personnel. The systems personnel are evaluated with respect to their expertise, dedication, judgment, ability to meet budgets, and inclinations to be either overly optimistic or overly pessimistic about time and personnel resource requirements for systems investigations.

Although there are no rigid rules about who should be part of a postaudit team, Exhibit 16.11 provides some suggestions. The team should be small, consisting of perhaps three to five persons. Objective outsiders, such as consultants and auditors, are often useful members of postaudit teams. The typical activities of the postaudit team are shown in Exhibit 16.12. The focus of these activities is preparation of a report to the systems

---

Purposes of the Systems Postaudit   EXHIBIT 16.10

1. To determine whether the system solves the problem or problems it is intended to solve

2. To determine the extent to which the system meets the needs as specified in the systems requirements specifications report

3. To determine, after experience with the system, whether there are new opportunities to improve it

4. To establish whether the system was completed within the time and resource budget and, if not, why not

5. To evaluate the performance of the systems investigation team members

---

Suggested Makeup of the Postaudit Team	EXHIBIT 16.11

1. One or more persons who were associated with the project over much of its life and who can provide this perspective

2. One or more nonparticipant users of the new system

3. One or more persons who are knowledgeable about systems but were not involved in the project in any way, such as an outside consultant

4. Someone with auditing experience or postaudit experience

steering committee and the information systems department. The typical postaudit is completed within 1 or 2 weeks.

SYSTEMS MAINTENANCE

After acceptance of the new system, the maintenance portion of the life cycle begins. During this period, which typically lasts from 3 to 8 years, the system is "maintained" by making minor changes or major modifications, as needed. At some point, a new systems investigation will be undertaken that will result in the replacement of the system. The need for a new investigation results from a combination of the following:

1. The environment has changed; thus the major functions performed by the system are no longer necessary or are not sufficient.

2. The changes to the system have made it a patchwork of changes, which causes processing inefficiency, errors, or frequent breakdowns. At this point the system is like an old tire tube; it has been patched so often that patches overlap patches, and further effective patching is difficult.

Activities of the Postaudit Team	EXHIBIT 16.12

1. Reviewing the original statement of the problem and the systems requirements specifications report

2. Reviewing system documentation

3. Measuring system performance (numbers of transactions, reporting delays, error rates, system reliability, and so on) and capacity, comparing it with each objective stated in the systems requirements specifications report, and seeking reasons for variances

4. Talking with user groups

5. Reviewing the work papers of the systems investigation (for example, minutes of meetings and work assignment briefs) and talking with members

6. Determining what modifications or enhancements might further improve the system

7. Reaching conclusions about the quality, benefits, and costs of the system and about the quality of the systems investigation and the performance of its developers and submiting a report about these to the systems steering committee

3. Technology has advanced. Even if the system is still performing efficiently, a new system employing new technology would nevertheless have a preferable costs/benefits tradeoff.

THE SYSTEMS INVESTIGATION ACTIVITIES: A SYNOPSIS

This section provides an overview of the systems investigation process, which has been explained in this chapter and the preceding two chapters. For ease of explanation, the discussion has been in terms of the phases of a systems investigation: the preliminary study phase, the analysis, phase, the design phase, and the implementation phase. Additionally, the post-audit has been discussed. The discussion below follows the format provided by Exhibit 16.13.

The preliminary study phase—and the entire life cycle of the system—begins with the discovery of a problem involving the existing information system or the need for an information system where none existed before. A short initial investigation follows, and the results of this are written up in a preliminary study brief. The purpose of this phase is to determine in a general way what is wrong and whether a systems project should be started. The phase ends with the decision of the systems steering committee (or of an information systems manager if there is no steering committee) either to start or not to start a systems investigation.

If the decision is to undertake an investigation, the analysis phase begins. The purpose of this phase is to determine exactly what a new system should accomplish. While carried out in a systematic manner, the activities of this phase are not highly structured, and they involve a great deal of talking with users as well as negotiation and compromise. The first step is project planning, which is followed by a "systems survey," or a study of the existing system to assess its status, strengths, and weaknesses. Good judgment is required here to gather enough information, but not more than is needed. The chief technique used in the systems survey is interviewing, which can be learned.

The information derived from the systems survey should enable the systems problem to be precisely and completely defined. This step is crucial. Often organizations expend too little time and effort on problem definition and proceed to solve the wrong problem. When the problem has been specified in written form, it is a good idea to try to get everyone involved to agree that it is indeed a systems problem and that it is the problem that the systems investigation should address.

The next step is systems analysis. Information about the existing system is studied in further detail, and users are interviewed, measurements are made, forecasts of future needs are developed, and all other necessary steps are taken to determine what the new system should be able to do. The results of this thorough activity lead to the systems re-

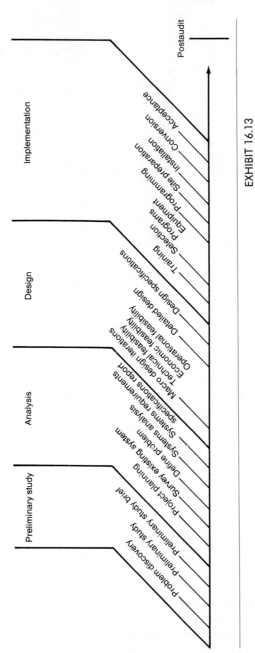

EXHIBIT 16.13
Outline of the systems
investigation activities.

quirements specifications report, which ends the systems analysis phase. (This is the earliest point in the system's life cycle at which a request for proposal, or RFP, is prepared. An RFP at this point would probably ask vendors to propose a turnkey system.)

The activities of the systems design phase are more structured than those of the preceding phases. The purpose of systems design is to determine what kind of system will best accomplish the systems specifications—in other words, *how* the new system will accomplish what it is intended to accomplish. A series of sets of macroalternative designs are evaluated in sequence; in general, the broader the original scope of the project, the greater the number of nested sets of macroalternatives that will be evaluated. This evaluation is in terms of the technical, operational, and economic feasibility of each alternative. Economic feasibility involves costs/benefits analysis, and intangible costs and benefits should not be overlooked.

Systems design requires imagination for establishing the sets of alternatives and a high level of technical knowledge for fully defining and evaluating them. Interpersonal skills are less important here than in the preceding phases. The progressive acceptance of increasingly more detailed alternatives leads to the development of a detailed microdesign for the new system, and the design phase ends with this microdesign captured in a formal set of design specifications. For projects that involve software or hardware vendors, the detailed design specifications may be prepared in the form of an RFP for distribution to selected vendors.

The purpose of the systems implementation phase is to develop and install the system described by the design specifications. Training of personnel to use and operate the new system is a major part of the implementation activities. The implementation phase also includes hardware and software selection, programming, site preparation, and installation, conversion, testing, and debugging of the new system. Conversion approaches include the parallel operations, direct cutover, phased cutover, and pilot study approaches. After system checkout and testing, the system is formally accepted as completed and becomes operational. The implementation activities end with formal acceptance of the new system.

When the system has reached a steady state (that is, when it is operating at a high level of efficiency but no major changes have yet been made to it), a postaudit is undertaken. The purpose of the postaudit is to determine whether the system has accomplished what it was intended to accomplish and whether it has done so within its time and cost budget. For this the systems requirements specifications report serves as a benchmark against which the system is measured.

A system typically remains in operation for from 3 to 8 years, during which time numerous minor changes are made to adapt it to changing needs for information. When the system requires replacement because it is outmoded or because of other reasons, a new life cycle begins.

SUMMARY

With a background in management information systems, computer systems, and systems investigations, the student is now in an excellent position to participate effectively in a systems investigation in any of several capacities. This background opens up job possibilities in information systems departments and in the computer industry.

Systems design activities are technical and structured in nature. Structued design involves reviewing the broadcast possible set of design alternatives that are still within the scope of the project, selecting one, reviewing a narrower set of design alternatives that are nested within the broadest one selected, and so on, until at the most detailed level, a microdesign has been established. At each layer in the alternatives hierarchy, the technical, economic, and operational feasibility of each alternative are considered.

Often, the detailed design approach utilized involves first designing the reports and documents that must be output from the new system. Then the data collection and input systems are designed. Finally, the processing and file system are designed. However, this sequence of activities is not suited to all projects. During detailed microdesign, controls over data processing are included as a part of the system.

One type of design activity involves first designing the data flows that will be needed and then evaluating the comparative advantages of software that would be purchased and software that would be developed by the organization. Increasingly, the decision is to purchase software rather than develop it; much of purchased software must be modified to suit the organization's needs.

If equipment is to be acquired, a request for proposal (RFP) is sent to vendors whose equipment is potentially suitable. Vendors then prepare bids and make a presentation to the soliciting organization. If the potential sale is large, vendors will devote a great deal of effort to developing a response to an RFP.

Most personnel training for use of the new system takes place during the implementation phase. One of the major activities of this phase for most projects is programming; because of its high cost and its tendency to greatly exceed budgeted time, the programming activity must be systematically and carefully controlled. Structured programming is one approach used to increase programmer productivity. Site preparation, software and equipment installation, file conversion, and final acceptance of the new system also take place during the implementation phase.

A new system can be phased in, run in parallel with the new system, or directly cutover to it, or it can be implemented first as a pilot project; the choice of which approach to use depends on the circumstances. Usually, the direct cutover approach is the fastest but the most risky, and the parallel operations and pilot study approaches are the least risky. The postaudit involves assessing how well the new system meets the preestablished systems requirements specifications as well as how efficiently the project was carried out.

KEY TERMS

structured design: beginning the systems design activities with the broadest possible set of design alternatives and proceeding through increasingly narrow sets of alternatives.

systems design specifications: the fully detailed statement of the structure and of the hardware and software components of a new system.

feasibility study: the examination of the technical, economic, and operational feasibility of a particular set of systems design alternatives and the comparison of the feasibility of each alternative.

general controls: systems control that are relevant for all applications.

applications controls: controls that are associated with a specific data processing job or program.

request for proposal (RFP): an invitation to vendors to bid on providing a system or part of a system; an RFP contains all of the information about the nature of the system sought that is needed by vendors for their bid preparation.

REFERENCES

Bryce, Milton, "Information Resources Mismanagement," *Infosystems,* February 1983.

Buss, Martin, D. J., and **Elaine Herman,** "Packaged Software—Purchase or Perish," *Financial Executive,* January 1983, p. 26.

Feidelman, Lawrence, "Buying Packaged Software for Micros and Minis," *Infosystems,* January 1981, p. 54.

Gane, Chris, and **Trish Sarson,** *Structured Systems Analysis: Tools and Techniques,* Improved Systems Technologies, Inc., 1977.

McCracken, Daniel D., "The Changing Face of Applications Programming," *Datamation,* November 1978, p. 25.

Sanders, G. Larry, Paul Minter, and **Ronald O. Reed,** "Selecting a Software Package," *Financial Executive,* September 1982.

Whipple, Donald, "Typical RFP vs. Vendor," *Production & Inventory Management Review and APICS News,* November 1981.

Withington, Frederic G., "The Golden Age of Packaged Software," *Datamation,* December 1980, p. 131.

Yourdon, Edward, and **Larry L. Constantine,** *Structured Design,* 2d ed. New York: Yourdon Press, 1978.

REVIEW QUESTIONS

1. Contrast systems analysis and systems design with respect to the nature of the processes and the expertise required for each type of activity.

2. What is structured design? What is structured programming? How do they differ from structured analysis, as discussed in the last chapter?

3. Explain the macro design concept. How does the scope of the systems investigation affect macro design?

4. What is a micro design? Is a micro design always done?

5. Explain technical feasibility and economic feasibility. Are these feasibilities evaluated only once during a systems investigation? Explain your answer.

6. What is operational feasibility? In the long run, if a system does not possess operational feasibility, can it be economically feasible?

7. What are general controls? Is a policy that all data processing employees be bonded a general control?

8. List several applications controls and explain each one.

9. A data file for payroll is processed by several separate payroll applications programs. Would controls over who can run these payroll programs be general controls or applications controls?

10. Why do user controls exist?

11. Why are error-correction controls considered so important?

12. How are systems investigations controlled?

13. What role or roles can auditors play in the following?
    (a) The preliminary study phase
    (b) The systems analysis phase
    (c) The design phase
    (d) The implementation phase
    (e) The postaudit

14. What are the advantages and disadvantages of buying programs?

15. What steps should be taken in the decision concerning whether a program should be bought or developed? If a program is to be bought, what steps should be taken in the decision concerning which one to buy?

16. How can an organization determine whether a program exists for sale that might meet its requirements?

17. Explain the process of developing an RFP and awarding a contract for equipment as a consequence of the RFP.

18. What tasks are accomplished as part of the implementation phase?

19. Why is it important for an organization to control programming activities carefully? How should these activities be controlled?

20. What tasks might be involved in site preparation? How will these differ for mainframes and microcomputers?

21. What are the four kinds of general approaches to systems conversion, and when would each probably be used?

22. Why is formal acceptance of a new system important?

23. Explain the purposes of the postaudit. Who should be members of a postaudit team?

CASE

The City of Framington

By George M. Scott with the assistance of Rob Rolfe

The city of Framington, Oregon, is audited annually by a local CPA firm. Along with its report, the CPA firm makes recommendations which it feels will improve the city's accounting system. In May 1980, the CPA firm recommended that the city purchase a computer to perform utility billing, tax statement preparation, tax collection, and payroll operations. The manual system then in use was not accurate, consistent, or reliable. The auditors noted, for example, that one case of absenteeism often caused delays and work stoppages, and they expressed their belief that a microcomputer could perform these clerical operations with much greater speed, accuracy, and reliability.

Shortly after receiving these recommendations and after checking with the mayor of a neighboring city about how well that city liked its computer system, the City Council of Framington voted to purchase a computer. After brief presentations by several microcomputer representatives, the council decided to purchase a Computatic IV computer. This decision was based primarily on the assurances provided by the Computatic Corporation salesperson that the model IV had been in service for several years ("long enough to get the bugs worked out") and there were more Computatic IVs in existence than the computers recommended by the other microcomputer representatives; indeed, the other representatives stated that the computers they recommended were very recent models and that not too many were in use yet.

None of the council members had seen the Computatic IV, but they were assured by the vendor that it was the most recent model produced by Computatic and was suitable for the city's needs. Since most of the installations of this micro were on the east coast and the midwest, no sites were visited, and none of the present users of this system were contacted. One reason for this was the fact that none of the present users were municipalities; thus the council members doubted that discussions with these users would have much relevance to Framington's situation.

Computatic was chosen as the vendor partly because it also had some applications packages available. While these programs had not been written specifically for utility billing and tax statement preparation, the council thought that they could be easily modified to perform these jobs. One of the new programmers to be selected by the city was expected to make this adaptation.

John Rushing, the director of finance, believed that the micro would reduce clerical costs and the number of clerical employees (however, he was not involved in the decision to acquire the Computatic IV). He thought that there would be little difficulty involved in training some of the clerical workers to become computer programmers. In August he administered an aptitude test to the employees and to himself to determine who had the necessary attributes for computer programming. Only three people had passing scores. These were Bill Richards, a posting machine operator; Dave Clark, a part-time clerical worker; and himself. Dave Clark said that he wasn't interested in computers, but Bill Richards was enthusiastic about the prospect of becoming a programmer, even though he had no background in EDP.

Bonnie Miller, the accounting department manager, had strongly opposed the acquisition of a computer and had refused to take the aptitude test; "Acquisition without representation!" was the way she expressed her displeasure. She resigned at the end of August, assuming a similar position, with a large raise in pay, in an adjacent town which had been seeking her services for several years. Bill Richards was promoted to accounting manager, which was an unusual move because Richards had no background in accounting and only a modest familiarity with the accounting system. Nevertheless, since he was the only remaining full-time employee, he received the promotion. He was taking courses at night, working toward a degree in management, and he believed that his courses would not interfere with the new job.

Since the old system was going to be replaced by the computer, Rushing and Richards did not believe that there was any need to "clean up" the old system to make it more accurate and efficient. They believed that all they had to do before the computer arrived was to learn how to program; given their aptitude test scores, they thought this would not be too much of a problem. The Computatic Corporation salesperson had supplied them with tape-cassette-recorded programming lessons and programmed texts, which he indicated would be sufficient to teach them how to program.

Bill Richards took over the accounting department at the most difficult period of the year. The accounting department had several responsibilities. First, there were the utility billings, which were a continuous, year-round activity. Second, the department had to prepare, print, assemble, and bind the city's budget document. It also had to prepare and mail tax statements. Of course, the department also had to keep the city's records, pay its vendors, and prepare the annual financial statements. Richards had to learn how the accounting system worked by himself since he had not been trained by his predecessor. This activity took so much time that he did not have an opportunity to study his programming material. He wasn't unduly concerned because he thought that he could rely on John Rushing to show him how to program.

In January 1981, Computatic Corporation had a display of its computer equipment in Portland, and Richards and Rushing went to look at the type of microcomputer they were to receive. The vendor told them that programming classes for purchasers of the Computatic IV were going to be offered at night starting the following week. Richards and Rushing decided to attend.

The first class was held on the night of January 20; after attending, Richards realized that these courses were intended for people who already had experience in EDP and knew how to program in at least one language. He was lost in the technical discussions. Rushing could follow parts of the lecture since he had done more preparation.

Since it was a long drive back to Framington, Richards decided that he would sleep in the back seat while Rushing drove. An hour later, Rushing dozed off to sleep and the car plowed into an embankment. Both were rushed to the hospital, and the prognosis was that Rushing would be hospitalized for at least 6 weeks, after which he would need about 6 to 9 months of recuperation at home; Richards had broken his arm. After the shock of the tragedy wore off, Richards began to realize that he now had a significantly increased burden placed upon him; he was the only person in the city government who had even the slightest bit of experience in EDP.

Chris Haney, the director of public works, was made the acting director of finance until John Rushing was able to return to work. The first thing Haney did as director was to create a new data processing department with Bill Richards as its manager; a new manager was hired for the accounting department.

In October the computer arrived, 5 months after the contracted delivery data and just at the inception of the busy part of the year. No one had time to give it any attention, so the manual system continued to be used. Richards was pressed into service to help accounting during this busy period.

In February 1982, Richards was ready to modify the applications programs provided by the vendor to make them suitable for utilities billing and collection. Their intended purpose had been for invoicing and updating accounts receivable and preparing customer statements. To his dismay, Richards discovered that the programs were not accompanied by documentation. After an urgent plea for help, Computatic Corporation agreed to provide one of its employees, John Young, to make the conversions. A daily consulting fee, plus expenses, was to be charged for this service.

Arriving in early April, Young was shocked to discover that no work had been done to convert the alphabetic system of classification used by the manual utilities billing system to the numeric system required by the packaged programs accompanying the Computatic IV. The ledger of accounts also needed to be rearranged. Young agreed to stay as long as necessary to convert the system and to modify the applications packages to perform the required duties.

After several months of work, the alphabetic manual system was converted, and the program was modified. After the modifications, the application package to perform utilities billing was 40 percent larger than the original program the vendor had provided.

In August 1982, in preparation for running the utilities billing programs, Richards dismantled the manual system by reassigning the clerical utility employees, since he felt the manual system would no longer be necessary, and by moving the Computatic IV from storage and installing it in what had been the utilities billing office. While the program was being run, a complication arose and the new system did not function. After a great deal of effort, Richards and Rushing (Rushing had assumed his old duties and was fully recovered) retrieved all the employees, machines, materials, and forms and were able to prepare the utility bills. However, the November 1982 bills were almost a month late and contained a very high rate of errors.

In his investigation to determine what had gone wrong, Young discovered that the modified application program was too large to fit into main memory. The program had to be rewritten into three separate programs, each of which could be processed separately.

After 2 months of rewriting and careful debugging, the application program was ready again (after the city complained, Computatic Corporation agreed to a 20 percent reduction of fees for these 2 months). This time the manual system and the new systems were run simultaneously. A very large number of discrepancies were discovered, and it was finally decided to send out the manual bills rather than the computer-prepared utility bills again for December 1982. During the following month, Young diligently traced each discrepancy and corrected the source of the problem. Most of the problems had been caused by minor errors in

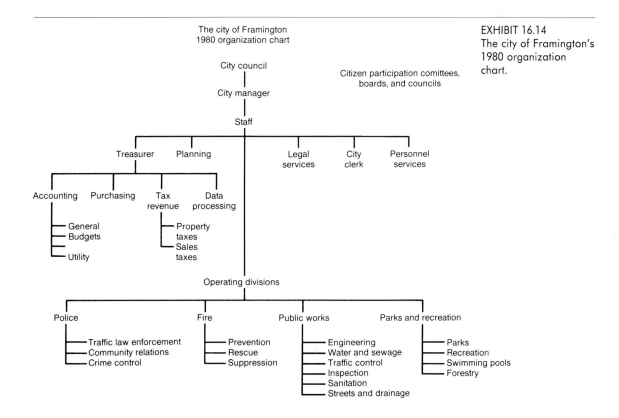

EXHIBIT 16.14
The city of Framington's 1980 organization chart.

the program logic or by inadequate programming controls. In January 1983, they followed the same dual-processing procedure and found the computer bills to be nearly error-free, and they used the computer for utility billing from then on. After almost 3 years, the computer was finally performing one of the applications which had been recommended by the CPA firm.

Because the processing of the utilities application took so long to run, since it was split into three parts, Richards began to wonder whether the Computatic IV would be too small when the other applications programs were added. One morning he asked Young, "Is Computatic developing a Computatic V, preferably one with a larger main memory?"

"No," Young replied, "the Computatic IV is our largest and last model, but in about 6 months we're going to announce a completely new system—a full-blown small business computer with one fixed hard disk and two flexible disks, remote terminal capability, and an entirely new operating system. The new system will be supported exclusively by our Report-Write language, which is now in the final stages of development. It will be a super system, the first of several related small business computer models. I'll make certain that we inform you about it when it's announced."

As he drove home from work that night, Richards thought, "I wonder if we will have as much trouble with the second application package as we had with the first? Have we bought a microcomputer whose capacity we have already exceeded? I hope we haven't made a big mistake!"

Postscript

Bill Richard's experience made him quite interested in computing. Within the next month he applied for a position in data processing with a major company in Portland. He was told that his background and training in EDP were not adequate. Shortly thereafter he gave notice to the city of Framington and entered a major west coast university to pursue a degree in computer science on a full-time basis. (See Framington's organization chart, which is shown in Exhibit 16.14).

Case Questions

1. What problems or constraints were associated with the new Computatic IV system?

2. What mistakes were made in the acquisition and implementation of the new system?

3. Assume that you were a member of the City Council and were considered by the other members to be knowledgeable about computers and systems investigations. As soon as the CPA firm made its recommendation, the City Council told you to "take charge and get us a computer." You interpreted this to mean that you were not to conduct the systems investigation, but were to ensure that it was conducted properly. Outline the steps you would have taken and the recommendations you would have made throughout the entire systems investigation.

Chapter 17

COMPUTER POWER: SOURCES AND SELECTION

PAYOFF THOUGHT

It should not be assumed that an organization should purchase its own computer system and use this system exclusively; there are several alternatives that should be explored each time an organization seeks additional computer power.

CHAPTER OBJECTIVES

1. To explain the advantages and disadvantages of the several ways in which computer power can be acquired

2. To present the general principles of computer selection

INTRODUCTION

The first part of this chapter considers several possible contractual arrangements for data processing capabilities. It discusses the advantages and disadvantages of each and analyzes the tradeoffs involved in the selection of one type rather than another. The alternatives are:

1. Computer purchase
2. Computer rental from the manufacturer
3. Computer lease from a third-party
4. Acquisition of a used computer
5. Computer service centers
6. Timesharing companies
7. Facilities management companies

The first four alternatives above involve operation of the computer by the acquiring organization; the organization therefore can control the schedule and use of the computer system. The other alternatives provide reduced control of data processing activities. A final alternative, not shown on the list, is some combination of those listed; combinations are widely employed in practice, but will not be discussed separately.

The last part of this chapter deals with the selection of a computer system and has the most relevance for the first four approaches in the above list, but it does have some relevance to the last three also. Computer selection is treated as a special type of systems investigation. Excluded are the selection and evaluation processes that are especially relevant to the selection of microcomputer systems; these are presented in the following chapter.

COMPUTER PURCHASE

Computer purchase is the most straightforward means of acquiring a data processing capability, and it is the means adopted by the majority of small computer users as well as by a substantial number of mainframe users. The typical arrangement is that the purchaser pays cash when the computer system is installed and is operating properly. The price is generally in the range of from 35 to 45 times what the monthly rental rate would have been. At the time of purchase, an operating system and other systems software packages usually are also purchased. Several applications programs for the computer system may also be purchased. The individual components of the total computer system are normally priced separately, a practice referred to as "unbundled" pricing, but are included in the same purchase contract. However, it is common for purchases of different components and software packages to be from different vendors, in which case contracts and payment arrangements are separate for each vendor.

A separate contract for service is usually available from the computer vendor, and this option is elected by most purchasers. The service contract can be written to meet the specific needs of the purchaser and may include, for example, provisions that maintenance engineers be on the site 24 hours a day or that service personnel be available for repairs within 4 hours after the system malfunctions. Service contracts are also available from independent computer service companies.

The purchase of a computer system is particularly advantageous for an organization which knows exactly what it needs and which expects to keep its computer for a long period of time, perhaps for 5 or more years. The purchase arrangement may be undesirable, however, if the organization is uncertain that the computer will satisfactorily fulfill its needs or if the organization's needs are expanding or changing rapidly, with the result that a computer system purchased now would soon be unsatisfactory. If an organization expects rapid future growth but nevertheless purchases a computer, it is especially important that the computer purchased be capable of being expanded substantially.

The purchase of a computer system can be disadvantageous for an organization that has not properly assessed changing needs within it or changing conditions in the external environment that will dictate the need for a computer system with different capabilities. Also, if a computer is purchased, there is a risk that new technology will make it obsolete in the near future; the resale and trade-in values of a purchased computer decline dramatically when computers with advanced new technology are introduced.

Another risk is involved in the purchase of a computer that has been only recently introduced. New computer systems, like new automobile models, may fail to gain market acceptance or may be unsatisfactory because of design or other shortcomings. Before purchasing a computer, an organization should be certain that the computer has been proved in actual operation. If in doubt, the organization may prefer to rent the computer for a period of time with a purchase option included in the rental contract; typically about 60 percent of the rent paid will count toward the purchase price of the computer system.

COMPUTER RENTAL FROM THE MANUFACTURER

This option is elected for the majority of large computers acquired by organizations, although many of the organizations subsequently purchase the computer they initially rent. Computers are rented directly from the manufacturer, typically under the terms of a contract that specifies that the organization is responsible for a minimum payment of rent and that the contract can be terminated, say, 90 days after written notice is given. The rental contract may also provide that the computer may be available for use for a certain number of hours per month and that additional usage

requires payment of additional rent. A service contract with the manufacturer is a normal requirement, since the manufacturer has a financial
interest in maintaining the value of the computer.

Computer rental is a flexible arrangement, which doubtless accounts
in good measure for its popularity in cases where large computer systems
costing millions of dollars are involved. Rental is an excellent arrangement
for an organization that anticipates changing computers in the fairly near
future or on short notice. For example, a fast-growth company or a company that is rapidly developing new computer applications may prefer the
flexiblility of a computer rental contract. Additionally, a company awaiting
delivery of a new computer that has been ordered may rent temporarily.
The major disadvantage of computer rental is that it is usually the most
expensive alternative if the computer is kept for a period of several years.

COMPUTER LEASE FROM A THIRD PARTY

Computers may also be leased from a third-party lessor. The arrangement
is nearly identical to that involved in rental from the manufacturer except
that the contract is for a longer period, perhaps for 3 years, which permits
the lease terms to be more favorable.

Third-party lessors are independent companies that purchase computers from the manufacturer and lease them on a long-term contract,
typically of 3 to 5 years' duration. The lessors are sometimes able to buy
several computers together for this purpose at a favorable price. A price
advantage to the leasing organization of from 10 to 30 percent below rental
cost is typically available, in part because of favorable provisions in the
tax code. Also, the lower price reflects the belief of some third-party lessors
that the computer systems will have a longer economic life than the
computer manufacturers believe they will have, and the lessors therefore
anticipate receiving lease fees for a longer period. During the last decade,
several third-party lessors have had low earnings performances because
their judgment about the economic life of the computers they leased was
incorrect.

A disadvantage of a third-party lease is that the lessee is committed
by contract for a much longer time than if the computer is rented from
the manufacturer. While there normally are provisions to "unwind" the
contract, lease cancellation can be accomplished only with a substantial
financial penalty to the lessee. In some instances an organization may
have less flexibility with a long-term lease arrangement than with the
purchase of a computer system; a purchased computer can sometimes be
sold without great loss, whereas the financial penalties for breaking a lease
contract are great.

Exhibit 17.1 uses a hypothetical example to illustrate the economic
tradeoff involved in the options of computer purchase, computer rental
from the manufacturer, and computer lease from a third party. It can be
seen that if an organization keeps a computer system for 6 months or less,

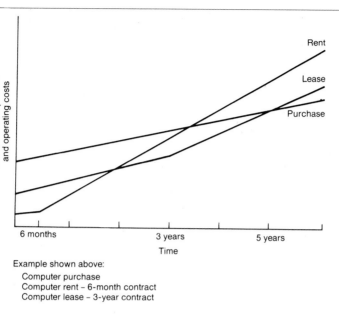

EXHIBIT 17.1
Approximate cost patterns of three computer acquisition options.

Example shown above:
Computer purchase
Computer rent – 6-month contract
Computer lease – 3-year contract

given the assumptions in the exhibit, the organization should rent the computer from the manufacturer. If the organization keeps the computer for 3 years, the least-cost alternative would be computer lease from a third party. If the computer is kept for 6 years, the least-cost option would be the purchase of the computer system. Given the assumptions of the exhibit, the crossover point at which it becomes more economical to purchase rather than rent from the manufacturer occurs at about 3½ years, and the point at which it becomes more economical to purchase rather than lease from a third party occurs at approximately the 5-year point.

When the organization has decided what computer system is to be installed, the two breakeven points between the three options of purchasing, renting from the manufacturer, and leasing from a third party can be calculated by examining the different contracts available. Considerably more analysis and a great deal of judgment are required, however, to determine how long the organization can reasonably expect to keep the computer system. The simplest circumstance is one in which the organization knows with a high degree of certainty that it will keep the computer for a definite period of time; then choosing from among the alternatives is a simple matter of consulting an analysis of breakeven points already prepared. However, few cases are so clear-cut.

ACQUISITION OF A USED COMPUTER

During the last decade, a well-developed used-computer market has emerged. Several firms actively participate as brokers in the used-computer market or purchase used computer systems for resale. Sometimes "used" computer systems have never been installed; for example, they may be minicomputer systems that were originally purchased in volume by systems houses to gain quantity discounts but have not been sold and so are marketed as used computers.

Used major peripheral devices are also available in this market. These peripheral devices include printers, tape decks, card equipment such as card input machines, channel devices of assorted varieties, front-end processors, and other types of communications equipment.

The used-computer market has many of the characteristics of the used-car market. The cost of a used computer typically is in the range of from 30 to 60 percent of the cost of a new computer. In general, the market quickly attaches a value to used computers primarily on the basis of their price/performance ratio (cost effectiveness) relative to the ratio for new computer equipment. This market price is somewhat lower for equivalent performance than the price for the newest and most technologically advanced equipment.

The typical purchaser in the used-computer market is an organization whose needs for a specific computer or for major peripheral component for a specific reason cannot be satisfied with a substitute. The seeker of used computer equipment is almost always quite experienced in computer data processing.

Used computers can be acquired by purchase or on a rental basis, but most commonly they are purchased. Typically the vendor will install the equipment and sometimes will make service contracts available to the acquiring organization.

Used computers provide good value to economy-minded organizations and to organizations that would prefer to have a new computer but would have to wait for an extended period for delivery of the new computer of their choice. Used computers are also bought by organizations that have one computer that is running out of processing capacity; acquiring a used computer that is identical to the existing one doubles the organization's processing capacity at a bargain-basement price. Even more important, all the experience that the organization has gained with the existing computer is fully applicable to the newly acquired used computer, and the programs that function on the existing computer will also function on the newly acquired one. Thus there is little hassle involved in the acquisition of a used computer, and the total cost of doubling processing capacity may be less than 50 percent of the total cost of doubling processing capacity by buying a larger computer or a second computer of a different type.

The major disadvantage of acquiring a used computer is that the organization is not staying on the frontier of computer technology, since it is usually acquiring a computer that is not among the most technologically advanced. This may mean that the organization will have to "catch up" quickly sometime in the future when the obsolete computer is replaced by a more advanced one.

COMPUTER SERVICE CENTERS

A computer service center, or service bureau, is an independent company that processes the data of other organizations on its own computer system. A service center may have purchased the computer for the exclusive purpose of running a service center, or it may have purchased it primarily for its own data processing but is selling the computer's excess capacity to other organizations. It is common for a bank, for example, to own a large computer for its data processing and also to use the computer as a service center for other organizations.

A service center usually provides standard accounting applications packages for its clients' use. Often, the center specializes in an industry and provides accounting and other applications programs tailored for that industry. The center may also have a programming staff that modifies programs or develops new programs for customers.

Data (usually consisting of the clients' transactions) is physically transported from the client to the service center for processing. This may be done by automobile, mail, or any other means of conveyance, and the transportation may be provided by the client or by the service center. The service center controls the data processing schedule. The client's data files are generally retained at the service center, and the reports are returned to the client.

The cost of data processing by a service center typically consists of at least five components. First, there is a monthly minimum charge; second, a rate is charged per unit of CPU time used (this is recorded by the computer's internal accounting system); third, a charge is levied for the amount of memory used during the period by the client's programs and files; fourth, there is a charge for the use of the major peripherals at the service center, such as for the use of printers on a number-of-lines-printed basis; and finally, charges are added for miscellaneous services, if any, such as for programming and data and report delivery costs.

The contract with a service center typically gives the client a great deal of flexibility; it can usually be cancelled on short notice, sometimes only 30 days. With a service center, users should be concerned that the contract provides that data processing be done in a timely fashion, perhaps even specifying a schedule for completion of critical reports. The contract should also contain specifics about data and file security provisions that will be kept in effect.

One frequently cited advantage of service centers is that they eliminate the hassle of developing a computer system. While this is true, it is also true that the user organization must exercise discipline to ensure that data submissions are correct and on schedule, and it must monitor the performance of the service center carefully to ensure that the charges are correct and that the terms of the contract are upheld in every respect. Additionally, any systems development performed for the user organization by the service center must be carefully coordinated by the organization. In sum, these responsibilities impose considerable demands on the user organization, which should have more than just a superficial understanding of computer information systems.

An advantage of a service center arrangement is that a customer can buy only as much computer processing and as many related services as are required for each time period. Another advantage in some circumstances is that use of a service center usually does not require justification on a capital budgeting basis before a commitment can be made; the monthly charges are expensed and are low enough to be authorized by lower-level managers.

The most common usage of service centers is by small organizations that do not have their own computers. A large organization is most likely to use a service center if there are temporary surges in data processing that exceed the capacity of its computer system or if the organization has peak loads each period that exceed the capacity of its own computer. In many organizations, however, these peaks occur at the end of the same accounting periods that are also the peak periods for the service center.

Service centers can also be used on a temporary basis until a new system is installed. Also, an organization can make contractual arrangements with a service center to provide backup data processing if the organization's computer system malfunctions. Computer centers may also be useful when a program or data base is larger than can be accommodated on the organization's computer or when, for technical reasons, the organization's computer cannot process certain programs that must be used.

Service centers also have disadvantages. One of the most important concerns administrative control of the files and programs. Because these typically remain with the service center, they may not be conveniently available to the organization when needed. A related control concern is that it is the service center, not the organization, that controls the schedule of the data processing, whereas if the organization used its own computer, the processing schedule could be altered at will to accommodate critical applications.

The security of programs and data of the organization is another concern. An organization cannot be certain that its files and programs are given adequate protection by the service center. The security of data and reports that are transported is also a problem with service centers; it is not rare, for example, for the reports of one user to be delivered in error to another user.

Another disadvantage of service centers is that the total cost for the amount of data processing done may be high relative to the cost of processing done on an organization's own computer. While a high rate can be justified if the service is viewed as a convenience, it may be excessive if the amount of data processing done is extensive. Special reports present another problem; if an organization has an unexpected need for reports because of an unanticipated operating problem, the data processing required may not be treated as urgent by the service center.

A final disadvantage of a service center arrangement is that programs developed for a client by a service center may not be transferable to another service center or to the client's own computer system. It is accepted marketing practice to attempt to "lock in" a client so that it is difficult for the client to discontinue use of the service center, and one technique that is used to accomplish this is developing programs that can be processed only on the service center's computer.

While there are many circumstances in which service centers provide valuable services to organizations, the economics of microcomputers and minicomputers generally mean that for many smaller organizations it is more cost-effective to purchase a computer system. Aside from economics, however, there are other considerations. For example, the hassle of implementing a computer system, particularly for a first-time user, may make a small organization prefer using a service center. Additionally, the probability of making a serious mistake in the choice or the implementation of a small computer is high for first-time uers, and the indirect cost of such a mistake can be many times greater than the direct monetary outlay associated with the computer system. Accordingly, when an organization is not confident that it can implement a cost-effective computer information system of its own, it may wisely elect to use a service center.

TIMESHARING COMPANIES

Timesharing companies are similar to service centers in that an organization subscribes to data processing provided by a company with a computer. The major difference is that the client organization enters transactions for processing via a computer terminal at its office, rather than physically transporting the transactions. The reports may be printed on a printer at the client's location or printed at the timesharing company and delivered.

Timesharing companies' pricing arrangements are similar to those of service centers except that (1) there are additional charges for terminal rental or purchase, and (2) there are additional charges for data communications. Usually, data is transmitted via telephone lines, so these charges appear as a part of the client's telephone costs.

The use of a remote terminal provides advantages to the timesharing user that are not available from a service center. First, timesharing can provide fast turnaround. The customer is on-line to the computer, and so its files may also usefully remain on-line (at an extra charge) for real-time transactions processing and file inquiries; also, some reports and documents (such as sales invoices) can be prepared in real-time mode.

Another advantage of timesharing is that many timesharing companies are regional, national, or international in scope, which enables their clients to use the timesharing network as a data communications system among geographically dispersed operations. For example, a company's branch could enter sales transactions for processing at the timesharing computer nearest it and have shipping instructions printed at a terminal at an inventory location several thousand miles distant. The development of its own internal computer communications network can be prohibitively costly for a smaller organization.

The larger timesharing companies also have numerous special-purpose programs available to clients for a fee—sometimes thousands of programs. These might be mathematical applications programs (such as for matrix inversion or logarithmic calculations), word processing programs, structural and electrical engineering programs, project management programs, operations research programs, nuclear research programs, learning curve programs, or graphics programs, as well as a variety of financial analysis programs. For many organizations, specific, specialized programs are needed on an occasional basis but would be too expensive to purchase. Specialized data bases such as economics and statistics data bases are also made available by some timesharing companies.

The largest of the timesharing systems are accessible by telephone over a broad geographic area. It is said that General Electric's Mark III system can be entered by a local telephone call from over 90 percent of the world's business telephones. The GE system is composed of more than 100 computers, including several large computers at a supercenter in Cincinnati, Ohio. These networks can be used to effectively link an in-house computer system of a multinational enterprise with operations that may range as far as southeast Asia and southern Europe.

Service centers and the smaller timesharing companies often specialize by industry. The organization with data processing needs that are unique to its industry should prefer a service center or timesharing company that specializes in that industry. Bowne Timesharing in New York City, for example, specializes in word processing. Computer Sharing Services in Denver specializes in savings and loan accounting services, and Comshare in Ann Arbor specializes in personnel management and CPA applications programs.

FACILITIES MANAGEMENT COMPANIES

Facilities management companies manage a client's computer facilities (hence the name) and assume responsibility for the client's data processing on a long-term contract basis. Facilities management companies emerged because a large proportion of organizations' data processing departments do generally unsatisfactory work. In many data processing centers, for example, report preparation is frequently late, nagging problems exist with equipment and software, and new applications are finished long after their deadlines and have large cost overruns. Additionally, systems are often improperly designed or installed and thus do not satisfy the needs of the users. Also, many of the equipment decisions, such as a decision to acquire a new computer, are ill-considered; typically, larger and more expensive computer systems are acquired than are necessary under the circumstances, and sometimes these computers do not possess the characteristics needed by the organization. Finally, personnel turnover in data processing has been high in most organizations, and this problem and other personnel problems are endemic.

These conditions exist in good part because the general managers of most organizations are not knowledgeable about data processing and systems project management. These managers are unable to discern which are the capable and which are the incompetent personnel, and they are unable to exert proper management control over data processing.

If conditions similar to these exist within an organization, a representative of a facilities management (FM) company may give a sales pitch like the following: "Your company is not in the data processing business; you should be concentrating on what you do best—providing the services [or products] that you are in business for. Think of data processing in the same way that you think of the company cafeteria. Your personnel don't run the cafeteria; instead, you call in an outside agency run by food services experts. You should do the same with data processing: call in experts such as our company to run your data processing facilities. Because we're professionals, we can lower your overall costs of doing business, and we'll write a contract to guarantee that we will meet schedules and perform other services for a set fee."

Many FM companies specialize by industry. Thus, not only are they professionals in data processing, but they also have a sound knowledge of the data processing problems of the particular industry. The typical contract specifies that the FM company will buy the computer equipment and software from the organization lock, stock, and barrel. The FM company usually agrees to employ the existing data processing personnel, or at least a significant proportion of them. The FM company will optimize the equipment it acquires by altering the computer system configuration, for example, or will sell or transfer equipment and, as necessary, replace it with equipment better suited to the circumstances. This may dramatically increase the efficiency of the client's data processing center, creating excess capacity and enabling the FM company to use it as a service center for the data processing of several other clients. Or the FM company may do the client's data processing at another of its computer sites. For industry-specific applications, the FM company is likely to utilize some of its own proprietary applications packages that are designed to process efficiently.

The FM firm will also leverage its personnel resources. Employees of the user organization who are less capable in data processing may elect to assume other positions within the organization rather than join the more demanding FM company. Those who elect to join the FM company are retrained as necessary and are put on notice that performance expectations are high. Additionally, the FM company assigns its own topflight personnel to key positions in the client organization's new data center. By providing better organization, better project management, and better equipment decisions and by using more productive personnel, the FM company processes the client's data in a more systematic and orderly way. The morale of the client's personnel who joined the FM company is enhanced because they are now employees of a professional data processing company, and this opens up new career paths that were not previously available to them. Over a period of time many of the original data processing personnel will be transferred to assist in the development of systems for other clients of the FM company.

The contract with the FM company can be flexibly written so that, in effect, the client can have any agreement desired, but at a negotiated price. This flexibility means that the client must give careful attention to the scope and quality of the services it wants from the FM company. A typical contract remains in effect for from 3 to 5 years.

FM company pricing procedures vary widely. For example, the price may be a fixed fee for fixed performance, it may be a fixed fee plus incentives for good performance and penalties for bad performance (such as missing schedules), or it may be a fixed fee plus a set rate per transaction processed. Typically, the FM company charges a certain amount for each transaction within a volume range, or a fixed amount for an activity level within that range, and a slightly lower amount for activity levels in each next higher volume range. Often, there is a minimum total price. The formula for establishing the cost is frequently based on a forecast by the organization of its operations during the term of the contract with the vendor.

The nature of FM company operations is shown in Exhibit 17.2. In this hypothetical example, the client organization has a composite average cost per transaction, as indicated by the curve in the leftmost portion of

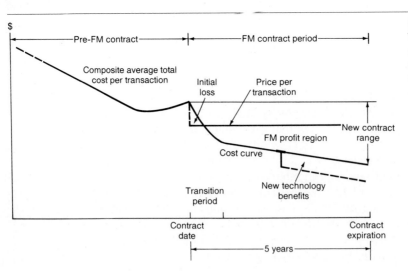

EXHIBIT 17.2
Typical costs and revenues before and during facilities management.

the exhibit. Note that the cost per transaction was increasing before the organization switched to the FM vendor, which naturally would be a matter of concern to the organization's management. A fixed-price-per-transaction contract is negotiated between the FM company and the client, as shown. The contract price per transaction usually is below that of the preceding average cost per transaction, which is the inducement to the organization to contract with the FM company. It can be seen that starting at the contract date, the FM company dramatically increases the efficiency of the data processing operations but nevertheless may accept a loss on the contract for a period of a few months.

As the efficiency of the facilities management data processing center continues to increase, the profit of the FM company also increases, as shown by the profit region in the exhibit. Note that if equipment with new technology is acquired by the FM company during the term of the contract (as indicated by the section labeled "new technology benefits"), the operating cost decreases associated with this equipment increase the FM company's profits. At the contract expiration point (assumed to be 5 years after the initiation of the contract), the contract will be renegotiated in approximately the range shown at the right of the exhibit. The new price per transaction may be above or below the old price, depending upon the negotiating positions and the abilities of the FM company and the client organization.

An FM company is likely to be used successfully primarily by organizations in certain industries. To have success with an FM company, the organization should be one in which procedures are fairly standard and applications are relatively static. Also, there should be "commonality" among the organizations in the industry so that the FM company can use programs it develops for several organizations in that industry. This commonality enables the FM company to use a high proportion of the applications packages that it develops with most of its clients, giving it economies of scale. Organizations with these traits include those in the insurance, banking, brokerage, distribution, and health care industries. There is also a great deal of commonality among companies in heavily regulated industries because of common reporting standards.

Additionally, organizations that benefit the most from FM companies usually are those for which the data processing function is not directly linked to their competitive strategies. For example, if an organization's marketing function is a major part of its competitive strategy and is also highly dependent upon data processing, it is unlikely that an FM company will be able to provide the intricate kinds of applications required to complement and supplement the organization's marketing strategy. This is due to the fact that the applications that are directly related to the organizations's strategy require frequent program changes and elaborately individualized applications programs, both of which are difficult for an FM company to provide. In general, FM companies are of more benefit to small and medium-sized organizations than to larger ones because it is the smaller organizations that are least able to provide the resources needed for effective development of their own data processing services.

Organizations should be concerned about certain aspects of FM company operations. One concern is that FM companies prefer to deal with applications that are fairly standard and relatively static, as noted. Accordingly, it is difficult to develop a workable relationship with an FM company that enables the client's management information systems (as opposed to its operations systems) to be properly developed. For example, an FM company will usually encounter difficulty in developing a long-range planning information system for a client.

Another major concern is that it may be difficult for an organization to reestablish its own data processing operations if it wishes to terminate or "unwind" from an FM company. After a period of years the most capable of the organization's data processing employees become thoroughly integrated into the FM company, and the least capable would be of little assistance to the organization. To combat this, the organization can include a carefully constructed clause in the contract providing that the FM company will assist fully in helping the organization reestablish its data processing should it desire to do so at the conclusion of the contract period; this approach has been successful in some instances in the past.

There also should be concern on the part of the organization about lack of control of the data processing operations after an FM company takes them over. If, for example, the FM company transfers the organization's data processing activities to another location, the data control and security concerns are much like those encountered with a service center or timesharing company. Also, the managers of the client organization are unable to exert the same degree of influence on the FM company's personnel that they could if these personnel were employees of the organization; one consequence is that if special or unusual data processing is required, the FM company's personnel may not respond satisfactorily. Also, if the services of the FM company deteriorate, the organization may not have adequate recourse. Courts of law often require overwhelming evidence that a contract has been breached, and quality of service is difficult to measure. As a precaution, the client organization should insist on an escape clause that permits cancellation of the contract without the necessity of demonstrating that the contract has been violated.

THE CRITERIA FOR CHOICE

Exhibit 17.3 summarizes the criteria of choice of a source of computer power from among the alternatives discussed in the preceding pages. With respect to item 1, if the organization is particularly concerned about its ability to maintain control of data processing, it should prefer one of the options that permit the computer to be physically at the organization's location and under its managerial control.

The Criteria for Choice of a Source of Computer Power — EXHIBIT 17.3

1. Control of data processing

2. Projected costs:
   Acquisition costs
   Implementation costs
   Continuing operations costs

3. The flexibility required for future growth, for changing computer systems, for new types of computing services, and so on

4. The organization's past experience with data processing

5. Management's willingness to devote attention to information systems development

6. The organization's competitive strategies

7. The organization's need for MIS development

8. The best prospects for software development

9. The pattern of data processing activities

10. The length of time for which the data processing is required

11. Accounting and tax considerations

Item 2 in the exhibit, projected costs, is a major concern in almost every selection process. When large volumes of data processing are involved, service centers and timesharing companies are probably the most costly alternatives. If flexiblity (item 3) is most important, all options involving a long-term contract as well as purchase of a computer system should be avoided.

If the organization's past experience with data processing has been largely unsatisfactory (item 4) and there is reason to believe that management is not willing or able to devote the necessary attention to the development of data processing (item 5) the preference should be for use of a service center, a timesharing company, or an FM company. It is often difficult for the managers of an organization to admit that they are unlikely to devote sufficient attention to the development of the information system; for this reason, an organization is most likely to err on the side of buying or renting a computer, when it might be better served by using a service center a timesharing company, or an FM company.

On the other hand, if the organization's strategic maneuvers in the pursuit of its long-term goals are highly dependent upon an information system that can be reshaped as necessary to support the strategic processes (item 6 in the exhibit), data processing by an outside company is probably least preferable, which precludes the exlusive use of a service center, a timesharing company, or an FM company. Similarly, if the organization has a pressing need for the development of an information system for management purposes (item 7), it should avoid these same sources of externally provided data processing.

With respect to item 8 in the exhibit, the best prospects for software development are generally present if the organization controls its own data processing, unless its data processing activities have been unsuccessful in the past and it is in an industry in which an FM company can provide a large number proven programs at a low cost. With respect to the pattern of data processing activities (item 9), if these activities are sporadic or intermittent, if they have peak periods, or if there are occasional very large data processing jobs, it is often advisable to use a service center or a timesharing company so that the organization pays only for the amount of data processing done and not for its own excess capacity. On the other hand, with respect to item 10, the length of time that data processing is required, if the organization has a temporary need for data processing—for example, if it is waiting for delivery of a computer—perhaps a computer should be rented, or a service center or a timesharing company should be used. Finally, accounting and tax considerations (item 11) can influence the choice. Depending on the circumstances, it may be undesirable to have the investment value of the computer appear on the organization's balance sheet (which it will if the computer is purchased), or it may be advantageous to have the investment tax credit that accrues to the purchase of a new computer.

It is clear that the criteria listed in Exhibit 17.3 can carry different weights in a variety of different circumstances. Each organization must assess its computer needs, along with all the criteria noted as a part of its systems investigation, and then choose the source of computer power that is best, considering its particular circumstances.

COMPUTER SYSTEM SELECTION

The software and computer equipment selection processes are conducted quite differently if a large computer system is needed from the way they are conducted if a microcomputer system is needed. In the case of a large computer system, the focus is first on selecting the equipment, with care given to ensuring that the systems software (including compilers) needed is available for the computer system selected. Then the organization's programmers develop or purchase applications software for the computer system acquired. Rarely does the availability or lack of availability of prewritten applications programs have a decisive effect on the selection of a large computer system.

For microcomputer systems an almost opposite approach is recommended. The critical applications software that will be needed, as well as the operating system, should be selected first. Then the microcomputers that will process this software should be identified, and the selection made from among the suitable ones on the basis of traditional computer systems acquisition analyses. Prewritten applications programs for microcomputers are so inexpensive that every attempt should be made to avoid writing major applications programs; it is therefore worthwhile first to select the programs that are most suitable and then to buy a microcomputer system that these programs operate on. Also, organizations or departments of organizations that typically purchase microcomputers rarely have professional programmers; therefore, the purchase of prewritten software is often the only logical alternative, which forces attention to focus more on software acquisition.

Certain important factors should be kept in mind when making any computer acquisition analysis. First, the equipment selected should not be approaching obsolescence, since this influences its economic life and the extent to which software and hardware enhancements will be available in the future. Another concern is the danger of becoming locked in to a particular vendor's equipment, that is, having expensive data files and programs that must be processed only on that vendor's equipment and cannot be converted fairly easily to another vendor's computer system if necessary. Avoiding lock-in requires selection of a computer system for which plug-compatible equipment is available from other vendors and which either utilizes ANSI standards for software or (in the case of microcomputers) employs a widely used operating system.

A third factor in equipment selection is avoiding a dead-end system. A system should be selected that will be enhanced by the vendor in the future with additional software programs and additional or more advanced hardware components; the contract should guarantee the availability of any programs or enhancements that significantly affect the acquisition decision.

Also, a computer system that is already configured to maximum capacity to accommodate initial needs generally should be avoided, since usually the amount of data processing done by a computer system increases substantially each year. Finally, the computer system selected should be part of a family of computers so that there will be upward compatibility if the system is outgrown and so that additional capabilities available only within the same family will be available if needed.

Two general questions having to do with acquisition strategies should be addressed. The first is whether to buy all or most of the computer system equipment from one manufacturer or to have a "mixed shop," in which plug-compatible equipment of multiple manufacturers is used. The advantages of one-brand shopping are (1) convenience, (2) the fact that a larger commitment to one manufacturer may result in better customer service from that manufacturer, (3) possibly fewer operating problems because the equipment components are initially designed to be mutually interfaced, and (4) a lack of opportunity for buck-passing, whereby each manufacturer claims that any problems encountered are the fault of another manufacturer's equipment. In general, the less technically sophisticated the personnel in the data processing center are and the less generously staffed the center is, the more advantageous a one-vendor data center approach becomes.

The advantages of a mixed-equipment data center are (1) lower total equipment cost (because the organization comparison-shops for equipment) and (2) higher systems performance (because other vendors' equipment with higher performance characteristics can be selected). A mixed-equipment data center may encounter interfacing problems and other problems that can be disastrous if the data processing personnel are not highly qualified. However, the cost savings and performance advantages of a mixed-equipment data center can be great.

The second question relates to whether to acquire equipment that has more capacity than is initially needed, for example, whether to acquire the next larger computer system. The alternative is to acquire a system initially that has little more capacity than is needed immediately. In general, it is preferable to defer acquisition of additional capacity until it is needed. Attached processors (additional CPUs), additional printers, and other peripheral equipment can be routinely added with little effort when needed. One reason to delay is that there is an excellent chance that either the performance of the peripherals will be increased or that their cost will be lower at a later time. What is necessary, however, is to ensure in advance that the devices will be available when needed and that there is enough space at the computer site for the additional equipment.

Turnkey Computer Systems

A turnkey computer system is a system that is purchased as a package; it includes all the necessary hardware, systems software, and applications programs. The term "turnkey" refers to the fact that the vendor often claims that all the purchaser must do after installation of the system is "turn on the key" and begin processing transactions data. In fact, it is seldom, if ever, as simple as this, and the incidence of problems with turnkey systems is high.

Turnkey minicomputer systems have been widely distributed for a decade. Now turnkey microcomputer systems are becoming important; hundreds of vendors specialize in providing turnkey microcomputer systems. Each vendor operates differently, but typically turnkey systems are provided as the result of a three-step sequence of events.

First, the organization specifies the reports and documents, along with their format, that must be produced by the system. Then the vendor's personnel work with the organization to determine what data must be gathered and input to the computer system.

Next, the vendor looks for suitable software programs, decides on a hardware configuration, and develops any programs that cannot be purchased. In general, the vendor prefers to provide prewritten programs because the cost is low, the profit margin is high, and the difficulties of writing, testing, and debugging programs are avoided. Because they have an intimate knowledge of the programs that are available in the marketplace, turnkey vendors are in a good position to identify suitable software for purchasers without engaging in time-consuming search and program evaluation activities.

The complete system is then delivered to the organization for use. The organization views the system more as a "problem solution" than as a computer system and has little or no understanding of the system components or of how the programs process data; to the organization, the system and its programs are a "black box" (a term used in electronics to mean a system that is not understood), as illustrated in Exhibit 17.4.

Turnkey microcomputer systems are usually sold to small organizations that do not have personnel who understand computers or who can do computer programming. These systems can be an inexpensive solution to such organizations' data processing problems, particularly if no programs must be written by the vendor for the system. Turnkey systems provide computer data processing for thousands of organizations that otherwise could not afford a computer system.

There are dangers with turnkey systems, however. First, the organization often has to change methods of operation to conform to the system's needs; this can be difficult and may cause operating problems. Also, if the system does not perform as promised by the vendor, the organization usually has no recourse except to the vendor, who may or may not provide a remedy. In addition, a turnkey system usually is not the result of a careful systems investigation, and there is a high likelihood of its being inadequate for future needs or having technical limitations which restrict its usefulness; it may even be based on obsolete or otherwise unsatisfactory equipment that the vendor happened to have available. Finally, because the organization is not sophisticated about computers and understands the system only as a black box, any modifications needed later must be done by the vendor, who normally charges consultants' rates for making these changes.

Choosing a Computer System

Large and medium-sized organizations generally can devote enough resources to a systems investigation to determine accurately whether new computer equipment is needed and, if it is needed, to avoid turnkey systems by conducting a thorough analysis of alternatives. These companies can find an appropriate computer and locate existing programs or

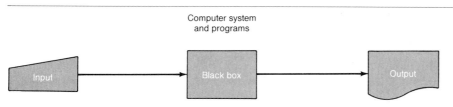

Computer system
and programs

Input   Black box   Output

EXHIBIT 17.4
An organization's view
of a turnkey system.

develop new ones as necessary. These activities demand a high level of specialized expertise, and many organizations use a consultant either to provide guidance to their personnel or to manage and conduct this part of the systems investigation.

Managers cannot expect to understand systems selection activities fully. However, it is useful for managers to have a general knowledge of these activities. The steps involved are:

1. Prepare the design specifications.
2. Prepare and distribute an RFP to selected computer vendors.
3. On the basis of an analysis of proposals, eliminate vendors whose proposals are inferior.
4. Have vendors present their proposals.
5. Conduct further analysis of the proposals.
6. Contact present users of the proposed systems.
7. Conduct equipment benchmark tests.
8. Select the equipment.

Steps 1, 2, and 4 were fully discussed in the preceding chapter. Step 3, analysis of submitted proposals and elimination of vendors whose proposals are inferior, is often referred to as "desk-checking the specifications." Typically, it is a two-stage process and is done before the vendor presentations (step 4) and again after the presentations (step 5). It consists of an analysis of the technical specifications of proposed equipment. Typical of the specifications evaluated are those which establish whether the proposed equipment has adequate capacity, can provide the specialized capabilities embodied in the original systems requirements specifications report (such as data base inquiry and high-resolution graphics), and has no obvious "bottlenecks" such as a particular component that operates more slowly than the equipment it interfaces, which will degrade the performance of the entire system. Also, the analyst must be alert to the possibility that certain components may be overpriced and that equivalent or better performance may be provided by components that are available from another vendor.

Desk-checking typically turns up many questions about the specifications and touted capabilities of the proposed system. These questions serve as the basis for penetrating questioning during the vendors' presentation (step 4).

The after-presentation equipment analysis is similar, but is carried out in even greater detail, and it involves the proposals of only those vendors who remain in the competition (typically only one or two). This second-stage desk-checking may produce further questions that will be answered less formally, or it may necessitate a second presentation by the vendor.

At this point the organization should be satisfied that the systems still being considered can solve its problems in a cost-effective manner. If this is not the case, the drastic steps of completely rewriting the design specifications and of submitting RFPs to other vendors must be considered. Assuming that one or more proposed configurations are deemed satisfactory, two questions remain: (1) Are present users of the system being considered satisfied with the system and the vendor's support? (2) Will the system actually perform as the vendor claims it will and as the specifications indicate that it should? With respect to the first question, usually preliminary inquiries are made to present users before the vendor is selected to receive an RFP. Even so, additional inquiries are likely to be made, perhaps to additional customers of the vendor and to the vendor's user association. Additionally, the financial condition of the vendor may be investigated through a credit rating agency or, more carefully, by means of a financial statements analysis. Vendors who are in poor financial condition are likely to skimp on services to purchasers and are less likely to provide hardware and software enhancements in the future. Also, continuing physical maintenance and spare parts can become major problems if the vendor is forced into bankruptcy.

If a vendor's other clients provide favorable reports and if the vendor's financial status is sound, there is reason to believe that the system offered will be satisfactory. However, it is impossible to detect every possible bottleneck and other system problem by desk-checking alone, and there may be unusual aspects of the organization's data processing activities that will cause problems with, and degrade the performance of, a particular computer system. Equipment benchmark tests protect the organization against such dangers; these tests consist of processing the organization's actual transactions using the proposed new computer system and copies of the organization's data files to see whether the transactions process properly and to determine how rapidly they process. Other aspects of processing can be tested too, such as the inquiry and telecommunications capabilities of the proposed system.

Usually, benchmark tests are done on equipment that is identical or very similar to the equipment that will be purchased; it is loaned by the vendor and operated by the organization's personnel. Tests may also be done on equipment borrowed from another client of the vendor. Benchmark testing may require adapting certain of the organization's programs to the new system. Because of the large amount of preparation effort involved, typically only the organization's most critical or highest-usage programs are tested, and how well the organization's other programs will run must be inferred from the results of these tests. Often, the vendor's personnel will assist in modifying the programs that will be tested.

Equipment benchmark testing as described is worth the immense effort involved only if the stakes are high—if the cost of the equipment is in the hundreds of thousands or millions of dollars or if the applications to be run on the new system are critical and a mistake in equipment acquisition would lead to high costs for the organization. Where the stakes are not high, the organization may rely on benchmark tests performed by independent testing companies using general types of transactions. The results of one such test are illustrated in Exhibit 17.5. Two types of processing were done by each computer—scientific and engineering processing and accounts receivable processing. It can be seen that the computers differed widely in terms of speed for these types of processing. If two other types of transactions had been chosen for the test, the results might have been completely different; the fact that a particular computer system is good at one kind of processing does not mean that it is good at all kinds.

Normally, only smaller systems are independently tested, and the results are either publicly reported in a systems journal or provided pri-

Series 1 results**** Systems up to $15,000	C-1 Scientific/ engineering Time	C-3 Accounts receivable Time
Pertec PCC 2000	28:48.4	6:04.3
North Star Horizon	12:01.9	1:57.7
Cromemco System Two	14:52.6	2:48.0
Texas Instruments 771	22:05.4	3:38.1
Vector Graphic System B	19:30.0	5:56.5
Decstation 78	22:35.6*	5:04.8*
Radio Shack TRS-80 Model II	20:00.7	3:38.6
Apple II	21:11.0	6:17.4

Series 2 results**** Systems $15,000 to $25,000	C-1	C-3
IBM 5110	29:47.2	4:11.0
Wang 2200VP	2:05.8	3:20.0
Texas Instruments FS990/10	**	3:18.6
Hewlett-Packard System 45	4:38.9	5:05.8
DEC PDP-11V03	14:43.4	4:14.0
Q1 Lite	6:50.7	5:03.3
Univac BC/7-610	12:09.2	10:37.0
Northern Telecom 405	**	**
Datapoint 1170	38:27.5	6:50.4
Randal 100	13:52.4	10:05.0
Hewlett-Packard 250	4:05.9	4:45.7
Texas Instruments DS990/2	**	2:48.3

*Results include both compile and run time.
**Test could not be run because of memory limitations.
***Test could not be run because of formatting limitations.
****Both Series 1 and Series 2 were run on the same programs.

EXHIBIT 17.5
The results of benchmark tests conducted by the Association of Computer Users (Boulder, Colorado).

(*Source: Computerworld*, Jan. 26, 1981.)

This is the 22nd in a series of articles giving the highlights of benchmark tests conducted on popular small computer systems. The full reports were originally published by the Association of Computer Users, a 4,000-member nonprofit organization.

vately for a fee. While benchmark tests are well worthwhile, from the vantage point of a particular organization they may have the shortcoming of usually not testing the types of transactions that the organization would prefer to have tested. Thus, independent benchmark tests may provide indications of a system's capabilities, but they do not tell an organization how quickly a particular computer system would process that organization's transactions or even whether it could meet the organization's unusual needs.

SUMMARY

This chapter considered the alternatives of purchasing a computer, renting a computer from the manufacturer, leasing a computer from a third-party lessor, acquiring a used computer, using the computer system of a service center or a timesharing company, employing a facilities management company that provides computing services, and acquiring a turnkey computer system. Several criteria for choice, including costs, organizational flexibility, the need to control data processing activities, and the role the computer system plays in the organization's competitive strategy, were examined as a basis for choosing from among these alternatives.

Equipment and software acquisition strategies are different for small and large computer systems. Whereas in the case of large computers, greater initial attention is given to the selection of the computer and the hardware, in the case of small computers, and especially microcomputers, the software needs should be considered first, and then a computer system should be selected that is compatible with the software. When selecting equipment, an organization should attempt to ensure that the computer it chooses will not become obsolete too quickly, that the vendor is financially strong and is willing to provide continuing services and enhancements, and that it retains the flexibility to expand the system and to select different vendors in the future.

The acquisition of a turnkey system involves the selection of a complete computer system and applications programs as one package from one vendor. No systems design is done by the organization—it tells the vendor what output the system must provide, and the vendor selects the needed hardware and software components.

Careful selection of a computer system by an organization is a complex and technical task that is performed best by computer systems specialists. Likely vendors are identified and are sent requests for proposals (RFPs). These vendors provide bids in the form of proposals which recommend certain equipment components and software packages and which include prices. Each vendor's proposal must be evaluated before one is accepted. Several techniques are used to evaluate proposed computer system configurations.

KEY TERMS

service center company: a company that uses its computer to provide batch data processing services to client companies.

timesharing company: a company that provides on-line, real-time transactions processing and data accessing services to client companies.

turnkey computer system: a computer system that, as delivered, includes all hardware and software and is ready to operate immediately.

benchmark tests: processing transactions with a particular computer or program to evaluate the efficiency and features of the equipment or software.

REFERENCES

Kafatou, Thalia, "Cutting the Hidden Costs in Time Sharing Services," *Small Systems World,* August 1980, p. 24.

Miller, Frederick W., "Used Computers: A Lower Cost Alternative," *Infosystems,* March 1980, p. 66.

Rockhold, Alan G., "A Changing and Maturing Market for Used Computers," *Infosystems,* March 1980, p. 66.

Szatrowski, Ted, "Rent, Lease, or Buy?" *Datamation,* February 1976, p. 59.

Thierauf, Robert J., and **George W. Reynolds,** *Effective Information Systems Management,* Columbus, OH: Merrill, 1982.

Timmreck, E. M., "Computer Selection Methodology," *Computing Surveys,* vol. 5, no. 4, December 1973, p. 199.

REVIEW QUESTIONS

1. What are the major alternatives for acquisition of computer power?

2. What criteria determine which source of computer power should be selected?

3. Name three or four sets of circumstances in which a combination of two sources of computer power would be logical.

4. If an organization's computer-based information system must be organized and managed so that it is able to be rapidly adapted to changing circumstances in a dynamic environment, which computer power sources should be considered, and why?

5. If the dominant consideration is that the computer-based information system must permit the data processing and report preparation activities to be rescheduled easily, which computer power sources should be considered, and why?

6. If the dominant consideration is that the computer-based information system must be organized and managed as an integral part of the organization's

competitive strategy, which computer power sources should be considered, and why?

7. If an organization needs supplemental computing capacity while it awaits delivery of its new, more powerful computer, which computer power sources should be considered, and why?

8. If a high level of program, data file, and report security is extremely important, which computer power sources should be considered, and why?

9. If an organization needs to use an extensive array of highly sophisticated engineering and scientific programs that are too expensive to purchase or to develop, which computer power sources should be considered, and why?

10. If the computer-based information system must provide a means of readily transmitting data to and from a wide variety of locations in the United States, Europe, and Asia, which computer power sources should be considered, and why?

11. If flexibility in terms of replacing its source of computer power on very short notice is important to an organization, which computer power sources should be considered, and why?

12. If the success of an organization requires that its computer-based information system be organized and managed well, but the data processing personnel have never been able to do this, which computer power sources should be considered, and why?

13. If an organization needs additional computing power but does not wish to convert its programs and files to a different computer system, which computer power sources should be considered, and why?

14. Explain in narrative form how a facilities management company operates and makes a profit. In what ways can this be good for an organization, and in what ways can it be harmful?

15. What kinds of needs can be met by a timesharing system similar to General Electric's MARK III?

16. When is it preferable to select computer equipment first, and when is it best to determine first which programs will be used? Why?

17. What factors should be considered in equipment selection?

18. What are the advantages and disadvantages of a "mixed shop," in which major equipment components from several different vendors are interconnected?

19. What are the advantages and disadvantages of a turnkey computer system?

20. How does the organization go about acquiring a turnkey computer system?

21. Explain the process of deciding whether a computer should be rented from the manufacturer, leased from a third party, or purchased.

22. What would you expect to find in an equipment RFP?

23. What is an equipment benchmark test, and in what ways may it be conducted?

24. Explain how each of the following activities relates to the systems design phase and systems implementation phase activities:

(a) Acquisition of a turnkey system

(b) Preparation of an RFP and selection of a vendor's proposed computer system

Chapter 18

ACQUIRING A SMALL
BUSINESS COMPUTER

PAYOFF THOUGHT

There is no magic formula for selecting a small computer system. A good choice requires having an extensive knowledge of the hardware and software available and of the needs of the organization, as well as following a few simple rules. This adds up to working hard and avoiding the big mistakes.

CHAPTER OBJECTIVES

1. To consider the circumstances in which small business computers are practical

2. To discuss the types of vendors from which small computers can be acquired

3. To present general rules for selecting small business computers

4. To examine the process of, and the criteria for, small business computer selection

INTRODUCTION

Computer systems of various sizes have been discussed in the preceding chapters. Minicomputers and microcomputers are small computers suitable for business usage; because of the increasing use of microcomputers for busines data processing, the focus of this chapter is on microcomputer acquisition, although most of the discussion is also relevant to minicomputer acquisition. Most of the discussion concerning selection of a business microcomputer is also applicable to the purchase of a personal computer by hobbyists and by persons who intend to use the computer for professional work in their homes. While minicomputers are frequently rented from the manufacturer or leased from a third party, microcomputers are almost always purchased, and the discussion in this chapter is in terms of purchasing.

This chapter is concerned primarily with computer acquisition by small organizations and by small units of large organizations. The preceding chapter dealt with the general aspects of computer evaluation and selection methodology, and these are also relevant to the acquisition of small computers. However, the acquisition of small computers is a sufficiently different activity to warrant additional treatment in this chapter.

Both large and small organizations acquire small computers. The small organization typically purchases only one small computer, and usually this is a business microcomputer. The large organization may acquire several, dozens, or even hundreds of small computers to perform a variety of functions, including the full range of busines data processing in sales branches. Increasingly, routine data processing activities that, in the past, would have been done on large central computers are now being done on microcomputers in user departments.

In a large organization, small computer acquisition should be coordinated, and the various departments should plead their cases to, and receive advice from, a central computer group. Often, department managers prefer to bypass the central computer group. However, if a distributed processing system exists or is contemplated in a large organization, the small computers acquired should be purchased with an eye toward their ability to interact with the host computer and other computers in the distributed processing network by exchanging data and utilizing the resources of the other computers. To assure this interaction, a central group must be given authority over microcomputer acquisition.

IS PURCHASE OF A SMALL BUSINESS COMPUTER JUSTIFIED?

Small organizations are most likely to seek one of two general types of small computers: a word processing computer or a small business computer. In general, the purchase of a word processing computer and that of a small business computer are justified in similar ways. The alternative of acquiring a combined small business computer and word processing computer is an increasingly attractive alternative.

The acquisition of a business microcomputer can be justified on several bases. Usually the system can be justified entirely on the basis of measurable cost savings (or revenue increases) if (1) the organization has one or more full-time accounting and clerical employees, (2) the monthly bill for data processing by a service center is $200 or more, (3) the microcomputer can save clerical employees 2 hours or more each day, or (4) the microcomputer can save managers an hour a day, or even less. There are very few organizations with more than 10 employees in which a microcomputer cannot be justified on a cost savings basis.

Cost savings, however, are only one means of justifying a business microcomputer, and in many situations cost savings are the least important benefit. If an existing manual system is inaccurate, inconsistent, or unreliable or if it cannot provide timely reports or certain kinds of information that would be useful, a business microcomputer may be justified even if it would increase the total data processing costs. For example, with a manual system, if one employee is absent for a day, often this causes a disruption of work flows that persists for a week or more, but if the microcomputer operator misses a day, the computer can usually be run more intensively for a day or two to catch up. Also, if programs are well developed and if control over the computer is good, more accurate information is provided than with a manual system. Procedural controls over a manual system may be overlooked from time to time or fall into disuse, and manual calculations are subject to frequent error, but procedural controls are not as extensive in a microcomputer system, and the computer does not err in its calculations.

A need for an interactive system is another way to justify microcomputer acquisition. For example, even a small company may want to monitor activities in process or look into the customer records to answer customers' questions. A microcomputer system makes this possible.

If the manual system does not provide managerial information quickly enough, a microcomputer system may be needed. Typically, for example, monthly financial statements produced by the manual system cannot be completed until at least the middle of the following month. A computerized system may reduce this delay, with the result that the financial statements and managerial reports are available 3 to 5 business days after the end of the month. If managers rely on these reports as an aid in their decision making, a microcomputer system can enable them to make more timely decisions.

As a practical matter, manual systems are unable to accomplish the type or the extent of data processing required for certain complex managerial statistical analyses. For example, numerous spreadsheet analysis tasks could not be done manually without an overwhelming effort, and present-value calculations, time-series analyses, and statistical correlations that are easily accomplished with financial analysis programs availble for microcomputers usually would not be done at all by small organizations if they had to be done manually. Further, these analyses may be only a part of more extensive models that are well within the capabilities of small organizations using microcomputer systems. A business microcomputer can add important new dimensions to the managerial information available in small organizations.

A business microcomputer may also appeal to a small organization if two or more of its branches must transfer data back and forth. An example is a small automobile parts retail store with multiple branches in the same city. Typically, these branches would regularly exchange inventory information by telephone and transfer inventory among themselves to provide better customer service and minimize the amount of inventory on hand. Microcomputers could be linked to form a distributed data processing system among the branches so that an inquiry through a microcomputer at one location could access the inventory files at other locations without disrupting local work activities; at the same time, each microcomputer at each location could maintain the inventory records at that location.

Similarly, the data base capability of microcomputers can be useful. For example, a small manufacturing company that produces a complex product can use the data base associative capabilities to relate raw materials with parts, parts with components, and components with finished products.

PRINCIPLES OF SELECTION

Many systems investigation principles have been discussed in the preceding chapters. This section presents those which are especially important to the acquisition of business microcomputers; all are easily overlooked by small organizations. Most major mistakes in acquiring a business microcomputer system can be avoided by adhering to the few simple principles discussed below.

• *Designate responsibility for acquisition to a key manager who will remain with the organization.* One manager in a small organization should take responsibility for acquiring the business microcomputer system. Often the most logical person is the proprietor or general manager; this manager is often the most capable member of the organization and the one who best understands the nature and purposes of the manual systems that will be computerized. Additionally, the small organization's resources are limited, and usually only one or two persons must be relied on to acquire knowledge about the computer system. These should be the persons who are least likely to leave the organization, one of whom is the proprietor. One other consideration is that, because of the difficulty of establishing adequate segregation of duties for data processing with small computers, overall management of the computer system by the owner greatly increases computer processing control and security.

• *Select a manager who understands the organization.* The person who will select and implement the computer system must also have an understanding of the organization's operations and its paper flows. This is essential to understanding the computer needs of the organization and will help ensure that all aspects of the computer system operate in a manner compatible with the operations of the organization.

• *Look for more benefits than just cost savings.* As has been noted, business microcomputer systems usually can be justified on a cost savings basis, but attention should be focused more on ensuring that the system will provide other, usually more important benefits. It is especially important for the small organization to take the occasion to assess the ways in which the computer can change the organization's mode of operations, for example, by providing a file inquiry capability, interactive processing, a cross-functional data base, or the ability to receive managerial reports sooner. Not to be overlooked are the possibilities of better service to customers in the form of faster shipments and better inventory control, accelerated cash flows from an improved or altered accounts receivable system, and enhanced control over production processes or service activities. In these and many other ways a business microcomputer system can provide a competitive advantage, and managers should be encouraged to think innovatively about ways in which to gain this advantage. Without this perspective, a small organization may err by acquiring a computer for routine data processing only and may simply computerize its existing manual systems. By seeking a broad range of possible benefits, however, an organization is more likely to substantially alter and improve the ways in which its operations are conducted.

• *Conduct a background analysis and start early.* The manager or team designated to select a computer should study the small computer segment of the marketplace and should also acquire a general knowledge of computers. Several months spent acquiring a background in computers should precede the active phase of computer acquisition. A crash program can result in too many shortcuts that can lead to disaster.

Microcomputer manufacturers, as well as other distribution outlets for microcomputers, provide promotional materials that describe their microcomputers and software programs. The responsible manager should attend computer trade shows, acquire these materials while watching demonstrations, and send for information offered in computer journals. Another important source of information is the yellow pages of the telephone books, which list vendors under "data processing" or "computers." Special attention should be given to vendors who advertise applications packages specialized to the purchaser's industry.

Articles in computer journals are another important source of information. These journals carry feature articles about specific microcomputer systems and sometimes publish comparative analyses. Computer journals include *Computerworld, Byte, Datamation, Infoworld, Mini-Micro Systems, Infosystems, Small Systems World,* and *Computer Decisions.* Specialized journals are devoted to the more popular microcomputers; for example, *Personal Computer Age,* and *PC World* report exclusively on the IBM Personal Computer and the IBM XT.

Data processing information services also provide information about microcomputers and other computer systems. These services provide special reports on particular data processing topics, such as microcomputer and software selection. Two of the better known of these have already been mentioned: Auerbach and Datapro.

• *Use a small computer consultant.* Large organizations employ personnel who have computer selection expertise; small organizations usually do not. Small organizations have neither the financial resources nor the computer expertise required for a thorough systems investigation and computer selection process, and so they are least able to effectively exercise the caution required. A qualified consultant can be of great help, given these circumstances. The moderate fees paid to a consultant are much less than the potential losses that could result from making selection mistakes, such as implementing an accounts receivable system that produces erroneous or late billings or acquiring a computer with a main memory that is too small to process the organization's larger applications programs.

A consultant can guide, participate in, or lead the selection activities and can help the small organization evaluate the tradeoffs involved in basic decisions. For example, the consultant can help determine whether an interactive system or a data base system would be worthwhile. The consultant can review a final list of five or six vendors and make recommendations and can attend vendors' presentations and ask penetrating questions; a consultant's evaluation of a presentation and of a vendor can be helpful and, in some cases, decisive. The consultant can also provide bases for the final comparison of computer systems. Finally, the consultant can assist in the actual implementation of the computer system. However, because the purchaser is likely to be the person who uses the microcomputer and because shopping for a business micro is itself an important learning experience, the purchaser should be deeply enough involved to form an independent judgment and should consider the consultant an adviser rather than someone who takes charge of the acquisition project.

Finding a qualified consultant is itself a high-risk project. One approach is to conduct a widespread inquiry among business associates, bankers and CPAs, and personal friends. If the names of certain nts are mentioned repeatedly and favorably in connection with uters, contact the organizations that used those consultants and ask for an evaluation of their suitability. In general, inquiries should not be made among persons who are potential consultants.

• *Consider acquiring an inexpensive "practice" computer.* A practice computer is not intended actually to process data, but only to provide one or two key employees with a general understanding of computer systems and with practice in their use.

• *Make some decisions early.* The number of options available with respect to microcomputers is large, and a full analysis of each would be enormously time-consuming and complex. To narrow the options somewhat, the organization should make some basic decisions early (perhaps with the assistance of a consultant), even if they are only tentative decisions. Early decisions should be made with respect to the expected mode of operation of the system (such as batch mode or single-transaction entry mode), the type of vendor to seek a system from, and the types of applications that will be processed by the system. Early tentative decisions would include, for example, the decision as to whether interactive data processing is required and, if it is, decisions about how many workstations will be needed, whether a data base is needed, and whether the organization will do its own programming. In making such tentative decisions, the organization should try to think several years ahead to anticipate future needs. These decisions are tentative in that the project participants should remain open to arguments from vendors or others about why other decisions would be preferable.

• *Specify the requirements of the system.* The organization should evaluate its data processing requirements carefully prior to acquiring a business microcomputer. This activity is roughly equivalent to preparing the systems requirements specifications report in the analysis phase, discussed in Chapter 15. The small organization that is seeking a business microcomputer seldom prepares an RFP because it is not worthwhile for a vendor to submit a formal proposal. In this respect, microcomputer selection is more like shopping carefully for an elaborate stereo system made up of components than like selecting a mainframe computer.

• *Build the system around the software.* If the organization plans to utilize prewritten applications programs, the evaluation processes should focus on the software, as was noted in the last chapter. Time and again organizations seeking a microcomputer commit the error of selecting a computer and related equipment and then choosing a set of applications programs to accompany the computer. In most situations, the reverse should occur; the applications programs should be evaluated and selected, and only then should a computer system be chosen. Applications programs that will meet a particular small organization's specialized needs may be few in number, whereas several different microcomputer systems can probably serve well.

Most small organizations have either two or three general classes of applications. The first class consists of applications that are similar in most small organizations, such as accounts receivable and payroll. The second class is more restrictive and consists of applications that are similar only in organizations in the same industry. Examples of such applications are production and cost accounting applications for small manufacturers in a particular manufacturing industry and project management applications for small construction firms. The third class consists of applications that are unique to the organization.

Almost all small organizations have the first two general classes of applications. For the first, prewritten applications programs are abundantly available from multiple software vendors and usually can be used effectively. Many of these programs have been tested in hundreds of organizations over a long period of time, and all are available at a small fraction of the cost of developing a similar program tailored precisely to the specific organization. The small organization should take advantge of these applications programs to the fullest extent possible.

Prewritten programs that are designed for specialized applications common to an organization's industry are less readily available. Because the vendor usually develops these programs for the relatively few companies in an industry, they may cost more than programs for applications in the first class, they may not be as well developed initially or improved as regularly, and they may be available for only one computer system. Nevertheless, if suitable industry-specific software programs are available, they can be quite cost-effective. Often programs are developed for one company in an industry and then made available by the vendor to others; these are seldom as satisfactory as programs that were flexibly developed initially to serve the entire industry.

If the organization has applications in the third category—that is, if unique data processing solutions are required because certain of the organization's operations are unique even within its industry—programs must be written specifically for these applications. The cost of developing these applications programs will be several times as great as the cost of purchasing prewritten programs of similar size and complexity.

The availability of suitable prewritten software programs usually should be the decisive factor in business microcomputer system selection. The small organization should direct its initial attention to locating and evaluating software programs.

• *Selecting a vendor carefully.* Typically, the business microcomputer purchaser has little expertise in data processing and, indeed, is often a first-time user of computer systems. However, while the cost of the microcomputer may not be great, the criticality of the system to the purchaser may be, and a major blunder in acquisition could cause chaos far out of proportion to the initial cost of the system. The inexperienced small purchaser usually relies to a high degree on vendor personnel for information and usually can perceive that different vendors provide different and often conflicting information; however, the purchaser may not realize how little a particular vendor's personnel know about the products they sell or about the purchaser's needs. The purchaser also may be unaware of vendors' widely differing sales and service policies and contracts.

For these and other reasons, the inexperienced purchaser should choose a well-established vendor with satisfied customers, if one can be found. Picking a vendor is particularly important to small organizations because of their lack of expertise and because for them, computer acquisition can be a high-risk project.

• *Seek just one vendor.* The organization should try to seek the services of just one vendor who provides the full range of the products and services needed. The two major reasons for this are simple and compelling. One is that the system components must be carefully matched in a number of dimensions. For example, as has already been mentioned, the computer's main memory usually must be large enough to contain multiple software programs along with data. When only one vendor is involved, that vendor is reasponsible for both hardware and software and is in a good position to match components properly and to integrate all aspects of the system. A second major reason is that with one vendor, the purchaser has no doubt about where to turn when a problem is encountered and assistance is needed, and the vendor cannot claim that the problem is the responsibility of another vendor.

In practice, each of these two reasons is more than enough justification to seek just one vendor. However, in some situations dual vendors may be necessary, for example, if the preferred programs and the most suitable computer for these programs are not distributed by the same vendor or if a vendor who is strongly preferred in other ways does not have a repair and maintenance facility. When two or more vendors are involved, the contract with each one should be as specific as possible in terms of establishing which vendor has the responsibility for what kinds of problems.

Exhibit 18.1 shows the types of products and services that a full-service vendor will provide. The backup computer indicated can be a "loaner" computer for use when the customer's computer is being repaired; this backup computer can be kept at the vendor's location and delivered to the borrowing organizations when needed.

• *Beware of salespersons.* The microcomputer marketplace is dynamic and is growing fast, and, as has already been noted, many of the salespersons are ill-trained in computing and have insufficient knowledge of their products. Salespersons are also inclined to make promises that they do not intend to keep or are later unable to keep. A small organization should err on the side of conservatism and deal with microcomputer salespersons as if they were selling used cars, adopting a "show me" attitude and insisting that all promises be included in the final contract.

**Products and Services Offered
by a Full-Service Vendor**

EXHIBIT 18.1

Computers
Peripheral equipment
Prewritten applications programs
Program development services
Service contracts
Repair facility
Backup computers
Customer training programs
Computer systems supplies

It is generally preferable to deal directly with the proprietor of the microcomputer store when possible. The owner or manager may be more knowledgeable about the product line and is a small businessperson with an understanding of small business problems. Often, the owner has a large stake in the local business community and is attempting to build a solid reputation among customers. Also, promises made by the owner are more likely to be fulfilled than those made by an errant salesperson who may soon be employed elsewhere.

Several nationwide and regional chains of microcomputer stores are already in existence. They have the advantages of being able to call on experts at other stores for assistance with difficult problems and of having readily available to them the inventory items of nearby stores. However, a particular store in a chain may be less willing to assist with the problems of individual customers than most independent vendors are. On balance, dealing with a chain store probably provides neither an inherent advantage nor an inherent disadvantage.

• *Be careful with the contract.* A contract for a microcomputer may consist only of a sales receipt and the manufacturers' warranties that attach to each component. However, if services such as contract programming, repairing the computer, setting up and checking out the system, and providing multiple computer systems over a period of time are involved, a formal contract will be used. Also, if performance of some type is guaranteed—for example, if it is guaranteed that a particular type of transaction can be processed by a particular program—a contract is needed. Among other things, a contract should define late delivery and implementation penalties and should specify an upper cost limit for any programming services associated with the development of tailored applications programs. Open-ended arrangements, whereby the purchaser is charged by the hour or in some other variable-cost manner that does not include a maximum cost, should be avoided. A related consideration is that the contract should stipulate specific performance criteria for each program developed by the vendor's personnel, such as by stating that the program must process a given number of transactions in a given period of time.

Many hardware components are warranted separately by the manufacturer (typically for 90 days), and many prewritten software packages also carry their own guarantees by the developing software house. However, these are independent warranties, and none ensure that the particular combination of hardware and software components will function together as an integrated system. Indeed, some hardware warranties are voided if the equipment is interconnected with equipment of other manufacturers. In some circumstances an additional warranty should be sought from the vendor to the effect that all aspects of the system are warranted to function effectively as a system and that the vendor will stand behind all warranties if for whatever reason they are not honored by the manufacturers and software houses. A consideration in vendor selection is the length of the warranty period, which is typically 6 months, although a year is preferable.

One additional provision should be considered if a contract is used. Often, the contract asks that the purchaser sign a release signifying acceptance of the business microcomputer system at the time the system is delivered. Once the system is accepted, no parts of it can be declared unacceptable and returned, and remedies thereafter are limited to adjustments, corrections, repairs, or replacements under the warranties. The purchaser should request a trial period of 2 weeks to a month, during which the system can be tested to ensure that it satisfies the needs of the purchaser. Preferably, this should be a part of the contract. Whatever their nature, however, contracts are often difficult to enforce, and the best protection is to deal only with a vendor who has an established reputation for integrity and good performance.

• *Elect the maintenance contract option.* Most busines microcomputer system vendors offer an extra-cost contract to provide routine maintenance and repairs. Although these systems require a minimum of service and repair and this contract is expensive, nevertheless it is generally worthwhile. Not only does this arrangement place a continuing responsibility on the original vendor, but it also assures that periodic preventive maintenance is provided for, and in most cases it also gives the purchaser a high priority for repairs. A user without a service contract usually must wait for repair service until repairs are completed on all other users' systems that are protected by service contracts. A service contract should provide that the computer will be repaired within a certain number of hours or days after the breakdown is reported, and it should include a clause stating that if repairs cannot be made within this time period, the vendor will loan a system to the purchaser. The period of time could be as little as 4 hours during a normal business day.

• *Acquire a modem with the system.* As has already been explained, a modem is a hardware device that permits digital data from a computer to be converted to analog signals for transmission via telecommunications lines. If the system has a modem, the vendor may be able to remote-diagnose the problem with a malfunctioning microcomputer by transmitting test commands to the microcomputer and receiving the test results back from it. The vendor may then be able to recommend by telephone what repairs or adjustments are needed, and often within a few minutes the user can make an adjustment or install a replacement part kept on hand for that purpose.

• *Negotiate the implementation and other initial costs.* The initial, one-time costs of installing a computer system may be substantial, in the range of from 10 to 15 percent of the total system purchase cost. Vendors are often more willing to negotiate these costs than the cost of the computer system because this type of "discounting" is least likely to lead future customers to expect comparable discounts. Software program prices are more likely to be negotiated than equipment prices, in part because software has a higher markup. Sometimes a vendor is willing to provide, free, or at a substantial discount, extensive additional software that is "nice to have but not necessary"—thousands of dollars' worth of software may be provided at a fraction of its retail cost even if the purchase cost of the business microcomputer system is itself only a few thousand dollars.

The purchaser's leverage for these discounts disappears, however, as soon as the sale is concluded. Therefore, the purchaser should bargain hard before agreeing to a purchase, and the willingness of a particular vendor to provide initial discounts may be the deciding factor in choosing between two vendors.

• *Clean up your manual system.* As can be inferred from the preceding chapters, it is necessary to specify carefully what the computer system must be able to accomplish in terms of types of transactions, processed throughout, and other considerations. Also important for small organizations is the need to improve or "clean up" their manual systems prior to establishing the need for a business microcomputer. Many small organizations seek a computer primarily because their existing manual systems are not of good quality. If they select prewritten software programs, these may replace poor-quality manual systems. However, if programs are written to replace inadequate manual systems and if these programs are based on the manual systems, these systems must be cleaned up so that they will operate efficiently when they are computerized. When a poorly designed and inefficient manual system is computerized, the result is an inefficient computerized system.

The important comparison in establishing the need for a small computer is that between an efficient, well-conceived manual system and the computer system that would replace it. To establish this comparison, an existing manual system should be tuned to peak performance.

• *Look for benchmark tests.* As was discussed in the preceding chapter, for the organization that is seeking a large computer, conducting benchmark tests is likely to be worthwhile. For small computer systems, independent organizations, such as the Association of Computer Users, perform comparative benchmark tests, conduct user satisfaction surveys about computers and software packages, and provide information in other forms that is useful in choosing from among small computer systems. As was noted in the preceding chapter, caution is warranted in the interpretation of published results of benchmark tests, however. The tests consider only certain aspects of the performance of the software and hardware. Additionally, considerations other than processing speed are important when selecting a microcomputer system.

• *If programmers are needed, seek the best.* Probably the most pervasive and often the most serious problem of small computer centers is incompetent programmers. Good programmers are rare, and good programmers in small organizations are rarer still because they usually prefer to work in large organizations, where the pay usually is higher and the programming assignments are more challenging.

One first-rate programmer is easily the equivalent, in terms of value, of two mediocre programmers and is preferable to an entire flock of bad programmers. An outstanding programmer is worth a 20 to 30 percent remuneration premium in terms of increased productivity and elimination of chaos in the systems area.

However, a willingness to provide this premium does not guarantee that a good programmer will be hired, since small enterprises generally do not have staff members who are experts at evaluating programmers' qualifications. Often, the best way for a small organization to hire a first-rate programmer is to utilize premium pay in conjunction with a programmer recruiting consultant who locates and evaluates candidates. Many of the least competent programmers in small organizations are former clerical personnel of the organization who have been retrained as programmers.

• *Consider efficiency of operations.* Often overlooked is the fact that an otherwise desirable small computer system may not have been engineered for efficient use. Systems should be checked for the efficiency with which they can be used by people. What seemed initially to be trivial matters, not worthy of consideration, may be important in the long run. For example, it is important to know how many steps are required to enter transactions, how easily error corrections can be made, how long it takes to place files on-line, how long it takes before the computer system is ready for operation after it is turned on, how much delay is involved in the completion of frequently used commands, how much time is required to activate the printer, and whether the printer can be operating while the computer is performing other tasks. With some types of tasks, the user of a slow microcomputer may be idle 30 percent or more of the time while waiting for the microcomputer to finish its processing. On this dimension of efficiency, microcomputers as well as the programs that are run on them vary widely. These and other, similar considerations can greatly influence the speed and accuracy of data processing and the morale of employees.

SOURCES OF BUSINESS MICROCOMPUTERS

Manufacturers of large computers market their computer systems directly to user organizations and provide continuing service to these organizations. However, microcomputers of all types, including business micros, can be acquired through a variety of distribution channels. Additionally, whereas large computer manufacturers are about a dozen in number and all have been in business for many years, microcomputers are manufactured by more than 150 companies (including almost all the manufacturers of large computers), and dozens of companies enter and leave the marketplace each year. Further, thousands of different vendors distribute microcomputers.

The market for microcomputers is also totally different with respect to the amount of attention that purchasers receive from vendors. Because the small computer market is fractured, most vendors have relatively small sales and service organizations. Vendors often do not help install the microcomputer, and some vendors do not provide continuing service of any type. Service may be provided on a pay-by-the-visit basis, similar to the way television sets are serviced, or the microcomputer owner may be required to bring the computer to a central service location.

One of the most dramatic differences between the merchandising of large computers and the merchandising of microcomputers is the expertise possessed by the salespersons. Microcomputer salespersons seldom have an intimate knowledge of either the technical intricacies—hardware and software—or the capabilities of the products they sell, although many may have a good working knowledge of a few of the products. Equally serious, most microcomputer salespersons have little knowledge of how organizations operate or of how micros should be used in an organization. The purchaser of a microcomputer system usually receives little real assistance from salespersons, either prior to the sale or afterward, when the novice purchaser has difficulty determining how the system operates and why it does not operate as expected. In part this is due to the fact that most salespersons handle a variety of products—too many to understand each one intimately—and in part it is due to the general scarcity of technically trained personnel in the computer field.

As has been noted, business microcomputers can be purchased through several different marketing channels. These are discussed below.

Computer Manufacturers

Microcomputer manufacturers sell microcomputers directly to large organizations by the dozens, hundreds, or even thousands, but few manufacturers make a serious attempt to sell microcomputers directly to small users. Manufacturers' sales personnel tend to be sophisticated technical personnel who work well with persons who have extensive computer experience, but they seldom understand the problems of small organizations. Generally, small organizations should look to other marketing channels to find vendors who are set up to provide more assistance, even if not enough assistance.

Package Dealers

Package dealers, sometimes termed "original equipment manufacturers," or OEMs (this is a misnomer because these companies are dealers, not manufacturers), purchase microcomputer equipment from one or more manufacturers at a 30 to 40 percent discount, combine the hardware with software packages, and provide completely functioning "turnkey systems" to users. Typically, several brands of microcomputers are available from these dealers, and the variety of applications programs available is also large.

Package dealers are independent companies, and many specialize in a particular industry. Although they are not restricted to one product line, they often do concentrate on one make of computer, as well as on the applications packages that have been developed for that computer family. These dealers may ask other vendors to provide peripheral equipment for their turnkey systems. Ideally, the package dealer can bring together preexisting components that are especially suited to a customer's needs. When purchasing a turnkey system as one package, the customer has the advantge of an investment tax credit on the entire cost because all components are charged for as just one product, whereas software programs purchased separately are not entitled to this tax credit.

Retail Computer Stores

The most important source of microcomputers for small organizations is the retail computer store. The acquisition of a business microcomputer from a retail computer store may be likened to the purchase of a stereo system. The store sells systems consisting of off-the-shelf hardware components and prewritten software packages, which are combined in a way determined by the purchaser. Most retail computer stores keep an inventory of several types of microcomputers, printers, monitors, and other types of peripheral equipment, as well as software packages. Retail computer stores differ from package dealers primarily in that while package dealers attempt to sell a "problem solution" thought to be suited to the customer's needs, and may even write (or have written) specialized software if necessary, a retail computer store may make suggestions but usually does no analysis of a customer's needs.

The retail store may or may not assume the responsibility of providing maintenance and repairs. Usually, however, the dealer answers questions about the operation of the system, and often a user's problem can be resolved quickly with a telephone call to the retail store. If the problem cannot be resolved quickly, however, it is frequently necessary to seek another source of assistance.

Microcomputer retail stores generally carry a full line of microcomputer supplies, such as printer paper and ribbons and mailing labels. While many independent computer retail stores exist, there are also several chains; one of the largest is ComputerLand. For most first-time users of microcomputers, and especially for hobbyists and other home computer users, a retail computer store offers convenient, price-competitive business microcomputer systems.

Manufacturers' Retail Outlets

Several manufacturers operate their own computer retail stores. Radio Shack sells its microcomputer systems through its nationwide network of electronics stores and also at over 100 specialized computer stores. Apple Computer also distributes its products through its system of retail stores as well as through other distribution outlets. IBM has office products retail stores that also sell IBM microcomputers. Other manufacturers also operate retail stores that sell their own microcomputers.

The advantage of dealing with a retail store is the sales and service personnel's depth of knowledge of the products. The disadvantage is that the sales personnel are unwilling to provide an objective comparative analysis of the characteristics of several different brands of microcomputer systems, as might be provided to customers of a computer retail store that sells several brands of microcomputers and peripheral devices.

Discount Mail-Order Stores

Microcomputers, peripheral units, software, and computer supplies are sold by discount mail-order stores. These stores can offer discounts because of volume sales and because salespersons are not needed to demonstrate or even describe the system. Also, usually no services of any type are provided. The manufacturers' warranties remain valid for mail-order purchases, and usually items returned under warranty will be accepted. For the customers who know exactly what they want, discount mail-order stores are convenient and are usually the least costly source of microcomputers, peripheral devices, business applications programs and other programs, and microcomputer supplies of most types. Discount mail-order stores advertise extensively in microcomputer journals, and one of the best known, 47th Street Photo, advertises periodically in *The Wall Street Journal*.

Convenience Software Stores

A large number of retail stores specialize in microcomputer software, supplies, books, and journals and do not sell hardware components. The concept of these stores is similar to that of stereo record and cassette music stores. Customers visit to browse or to select programs that have been reviewed in microcomputer journals, and the stores provide a convenient way for customers to see what new items are available and to purchase programs.

User Clubs

Local and regional clubs have developed that are composed of members who use one of the better-known microcomputers. While most clubs do not sell products to their members in an organized way (but some do!), individual members often have for sale, at bargain prices, components that they have abandoned because of an upgrade of their system. Additional memory, special-purpose circuit boards, modems, disk drives, and printers are among the components most frequently sold by members.

Typically, a club dedicated to a specific microcomputer meets monthly, and each meeting is organized around a theme, such as an equipment demonstration by a vendor. Most members find that the real advantage of belonging to a club is not the equipment they can buy cheaply or the presentations made at monthly meetings, but rather the opportunity to meet and talk with people who are intimately acquainted with the kind of system they use. Fellow members are often quite helpful in solving problems which have baffled a user and which the vendor has not dealt with satisfactorily. Clubs are often listed by location and by contact person in the journals dedicated to the particular computer system.

THE SELECTION PROCESS

The environments of small organizations that acquire microcomputers are quite different from those of large organizations. One difference is the degree of organizational and financial stability. Small organizations often cannot afford to make a mistake in the selection of a computer because one error could destroy the administrative systems of the organization. It is because they recognize the consequences of a mistake that some small organizations have deferred acquisition of their first computer far beyond the point where it would be beneficial, if successfully implemented.

Another difference is that small organizations must be especially careful to select a business microcomputer that is user-friendly. In most cases the system will be operated by clerical personnel rather than by data processing professionals, and a small organization may have few employees with the aptitude to work effectively with computers.

The step-by-step activities involved in selecting a computer system were detailed in the preceding chapter. This section describes the aspects of computer selection that are significantly different in small organizations. Two differences are that the selection effort is scaled down to be somewhat proportional to the cost of the microcomputer system and that the selection process is normally carried out much less formally and not so much "by the book." A small task team is more typical of a small organization than a detailed project plan and a systems steering committee. However, small organizations should recognize the value of a careful computer acquisition project system and plan, as described in preceding chapters.

The number of possible microcomputers that a small organization can afford to purchase is limited, but hundreds of alternatives appear in journal, newspaper, and television advertisements; are touted by salespersons; and are recommended by acquaintences who have some knowledge of microcomputer systems. Most of the 150 microcomputer manufacturers provide multiple computer models, and thousands of components are available from other sources.

A small organization should establish initial requirements for a new system that effectively eliminate most microcomputers from consideration. It is reasonable, for example, to eliminate those systems for which only a few suitable prewritten applications packages are available; this can be done by selecting all programs that are expected to be needed before considering the equipment. Additionally, those systems which do not have a clear upward migration path—which cannot be readily expanded or replaced with a larger but compatible computer—usually should be eliminated from consideration. Companies whose product lines are oriented toward another market should also be eliminated; many systems specialized to engineering applications, for example, probably will never have components or programs that are designed for business applications.

The organization that is seeking one or two microcomputers is unlikely to send an RFP to vendors of a microcomputer system that is being considered because few vendors would believe that the value of the sale would be worth the effort of responding to a formal RFP. Instead, the person or team making the selection typically begins visiting retail stores and talking with salespersons about the performance characteristics of various microcomputers and applications programs. After the purchaser visits several stores, the list of possibilities is likely to be narrowed to three or four software and hardware combinations, each sold by a vendor that the purchaser believes is a likely candidate. Usually, the programs being considered can be run on the microcomputer system right at the store; the purchaser should pay careful attention to how easily the system would be operated by the organization's clerical personnel and the managers who will be using it. Once a decision is made, the business microcomputer may usually be removed from the store and installed at the purchaser's organization the same day; sometimes a delay in delivery of days or weeks may be caused by the need to order some or all of the components.

The organization should not assume that a higher-cost microcomputer is a higher-quality one. As indicated in Exhibit 17.5, testing showed that several computers in the under-$15,000 range outperformed systems costing $15,000 to $25,000 in an accounts receivable benchmark test. The careful buyer of a microcomputer system can often find one system that serves better than another, more costly computer system. On the other hand, if one system that is clearly better, in terms of meeting the organization's needs, costs substantially more than the next best system, the additional money is usually well spent. A few thousand dollars of extra purchase cost can seem trivial by comparison with the frustration experienced by users, the extra attention that managers must give to data processing and other computer problems, and the chaos that can result in an organization when a business computer system does not function as it should.

SUMMARY

This chapter examined the acquisition of business microcomputer systems from the perspective of small organizations, but most of the discussion is also relevant to large organizations and to individuals seeking microcomputers. Often a business microcomputer system can be justified on a cost savings basis if the organization has one or more clerical or accounting employees, but in many organizations it is the additional capabilities provided by the system, rather than the cost savings, that are the greatest benefit of a business micro.

There are many more vendors of microcomputers than vendors of large computers. The number of vendors from whom the organization is considering purchasing a business microcomputer system should be sharply reduced at an early point and then progressively further reduced as the selection activities proceed.

Business microcomputer selection principles include assigning to the selection task a key manager who will remain with the organization and being wary of microcomputer salespersons. Sales outlets for business microcomputers are varied and include computer retail stores and discount mail-order stores. The selection process is significantly different for microcomputers and for large computers. A key step in the selection process is visiting several computer stores to examine and try out various business microcomputer systems.

REFERENCES

Frankenhuis, Jean Pierre, "How to Get a Good Mini," *Harvard Business Review*, May–June 1982, p. 139.

The Insider's Guide to Small Business Computers, Westboro, MA: Data General Computer Co., 1980.

Isshiki, Koichiro R., *Small Business Computers*. Englewood Cliffs, NJ: Prentice-Hall, 1982.

Lipsher, Laurence E., "Selecting a Minicomputer," *The Journal of Accountancy*, June 1979.

Shaw, Donald, *Your Small Business Computer*, Princeton, NJ: Van Nostrand/Reinhold, 1981.

Silver, Gerald, *Small Computer Systems for Business*, New York: McGraw-Hill, 1978.

Comparison of Large and Small Computer System Acquisition by Large and Small Companies EXHIBIT 18.2

Computer System Acquisition Considerations	Large Company—Large Computer System	Small Company—Small Computer System
1. Computer system investment relative to company size: ratio of system cost to company size	Usually lower	Usually higher
2. Company financial stability	Usually greater	Usually less
3. General expertise and training levels of personnel	Usually higher	Usually lower
4. EDP expertise level	Usually substantial	Often none
5. Legal expertise relevant to contract that is readily available	Some (but not sufficient)	Much less or none
6. Control environment	Control consciousness, good control policies and procedures, and separation of duties	Poor environment, including little separation of duties
7. Quality of the existing system	Probably efficient and well controlled	Probably manual and more likely to be haphazard, inefficient, and dependent on human memory and ad hoc procedures for control
8. Sophistication of the system needed	Very sophisticated	Primarily for basic accounting applications
9. Company expectations of the computer system	Generally reasonable, based on past experience	Varies widely from completely unknown to unrealistically high expectations
10. Applications software	Mostly uses its own programmers	Cannot afford extensive programming and prefers not to have programmers
11. Applications' growth rate—number and size	Predictable and high in number	May be unpredictable; could be very high in number as new uses are found and large in size as company grows rapidly
12. Hardware—CPU and peripheral equipment	Careful technical evaluation, including benchmark testing	Less attention to technical capabilities and decreased ability to benefit from suitable benchmark tests

Computer System Acquisition Considerations	Large Company—Large Computer System	Small Company—Small Computer System	EXHIBIT 18.2 (continued)
13. Variety of computers available	Only about 10 major vendors, each with a limited number of large CPU models	Over 150 manufacturers of small computers, many of whom sell several models	
14. Types of vendors	Acquisition from the manufacturer	Acquisition from one or more of several types of resellers	
15. Computer selection procedures	Usually well developed and formal	Usually non-existent and developed informally	
16. Vendor size	Large size for large computer systems	Much smaller or even very small	
17. Computer cost	Usually high—$150,000 and over	Usually low—$30,000 or less	

KEY TERMS

full service vendor: a computer dealer who provides a full range of products and services required for a small business computer system.

user club: an association of users of a particular brand or model of computer that is dedicated to providing knowledge and assistance in the use of that computer.

REVIEW QUESTIONS

1. Explain the ways in which a business microcomputer system can be justified.

2. Why should a central group of a large organization coordinate acquisition of that organization's business microcomputers?

3. What kind of background information should be acquired prior to making a serious effort to select a business microcomputer system? What are the sources of background information?

4. Why is a consultant important in the acquisition of a business microcomputer? How can a consultant be found?

5. In what ways is the computer selection process different for business microcomputers and for large computers?

6. Why do you think small organizations often overlook many of the general principles of selection discussed in the chapter?

7. What features would you look for in a practice computer, and why?

8. Of the several types of microcomputer vendors, which would be your first choice as the place to initiate your search if you were looking for a small business computer, and why? Which would you avoid, and why?

9. Describe the products and services that a full-service vendor provides.

10. What characteristics other than full services should a business microcomputer purchaser look for in a vendor?

11. Why is caution warranted in relying on published benchmark tests as the basis for a decision about a business microcomputer system?

12. What are the advantages and disadvantages of visiting a manufacturer's retail computer store rather than a retail computer store that sells several brands of products?

13. Assume that you have just been selected to head a small task team to recommend a business microcomputer for your company. Outline the steps you would take, in about the sequence you would take them. Base your outline on the material in both this chapter and the preceding ones.

PROBLEMS

1. Select five business microcomputer system vendors in your locale and prepare an anlysis of the extent and nature of the small computer products and services they offer. Which, if any, are full-service vendors? On the basis of only the above analysis, which vendor would you select, and why? What other considerations besides the nature and extent of the products and services offered should affect the selection of a vendor?

2. As a sales approach, a consultant specializing in assisting small businesses choose a computer system wants to prepare a document that explains to small businesses why they need the consultant's services. The consultant has prepared the table shown in Exhibit 18.2 and wants you to complete the column headed "Implications for the Small Company."

CASE

Benchmark Tests

One of the industry's most popular personal computers, Apple Computer, Inc.'s Apple II, did not match benchmark times of more expensive systems, but does appear headed for victory in the "least expensive" category. The Apple underwent testing in the Association of Computer Users' (ACU) Series I Benchmark Reports.

Priced under $4,300 for a complete system with dual minidiskettes and Centronics Data Computer Corp. 779 printer, the Apple II can be configured more cheaply than that and features an entry-level price below $1,000.

While the system's benchmark test results were slower than some others we've looked at, they were not unreasonably so, especially considering the fact that this is a minimum-cost setup. However, potential busines users should be aware that systems in this price bracket may lack sufficient diskette storage, memory capacity and system expandability for use in a general accounting application, except in a very small business environment.

Instead, the Apple finds applications where less computing power is needed. In the business field, Apple finds more use in management planning and personal financial planning. While an accounting package is offered, the firm states that it is designed for use in businesses having fewer than 500 customer accounts, 100 vendors and less than

$1 million in total dollar volume annually. Some dealers are even more conservative than this in recommending the Apple as a general-purpose bookkeeping system.

Source: Excerpted from *Computerworld,* Jan. 26, 1981. (This article accompanied the benchmark tests shown in Exhibit 17.5.)

Case Questions

1. Consider several local small businesses and state whether the Apple II might be a suitable business data processing computer for them.

2. How satisfactory would the Apple II probably be as a "practice computer"? How would it be used for this purpose?

INDEX